GREEK MYTHS

Imitation in Writing Series
Book 3

Matt Whitling

Logos School Materials
Moscow, Idaho

IMITATION IN WRITING

This *Greek Myths* text is the third book in a growing series of Imitation in Writing materials designed to teach aspiring writers the art and discipline of crafting delightful prose and poetry.

Aesop's Fables
Fairy Tales
Greek Myths
Greek Heroes
Medieval Legends
The Grammar of Poetry

C085 Imitation in Writing - Greek Myths
ISBN 1-930443-12-9   20.00
I. Bulfinch, Thomas. *The Age of Fable* II. Hawthorne, Nathaniel. *A Wonder Book for Girls and Boys*. III. Cruse, Amy. *The Book of Myths*. IV. Hawthorne, Nathaniel. *Tanglewood Tales*.

Logos School Materials
110 Baker Street, Moscow, Idaho 83843
Toll Free 866-562-2174
www.logosschool.com or materials@logosschool.com

Call, write, or email for a free catalog of our Classical, Christian educational materials for schools and home schools.

CONTENTS

Imitation In Writing

Background:

We are commanded in Scripture to imitate the Lord Jesus Christ. We are also commanded to imitate those brothers and sisters who, through faith and patience, have inherited the promises. To imitate something or someone means:

- To do or try to do after the manner of; to follow the example of; to copy in action.
- To make or produce a copy or representation of; to copy, reproduce.
- To be, become, or make oneself like; to assume the aspect or semblance of; to simulate.

This God-sanctioned method of learning is an essential tool for educating young people. For example, how is it that we teach a child to perform simple physical skills such as throwing and catching? "Hold your hands like this. Step forward as you throw like this." Imitation. How is it that we teach a child how to form his letters correctly? "Hold your pencil like this. Look at this 'a'. Trace this letter. Now, you try to make an 'a' like this one." Imitation. How is it that we teach art? At Logos School students learn how to paint by imitating master painters of the past. "This is a good painting. Let's see if you can reproduce it." Imitation. How is it that music is taught, or reading, or math? Very often the best instruction in any of these areas necessarily includes imitation. Why, when it comes to teaching young people writing, do we educators regularly neglect this effective tool?

Educators in seventeenth century England knew the value of imitation as a tool through which they could teach style, particularly in the area of writing. The primary method of imitation in these English grammar schools was called Double Translation. In a double translation the teacher would translate a Latin work into English. The student was to copy this English translation over, paying close attention to every word and its significance. Then the student was to write down the English and Latin together, one above the other, making each language answer to the other. Afterwards the student translated the original Latin to English on his own. This was the first part of the translation. The second part took place ten days afterward when the student was given his final English translation and required to turn it back into good Latin.

Benjamin Franklin wrote of a similar exercise that he employed to educate himself a century later. When he was a young man, he came across a particular piece of writing that he delighted in, The Spectator. The Spectator is a series of 555 popular essays published in 1711 and 1712. These essays were intended to improve manners and morals, raise the cultural level of the middle-class reader, and popularize serious ideas in science and philosophy. They were written well, the style was excellent, and Franklin wanted to imitate it. Here is Franklin's method of "double translation" regarding The Spectator:

With that view (imitating this great work) I took some of the papers, and making short hints of the sentiments in each sentence, laid them by a few days, and then, without looking at the book, tried to complete the papers again, by expressing each hinted sentiment at length, and as fully as it had been expressed before, in any suitable words that should occur to me. Then I compared my Spectator with the original, discovered some of my faults, and corrected them.

But he realized that he needed a greater stock of words in order to add variety and clarity of thought to his writing.

Therefore I took some of the tales in the Spectator, and turned them into verse; and, after a time, when I had pretty well forgotten the prose, turned them back again. I also sometimes jumbled my collection of hints into confusion, and after some weeks endeavored to reduce them into the best order, before I began to form the sentences and complete the subject. This was to teach me method in the arrangement of thoughts. By comparing my work with the original, I discovered many faults and corrected them; but I sometimes had the pleasure to fancy that, in particulars of small consequence, I had been fortunate enough to improve the method or the language, and this encouraged me to think that I might in time become to be a tolerable English writer, of which I was extremely ambitious.

Now the question is; "How can we employ a similar methodology?"

Imitation In Writing
GREEK MYTHS

<u>Instructions:</u>

1. READ SILENTLY: Have the students read the myth quietly to themselves, paying close attention to the story line. When they are done, they should underline the vocabulary words and describe the characters. Discuss, by means of questioning, who the characters are in the myth and what took place.

2. STUDENT READS MYTH: Choose a student to come to the front of the class and read the entire myth while the class follows along. (Variation: To develop listening and note taking skills try reading the myth to your students without giving them a copy of it.)

3. ORAL RETELLING: The teacher calls on individual students to retell the myth in their own words. These oral summaries should be short and to the point.

4. VOCABULARY: Call on one student for each of the vocabulary words. That student will read the sentence in which the word is found, providing context, and then define the word for the class. Occasionally the student definition will need to be modified by the teacher so that it is an exact match with the vocabulary word in the myth. One word definitions work well. The idea here is to provide the students with a synonym for each vocabulary word which could be substituted into the sentence without distorting the meaning. Have the students write the definition of each word on the blank provided.

5. OUTLINE THE PLOT: Initially this activity should be guided by the teacher and completed as a class. Providing every other simple sentence or phrase for each scene is helpful for younger students. There is some room for variation in the exact wording of the sentence or phrase. The rules are that each sentence or phrase must be three to four words long and represent a significant chronological event in that scene. From time to time the students will come up with a better sentence or phrase than the one provided in the Suggested Plot Summaries at the back of this book. Use it, by all means.

6. CHARACTERS: At this point the students will list the main characters in the story and write a few descriptive words about each.

7. ADDITIONAL REQUIREMENTS: Discuss any additional requirements and have the students write them on the blanks provided at the bottom of each worksheet. For examples of additional requirements see EXCELLENCE IN WRITING @ 800-856-5815 (stylistic techniques, dress-ups, sentence openers, etc...) or teach your students figures of speech and require that they use them in their own writing (metaphor, simile, synecdoche, hyperbole, onomatopoeia, rhetorical question, personification, pun, oxymoron, alliteration).

8. PASS IN ORIGINAL MYTH: Before the students begin rewriting the myth, they must pass the original one in. Some students will want to read through the myth one more time to better understand what the whole thing is all about.

9. WRITE FIRST DRAFT: The students are now ready to rewrite the myth using their outlines to guide them. I allow my students to change the characters and some of the incidentals of the story in their rewrites as long as the plot is identifiable. The exceptionally good writers in the class will thrive off of this opportunity to be innovative. The students who are less comfortable with writing will tend to stick to the same characters and incidentals, which is fine. All of the vocabulary words must be used correctly and underlined in the rewrite. The students should skip lines on the first draft to allow room for editing.

10. PARENTS EDIT: Students take their rewrites home to complete the first draft and then they have their parents edit it. This is most profitable when the parents sit down with the student and edit the myth together. Guidelines for editing can be sent home at the beginning of the year or communicated at "Back to School Night" so that parents know what is expected.

11. FINAL DRAFT: Time in class can be provided for the students to work on the final draft. The students should not skip lines. I allow the students to draw an illuminated letter at the beginning of their story if they like.

12. GRADING: There is a grading sheet included which can be duplicated, cut out, completed, and stapled to each student's rewrite. This will help the teacher to focus on the essential aspects of the composition as he is grading it and will provide specific feedback to the student and parents regarding which areas will need more attention in the future. If you have a different policy for grading writing assignments then simply disregard the grading sheet.

GREEK MYTHS

1st Draft/Worksheet	10	_____
Handwriting	10	_____
Vocab. Usage	20	_____
Content (style, structure...)	30	_____
Mechanics (spell, punct...)	30	_____
Total	100	_____

GREEK MYTHS

1st Draft/Worksheet	10	_____
Handwriting	10	_____
Vocab. Usage	20	_____
Content (style, structure...)	30	_____
Mechanics (spell, punct...)	30	_____
Total	100	_____

GREEK MYTHS

1st Draft/Worksheet	10	_____
Handwriting	10	_____
Vocab. Usage	20	_____
Content (style, structure...)	30	_____
Mechanics (spell, punct...)	30	_____
Total	100	_____

GREEK MYTHS

1st Draft/Worksheet	10	_____
Handwriting	10	_____
Vocab. Usage	20	_____
Content (style, structure...)	30	_____
Mechanics (spell, punct...)	30	_____
Total	100	_____

GREEK MYTHS

1st Draft/Worksheet	10	_____
Handwriting	10	_____
Vocab. Usage	20	_____
Content (style, structure...)	30	_____
Mechanics (spell, punct...)	30	_____
Total	100	_____

GREEK MYTHS

1st Draft/Worksheet	10	_____
Handwriting	10	_____
Vocab. Usage	20	_____
Content (style, structure...)	30	_____
Mechanics (spell, punct...)	30	_____
Total	100	_____

Name: <u>Seth Bloomsburg</u>

Date: <u>January 12, 2000</u>

PANDORA

I. Vocabulary: Underline the following words in the myth and define them below.

- ○ vexation: <u>annoyance</u>
- ○ contrivance: <u>invention</u>
- ○ sage: <u>wise</u>
- ○ lamentable: <u>regrettable or mournful</u>
- ○ personage: <u>notable person</u>

II. Plot: Write a simple sentence or phrase to describe the main actions that take place in each scene.

THAT TEMPTING BOX	PANDORA GIVES IN	TROUBLES ESCAPE
1. Pandora enters cottage.	1. Pandora unties knot.	1. Pandora opens box.
2. Pandora sees box.	2. Epimetheus gathers flowers.	2. People are stung.
3. Epimetheus warns Pandora.	3. Epimetheus watches Pandora.	3. Hopes cures wounds.

III. Characters: List and briefly describe the main characters in this myth.

<u>Pandora: curious, unwise</u>

<u>Epimetheus: guilty, foolish</u>

<u>Hope: nice, diminutive</u>

IV. Rewrite this myth. Be sure to:

- ○ Include and underline all of the vocabulary words in your rewrite.
- ○ Write at least three separate paragraphs, one for each scene.
- ○ Include the following additional requirements:

PANDORA

(Rewritten by Seth Bloomsburg - 6th Grade)

There once lived a boy named Epimetheus, who was parentless. All he had was a box which he was told never to open. The box was beautifully crafted. Its lock was quite a contrivance; it was made of gold cord and the knot apparently had no end nor beginning. Anyway, there was another child named Pandora, who was likewise parentless. Pandora soon came to live in Epimetheus' house. Coming into the house, the box caught her eye. Epimetheus gave sage speeches telling her not to open the box. Living there with the box, though, made her vexations with it grow. She wished to open it more everyday. Angrily, she cursed it and called it ugly more than once.

Unfortunately, one day it got to be too much. She had to open it. Quietly she crept into Epimetheus' room and walked towards the box. She had barely touched the knot when, like magic, the cord untied itself. She tried to retie it, but to no avail. During this time Epimetheus was gathering flowers to make a wreath for Pandora's head. He was thinking of creeping in very quietly to surprise her, but he may as well have stomped through like a ragging storm for it would not have made a difference. She was so enraptured by the box that she didn't notice her surroundings. When he opened the door, he saw a very different sight than he anticipated. He saw that Pandora had untied the cord. Since he didn't even try to stop her from opening the box, he was probably just as guilty. She opened it.

The next moment something very lamentable happened. Swarms of vile, winged creatures spilled forth. Pandora instantly shut the box. Pandora and Epimetheus were both stung. One time Epimetheus saved Pandora by brushing a creature away. They were finally able to open some windows, hoping to get rid of the creatures, yet this only spread them throughout the world. These Troubles and Angers and Passions would wreak havoc on the world. Neither of the two smiled for days, but one day Pandora heard a knock on the lid of the box, with a voice saying, "Let me out!" "Should I open it?" Pandora asked. "You've already done so much damage. What difference could another evil make?" Epimetheus stated. So, Pandora opened the box and out came a small personage that looked like a fairy. "Who are you?" inquired Pandora. "I am Hope," the fairy said. Then it kissed Pandora on the head and touched Epimetheus' wounds and they were healed. "I was put in that box because it was destined to be opened someday and when it was I would heal the wounds of those afflicted by the evils. Sometimes it will seem that I have utterly vanished, but I'm always here."

PROMETHEUS

I

Prometheus was one of the Titans, a gigantic race who had fought with the gods of Olympus and were conquered. To him and his brother Epimetheus was committed the office of providing man and all the animals with the faculties necessary for their preservation. Jupiter, king of the gods, put a great store of gifts at their disposal, and Epimetheus at once set to work to allot these to the different animals while Prometheus overlooked and directed his work. Epimetheus accordingly proceeded to bestow upon the various animals the gifts of courage, strength, swiftness, sagacity, and patience. He gave wings to one, claws to another, a shell covering to a third. To some he gave teeth, to some beaks, and to some tusks. Each animal was endowed with characteristics as Epimetheus saw fit. Soon it became apparent that he had been too generous with the store entrusted to him by Jupiter. Great as the store had been, it was now exhausted; and man had not yet received his gift.

Prometheus regretted this error deeply. He longed to give man a gift worthy of his upright stature. He thought long of what he could bestow upon man, and at last a great and terrible idea came into his mind. "In the dwelling of the gods," he thought, "is the divine fire which helps to make them all-powerful. On the earth no fire exists; if only I could obtain some and bestow it upon men, all that I desire might be accomplished." Then he reminded himself, "Jupiter would never consent to give to man a portion of fire. I must not dream of such a thing."

Yet Prometheus could not drive the idea from his mind. By day and by night he brooded over it, debating how the fire could be obtained. Could he steal it from the abode of the gods? The very thought brought terror. Swift and merciless would be the vengeance of Jupiter on such a thief. Yet, once the fire was given to man, even Jupiter could not take it back. Man would be raised forever above the beasts. If this could be done it would not matter what tortures Jupiter would inflict. Would not the thought of his deed comfort him in his pain so that he would triumph still?

II

For many days Prometheus brooded over his great plan, until he quite lost sight of his own certain punishment in the splendid vision that rose before him of man inspired and ennobled by fire. At last he determined to undertake the great adventure. He chose a night when heavy clouds hung across the sky. In the thick darkness he set out, going softly and stealthily across the plains lest anyone should meet and question him. At the foot of Olympus he paused and looked upward to where he knew the shining city of the gods stood. Then with dogged courage he went up and up, climbing steadily until he passed through the dark enfolding clouds and stood in the clear and lovely light that shone upon the dwelling-place of the gods. Prometheus remembered the peril and greatness of his errand and wasted not another instant in gazing on the glories of that heavenly realm. Everything was quiet, and he could see no watchmen on the shining walls. Treading quickly and lightly for all his great stature, he passed into the city which none except the gods might enter, on pain of death.

In a moment he was out again, carrying a reed which he had lighted at the fire of the immortals. The great deed was done.

Back by the way he had come went Prometheus, guarding with fearful care that wavering flame. If anyone had seen that small point of light traveling through the night's blackness there would have been great marvel and questioning, for no light save that of the sun and moon and stars had ever shone on the earth. But none saw him, and he returned safely with the flame.

Yet Prometheus knew that he had not escaped and that his punishment was certain. It could not be long before Jupiter would discover that there was fire upon the earth and to find the thief would be an easy task. Then his swift and terrible bolt would fall. The assurance of this did not frighten Prometheus or lead him to extinguish the fire. He had counted the cost beforehand and was prepared to pay to the uttermost. Now he only felt a great desire to spread the fire through all the world.

So he began and labored without ceasing. He revealed to man the divine fire and showed him how it would help him in his work, how it would burn wood and melt metals and fashion tools, how it would cook food and make life bearable in the frozen days of winter, and how it would give light in darkness so that men might labor and travel in the night-time as well as by day.

And fire did also a greater work than all these. It gave inspiration and enthusiasm and urged men on to gain higher and greater things. The whole earth thrilled with man's activities, and in the midst moved Prometheus, teaching, guiding, opening out before men's delighted eyes fresh fields for effort and attainment.

Jupiter, being occupied with other things, looked but little upon the earth at that time, but there came a day when the points of light scattered over its surface caught his attention, and with a shock of terrible anger he realized that daring hands had stolen heaven's fire. In a voice that sent echoing thunders throughout the earth Jupiter made his accusation and heaven and earth trembled. Jupiter was certain that no mortal could have put his foot over the shining threshold of the gods, and very soon his suspicions rested on the mighty Titan Prometheus. Prometheus was summoned and appeared before him. "Who is it that has stolen fire from heaven?" thundered Jupiter; and the Titan calmly answered, "It is I."

III

Then the anger of Jupiter turned to fury, and he seized a thunderbolt to destroy the daring thief; but Prometheus stood so calmly, holding his head high and looking at death with such fearless eyes, that Jupiter dropped his bolt and asked in wonder, "Why did you do this thing?"

"Because," answered Prometheus, "I loved man; I longed to give him some gift that would raise him high above the brute creation. I knew of nought else that could do this save fire from heaven, and to ask the boon from you, O Jupiter, would have been to ask in vain. So I scaled the walls of your city and lit my reed at the flame, and now all over the earth fires are kindled. Not all your power can put out those fires or bring men back to the easy content which marks the beasts of the field."

As Jupiter listened to these proud words his fury died, and there came in its place a cold and bitter hatred of the being who had thus defied his power; so that he no longer thought of hurling a thunderbolt, deeming that it would bring a death too easy for the deserving of such a rebel. He wished to see Prometheus suffer slow and awful and unending tortures, that would not only wring his body but would seize on his proud spirit and lay it low in agony. So he called to his son, Vulcan, the god of the forge who had marvelous skill in the working of metals.

"Take this Titan, this Prometheus, and stretch him upon a rock and fasten him to it with chains that cannot be broken. There shall he lie through endless ages, and none shall succor him. Also I will send an eagle who each day shall devour his liver, causing him fearful torments; and each night the liver shall grow again, so that in the morning his sufferings may be renewed."

The gods of Olympus were used to Jupiter's fits of passion and to the terrible punishments that he ordered for those who resisted his will; but at this sentence, which condemned Prometheus to unending agony, even they were aghast. But the Titan himself stood calm and proud, never flinching as he heard the dreadful words.

"Let it be so, O tyrant," he said; "because you are strong you are merciless. My theft has done you no harm; there is still fire to spare on Olympus. Chain me to the rock and leave me to my cruel fate."

By this time Vulcan had come with his dusky servants, the Cyclopes, to carry out his father's will. Prometheus did not resist but allowed the god to bear him to his place of punishment. There they fastened him to the rock with chains that could not be broken, and left him to lie without shelter from the sun or the rain and with none to succor him through countless ages.

PROMETHEUS

I. Vocabulary: Underline the following words in the myth and define them below.

- sagacity: _? being wise have ing good jugement_
- ennobled: _Put higher in rank to a noble rank._
- realm: _Kingdom, a place that is owned by someone_
- succor: _? cumfort, or talk to_
- aghast: _suprised, amazed, confused._

II. Plot: Write a simple sentence or phrase to describe the main actions that take place in each scene.

GIFT FOR MAN?	THE CRIME COMMITTED	THE PUNISHMENT
1. fire	1. Stealing fire	1. chained to a rock
2.	2.	2. no food or water
3.	3.	3. torture

III. Characters: List and briefly describe the main characters in this myth.

Prometheus: a Titan, who is incharge of giving gifts to animals. Jupiter: The king of the Gods.
Man: the reciever of the gift of fire.
Vulcan: Jupiters son who craft chains to hold Prometheus.

IV. Rewrite this myth. Be sure to:

- Include and underline all of the vocabulary words in your rewrite.
- Write at least three separate paragraphs, one for each scene.
- Include the following additional requirements:

_____

_____

_____

_____

_____

PANDORA

I

Long, long ago, there was a child, named Epimetheus, who didn't have a father or mother; and, that he might not be lonely, another child, fatherless and motherless like himself, was sent from a far country to live with him and be his playfellow and helpmate. Her name was Pandora.

The first thing that Pandora saw, when she entered the cottage where Epimetheus dwelt, was a great box. And the first question which she put to him was this, "Epimetheus, what have you in that box?"

"My dear little Pandora," answered Epimetheus, "that is a secret, and you must be kind enough not to ask any questions about it. The box was left here to be kept safely, and I do not myself know what it contains."

"But who gave it to you?" asked Pandora. "And where did it come from?"

"That is a secret, too," replied Epimetheus.

"How provoking!" exclaimed Pandora. "I wish the great ugly box were out of the way!"

"Oh come, don't think of it any more," cried Epimetheus. "Let us run out of doors and play with the other children."

Pandora played for a while but when she came in there was the box. Every day Pandora's vexation with the box increased until the cottage of Epimetheus and Pandora was less sunshiny than those of other children.

"Whence can the box have come?" Pandora continually kept saying to herself and to Epimetheus. "And what in the world can be inside of it?"

One day, after Epimetheus had gone out to play, Pandora stood gazing at the box. She had called it ugly, above a hundred times; but, in spite of all that she had said against it, it was positively a very handsome article of furniture and would have been quite an ornament to any room in which it should be placed. It was made of a beautiful kind of wood, with dark and rich veins spreading over its surface, which was so highly polished that little Pandora could see her face in it.

The box, I had almost forgotten to say, was fastened, not by a lock nor by any other such contrivance, but by a very intricate knot of gold cord. There appeared to be no end to this knot, and no beginning. By the very difficulty that there was in it, Pandora was the more tempted to examine the knot and just see how it was made.

"I really believe," said she to herself, "that I begin to see how it was done. Nay, perhaps I could tie it up again, after undoing it. There would be no harm in that, surely. I need not open the box and should not, of course, without the consent of Epimetheus, even if the knot were untied."

It might have been better for Pandora if she had had a little work to do so as not to be so constantly thinking of this one subject. But children led so easy a life then that they had really a great deal too much leisure. When life is all sport, toil is the real play.

II

On this particular day, however, her curiosity grew so great that, at last, she approached the box. She was more than half determined to open it, if she could. Ah, naughty Pandora!

She took the golden knot in her fingers and pried into its intricacies as sharply as she could. Almost without intending it, or quite knowing what she was about, she was soon busily engaged in attempting to undo it. Then, by the merest accident, she gave the knot a kind of a twist, which produced a wonderful result. The gold cord untwined itself, as if by magic, and left the box without a fastening.

"This is the strangest thing I ever knew! " said Pandora. "What will Epimetheus say?"

She made one or two attempts to restore the knot but soon found it quite beyond her skill.

Nothing was to be done, therefore, but to let the box remain until Epimetheus should come in.

"But," said Pandora, "when he finds the knot untied, he will know that I have done it. How shall I make him believe that I have not looked into the box?"

And then the thought came into her naughty little heart, that, since she would be suspected of having looked into the box, she might just as well do so at once. Oh, foolish Pandora!

But it is now time for us to see what Epimetheus was doing.

Epimetheus had been playing with other children and at length judged it time to return home to Pandora. With a hope of giving her pleasure, he gathered some flowers and made them into a wreath which he meant to put upon Pandora's head.

Epimetheus entered the cottage softly; for he meant to steal behind Pandora and fling the wreath of flowers over her head before she should be aware of his approach. As it happened, there was no need of his treading so very lightly. He might have trod as heavily as he pleased, as heavily as an elephant, without much probability of Pandora's hearing his footsteps. She was too intent upon her purpose. At the moment of his entering the cottage, the naughty child had put her hand to the lid and was on the point of opening the mysterious box. Epimetheus beheld her. If he had cried out, Pandora would probably have withdrawn her hand, and the mystery of the box might never have been known.

But Epimetheus himself had his own share of curiosity to know what was inside. Perceiving that Pandora was resolved to find out the secret, he determined that his playfellow should not be the only wise person in the cottage. Thus, after all his sage speeches to Pandora about restraining her curiosity, Epimetheus turned out to be quite as foolish, and nearly as much in fault, as she.

III

Epimetheus watched as Pandora lifted the lid nearly upright and looked inside. It seemed as if a sudden swarm of winged creatures brushed past her, taking flight out of the box, while, at the same instant, she heard the voice of Epimetheus, with a lamentable tone, as if he were in pain.

"Oh, I am stung!" cried he. "Naughty Pandora! why have you opened this wicked box?"

Pandora let fall the lid and, starting up, looked about her to see what had befallen Epimetheus. She heard a disagreeable buzzing, as if a great many huge flies or gigantic mosquitoes were darting about. Then she saw a crowd of ugly little shapes, with bats' wings, looking abominably spiteful and armed with terribly long stings in their tails. It was one of these that had stung Epimetheus. Nor was it a great while before Pandora herself began to scream, in no less pain than her playfellow. An odious little monster had settled on her forehead and would have stung her if Epimetheus had not run and brushed it away.

Now, if you wish to know what these ugly things might be, which had made their escape out of the box, I must tell you that they were the whole family of earthly Troubles. There were evil Passions; a great many species of Cares; more than a hundred and fifty Sorrows; Diseases; and more kinds of Naughtiness than it would be of any use to talk about. In short, everything that has since afflicted the souls and bodies of mankind had been shut up in the mysterious box and given to Epimetheus and Pandora to be kept safely, in order that the world might never be molested by them. Had they been faithful to their trust, all would have gone well.

But these Troubles have obtained a foothold among us and do not seem very likely to be driven away in a hurry. For it was impossible, as you will easily guess, that the two children should keep the ugly swarm in their own little cottage. On the contrary, the first thing that they did was to fling open the doors and windows in hopes of getting rid of them; and, sure enough, away flew the winged Troubles all abroad and so pestered and tormented people everywhere, that none of them so much as smiled for many days afterwards.

Meanwhile, the naughty Pandora, and hardly less naughty Epimetheus, remained in their cottage. Both of them had been grievously stung and were in a good deal of pain.

Suddenly there was a gentle little tap on the inside of the lid.

"What can that be?" cried Pandora, lifting her head.

Again the tap! It sounded like the tiny knuckles of a fairy's hand knocking lightly and playfully on the inside of the box.

"Who are you?" asked Pandora with a little of her former curiosity. "Who are you inside of this naughty box?"

A sweet little voice spoke from within, "Only lift the lid, and you shall see."

And, indeed, there was a kind of cheerful witchery in the tone that made it almost impossible to refuse anything which this little voice asked.

"My dear Epimetheus," cried Pandora, "have you heard this little voice?"

"Yes, to be sure I have," answered he, but in no very good-humor as yet. "And what of it?"

"Shall I lift the lid again?" asked Pandora.

"Just as you please," said Epimetheus. " You have done so much mischief already, that perhaps you may as well do a little more. One other Trouble in such a swarm as you have set adrift about the world can make no very great difference."

So Pandora again lifted the lid. Out flew a sunny and smiling little personage. She flew to Epimetheus and laid the least touch of her finger on the inflamed spot where the Trouble had stung him, and immediately the anguish of it was gone. Then she kissed Pandora on the forehead, and her hurt was cured likewise.

After performing these good offices, the bright stranger fluttered sportively over the children's heads and looked so sweetly at them that they both began to think it not so very much amiss to have opened the box, since, otherwise, their cheery guest must have been kept a prisoner among those naughty imps with stings in their tails.

"Pray, who are you, beautiful creature?" inquired Pandora.

"I am to be called Hope!" answered the sunshiny figure. "And because I am such a cheery little body, I was packed into the box to make amends to the human race for that swarm of ugly Troubles which was destined to be let loose among them.

"And will you stay with us," asked Epimetheus, "forever and ever?"

"As long as you need me," said Hope with her pleasant smile. "There may come times and seasons when you will think that I have utterly vanished. But again and again, when you least dream of it, you shall see the glimmer of my wings on the ceiling of your cottage."

And so it is that, whatever evils are abroad, hope never entirely leaves us; and while we have that, no amount of other ills can make us completely wretched.

PANDORA

I. Vocabulary: Underline the following words in the myth and define them below.

- ☉ vexation: *Anger Annoying*
- ☉ contrivance: *invention.*
- ☉ sage: *wise*
- ☉ lamentable: *regrettable*
- ☉ personage: *notable person*

II. Plot: Write a simple sentence or phrase to describe the main actions that take place in each scene.

THAT TEMPTING BOX	PANDORA GIVES IN	TROUBLES ESCAPE
1. *Pandora arives*	1. *Pandora unties knot*	1. *Swarm around*
2. *Pandora sees box*	2. *Pandora tries to put back*	2. *sting People*
3. *Pandora is told not to open*	3. *Pandora opens box*	3. *Hope is discovered.*

III. Characters: List and briefly describe the main characters in this myth.

Pandora: naughty little girl who is parentless
Epimetheus: a boy who is also parentless
troubles: diseses, etc.
Hope: hope dhu.

IV. Rewrite this myth. Be sure to:

- ○ Include and underline all of the vocabulary words in your rewrite.
- ○ Write at least three separate paragraphs, one for each scene.
- ○ Include the following additional requirements:

_____

_____

_____

_____

_____

_____

APOLLO AND DAPHNE

I

One day after Apollo had killed the enormous serpent Python with his arrows, he was strolling through the woods and spied Cupid. Apollo noticed that the boy was playing with his bow and arrows; and, being himself elated with his recent victory over Python, he taunted him, "What have you to do with warlike weapons you young boy? Leave them for hands worthy of them. Be content with your torch, child, and kindle up your flames, as you call them, where you will, but presume not to meddle with my weapons with which I slew the great serpent."

Venus's boy heard these words and rejoined, "Your arrows may strike all things else, Apollo, but mine shall strike you."

II

So saying, he took his stand on a high rock and drew from his quiver two arrows of different workmanship, one to excite love, the other to repel it. The former was of gold and sharp pointed. Anyone struck with this arrow would fall in love with the first person he saw instantly. The second arrow was blunt and tipped with lead. A person struck with this arrow would run from love. With the leaden shaft he struck the nymph Daphne and with the golden one Apollo, through the heart. Forthwith the god was seized with love for the maiden, and she abhorred the thought of loving.

Her delight was in woodland sports and in the spoils of the chase. Lovers sought her, but she spurned them all. Her father, who was the river god Peneus, often said to her, "Daughter, you owe me a son-in-law; you owe me grandchildren." She would throw her arms around her father's neck and say, "Dearest father, grant me this favor, that I may always remain unmarried, like Diana." At last Peneus consented to help her avoid potential suitors and to never make her marry.

Now Apollo loved her and longed to obtain her for his wife. He followed her, but she fled, swifter than the wind, and delayed not a moment at his entreaties. "Stay," said he, "I am not a foe. Do not fly me as a lamb flies the wolf or a dove the hawk. It is for love I pursue you. You make me miserable, for fear you should fall and hurt yourself on these stones, and I should be the cause. Remember, I am no clown and no rude peasant. Jupiter is my father and I am the god of song and the lyre. My arrows fly true to the mark; but, alas! an arrow more fatal than mine has pierced my heart! I suffer a malady that no balm can cure!"

III

The nymph continued her flight and left his plea half uttered. And even as she fled she charmed him. The god grew impatient to find his wooings thrown away and gained upon her in the race. Her strength began to fail, and, ready to sink, she called upon her father the river god, "Help me, Father! open the earth to enclose me or change my form which has brought me into this danger!" Scarcely had she spoken when a stiffness seized all her limbs; her body began to be enclosed in a tender bark; her hair became leaves; her arms became branches; her foot stuck fast in the ground as a root; her face became a tree-top, retaining nothing of its former self but its beauty; Apollo stood amazed. He touched the stem and felt the flesh tremble under the new bark. He embraced the branches and kissed the wood. The branches shrank from his lips. "Since you cannot be my wife," said he, "you shall assuredly be my tree. I will wear you for my crown; I will use your wood for my harp and my quiver; and when the great Roman conquerors lead up the triumphal pomp to the Capitol, you shall be woven into wreaths for their brows. As eternal youth is mine, you also shall be always green, and your leaf know no decay." The nymph, now changed into a Laurel tree, bowed its head in grateful acknowledgment.

APOLLO AND DAPHNE

I. Vocabulary: Underline the following words in the myth and define them below.

- spied: _Saw_
- forthwith: _after? immediately after_
- potential: _might happen_
- entreaties: _pleadings_
- malady: ~~my lady~~ _sickness_

II. Plot: Write a simple sentence or phrase to describe the main actions that take place in each scene.

THE TAUNT	CUPID STRIKES	THE TRANSFORMATION
1. _Apollo sees cupid_	1. _Cupid talks_	1. _Apollo loves Daphne_
2. _Apollo taunts cupid_	2. _Cupid selects arows_	2. _Daphne hates love_
3. _Cupid is angry_	3. _Cupid shoots_	3. _Apollo chases Daphne_

III. Characters: List and briefly describe the main characters in this myth.

Apollo: God of song and lyre
Daphne: Apollos love the nymph
Cupid: boy who shoots Apollo and Daphne
Peneus: The river God Daphne's father.

IV. Rewrite this myth. Be sure to:

- Include and underline all of the vocabulary words in your rewrite.
- Write at least three separate paragraphs, one for each scene.
- Include the following additional requirements:

_____

_____

_____

_____

_____

_____

PYRAMUS AND THISBE

I

Pyramus was the handsomest youth and Thisbe the fairest maiden in all Babylonia. Their parents occupied adjoining houses. The neighborhood brought the young people together, and the acquaintance ripened into love. They would gladly have married, but their parents forbade it. One thing, however, they could not forbid - that love should glow with equal ardor in the bosoms of both. They conversed by signs and glances, and the fire burned more intensely for being covered up. In the wall that parted the two houses there was a crack, caused by some fault in the structure. No one had remarked it before, but the lovers discovered it. What will not love discover! It afforded a passage to the voice; and tender messages used to pass backward and forward through the gap. As they stood, Pyramus on this side, Thisbe on that, their breaths would mingle. "Cruel wall," they said, "why do you keep two lovers apart? But we will not be ungrateful. We owe you, we confess, the privilege of transmitting loving words to willing ears." Such words they uttered on different sides of the wall; and when night came and they had to say farewell, they pressed their lips upon the wall, she on her side, he on his, as they could come no nearer.

II

One morning, when Aurora had put out the stars and the sun had melted the frost from the grass, they met at their accustomed spot. Then, after lamenting their hard fate, they agreed that the next night, when all was still, they would slip away from watchful eyes, leave their dwellings, and walk out into the fields. To insure a meeting, they would meet at a well-known edifice standing without the city's bounds, called the Tomb of Ninus, and the one who came first would await the other at the foot of a certain tree. It was a white mulberry tree and stood near a cool spring. All was agreed on, and they waited impatiently for the sun to go down beneath the waters and night to rise up from them. Then cautiously Thisbe stole forth, unobserved by the family, her head covered with a veil, made her way to the monument, and sat down under the tree. As she sat alone in the dim light of the evening she descried a lioness, her jaws reeking with recent slaughter, approaching the fountain to slake her thirst. Thisbe fled at the sight and sought refuge in the hollow of a rock. As she fled she dropped her veil. The lioness, after drinking at the spring, turned to retreat to the woods and, seeing the veil on the ground, tossed and rent it with her bloody mouth.

III

Pyramus, having been delayed, now approached the place of meeting. He saw in the sand the footsteps of the lion and the color fled from his cheeks at the sight. Presently he found the veil all rent and bloody. "O hapless girl," said he, "I have been the cause of thy death! Thou, more worthy of life than I, hast fallen the first victim. I will follow. I am the guilty cause, in tempting thee forth to a place of such peril and not being myself on the spot to guard thee. Come forth, ye lions, from the rocks and tear this guilty body with your teeth." He took up the veil, carried it with him to the appointed tree, and covered it with kisses and with tears. "My blood also shall stain your texture," said he and, drawing his sword, plunged it into his heart. The blood spurted from the wound and tinged the white mulberries of the tree all red; and sinking into the earth reached the roots so that the red color mounted through the trunk to the fruit.

By this time Thisbe, still trembling with fear yet wishing not to disappoint her lover, stepped cautiously forth, looking anxiously for the youth, eager to tell him the danger she had escaped. When she came to the spot and saw the changed color of the mulberries she doubted whether it was the same place. While she hesitated she saw the form of one struggling in the agonies of death. She started back, a shudder ran through her frame as a ripple on the face of the still water when a sudden breeze sweeps over it. But as soon as she recognized her lover, she screamed and beat her breast, embracing the lifeless body, pouring tears into its wounds, and imprinting kisses on the cold lips. "O Pyramus," she cried, "what has done this? Answer me, Pyramus; it is your own Thisbe that speaks. Hear me, dearest, and lift that drooping head!" At the name of Thisbe Pyramus opened his eyes then closed them again. She saw her veil stained with blood and the scabbard empty of its sword. "Thy own hand has slain thee, and for my sake," she said. "I too can be brave for once, and my love is as strong as thine. I will follow thee in death, for I have been the cause; and death which alone could part us shall not prevent my joining thee. And ye, unhappy parents of us both, deny us not our united request. As love and death have joined us, let one tomb contain us. And thou, tree, retain the marks of slaughter. Let thy berries still serve for memorials of our blood. " So saying she plunged the sword into her breast. Her parents ratified her wish; the gods also ratified it. The two bodies were buried in one sepulcher, and the tree ever after brought forth purple berries, as it does to this day.

Name: Emily Stiles

Date: 4-8-19

PYRAMUS AND THISBE

I. Vocabulary: Underline the following words in the myth and define them below.

- ① lamenting: ?? mourn
- ② edifice: place large building
- ③ descried: saw? catch sight of
- ④ scabbard: sword holder - sheath?
- ⑤ sepulchre: Tomb?

II. Plot: Write a simple sentence or phrase to describe the main actions that take place in each scene.

LOVE DENIED	THISBE ARRIVES	THE DEATHS
1. Thisbe meets Pyramus.	1. They are to meet at a tomb	1. Pyramus sees a bloodie veil
2. They fall in love	2. Thisbe sit under a white mullbeery	2. Ausums Thisbe is dead and kills himself
3. The parents denie their marriage.	3. Thisbe sees a liones and hides.	3. Thisbe sees dead pyramus and also killsself.

III. Characters: List and briefly describe the main characters in this myth.

Pyramus: loves Thisbe, very handsom. Thisbe: loves Pyramus - very pretty. Parents of both: wont let them marry. Lioness: scares Thisbe, and plays with her vail.

IV. Rewrite this myth. Be sure to:

○ Include and underline all of the vocabulary words in your rewrite.

○ Write at least three separate paragraphs, one for each scene.

○ Include the following additional requirements:

PAN

I

Pan was the son of Mercury and Penelope, a nymph of the woods. When he was a tiny, newborn baby he was such a curious little creature that his mother ran away from him in fear. His body was covered with fur; and he had little, furry, pointed ears, a tail, and feet like the hoofs of a goat.

II

His father carried him up to Olympus to show him to the gods, and they were all delighted with him. They laughed at him and praised his quaint ways and his funny bounding movements. But Pan did not care to dwell on Olympus; he loved better the woodland places of the earth where he could wander freely and sport with the satyrs and fauns and forest nymphs and startle travelers by jumping out upon them from behind a tree and dance and sing through the long sunny days.

III

Once he loved a nymph named Syrinx, but she, frightened at his curious appearance, fled from him in terror. He followed her, his hoofed feet pattering on the ground. Coming to the banks of a river, Syrinx called piteously upon the water nymphs to help her. They heard and hurried to her assistance so that Pan, coming up and clasping what he thought was his loved Syrinx, found that he was embracing a tuft of reeds. He sighed deeply, and his sigh breathed through the reeds, brining out from them a sweet, low sound. "I will at least have something that will remind me of my love," he said. He cut seven pieces of different lengths from the reeds and fashioned them into a pipe which was called the Syrinx pipes and on which he played the most delightful music.

PAN

I. Vocabulary: Underline the following words in the myth and define them below.

- ○ nymph:_____
- ○ quaint:_____
- ○ bounding:_____
- ○ satyrs:_____
- ○ piteously:_____

II. Plot: Write a simple sentence or phrase to describe the main actions that take place in each scene.

PAN BORN	MT. OLYMPUS	ADVENTURE WITH SYRINX
1._____	1._____	1._____
2._____	2._____	2._____
3._____	3._____	3._____

III. Characters: List and briefly describe the main characters in this myth.

_____

_____

_____

_____

IV. Rewrite this myth. Be sure to:

- ○ Include and underline all of the vocabulary words in your rewrite.
- ○ Write at least three separate paragraphs, one for each scene.
- ○ Include the following additional requirements:

_____

_____

_____

_____

_____

_____

IO

I

Juno one day perceived it suddenly grow dark and suspected that her husband had raised a cloud to hide some of his doings. She brushed away the cloud and saw her husband on the banks of a glassy river with a beautiful heifer standing near him. Juno suspected the heifer's form concealed some fair nymph of mortal mold - as was, indeed, the case; for it was Io, whom Jupiter had been conversing with. When he became aware of the approach of his wife, he had changed her into a cow.

Juno joined her husband and, noticing the heifer, praised its beauty and asked whose it was and of what herd. Jupiter, to stop questions, replied that it was a fresh creation from the earth. Juno asked to have it as a gift. What could Jupiter do? He was loath to give Io to his wife; yet how could he refuse so trifling a present as a simple heifer? He could not, without exciting suspicion, so he consented. The goddess was not yet relieved of her suspicions; so she delivered the heifer into the charge of Argus, to be strictly watched.

II

Now Argus was a giant who had a hundred eyes in his head and never went to sleep with more than two at a time, so that he kept watch of Io constantly. He suffered her to feed through the day and at night tied her up with a vile rope round her neck. She would have stretched out her arms to implore freedom of Argus, but she had no arms to stretch out, and her voice was a bellow that frightened even herself. She saw her father and her sisters, went near them, and suffered them to pat her back and heard them admire her beauty. Her father reached to her with a tuft of grass, and she licked the outstretched hand. She longed to make herself known to him and would have uttered her wish; but, alas! words were wanting. At length she bethought herself of writing and inscribed her name - it was a short one - with her hoof on the sand. Her father recognized it and, discovering that his daughter whom he had long sought in vain was hidden under this disguise, mourned over her and, embracing her white neck, exclaimed, "Alas! my daughter, it would have been a less grief to have lost you altogether!" While he thus lamented, Argus, observing, came and drove Io away and took his seat on a high bank from whence he could see all round in every direction.

Jupiter was troubled at beholding the sufferings of Io and at last called Mercury and bade him to try to make a plan to rescue the maiden. Mercury made haste, put his winged slippers on his feet and cap on his head, took his sleep-producing wand, and leaped down from the heavenly towers to the earth. There he laid aside his wings and kept only his wand, with which he presented himself as a shepherd driving his flock. As he approached the place where Argus sat watching the white heifer, Mercury blew upon his pipes. Argus listened to the Syrinx pipes with delight, for he had never seen the instrument before. "Young man," said he, "come and take a seat by me on this stone. There is no better place for your flocks to graze in than hereabouts, and here is a pleasant shade such as shepherds love." Mercury sat down, talked, told stories till it grew late, and played upon his pipes his most soothing strains, hoping to lull the watchful eyes to sleep, but all in vain; for Argus still contrived to keep some of his eyes open though he shut the rest.

III

Mercury droned on and on telling the story of how Pan had invented the Syrinx whose music had charmed Argus a little while before. Before Mercury had finished his story he saw with delight that all Argus's eyes slept. As his head nodded forward on his breast, Mercury with one stroke cut his neck through, and his head tumbled down the rocks. Mercury did not stay to triumph but bounded toward the white heifer and began to lead her quickly away. Swift as his movements had been, they had not been swift enough to outwit Juno. From Olympus she had seen the slaying of Argus, and now she sent a gadfly to torment Io, who fled over the whole world from its pursuit. She swam through the Ionian Sea, which derived its name from her, then roamed from country to country till she crossed the Thracian Strait, thence named the Bosphorus. She rambled on till at last she arrived on the banks of the Nile. At length Jupiter interceded for her, and upon his promising not to pay her any more attentions Juno consented to restore her to her form. It was curious to see her gradually recover her former self. The coarse hairs fell from her body, her horns shrank up, her eyes grew narrower, her mouth shorter; hands and fingers came instead of hoofs to her forefeet; in time there was nothing left of the heifer, except her beauty. At first she was afraid to speak, for fear she should low, but gradually she recovered her confidence and was restored to her father and sisters. As for Argus, who had met such a sad fate in her service, his hundred eyes were taken by Hera and set in the tail of the peacock; and she took this bird as her emblem in memory of her faithful servant.

IO

I. Vocabulary: Underline the following words in the myth and define them below.

○ loath:_____

○ trifling:_____

○ lull:_____

○ contrived:_____

○ droned:_____

II. Plot: Write a simple sentence or phrase to describe the main actions that take place in each scene.

IO TRANSFORMED	ARGUS WATCHES	THE RESCUE
1._____	1._____	1._____
2._____	2._____	2._____
3._____	3._____	3._____

III. Characters: List and briefly describe the main characters in this myth.

_____

_____

_____

_____

IV. Rewrite this myth. Be sure to:

○ Include and underline all of the vocabulary words in your rewrite.

○ Write at least three separate paragraphs, one for each scene.

○ Include the following additional requirements:

_____

_____

_____

_____

_____

_____

CALLISTO

I

Jupiter, king of the gods, once admired the young maiden Callisto, who enjoyed hunting and was a companion of Diana in the mountains of Arcadia.   Jupiter's wife Juno heard this and was jealous of Callisto. Soon Juno set out to find her rival. When she found Callisto, Juno exclaimed, "So, my husband admires your beauty. Let us see if he still likes you this way!"

With that Callisto fell on her hands and knees; she tried to stretch out her arms in supplication but they were already beginning to be covered with black hair. Her hands grew rounded, became armed with crooked claws, and served for feet; her mouth became a horrid pair of jaws; her voice, which if unchanged would have moved the heart to pity, became a growl more fit to inspire terror. The transformation was complete - Callisto was no longer a beautiful maiden. She was a bear.

When Callisto went home to her son Arcas she tried to reveal herself to him but he screamed in terror and ran away. The worst of it was that her former disposition remained, and with continual groaning, she bemoaned her fate and stood upright as well as she could. Ah, how often, afraid to stay in the woods all night alone, she wandered about the neighborhood of her former haunts; how often, frightened by the dogs, did she, so lately a huntress, fly in terror from the hunters! Often she fled from the wild beasts, forgetting that she was now a wild beast herself, and, bear as she was, was afraid of the bears.

II

One day a handsome youth espied her as he was hunting. She saw him and recognized him as her own son, Arcas, now grown a young man. She stopped and felt inclined to embrace him. As she was about to approach, he, thinking that the bear was about to attack, raised his hunting spear. Arcas was on the point of hurling the spear at her, when Jupiter stopped the crime, by turning Arcas into a bear also. Then Jupiter grabbed each bear by the tail and flung them into the sky, placing them in the heavens. (This tugging of the tails by Jupiter explains why the celestial bears have long tails, unlike the bears that we have here on earth.)

III

Juno was in a rage to see her rival set in honor, so she hastened to ancient Tethys and Oceanus, the powers of the ocean. In answer to their inquiries she thus told the cause of her coming. "Do you ask why I, the queen of the gods, have left the heavenly plains and sought your depths? Learn that I am supplanted in heaven- my place is given to another. You will hardly believe me; but look when night darkens the world, and you shall see why I have so much reason to complain. Why should any one hereafter tremble at the thought of offending Juno when a place in the heavens is the reward of my displeasure? See what I have been able to effect! I forbade her to wear the human form- she is placed among the stars! So do my punishments result! Better that she should have resumed her former shape. If you feel for me and see with displeasure this unworthy treatment of me, show it, I beseech you, by forbidding this couple from coming into your waters."

The powers of the ocean assented and consequently the Great and Little Bear are the only two constellations that move round and round in heaven but never sink, as the other stars do, beneath the ocean.

CALLISTO

I. Vocabulary: Underline the following words in the myth and define them below.

○ rival:_____

○ supplication:_____

○ disposition:_____

○ espied:_____

○ assented:_____

II. Plot: Write a simple sentence or phrase to describe the main actions that take place in each scene.

THE TRANSFORMATION	CONSTELLATIONS	JUNO'S REVENGE
1._____	1._____	1._____
2._____	2._____	2._____
3._____	3._____	3._____

III. Characters: List and briefly describe the main characters in this myth.

_____

_____

_____

_____

IV. Rewrite this myth. Be sure to:

○ Include and underline all of the vocabulary words in your rewrite.

○ Write at least three separate paragraphs, one for each scene.

○ Include the following additional requirements:

_____

_____

_____

_____

_____

_____

_____

PHAETON

I

Phaeton was the son of Apollo and the nymph Clymene. One day a schoolfellow laughed at the idea of his being the son of the god, and Phaeton went in rage and reported it to his mother. "If," said he, "I am indeed of heavenly birth, give me, Mother, some proof of it and establish my claim to the honor." Clymene stretched forth her hands towards the skies and said, "I call to witness the Sun, which looks down upon us, that I have told you the truth. Go and inquire for yourself and demand of Apollo whether he will own you as a son." Phaeton heard this with delight. Full of hope, he traveled to the regions of sunrise.

The palace of the Sun stood reared aloft on columns, glittering with gold and precious stones. Over all was carved the likeness of the glorious heaven; and on the silver doors the twelve signs of the zodiac, six on each side.

Phaeton advanced up the steep ascent and entered the halls of his disputed father. He approached the paternal presence but stopped at a distance, for the light was more than he could bear. Apollo sat on a throne which glittered as with diamonds. On his right hand and his left stood the Day, the Month, and the Year, and, at regular intervals, the Hours. Spring, Summer, Autumn, and Winter also stood in attention. Surrounded by these attendants, Apollo beheld the youth, dazzled with the novelty and splendor of the scene, and inquired the purpose of his errand. The youth replied, "O light of the boundless world, Apollo, my father, if you permit me to use that name, give me some proof, I beseech you, by which I may be known as yours."

II

He ceased; and his father, laying aside the beams that shone all around his head, bade him approach and said, "My son, you deserve not to be disowned, and I confirm what your mother has told you. To put an end to your doubts, ask what you will, the gift shall be yours." Phaeton immediately asked to be permitted for one day to drive the chariot of the sun.

The father repented of his promise; thrice and four times he shook his radiant head in warning. "I have spoken rashly," said he; "this only request I would fain deny. I beg you to withdraw it. It is not a safe boon, nor one, my Phaeton, suited to your youth and strength. Your lot is mortal, and you ask what is beyond a mortal's power. In your ignorance you aspire to do that which not even the gods themselves may do. None but myself may drive the flaming car of day. The first part of the way is steep and such as the horses can hardly climb; the middle is high up in the heavens, whence I myself can scarcely, without alarm, look down and behold the earth and sea stretched beneath me. The last part of the road descends rapidly and requires most careful driving. Add to all this, the heaven is all the time turning round and carrying the stars with it. Suppose I should lend you the chariot, what would you do? Could you keep your course while the sphere was revolving under you? You will not find it easy to guide those horses. I can scarcely govern them myself. Beware, my son, lest I be the donor of a fatal gift; recall your request while yet you may. Do you ask me for a proof that you are sprung from my blood? I give you a proof in my fears for you. Finally," he continued, "look round the world and choose whatever you will of what earth or sea contains, ask it and fear no refusal. This only I pray you not to urge. It is not honor but destruction you seek. Why do you hang round my neck and still entreat me? You shall have it if you persist, the oath is sworn and must be kept, but I beg you to choose more wisely."

He ended; but the youth rejected all admonition and held to his demand. So, having resisted as long as he could, Apollo at last led the way to where stood the lofty chariot.

It was of gold, the gift of Vulcan; and the seats were covered with diamonds to reflect the brightness of the sun. While the daring youth gazed in admiration, the early Dawn threw open the purple doors of the east and showed the pathway strewn with roses. Then stars withdrew. Apollo, when he saw the earth beginning to glow, ordered the Hours to harness up the horses. They obeyed and led forth from the lofty stalls the Steeds and attached the reins. Then the father bathed the face of his son with a powerful unguent and made him capable of enduring the brightness of the flame. He set the rays on his head and, with a foreboding sigh, said, "If, my son, you will in this at least heed my advice, spare the whip and hold tight the reins. They go fast enough of their own accord; the labor is to hold them in. Keep within the limit of the middle zone and avoid the northern and the southern alike. You will see the marks of the wheels, and they will serve to guide you. That the skies and the earth may each receive their due share of heat, go not too high, or you will burn the heavenly dwellings, nor too low, or you will set the earth on fire; the middle course is safest and best. And now I leave you to your chance. We can delay no longer. Take the reins; but if at last your heart fails you, stay where you are in safety and suffer me to light and warm the earth." The agile youth sprang into the chariot, stood erect, and grasped the reins while pouring out thanks to his reluctant parent.

III

Meanwhile the horses filled the air with their snorting and stomped the ground impatiently. Then the bars were let down and the boundless plain of the universe lay open before them. The horses darted forward and outran the morning breezes. Soon the steeds perceived that the load they drew was lighter than usual; and as a ship without ballast is tossed hither and thither on the sea, so the chariot, without its accustomed weight, was dashed about as if empty. They ran headlong and left the traveled road.

When hapless Phaeton looked down upon the earth, now spreading in vast extent beneath him, he grew pale and his knees shook with terror. He wished he had never touched his father's horses, never learned his parentage, never prevailed in his request. He was born along like a vessel that flies before a tempest when the pilot can do no more and betakes himself to his prayers. What should he do? Much of the heavenly road was left behind, but more remained before. Phaeton knew not what to do, whether to draw tight the reins or throw them loose. He saw with terror the monstrous forms scattered over the surface of heaven. In fear the reins fell from his hands. The horses, when they felt them loose on their backs, dashed headlong and unrestrained went off into unknown regions of the sky. The clouds began to smoke, and the mountain tops took fire; the fields were parched with heat, the plants withered, the tree branches burned, the harvest was ablaze! But these were small things. Great cities perished with their walls and towers; whole nations with their people were consumed to ashes!

Then Phaeton beheld the world on fire and felt the heat intolerable. He dashed forward he knew not whither. Then, it is believed, the people of AEthiopia became black by the blood being forced so suddenly to the surface, and the Libyan desert was dried up to the condition in which it remains to this day. Where before was water, it became a dry plain; and the mountains that laid beneath the waves lifted up their heads and became islands. The fish sought the lowest depths, and the dolphins no longer ventured to sport on the surface. Earth, screening her face with her hand, looked up to heaven and, with a husky voice, called on Jupiter: "O ruler of the gods, if I have deserved this treatment and it is your will that I perish with fire, why withhold your thunderbolts? Let me at least fall by your hand. Is this the reward of my fertility, of my service? But if I am unworthy of regard, what has my brother Ocean done to deserve such a fate? Save what yet remains of us from the devouring flame. Take thought for our deliverance in this awful moment!"

Thus spoke Earth and, overcome with heat and thirst, could say no more. Then Jupiter called to witness all the gods, including him who had lent the chariot, and showed them that all was lost unless some speedy remedy were applied. Then he mounted the lofty tower and brandishing a lightning bolt in his right hand launched it against the charioteer and struck him at the same moment from his seat and from existence! Phaeton, with his hair on fire, fell headlong, like a shooting star which marks the heavens with its brightness as it falls, and Eridanus, the great river, received him and cooled his burning frame.

His sisters, the Heliades, as they lamented his fate, were turned into poplar trees on the banks of the river, and their tears, which continued to flow, became amber as they dropped into the stream.

Phaeton had a true friend named Cygnus. Upon hearing of Phaeton's death, Cygnus traveled to the Eridanus. There he plunged himself into the waters repeatedly and swam back and forth trying to find Phaeton's body. Cygnus' diving so resembled the motions of a swan searching for food that, when Cygnus had died of grief, the gods raised him to the skies.

PHAETON

I. Vocabulary: Underline the following words in the myth and define them below.

- ○ ascent:_____

- ○ unguent:_____

- ○ hapless:_____

- ○ prevailed:_____

- ○ brandishing:_____

II. Plot: Write a simple sentence or phrase to describe the main actions that take place in each scene.

PHAETON MEETS FATHER	PHAETON ASKS PERMISSION	FATAL JOURNEY
1._____	1._____	1._____
2._____	2._____	2._____
3._____	3._____	3._____

III. Characters: List and briefly describe the main characters in this myth.

_____

_____

_____

_____

IV. Rewrite this myth. Be sure to:

- ○ Include and underline all of the vocabulary words in your rewrite.

- ○ Write at least three separate paragraphs, one for each scene.

- ○ Include the following additional requirements:

_____

_____

_____

_____

_____

_____

KING MIDAS - THE GOLDEN TOUCH

I

Once upon a time there lived a very rich man, and a king besides, whose name was Midas; and he had a little daughter whose name I have entirely forgotten. So, because I love odd names for little girls, I choose to call her Marygold.

This King Midas was fonder of gold than of anything else in the world. If he loved anything better, or half so well, it was the one little maiden who played so merrily around her father's footstool. But the more Midas loved his daughter, the more did he desire and seek for wealth. He thought that the best thing he could possibly do for this dear child would be to bequeath her the largest pile of yellow, glistening coin, that had ever been heaped together since the world was made. Thus, he gave all his thoughts and all his time to this one purpose. When little Marygold ran to met him with a bunch of buttercups and dandelions, he used to say, "Poh, poh, child! If these flowers were as golden as they look, they would be worth the plucking!"

At length (as people always grow more and more foolish, unless they take care to grow wiser and wiser), Midas had got to be so exceedingly unreasonable that he could scarcely hear to see or touch any object that was not gold. He made it his custom, therefore, to pass a large portion of every day in a dark and dreary apartment, underground, at the basement of his palace. It was here that he kept his wealth. Here, after carefully locking the door, he would bring his gold from the obscure corners of the room into the one bright and narrow sunbeam that fell from the dungeon-like window. He valued the sunbeam for no other reason but that his treasure would not shine without its help.

Midas called himself a happy man but felt that he was not yet quite so happy as he might be. The very tiptop of enjoyment would never be reached, unless the whole world were to become his treasure-room and be filled with yellow metal which should be all his own.

Midas was enjoying himself in his treasure-room one day, as usual, when he perceived a shadow fall over the heaps of gold; and, looking suddenly up, what should he behold but the figure of a stranger standing in the bright and narrow sunbeam! It was a young man with a cheerful and ruddy face.

As Midas knew that he had carefully turned the key in the lock and that no mortal strength could possibly break into his treasure-room, he, of course, concluded that his visitor must be something more than mortal. The stranger's aspect, indeed, was so good-humored and kindly, if not beneficent, that it would have been unreasonable to suspect him of intending any mischief. It was far more probable that he came to do Midas a favor. And what could that favor be unless to multiply his heaps of treasure?

The stranger gazed about the room; and when his lustrous smile had glistened upon all the golden objects that were there, he turned again to Midas.

"You are a wealthy man, friend Midas!" he observed. "I doubt whether any other four walls on earth contain so much gold as you have contrived to pile up in this room."

"I have done pretty well – pretty well," answered Midas, in a discontented tone. "But, after all, it is but a trifle when you consider that it has taken me my whole life to get it together.

"What!" exclaimed the stranger. "Then you are not satisfied?"

Midas shook his head.

"And pray what would satisfy you?" asked the stranger.

Midas paused and meditated. He felt that this stranger, with such a golden luster in his good-humored smile, had come hither to gratify his utmost wishes. So he thought and thought and thought. At last a bright idea occurred to King Midas. Raising his head, he looked the lustrous stranger in the face.

"Well, Midas," observed his visitor, "I see that you have at length hit upon something that will satisfy you. Tell me your wish."

"It is only this," replied Midas. "I wish everything that I touch to be changed to gold!"

The stranger's smile grew so very broad that it seemed to fill the room like an outburst of the sun. "The Golden Touch!" exclaimed he. "You certainly deserve credit, friend Midas, for striking out so brilliant a conception. But are you quite sure that this will satisfy you?"

"How could it fail?" said Midas.

"And will you never regret the possession of it?"

"What could induce me?" asked Midas. "I ask nothing else to render me perfectly happy."

"Be it as you wish, then," replied the stranger, waving his hand in token of farewell. "Tomorrow, at sunrise, you will find yourself gifted with the Golden Touch."

The figure of the stranger then became exceedingly bright, and Midas involuntarily closed his eyes. On opening them again, he beheld only one yellow sunbeam in the room and, all around him, the glistening of the precious metal which he had spent his life in hoarding up.

II

Whether Midas slept as usual that night, the story does not say. At any rate, day had hardly peeped over the hills when King Midas was broad awake and, stretching his arms out of bed, began to touch the objects that were within reach. He seized one of the bed-posts, and it became immediately a fluted golden pillar. He hurriedly put on his clothes and was enraptured to see himself in a magnificent suit of gold cloth which retained its flexibility and softness, although it burdened him a little with its weight.

Wise King Midas was so exalted by his good fortune that the palace seemed not sufficiently spacious to contain him. He, therefore, went down into the garden. Here, as it happened, he found a great number of beautiful roses in full bloom. Very delicious was their fragrance in the morning breeze.

But Midas knew a way to make them far more precious, according to his way of thinking, than roses had ever been before. So he took great pains in going from bush to bush, and exercised his magic touch most indefatigably; until every individual flower and bud were changed to gold. By the time this good work was completed, King Midas was summoned to breakfast; and, as the morning air had given him an excellent appetite, he made haste back to the palace.

Little Marygold had not yet made her appearance. Her father ordered her to be called and, seating himself at the table, awaited the child's coming, in order to begin his own breakfast. To do Midas justice, he really loved his daughter and loved her so much the more this morning on account of the good fortune which had befallen him. It was not a great while before he heard her coming along the passageway crying bitterly. This circumstance surprised him because Marygold was one of the most cheerful little people whom you would see in a summer's day and hardly shed a thimbleful of tears in a twelvemonth.

Finally Marygold slowly and disconsolately opened the door and showed herself with her apron at her eyes, still sobbing as if her heart would break.

"How now, my little lady!" cried Midas. "Pray what is the matter with you this bright morning?"

Marygold, without taking the apron from her eyes, held out her hand, in which was one of the roses which Midas had so recently transmuted.

"Beautiful!" exclaimed her father. "And what is there in this magnificent golden rose to make you cry?"

"Ah, dear father!" answered the child, as well as her sobs would let her; "it is not beautiful, but the ugliest flower that ever grew! As soon as I was dressed I ran into the garden to gather some roses for you because I know you like them. But, oh dear, dear me! What do you think has happened? Such a misfortune! All the beautiful roses that smelled so sweetly are blighted and spoilt! They are grown quite yellow, as you see this one, and have no longer any fragrance! What can have been the matter with them?"

"Poh, my dear little girl – pray don't cry about it!" said Midas, who was ashamed to confess that he himself had wrought the change which so greatly afflicted her. "Sit down and eat your bread and milk. You will find it easy enough to exchange a golden rose like that (which will last hundreds of years) for an ordinary one which would wither in a day."

"I don't care for such roses as this!" cried Marygold, tossing it contemptuously away. "It has no smell, and the hard petals prick my nose!"

The child now sat down to table. Midas, meanwhile, had poured out a cup of coffee, and, as a matter of course, the coffee-pot was gold when he set it down. He thought to himself that it was rather an extravagant style of splendor to breakfast off a service of gold and began to be puzzled with the difficulty of keeping his treasures safe. The cupboard and the kitchen would no longer be a secure place of deposit for articles so valuable as golden bowls and coffee pots.

Amid these thoughts, he lifted a spoonful of coffee to his lips and, sipping it, was astonished to perceive that, the instant his lips touched the liquid, it became molten gold and, the next moment, hardened into a lump!

"Ha!" exclaimed Midas, rather aghast.

"What is the matter, father?" asked little Marygold, gazing at him with the tears still standing in her eyes.

"Nothing, child, nothing!" said Midas. "Eat your milk before it gets quite cold."

He took one of the nice little trouts on his plate and, by way of experiment, touched its tail with his finger. To his horror, it was immediately transmuted from an admirably fried brook-trout into a gold-fish, though not one of those gold-fishes which people often keep live in glass globes.

"I don't quite see," thought he to himself, "how I am to get any breakfast!"

He took one of the smoking-hot cakes and had scarcely broken it, when, to his cruel mortification, though, a moment before, it had been of the whitest wheat, it assumed the yellow hue of Indian meal. Almost in despair, he helped himself to a boiled egg which immediately underwent a change similar to those of the trout and the cake.

"Well, this is a quandary!" thought he, leaning back in his chair and looking quite enviously at little Marygold, who was now eating her bread and milk with great satisfaction. "Such a costly breakfast before me, and nothing that can be eaten!"

Hoping that, by dint of great dispatch, he might avoid what he now felt to be a considerable inconvenience, King Midas next snatched a hot potato and attempted to cram it into his mouth and swallow it in a hurry. But the Golden Touch was too nimble for him. He found his mouth full, not of mealy potato, but of solid metal, which so burnt his tongue that he roared aloud and, jumping up from the table, began to dance and stamp about the room, both with pain and affright.

"Father, dear father!" cried little Marygold, who was a very affectionate child, "pray what is the matter? Have you burnt your mouth?"

"Ah, dear child," groaned Midas, "I don't know what is to become of your poor father!"

King Midas had began to doubt whether, after all, riches are the one desirable thing in the world, or even the most desirable. So great was his hunger and the perplexity of his situation, that he again groaned aloud, and very grievously too. Our pretty Marygold could endure it no longer. She sat a moment, gazing at her father, and trying, with all the might of her little wits, to find out what was the matter with him. Then, with a sweet and sorrowful impulse to comfort him, she started from her chair and, running to Midas, threw her arms affectionately about his knees. He bent down and kissed her. He felt that his little daughter's love was worth a thousand times more than he had gained by the Golden Touch.

"My precious, precious Marygold!" cried he.

But Marygold made no answer.

Alas, what had he done? How fatal was the gift which the stranger bestowed! The moment the lips of Midas touched Marygold's forehead, a change had taken place. Her sweet, rosy face assumed a glittering yellow color, with yellow tear-drops congealing on her cheeks. Her beautiful brown ringlets took the same tint. Her soft and tender little form grew hard and inflexible within her father's encircling arms. Oh, terrible misfortune! The victim of his insatiable desire for wealth, little Marygold was a human child no longer, but a golden statue!

It had been a favorite phrase of Midas, whenever he felt particularly fond of the child, to say that she was worth her weight in gold. And now the phrase had become literally true. And now, at last, when it was too late, he felt how infinitely a warm and tender heart that loved him exceeded in value all the wealth that could be piled up betwixt the earth and sky!

It would be too sad a story, if I were to tell you how Midas, in the fullness of all his gratified desires, began to wring his hands and bemoan himself and how he could neither bear to look at Marygold nor yet to look away from her.

III

While he was in this tumult of despair, he suddenly beheld a stranger standing near the door. Midas bent down his head without speaking, for he recognized the same figure which had appeared to him the day before in the treasure-room and had bestowed on him this disastrous faculty of the Golden Touch. The stranger's countenance still wore a smile which seemed to shed a yellow luster all about the room.

"Well, friend Midas," said the stranger, "pray how do you succeed with the Golden Touch?"

Midas shook his head.

"I am very miserable," said he.

"Very miserable, indeed!" exclaimed the stranger. "And how happens that? Have I not faithfully kept my promise with you? Have you not everything that your heart desired?"

"Gold is not everything," answered Midas. "And I have lost all that my heart really cared for."

"Ah! So you have made a discovery since yesterday?" observed the stranger. "Let us see then. Which of these two things do you think is really worth the most – the gift of the Golden Touch or one cup of clear cold water?"

"O blessed water!" exclaimed Midas. "It will never moisten my parched throat again!"

"The Golden Touch," continued the stranger, "or a crust of bread?"

"A piece of bread," answered Midas, "is worth all the gold on earth!"

"The Golden Touch," asked the stranger, "or your own little Marygold, warm, soft, and loving as she was an hour ago?"

"Oh my child, my dear child!" cried poor Midas wringing his hands.

"You are wiser than you were King Midas!" said the stranger, looking seriously at him. "Your own heart, I perceive, has not been entirely changed from flesh to gold. Were it so, your case would indeed be desperate. But you appear to be still capable of understanding that the commonest things are more valuable than the riches which so many mortals sigh and struggle after. Tell me, now, do you sincerely desire to rid yourself of this Golden Touch?"

"It is hateful to me!" replied Midas.

A fly settled on his nose but immediately fell to the floor; for it, too, had become gold. Midas shuddered.

"Go, then," said the stranger, "and plunge into the river that glides past the bottom of your garden. Take likewise a vase of the same water, and sprinkle it over any object that you may desire to change back again from gold into its former substance. If you do this in earnestness and sincerity, it may possibly repair the mischief which your avarice has occasioned."

King Midas bowed low; and when he lifted his head, the lustrous stranger had vanished.

You will easily believe that Midas lost no time in snatching up a great earthen pitcher (but, alas me! it was no longer earthen after he touched it) and hastening to the river-side. On reaching the river's brink, he plunged headlong in, without waiting so much as to pull off his shoes.

"Poof! poof! poof!" snorted King Midas, as his head emerged out of the water. "Well; this is really a refreshing bath, and I think it must have quite washed away the Golden Touch. And now for filling my pitcher!"

As he dipped the pitcher into the water, it gladdened his very heart to see it change from gold into the same good, honest earthen vessel which it had been before he touched it. Perceiving a violet, that grew on the bank of the river, Midas touched it with his finger and was overjoyed to find that the delicate flower retained its purple hue instead of undergoing a yellow blight. The curse of the Golden Touch had, therefore, really been removed from him.

King Midas hastened back to the palace; and, I suppose, the servants knew not what to make of it when they saw their royal master so carefully bringing home an earthen pitcher of water. But that water, which was to undo all the mischief that his folly had wrought, was more precious to Midas than an ocean of molten gold could have been. The first thing he did, as you need hardly be told, was to sprinkle it by handfuls over the golden figure of little Marygold.

No sooner did it fall on her than you would have laughed to see how the rosy color came back to the dear child's cheek and how she began to sneeze and sputter!--and how astonished she was to find herself dripping wet and her father still throwing more water over her!

"Pray do not, dear father!" cried she. "See how you have wet my nice frock which I put on only this morning!"

For Marygold did not know that she had been a little golden statue, nor could she remember anything that had happened since the moment when she ran with outstretched arms to comfort poor King Midas.

Her father did not think it necessary to tell his beloved child how very foolish he had been but contented himself with showing how much wiser he had now grown. For this purpose, he led little Marygold into the garden, where he sprinkled all the remainder of the water over the rose-bushes, and with such good effect that above five thousand roses recovered their beautiful bloom. There were two circumstances, however, which, as long as he lived, used to put King Midas in mind of the Golden Touch. One was, that the sands of the river sparkled like gold; the other, that little Marygold's hair had now a golden tinge, which he had never observed in it before she had been transmuted by the effect of his kiss. This change of hue was really an improvement and made Marygold's hair richer than in her babyhood.

When King Midas had grown quite an old man and used to trot Marygold's children on his knee, he was fond of telling them this marvelous story, pretty much as I have now told it to you. And then would he stroke their glossy ringlets and tell them that their hair, likewise, had a rich shade of gold, which they had inherited from their mother.

"And to tell you the truth, my precious little folks," quoth King Midas, diligently trotting the children all the while, "ever since that morning, I have hated the very sight of all other gold, save this!"

KING MIDAS - THE GOLDEN TOUCH

I. Vocabulary: Underline the following words in the myth and define them below.

⭕ bequeath:_____

⭕ obscure:_____

⭕ disconsolately:_____

⭕ insatiable:_____

⭕ avarice:_____

II. Plot: Write a simple sentence or phrase to describe the main actions that take place in each scene.

MIDAS LOVES GOLD	THE GOLDEN TOUCH	MIDAS LOSES TOUCH
1._____	1._____	1._____
2._____	2._____	2._____
3._____	3._____	3._____

III. Characters: List and briefly describe the main characters in this myth.

_____

_____

_____

_____

IV. Rewrite this myth. Be sure to:

⭕ Include and underline all of the vocabulary words in your rewrite.

⭕ Write at least three separate paragraphs, one for each scene.

⭕ Include the following additional requirements:

_____

_____

_____

_____

_____

_____

KING MIDAS - THE MUSIC CONTEST

I

After King Midas had rid himself of the "golden touch," he dwelt in the country and became a follower of Pan, the god of the fields. Midas loved the music of Pan's pipes and would lie in the woods listening to it the whole of a summer afternoon. Pan himself was very proud of his skill; he even boasted that the music he made on his pipes was sweeter than that made by Apollo, and one day he challenged the sun-god to a contest. The challenge was accepted, and Tmolus, the mountain god, was chosen umpire. He took his seat and cleared away the trees from his ears to listen. All the inhabitants of the woodland gathered round to hear.

II

At a given signal Pan blew on his pipes and with his rustic melody gave great satisfaction to himself and his faithful follower Midas, who happened to be present. Then Tmolus turned his head toward the Sun-god, and all his trees turned with him. Apollo rose, his brow wreathed with laurel, while his robe of purple swept the ground. In his left hand he held the lyre, and with his right hand struck the strings. Although Pan had played very sweetly, there was no doubt that Apollo's music excelled his. Ravished with the harmony, Tmolus at once awarded the victory to the god of the lyre, and all but Midas acquiesced in the judgment.

Midas obstinately persisted in his opinion, though all the others exclaimed loudly at his strange lack of musical taste. At last Apollo grew angry.

"Is it possible," he said, "that anyone with ears can have so little power to use them? I will give you a new pair of ears with which you may perhaps do better."

Then Midas, to his dismay, felt his ears grow long and hairy, within and without, and he found that he was able to move them about as he had seen asses do. He was, indeed, furnished with a pair of ass's ears!

III

Mortified enough was King Midas at this mishap, but he consoled himself with the thought that it was possible to hide his misfortune, which he attempted to do by means of an ample turban or head-dress. But his hair-dresser, of course, knew the secret. He was charged not to mention it and threatened with death if he presumed to disobey. But he found it too much for his discretion to keep such a secret; so he went out into the meadow, dug a hole in the ground, and, stooping down, whispered aloud: "King Midas has the ears of an ass. I myself have seen them." This act gave him the relief that he desired, and he filled up the hole and went back to his work in the palace. Before long a thick bed of reeds appeared on the place where the barber had filled up the hole, and when the wind blew through them they whispered, "King Midas has the ears of an ass"; and all the people passing by heard and repeated the marvel. So that after all the great secret became known through the land.

KING MIDAS - THE MUSIC CONTEST

I. Vocabulary: Underline the following words in the myth and define them below.

○ inhabitants:_____

○ lyre:_____

○ acquiesced:_____

○ persisted:_____

○ mortified:_____

II. Plot: Write a simple sentence or phrase to describe the main actions that take place in each scene.

THE CHALLENGE	CONTEST AND CONSEQUENCES	THE SECRET REVEALED
1._____		1._____
2._____	1._____	2._____
3._____	2._____	3._____
	3._____	

III. Characters: List and briefly describe the main characters in this myth.

_____

_____

_____

_____

IV. Rewrite this myth. Be sure to:

○ Include and underline all of the vocabulary words in your rewrite.

○ Write at least three separate paragraphs, one for each scene.

○ Include the following additional requirements:

_____

_____

_____

_____

_____

_____

_____

BAUCIS AND PHILEMON

I

One evening, in times long ago, old Philemon and his old wife Baucis sat at their cottage-door enjoying the sunset. They had already eaten their frugal supper and intended now to spend a quiet hour or two conversing before bedtime. But the rude shouts of children and the fierce barking of dogs in the village near at hand grew louder and louder, until, at last, it was hardly possible for Baucis and Philemon to hear each other speak.

"Ah, wife," cried Philemon, "I fear some poor traveler is seeking hospitality among our neighbors yonder, and, instead of giving him food and lodging, they have set their dogs on him.

"Well-a-day!" answered old Baucis, "I do wish our neighbors felt a little more kindness for their fellow-creatures. And only think of bringing up their children in this naughty way and patting them on the head when they fling stones at strangers!"

"Those children will never come to any good," said Philemon, shaking his white head. "To tell you the truth, wife, I should not wonder if some terrible thing were to happen to the people in the village unless they mend their manners. But, as for you and me, so long as Providence affords us bread, let us be ready to give to any poor, homeless stranger that may come along and need it."

"That's right, husband!" said Baucis. "So we will!"

These old folks, you must know, were quite poor and had to work pretty hard for a living. Their food was seldom anything but bread, milk, and vegetables. But they were two of the kindest old people in the world and would cheerfully have gone without their dinners rather than refuse food to any weary traveler who might pause before their door.

Their cottage stood on a rising ground, at some short distance from a village which lay in a beautiful valley. But, we are sorry to say, the people of this village were not worthy to dwell in such a lovely spot. They were a very selfish people and had no pity for the poor nor sympathy with the homeless. These naughty people taught their children to be no better than themselves. They kept large fierce dogs, and whenever a traveler ventured to show himself in the village, this pack of disagreeable curs scampered to meet him, barking, snarling, and showing their teeth. Travelers would go miles and miles out of their way rather than try to pass through this village.

What made the matter seem worse, if possible, was that when rich persons came in their chariots nobody could be more civil and obsequious than the inhabitants of the village. They would take off their hats and make the humblest bows you ever saw.

So now you can understand why old Philemon spoke so sorrowfully when he heard the shouts of the children and the barking of the dogs at the farther extremity of the village street.

They sat shaking their heads, one to another, while the noise came nearer and nearer; until, at the foot of the little eminence on which their cottage stood, they saw two travelers approaching on foot. Close behind them came the fierce dogs, snarling at their very heels. A little farther off ran a crowd of children who sent up shrill cries and flung stones at the two strangers with all their might. Once or twice, the younger of the two men (he was a slender and very active figure) turned about and drove back the dogs with a staff which he carried in his hand. His companion, who was a very tall person, walked calmly along, as if disdaining to notice either the naughty children or the pack of curs, whose manners the children seemed to imitate.

Both of the travelers were very humbly clad and looked as if they might not have money enough in their pockets to pay for a night's lodging. And this, I am afraid, was the reason why the villagers had allowed their children and dogs to treat them so rudely.

"Come, wife," said Philemon to Baucis, "let us go and meet these poor people. No doubt they feel almost too heavy-hearted to climb the hill."

"Go you and meet them," answered Baucis, "while I make haste within doors and see whether we can get them anything for supper."

Accordingly, she hastened into the cottage. Philemon, on his part, went forward and extended his hand while saying, in the heartiest tone imaginable, "Welcome, strangers! welcome!"

"Thank you!" replied the younger of the two, in a lively kind of way, notwithstanding his weariness and trouble. "This is quite another greeting than we have met with yonder in the village. Pray, why do you live in such a bad neighborhood?"

"Ah!" observed old Philemon, with a quiet and benign smile, "Providence put me here, I hope, in order that I may make you what amends I can for the inhospitality of my neighbors."

"Well said, old father!" cried the traveler, laughing; "and, if the truth must be told, my companion and myself need some amends. Those children (the little rascals!) have bespattered us finely with their mud-ball; and one of the curs has torn my cloak which was ragged enough already. By this time, Philemon and his two guests had reached the cottage door.

II

While Baucis was getting the supper, the travelers both began to talk very sociably with Philemon. The younger, indeed, was extremely loquacious and made such shrewd and witty remarks that the good old man continually burst out a-laughing and pronounced him the merriest fellow whom he had seen for many a day.

Before Baucis served dinner she began to make apologies for the poor fare which she was forced to set before her guests.

"Had we known you were coming," said she, "my good man and myself would have gone without a morsel, rather than you should lack a better supper. Ah me! I never feel the sorrow of being poor, save when a poor traveler knocks at our door."

"All will be very well; do not trouble yourself, my good dame," replied the elder stranger kindly. "An honest, hearty welcome to a guest works miracles with the fare."

As Baucis had said, there was but a scanty supper for two hungry travelers. In the middle of the table was the remnant of a brown loaf, with a piece of cheese on one side of it and a dish of honeycomb on the other. An earthen pitcher, nearly full of wine, stood at a corner of the board; and when Baucis had filled two cups and set them before the strangers, only a little wine remained in the bottom of the pitcher. Poor Baucis kept wishing that she might starve for a week to come, if it were possible, by so doing, to provide these hungry folks a more plentiful supper.

The strangers quickly drained their cups and the younger politely asked, "A little more wine, kind Mother Baucis, if you please. The day has been hot, and I am very much athirst."

"Now, my dear people," answered Baucis, in great confusion, "I am so sorry and ashamed! But the truth is there is hardly a drop more in the pitcher."

"Why, it appears to me," cried the young traveler, "it really appears to me that matters are not quite so bad as you represent them. Here is certainly more wine in the pitcher."

So saying, and to the vast astonishment of Baucis, he proceeded to fill not only his own cup but his companion's likewise from the pitcher that was supposed to be almost empty. The good woman could scarcely believe her eyes. She had certainly poured out nearly all the wine and had peeped in afterwards and seen the bottom of the pitcher as she set it down upon the table.

"But I am old," thought Baucis to herself, "and apt to be forgetful. I suppose I must have made a mistake. At all events, the pitcher cannot help being empty now, after filling the bowls twice over."

"What excellent wine!" observed the young traveler, after quaffing the contents of the second bowl. "Excuse me, my kind hostess, but I must really ask you for a little more."

Now Baucis had seen, as plainly as she could see anything, that the traveler had turned the pitcher upside down and consequently had poured out every drop of wine in filling the last bowl. Of course, there could not possibly be any left. However, in order to let him know precisely how the case was, she lifted the pitcher and made a gesture as if pouring into the bowl. What was her surprise, therefore, when such an abundant cascade fell bubbling into the bowl that it was immediately filled to the brim and overflowed upon the table!

Although good Mother Baucis was a simple old dame, she could not but think that there was something rather out of the common way in all that had been going on. So she sat down by Philemon and told him what she had seen, in a whisper.

"Did you ever hear the like?" asked she.

"No, I never did," answered Philemon with a smile. "And I rather think, my dear old wife, you have been walking about in a sort of a dream. There happened to be a little more in the pitcher than you thought; that is all."

"Ah, husband," said Baucis, "say what you will, these are very uncommon people."

"Well, well," replied Philemon, still smiling, "perhaps they are. They certainly do look as if they had seen better days; and I am heartily glad to see them making so comfortable a supper."

Each of the guests had been diligently partaking of his dinner during this conversation between husband and wife. The younger traveler now called out, "Another cup of this delicious wine, if you please, and I shall then have supped better than a prince."

This time, old Philemon bestirred himself and took up the pitcher; for he was curious to discover whether there was any reality in the marvels which Baucis had whispered to him. He knew that his good old wife was incapable of falsehood, but this was so very singular a case that he wanted to see into it with his own eyes. On taking up the pitcher, therefore, he slyly peeped into it and was fully satisfied that it contained not so much as a single drop. All at once, however, he beheld a little fountain which gushed up from the bottom of the pitcher and speedily filled it to the brim with wine. It was lucky that Philemon, in his surprise, did not drop the miraculous pitcher from his hand.

"Who are ye, wonder-working strangers!" cried he, even more bewildered than his wife had been.

"Your guests, my good Philemon, and your friends," replied the elder traveler in his mild, deep voice that had something at once sweet and awe-inspiring in it.

The supper being now over, the strangers requested to be shown to their place of repose. When left alone, the good old couple spent some time in conversation about the events of the evening and then lay down on the floor and fell fast asleep. They had given up their sleeping-room to the guests and had no other bed for themselves, save these planks which I wish had been as soft as their own hearts.

III

The old man and his wife were stirring, betimes, in the morning, and the strangers likewise arose with the sun and made their preparations to depart. Philemon hospitably entreated them to remain a little longer. The guests, however, persisted in setting out immediately, but they asked Philemon and Baucis to walk forth with them a short distance and show them the road which they were to take.

So they all four issued from the cottage, chatting together like old friends. It was very remarkable, indeed, how familiar the old couple insensibly grew with the elder traveler. As for the younger stranger, with his keen, quick, laughing wits, he appeared to discover every little thought that but peeped into their minds, before they suspected it themselves.

"Ah me! Well-a-day!" exclaimed Philemon, when they had walked a little way from their door. "If our neighbors only knew what a blessed thing it is to show hospitality to strangers, they would tie up all their dogs and never allow their children to fling another stone."

As the group reached the crest of a hill, Philemon and his wife turned towards the valley where, only the day before, they had seen the village. But what was their astonishment! There was no longer any appearance of it! In its stead, they beheld the broad, blue surface of a lake which filled the great basin of the valley from brim to brim.

"Alas!" cried these kind-hearted old people, "what has become of our poor neighbors?"

"They exist no longer as men and women," said the elder traveler, in his grand and deep voice, while a roll of thunder seemed to echo it at a distance.

"They are all transformed to fishes," explained the young traveler.

"As for you, good Philemon," continued the elder traveler, "and you, kind Baucis, you, with your scanty means, have mingled so much heartfelt hospitality with your entertainment of the homeless stranger that the divinities Jupiter and Mercury have feasted at your board. You have done well, my dear old friends. Wherefore, request whatever favor you have most at heart, and it is granted."

Philemon and Baucis looked at one another and then, I know not which of the two it was who spoke, one uttered the desire of both their hearts.

"Let us live together, while we live, and leave the world at the same instant when we die! For we have always loved one another!"

"Be it so!" replied the stranger with majestic kindness. "Now, look towards your cottage!"

They did so. But what was their surprise on beholding a tall edifice of white marble with a wide-open portal, occupying the spot where their humble residence had so lately stood!

"There is your home," said the stranger, beneficently smiling on them both. "Exercise your hospitality in yonder palace as freely as in the poor hovel to which you welcomed us last evening."

The old folks fell on their knees to thank him; but, behold! neither traveler was there.

So Philemon and Baucis took up their residence in the marble palace and spent their time, in making everybody jolly and comfortable who happened to pass that way.

Thus the old couple lived in their palace a great, great while and grew older and older and very old indeed. At length, however, there came a summer morning when Philemon and Baucis failed to make their appearance to invite the guests of over-night to breakfast. The guests searched everywhere and all to no purpose. After a great deal of perplexity, they espied, in front of the portal, two venerable trees which nobody could remember to have seen there the day before. Yet there they stood, with their roots fastened deep into the soil, and a huge breadth of foliage overshadowing the whole front of the edifice. One was an oak and the other a linden-tree. Their boughs were intertwined together and embraced one another, so that each tree seemed to live in the other tree's bosom much more than in its own.

While the guests were marveling how these trees, that must have required at least a century to grow, could have come to be so tall and venerable in a single night, a breeze sprang up and set their intermingled boughs astir. And then there was a deep, broad murmur in the air, as if the two mysterious trees were speaking.

"I am old Philemon!" murmured the oak.

"I am old Baucis!" murmured the linden-tree.

So it was, Philemon was an oak, and Baucis a linden-tree. And oh, what a hospitable shade did they fling around them. Whenever a wayfarer paused beneath it, he heard a pleasant whisper of the leaves above his head and wondered how the sound should so much resemble words like these:

"Welcome, welcome, dear traveler, welcome!

BAUCIS AND PHILEMON

I. Vocabulary: Underline the following words in the myth and define them below.

○ obsequious:_____

○ amends:_____

○ loquacious:_____

○ quaffing:_____

○ edifice:_____

II. Plot: Write a simple sentence or phrase to describe the main actions that take place in each scene.

TRAVELERS ARRIVE	THE MEAL	STRANGERS DEPART
1._____	1._____	1._____
2._____	2._____	2._____
3._____	3._____	3._____

III. Characters: List and briefly describe the main characters in this myth.

_____

_____

_____

_____

IV. Rewrite this myth. Be sure to:

○ Include and underline all of the vocabulary words in your rewrite.

○ Write at least three separate paragraphs, one for each scene.

○ Include the following additional requirements:

_____

_____

_____

_____

_____

_____

PROSERPINA

I

Mother Ceres was exceedingly fond of her daughter Proserpina and seldom let her go alone into the fields. But, just at the time when my story begins, the good lady was very busy because she had the care of the crops of every kind all over the earth; and as the season had thus far been uncommonly backward, it was necessary to make the harvest ripen more speedily than usual. So she put on her turban, got into her chariot, and was just ready to set off.

"Dear mother," said Proserpina, "I shall be very lonely while you are away. May I not run down to the shore and ask some of the sea nymphs to come up out of the waves and play with me?"

"Yes, child," answered Mother Ceres. "But you must take care not to stray away from them nor go wandering about the fields by yourself. Young girls without their mothers to take care of them are very apt to get into mischief."

The child promised to be as prudent as if she were a grown-up woman; and, by the time Ceres' chariot was out of sight, Proserpina was on the shore, calling to the sea nymphs to come and play with her. They knew her voice and were not long in showing their glistening faces and sea-green hair above the water. They brought along with them a great many beautiful shells; and, sitting down on the moist sand, they busied themselves in making a necklace for Proserpina. By way of showing her gratitude, the child besought them to go with her a little way into the fields so that they might gather abundance of flowers with which she would make each of her kind playmates a wreath.

"O no, dear Proserpina," cried the sea nymphs; "we dare not go with you upon the dry land. We are apt to grow faint unless we let the surf wave break over us every moment or two so as to keep ourselves comfortably moist."

"It is a great pity," said Proserpina. "But do you wait for me here, and I will run and gather my apron full of flowers and be back again before the surf wave has broken ten times over you."

"We will wait, then," answered the sea nymphs. "But while you are gone, we will lie down under the water. The air today is a little too dry for our comfort. But we will pop up our heads every few minutes to see if you are coming."

The young Proserpina ran quickly to a spot where, only the day before, she had seen a great many flowers. These, however, were now a little past their bloom; and wishing to give her friends the freshest and loveliest blossoms, she strayed farther into the fields and found some that made her scream with delight. Two or three times, moreover, she could not help thinking that a tuft of most splendid flowers had suddenly sprouted out of the earth before her very eyes, as if on purpose to tempt her a few steps farther. Proserpina's apron was soon filled and brimming over with delightful blossoms. She was on the point of turning back in order to rejoin the sea nymphs, but, a little farther on, what should she behold? It was a large shrub, completely covered with the most magnificent flowers in the world.

Proserpina thought to herself, "I was just looking at that spot. How strange it is that I did not see the flowers!"

The nearer she approached the shrub, the more attractive it looked.

"It is really the most beautiful shrub that ever sprang out of the earth. I will pull it up by the roots and carry it home and plant it in my mother's garden," she concluded.

Holding up her apron full of flowers with her left hand, Proserpina seized the large shrub with the other and pulled and pulled but was hardly able to loosen the soil about its roots. Again the girl pulled with all her might and observed that the earth began to stir and crack to some distance around the stem. She gave another pull but relaxed her hold, fancying that there was a rumbling sound right beneath her feet. Then laughing at herself for so childish a notion, she made another effort; up came the shrub, and Proserpina staggered back, holding the stem triumphantly in her hand, and gazing at the deep hole which its roots had left in the soil.

Much to her astonishment, this hole kept spreading wider and wider and growing deeper and deeper; and all the while, there came a rumbling noise out of its depths, louder and louder and nearer and nearer. Too much frightened to run away, she stood straining her eyes into this wonderful cavity and soon saw a team of four sable horses, snorting smoke out of their nostrils and tearing their way out of the earth with a splendid golden chariot whirling at their heels. They leaped out of the bottomless hole, chariot and all, close by the spot where Proserpina stood. In the chariot sat the figure of a man, richly dressed, with a crown on his head, all flaming with diamonds. He was of a noble aspect, and rather handsome, but looked sullen and discontented; and he kept rubbing his eyes and shading them with his hand, as if he did not live enough in the sunshine to be very fond of its light.

As soon as this personage saw the affrighted Proserpina, he beckoned her to come a little nearer.

"Do not be afraid," said he with as cheerful a smile as he knew how to put on. "Come! Will you not like to ride a little way with me in my beautiful chariot?"

But Proserpina was so alarmed that she wished for nothing but to get out of his reach. As is always the case with children in trouble, Proserpina's first thought was to call for her mother.

"Mother, Mother Ceres!" cried she, all in a tremble. "Come quickly and save me."

But her voice was too faint for her mother to hear, and no sooner did Proserpina begin to cry out, than the stranger leaped to the ground, caught the child in his arms, and again mounted the chariot, shook the reins, and shouted to the four black horses to set off. They immediately broke into so swift a gallop that it seemed rather like flying through the air than running along the earth. But still the poor child screamed and scattered her apron full of flowers along the way; and many mothers, to whose ears it came, ran quickly to see if any mischief had befallen their children. But Mother Ceres was a great way off and could not hear the cry.

As they rode on, the stranger did his best to soothe her.

"Why should you be so frightened, my pretty child?" said he, trying to soften his rough voice. "I promise not to do you any harm. They call my name Pluto; and I am the king of diamonds and all other precious stones. O, we shall be very good friends, and you will find me more agreeable than you expect when once we get out of this troublesome sunshine."

"Let me go home!" cried Proserpina. "Let me go home!"

"My home is better than your mother's," answered King Pluto. "It is a palace, all made of gold, and you never saw anything half so magnificent as my throne. If you like, you may sit down on it and be my little queen, and I will sit on the footstool. The one thing my palace needs is a merry little maid to run upstairs and down and cheer up the rooms with her smile. And this is what you must do for King Pluto."

"Never!" answered Proserpina, looking as miserable as she could. "I shall never smile again till I am home."

But she might just as well have talked to the wind that whistled past them, for Pluto urged on his horses and went faster than ever. Proserpina continued to cry out and screamed so long and so loudly that her poor little voice was almost screamed away; and when it was nothing but a whisper, she happened to cast her eyes over a great broad field of waving grain--and whom do you think she saw? Who, but Mother Ceres, making the corn grow, and too busy to notice the golden chariot as it went rattling along. The child mustered all her strength and gave one more scream but was out of sight before Ceres had time to turn her head.

King Pluto had taken a road which now began to grow excessively gloomy. By and by the air became obscured with a gray twilight, and the duskier it grew, the more did Pluto's visage assume an air of satisfaction. Proserpina peeped at his face through the gathering dusk and hoped that he might not be so very wicked as she at first thought him.

"Ah, this twilight is truly refreshing," said King Pluto, "after being so tormented with that ugly and impertinent glare of the sun. How much more agreeable is lamplight or torchlight, more particularly when reflected from diamonds! It will be a magnificent sight, when we get to my palace."

"Is it much farther?" asked Proserpina. "And will you carry me back when I have seen it?"

"We will talk of that by and by," answered Pluto. "We are just entering my dominions. Do you see that tall gateway before us? When we pass those gates, we are at home. And there lies my faithful mastiff at the threshold. Cerberus! Cerberus! Come hither, my good dog!"

So saying, Pluto pulled at the reins and stopped the chariot right between the tall, massive pillars of the gateway. The mastiff of which he had spoken got up from the threshold and stood on his hinder legs, so as to put his fore paws on the chariot wheel. But, my stars, what a strange dog it was! Why, he was a big, rough, ugly-looking monster, with three separate heads, and each of them fiercer than the two others; but fierce as they were, King Pluto patted them all. He seemed as fond of his three-headed dog as if it had been a sweet little spaniel.

"Will the dog bite me?" asked Proserpina, shrinking closer to Pluto. "What an ugly creature he is!"

"O, never fear," answered her companion. "He never harms people, unless they try to enter my dominions without being sent for or to get away when I wish to keep them here. Now, my pretty Proserpina, we will drive on."

On went the chariot, and King Pluto seemed greatly pleased to find himself once more in his own kingdom. Not far from the gateway they came to a bridge. Pluto stopped the chariot and bade Proserpina look at the stream which was gliding so lazily beneath it. Never in her life had she beheld so torpid, so black, so muddy-looking a stream; and it moved as sluggishly as if it had quite forgotten which way it ought to flow.

"This is the River Lethe," observed King Pluto. "Is it not a very pleasant stream?"

"I think it a very dismal one," answered Proserpina.

"It suits my taste, however," answered Pluto, who was apt to be sullen when anybody disagreed with him. "At all events, its water has one excellent quality; for a single draught of it makes people forget every care and sorrow that has hitherto tormented them. Only sip a little of it, my dear Proserpina, and you will instantly cease to grieve for your mother and will have nothing in your memory that can prevent your being perfectly happy in my palace. I will send for some, in a golden goblet, the moment we arrive."

"O, no, no, no!" cried Proserpina, weeping afresh. "I had a thousand times rather be miserable with remembering my mother, than be happy in forgetting her. That dear, dear mother! I never, never will forget her."

"We shall see," said King Pluto. "You do not know what fine times we will have in my palace. Here we are just at the portal. These pillars are solid gold, I assure you."

He alighted from the chariot and, taking Proserpina in his arms, carried her up a lofty flight of steps into the great hall of the palace. It was splendidly illuminated by means of large precious stones of various hues which seemed to burn like so many lamps. And yet there was a kind of gloom in the midst of this enchanted light; nor was there a single object in the hall that was really agreeable to behold, except the little Proserpina herself, a lovely child, with one earthly flower which she had not let fall from her hand. It is my opinion that even King Pluto had never been happy in his palace and that this was the true reason why he had stolen away Proserpina, in order that he might have something to love, instead of cheating his heart any longer with this tiresome magnificence.

Pluto now summoned his domestics and bade them lose no time in preparing a most sumptuous banquet and, above all things, not to fail of setting a golden beaker of the water of Lethe by Proserpina's plate.

"I will neither drink that nor anything else," said Proserpina. "Nor will I taste a morsel of food in your palace."

"I should be sorry for that," replied King Pluto; for he really wished to be kind, if he had only known how.

Then, sending for the head cook, he gave strict orders that all sorts of delicacies, such as young people are usually fond of, should be set before Proserpina. He had a secret motive in this; for, you are to understand, it is a fixed law that when persons are carried off to the land of magic, if they once taste any food there, they can never get back to their friends. Now, if King Pluto had been cunning enough to offer Proserpina some fruit or bread and milk (which was the simple fare to which the child had always been accustomed), it is very probable that she would soon have been tempted to eat it. But he left the matter entirely to his cook who, like all other cooks, considered nothing fit to eat unless it were rich pastry or highly-seasoned meat or spiced sweet cakes--things which Proserpina's mother had never given her, and the smell of which quite took away her appetite instead of sharpening it.

II

But my story must now clamber out of King Pluto's dominions and see what Mother Ceres had been about since she was bereft of her daughter. We had a glimpse of her, as you remember, half hidden among the waving grain while the four black steeds were swiftly whirling along the chariot in which her beloved Proserpina was so unwillingly borne away. You recollect, too, the loud scream which Proserpina gave, just when the chariot was out of sight.

Of all the child's outcries, this last shriek was the only one that reached the ears of Mother Ceres. She had mistaken the rumbling of the chariot wheels for a peal of thunder and imagined that a shower was coming up. But, at the sound of Proserpina's shriek, she started and looked about in every direction, not knowing whence it came but feeling almost certain that it was her daughter's voice. It seemed so unaccountable, however, that the girl should have strayed over so many lands and seas, that the good Ceres tried to believe that it must be the child of some other parent, and not her own darling Proserpina, who had uttered this lamentable cry. Nevertheless, it troubled her with a vast many tender fears so she quickly left the field in which she had been so busy.

In less than an hour, Mother Ceres had alighted at the door of her home and found it empty. Next she hastened to the sea-shore as fast as she could, and there beheld the wet faces of the poor sea nymphs peeping over a wave. All this while, the good creatures had been waiting on the bank of sponge, and once, every half minute or so, had popped up their four heads above water to see if their playmate were yet coming back. When they saw Mother Ceres, they sat down on the crest of the surf wave and let it toss them ashore at her feet.

"Where is Proserpina?" cried Ceres. "Tell me, you naughty sea nymphs, have you enticed her under the sea?"

"O, no, good Mother Ceres," said the innocent sea nymphs. "We never should dream of such a thing. Proserpina has been at play with us, it is true; but she left us a long while ago, meaning only to run a little way upon the dry land and gather some flowers for a wreath. This was early in the day, and we have seen nothing of her since."

Ceres scarcely waited to hear what the nymphs had to say before she hurried off to make inquiries all through the neighborhood. But nobody told her anything that would enable the poor mother to guess what had become of Proserpina. A fisherman, it is true, had noticed her little footprints in the sand; a rustic had seen the child stooping to gather flowers; several persons had heard the rattling of chariot wheels; and one old woman had heard a scream but did not take the trouble to look up. The stupid people! It took them such a tedious while to tell the nothing that they knew that it was dark night before Mother Ceres found out that she must seek her daughter elsewhere. So she lighted a torch and set forth, resolving never to come back until Proserpina was discovered.

All night long, at the door of every cottage and farm-house, Ceres knocked and called up the weary laborers to inquire if they had seen her child; and they stood, gaping and half asleep at the threshold, and answered her pityingly and besought her to come in and rest. Thus passed the night; and still she continued her search without sitting down to rest or stopping to take food.

It was not merely of human beings that she asked tidings of her daughter. Often she encountered fauns who looked like sunburnt country people, except that they had hairy ears and little horns upon their foreheads and the hinder legs of goats, on which they gamboled merrily about the woods and fields. They were a frolicsome kind of creature but grew as sad as their cheerful dispositions would allow, when Ceres inquired for her daughter, and they had no good news to tell. But sometimes she same suddenly upon a rude gang of satyrs, who had faces like monkeys and horses' tails behind them and who were generally dancing in a very boisterous manner with shouts of noisy laughter. When she stopped to question them, they would only laugh the louder and make new merriment out of the lone woman's distress. How unkind of those ugly satyrs!

Thus Mother Ceres went wandering about for long days and nights, finding no trace of Proserpina. All day she traveled onward through the hot sun; and at night she continued her search, without ever sitting down to rest.

One day, as she traveled, a thought struck Ceres. "There is one person," she exclaimed to herself, "who must have seen my poor child and can doubtless tell what has become of her. Why did not I think of him before? I must speak with Phoebus."

Accordingly, she went along in quest of Phoebus. By and by, after a pretty long journey, she arrived at the sunniest spot in the whole world. There they beheld a beautiful young man with long, curling ringlets which seemed to be made of golden sunbeams. Phoebus (for this was the very person whom she was seeking) had a lyre in his hands and was making its chords tremble with sweet music; at the same time singing a most exquisite song.

"Phoebus!" exclaimed Ceres, "I am in great trouble and have come to you for assistance. Can you tell me what has become of my dear child Proserpina?"

"Proserpina! Proserpina, did you call her name?" answered Phoebus, endeavoring to recollect; for there was such a continual flow of pleasant ideas in his mind, that he was apt to forget what had happened no longer ago than yesterday. "Ah, yes, I remember her now. I am happy to tell you, my dear madam, that I did see the little Proserpina not many days ago. You may make yourself perfectly easy about her. She is safe and in excellent hands."

"O, where is my dear child?" cried Ceres, clasping her hands and flinging herself at his feet.

"Why," said Phoebus, "as the little damsel was gathering flowers, she was suddenly snatched up by King Pluto and carried off to his dominions. I have never been in that part of the universe; but the royal palace, I am told, is built in a very noble style of architecture and of the most splendid and costly materials. I recommend to you, my dear lady, to give yourself no uneasiness. Proserpina's sense of beauty will be duly gratified, and even in spite of the lack of sunshine, she will lead a very enviable life."

"Hush! Say not such a word!" answered Ceres, indignantly. "What is there to gratify her heart? What are all the splendors you speak of without affection? I must have her back again. Will you go with me, Phoebus, to demand my daughter of this wicked Pluto?"

"Pray excuse me," replied Phoebus, with an elegant obeisance. "I certainly wish you success and regret that my own affairs are so immediately pressing that I cannot have the pleasure of attending you."

"Ah, Phoebus," said Ceres, with bitter meaning in her words, "you have a harp instead of a heart. Farewell."

"Will not you stay a moment," asked Phoebus, "and hear me turn the pretty and touching story of Proserpina into extemporary verses?"

But Ceres shook her head and hastened away. Poor Mother Ceres had now found out what had become of her daughter but was not a whit happier than before. Her case, on the contrary, looked more desperate than ever. As long as Proserpina was above ground, there might have been hopes of regaining her. But now that the poor child was shut up within the iron gates of the king of the mines, at the threshold of which lay the three-headed Cerberus, there seemed no possibility of her ever making her escape. Ceres at last concluded that she must wander about the earth in quest of the entrance to King Pluto's dominions.

Poor Mother Ceres! It is melancholy to think of her, pursuing her toilsome way all alone. So much did she suffer that she grew to look like an elderly person in a very brief time. She cared not how she was dressed. She roamed about in so wild a way, and with her hair so disheveled, that people took her for some distracted creature and never dreamed that this was Mother Ceres, who had the oversight of every seed which the husbandman planted. At length, in her despair, she came to the dreadful resolution that not a stalk of grain, nor a blade of grass, not a potato, nor a turnip, nor any other vegetable that was good for man or beast to eat should be suffered to grow until her daughter were restored. She even forbade the flowers to bloom, lest somebody's heart should be cheered by their beauty.

Now, as not so much as a head of asparagus ever presumed to poke itself out of the ground without the especial permission of Ceres, you may conceive what a terrible calamity had here fallen upon the earth. The husbandmen plowed and planted as usual; but there lay the rich black furrows, all as barren as a desert of sand. The pastures looked as brown in the sweet month of June as ever they did in chill November. Things were very desperate and everybody that was acquainted with her power besought her to have mercy on the human race and, at all events, to let the grass grow. But Mother Ceres, though naturally of an affectionate disposition, was now inexorable.

"Never," said she. "If the earth is ever again to see any verdure, it must first grow along the path which my daughter will tread in coming back to me."

III

Finally, as there seemed to be no other remedy, our old friend Quicksilver was sent post-haste to King Pluto, in hopes that he might be persuaded to undo the mischief he had done and to set everything right again by giving up Proserpina. When he arrived, Quicksilver requested to be shown immediately into the king's presence; and Pluto, who heard his voice from the top of the stairs and who loved to recreate himself with Quicksilver's merry talk, called out to him to come up. And while they settle their business together, we must inquire what Proserpina had been doing ever since we saw her last.

The child had declared, as you may remember, that she would not taste a mouthful of food as long as she should be compelled to remain in King Pluto's palace. How she contrived to maintain her resolution and at the same time to keep herself tolerably plump and rosy is more than I can explain; but some young ladies, I am given to understand, possess the faculty of living on air, and Proserpina seems to have possessed it too. At any rate, it was now six months since she left the outside of the earth; and not a morsel had yet passed between her teeth.

All this time, being of a cheerful and active disposition, the little damsel was not quite so unhappy as you may have supposed. There was a never-ceasing gloom, it is true. But still, whenever the girl went among those gilded halls and chambers, it seemed as if she carried nature and sunshine along with her. After Proserpina came, the palace was no longer the same abode of stately artifice and dismal magnificence that it had before been. The inhabitants all felt this, and King Pluto more than any of them.

"My own little Proserpina," he used to say. "I wish you could like me a little better. We gloomy and cloudy-natured persons have often as warm hearts, at bottom, as those of a more cheerful character. If you would only stay with me of your own accord, it would make me happier than the possession of a hundred such palaces as this."

"Well, I do love you a little," whispered she one day, looking up in his face as he spoke to her.

"Do you, indeed, my dear child?" cried Pluto. "Well, I have not deserved it, after keeping you a prisoner for so many months and starving you besides. Are you not terribly hungry? Is there nothing which I can get you to eat?"

In asking this question, the king of the mines had a very cunning purpose; for, you will recollect, if Proserpina tasted a morsel of food in his dominions, she would never afterwards be at liberty to quit them.

"No indeed," said Proserpina. "Your head cook is always contriving one dish or another, which he imagines may be to my liking. But he might just as well save himself the trouble, poor, fat little man that he is. I have no appetite for anything in the world, unless it were a slice of bread, of my mother's own baking or a little fruit out of her garden."

When Pluto heard this, he began to see that he had mistaken the best method of tempting Proserpina to eat. Wondering that he had never thought of it before, the king now sent one of his trusty attendants with a large basket, to get some of the finest fruit which could anywhere be found in the upper world. Unfortunately, however, this was during the time when Ceres had forbidden any fruits or vegetables to grow; and, after seeking all over the earth, King Pluto's servant found only a single pomegranate, and that so dried up as not to be worth eating. Nevertheless, since there was no better to be had, he brought this dry, old withered pomegranate home to the palace, put it on a magnificent golden salver, and carried it up to Proserpina. Now, it happened, curiously enough, that, just as the servant was bringing the pomegranate into the back door of the palace, our friend Quicksilver had gone up the front steps, on his errand to get Proserpina away from King Pluto.

As soon as Proserpina saw the pomegranate, she told the servant he had better take it away again.

"I shall not touch it," said she. "I should never think of eating such a miserable, dry pomegranate as that."

"It is the only one in the world," said the servant.

He set down the golden salver and left the room. When he was gone, Proserpina could not help coming close to the table and looking at this poor specimen of dried fruit with a great deal of eagerness; for, to say the truth, on seeing something that suited her taste, she felt all the six months' appetite taking possession of her at once.

"At least I may smell it," thought Proserpina.

So she took up the pomegranate and applied it to her nose; and, somehow or other, being in such close neighborhood to her mouth, the fruit found its way into that little red cave. Dear me! what an everlasting pity! Before Proserpina knew what she was about, her teeth had actually bitten it. Just as this fatal deed was done, the door of the apartment opened, and in came King Pluto, followed by Quicksilver, who had been urging him to let his little prisoner go. At the first noise of their entrance, Proserpina withdrew the pomegranate from her mouth. But Quicksilver perceived that the child was a little confused; and seeing the empty salver, he suspected that she had been taking a sly nibble of something or other. As for honest Pluto, he never guessed at the secret.

"My little Proserpina," said the king, sitting down and affectionately drawing her between his knees, "here is Quicksilver, who tells me that a great many misfortunes have befallen innocent people on account of my detaining you in my dominions. To confess the truth, I myself had already reflected that it was an unjustifiable act to take you away from your good mother. But, then, you must consider, my dear child, that this vast palace is apt to be gloomy and that I am not of the most cheerful disposition and that, therefore, it was a natural thing enough to seek for the society of some merrier creature than myself. An iron heart I should surely have, if I could detain you here any longer, when it is now six months since you tasted food. I give you your liberty. Go with Quicksilver. Hasten home to your dear mother."

Now, although you may not have supposed it, Proserpina found it impossible to take leave of poor King Pluto without some regrets and a good deal of compunction for not telling him about the pomegranate. She even shed a tear or two, thinking how lonely and cheerless the great palace would seem to him after she herself--his one little ray of natural sunshine, should have departed. I know not how many kind things she might have said to the disconsolate king of the mines, had not Quicksilver hurried her way.

"Come along quickly," whispered he in her ear, "or his majesty may change his royal mind. And take care, above all things, that you say nothing of what was brought you on the golden salver."

In a very short time, they had passed the great gateway and emerged upon the surface of the earth. It was delightful to behold, as Proserpina hastened along, how the path grew verdant behind and on either side of her. Wherever she set her blessed foot, there was at once a dewy flower. The grass and the grain began to sprout with tenfold vigor and luxuriance, to make up for the dreary months that had been wasted in barrenness. The starved cattle immediately set to work grazing, after their long fast, and ate enormously all day and got up at midnight to eat more.

Mother Ceres had returned to her deserted home and was sitting disconsolately on the doorstep when, lifting her eyes, she was surprised to see a sudden verdure flashing over the brown and barren fields.

"Does the earth disobey me?" exclaimed Mother Ceres, indignantly. "Does it presume to be green, when I have bidden it be barren until my daughter shall be restored to my arms?"

"Then open your arms, dear mother," cried a well-known voice, "and take your little daughter into them."

And Proserpina came running and flung herself upon her mother's bosom. Their mutual transport is not to be described. When their hearts had grown a little more quiet, Mother Ceres looked anxiously at Proserpina.

"My child," said she, "did you taste any food while you were in King Pluto's palace?"

"Dearest mother," exclaimed Proserpina, "I will tell you the whole truth. Until this very morning, not a morsel of food had passed my lips. But today, they brought me a pomegranate and, having seen no fruit for so long a time and being faint with hunger, I was tempted just to bite it. The instant I tasted it, King Pluto and Quicksilver came into the room. I had not swallowed a morsel; but--dear mother, I hope it was no harm--but six of the pomegranate seeds, I am afraid, remained in my mouth."

"Ah, unfortunate child, and miserable me!" exclaimed Ceres. "For each of those six pomegranate seeds you must spend one month of every year in King Pluto's palace. You are but half restored to your mother. Only six months with me, and six with that good-for-nothing King of Darkness!"

"Do not speak so harshly of poor King Pluto," said Prosperina, kissing her mother. "He has some very good qualities; and I really think I can bear to spend six months in his palace, if he will only let me spend the other six with you. He certainly did very wrong to carry me off; but then, as he says, it was but a dismal sort of life for him to live in that great gloomy place all alone; and it has made a wonderful change in his spirits to have a little girl to run up stairs and down. There is some comfort in making him so happy; and so, upon the whole, dearest mother, let us be thankful that he is not to keep me the whole year round."

PROSERPINA

I. Vocabulary: Underline the following words in the myth and define them below.

○ sullen:_____

○ lamentable:_____

○ extemporary:_____

○ salver:_____

○ verdant:_____

II. Plot: Write a simple sentence or phrase to describe the main actions that take place in each scene.

PLUTO TAKES PROSERPINA	CERES SEARCHES	PROSERPINA RETURNS
1._____	1._____	1._____
2._____	2._____	2._____
3._____	3._____	3._____

III. Characters: List and briefly describe the main characters in this myth.

_____

_____

_____

_____

IV. Rewrite this myth. Be sure to:

○ Include and underline all of the vocabulary words in your rewrite.

○ Write at least three separate paragraphs, one for each scene.

○ Include the following additional requirements:

_____

_____

_____

_____

_____

_____

GLAUCUS AND SCYLLA

I

Glaucus was a fisherman. One day he had drawn his nets full of various fish to land and had emptied them on the shore. Next he proceeded to sort the fish on the grass. The place where he stood was a beautiful island in the river, a solitary spot, uninhabited, and not ever visited by any but himself. All of a sudden, the fishes, which had been laid on the grass, began to revive and move their fins as if they were in the water. While he looked on astonished, they one and all moved off to the water, plunged in, and swam away. He did not know what to make of this, whether some god had done it or some secret power in the herbage.

"What herb has such a power?" he exclaimed; and gathering some of it, he tasted it. Scarce had the juices of the plant reached his palate when he found himself agitated with a longing desire for the water. He could no longer restrain himself, but bidding farewell to earth, he plunged into the stream. As the water covered him he lost consciousness. When he recovered, he found himself changed in form and mind. His hair was sea-green and trailed behind him on the water; his shoulders grew broad, and what had been thighs and legs assumed the form of a fish's tail. The sea-gods complimented him on the change of his appearance, and he fancied himself rather a good-looking personage.

II

One day Glaucus saw the beautiful maiden Scylla, rambling on the shore. He fell in love with her and, showing himself on the surface, spoke to her, saying such things as he thought most likely to win her to stay; for she turned to run immediately on the sight of him and ran till she had gained a cliff overlooking the sea. Here she stopped and turned round to see whether it was a god or a sea animal and observed with wonder his shape and color. Glaucus partly emerging from the water and, supporting himself against a rock, said, "Maiden, I am no monster, nor a sea animal, but a god. Once I was a mortal and followed the sea for a living; but now I belong wholly to it." Then he told the story of his metamorphosis and how he had been promoted to his present dignity and added, "But what avails all this if it fails to move your heart?" He was going on in this strain, but Scylla turned and hastened away.

Glaucus was in despair, but it occurred to him to consult the enchantress Circe. Accordingly he repaired to her island. After mutual salutations, he said, "Goddess, I entreat your pity; you alone can relieve the pain I suffer. I love Scylla. I want to marry her but I am ashamed to tell you how scornfully she has treated me. I beseech you to use your incantations or potent herbs, if they are more prevailing, not to cure me of my love, for that I do not wish, but to make her share it and yield me a like return." To which Circe replied, for she was not insensible to the attractions of the sea-green deity, "You had better pursue a willing object; you are worthy to be sought, instead of having to seek in vain. Be not diffident; know your own worth. I protest to you that even I, goddess though I be and learned in the virtues of plants and spells, should not know how to refuse you. If she scorns you scorn her; meet one who is ready to meet you half way and thus make a due return to both at once." To these words Glaucus replied, "Sooner shall trees grow at the bottom of the ocean and sea-weed on the top of the mountains, than I will cease to love Scylla, and her alone."

III

The goddess was indignant, but she could not punish him, neither did she wish to do so, for she liked him too well; so she turned all her wrath against her rival, poor Scylla. She took plants of poisonous powers and mixed them together with incantations and charms. Then she proceeded to the coast of Sicily where Scylla lived. There was a little bay on the shore to which Scylla used to resort in the heat of the day to breathe the air of the sea and to bathe in its waters. Here the goddess poured her poisonous mixture. Scylla came as usual and plunged into the water up to her waist. What was her horror to perceive a brood of serpents and barking monsters surrounding her! At first she could not imagine they were a part of herself and tried to run from them and to drive them away; but as she ran she carried them with her, and when she tried to touch her limbs, she found her hands touch only the yawning jaws of monsters. Scylla remained rooted to the spot. Her temper grew as ugly as her form, and she took pleasure in devouring hapless mariners who came within her grasp. Thus she destroyed six of the companions of Ulysses and tried to wreck the ships of Aeneas, till at last she was turned into a rock, and as such still continues to be a terror to mariners.

GLAUCUS AND SCYLLA

I. Vocabulary: Underline the following words in the myth and define them below.

◯ uninhabited:_____

◯ herbage:_____

◯ palate:_____

◯ metamorphosis:_____

◯ indignant:_____

II. Plot: Write a simple sentence or phrase to describe the main actions that take place in each scene.

GLAUCUS TRANSFORMED	GLAUCUS SEES SCYLLA	CIRCE "HELPS"
1._____	1._____	1._____
2._____	2._____	2._____
3._____	3._____	3._____

III. Characters: List and briefly describe the main characters in this myth.

_____

_____

_____

_____

IV. Rewrite this myth. Be sure to:

◯ Include and underline all of the vocabulary words in your rewrite.

◯ Write at least three separate paragraphs, one for each scene.

◯ Include the following additional requirements:

_____

_____

_____

_____

_____

_____

CEYX AND HALCYONE

I

Ceyx, son of Hesperus, was king of Thessaly. There he reigned in peace, without violence or wrong. Halcyone, the daughter of Aeolus, was his wife and devotedly attached to him. Now Ceyx needed to make a voyage to consult the oracle of Apollo. As soon as he disclosed his intention to his wife Halcyone, a shudder ran through her frame and her face grew deadly pale. She knew the dangers of the sea and endeavored to discourage him by describing the violence of the winds which she had known familiarly when she lived at home in her father's house; for Aeolus, her father, was the god of the winds. "They rush together," said she, "with such fury that fire flashes from the conflict. But if you must go," she added, "dear husband, let me go with you, otherwise I shall suffer not only the real evils which you must encounter but those also which my fears suggest."

These words weighed heavily on the mind of King Ceyx, and it was no less his own wish than hers to take her with him, but he could not bear to expose her to the dangers of the sea. He, therefore, consoled her as well as he could and finished with these words: "I promise, by the rays of my father the Day-star, that if fate permits I will return before the moon shall have twice rounded her orb." When he had thus spoken, he ordered the vessel to be drawn out of the ship house and the oars and sails to be put aboard. When Halcyone saw these preparations she shuddered, as if with a presentiment of evil. With tears and sobs she said farewell and then fell senseless to the ground.

Ceyx would still have lingered, but now the young men grasped their oars and pulled vigorously through the waves with long and measured strokes. Halcyone raised her streaming eyes and saw her husband standing on the deck, waving his hand to her. She answered his signal till the vessel had receded so far that she could no longer distinguish his form from the rest. Then, retiring to her chamber, she threw herself on her solitary couch.

Meanwhile, Ceyx and his men glided out of the harbor. The seamen drew in their oars and hoisted their sails. When half or less of their course was passed, as night drew on, the sea began to whiten with swelling waves and the east wind to blow a gale. The master gave the word to take in sail, but because of the roar of the winds and waves his orders were unheard. The men, of their own accord, busied themselves to secure the oars and to reef the sail. While they did this the storm increased.

Rain fell in torrents, as if the skies were coming down to unite with the sea. When the lightning ceased for a moment, the night seemed to add its own darkness to that of the storm. Skill failed, courage sank, and death seemed to come on every wave. The men were stupefied with terror. The thought of parents and kindred, left at home, came over their minds. Ceyx thought of Halcyone. No name but hers was on his lips, and while he yearned for her, he yet rejoiced in her absence. Presently the mast was shattered by a stroke of lightning, the rudder broken, and the triumphant surge curled over upon the wreck, then fell, and crushed it to fragments. Some of the seamen, stunned by the stroke, sank, and rose no more; others clung to fragments of the wreck. Ceyx held fast to a plank and called for help from his father and father-in-law. But oftenest on his lips was the name of Halcyone. To her his thoughts clung. At length the waters overwhelmed him, and he sunk.

II

In the meanwhile Halcyone, ignorant of all these horrors, counted the days till her husband's promised return. To all the gods she offered frequent incense, but more than all to Juno. For her husband, who was no more, she prayed incessantly that he might be safe and that he might come home. Juno at length could not bear any longer to be pleaded with for one already dead. So, calling Iris, she said, "Iris, my faithful messenger, go to the drowsy dwelling of Somnus, and tell him to send a vision to

Halcyone in the form of Ceyx to make known to her the event."

Iris put on her robe of many colors and, tinging the sky with her bow, sought the palace of the King of Sleep. A mountain cave was the abode of the dull god Somnus. Here no man or animal makes a sound but silence reigns. Poppies grow abundantly before the door of the cave, as well as other herbs from whose juices Night collects slumbers which she scatters over the darkened earth. There is no gate to the mansion to creak on its hinges nor any watchman; but in the midst of it is a couch of black ebony, adorned with black plumes and black curtains. There the god reclines, his limbs relaxed with sleep. Around him lie dreams, resembling various forms, as many as the forest leaves or the sand on the sea.

As soon as the goddess entered and brushed away the dreams that hovered around her, her brightness lit up all the cave. The god scarcely opened his eyes and ever and anon dropped his beard upon his breast. At last he shook himself free from himself and inquired her errand - for he knew who she was. She answered, "Somnus, gentlest of the gods, tranquillizer of minds and soother of care-worn hearts, Juno sends you her command that you despatch a dream to Halcyone, in the city of Trachine, representing her lost husband and all the events of the wreck."

Having delivered her message, Iris hastened away, for she could not longer endure the stagnant air, and she felt drowsiness creeping over her. She made her escape and returned by her bow the way she came. Then Somnus called one of his numerous sons, Morpheus, and told him to perform the command of Iris. Now Morpheus was the most expert in counterfeiting forms and in imitating the walk, the countenance, and mode of speaking of men. After Somnus had dispatched his son, he laid his head on his pillow and yielded himself to grateful repose.

Morpheus flew, making no noise with his wings, and soon came to the home of Halcyone. There he laid aside his wings and assumed the form of Ceyx. Under that form, but pale like a dead man, he stood before the couch of the wretched wife. His beard seemed soaked with water, and water trickled from his drowned locks. Leaning over the bed, tears streaming from his eyes, he said, "Do you recognize your Ceyx, unhappy wife, or has death too much changed my visage? Behold me, know me, your husband's shade, instead of himself. Your prayers, Halcyone, availed me nothing. I am dead. No more deceive yourself with vain hopes of my return. The stormy winds sunk my ship and waves filled my mouth while it called aloud on you. Arise! give me tears, give me lamentations, let me not go down to Tartarus unwept." To these words Morpheus added the voice, which seemed to be that of her husband; he seemed to pour forth genuine tears; his hands had the gestures of Ceyx.

Halcyone wept, groaned, and stretched out her arms in her sleep, striving to embrace his body but grasping only the air. "Stay!" she cried; "whither do you fly? let us go together." Her own voice awakened her. Starting up, she gazed eagerly around to see if he was still present, for the servants, alarmed by her cries, had brought a light. When she found him not, she smote her breast and rent her garments. Her nurse asked what was the cause of her grief. "Ceyx is no more," she answered. "Utter not words of comfort, he is shipwrecked and dead. I have seen him; I have recognized him. I stretched out my hands to seize him and detain him. His shade vanished, but it was the true shade of my husband. Here, in this very spot, the sad vision stood," and she looked to find the mark of his footsteps. "This it was, this that my presaging mind foreboded, when I implored him not to leave me to trust himself to the waves. Oh, how I wish, since thou wouldst go, thou hadst taken me with thee! In death, if one tomb may not include us, one epitaph shall." Her grief forbade more words, and these were broken with tears and sobs.

III

It was now morning. She went to the seashore and sought the spot where she last saw him on his departure. While she reviewed every object and tried to recall every incident, she looked out over the sea and descried an indistinct object floating in the water. At first she was in doubt what it was, but by degrees the waves bore it nearer, and it was plainly the body of a man. Though unknowing of whom, yet, as it was of some shipwrecked one, she was deeply moved and gave it her tears, saying, "Alas! unhappy one, and unhappy, if such there be, thy wife!" Borne by the waves, it came nearer. As she more and more nearly viewed it, she trembled more and more. As it approached the shore, she recognized the body. It was her husband! She stretched out her arms and exclaimed, "O dearest husband, is it thus you return to me?"

There was built out from the shore a mole, constructed to break the assaults of the sea and stem its violent ingress. She leaped upon this barrier and she flew, and striking the air with wings produced on the instant, skimmed along the surface of the water, an unhappy bird. As she flew, her throat poured forth sounds full of grief and like the voice of one lamenting. When she touched the mute and bloodless body, she enfolded its beloved limbs with her new-formed wings and tried to give kisses with her horny beak. Then, by the pitying gods, both of them were changed into birds. They mate and have their young ones. For seven placid days, in winter time, Halcyone broods over her nest which floats upon the sea. Then the way is safe to seamen. Aeolus guards the winds and keeps them from disturbing the deep. The sea is given up, for the time, to his grandchildren.

CEYX AND HALCYONE

I. Vocabulary: Underline the following words in the myth and define them below.

◯ solitary:_____

◯ visage:_____

◯ smote:_____

◯ epitaph:_____

◯ mole:_____

II. Plot: Write a simple sentence or phrase to describe the main actions that take place in each scene.

CEYX DIES	THE DREAM	HALCYONE REACTS
1._____	1._____	1._____
2._____	2._____	2._____
3._____	3._____	3._____

III. Characters: List and briefly describe the main characters in this myth.

_____

_____

_____

_____

IV. Rewrite this myth. Be sure to:

◯ Include and underline all of the vocabulary words in your rewrite.

◯ Write at least three separate paragraphs, one for each scene.

◯ Include the following additional requirements:

_____

_____

_____

_____

_____

_____

_____

CUPID AND PSYCHE

I

A certain king and queen had three daughters. The charms of the two elder were more than common, but the beauty of the youngest was so wonderful that the poverty of language is unable to express its due praise. The fame of her beauty was so great that strangers from neighboring countries came in crowds to enjoy the sight and looked on her with amazement, paying her that homage which is due only to Venus herself. As she passed along, the people sang her praises and strewed her way with chaplets and flowers.

This homage to a mere mortal gave great offence to Venus. Shaking her ambrosial locks with indignation, she exclaimed, "Am I then to be eclipsed in my honors by a mortal girl? She shall not so quietly usurp my honor. I will give her cause to repent of so unlawful a beauty."

Thereupon she called her winged son Cupid. She pointed out Psyche to him and said, "My dear son, punish that contumacious beauty; give thy mother a revenge as sweet as her injuries are great; infuse into the bosom of that haughty girl a passion for some low, mean, unworthy being, so that she may reap a mortification as great as her present exultation and triumph."

Cupid prepared to obey the commands of his mother. Thence he hastened to the chamber of Psyche, whom he found asleep. The sight of her almost moved him to pity. As Cupid got out his arrow she stirred. This so startled him that in his confusion he wounded himself with his own arrow and flew away hurriedly so as to not be seen. But the work was done; Cupid was in love with Psyche.

For some time Cupid was tormented by his feelings for Psyche. At last he went to Apollo for help. Soon after this all Psyche's suitors mysteriously disappeared. True, all eyes were cast eagerly upon her, and every mouth spoke her praises; but neither king, royal youth, nor plebeian presented himself to demand her in marriage. Her two elder sisters of moderate charms had now long been married to two royal princes; but Psyche, in her lonely apartment, deplored her solitude, sick of that beauty which, while it procured abundance of flattery, had failed to awaken love.

Her parents, afraid that they had unwittingly incurred the anger of the gods, consulted the oracle of Apollo, and received this answer: "Perhaps you daughter is destined to be the bride of no mortal lover but is destined to marry a god. Leave her on top of a mountain to see if one wants her for a wife."

This decree of the oracle filled her parents with dismay, but Psyche said, "Why, my dear parents, do you now lament me? I submit. Lead me to that rock to which my fate has destined me." Accordingly, all things being prepared, the royal maid took her place in a procession which more resembled a funeral than a nuptial pomp, and she with her parents ascended the mountain, on the summit of which they left her alone.

Psyche stood on the ridge of the mountain with eyes full of tears and wept until sleep came. While she slept, the gentle Zephyr raised her from the earth and bore her with an easy motion into a flowery dale. When she awoke refreshed, she looked round and beheld near by a pleasant grove of tall and stately trees. She entered it, and in the midst discovered a magnificent palace which impressed the spectator that it was not the work of mortal hands but the happy retreat of some god. Drawn by admiration and wonder, she approached the building and ventured to enter. Every object she met filled her with pleasure and amazement. Golden pillars supported the vaulted roof, and the walls were enriched with carvings and paintings which delighted the eye of the beholder. Proceeding onward, she perceived that besides the apartments of state there were others filled with all manner of treasures and beautiful and precious productions of nature and art.

While her eyes were thus occupied, a voice addressed her, though she saw no one, uttering these words: "Sovereign lady, all that you see is yours. We whose voices you hear are your servants and shall obey all your commands with our utmost care and diligence. Retire, therefore, to your chamber and repose on your bed of down, and when you see fit repair to the bath. Supper awaits you in the adjoining alcove when it pleases you to take your seat there."

Psyche gave ear to the admonitions of her vocal attendants, and after repose and the refreshment of the bath, she seated herself in the alcove, where a table immediately presented itself, without any visible aid from waiters or servants, and it was covered with the greatest delicacies of food and the most nectareous wines. Her ears too were feasted with music from invisible performers; of whom one sang, another played on the lute, and all closed in the wonderful harmony of a full chorus.

II

She had not yet seen her destined husband. He came only in the hours of darkness and fled before the dawn of morning, but his accents were full of love and inspired a like passion in her. She often begged him to stay and let her behold him, but he would not consent. On the contrary he charged her to make no attempt to see him, for it was his pleasure, for the best of reasons, to keep concealed. "Why should you wish to behold me?" he said; "have you any doubt of my love? have you any wish ungratified? If you saw me, perhaps you would fear me, perhaps adore me, but all I ask of you is to love me. I would rather you would love me as an equal than adore me as a god."

This reasoning quieted Psyche for a time, and while the novelty lasted she felt quite happy. But at length the thought of her parents, left in ignorance of her fate, and of her sisters, precluded from sharing with her the delights of her situation, preyed on her mind and made her begin to feel her palace as but a splendid prison. When her husband came one night, she told him her distress, and at last drew from him an unwilling consent that her sisters should be brought to see her.

So, calling Zephyr, she acquainted him with her husband's commands, and he, promptly obedient, soon brought them across the mountain down to Psyche's valley. They embraced her and she returned their caresses. "Come," said Psyche, "enter with me my house and refresh yourselves with whatever your sister has to offer." Then taking their hands she led them into her golden palace and committed them to the care of her numerous train of attendant voices, to refresh them in her baths and at her table and to show them all her treasures. The view of these celestial delights caused envy to enter their bosoms, at seeing their young sister possessed of such state and splendor so much exceeding their own.

They asked her numberless questions, among others what sort of a person her husband was. Psyche replied that he was a beautiful youth who generally spent the daytime in hunting upon the mountains. The sisters, not satisfied with this reply, soon made her confess that she had never seen him. Then they proceeded to fill her bosom with dark suspicions. "The inhabitants of this valley say that your husband is a terrible and monstrous serpent who nourishes you for a while with dainties that he may by and by devour you. Take our advice," they said. "Provide yourself with a lamp and a sharp knife; put them in concealment that your husband may not discover them, and when he is sound asleep, slip out of bed, bring forth your lamp, and see for yourself whether what they say is true or not. If it is, hesitate not to cut off the monster's head and thereby recover your liberty."

Psyche resisted these persuasions as well as she could, but they did not fail to have their effect on her mind, and when her sisters were gone, their words and her own curiosity were too strong for her to resist. So she prepared her lamp and a sharp knife and hid them out of sight of her husband. When he had fallen asleep, she silently rose and uncovering her lamp beheld not a hideous monster, but the most beautiful and charming of the god's. As she leaned the lamp over to have a nearer view of his face, a drop of burning oil fell on the shoulder of the god. This startled him and he opened his eyes and fixed them full upon her; then, without saying one word, he spread his white wings and flew out of the window. Psyche, in vain endeavoring to follow him, fell from the window to the ground. Cupid, beholding her as she lay in the dust, stopped his flight for an instant and said, "O foolish Psyche, is it thus you repay my love? After

61

having disobeyed my mother's commands and made you my wife, will you think me a monster and cut off my head? But go; return to your sisters whose advice you seem to think preferable to mine. I inflict no other punishment on you than to leave you forever. Love cannot dwell with suspicion." So saying, he fled away, leaving poor Psyche prostrate on the ground, filling the place with mournful lamentations.

When she had recovered some degree of composure she looked around her, but the palace and gardens had vanished and she found herself in the open field not far from the city where her sisters dwelt. She repaired thither and told them the whole story of her misfortunes, at which, pretending to grieve, those spiteful creatures inwardly rejoiced.

From then on Psyche wandered day and night, without food or repose, in search of her husband. Casting her eyes on a lofty mountain having on its brow a magnificent temple, she sighed and said to herself, "Perhaps my love, my lord, inhabits there," and directed her steps thither.

She had no sooner entered than she saw heaps of corn, some in loose ears and some in sheaves with mingled ears of barley. Scattered about, lay sickles and rakes and all the instruments of harvest, as if thrown carelessly out of the weary reapers' hands in the sultry hours of the day.

This unseemly confusion the pious Psyche put an end to by separating and sorting everything to its proper place and kind. The holy Ceres, whose temple it was, finding her so religiously employed, thus spoke to her: "O Psyche, though I cannot shield you from the frowns of Venus, yet I can teach you how best to allay her displeasure. Go, then, and voluntarily surrender yourself to her and try by modesty and submission to win her forgiveness, and perhaps her favor will restore you the husband you have lost."

Psyche obeyed the commands of Ceres and took her way to the temple of Venus, endeavoring to fortify her mind and ruminating on what she should say and how best propitiate the angry goddess.

III

Venus received her with angry countenance. "Most faithless of servants," said she, "do you at last remember me? Or have you rather come to see your husband? You are so ill-favored and disagreeable that the only way you can merit your lover must be by dint of industry and diligence. I will make trial of your housewifery." Then she ordered Psyche to be led to one of her storehouses where was laid up a great quantity of wheat, barley, millet, vetches, beans, and lentils prepared for food for her pigeons and said, "Take and separate all these grains, putting all of the same kind in a parcel by themselves, and see that you get it done before evening." Then Venus departed and left her to her task.

But Psyche, in a perfect consternation at the enormous work, sat stupid and silent, without moving a finger to the inextricable heap.

While she sat despairing, Cupid stirred up the little ant, a native of the fields, to take compassion on her. The leader of the ant-hill, followed by whole hosts of his six-legged subjects, approached the heap, and with the utmost diligence taking grain by grain, they separated the pile, sorting each kind to its parcel; and when it was all done, they vanished out of sight in a moment.

Venus at the approach of twilight returned to the storehouse. Seeing the task done, she exclaimed, "This is no work of yours, wicked one, but the work of an immortal." So saying, she threw her a piece of black bread for her supper and went away.

Next morning Venus ordered Psyche to be called and said to her, "Behold yonder grove which stretches along the margin of the water. There you will find sheep feeding without a shepherd, with golden-shining fleeces on their backs. Go, fetch me a sample of that precious wool gathered from every one of their fleeces."

Psyche obediently went to the riverside, prepared to do her best to execute the command. But the river god inspired the reeds with harmonious murmurs which seemed to say, "O maiden, venture not among the formidable rams on the other side, for as long as they are under the influence of the rising sun, they burn with a cruel rage to destroy mortals with their sharp horns or rude teeth. But when the noontide sun has driven them to the shade, you may then cross in safety, and you will find the woolly gold sticking to the bushes and the trunks of the trees."

Thus the compassionate river god gave Psyche instructions how to accomplish her task, and by observing his directions she soon returned to Venus with her arms full of the golden fleece; but she received not the approbation of her implacable mistress, who said, "I know very well it is by none of your own doings that you have succeeded in this task, and I am not satisfied yet that you have any capacity to make yourself useful. But I have another task for you. Here, take this box and go your way to the infernal shades and give this box to Proserpine and say, 'My mistress Venus desires you to send her a little of your beauty, for in tending her sick son she has lost some of her own.' Be not too long on your errand, for I must paint myself with it to appear at the circle of the gods and goddesses this evening."

Psyche was now satisfied that her destruction was at hand. Wherefore, to make no delay of what was not to be avoided, she went to the top of a high tower in order to throw herself headlong and thus descend the shortest way to the shades below. But a voice from the tower said to her, "Why, unlucky girl, dost thou design to put an end to thy days in so dreadful a manner? And what cowardice makes thee sink under this last danger who hast been so miraculously supported in all thy former?" Then the voice told her how by a certain cave she might reach the realms of Pluto and how to avoid all the dangers of the road, to pass by Cerberus, the three-headed dog, and prevail on Charon, the ferryman, to take her across the black river and bring her back again. But the voice added, "When Proserpine has given you the box filled with her beauty, of all things this is chiefly to be observed by you, that you never once open or look into the box nor allow your curiosity to pry into the treasure of the beauty of the goddesses."

Psyche, encouraged by this advice, obeyed it in all things and traveled safely to the kingdom of Pluto. She was admitted to the palace of Proserpine and delivered her message from Venus. Presently the box was returned to her, shut and filled with the precious commodity. Then she returned the way she came, and glad was she to come out once more into the light of day.

But having got so far successfully through her dangerous task a longing desire seized her to examine the contents of the box, "What," said she, "shall I, the carrier of this divine beauty, not take the least bit to put on my cheeks to appear to more advantage in the eyes of my beloved husband!" So she carefully opened the box but found nothing there of any beauty at all but an infernal, deep sleep which took possession of her, and she crumpled down in the midst of the road, a sleepy corpse without sense or motion.

But Cupid, being now recovered from his wound and not able longer to bear the absence of his beloved Psyche, flew to the spot where Psyche lay and, gathering up the sleep from her body, closed it again in the box and waked Psyche with a light touch of one of his arrows. "Again," said he, "hast thou almost perished by the same curiosity. But now perform exactly the task imposed on you by my mother, and I will take care of the rest.

Then Cupid, as swift as lightning penetrating the heights of heaven, presented himself before Jupiter with his supplication. Jupiter lent a favoring ear and pleaded the cause of the lovers so earnestly with Venus that he won her consent. On this he sent Mercury to bring Psyche up to the heavenly assembly, and when she arrived, handing her a cup of ambrosia, he said, "Drink this, Psyche, and be immortal; nor shall Cupid ever break away from the knot in which he is tied, but these nuptials shall be perpetual."

Thus Psyche became at last united to Cupid, and in due time they had a daughter born to them whose name was Pleasure.

CUPID AND PSYCHE

I. Vocabulary: Underline the following words in the myth and define them below.

○ ambrosial:_____

○ plebeian:_____

○ novelty:_____

○ ruminating:_____

○ implacable:_____

II. Plot: Write a simple sentence or phrase to describe the main actions that take place in each scene.

JEALOUS VENUS	PALACE LIFE	THE TASKS
1._____	1._____	1._____
2._____	2._____	2._____
3._____	3._____	3._____

III. Characters: List and briefly describe the main characters in this myth.

_____

_____

_____

_____

IV. Rewrite this myth. Be sure to:

○ Include and underline all of the vocabulary words in your rewrite.

○ Write at least three separate paragraphs, one for each scene.

○ Include the following additional requirements:

_____

_____

_____

_____

_____

_____

CADMUS

I

Jupiter, under the disguise of a bull, had carried away Europa, the daughter of Agenor, king of Phoenicia. Agenor commanded his son Cadmus to go in search of his sister and not to return without her. Cadmus went and sought long and far for his sister but could not find her, and not daring to return unsuccessful, consulted the oracle of Apollo to know what country he should settle in. The oracle informed him that he should find a cow in the field and should follow her wherever she might wander, and where she stopped, he should build a city and call it Thebes. Cadmus had hardly left the cave, from which the oracle was delivered, when he saw a young cow slowly walking before him. He followed her closely and the cow went on till she came out into the plain of Panope. There she stood still and raising her broad forehead to the sky, filled the air with her lowings. Cadmus gave thanks and, stooping down kissed the foreign soil, then lifting his eyes, greeted the surrounding mountains. Wishing to offer a sacrifice, he sent his servants to seek pure water for a libation. Near by there stood an ancient grove which had never been profaned by the axe, in the midst of which there was a cave that was thickly covered with the growth of bushes. Its roof formed a low arch, from beneath which burst forth a fountain of purest water. In the cave lurked a horrid serpent with a crested head and scales glittering like gold. His eyes shone like fire, his body was swollen with venom, he vibrated a triple tongue, and he showed a triple row of teeth. No sooner had the servants dipped their pitchers in the fountain and the in-gushing waters made a sound, than the glittering serpent raised his head out of the cave and uttered a fearful hiss. The vessels fell from their hands, the blood left their cheeks, and they trembled in every limb. The serpent, twisting his scaly body in a huge coil, raised his head over the tallest trees and, while the servants from terror could neither fight nor fly, slew some with his fangs, others in his folds, and others with his poisonous breath.

II

Cadmus, having waited for the return of his men till midday, went in search of them. His covering was a lion's hide, and besides his javelin he carried in his hand a lance and in his breast a bold heart, a surer reliance than either. When he entered the wood and saw the lifeless bodies of his men and the monster with his bloody jaws, he exclaimed, "O faithful friends, I will avenge you or share your death."

So saying he lifted a huge stone and threw it with all his force at the serpent. Such a block would have shaken the wall of a fortress, but it made no impression on the monster. Cadmus next threw his javelin which met with better success, for it penetrated the serpent's scales and pierced through to his entrails. Fierce with pain, the monster turned back his head to view the wound and attempted to draw out the weapon with his mouth but broke it off, leaving the iron point rankling in his flesh. His neck swelled with rage, bloody foam covered his jaws, and the breath of his nostrils poisoned the air around. Now he twisted himself into a circle, then stretched himself out on the ground like the trunk of a fallen tree. As he moved onward, Cadmus retreated before him, holding his spear opposite to the monster's opened jaws. The serpent snapped at the weapon and attempted to bite its iron point. At last Cadmus, watching his chance, thrust the spear at a moment when the animal's head was thrown back against the trunk of a tree, and so succeeded in pinning him to the tree. The serpent's weight bent the tree as he struggled in the agonies of death.

III

While Cadmus stood over his conquered foe, contemplating its vast size, a voice was heard (from whence he knew not, but he heard it distinctly) commanding him to take the dragon's teeth and sow them in the earth. He obeyed. He made a furrow in the ground and planted the teeth. Scarce had he done so when the clods began to move, and the points of spears to appear above the surface. Next helmets with their nodding plumes came up, and next the shoulders and breasts and limbs of men with weapons, and in time a harvest of armed warriors. Cadmus, alarmed, prepared to encounter a new enemy, but one of them said to him, "Meddle not with our civil war." With that he who had spoken smote one of his earth-born brothers with a sword, and he himself fell pierced with an arrow from another. The latter fell victim to a fourth, and in like manner the whole crowd dealt with each other till all fell, slain with mutual wounds, except five survivors. One of these cast away his weapons and said, "Brothers, let us live in peace!" These five joined with Cadmus in building his city, to which they gave the name of Thebes.

CADMUS

I. Vocabulary: Underline the following words in the myth and define them below.

○ stooping:_____

○ profaned:_____

○ javelin:_____

○ rankling:_____

○ contemplating:_____

II. Plot: Write a simple sentence or phrase to describe the main actions that take place in each scene.

ORACLE'S ADVICE	CADMUS FIGHTS SERPENT	SOLDIERS FROM TEETH
1._____	1._____	1._____
2._____	2._____	2._____
3._____	3._____	3._____

III. Characters: List and briefly describe the main characters in this myth.

_____

_____

_____

_____

IV. Rewrite this myth. Be sure to:

○ Include and underline all of the vocabulary words in your rewrite.

○ Write at least three separate paragraphs, one for each scene.

○ Include the following additional requirements:

_____

_____

_____

_____

_____

_____

ECHO AND NARCISSUS

I

Echo was a beautiful nymph, fond of the woods and hills, where she devoted herself to woodland sports with the companions of Diana. Echo had one failing; she was fond of talking and, whether in chat or argument, would always have the last word. Finally Echo succeeded in offending Juno with her chattering tongue. Juno passed sentence upon Echo in these words: "You shall forfeit the use of that tongue with which you have cheated me, except for that one purpose you are so fond of – reply. You shall still have the last word, but no power to speak first."

From then on all Echo could do was repeat the last few words that someone else had spoken. Sometimes she even imitated the animals.

"Whoo," she would say after the owl spoke.

"Honk, honk," she would say after the goose.

"Moo," she copied the cattle.

"Croak," she replied after the frog.

II

This nymph saw Narcissus, a beautiful youth, as he pursued the chase upon the mountains. She wished to speak with him and followed his footsteps. O how she longed to converse with him! but it was not in her power. She waited with impatience for him to speak first and had her answer ready. One day the youth, being separated from his companions, shouted aloud, "Who's here?"

Echo replied, "Here."

Narcissus looked around and saw Echo approaching. He called out, "Come here."

Echo answered, "Come here."

Narcissus replied, "Stop that repeating!"

Echo could not help but answer with the same words.

By this time Narcissus, a very self-centered young man, was weary of hearing himself apparently mocked. He turned away from her and disgustingly murmured, "I have no time for this parroting woman and her senseless repeating."

Echo realized that her approaching was all in vain. Narcissus had left her, and she went to hide her blushes in the recesses of the woods. From that time forth she lived in caves and among mountain cliffs. Her form faded with grief, till at last all her flesh shrank away. Her bones were changed into rocks and there was nothing left of her but her voice. With that she is still ready to reply to any one who calls her and keeps up her old habit of having the last word.

Meanwhile Narcissus continued on his way thinking of himself. He had a habit of not thinking of others unless they bestowed a compliment or favor upon him. The gods of Olympus watched Narcissus and decided to punish his vanity.

III

Now there was a clear fountain with water like silver to which the shepherds never drove their flocks, nor the mountain goats resorted, nor any of the beasts of the forests; neither was it defaced with fallen leaves or branches; but the grass grew fresh around it, and the rocks sheltered it from the sun. Hither came one day the youth, fatigued with hunting, heated and thirsty. He stooped down to drink and saw his own image in the water; he thought it was some beautiful water-spirit living in the fountain. He stood gazing with admiration at those bright eyes, those locks curled like the locks of Bacchus or Apollo, the rounded cheeks, the ivory neck, the parted lips, and the glow of health and exercise over all. He fell in love with himself. He could not tear himself away; he lost all thought of food or rest while he hovered over the brink of the fountain gazing upon his own image. With this and much more of the same kind, he cherished the flame that consumed him, so that by degrees he lost his color, his vigor, and the beauty which formerly had so charmed the nymph Echo. Finally he pined away and died. The nymphs mourned for him. They prepared a funeral pile and would have burned the body, but it was nowhere to be found. In its place was a flower, purple within and surrounded with white leaves, which bears the name and preserves the memory of Narcissus.

ECHO AND NARCISSUS

I. Vocabulary: Underline the following words in the myth and define them below.

○ forfeit:_____

○ converse:_____

○ apparently:_____

○ fatigued:_____

○ pined:_____

II. Plot: Write a simple sentence or phrase to describe the main actions that take place in each scene.

ECHO TRANSFORMED	ECHO SEES NARCISSUS	NARCISSUS PUNISHED
1._____	1._____	1._____
2._____	2._____	2._____
3._____	3._____	3._____

III. Characters: List and briefly describe the main characters in this myth.

_____

_____

_____

_____

IV. Rewrite this myth. Be sure to:

○ Include and underline all of the vocabulary words in your rewrite.

○ Write at least three separate paragraphs, one for each scene.

○ Include the following additional requirements:

_____

_____

_____

_____

_____

_____

MINERVA AND ARACHNE

I

Arachne was a proud maiden who had attained such skill in the arts of weaving and embroidery that the nymphs themselves would leave their groves and fountains to come and gaze upon her work. It was not only beautiful when it was done, but beautiful also in the doing. To watch her, as she sat at the spinning-wheel and spun the soft, many-colored wools into fine, even threads and then wove them on her loom into a web enchanting both to the sight and to the touch, one would have said that Minerva herself had taught her. But this she denied and could not bear to be thought a pupil even of a goddess.

"Ha!" she would boast, "I have taught myself everything I know. Let Minerva try her skill with mine," said she. "If beaten I will pay the penalty."

Minerva heard this and was displeased. She assumed the form of an old woman and went and gave Arachne some friendly advice. "I have had much experience," said she, "and I hope you will not despise my counsel. Challenge your fellow-mortals as you will, but do not compete with a goddess. On the contrary, I advise you to ask her forgiveness for what you have said, and as she is merciful perhaps she will pardon you."

Arachne stopped her spinning and looked at the old dame with anger in her countenance. "Keep your counsel," said she, "for your daughters or handmaids; for my part I know what I say, and I stand to it. I am not afraid of the goddess; let her try her skill, if she dare venture."

"Minerva is here," said the old woman; and dropping her disguise she stood confessed. The nymphs present bent low in homage, and all the bystanders paid reverence. Arachne alone was not terrified. She blushed, indeed; a sudden color dyed her cheek, and then she grew pale. But she stood to her resolve and with a foolish conceit of her own skill rushed on her fate. Minerva forbore no longer nor interposed any further advice.

II

Hurriedly Arachne's servants prepared two looms. The weavers then proceeded to the contest. Each took her station and attached the web to the beam. Both worked with speed; their skillful hands moved rapidly, and the excitement of the contest made the labor light.

Minerva wrought on her web the scene of her contest with Neptune. Twelve of the heavenly powers were represented in the central circle; and in the four corners were represented incidents illustrating the displeasure of the gods at such presumptuous mortals as had dared to contend with them. These were meant as warnings to her rival to give up the contest before it was too late.

Arachne filled her web with subjects designedly chosen to exhibit the failings and errors of the gods. One scene represented Danae, in the brazen tower in which her father had imprisoned her but where the god effected his entrance in the form of a golden shower. Still another depicted Europa deceived by Jupiter under the disguise of a bull. You would have thought it was a real bull, so naturally was it wrought and so natural the water in which it swam.

III

Thus Arachne filled her canvas with subjects, wonderfully well done but strongly marking her presumption and impiety. Minerva could not forbear to admire, yet felt indignant at the insult. She struck the web with her shuttle and rent it in pieces; she then touched the forehead of Arachne and made her feel her guilt and shame. Arachne could not endure it.

Minerva was moved to pity as she watched Arachne crawl away. "Live," she said, "guilty woman! and that you may preserve the memory of this lesson, continue to weave, both you and your descendants, to all future times."

She sprinkled her with the juices of aconite and immediately Arachne's hair fell off and her nose and ears likewise. Her form shrank up, and her head grew smaller yet, till she was mostly a large, soft, belly; her fingers cleaved to her side and served for legs. Out of her belly Arachne spins her thread, often hanging suspended by it, in the same attitude as when Minerva touched her and transformed her into a spider.

MINERVA AND ARACHNE

I. Vocabulary: Underline the following words in the myth and define them below.

- ○ reverence:_____

- ○ interposed:_____

- ○ presumptuous:_____

- ○ indignant:_____

- ○ aconite:_____

II. Plot: Write a simple sentence or phrase to describe the main actions that take place in each scene.

MINERVA DISPLEASED	THE CONTEST	ARACHNE TRANSFORMED
1._____	1._____	1._____
2._____	2._____	2._____
3._____	3._____	3._____

III. Characters: List and briefly describe the main characters in this myth.

_____

_____

_____

_____

IV. Rewrite this myth. Be sure to:

- ○ Include and underline all of the vocabulary words in your rewrite.

- ○ Write at least three separate paragraphs, one for each scene.

- ○ Include the following additional requirements:

_____

_____

_____

_____

_____

_____

OEDIPUS

I

Laius, king of Thebes, was warned by an oracle that there was danger to his throne and life if his new-born son should be suffered to grow up. He therefore committed the child to the care of a herdsman with orders to destroy him. Now the herdsman was moved with pity, but he dare not entirely disobey, so he tied up the child by the feet and left him hanging to the branch of a tree. It was in this condition that the infant was found by a peasant who carried him to his master and mistress. These kind people adopted the boy and called him Oedipus or Swollen-foot.

Many years afterwards King Laius was riding in his chariot on his way to Delphi, accompanied only by one attendant. In a narrow part of the road they met a young man also driving in a chariot. On his refusal to leave the way at their command, the attendant killed one of the young man's horses, and the stranger, filled with rage, slew both Laius and his attendant. The young man was Oedipus, who thus unknowingly became the slayer of his own father.

II

Shortly after this event the city of Thebes was afflicted with a monster which infested the highroad. It was called the Sphinx. It had the body of a lion and the upper part of a woman. It lay crouched on the top of a rock and arrested all travelers who came that way, proposing to them a riddle, with the condition that those who could solve it should pass safe but those who failed should be killed. Not one had yet succeeded in solving it, and all had been slain. Oedipus was not daunted by these alarming accounts but boldly advanced to the trial. The Sphinx asked him, "What animal is it which in the morning goes on four feet, at noon on two, and in the evening upon three?" Oedipus thought a while and replied, "Man, who in childhood creeps on hands and knees, in manhood walks erect, and in old age with the aid of a staff." The Sphinx was so mortified at the solving of her riddle that she cast herself down from the rock and perished.

III

The gratitude of the people for their deliverance was so great that they made Oedipus their king, giving him in marriage their queen Jocasta. Oedipus, ignorant of his parentage, had already become the slayer of his father; in marrying the queen he became the husband of his mother. These horrors remained undiscovered, till at length Thebes was afflicted with famine and pestilence, and the oracle was consulted. Then the double crime of Oedipus came to light. Jocasta put an end to her own life, and Oedipus, seized with madness, tore out his eyes and wandered away from Thebes, dreaded and abandoned by all except his daughters who faithfully adhered to him, till after a tedious period of miserable wandering he found the termination of his wretched life.

OEDIPUS

I. Vocabulary: Underline the following words in the myth and define them below.

○ infested:_____

○ proposing:_____

○ daunted:_____

○ famine:_____

○ pestilence:_____

II. Plot: Write a simple sentence or phrase to describe the main actions that take place in each scene.

SWOLLEN FOOT	THE SPHINX	DOUBLE CRIME
1._____	1._____	1._____
2._____	2._____	2._____
3._____	3._____	3._____

III. Characters: List and briefly describe the main characters in this myth.

_____

_____

_____

_____

IV. Rewrite this myth. Be sure to:

○ Include and underline all of the vocabulary words in your rewrite.

○ Write at least three separate paragraphs, one for each scene.

○ Include the following additional requirements:

_____

_____

_____

_____

_____

_____

ATALANTA

I

Atalanta was a maiden whose face you might truly say was boyish for a girl yet too girlish for a boy. Her fortune had been told by Apollo, and it was to this effect: "Atalanta, do not marry; marriage will be your ruin." Terrified by this oracle, she fled the society of men and devoted herself to the sports of the chase. To all suitors (for she had many) she imposed a condition which was generally effectual in relieving her of their persecutions- "I will be the prize of him who shall conquer me in the race; but death must be the penalty of all who try and fail." In spite of this hard condition some would try. A young man named Hippomenes planned to watch one such race. "Can it be possible that any will be so rash as to risk so much for a wife?" said he. But when he saw Atalanta and her beauty and grace, he changed his mind and said, "Pardon me, youths, I knew not the prize you were competing for."

As he surveyed them he wished them all to be beaten and swelled with envy of any one that seemed at all likely to win. While such were his thoughts, the virgin darted forward. As she ran she looked more beautiful than ever. The breezes seemed to give wings to her feet, her hair flew over her shoulders, and the gay fringe of her garment fluttered behind her. A ruddy hue tinged the whiteness of her skin, such as a crimson curtain casts on a marble wall. All her competitors were distanced and were put to death without mercy. Hippomenes, not daunted by this result, fixing his eyes on the virgin, said, "Why boast of beating those laggards? I offer myself for the contest." Atalanta looked at him with a pitying countenance and hardly knew whether she would rather conquer him or not. "What god can tempt one so young and handsome to throw himself away? I pity him, not for his beauty (yet he is beautiful) but for his youth. I wish he would give up the race, or if he will be so mad, I hope he may outrun me." While she hesitated, the spectators grew impatient for the race and urged her to compete. Thus with a heavy heart Atalanta consented to race Hippomenes on the next day. That evening Hippomenes addressed a prayer to Venus: "Help me, Venus, for you have led me on." Venus heard and was propitious.

II

In the garden of her temple in her own island of Cyprus is a tree with yellow leaves and yellow branches and golden fruit. Hence she gathered three golden apples and, unseen by any one else, gave them to Hippomenes and told him how to use them. The next day the competitors lined up for the race. The signal was given; each started from the goal and skimmed over the sand. So light was their tread that you would almost have thought they might run over the river surface or over the waving grain without sinking. The cries of the spectators cheered Hippomenes, "Now, now, do your best! haste, haste! you gain on her! relax not! one more effort!" It was doubtful whether the youth or the maiden heard these cries with the greater pleasure. But his breath began to fail him, his throat was dry, and the goal yet far off. At that moment he threw down one of the golden apples. The virgin was all amazement. She stopped to pick it up. Hippomenes shot ahead. Shouts burst forth from all sides. She redoubled her efforts and soon overtook him. As he thought his chest would burst he again he threw an apple. She stopped again but again came up with him again. The goal was near; one chance only remained. "Now, goddess," said he, "prosper your gift!" and threw the last apple off at one side. She looked at it and hesitated, trying to decide if she should run after it. Venus impelled her to turn aside for it. She did so, and he sprinted to the finish. Atalanta was vanquished. The youth carried off his prize.

III

Hippomenes had won Atalanta for his bride but in his bliss he forgot to thank Venus, who had helped him. She was enraged and called upon Cybele to help her. As Cybele watched the two proudly strolling through the woods she took from them their human form and turned them into the animals whose characters they most resembled—of the huntress-heroine, triumphing in the blood of her lovers, she made a lioness and of her lord and master a lion—and yoked them to her car, where they are still to be seen in all representations, in statuary or painting, of the goddess Cybele.

ATALANTA

I. Vocabulary: Underline the following words in the myth and define them below.

○ laggards:_____

○ propitious:_____

○ impelled:_____

○ bliss:_____

○ enraged:_____

II. Plot: Write a simple sentence or phrase to describe the main actions that take place in each scene.

THE CHALLENGE	THE RACE	THE TRANSFORMATION
1._____	1._____	1._____
2._____	2._____	2._____
3._____	3._____	3._____

III. Characters: List and briefly describe the main characters in this myth.

_____

_____

_____

_____

IV. Rewrite this myth. Be sure to:

○ Include and underline all of the vocabulary words in your rewrite.

○ Write at least three separate paragraphs, one for each scene.

○ Include the following additional requirements:

_____

_____

_____

_____

_____

_____

DAEDALUS

I

Daedalus was a skillful inventor. One of his most famous accomplishments was the labyrinth that he built for King Minos. After the job was completed, he lost the favor of the king and was shut up with his son Icarus in a tower. He contrived to make an escape from his prison but could not leave the island by sea, as the king kept strict watch on all the vessels and permitted none to sail without being carefully searched.

"Minos may control the land and sea," said Daedalus, "but not the regions of the air. I will try that way." So he set to work to fabricate wings for himself and his young son Icarus. He wrought feathers together, beginning with the smallest and adding larger, so as to form an increasing surface. The larger ones he secured with thread and the smaller with wax and gave the whole a gentle curvature like the wings of a bird. Icarus, the boy, stood and looked on, sometimes running to gather up the feathers which the wind had blown away and then handling the wax and working it over with his fingers, by his play impeding his father in his labors. When at last the work was done, the artist, waving his wings, found himself buoyed upward and hung suspended, poising himself on the beaten air. He next equipped his son in the same manner and taught him how to fly, as a bird tempts her young ones from the lofty nest into the air.

II

When all was prepared for flight he said, "Icarus, my son, I charge you to keep at a moderate height, for if you fly too low the damp will clog your wings, and if too high the heat will melt them. Keep near me and you will be safe." While he gave him these instructions and fitted the wings to his shoulders, the face of the father was wet with tears and his hands trembled. He kissed the boy, not knowing that it was for the last time. Then rising on his wings, he flew off, encouraging him to follow, and looked back from his own flight to see how his son managed his wings. As they flew the ploughman stopped his work to gaze, and the shepherd leaned on his staff and watched them, astonished at the sight and thinking they were gods who could thus cleave the air.

III

Things were going well when the boy, exulting in his flight, began to leave the guidance of his father and soar upward as if to reach heaven. The nearness of the blazing sun softened the wax which held the feathers together, and they came off. He fluttered with his arms, but no feathers remained to hold the air. While his mouth was uttering cries to his father it was submerged in the blue waters of the sea (which thenceforth was called by his name). His father cried, "Icarus, Icarus, where are you?" At last he saw the feathers floating on the water, and bitterly lamenting his own arts, he buried the body and called the land Icaria in memory of his child.

DAEDALUS

I. Vocabulary: Underline the following words in the myth and define them below.

○ accomplishments:_____

○ labyrinth:_____

○ vessels:_____

○ suspended:_____

○ exulting:_____

II. Plot: Write a simple sentence or phrase to describe the main actions that take place in each scene.

REGIONS OF THE AIR	MODERATE HEIGHT	SUBMERGED
1._____	1._____	1._____
2._____	2._____	2._____
3._____	3._____	3._____

III. Characters: List and briefly describe the main characters in this myth.

_____

_____

_____

_____

IV. Rewrite this myth. Be sure to:

○ Include and underline all of the vocabulary words in your rewrite.

○ Write at least three separate paragraphs, one for each scene.

○ Include the following additional requirements:

_____

_____

_____

_____

_____

_____

_____

ORPHEUS AND EURYDICE

I

Orpheus was the son of Apollo and the Muse Calliope. He was presented by his father with a lyre and taught to play upon it, which he did to such perfection that nothing could withstand the charm of his music. Not only his fellow-mortals, but wild beasts were softened by his strains, and gathering round him they laid aside their fierceness and stood entranced by his playing. Nay, the very trees and rocks were sensible to the charm.

Orpheus eventually met the lovely nymph Eurydice and loved her and wooed her with enchanting strains that could not be resisted. Apollo arranged a grand marriage feast for his son, and many of the gods came as guests in splendid array. But the one to whom everybody looked most anxiously was a tall and handsome youth who carried a torch in his hand. This was Hymen, the god of marriage, and according as his torch burned bright or dimly would be the fortunes of the bride and bridegroom. Imagine, therefore, the dismay of the guests when they saw that no clear flame rose from the torch–hardly even a glimmer of light, but thick, acrid smoke which spread through the air until it brought tears–ill omens for a marriage–into everyone's eyes. A gloom fell on the festivities, but soon Orpheus and Eurydice forgot the evil omen in bright visions of the happiness in store for them.

II

For a short time they were, indeed, very happy, and Orpheus made more wonderful music than ever before. Then one day Eurydice went to join in the games of the woodland nymphs, as she had been used to doing before her marriage. As she wandered, she trod upon a snake in the grass, was bitten in the foot, and died. Orpheus sang his grief to all who breathed the upper air, both gods and men. Finally he resolved to seek his wife in the regions of the dead (Hades). He descended by a cave and arrived at the Stygian realm. He passed through crowds of ghosts and presented himself before the throne of Pluto and Proserpine. Accompanying the words with the lyre, he sung:

"O deities of the under-world, to whom all we who live must come, hear my words, for they are true. I come to seek my wife whose opening years the poisonous viper's fang has brought to an untimely end. Love has led me here. I implore you by these abodes full of terror, these realms of silence and uncreated things, unite again the thread of Eurydice's life. We all are destined to you and sooner or later must pass to your domain. She too, when she shall have filled her term of life, will rightly be yours. But till then grant her to me, I beseech you. If you deny me, I cannot return alone; you shall triumph in the death of us both."

III

As he sang these tender strains, the very ghosts shed tears. Proserpine could not resist, and Pluto himself gave way. Eurydice was called. She came from among the new-arrived ghosts, limping with her wounded foot. Orpheus was permitted to take her away with him on one condition, that he should not turn around to look at her till they should have reached the upper air. Under this condition they proceeded on their way, he leading, she following, through passages dark and steep, in total silence, till they had nearly reached the outlet into the cheerful upper world. Then Orpheus, in a moment of forgetfulness, to assure himself that she was still following, cast a glance behind him, when instantly she was borne away. Stretching out their arms to embrace each other, they grasped only the air! Dying now a second time, she yet could not reproach her husband, for how could she blame his impatience to behold her? "Farewell," she said, "a last farewell," and was hurried away, so fast that the sound hardly reached his ears.

Orpheus endeavored to follow her and besought permission to return and try once more for her release; but the stern ferryman (Charon) repulsed him and refused passage. Seven days he lingered about the brink, without food or sleep; then he turned and sang his complaints to the rocks and mountains, melting the hearts of tigers and moving the oaks from their stations. Finally Orpheus died in grief. His lyre was placed by Jupiter among the stars and his shade passed a second time to Tartarus where he sought out his Eurydice and embraced her with eager arms. They roam the happy fields together now, and Orpheus gazes as much as he will upon her, no longer incurring a penalty for a thoughtless glance.

ORPHEUS AND EURYDICE

I. Vocabulary: Underline the following words in the myth and define them below.

  ○ lyre:_____

  ○ mortals:_____

  ○ descended:_____

  ○ permitted:_____

  ○ repulsed:_____

II. Plot: Write a simple sentence or phrase to describe the main actions that take place in each scene.

ACRID SMOKE	HADES	A GLANCE
1._____	1._____	1._____
2._____	2._____	2._____
3._____	3._____	3._____

III. Characters: List and briefly describe the main characters in this myth.

_____

_____

_____

_____

IV. Rewrite this myth. Be sure to:

  ○ Include and underline all of the vocabulary words in your rewrite.

  ○ Write at least three separate paragraphs, one for each scene.

  ○ Include the following additional requirements:

_____

_____

_____

_____

_____

_____

_____

DIANA AND ORION

I

Diana, the moon-goddess, was the sister of Apollo and, like him, loved all woodland pastimes, so that she became also the goddess of hunting. She was tall and straight and strong and very beautiful, and she had many suitors; but she would not marry, declaring that she loved best to be free and live with her nymphs in the forest. Her nymphs also vowed to remain unmarried.

It was a fair sight to see the train of lovely maidens who, dressed in short green tunics and carrying each a bow and sheaf of arrows, ranged gaily through the forest glades. Diana went in front, a shining crescent on her head to mark her out as moon-goddess and leader of the band.

One day seven of the nymphs–the daughters of Atlas and known as the Pleiades–had left the others and were walking by themselves through the shady woodland, when they heard a shout and saw coming toward them a gigantic youth, comely and handsome in his hunter's dress. This was Orion, son of Neptune, and he was followed by his dog, Sirius. The Pleiades turned quickly and ran away in the opposite direction, for the nymphs of Diana were vowed to shun the society of man. The hunter caught only a glimpse of their faces before they turned from him, but in that one glimpse he saw that they were young and beautiful and that their eyes sparkled and their lips smiled. He followed quickly, calling to them to stop, but they only fled the faster. They were strong and lithe and trained to run, so that Orion found it very difficult to catch up to them. On and on they ran, speeding down forest paths and across open glades, and still Orion followed, until at length the strength of the nymphs began to fail, and they called upon Diana to help them.

Orion saw them flag and came on triumphantly; but the goddess heard the prayer of her followers, and when Orion put out his hand, thinking to touch a maiden, a white pigeon fluttered from his grasp and flew swiftly, with six companions like itself, toward the heavens. Orion watched them in amazement as they mounted higher and higher until they became seven white dots against the blue sky. Then, to his astonishment, the white dots turned to points of light, and there, shining in the heavens above him, he saw a group of seven stars.

II

Orion turned away in great vexation, but he soon forgot his disappointment and went off on other adventures. Some time after he met Diana herself, and the two became great friends. Both loved hunting and were daring and fearless in their favorite sport. Diana found all her pastimes far more enjoyable when they were shared with this mighty hunter than when her more timid nymphs were her only companions.

Apollo looked with great disfavor upon his sister's friendship with Orion. He feared that she was about to forget her vows as a maiden-goddess and marry this son of Neptune who had just the qualities to win her love. He laid his plans very carefully, resolving to put an end to the friendship. He knew that Neptune had given his son the power of wading or walking through the waves and that Orion might often be seen far out at sea. He waited for one of these occasions, and then he went to his sister and, talking pleasantly to her, drew her toward the seashore. Then he began to talk of the wonderful marksmanship of himself and his companions, and Diana, jealous for the honor of her maiden-band, told in her turn of the feats that they had performed.

III

"All very well" said Apollo, pretending doubt, "but show me what you can do. Can you hit that black spot far out at sea?" and he pointed to Orion's head, which showed dark above the waters.

Eager to prove her skill, Diana at once took her bow and shot with such exactness of aim that the black spot disappeared beneath the waves. The goddess turned triumphantly to her brother, who praised her warmly, being delighted that his scheme had succeeded so well.

But the waves lifted the body of Orion and bore it toward the shore, where they laid it gently down in the sight of Diana; and there, piercing the dark head, was her own arrow.

Diana wept bitterly, reproaching her brother and reproaching herself also that she had fallen so readily into his trap, but she could not bring Orion back to life. So she placed him among the stars, and there he shines to this day with his dog Sirius following and the Pleiades flying before him.

DIANA AND ORION

I. Vocabulary: Underline the following words in the myth and define them below.

○ pastimes:_____

○ crescent:_____

○ timid:_____

○ marksmanship:_____

○ triumphantly:_____

II. Plot: Write a simple sentence or phrase to describe the main actions that take place in each scene.

ORION AND PLEIADES	GREAT FRIENDS	THE TRAP
1._____	1._____	1._____
2._____	2._____	2._____
3._____	3._____	3._____

III. Characters: List and briefly describe the main characters in this myth.

_____

_____

_____

_____

IV. Rewrite this myth. Be sure to:

○ Include and underline all of the vocabulary words in your rewrite.

○ Write at least three separate paragraphs, one for each scene.

○ Include the following additional requirements:

_____

_____

_____

_____

_____

_____

THE APPLE OF DISCORD

I

It happened very often that Venus and Minerva were opposed to one another in the affairs of men. Venus nearly always sympathized with the young and beautiful, while Minerva had more regard to thoughtfulness and nobility of character. So a sort of rivalry in power grew up between them, and at last they came to an open quarrel.

It happened that a great feast was made at the marriage of Thetis, a beautiful sea-nymph, with King Peleus. Jupiter, with all the gods of Olympus, was present. He brought his splendid train to the coral caves under the sea where the wedding was to take place, and the banquet was begun with much rejoicing. In the midst of the merriment there walked into the hall an uninvited guest. It was Discordia, the goddess of discord. She had not been asked with the other deities because she was so sour and bad-tempered that wherever she went merriment and good fellowship were changed into bitter strife. She was very angry at having been slighted and was bent on revenge. Her venomous looks made everybody feel uncomfortable, and when, after a few minutes, she went rudely away, she left discord behind her; for she threw upon the table a golden apple upon which was written "To the fairest."

II

At once many voices claimed the apple, for there were maidens and nymphs and goddesses present at the feast whose title to be considered beautiful none could dispute; but after a time all save Juno, Minerva, and Venus withdrew from the contest. Juno claimed the apple as the right of the acknowledged queen of Olympus; Minerva urged that there was no beauty so precious as the beauty of mind and spirit; while Venus lifted up her fair face, surprised that there should be any question, for was she not, by the consent of all, queen of beauty?

Bitter words were said and angry looks exchanged. Each claimant called on one after another of the guests to give judgment in the matter, but all shrank from offering an opinion, for to please one must mean that the other two would be offended. At last Jupiter, to end the dispute, bade his messenger, Mercury, to take the three goddesses to Mount Ida and call upon the shepherd whom they should find there to decide the question. The shepherd was really Paris, son of Priam, King of Troy. At his birth an oracle had predicted that he would bring great misfortune to his family and his native city, and to avoid this he had been taken to Mount Ida and left there to die. But a shepherd had found him and had taken him home and brought him up as his son. When Paris grew to be a man he also became a shepherd. He was a very beautiful youth and all three goddesses were at once charmed with him.

III

Paris could not resist this appeal. Venus's face made him forget wisdom and glory and riches and power and think only of love. Here was the fairest. He would give her the apple.

So Paris gave judgment in favor of Venus, and henceforward Juno and Minerva hated their successful rival and hated Paris too. The decision which he made that day brought about the fulfilment of the oracle's prophecy that he should bring great woe upon his family and his native city, as you will see when some day you read the famous story of the siege of Troy.

THE APPLE OF DISCORD

I. Vocabulary: Underline the following words in the myth and define them below.

○ train:_____

○ banquet:_____

○ claimant:_____

○ bade:_____

○ native:_____

II. Plot: Write a simple sentence or phrase to describe the main actions that take place in each scene.

TO THE FAIREST	THE CLAIMANTS	PARIS
1._____	1._____	1._____
2._____	2._____	2._____
3._____	3._____	3._____

III. Characters: List and briefly describe the main characters in this myth.

_____

_____

_____

_____

IV. Rewrite this myth. Be sure to:

○ Include and underline all of the vocabulary words in your rewrite.

○ Write at least three separate paragraphs, one for each scene.

○ Include the following additional requirements:

_____

_____

_____

_____

_____

_____

_____

ULYSSES AND THE CYCLOPS

I

The Cyclopses were giants who inhabited an island of which they were the only possessors. The name means round eye, and these giants were so called because they had but one eye, and that placed in the middle of the forehead. They dwelt in caves and fed on the wild productions of the island and on what their flocks yielded, for they were shepherds. Ulysses left the main body of his ships at anchor, and with one vessel went to the Cyclopses' island to explore for supplies. He landed with his companions, carrying with them a jar of wine for a present, and, coming to a large cave, they entered it and, finding no one within, examined its contents. They found it stored with the richest of the flock, quantities of cheese, pails and bowls of milk, lambs and kids in their pens, all in nice order. Presently arrived the master of the cave, Polyphemus, bearing an immense bundle of firewood which he threw down before the cavern's mouth. He then drove into the cave the sheep and goats to be milked and, entering, rolled to the cave's mouth an enormous rock that twenty oxen could not draw. Next he sat down and milked his ewes, preparing a part for cheese and setting the rest aside for his customary drink.

II

Then, turning round his great eye, he discerned the strangers and growled out to them, demanding who they were and where from. Ulysses replied most humbly, stating that they were Greeks from the great expedition that had lately won so much glory in the conquest of Troy, that they were now on their way home, and finished by imploring his hospitality in the name of the gods. Polyphemus deigned no answer but, reaching out his hand, seized two of the Greeks, whom he hurled against the side of the cave, and dashed out their brains. He proceeded to devour them with great relish and, having made a hearty meal, stretched himself out on the floor to sleep. Ulysses was tempted to seize the opportunity and plunge his sword into him as be slept but recollected that it would only expose them all to certain destruction, as the rock with which the giant had closed up the door was far beyond their power to remove, and they would therefore be in hopeless imprisonment. Next morning the giant seized two more of the Greeks and despatched them in the same manner as their companions, feasting on their flesh till no fragment was left. He then moved away the rock from the door, drove out his flocks, and went out, carefully replacing the barrier after him. When he was gone Ulysses planned how he might take vengeance for his murdered friends and effect his escape with his surviving companions. He made his men prepare a massive bar of wood cut by the Cyclops for a staff, which they found in the cave. They sharpened the end of it and seasoned it in the fire and hid it under the straw on the cavern floor. Then four of the boldest were selected, with whom Ulysses joined himself as a fifth. The Cyclops came home at evening, rolled away the stone, and drove in his flock as usual. After milking them and making his arrangements as before, he seized two more of Ulysses' companions and dashed their brains out and made his evening meal upon them as he had on the others. After he had supped, Ulysses, approaching him, handed him a bowl of wine, saying, "Cyclops, this is wine; taste and drink after thy meal of men's flesh." He took and drank it and was hugely delighted with it and called for more. Ulysses supplied him once again, which pleased the giant so much that he promised him as a favour that he should be the last of the party devoured. He asked his name, to which Ulysses replied, "My name is Noman."

III

After his supper the giant lay down to repose and was soon found asleep. Then Ulysses with his four select friends thrust the end of the stake into the fire till it was all one burning coal, then poising it exactly above the giant's only eye, they buried it deeply into the socket, twirling it round as a carpenter does his auger.

The howling monster with his outcry filled the cavern, and Ulysses with his aides nimbly got out of his way and concealed themselves in the cave. He, bellowing, called aloud on all the Cyclopses dwelling in the caves around him, far and near. They on his cry flocked round the den and inquired what grievous hurt had caused him to sound such an alarm and break their slumbers. He replied, "O friends, I die, and Noman gives the blow." They answered, "If no man hurts thee it is the stroke of Jove, and thou must bear it." So saying, they left him groaning.

Next morning the Cyclops rolled away the stone to let his flock out to pasture but planted himself in the door of the cave to feel of all as they went out, that Ulysses and his men should not escape with them. But Ulysses had made his men harness the rams of the flock three abreast, with osiers which they found on the floor of the cave. To the middle ram of the three one of the Greeks suspended himself, so protected by the exterior rams on either side. As they passed, the giant felt of the animals' backs and sides but never thought of their bellies; so the men all passed safe, Ulysses himself being on the last one that passed. When they had got a few paces from the cavern, Ulysses and his friends released themselves from their rams and drove a good part of the flock down to the shore to their boat. They put them aboard with all haste, then pushed off from the shore, and when at a safe distance Ulysses shouted out, "Cyclops, the gods have well requited thee for thy atrocious deeds. Know it is Ulysses to whom thou owest thy shameful loss of sight." The Cyclops, hearing this, seized a rock that projected from the side of the mountain, and, rending it from its bed, he lifted it high in the air then, exerting all his force, hurled it in the direction of the voice. Down came the mass, just clearing the vessel's stern. The ocean, at the plunge of the huge rock, heaved the ship towards the land, so that it barely escaped being swamped by the waves. When they had with the utmost difficulty pulled off shore, Ulysses was about to hail the giant again, but his friends besought him not to do so. He could not forbear, however, letting the giant know that they had escaped his missile, but he waited till they had reached a safer distance than before. The giant answered them with curses, but Ulysses and his friends plied their oars vigorously and soon regained their companions.

ULYSSES AND THE CYCLOPS

I. Vocabulary: Underline the following words in the myth and define them below.

○ ewes:_____

○ customary:_____

○ discerned:_____

○ imploring:_____

○ poising:_____

II. Plot: Write a simple sentence or phrase to describe the main actions that take place in each scene.

THE CAVE	THE CYCLOPS	ESCAPE
1._____	1._____	1._____
2._____	2._____	2._____
3._____	3._____	3._____

III. Characters: List and briefly describe the main characters in this myth.

_____

_____

_____

_____

IV. Rewrite this myth. Be sure to:

○ Include and underline all of the vocabulary words in your rewrite.

○ Write at least three separate paragraphs, one for each scene.

○ Include the following additional requirements:

_____

_____

_____

_____

_____

_____

CIRCE'J PALACE

I

Some of you have heard, no doubt, of the wise King Ulysses and how he went to the siege of Troy and how, after that famous city was taken, he spent ten long years in trying to get back to his own kingdom of Ithaca. At one time in the course of his weary voyage, he arrived at a green and pleasant island upon which a large palace could be seen from a distance. Ulysses and his men had encountered so many dangers that they could not help dreading some mischief, even in this pleasant spot. For two days, therefore, the poor weather-worn voyagers kept quiet, and either staid on board of their vessel or merely crept along under the cliffs that bordered the shore. To keep themselves alive, they dug shellfish out of the sand and sought for any little rill of fresh water that might be running towards the sea.

Before the two days were spent, they grew very weary of this kind of life; for the followers of King Ulysses were terrible gormandizers and pretty sure to grumble if they missed their regular meals, and their irregular ones besides. Their stock of provisions was quite exhausted so that they had now to choose between starving to death or venturing into the interior of the island, where perhaps some huge horrible monster had his den.

But King Ulysses was a bold man, as well as a prudent one, and on the third morning he called his men together. "My proposal is that we divide ourselves into two equal parties and ascertain, by drawing lots, which of the two shall go inland and beg for food and assistance," he explained. "If these can be obtained, all is well. If not, then there will but half of us perish, and the remainder may set sail and escape."

As nobody objected to this scheme, Ulysses proceeded to count the whole band and then numbered off twenty-two of them and put Eurylochus at their head. Ulysses took command of the remaining twenty-two men, in person. Then, taking off his helmet, he put two shells into it, on one of which was written, "Go," and on the other "Stay." Another person held the helmet, while Ulysses and Eurylochus drew out each a shell. The word "Go" was found written on that which Eurylochus had drawn. Thus Eurylochus immediately set forth at the head of his twenty-two followers.

No sooner had they clambered up the cliff, than they discerned the tall marble towers of a palace, ascending out of the lovely green shadow of the trees which surrounded it. A gush of smoke came from a chimney in the rear.

"That smoke comes from the kitchen!" cried one of them, "and I smell roast meat in it."

"Let us make haste," cried the others, "or we shall be too late for the good cheer!"

Then they quickened their pace and capered for joy at the thought of the savory banquet at which they hoped to be guests. But Eurylochus warned them to be wary.

At length they came within full sight of the palace which proved to be very large and lofty. They hastened their steps towards the portal but had not got half way across the wide lawn, when a pack of lions, tigers, and wolves came bounding to meet them. The terrified mariners started back, expecting no better fate than to be torn to pieces and devoured. To their surprise and joy, however, these wild beasts merely capered around them, wagging their tails and behaving like so many well-bred house dogs.

Eurylochus and his followers continued on and passed under a lofty portal and looked through the open doorway into the interior of the palace. Before the strangers had time to look closely at the sight, their attention was drawn off by a very sweet and agreeable sound. A woman's voice was singing melodiously in another room of the palace, and with her voice was mingled the noise of a loom.

By and by, the song came to an end; and then, all at once, there were several feminine voices, talking airily and cheerfully, with now and then a merry burst of laughter such as you may always hear when women sit at work together.

"What a sweet song that was!" exclaimed one of the voyagers.

"Too sweet, indeed," answered Eurylochus, shaking his head.

"But how innocently those women are babbling together! Let us show ourselves at once," said another.

Thus the companions went up to a pair of folding doors at the farther end of the hall and, throwing them wide open, passed into the next room. Eurylochus, meanwhile, had stepped behind a pillar. In the short moment while the folding doors opened and closed again, he caught a glimpse of a very beautiful woman rising from the loom and coming to meet the poor weather-beaten wanderers with a hospitable smile. He also glimpsed four other young women who were only less beautiful than the lady who seemed to be their mistress.

The folding doors swung quickly back and left him standing behind the pillar in the solitude of the outer hall. There Eurylochus waited until he was quite weary and listened eagerly to every sound but without hearing anything that could help him to guess what had become of his friends. Footsteps, it is true, seemed to be passing and repassing, in other parts of the palace. Then there was a clatter of dishes which made him imagine a rich feast in a splendid banqueting hall. By and by he heard a tremendous grunting and squealing and then a sudden scampering, like that of small, hard hoofs over a marble floor.

II

But we must leave the prudent Eurylochus waiting in the outer hall and follow his friends into the inner secrecy of the palace. As soon as the beautiful woman saw them, she arose from the loom, as I have told you, and came forward. She took the hand of the foremost among them and bade him and the whole party welcome.

"You have been long expected, my good friends," said she. "I and my maidens are well acquainted with you."

"You see," she said, "that I know all about your troubles; and you cannot doubt that I desire to make you happy for as long a time as you may remain with me. For this purpose, my honored guests, I have ordered a banquet to be prepared. Fish, fowl, and flesh, roasted and in luscious stews and seasoned, I trust, to all your tastes are ready to be served up. If your appetites tell you it is dinner time, then come with me to the festal saloon."

At this kind invitation, the hungry mariners were quite overjoyed; and one of them, taking upon himself to be spokesman, assured their hospitable hostess that any hour of the day was dinner time with them. So the beautiful woman led the way; and the four maidens followed behind and hurried the guests along, until they entered a magnificent saloon. It was built in a perfect oval and lighted from a crystal dome above. Around the walls were ranged two and twenty thrones, overhung by canopies of crimson and gold, and provided with the softest of cushions. Each of the strangers was invited to sit down; and there they were, two and twenty storm-beaten mariners in worn and tattered garb, sitting on two and twenty cushioned and canopied thrones.

"Our good hostess has made kings of us all," said one. "Ha! do you smell the feast? I'll engage it will be fit to set before two and twenty kings."

"I hope," said another, "it will be good substantial sirloins, spareribs, and hinder quarters, without too many kickshaws. If I thought the good lady would not take it amiss, I should call for a fat slice of fried bacon to begin with."

Ah, the gormandizers! You see how it was with them. They could think of nothing but their greedy appetite.

But the beautiful woman now clapped her hands; and immediately there entered a train of serving men, bringing dishes of the richest food, all hot from the kitchen fire. Other attendants came next bringing great flagons of wine, of various kinds. While the servants supplied the guests with food and drink, the hostess and her four maidens went from one throne to another, exhorting them to eat and drink their fill and thus to recompense themselves, at this one banquet, for the many days when they had gone without a dinner. But whenever the mariners were not looking at them (which was pretty often, as they looked chiefly into the basins and platters), the beautiful woman and her damsels turned aside and laughed. Even the servants, as they knelt down to present the dishes, might be seen to grin and sneer, while the guests were helping themselves to the offered dainties.

These two and twenty guests sat at dinner a prodigiously long while; and it would really have made you ashamed to see how they swilled down the liquor and gobbled up the food. They sat on golden thrones, to be sure; but they behaved like pigs in a sty. At length they began to give over, from mere incapacity to hold any more.

Finally they all left off eating and leaned back on their thrones with such a stupid and helpless aspect as made them ridiculous to behold. When their hostess saw this, she laughed aloud; so did her four damsels; so did the serving men that bore the dishes, and those that poured out the wine. And the louder they all laughed, the more stupid and helpless did the two and twenty gormandizers look. Then the beautiful woman took her stand in the middle of the saloon, and stretching out a slender rod (it had been all the while in her hand, although they never noticed it till this moment), she turned it from one guest to another until each had felt it pointed at himself. Beautiful as her face was, and though there was a smile on it, it looked just as wicked and mischievous as the ugliest serpent that ever was seen.

"Wretches," cried she, "you have abused a lady's hospitality; and in this princely saloon your behavior has been suited to a hog-pen. You are already swine in everything but the human form, which you disgrace. But it will require only the slightest exercise of magic to make the exterior conform to the hoggish disposition. Assume your proper shapes, gormandizers, and begone to the sty!"

Uttering these last words, she waved her wand; and stamping her foot imperiously, each of the guests was struck aghast at beholding, instead of his comrades in human shape, one and twenty hogs sitting on the same number of golden thrones. Each man (as he still supposed himself to be) essayed to give a cry of surprise but found that he could merely grunt. It looked so intolerably absurd to see hogs on cushioned thrones, that they made haste to wallow down upon all fours like other swine. They tried to groan and beg for mercy, but forthwith emitted the most awful grunting and squealing that ever came out of swinish throats. Dear me! what pendulous ears they had! what little red eyes, half buried in fat! and what long snouts, instead of Grecian noses!

"Begone to your sty!" cried the enchantress, giving them some smart strokes with her wand; and then she turned to the serving men— "Drive out these swine, and throw down some acorns for them to eat."

The door of the saloon being flung open, the drove of hogs ran in all directions save the right one but were finally driven into the back yard of the palace. It was a sight to bring tears into one's eyes (and I hope none of you will be cruel enough to laugh at it) to see the poor creatures go snuffing along. In their sty, moreover, they behaved more piggishly than the pigs that had been born so; for they bit and snorted at one another, put their feet in the trough, and gobbled up their victuals in a ridiculous hurry; and, when there was nothing more to be had, they made a great pile of themselves among some unclean straw and fell fast asleep.

III

Meantime, as I told you before, Eurylochus had waited and waited and waited in the entrance hall of the palace without being able to comprehend what had befallen his friends. At last, when the swinish uproar resounded through the palace, he thought it best to hasten back to the vessel and inform the wise Ulysses of these marvelous occurrences. So he ran as fast as he could down the steps and never stopped to draw breath till he reached the shore.

"Why do you come alone?" asked King Ulysses. "Where are your two and twenty comrades?"

At these questions, Eurylochus burst into tears.

"Alas!" he cried, "I greatly fear that we shall never see one of their faces again."

Then he told Ulysses all that had happened, as far as he knew it. When they heard his story, all the voyagers were greatly affrighted. But Ulysses lost no time in girding on his sword and taking a spear in his right hand.

"As I am your king," explained Ulysses, " it is my duty to see what has befallen our comrades and whether anything can yet be done to rescue them. Wait for me here until tomorrow. If I do not return, you must hoist sail and endeavor to find your way to our native land. For my part, I am answerable for the fate of these poor mariners. I will either bring them back with me or perish."

Had his followers dared, they would have detained him by force. But seeing him so determined, they let him go and sat down on the sand, waiting and praying for his return.

It happened to Ulysses that after he had gone a good way along the pleasant wood path, he met him a young man clad in a rather singular garb. He wore a short cloak and a sort of cap that seemed to be furnished with a pair of wings. To enable him to walk better he carried a winged staff, around which two serpents were wriggling and twisting. In short, I have said enough to make you guess that it was Quicksilver; and Ulysses recognized him in a moment.

"Whither are you going in such a hurry, wise Ulysses?" asked Quicksilver. "Do you not know that this island is enchanted? The wicked enchantress Circe dwells in the marble palace which you see yonder among the trees. By her magic arts she changes every human being into the brute, beast, or fowl whom he happens most to resemble. Some kings who were too proud of their purple robes have been turned to gaudy-feathered birds. The lions and wolves and tigers who will come running to meet you in front of the palace were formerly fierce and cruel men."

"And my poor companions," said Ulysses. "Have they undergone a similar change?"

"You well know what gormandizers they were," replied Quicksilver; and rogue that he was, he could not help laughing at the joke. "So you will not be surprised to hear that they have all taken the shapes of swine! If Circe had never done anything worse, I really should not think her so very much to blame."

"But can I do nothing to help them?" inquired Ulysses.

"It will require all your wisdom," said Quicksilver, "and a little of my own into the bargain, to keep your royal and sagacious self from being transformed into a fox. Do as I bid you, and the matter may end better than it has begun."

While he was speaking, Quicksilver seemed to be in search of something; he went stooping along the ground and soon laid his hand on a little plant with a snow-white flower which he plucked and smelt of.

"Take this flower, King Ulysses," said he. "Guard it as you do your eyesight; for I can assure you it is exceedingly rare and precious. Keep it in your hand and smell of it frequently after you enter the palace and while you are talking with the enchantress. Especially when she offers you food or a draught of wine out of her goblet, be careful to fill your nostrils with the flower's fragrance. Follow these directions, and you may defy her magic arts to change you into a fox."

After listening attentively, Ulysses thanked his friend and resumed his way.

On entering the hall of the palace, Ulysses heard the sweet melody of the beautiful woman's song and then the pleasant voices of herself and the four maidens talking together. But Ulysses did not waste much time in listening to them. He leaned his spear against one of the pillars of the hall and then, after loosening his sword in the scabbard, stepped boldly forward, and threw the folding doors wide open. The moment she beheld his stately figure standing in the doorway, the beautiful woman rose from the loom and ran to meet him with both her hands extended.

"Welcome, brave stranger!" cried she. "We were expecting you. Your companions have already been received into my palace. If such be your pleasure, you shall first take some refreshment and then join them in the elegant apartment which they now occupy. Deign to follow me, and you shall be treated as befits your rank."

So Ulysses followed her into the saloon. But, all this while, he held the snow-white flower in his hand and constantly smelt of it while Circe was speaking. Instead of two and twenty thrones, there was now only a single throne in the center of the apartment. The enchantress took Ulysses by the hand and made him sit down upon this dazzling throne. Then, clapping her hands, she summoned the chief butler.

"Bring hither," said she, "the goblet that is set apart for kings to drink out of."

The chief butler liked nothing better than to see people turned into swine, so he made haste to bring the royal goblet, filled with a liquid as bright as gold, and which kept sparkling upward and throwing a sunny spray over the brim. But, delightfully as the wine looked, it was mingled with the most potent enchantments that Circe knew how to concoct. The mere smell of the bubbles which effervesced at the brim was enough to turn a man's beard into pig's bristles or make a lion's claws grow out of his fingers or a fox's brush behind him.

"Drink, my noble guest," said Circe, smiling, as she presented him with the goblet. "You will find in this draught a solace for all your troubles."

King Ulysses took the goblet with his right hand, while with his left he held the snow-white flower to his nostrils and drew in so long a breath that his lungs were quite filled with its pure and simple fragrance. Then, drinking off all the wine, he looked the enchantress calmly in the face.

"Wretch," cried Circe, giving him a smart stroke with her wand, "how dare you keep your human shape a moment longer! Take the form of the brute whom you most resemble. Thou canst be man no longer."

But, such was the virtue of the snow-white flower that Ulysses looked even more manly and king-like than before. He gave the magic goblet a toss. Then, drawing his sword, he seized the enchantress by her beautiful ringlets and made a gesture as if he meant to strike off her head at one blow.

"Wicked Circe," cried he in a terrible voice, "this sword shall put an end to thy work. Thou shalt die, vile wretch, and do no more mischief in the world by tempting human beings into the vices which make beasts of them."

The tone and countenance of Ulysses were so awful and his sword gleamed so brightly that Circe was almost killed by the mere fright, without waiting for a blow. The chief butler scrambled out of the saloon; and the enchantress and the four maidens fell on their knees, wringing their hands and screaming for mercy.

"Spare me!" cried Circe. "Spare me, royal and wise Ulysses. For now I know that thou art he of whom Quicksilver forewarned me, the most prudent of mortals, against whom no enchantments can prevail. Spare me!"

But Ulysses would not be pacified until Circe had taken a solemn oath to change back his companions and as many others as he should direct from their present forms of beast or bird into their former shapes of men.

"On these conditions," said he, "I consent to spare your life. Otherwise you must die upon the spot."

With a drawn sword hanging over her, the enchantress led Ulysses out of the back entrance of the palace and showed him the swine in their sty. There were about fifty beasts in the whole herd; and though the greater part were hogs by birth, there was wonderfully little difference to be seen betwixt them and their new brethren. To speak critically, indeed, the latter rather carried the thing to excess and seemed to make it a point to wallow in the miriest part of the sty and otherwise to outdo the original swine in their own natural vocation.

The comrades of Ulysses, however, had not quite lost the remembrance of having formerly stood erect. When he approached the sty, two and twenty enormous swine separated themselves from the herd and scampered towards him with such a chorus of horrible squealing as made him clap both hands to his ears.

"These must certainly be my comrades," said Ulysses. "I recognize their dispositions. They are hardly worth the trouble of changing them into the human form again. Nevertheless, we will have it done, lest their bad example should corrupt the other hogs. Let them take their original shapes, therefore, Dame Circe, if your skill is equal to the task."

So Circe waved her wand again and repeated a few magic words, at the sound of which the two and twenty hogs pricked up their pendulous ears. It was a wonder to behold how their snouts grew shorter and shorter, and their mouths smaller and smaller, and how one and another began to stand upon his hind legs and scratch his nose with his fore trotters. At first the spectators hardly knew whether to call them hogs or men, but by and by came to the conclusion that they rather resembled the latter. Finally, there stood the twenty-two comrades of Ulysses, looking pretty much the same as when they left the vessel.

"Thanks, noble Ulysses!" they cried. "From brute beasts you have restored us to the condition of men again."

"Do not put yourselves to the trouble of thanking me," said the wise king. "I fear I have done but little for you."

To say the truth, there was a suspicious kind of a grunt in their voices, and, for a long time afterwards, they spoke gruffly and were apt to set up a squeal.

As for the lions, tigers, and wolves (though Circe would have restored them to their former shapes at his slightest word), Ulysses thought it advisable that they should remain as they now were instead of going about under the guise of men. And, when everything was settled according to his pleasure, he sent to summon the remainder of his comrades, whom he had left at the sea-shore. These being arrived, with the prudent Eurylochus at their head, they all made themselves comfortable in Circe's enchanted palace until quite rested and refreshed from the toils and hardships of their voyage.

CIRCE'J PALACE

I. Vocabulary: Underline the following words in the myth and define them below.

○ gormandizers:_____

○ crimson:_____

○ recompense:_____

○ imperiously:_____

○ effervesced:_____

II. Plot: Write a simple sentence or phrase to describe the main actions that take place in each scene.

ARRIVAL AT PALACE	MEN TO SWINE	RESCUE
1._____	1._____	1._____
2._____	2._____	2._____
3._____	3._____	3._____

III. Characters: List and briefly describe the main characters in this myth.

_____

_____

_____

_____

IV. Rewrite this myth. Be sure to:

○ Include and underline all of the vocabulary words in your rewrite.

○ Write at least three separate paragraphs, one for each scene.

○ Include the following additional requirements:

_____

_____

_____

_____

_____

_____

ULYSSES RETURNS HOME

I

After staying at Circe's palace for some time, Ulysses and his men decided to continue on in their journey home. Circe aided their departure and instructed them how to pass safely by the coast of the Sirens. The Sirens were sea-nymphs who had the power of charming by their song all who heard them so that the unhappy mariners were irresistibly impelled to cast themselves into the sea to their destruction. Circe directed Ulysses to fill the ears of his seamen with wax so that they should not hear the strain and to cause himself to be bound to the mast and his people to be strictly enjoined, whatever he might say or do, by no means to release him till they should have passed the Sirens' island. Ulysses obeyed these directions. He filled the ears of his people with wax and suffered them to bind him with cords firmly to the mast. As they approached the Sirens' island, the sea was calm, and over the waters came the notes of music so ravishing and attractive that Ulysses struggled to get loose, and by cries and signs to his people begged to be released; but they, obedient to his previous orders, sprang forward and bound him still faster. They held on their course, and the music grew fainter till it ceased to be heard, when with joy Ulysses gave his companions the signal to unseal their ears, and they relieved him from his bonds.

II

Ulysses had been warned by Circe of the two monsters Scylla and Charybdis. Scylla was once a beautiful maiden and was changed into a snaky monster by Circe. She dwelt in a cave high up on the cliff, from whence she was accustomed to thrust forth her long necks (for she had six heads), and in each of her mouths seize one of the crew of every vessel passing within reach. The other terror, Charybdis, was a gulf, nearly on a level with the water. Thrice each day the water rushed into a frightful chasm, and thrice was disgorged. Any vessel coming near the whirlpool when the tide was rushing in must inevitably be engulfed; not Neptune himself could save it.

On approaching the haunt of the dread monsters, Ulysses kept strict watch to discover them. The roar of the waters as Charybdis engulfed them, gave warning at a distance, but Scylla could nowhere be discerned. While Ulysses and his men watched with anxious eyes the dreadful whirlpool, they were not equally on their guard from the attack of Scylla, and the monster, darting forth her snaky heads, caught six of his men and bore them away, shrieking, to her den. It was the saddest sight Ulysses had yet seen, to behold his friends thus sacrificed and hear their cries yet unable to afford them any assistance.

III

Circe had warned him of another danger. After passing Scylla and Charybdis the next land he would make was Thrinakia, an island whereon were pastured the cattle of Hyperion, the Sun, tended by his daughters Lampetia and Phaethusa. These flocks must not be violated, whatever the wants of the voyagers might be. If this injunction were transgressed destruction was sure to fall on the offenders.

Ulysses would willingly have passed the island of the Sun without stopping, but his companions so urgently pleaded for the rest and refreshment that would be derived from anchoring and passing the night on shore that Ulysses yielded. He bound them, however, with an oath that they would not touch one of the animals of the sacred flocks and herds but content themselves with what provision they yet had left of the supply which Circe had put on board. So long as this supply lasted the people kept their oath, but contrary winds detained them at the island for a month, and after consuming all their stock of provisions, they were forced to rely upon the birds and fishes they could catch. Famine pressed them, and at length one day, in the absence of Ulysses, they slew some of the cattle, vainly attempting to make amends for the deed by offering from them a portion to the offended powers. Ulysses, on his return to the shore, was horror-struck at perceiving what they had done, and the more so on account of the portentous signs which followed. The skins crept on the ground, and the joints of meat lowed on the spits while roasting.

The wind becoming fair they sailed from the island. They had not gone far when the weather changed, and a storm of thunder and lightning ensued. A stroke of lightning shattered their mast, which in its fall killed the pilot. At last the vessel itself came to pieces. The keel and mast floating side by side, Ulysses formed of them a raft, to which he clung, and, the wind changing, the waves bore him to Calypso's island. All the rest of the crew perished.

Calypso was a sea-nymph, one of a numerous class of female divinities of lower rank, yet sharing many of the attributes of the gods. Calypso received Ulysses hospitably, entertained him magnificently, became enamored of him, and wished to retain him forever, conferring on him immortality. But he persisted in his resolution to return to his country and his wife and son. Calypso at last received the command of Jove to dismiss him. Mercury brought the message to her and found her in her grotto. Calypso, with much reluctance, proceeded to obey the commands of Jupiter. She supplied Ulysses with the means of constructing a raft, provisioned it well for him, and gave him a favoring gale. He sped on his course prosperously for many days, till at length, when in sight of land, a storm arose that broke his mast and threatened to rend the raft asunder. In this crisis he was seen by a compassionate sea-nymph who, in the form of a cormorant, alighted on the raft and presented him a girdle, directing him to bind it beneath his breast, and if he should be compelled to trust himself to the waves, it would buoy him up and enable him by swimming to reach the land.

After other adventures in the land upon which he arrived, Ulysses finally returned home only to find his home overrun by suitors hoping to marry his wife Penelope. How Ulysses defeated the suitors and became master of his own kingdom again is more than I can tell here. Some day soon you must read Homer's Odyssey and find out for yourself.

ULYSSES RETURNS HOME

I. Vocabulary: Underline the following words in the myth and define them below.

○ mariners:_____

○ irresistibly:_____

○ dwelt:_____

○ derived:_____

○ portentous:_____

II. Plot: Write a simple sentence or phrase to describe the main actions that take place in each scene.

SIRENS	SCYLLA AND CHARIBDIS	HOMEWARD BOUND
1._____	1._____	1._____
2._____	2._____	2._____
3._____	3._____	3._____

III. Characters: List and briefly describe the main characters in this myth.

_____

_____

_____

_____

IV. Rewrite this myth. Be sure to:

○ Include and underline all of the vocabulary words in your rewrite.

○ Write at least three separate paragraphs, one for each scene.

○ Include the following additional requirements:

_____

_____

_____

_____

_____

_____

PROMETHEUS

1. Brothers give gifts. 2. Man receives none. 3. Prometheus schemes for fire.	1. Prometheus raids Olympus. 2. Fire spreads and ennobles. 3. Light catches Jupiter's attention.	1. Jupiter's bitter hatred. 2. Unending tortures planned. 3. Prometheus chained, no succor.

PANDORA

1. Pandora sent as helpmate. 2. Pandora vexed about box. 3. Pandora ponders knot.	1. Pandora tries knot. 2. Pandora justifies opening. 3. Epimetheus watches silently.	1. Earthly troubles escape. 2. A tapping is heard. 3. Hope is discovered.

APOLLO AND DAPHNE

1. Apollo kills Python. 2. Apollo taunts Cupid. 3. Cupid threatens Apollo.	1. Apollo hit by gold. 2. Daphne hit by lead. 3. Apollo pursues Daphne.	1. Apollo gains on Daphne. 2. Daphne cries for help. 3. Daphne changed to Laurel.

PYRAMUS AND THISBE

1. Parents forbid marriage. 2. Lovers find crack. 3. Lovers kiss wall.	1. Lovers plan escape. 2. Lioness "kills" Thisbe. 3. Lioness tears veil.	1. Pyramus sees veil. 2. Pyramus punctures heart. 3. Thisbe follows after.

PAN .

1. Mercury and Penelope love. 2. Pan resembles gnat. 3. Penelope flees from fear.	1. Pan taken to Olympus. 2. Pan delights gods. 3. Pan loves woodland.	1. Pan pursues Syrinx. 2. Nymphs give assistance. 3. Pan plays pipes.

IO

1. Juno brushes cloud away. 2. Jupiter seen with cow. 3. Io given to Argus.	1. Io's name in sand. 2. Jupiter employs Mercury. 3. Mercury attempts to lull.	1. Mercury kills Argus. 2. Gadfly torments Io. 3. Io is restored.

CALLISTO

1. Jupiter admires Callisto. 2. Juno becomes jealous. 3. Callisto turned into bear.	1. Arcas raises spear. 2. Jupiter transforms Arcas. 3. Bears flung into sky.	1. Juno seeks Tethys, Oceanus. 2. Juno pleads case. 3. Ocean powers assent.

PHAETON

1. Schoolfellow disbelieves Phaeton. 2. Phaeton enters Palace. 3. Phaeton asks proof.	1. Apollo invites wish. 2. Phaeton seeks to pilot. 3. Apollo warns then prepares.	1. Steeds rage uncontrolled. 2. Heaven and earth damaged. 3. Jupiter strikes Phaeton.

KING MIDAS - THE GOLDEN TOUCH

1. Midas ponders treasure. 2. Stranger suddenly appears. 3. Midas desires Golden Touch.	1. The wish is granted. 2. Midas cannot eat. 3. Midas transforms Marygold.	1. Stranger appears again. 2. Stranger gives antidote. 3. Midas learns lesson.

KING MIDAS - THE MUSIC CONTEST

1. Midas follows Pan. 2. Pan boasts proudly. 3. Inhabitants attend competition.	1. Pan and Apollo compete. 2. Midas maintains opinion. 3. Apollo transforms ears.	1. Midas hides ears. 2. Hair-dresser digs hole. 3. Reeds grow and whisper.

BAUCIS AND PHILEMON

1. Baucis, Philemon hear noise. 2. Neighbors are inhospitable. 3. Travelers are welcomed.	1. Meager meal is served. 2. Travelers quaffing wine. 3. Wine is replenished.	1. Village is drowned. 2. Hospitality is rewarded. 3. Couple become linden, oak.

PROSERPINA

1. Proserpina picks flowers. 2. Pluto snatches Proserpina. 3. Proserpina enters dominion.	1. Ceres scours world. 2. Phoebus unfolds mystery. 3. Ceres denies verdure.	1. Servant brings pomegranate. 2. Quicksilver visits Pluto. 3. Proserpina eats 6 seeds.

GLAUCUS AND SCYLLA

1. Glaucus catches fish. 2. Fish revive and return. 3. Herb transforms Glaucus.	1. Glaucus loves Scylla. 2. Love is not returned. 3. Glaucus entreats Circe.	1. Circe seeks revenge. 2. Circe poisons waters. 3. Scylla is transformed.

CEYX AND HALCYONE

1. Ceyx must voyage. 2. Waves arise. 3. Ceyx slips below surface.	1. Halcyone entreats gods. 2. Juno - Somnus - Morpheus sent. 3. "Ceyx" appears to Halcyone.	1. Body returns home. 2. Halcyone leaps in air. 3. Husband and wife transformed.

CUPID AND PSYCHE

1. Venus seeks revenge. 2. Cupid makes mistake. 3. Psyche brought to palace.	1. Never sees husband. 2. Sisters plant suspicions. 3. Psyche loses all.	1. Psyche makes amends. 2. Venus assigns tasks. 3. Psyche and Cupid united.

CADMUS

1. Jupiter steals Europa. 2. Cadmus locates cow. 3. Serpent attacks servants.	1. Stone bounces off. 2. Javelin enters in. 3. Spear pins serpent.	1. Cadmus sows teeth. 2. All but 5 die. 3. Cadmus builds Thebes.

ECHO AND NARCISSUS

1. Echo speaks overmuch. 2. Echo offends Juno. 3. Juno passed sentence.	1. Echo "echos" Narcissus. 2. Narcissus selfishly leaves. 3. Nothing left but voice.	1. Narcissus finds fountain. 2. Narcissus loves himself. 3. Narcissus dies into flower.

MINERVA AND ARACHNE

1. Arachne boasts of weaving. 2. Minerva gives advice. 3. Arachne stiffens her neck.	1. Weaving competition begins. 2. Minerva's exalts gods. 3. Arachne's chides gods.	1. Minerva humbles Arachne. 2. Minerva sprinkles aconite. 3. Arachne becomes spider.

OEDIPUS

1. Laius heeds oracle. 2. Oedipus is adopted. 3. Fight after collision.	1. Thebes afflicted by Sphinx. 2. Sphinx proposes riddle. 3. Oedipus answers "man."	1. Oedipus marries Jocasta. 2. Oracle reveals horrors. 3. Oedipus removes eyes.

ATALANTA

1. Apollo tells fortune. 2. Atlanta imposes condition. 3. Hippomenes volunteers.	1. Venus gives apples. 2. Hippomenes distracts and wins. 3. Youth carries off prize.	1. No thanks given. 2. Venus is enraged. 3. Lovers are transformed.

DAEDALUS

1. Daedalus builds labyrinth. 2. Favor is lost. 3. Daedalus makes wings.	1. Father gives instructions. 2. Daedalus kisses Icarus. 3. Off they go.	1. Icarus flies high. 2. Sun melts wax. 3. Land, sea named Icaria.

ORPHEUS AND EURYDICE

1. Apollo, Calliope have son. 2. Orpheus woos Eurydice. 3. Hymen's torch is dim.	1. Eurydice joins games. 2. Killed by serpent. 3. Orpheus enters Hades.	1. Singing persuades gods. 2. Conditions are broken. 3. Lyre becomes constellation.

DIANA AND ORION

1. Diana loves hunting. 2. Pleiades take vow. 3. Orion chases - doves - stars.	1. Orion, Diana are friends. 2. Apollo isn't pleased. 3. Diana is made jealous.	1. Apollo challenges Diana. 2. Diana hits "spot." 3. Orion becomes constellation.

THE APPLE OF DISCORD

1. Great wedding is held. 2. Discordia is not invited. 3. "To the fairest."	1. Juno- queen of Olympus. 2. Minerva- mind and spirit. 3. Venus- queen of beauty.	1. Paris chooses Venus. 2. Juno and Minerva hate. 3. Prophecy will be fulfilled.

ULYSSES AND THE CYCLOPS

1. Ulysses at Cyclops' island. 2. All enter cave. 3. Polyphemus rolls stone.	1. Ulysses explains situation. 2. Cyclops eats 2 Greeks. 3. Ulysses plots revenge.	1. Greeks gore eye. 2. "Noman gives blow." 3. Sheep smuggle Greeks.

CIRCE'S PALACE

1. Men are hungry. 2. Half enter palace. 3. Eurylachus hears squealing.	1. Greeks eat piggishly. 2. Circe waves wand. 3. Men snort out.	1. Quicksilver gives flower. 2. Ulysses overcomes magic. 3. Men are restored.

ULYSSES RETURNS HOME

1. Circe gives advice. 2. Ulysses is bound. 3. Greeks are obedient.	1. Greeks approach monsters. 2. Greeks avoid Charybdis. 3. Scylla eats six.	1. Greeks slay cattle. 2. Storm engulfs men. 3. Ulysses returns to suitors.

ROMAN / GREEK NAME CHART

Below is a chart that shows which Greek gods the Romans associated with their own gods. Because the Roman names are more common in our language we use the Roman names in this book.

ROMAN / LATIN NAME	GREEK NAME	DESCRIPTION
Jupiter, Jove	Zeus	King of Gods and Men
Neptune	Poseidon	God of the Sea
Pluto	Pluto or Hades	God of the Underworld
Juno	Hera	Goddess of Marriage
Apollo	Phoebus Apollo	God of Sun, Music and Poetry
Minerva	Pallas Athena	Goddess of Wisdom, Crafts and War
Diana	Artemis	Goddess of the Hunt and Childbirth
Venus	Aphrodite	Goddess of Love and Beauty
Mercury	Hermes	God of Commerce and Science, Jupiter's Messenger
Mars	Ares	God of War
Vulcan	Hephaestus	God of the Forge and Fire, Smith to the Gods
Cupid	Eros	God of Love
Proserpine	Persephone	Goddess of the Underworld
Ceres	Demeter	Goddess of the Harvest and Growing Things
Bacchus	Dionysus	God of the Vine, Wine and Merriment
Aurora	Eos	Goddess of the Dawn
Somnus	Hypnus	God of Sleep
Hercules	Heracles	Son of Jupiter and Alcmena

A GLOSSARY OF MYTHOLOGICAL TERMS AND GODS

GREEK MYTHS

Aeolus (EE uh luhs) – Aeolus was the master of the winds and a son of Neptune. The gods gave him dominion over the winds, which he kept in vast caves on his floating island. The Aeolian Islands near Sicily are named for him. Aeolus gave Ulysses a bag of winds to help him on his voyage back home, but his crew opened the bag and the winds escaped. Aeolus was the father of Halcyone.

Apollo – Apollo was considered the god of the sun. He was in charge of driving the chariot of the sun across the sky daily to light the earth. He was known for killing an enormous serpent named Python. In commemoration of this conquest, he instituted the Pythian games in which the victor was crowned with a wreath of leaves. Apollo brought the warm spring and summer and the harvest. He was also thought to heal the sick and he was patron of music and poetry. Apollo had an oracle at Delphi where he made the future known. Diana was the twin sister of Apollo and Aesculapius was his son. (see Lyre)

Arachne (uh RAK nee) – Arachne was a mortal who entered into a weaving contest with Minerva. Arachne is the Greek word for spider. Even today in the field of zoology, spiders and their relatives are put into the class Arachnida. The word arachnoid is used as an adjective to describe something resembling or related to the arachnids. Something flimsy and thin like a spider's web can be described as arachnoid also. In the medical field, there is a thin membrane of the brain and spinal cord that is called the arachnoid membrane.

Argus (AHR guhs) – Argus was a monster with one hundred eyes in his head. After his death it is said that Juno placed his eyes in the tail of the peacock. It is interesting to note that there is a species of bird which is closely related to the peacock which bears the name Argus pheasant.

Aurora – The Romans associated their goddess Aurora with Eos. Both were considered the goddess of the dawn. The English word east resembles the word Eos where the dawn begins. The Northern Lights or Aurora Borealis are named after Aurora because they resemble lights like the light of dawn.

Cadmus – Cadmus supposedly invented the alphabet which is sometimes called the "Cadmean letters." There are a couple of phrases in English which originate with this myth. To "sow dragon's teeth" can mean to stir up war or dissension and a "Cadmean Victory" is a victory in which hardly anyone survives.

Caduceus – The caduceus is a rod or pole around which are entwined two snakes. Sometimes caduceus have wings near the top. The caduceus was the badge of Mercury the messenger of Jupiter. Before modern medicine, doctors treated an infection of parasitic worms by using a stick and a knife. The doctor would cut a slit in the patient's skin just in front of the moving worm, and as the worm would crawl out the cut, it was wound around the stick until the entire worm was removed from the patient. Because of this practice, doctors would promote their services by means of a sign on which was painted a stick with worms entwined around it. This caduceus symbolizes medicine today and is the insignia of the U.S. Army Medical Corps.

Callisto – The Greeks believed that Callisto was turned into the constellation Ursa Major or "the Great Bear" and her son Arcas into Ursa Minor or "the Little Bear." The constellation Ursa minor contains the North Star. It is interesting to note that the Greek word for bear is "arkto" and the Greeks called the northern region "arktikos." This explains why we today refer to the area around the North Pole as the "Arctic Circle" and why the ocean in the arctic zone is called the "Arctic Ocean." The prefix "ant" means opposite. The South Pole is bounded by the "Antarctic circle." The continent contained in the Antarctic circle is called "Antarctica" and the water surrounding Antarctica is the "Antarctic Ocean." There is yet one other remnant of this myth in the sky. Near Ursa Major and Ursa Minor there is a star that appears to watch over the constellations. This star is called "Arcturus" which comes from the Greek words which mean "to guard the bears." The Bible also mentions these constellations. God said to Job in chapter 38:31,32,

> "Can you bind the chains of the Pleiades,
> Or loose the cords of Orion?
> Can you lead forth a constellation in its season,
> And guide the Bear with her satellites?"

Canis Major and **Canis Minor** – Canis Major and Minor are known as the hunting dogs of Orion. These two constellations contain two of the brightest stars visible. Sirius is the brightest star in the night sky and can be seen as the nose of Canis Major. The Romans sacrificed a dog to the star Sirius once a year in hopes that the hot star would not scorch the earth and dry the crops. Canis Major is best seen from January through March. The star Procyon is also a bright star and is found in the constellation Canis Minor which is best seen from December through May.

Ceres (SIHR eez) – Ceres was the daughter of Saturn and Rhea. She had a daughter named Proserpine, who became the wife of Pluto, and queen of the realms of the dead. Ceres presided over agriculture, particularly the grains. We call a group of breakfast foods cereal after Ceres. Ceres is also the name of an asteroid or planetoid between Jupiter and Mars. The element cerium was named to honor Ceres.

Circe (SUR see) – Circe was the daughter of Apollo. She was an enchantress especially remembered for turning Ulysses' men into swine.

Cupid – Cupid, the god of love, was the son of Venus and Mars. Cupid was the constant companion of Venus. He was often represented with his eyes covered because of the blindness of his actions. Armed with bow and arrows, he shot the darts of desire into the bosoms of both gods and men. In 1898 a planetoid was discovered between Mars and Earth. It was named Eros. The word cupidity has come to mean "strong desire" or greed, and describes too much love of money or material things.

Cyclops – Cyclops in Greek means round-eye. Cyclopes were giant creatures with one eye in the middle of their forehead. The Cyclopes worked forges in volcanos and manufactured lightning bolts. The Greeks believed that when the fires of their forges grew too high, molten rock and ash spewed out. The first three Cyclopes born to Uranus and Terra were Brontes, Steropes, and Arges; which happen to be the Greek words for thunder, lightning, and brightness. There is a type of dinosaur called the brontosaurus, or "thunder lizard," after Brontes the Cyclops. Strangely enough, there is a tiny water flea named Cyclops, not for its size, but for the fact that it appears to have only one eye in the middle of its head.

Cygnus (SIHG nuhs) – Cygnus was the name of Phaeton's friend who was turned into a swan and placed in the skies. The constellation Cygnus is best seen during the month of September flying along the section of sky which was scorched by Phaeton's trip, the Milky Way.

Daedalus (DEHD uh luhs) – Daedalus was so proud of his achievements that he could not bear the idea of a rival. His sister had placed her son Perdix under his charge to be taught the mechanical arts. He was an apt scholar and gave striking evidences of ingenuity. Daedalus was so envious of his nephew's performance that he took an opportunity, when they were together one day on the top of a high tower to push him off. But Minerva , who favors ingenuity, saw him falling, and arrested his fate by changing him into a bird called after his name, the Partridge. This bird does not build his nest in the trees, nor take lofty flights, but nestles in the hedges, and mindful of his fall, avoids high places. (The Latin word for partridge is perdix.)

Daphne (DAF nee) – Daphne was a nymph who, to escape Apollo, was turned into a laurel tree. It is interesting to note that the genus of plants that the laurel tree belongs to is called "Daphne" by botanists. The word "daphnean" means shy or bashful.

Diana – Diana was the goddess of the hunt and also the moon. She was the sister of Apollo and considered the ideal of modesty, grace, and maidenly vigor. Diana despised the "weakness" of love and imposed upon her nymphs vows of perpetual maidenhood. She was not only a huntress, but a guardian of wild beasts. When she was weary of the chase she turned to music and dancing, for the lyre and flute and song were dear to her. Though naturally gracious, gentle, and a healer of ills, Diana was, like her brother, quick to resent injury to her sacred herds or insult to herself. The cypress tree was sacred to her and her favorite animals were the bear, the boar, the dog, the goat, and specially the hind.

Epimetheus – Epimetheus was a Titan and the brother of Prometheus. His name means "hind thought." He tended to be foolish and only saw the consequences of his actions after they had occurred.

Eridanus – Eridanus is the name of the river into which Phaeton fell after being struck with a thunderbolt thrown by Jupiter. The river Eridanus is represented in the sky as the constellation Eridanus which is best seen in the month of December between the constellations Pegasus and Draco. Even today some say that the amber tears of Phaeton's sisters can still be found mixed in the sand along the Eridanus.

Halcyone (HAL see uhn) – Halcyone was the daughter of Aeolus and the wife of Ceyx. Halcyone was turned into a bird as she was mourning for Ceyx. The word Halcyone denotes a bird that is identified with the kingfisher. It can also mean calm or peaceful.

Icarus – Icarus is remembered also as a planetoid. This planetoid, named Icarus, travels at some points farther from the sun than Mars but then swoops toward the sun and gets closer to it than the planet Mercury. Interestingly enough, the death of Icarus is told in the following lines by Darwin:

> "...with melting wax and loosened strings
> Sunk hapless Icarus on unfaithful wings;
> Headlong he rushed through the affrighted air,
> With limbs distorted and dishevelled hair;
> His scattered plumage danced upon the wave,
> And sorrowing Nereids decked his watery grave;
> O'er his pale corse their pearly sea-flowers shed,
> And strewed with crimson moss his marble bed;
> Struck in their coral towers the passing bell,
> And wide in ocean tolled his echoing knell."

Io – Io was a nymph who was turned into a cow by Jupiter. There are two words in geography which received their names from the myth concerning Io. The portion of the Mediterranean sea that separates Greece from southern Italy is called the Ionian Sea. The straits which separate Europe and Asia where Istanbul is located are called Bosporus which means "cow crossing." One story states that Jupiter raised Io to the skies after her death as the constellation Taurus or "the bull." The best time to see Taurus is October through March. Some think that Taurus may have been the first constellation.

Iris – Iris was a minor goddess who was a messenger and attendant of Juno. She used a rainbow to travel from heaven to earth to deliver messages to mortals. Iris is the Greek word for rainbow. The colored part of our eyes is called the iris in her honor. The plural form of iris in Greek is irides. This is where the adjective iridescent comes from. There is also an element which combines with other elements to form colorful substances. This element is named iridium.

Juno – Juno was the wife of Jupiter, and queen of the gods. Iris, the goddess of the rainbow, was her attendant and messenger. The peacock was her favorite bird. The sixth month of the year is named after Juno who was considered the goddess of marriage. June is still a popular month for weddings.

Jupiter – Jupiter was king of gods and men and considered god of the sky. He was the supreme ruler of the universe, and the wisest and most glorious of the divinities. Jupiter gathered the clouds and snows, dispensed the gentle rains and winds and moderated the light and heat of the seasons. The thunder was his weapon. The eagle was his favorite bird, which bore his thunderbolts. The Romans identified their god of the sky, Jupiter, with the Greek god Zeus. The Greeks had named the fifth planet after Zeus. Naturally, the Romans used their version of the name and we today call the planet Jupiter. The planet Jupiter accurately reflects the god Jupiter - the planet has the largest family of satellites in the Solar System. There are twelve altogether and each is named after some person connected with Jupiter in mythology. Four of these satellites happen to be the first objects in the solar system that were discovered by the telescope. They were discovered in 1610 by Galileo Galilei. These four satellites were are named Io, Europa, Ganymede, and Callisto. The fifth satellite discovered is often referred to as Amaltheia after the goat which nursed Jupiter as an infant. The last seven satellites have yet to be named. Jupiter was also referred to as Jove. When people today say, "by Jove," they are referring to Jupiter. Jove is used as an adjective to refer to things associated with Jupiter. Thus the satellites of Jupiter are called the Jovian satellites.

Lyre – Mercury is said to have invented the lyre. He found, one day, a tortoise, of which he took the shell, made holes in the opposite edges of it, and drew cords of linen through them, and the instrument was complete. The cords were nine, in honor of the nine Muses. Mercury gave the lyre to Apollo, and received from him in exchange the caduceus. Later Apollo gave the lyre to his son Orpheus. When Orpheus died Jupiter placed the lyre in the sky as the constellation Lyra. The constellation Lyra is located next to Cygnus and is best seen from May to November. (See Mercury, Apollo, Orpheus)

Mercury – Mercury was the son of Jupiter and Maia. He presided over commerce, wrestling, and other gymnastic exercises, even over thieving, and everything, in short, which required skill and dexterity. He is also thought of as presiding over chemistry and medicine. Today when chemists seal off a vessel to keep the contents from being exposed to the air, we call the vessel hermitically sealed (see Roman / Greek Name Chart for the connection). He was the messenger of Jupiter, and wore a winged cap and winged shoes. He bore in his hand a rod entwined with two serpents, called the caduceus (See caduceus). The planet which moves the fastest is naturally named Mercury. It is interesting to note that the symbol for the planet Mercury is - a caduceus with two wings on top and snakes twining the sides. Mercury is said to have invented the lyre (See Lyre, Muses). Mercury is the name of a metallic element which is also called quicksilver.

Midas – Midas was king of Phrygia and the son of Gordius, a poor countryman, who was taken by the people and made king. They did this in obedience to the command of the oracle, which had said that their future king should come in a wagon. While the people were deliberating the prophecy, Gordius with his wife and son came riding into the public square in a wagon. Gordius, being made king, dedicated his wagon to the deity of the oracle, and tied it up in its place with a fast knot. This was the celebrated Gordian Knot, which, in after times it was said, whoever should untie should become lord of all Asia. Many tried to untie it, but none succeeded, till Alexander the Great, in his career of conquest, came to Phrygia. He tried his skill with as ill success as others, till growing impatient he drew his sword and cut the knot. When he afterwards succeeded in subjecting all Asia to his sway, people began to think that he had complied with the terms of the oracle according to its true meaning.

Minerva – The Romans identified their goddess Minerva with the Greek goddess Athena. Minerva comes from the Latin word *mens*, meaning mind. Minerva, the goddess of wisdom, was the daughter of Jupiter. She was said to have leaped forth from his brain, mature, and in complete armor. Her favorite bird was the owl, and the plant sacred to her the olive. She presided over the useful and ornamental arts, both those of men - such as agriculture and navigation, and those of women - spinning, weaving, and needlework. She was also a warlike divinity, but it was defensive war only that she patronized. Athens was her chosen seat, her own city, awarded to her as the prize of a contest with Neptune (Poseidon), who also aspired to it. The tale runs that in the reign of Cecrops, the first king of Athens, the two deities contended for the possession of the city. The gods decreed that it should be awarded to that one who produced the gift most useful to mortals. Neptune gave the horse; Minerva produced the olive. The gods gave judgment that the olive was the more useful of the two, and awarded the city to the goddess; and it was named Athens after her, her name in Greek being Athena. In the ancient world, Athens was the most powerful and richest and civilized of all the cities of Greece. It is still the capital Greece today.

Another name used for Athena is Pallas. At one time, it is said that Athena killed a giant named Pallas and then adopted his name. Thus Athena is frequently referred to as Pallas Athena. References to Pallas Athena show up many places in our modern language. The second planetoid that was discovered (in 1802) was named Pallas. It is also the second largest of the known asteroids with a diameter of 304 miles. In 1803 a new element was discovered by an English chemist. He named it palladium after Pallas. Palladium is especially used in electrical contacts and in alloys. There are other tales that contain the word palladium. The ancient city of Troy had a statue of Athena called a palladium. Legend had it that the city of Troy would be safe as long as the statue was preserved in the city. The statue was eventually lost and the city of Troy fell. In the modern world a palladium has come to mean a safeguard. Our constitution can be considered a palladium of our freedoms.

Athena was often referred to by the Greeks as Athena Parthenos (Athena the Virgin) because she never married. In 437 B.C. a temple to Athena was completed in Athens. The Greeks called it the Parthenon. Its remains can still be seen today as a reminder of the glories of ancient Greece. Because of all the words we use today that originated with Pallas Athena, this is one case where the Greek name of the goddess is more commonly known today than the Roman.

Morpheus – The Greek god of dreams is Morpheus. He lies on an ebony bed in a dim-lit cave, surrounded by poppies. He appears to humans in their dreams in the shape of a man. He is responsible for shaping dreams, or giving shape to the beings which inhabit dreams. Morpheus, known from Ovid's Metamorphoses, plays no part in Greek mythology. His name means "he who forms, or molds", and is mentioned as the son of Hypnos or Somnus, the god of sleep. The first chemical to be obtained from a plant was a powerful hypnotic which brought sleep and relief to those treated with it. It was named "morphine" because it's effects were like that of Morpheus coming and bringing rest.

Muses – The Muses were the daughters of Jupiter and Mnemosyne (Memory). The name Mnemosyne which means memory in Greek is represented today in our word mnemonic. They presided over song, and prompted the memory. Poets considered the muses as the goddesses of poetic inspiration. Many times poets called on the Muses for inspiration. They were nine in number, to each of whom was assigned the presidence over some particular department of literature, art, or science. Calliope was the muse of epic poetry, Clio of history, Euterpe of lyric poetry, Melpomene of tragedy, Terpsichore of choral dance and song, Erato of love poetry, Polyhymnia of sacred poetry, Urania of astronomy, Thalia of comedy. Our word Music is related to the Muses and places which are dedicated to the learning of history of types are called Museums. Three planitoids are named Melpomene, Calliope, and Thalia.

Narcissus (nahr SIHS uhs) – Narcissus was a human who fell in love with his own reflection. The word narcissist denotes a person who is absorbed in himself. Narcissus represents a family of flowers which includes daffodils and jonquils.

Neptune – Neptune was god of the waters. The Romans identified their god of springs and rivers named Neptune with the Greek god Poseidon. When, in the 1800's scientists observed Uranus to discover its exact orbit they realized that there must be another planet beyond Uranus which was affecting its orbit. When they had calculated where such a planet must be, astronomers looked into the sky and there was Neptune. Neptune carried a trident which was given him by the Cyclopes. The two satellites of Neptune are named Triton and Nereid. Triton was Poseidon's son who was half man and half fish. After a storm it was his job to blow a horn made of a large shell to calm the sea. There is a type of large sea snail that is called Triton after the shell that he was supposed to have blown. Nereid refers to the fifty sea nymphs that accompanied Poseidon on his travels. Element number 93 of the periodic table is known as neptunium after Neptune.

Nymph – Nymphs were minor goddesses that were pictured as young girls. The word nymph was Greek for "young girl" and even today zoologists call the young forms of some insects "nymphs." Nymphs were representative of various objects of nature. There were nymphs in trees, rocks, mountains, forests, lakes and rivers. They represented the spirit of these things to the Greeks. The word Atlantic comes from a group of nymphs called the Atlantides who were the daughters of Atlas and were associated with the far western waters. The Oceanids were nymphs who were the daughters of Oceanus and the Nereids were the daughters of Nereus.

Oedipus (EHD uh puhs) – Oedipus was the king of Thebes known for killing his father and marrying his mother. The most famous version of the story of Oedipus is in the form of a tragedy written by Sophocles called *Oedipus Rex*.

Olympus – Mount Olympus is the highest mountain in Greece. The abode of the gods was on the summit of Mount Olympus, in Thessaly. A gate of clouds, kept by the goddesses named the Seasons, opened to permit the passage of the Celestials to earth, and to receive them on their return. The gods had their separate dwellings; but all, when summoned, repaired to the palace of Jupiter, as did also those deities whose usual abode was the earth, the waters, or the under-world. It was also in the great hall of the palace of the Olympian king that the gods feasted each day on ambrosia and nectar, their food and drink. Here they conversed of the affairs of heaven and earth. As they quaffed their nectar, Apollo, the god of music, delighted them with the tones of his lyre, to which the Muses sang in responsive strains. When the sun was set, the gods retired to sleep in their respective dwellings.

The word Olympics comes from the word Olympus. It was said that these games were founded by Jupiter himself. They were celebrated at Olympia in Elis. Vast numbers of spectators flocked to them from every part of Greece, and from Asia, Africa and Sicily. They were repeated every four years in midsummer, and continued five days. The exercises in these games were of five sorts: running, leaping, wrestling, throwing the quoit, and hurling the javelin, or boxing. Besides these exercises of bodily strength and agility there were contests in music, poetry and eloquence or literature. Thus the games furnished poets, musicians and authors the best opportunities to present their productions to the public, and the fame of the victors was diffused far and wide. The winner's prize was a crown of wild olive. The first Olympiad is generally considered as corresponding with the year 776 B.C. The games continued every four years until A.D. 394 when the Roman Emperor Theodosius put and end to them. They were revived and renamed the "Olympic Games" in 1896. They have continued every four years except for interruptions during World War I and World War II.

Orion – One myth states that Orion's friend Diana was tricked into shooting Orion by her brother Apollo. After Diana realized what had happened she placed the body of Orion in her moon-chariot and in sadness drove him into the darkest part of the sky. There she placed him so that he would shine brighter than the surrounding stars. Another myth concerning the death of Orion states that he once boasted that he was so great a hunter that he could kill all the animals on the face of the earth. This so concerned Gaea - the goddess of the earth that she sent a giant scorpion to sting Orion. The scorpion succeeded and both were placed in the night sky. The constellation Scorpius is part of the Zodiac and is best seen in the southern hemisphere during July and August. The constellation Orion is best seen from December through March.

Orpheus (OHR fee uhs) – Orpheus was the son of Apollo and the Muse Calliope. (See Lyre)

Pan – Pan was the god of flocks and shepherds. His favourite residence was in Arcadia. Pan gets his name from the Greek word meaning all. He is usually pictured playing a simple pipe instrument and dancing happily. Pan was known as a son of the god Mercury. He is considered a god of the fields and woods. Pan is depicted as having the hindquarters, legs, ears, and horns of a goat and the rest of him is man. Pan was considered by early Christians as immoral. This is where our modern picture of the devil with horns, hoofs, and tail comes from. The Greeks thought that Pan could strike terror in people, and thus our word panic.

Pandora – Pandora was the first woman. She was made by Jupiter and sent to Prometheus and his brother to punish them for their presumption in stealing fire from heaven; and to punish man, for accepting the gift. She was made in heaven, and every god contributed something to perfect her. Venus gave her beauty, Mercury persuasion, Apollo music, etc. They then named her Pandora, "the gift of all the gods." Thus equipped, she was conveyed to earth, and presented to Epimetheus, who gladly accepted her, though cautioned by his brother to beware of Jupiter and his gifts. The caution was not groundless. Pandora had been given a box from the immortals which she was forbidden to open. Overcome with curiosity to know what it contained she one day opened the lid and looked in. Forthwith there escaped a multitude of plagues for man - diseases for the body, envy spite, and revenge for his mind etc. Pandora hastened to replace the lid but one thing remained in the box - Hope. Through "Pandora's box" all the evils in the world came about, thus today anything which is harmless when undisturbed but which becomes troublesome when tampered with is called a "Pandora's Box."

Phaeton (FAY uh thahn) – Phaeton was the son of the god of the sun. A phaeton was an open carriage used in the 19th century. Some say that the chariot of the sun god, while driven by Phaeton, scorched a great streak across the sky which we call the Milky Way.

Pleiades – The Pleiades were the nymph daughters of Atlas who ran from Orion and were changed into stars just as he was about to catch them. The Pleiades are represented as a small cluster of stars forming the left shoulder of Taurus the bull.

Pluto or Hades – Pluto is the god of the underworld. The Romans had a god of the dead named Dis, but in this instance the name that has stuck with us has been the Greek one - Pluto. In 1931 the ninth planet was discovered and named Pluto. It is the only planet named after a Greek god and not a Roman one. Element number 94 of the periodic table is known as plutonium after Pluto.

Prometheus (proh MEE thee uhs) – Prometheus was a Titan whose name comes from the Greek words meaning "forethought," and indeed he was wise and saw where actions would lead. When the Titans and Olympians were at war, Prometheus foresaw that the Olympians would win. He thus convinced his brother, Epimetheus to abandon the Titan cause with him. Thus the two brothers were spared the punishment that fell on the other Titans when they lost. Prometheus was so defiant in his theft of fire that the adjective "Promethean" is used to describe a daring, original, creative action. There is a radioactive metallic element (Atomic number 61) which is named promethium after this famous Titan.

Proserpine (Proh SUR puh nuh) – There are some who say that the constellation Virgo is Proserpine. This is why she is seen in the sky half of the year and descends to Tartarus the other half. The best time of year to see Virgo is April through June.

Psyche – The fable of Cupid and Psyche is usually considered allegorical. Psyche was made immortal and joined Cupid in the end. The Greek name for a butterfly is Psyche, and the same word means the soul. There is no illustration so striking and beautiful as the butterfly, bursting on brilliant wings from the tomb in which it has lain, after a dull, groveling, caterpillar existence, to flutter in the blaze of day and feed on the most fragrant and delicate productions of the spring. Psyche, then, has been considered to represent the human soul, which is purified by sufferings and misfortunes, and is thus prepared for the enjoyment of true and pure happiness. In works of art Psyche is represented as a maiden with the wings of a butterfly. This also led to fairies being pictured with wings. The relationship between Psyche and butterflies is also shown in the fact that there is a group of moths that belong to the family "Psychidae."

Satyrs (SAT uhr) – Satyrs were deities of the woods and fields. They were covered with bristly hair, their heads decorated with short, sprouting horns, and their feet like goats' feet.

Scylla (SIHL uh) – Scylla is pictured as having a human body with six long necks. At the end of each neck is a growling dog's head.

Somnus – Somnus was the Roman god of sleep. He is the father of Morpheus. The word "somnambulism" in Latin means sleepwalking and it is another word for sleepwalking in English. When we are sleepy it can be said that we are somnolent.

Syrinx – Syrinx was a nymph that was chased by Pan and turned into reeds just before she was caught. Pan made a flute or pipe from these reeds. Syrinx is also Greek word which means pipe. It is interesting to note that there is a special region in the windpipe of songbirds named after the nymph. This region is called the syrinx. The word syringe is the plural form of the word syrinx. Syringes are also pipes but less musical in nature, they convey fluids either in or out of a reservoir.

Titans and Titanesses – Titans and Titanesses were the most important children of Uranus and Gaea. They were beings of tremendous size who were defeated in a war against the Olympians. In our language the word titanic is used to describe something of enormous size. In 1911 the largest ship in existence was launched. It was named the Titanic. If the owners of the Titanic had considered mythology more, they may have chosen a different name. In 1912 the Titanic sank in three hours. Over 1500 of the 2206 passengers were killed. In 1791 a newly discovered metal was named titanium. Pure titanium has been shown to be one of the strongest metals known. Many dinosaurs also take their name from the giants or Titans. Titanosaurus, gigantosaurus, and titanotherium, all have their name beginnings in the Titans.

Venus – Venus the goddess of love and beauty, was the daughter of Jupiter. Others say that Venus sprang from the foam of the sea. The zephyr wafted her along the waves to the Isle of Cyprus, where she was received and attired by the Seasons, and then led to the assembly of the gods. All were charmed with her beauty, and each one demanded her for his wife. Jupiter gave her to Vulcan, in gratitude for the service he had rendered in forging thunderbolts. So the most beautiful of the goddesses became the wife of the only deformed god. The Romans respected Venus so much that the word venerate has come to mean to honor or respect. Venus possessed an embroidered girdle called Cestus, which had the power of inspiring love. There is a type of flatworm that resides in the sea which is shaped like a belt. Zoologists have named these worms cestus. The only planet named after a goddess is Venus. It is far brighter than any star. In fact it is the next brightest thing after the sun and moon. The symbol for Venus is ♀ a mirror or looking glass. Something easily identified with the goddess of beauty. This symbol has also come to indicate females in general. Her favorite birds were swans and doves, and the plants sacred to her were the rose and the myrtle.

Vulcan – Vulcan was the son of Jupiter and Juno. He was born lame, and his mother was so displeased at the sight of him that she flung him out of heaven. Other accounts say that Jupiter kicked him out for taking part with his mother in a quarrel which occurred between them. Vulcan's lameness, according to this account, was the consequence of his fall. He was a whole day falling, and at last alighted in the Island of Lemnos, which was thenceforth sacred to him.

Vulcan was the god of fire. He was architect, smith, armorer, chariot builder, and artist of all work in Olympus. He built of brass the houses of the gods; he made for them the golden shoes with which they trod the air or the water, and moved from place to place with the speed of the wind, or even of thought. He also shod with brass the celestial steeds, which whirled the chariots of the gods through the air, or along the surface of the sea. Vulcan made the scepter of Jove, the shields and spears of the Olympians, the arrows of Apollo and Diana, the breastplate of Hercules and the shield of Achilles. He was able to bestow on his workmanship self-motion, so that the chairs and tables could move of themselves in and out of the celestial hall. Vulcan even endowed with intelligence the golden handmaidens whom he made to wait on himself.

Vulcan was the god of smiths and the Romans pictured him as working in the depths of the volcano Mount Etna. In 1839 a man named Charles Goodyear discovered how to heat rubber and sulfur to make rubber more useful. Men wanted to use rubber waterproof clothing but the rubber got soft in the hot weather and too hard in the cold. The method discovered by Goodyear allowed rubber to be put to many uses. This process is now called vulcanization after Vulcan.

Vulcan was a good natured god, loved and honored among men. When he choose, he was the cause of "inextinguishable laughter" to the gods, but he was by no means a fool. The famous god of the strong arms could be cunning, even vengeful, when the emergency demanded.

Some say that Vulcan invented a better kind of chariot and is honored in the sky as Auriga or the charioteer. Others say that because Vulcan was lame he invented the chariot so that he could get around. The constellation Auriga is best seen during February.

F I N I S

MICROBIOLOGY

Custom Publication

MCGRAW-HILL RYERSON LIMITED

Toronto • New York • Burr Ridge • Bangkok • Bogotá • Caracas • Lisbon
London • Madrid • Mexico City • Milan • New Delhi • Seoul
Singapore • Sydney • Taipei

Chapters selecetd from:

Microbiology, second edition, by Daniel Lim
Copyright © 1998 by the McGraw-Hill Companies, Inc

ISBN: 0-07-560432-9

Printed and bound in Canada

BRIEF CONTENTS

chapter one

FOUNDATIONS OF MODERN MICROBIOLOGY

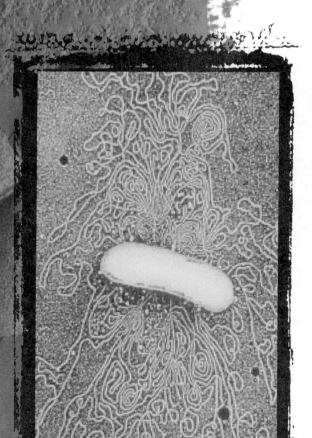

Electron micrograph of DNA released from *Escherichia coli* (colorized, ×56,000).

Historical Perspectives
Microorganisms and Spontaneous Generation
The Germ Theory of Disease
Immunology
Viruses as Submicroscopic Filterable Agents

Modern Microbiology
Recombinant DNA Technology
The Polymerase Chain Reaction
Important Roles of Microorganisms

PERSPECTIVE
Disproving the Doctrine of Spontaneous Generation

EVOLUTION AND BIODIVERSITY

Imagine a world in which life-threatening diseases are diagnosed in minutes using a genetic road map to locate and identify the microscopic pathogen. Picture a society in which highly specific antibodies are used as magic bullets to target drugs to cancerous cells and where recombinant DNA in viruses is used as live vaccines, for cancer immunotherapy, and to treat cystic fibrosis through gene therapy. In this world, "superbugs" devour toxic pollutants, clean up oil spills, and eliminate agricultural pests without harm to animals, humans, and plants. Agricultural crops are protected from frost damage, saving farmers millions of dollars in potential economic loss and providing the public with year-round produce and fruits; genetically engineered bacteria fertilize crops and significantly increase agricultural production; and plants are genetically modified to protect them from insects, drought, and disease.

The world described in this scenario is not in the future—it exists today and was made possible through a series of technological advances. At the forefront of these exciting discoveries is the traditional discipline of **microbiology.** Microbiology is the study of agents too small to be seen with the unaided eye, specifically bacteria (bacteriology), viruses (virology), fungi (mycology), protozoa (protozoology), and algae (phycology) (Figure 1.1). Through the techniques developed in microbiology, it is now possible, at least in principle, to use microorganisms as living factories capable of producing any biochemical a person desires. These minute organisms also provide scientists with the capability of understanding in greater detail the genetic composition of all forms of life.

Microbes play indispensible roles in our daily lives. They are important not only in molecular biology and biotechnology, but also in medicine, ecology, agriculture, and industry. This knowledge of microorganisms did not emerge overnight, but resulted from about a century of careful and deliberate scientific advances in the field of microbiology.

Historical Perspectives

Microbiology as a science began with the development of the microscope. No one knows who invented the microscope. In A.D. 60, Seneca, a Roman philosopher and statesman, noted in his writings that "letters, however small and indistinct, are seen enlarged and more clearly through a globe of glass filled with water." Early observations of this kind led to the use of crude lenses made of certain clear minerals. Eventually glass was set in frames to help older people see better.

The invention of the modern microscope is often attributed to Zacharias Janssen (1580–c. 1638), a Dutch maker of spectacles who, as a young boy, combined two lenses to form a crude compound microscope in 1590. The microscope was subsequently improved by the German mathematician and astronomer Johann Kepler (1571–1630), the noted Italian astronomer Galileo (1564–1642), and the English physicist and mathematician Robert Hooke (1635–1703). Hooke experimented extensively with the microscope and illustrated his written observations with detailed drawings of plant tissues. It was Hooke who first described the small cavities separated by walls as "cells" in *Micrographia*, a book commissioned in 1665 by King Charles II of England because of his interest in Hooke's microscopic observations.

However, it was not until the late 1600s that microscopes became popular as instruments to observe objects normally not visible to the naked eye. A Dutch linen draper and town civil servant named Anton van Leeuwenhoek (1632–1723) became interested in the microscope and made hundreds of them in his lifetime (Figure 1.2). Leeuwenhoek's microscopes were noted for their lenses, which were meticulously ground and highly polished. These early single-lens instruments gave magnifications of only 50 to 300 diameters, or approximately one-third the magnification of modern light microscopes (Figure 1.3). Nonetheless, these microscopes provided glimpses into an entirely new world consisting of microbes—small organisms that Leeuwenhoek called "animalcules" in a letter written to the Royal Society of London in 1674:

> I found floating (in lake water) therin divers earthly particles, some green streaks, spirally wound serpent-wise, and orderly arranged, after the manner of the copper or tin worms... The whole circumstance of each of these streaks was about the thickness of a hair on one's head... These animalcules had divers coulors, some being whitish and transparent; others with green and very glittering little scales; others again were green in the middle, and before and behind white.

In this and other communications to the scientific community, Leeuwenhoek described in detail many of the different types of microbial shapes that we recognize today (Figure 1.4). Because of his accomplishments, Leeuwenhoek is considered to be the "father of microbiology."

Microorganisms Were Once Thought to Arise Spontaneously

The invention of the microscope paved the way for other significant discoveries in microbiology. One of these discoveries was initiated because of the theory of **spontaneous generation,** which proposed that life could arise spontaneously from nonliving matter. This was a longheld belief, dating back hundreds of years. People commonly believed that mice, toads, flies, maggots, and other forms of life could appear spontaneously from piles of litter, dirt, and manure. A recipe for generating mice from soiled undergarments, written by the prominent physician, chemist, and physicist J. B. van Helmont (1577–1644), echoed these sentiments:

> If a dirty undergarment is squeezed into the mouth of a vessel containing wheat, within a few days (say 21) a ferment drained from the garments and transformed by the smell of the grain, encrusts the wheat itself with its own skin and turns it into mice. And what is more remarkable, the mice from the grain and undergarments are neither weanlings or sucklings nor premature but they jump out fully formed.

a.

b.

c.

d.

e.

figure 1.1

Representative Types of Microorganisms
a. Scanning electron micrograph of *Escherichia coli,* a bacterium (colorized, ×12,000).
b. Electron micrograph of poliovirus, a virus (colorized, ×34,000). c. Scanning electron micrograph of *Aspergillus flavus,* a fungus (colorized, ×160). d. Scanning electron micrograph of *Tetrahymena pyriformis,* a protozoan (colorized, ×8,000). e. Scanning electron micrograph of *Cyclotella meneghiniana,* an alga (colorized, ×750).

figure 1.2
Anton van Leeuwenhoek (1632–1723)
Leeuwenhoek opened the doors to a new world of microorganisms with his early microscopes.

Francesco Redi (1626–1698), an Italian physician, was one of the first persons to challenge the theory of spontaneous generation. He showed that meat placed in glass-covered or gauze-covered containers remained free of maggots, whereas meat in uncovered containers eventually became infested with maggots from flies laying their eggs on the meat. This and similar experiments by others dispelled the idea that organisms such as insects and mice could arise spontaneously. Despite these findings disproving spontaneous generation of macroorganisms, people still believed that microorganisms could arise this way.

With the discovery of microscopic organisms by Leeuwenhoek, the controversy surrounding spontaneous generation was renewed. A common argument used by proponents of spontaneous generation was that fresh food contained few if any microorganisms. However, if such food were allowed to sit at room temperature and spoil, large numbers of microscopic organisms would appear in the putrefied food. It was therefore only logical to assume that these spoilage organisms arose spontaneously within the food. John Needham (1713–1781), an English priest, fueled this argument by showing in 1749 that heated nutrient solutions poured into flasks that were subsequently stoppered soon became cloudy with microorganisms. The Italian priest and scientist Lazzaro Spallanzani (1729–1799) attempted to counter these arguments in 1776 by showing that no growth occurred in a wide variety of liquid nutrients that were boiled in flasks *after* sealing. However, supporters of spontaneous generation contended either that heating the liquids destroyed their ability to support life or sealing the flasks excluded oxygen that was required for life.

The controversy surrounding the theory of spontaneous generation remained unresolved until 1861 when Louis Pasteur, a French chemist (1822–1895), showed that microorganisms found in spoiled food were similar to those commonly found in the air.

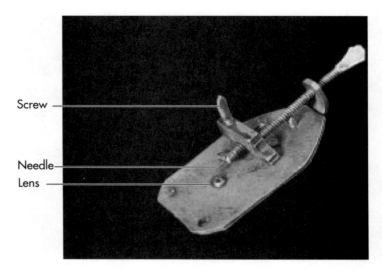

Screw

Needle
Lens

figure 1.3
Photograph of an Early Leeuwenhoek Microscope
The sample is placed at the tip of the needle and brought into focus by turning the screw. The sample is then viewed through the lens. Illumination is by light from a candle or sunlight.

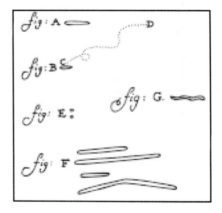

figure 1.4
Examples of Bacteria Drawn by Leeuwenhoek
Leeuwenhoek's drawings included rod-shaped bacteria (A, B, F, and G) and spherical, or coccus-shaped, bacteria (E).

(Figure 1.5). He passed large amounts of air through guncotton (nitrocellulose) filters and observed with a microscope entrapped particles of inorganic matter and also microbes that were indistinguishable from those seen in putrefying foods. Pasteur furthermore showed that nutrient solutions boiled in swan-necked flasks that were exposed to the air remained sterile and untouched by microorganisms present in the environment. However, when the necks of these flasks were broken, the liquids inside quickly came in contact with microbes in the air and became contaminated. Pasteur concluded that these microorganisms found commonly in the air were responsible for the decomposition of foods and did not arise spontaneously. These simple but fundamental experiments by Pasteur were instrumental in disproving the theory of spontaneous generation.

figure 1.5
Louis Pasteur (1822–1895)
Pasteur was responsible for many accomplishments in microbiology, including disproving the theory of spontaneous generation, developing vaccines for anthrax and rabies, and developing a process (pasteurization) to destroy spoilage organisms in wine.

figure 1.6
Robert Koch (1843–1910)
Koch established the microbial cause for many infectious diseases through his postulates.

The Germ Theory of Disease States That Infectious Diseases Are Caused by Microorganisms

After Pasteur had shown that microorganisms existed in the environment and did not arise spontaneously, some other scientists focused their attention on the role of these organisms in disease. The belief that microorganisms might cause disease was known as the **germ theory of disease.**

During the latter part of the nineteenth century a German country physician named Robert Koch (1843–1910) investigated the nature of disease transmission from person to person (Figure 1.6). Koch conducted a series of experiments on animals he had infected with the spores of anthrax bacilli. Anthrax was a lethal, highly contagious bacterial disease of livestock that killed large numbers of animals and caused great economic losses to European farmers during Koch's time. In his meticulous studies reported in 1876, Koch discovered that anthrax could be transmitted from ani-

mal to animal by injecting blood from a diseased animal into a healthy animal. This process could be repeated as many as 20 times, with similar symptoms appearing in each newly infected animal (Figure 1.7).

Furthermore, Koch showed that blood from infected animals contained large numbers of bacteria that were directly responsible for the disease. He transformed his observations and experiments into a series of criteria necessary for the logical association of specific microbes with specific diseases; these criteria are now known as **Koch's postulates.** Koch's postulates state that the following are needed to prove an organism causes a specific disease:

1. The specific microorganism should be shown to be present in all cases of the disease.

2. The specific microorganism should be isolated from the diseased host and grown in pure culture.

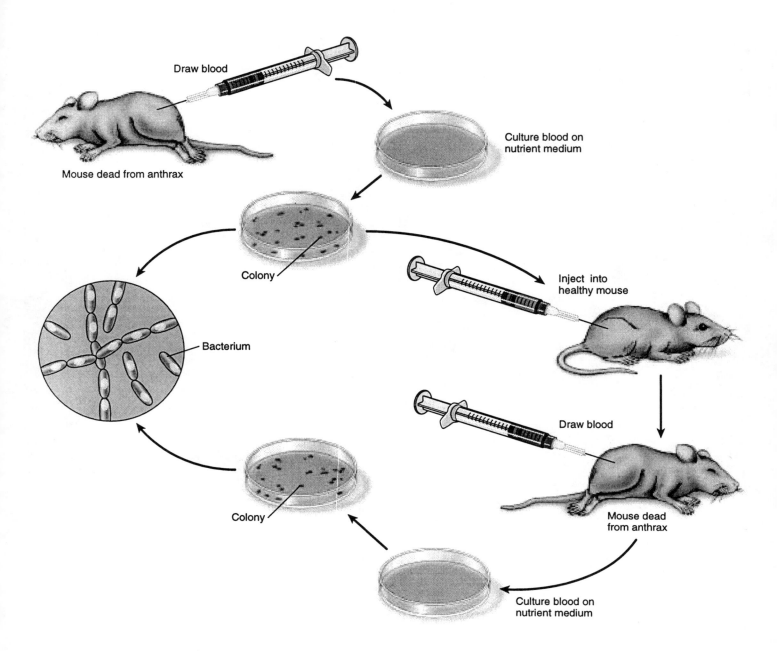

Draw blood

Mouse dead from anthrax

Culture blood on nutrient medium

Colony

Bacterium

Inject into healthy mouse

Draw blood

Mouse dead from anthrax

Colony

Culture blood on nutrient medium

figure 1.7
Koch's Postulates

Koch's postulates describe the steps required for logical proof that a microorganism causes a disease. The suspected microbe is isolated in pure culture from a diseased animal and then injected into a healthy animal. The infected animal should develop the same disease symptoms, and identical microorganisms should be isolated from this inoculated animal.

Dates During the Golden Age of Microbiology (1876–1906) When Infectious Diseases Were Associated with Specific Microorganisms

Disease	Year	Infectious Agent[a]	Discoverer(s)
Anthrax	1876	Bacillus anthracis	Koch
Pear fire blight	1877	Erwinia amylovora	Burrill
Gonorrhea	1879	Neisseria gonorrhoeae	Neisser
Malaria	1880	Plasmodium malariae	Laverans
Wound infections	1881	Staphylococcus aureus	Ogston
Tuberculosis	1882	Mycobacterium tuberculosis	Koch
Erysipelas	1882	Streptococcus pyogenes	Fehleisen
Diphtheria	1883	Corynebacterium diphtheriae	Klebs and Loeffler
Cholera	1883	Vibrio cholerae	Koch
Typhoid fever	1884	Salmonella typhi	Eberth and Gaffky
Bladder infections	1885	Escherichia coli	Escherich
Salmonellosis	1888	Salmonella enteritidis	Gaertner
Tetanus	1889	Clostridium tetani	Kitasato
Gas gangrene	1892	Clostridium perfringens	Welch and Nuttall
Plague	1894	Yersinia pestis	Yersin and Kitasato
Botulism	1897	Clostridium botulinum	Van Ermengem
Shigellosis	1898	Shigella dysenteriae	Shiga
Syphilis	1905	Treponema pallidum	Schaudinn and Hoffmann
Whooping cough	1906	Bordetella pertussis	Bordet and Gengou

[a]The names for the infectious agents are those in current use rather than those given at the time of their discovery.

3. This freshly isolated microorganism, when inoculated into a healthy, susceptible host, should cause the same disease seen in the original host.

4. The microorganism should be reisolated in pure culture from the experimental infection.

Koch's postulates initiated the **Golden Age of Microbiology** (1876–1906), an era during which the causes of most bacterial diseases were discovered. With Koch's criteria scientists were able to identify major microbial pathogens. It should be recognized that whereas Koch's postulates are invaluable for identifying specific microbial agents of diseases, they are not applicable to all microorganisms; there are technical limitations in using these criteria for all infectious diseases. Some transmissible microorganisms cannot readily be cultured on artificial media at this time because they are obligate intracellular parasites (for example, viruses; *Rickettsia rickettsii,* the causative agent of Rocky Mountain spotted fever; and *Chlamydia trachomatis,* the causative agent of trachoma and one of the causes of the sexually transmitted disease nongonococcal urethritis, or NGU). Other transmissible microorganisms cannot be grown in vitro (outside a living organism) and thus cannot be artificially cultured (for example, *Treponema pallidum,* the causative agent of syphilis). Clinical signs and symptoms of some infectious diseases are manifested differently in experimental laboratory animals and in

humans (for example, *Neisseria gonorrhoeae,* which causes gonorrhea in humans but not in animals). It should also be noted that not all diseases are infectious (for example, cardiovascular diseases, diabetes, black lung disease, and certain types of cancer), and knowing which are infectious can be very difficult (for example, duodenal and gastric ulcers, previously thought to be induced by stress, emotional disturbance, and other noninfectious factors, are now known to be caused by the bacterium *Helicobacter pylori*).

Despite these limitations, Koch's postulates have been instrumental in showing the relationships between microorganisms and the diseases they cause. The importance of Koch's work as a foundation of modern microbiology is evident in the numerous diseases that were proven to be caused by specific microbes in the few years immediately after his historical studies of anthrax (Table 1.1).

Immunology Is the Study of Resistance of Organisms to Infection

While Koch was demonstrating the infectious nature of many diseases, other scientists were making discoveries that would significantly reduce the incidence of these diseases in the world. In 1884 the Russian zoologist Élie Metchnikoff (1845–1916) discovered that certain cells in the blood could engulf foreign particles such as

figure 1.8
Paul Ehrlich (1854–1915)
Ehrlich proposed that proteins (antibodies) in serum could combine with and destroy foreign substances (antigens). For his work in immunology he shared with Élie Metchnikoff the 1908 Nobel Prize in physiology and medicine.

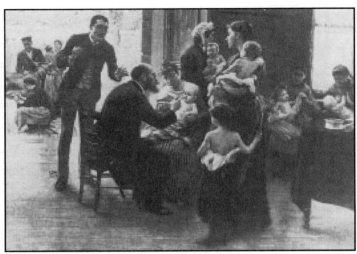

figure 1.9
Edward Jenner (1749–1823)
Jenner's experiment with vaccination proved that cowpox conferred immunity against smallpox, and laid the foundation of modern immunology as a science.

bacterial cells and protect the body against infectious diseases. Metchnikoff called these cells *phagocytes*. This discovery formed the basis for the field of **immunology,** the study of resistance of organisms to infection.

Other scientists believed that noncellular components of the blood could also be protective (humoral immunity). Two of these scientists, Paul Ehrlich (1854–1915) and Emil von Behring (1854–1917), worked together to show that specific antitoxins (antibodies, or protein molecules in the blood of an immunized individual) effectively neutralized potent diphtheria toxin (antigen). In the 1890s Ehrlich conducted further experiments to demonstrate that immunity to toxins could be transferred from one animal to another by injection of immune serum (serum containing antibodies). These and other observations led Ehrlich to hypothesize that a toxin or other foreign substance entering the body induced the formation of protein molecules (antitoxins or antibodies) that combined specifically with the foreign substance inducing their formation (Figure 1.8).

The field of immunology actually began with an experiment performed in 1798 by Edward Jenner (1749–1823). Jenner was an English country doctor who showed that immunity could be conferred by vaccination (Figure 1.9). During the eighteenth century, smallpox frequently occurred in epidemic proportions in continental Europe and England. It was observed at the time that individuals who at one point had cowpox (a similar, less serious disease than smallpox that was contracted from cows) seldom contracted the disease agent of smallpox. In a classical experiment, Jenner inoculated an eight-year-old boy with pus taken from the lesion of a dairymaid with cowpox. The boy was later inoculated with material from a smallpox patient but did not develop smallpox. Jenner repeated this experiment several times with different people, and the results of these experiments led Jenner to propose the procedure that came to be known as **vaccination** [Latin *vacca,* cow].

Viruses Are Submicroscopic Filterable Agents Consisting of Nucleic Acid Surrounded by a Protein Coat

The word **virus** [Latin *virus,* poison] was originally used by the ancient Romans to describe any type of poisonous material. Later, when microbiology began to emerge as a discipline, the word *virus* implied any infectious microbe. It was not until the late 1800s that viruses were described as distinct submicroscopic filterable entities capable of replication and infection.

The first evidence that organisms smaller than bacteria might exist and be associated with disease was proposed in 1892 by a Russian scientist, Dmitri Ivanowsky (1864–1920). In his studies of mosaic disease of tobacco plants, Ivanowsky observed that the agent responsible for the disease easily passed through filters that stopped all known bacteria. Ivanowsky surmised that the infectious agent was a filterable microorganism that could not be seen with a light microscope. These observations established filterability as an early criterion for distinguishing viruses from bacteria and other microorganisms.

Martinus Willem Beijerinck (1851–1931), a Dutch soil microbiologist, studied the infectious agent of tobacco mosaic disease in the 1890s and discovered that not only was it filterable, but, unlike bacteria, it could also easily diffuse through solid growth

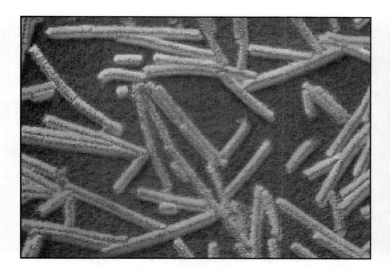

figure 1.10
Electron Micrograph of Tobacco Mosaic Viruses
The virus consists of a single long RNA molecule enclosed in a cylindrical protein coat (colorized, ×220,000).

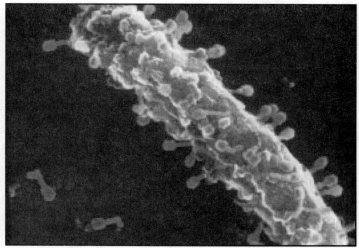

figure 1.11
Scanning Electron Micrograph of Bacteriophages Attached to a Bacterium
Bacteriophages (blue) are shown attached to an *Escherichia coli* cell (colorized, ×36,000).

media. He used the term *contagium vivum fluidum* (fluid infectious principle), or **virus,** to describe the agent. A major contribution to the understanding of viruses was made by chemist Wendell Stanley (1904–1971) of the University of California, Berkeley, who crystallized the tobacco mosaic virus (TMV) in 1935 (Figure 1.10). Crystallization of the TMV was a first step in elucidating the chemical structure and composition of viruses. Within a few years of Stanley's work, viruses were found to be composed mainly of nucleic acid contained within a protein coat.

The observations of Ivanowsky, Beijerinck, and Stanley were all made on the TMV, a plant virus. The first animal virus characterized was the virus responsible for bovine foot-and-mouth disease. This virus was isolated in 1898 from infected cattle by Friedrich Loeffler (1852–1915) and Paul Frosch (1860–1928). Like Ivanowsky, Loeffler and Frosch found that the virus causing foot-and-mouth disease was filterable. They concluded that the responsible agent was not a bacterium, but a filterable particle.

Bacterial viruses, more commonly called **bacteriophages,** or **phages** [Greek *phagein,* to devour], were discovered by Frederick W. Twort (1877–1950), a British scientist, and Felix d'Hérelle (1873–1949), a French scientist, in the early 1900s. Twort, in 1915, and d'Hérelle, in 1917, both reported observing a filterable agent that destroyed bacteria growing on solid media. D'Hérelle considered this filterable agent to be a parasite of bacteria and named it *bacteriophage* (Figure 1.11). Despite d'Hérelle's extensive work on the growth and infectious nature of bacteriophages, few scientists at the time accepted his findings. It was not until later in the 1930s, when the German biochemist Martin Schlesinger purified and characterized bacteriophages, that these viruses established their own unique place in the microbial world.

Through the early work of these and many other scientists, microbiology began to emerge as a distinct discipline. A new classification of scientists, **microbiologists,** and new terminology appeared in the scientific world. Microbiology began to play an important and vital role in many areas. This role has expanded as microbiologists continue to make significant contributions to science. In recent years, with the discovery of new techniques in molecular biology and the application of these techniques to microorganisms, microbiology has entered a new golden age.

Recombinant DNA Technology Involves the Manipulation of Genes in Organisms

Several significant discoveries led to this new golden age of microbiology. In the early 1960s Werner Arber, a Swiss microbiologist, discovered that certain bacteria produced enzymes that cleaved viral DNA at specific sites to protect the bacteria from viral infection. These enzymes, called **restriction endonucleases,** were later purified and characterized by Hamilton Smith and Daniel Nathans. The discovery led to the development of laboratory techniques to manipulate genes in living organisms, called **recombinant DNA technology,** and genetic engineering. Using these enzymes, it now was possible to isolate and move genes from one organism to another. Arber, Smith, and Nathans were awarded the Nobel Prize in physiology or medicine in 1978 for their discovery and studies of restriction endonucleases.

In 1972 Paul Berg of Stanford University created the first recombinant DNA molecule by successfully splicing DNA from

An exciting recent development in microbiology has been the study of the presence and spread of microorganisms in the closed microgravity environment of space-

Microbes in Space

crafts. On earth, gravity is an important physical force in reducing aerosols and thus the spread of infectious microorganisms. However, under the microgravity conditions of outer space, droplets of microorganisms generated by coughing, sneezing, and talking may remain suspended for hours in the air and be a source of infection. Consequently, microorganisms that normally would not be considered a problem on earth could potentially be harmful to astronauts in the closed environment of space vehicles and the proposed international space station. Evidence of this potential health hazard was seen in the early *Apollo* missions in which crew members experienced upper respiratory illnesses (influenza, rhinitis, and pharyngitis), gastroenteritis, and mild dermatological problems. On the *Apollo 13* mission, an in-flight malfunction in the service module resulted in a cold, moist environment, which led to a severe *Pseudomonas aeruginosa* urinary tract infection in one of the crew members. In-flight antibiotic therapy was ineffective until he could be returned to earth, where bacterial isolation was possible.

Because of these problems and to minimize future health hazards due to microorganisms, the National Aeronautics and Space Administration (NASA) initiated extensive preflight quar-

antine measures for astronauts, starting with the *Apollo 14* mission. During the quarantine period, astronauts are restricted to limited-access areas to reduce contact with contaminated objects. Only individuals screened for the presence of potential pathogens may come in contact with the crew members. These quarantine procedures have been successful, and no major illnesses have been reported during the *Apollo 14* through *Apollo 17* or space shuttle missions.

These early space missions have been short, typically lasting only a few days or weeks. In comparison, the space station will be a permanent platform, with confinements as long as 90 days planned for each team of astronauts. To prevent gross contamination of the space station environment by pathogenic microorganisms, NASA plans to require a minimum 14-day isolation period (the incubation time for most pathogenic microorganisms) for astronauts prior to launch. Family members of the crew will be monitored for infectious diseases during the 30 to 60 day preflight period, and all crew members will be immunized against infectious disease agents. The environment of the space station will be monitored continuously with air, water, and surface samples. Although it will be impractical to have a sterile, noncontaminated environment on the space station, these measures by NASA will ensure an environment that is safe for human habitation (Figure 1.12).

figure 1.12

An Astronaut Demonstrates the Shirtsleeve Environment of Life Aboard the Space Station
The astronaut is taking notes at the NASA health maintenance facility, which has capabilities for diagnostic and environmental microbiology tests.

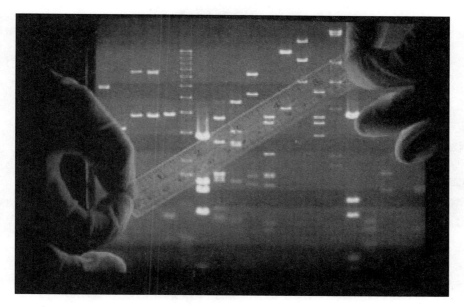

figure 1.13

Examining DNA Fragments on a Gel

DNA fragments can be separated by electric current into distinct patterns on a gel. These patterns are unique to each organism.

a virus into a bacterial chromosome. Berg was honored as a co-recipient of the 1980 Nobel Prize in chemistry for this work. Berg's studies were followed in 1973 by elegant experiments conducted by Herbert Boyer of the University of California in San Francisco and Stanley Cohen of Stanford University in which foreign genes were inserted into a plasmid, or extrachromosomal piece of DNA, which could then be transferred into a bacterium (Figure 1.13). With these techniques and genetic tools, it was now possible to isolate a gene from one organism, splice it into a plasmid, and insert the plasmid with the foreign gene into a bacterium. The process of **gene cloning** was thus born.

The Polymerase Chain Reaction Permits Rapid Amplification of Genes Outside the Cell

The most recent technique developed in the area of recombinant DNA technology is the **polymerase chain reaction (PCR),** developed by Kary Mullis in 1985. This innovative laboratory procedure, which was conceived by Mullis two years earlier during an evening drive through the mountains of northern California, amplifies a gene a billionfold in as little as one hour without the need for a living cell. The PCR technique has wide applications in microbiology, including rapid and accurate diagnosis of infectious diseases using genetic probes to identify amplified genes from microbial pathogens, and amplification of microbial genes for further study and characterization. Kary Mullis received the 1993 Nobel Prize in chemistry for his discovery of PCR.

Microorganisms Have Important Roles in Medicine, the Environment, Agriculture, and Industry

As we enter the next century, microbiology continues to play important roles in our world. In *medical microbiology,* new and emerging infections such as the Ebola virus and drug-resistant bacteria continue to plague and perplex scientists. Although smallpox and a few other diseases have been effectively eliminated, there has been a resurgence of tuberculosis, polio, and other diseases that once were thought conquered. Infectious diseases remain the leading cause of death in the world. Diseases such as Acquired Immune Deficiency Syndrome (AIDS), caused by the human immunodeficiency virus (HIV), destroy our body's immune system and affect millions of people worldwide.

Microbes are indispensable in the recycling of chemical elements, interaction with other organisms in ecosystems, and sewage treatment—a field called *microbial ecology.* In recent years microorganisms have especially been useful in the biodegradation of chemical pesticides, pollutants, and petroleum products. Such bioremediation benefits the environment because it not only removes the toxic chemical, but also does it in such a manner as to minimize additional environmental damage. The 1989 oil spill by the supertanker *Exxon Valdez,* which contaminated Prince William Sound, Alaska, with 11 million gallons of oil, provided scientists with an opportunity to use microorganisms for cleanup of the spill. Nutrients added to shorelines contaminated by oil stimulated growth of indigenous oil-degrading bacteria, resulting in

a.

b.

figure 1.14
Contamination Caused by the _Exxon Valdez_ Oil Spill
a. Example of a contaminated beach on Knight Island and Prince William Sound, Alaska, after the oil spill. b. Cleanup operation on Knight Island and Prince William Sound.

significantly increased bioremediation rates (Figure 1.14). These results suggested that naturally occurring microbes may be adequate for the bioremediation of oil spills, if these microbes are provided with sufficient nutrients for growth and metabolism.

Microbiology is important to _agriculture_ and the _food industry_. Certain bacteria (for example, _Rhizobium_ and _Bradyrhizobium_) live in symbiotic associations with plants called legumes (soybeans, alfalfa, clover, peas, and so forth). In these associations, the bacterium converts (fixes) atmospheric nitrogen into nitrogen-containing chemical compounds, which can then be used by the plant as a source of nitrogen. Crop rotation between legumes and nonlegumes is one method by which farmers replenish the soil with nitrogen without using expensive chemical fertilizers that may be environmentally damaging. Cheeses, yogurt, buttermilk, sauerkraut, pickles, and beer are examples of foods and beverages prepared using microorganisms. Yeasts, a rich source of protein, are being considered as a possible major source of food for human consumption in a world where traditional food supplies may become inadequate for a rapidly growing population.

Microorganisms are important in _industry_ as producers of antibiotics, vitamins, and chemicals. Monosodium glutamate, a flavor enhancer in foods, is commercially produced using the bacterium _Corynebacterium glutamicum_. Enzymes such as amylases (starch digestion), used in desizing agents and detergents, and proteases (protein digestion), used for spot removal, meat tenderizing, and wound cleansing, are commercially produced by bacteria and fungi. The multibillion-dollar pharmaceutical industry is based on microbial production of antibiotics such as bacitracin, chloramphenicol, neomycin, streptomycin, and tetracycline.

In the eighteenth and nineteenth centuries, many of the world's leading scientists believed that microorganisms arose spontaneously from nonliving matter. This doctrine of spontaneous generation originated from ancient beliefs that maggots that appeared on decaying meat and flies found on manure arose spontaneously. Several scientists, including Francesco Redi (1626–1697), Lazzaro Spallanzani (1729–1799), and Theodor Schwann (1810–1882), challenged the idea of spontaneous generation. Redi, an Italian physician, conducted a simple experiment in which meat was placed in three containers. One was covered with paper, a second covered with a fine gauze that excluded flies from entering, and a third was left uncovered. Flies laid their eggs on the meat in the uncovered container, and maggots, the larvae of flies, subsequently developed from the eggs. Meat in the other two containers did not generate maggots spontaneously, although flies attracted to meat in the gauze-covered container laid eggs on the gauze and the eggs subsequently produced maggots on the gauze. Spallanzani, an Italian naturalist, and Schwann, a German physiologist, provided further evidence that microorganisms do not arise spontaneously. Spallanzani showed that heating animal and vegetable juices, called infusions, in hermetically sealed flasks prevented the appearance of microorganisms (which he called *animalcula*). Breaking the seals exposed the flasks' contents to the air and resulted in microbial growth. Schwann repeated Spallanzani's experiments, but he heated air entering the flask through a bent tube to kill any microorganisms in the air (Figure 1P.1). Although the experiments of these three scientists showed that contaminating microorganisms originated from air, the results could not be reproduced by other scientists, and the controversy concerning spontaneous generation continued.

In 1861 Louis Pasteur convincingly showed that microorganisms could not arise spontaneously. Pasteur designed an ingenious series of experiments demonstrating that microorganisms from the air were responsible for contaminating heated infusions. Pasteur first filtered large volumes of air through guncotton to collect any microorganisms that might be in the air. The guncotton was dissolved in a mixture of alcohol and ether, and the entrapped microorganisms were examined under a microscope. Pasteur observed that microorganisms in the air had various sizes and shapes, and some contained starch granules, which could be stained with iodine.

To show that these airborne microbes were capable of contaminating infusions, Pasteur designed long-necked flasks that allowed the contents to be effectively heated, while at the same time let air in. Infusions such as yeast water, sugared yeast water, sugar beet juice, or pepper water were placed into the flasks and boiled for several minutes to kill any microorganisms already present. The flasks were allowed to cool. Although the infusions were exposed to air, no growth appeared in the flasks. Pasteur concluded that the curved necks of the flasks slowed the movement of airborne microorganisms and prevented their contamination of the infusions. Pasteur furthermore observed that when the necks of the flasks were broken, the infusions became contaminated (Figure 1P.2). Several of Pasteur's original swan-necked flasks have been preserved at the Pasteur Institute in Paris and still contain their original nutrient solutions—untouched by microorganisms and uncontaminated.

Pasteur's experiments were logical, simple, and easily reproducible. As a result, they left little doubt that the doctrine of spontaneous generation was untenable.

References

Pasteur, L. 1861. Mémoire sur les corpuscles organisés qui existent dans l'atmosphére. Examen de la doctrine des générations spontanées. *Annales des sciences naturelles,* 4th series 16:5–98.

Schwann, T. 1837. Vorläufige Mittheilung betreffend Versuche über die Weingahrung und Fäulnis. *Annalen der Physik und Chemie* 41:184–193.

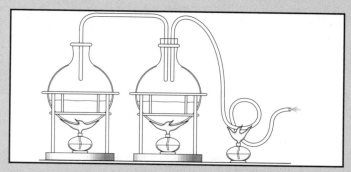

figure 1P.1
Schwann's Experimental System

The stoppered center flask containing infusion is heated to boiling. Air entering the center flask from the right is heated through a bent tube to kill any microorganisms in the air. Air leaving the center flask to the left is sent through a second heated infusion to prevent contamination of the center flask from backflow.

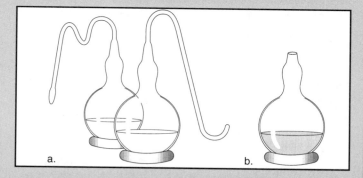

figure 1P.2
Pasteur's Experimental System

a. Infusions in swan-necked flasks are heated and then cooled. No growth appears in the infusions, even though they are exposed to the environment. b. Growth occurs if the flask necks are broken, allowing the infusions to become contaminated.

Summary

1. Microbiology is the study of agents too small to be seen with the unaided eye, specifically bacteria (bacteriology), viruses (virology), fungi (mycology), protozoa (protozoology), and algae (phycology).

2. Zacharias Janssen combined two lenses to form the first crude compound microscope. Robert Hooke made detailed drawings of plant tissues from his observations with the microscope. Anton van Leeuwenhoek is considered to be the father of microbiology because he constructed hundreds of microscopes and described in detail many of the microbial shapes he saw with his microscopes.

3. The theory of spontaneous generation was disproved by the work of scientists such as Lazzaro Spallanzani and Louis Pasteur, who showed that microorganisms could not arise spontaneously and grow in properly sterilized nutrient solutions.

4. Robert Koch established a series of criteria necessary for association of specific microorganisms with specific diseases in 1876. These criteria, known as Koch's postulates, initiated the Golden Age of Microbiology (1876-1906), a period during which the causes of most bacterial diseases were discovered.

5. Élie Metchnikoff discovered in 1884 that cells in the blood could engulf foreign particles and protect the body against infectious diseases. Earlier, in 1798, Edward Jenner showed that immunity could be conferred by vaccination. These two discoveries were instrumental in the development of the field of immunology.

6. Virology developed as a field of study with Dmitri Ivanowsky's discovery in 1892 that filterable agents were responsible for tobacco mosaic disease. The term virus was later coined by Martinus Willem Beijerinck to describe this filterable infectious agent. Bacterial viruses, or bacteriophages, were discovered by Frederick W. Twort and Felix d'Hérelle in the early 1900s in their observations of filterable agents that were parasites of bacteria.

7. A new golden age of microbiology has emerged in recent years with the discovery of new techniques in molecular biology and the applications of these techniques to microorganisms. The first recombinant DNA molecule was created by Paul Berg in 1972 when he successfully spliced DNA virus into a bacterial chromosome. In 1985, Kary Mullis developed the polymerase chain reaction, a process that amplifies a gene a billionfold in as little as one hour.

8. Today microbiology plays an important role in medicine, ecology, agriculture, food production, and industry. As we enter the twenty-first century, microorganisms will continue to be important in solving environmental problems and the intricate mysteries of the living cell.

EVOLUTION *and* BIODIVERSITY

 Microbiology is a relatively young discipline that has evolved from the minuscule microbes observed through Leeuwenhoek's single-lens microscopes three centuries ago, to the discovery during the Golden Age of Microbiology that specific microorganisms cause infectious diseases, to the genetic engineering of microbes to benefit humankind and society in a new golden age of microbiology. As microbiology has evolved, it also has diversified into a discipline that significantly impacts many other fields. The foundations of molecular biology are based on detailed investigations of DNA, RNA, and proteins in bacteria and viruses. Many of the early, definitive studies in genetics were conducted using the bread mold *Neurospora crassa*. Microbes are indispensable in the recycling of chemical elements and have been instrumental in recent advances in the bioremediation of chemical pollutants and toxic wastes. The modern multibillion-dollar pharmaceutical industry developed after World War II, based on the earlier discoveries of the antibiotic penicillin, produced by the mold *Penicillium notatum*, in 1928 by the Scottish physician and bacteriologist Alexander Fleming (1881–1955) and of the antibiotics gramicidin and tyrocidine, produced by the soil bacterium *Bacillus brevis*, in 1939 by the French microbiologist René Dubos. In the same manner as microbiology is interwoven in the fabric of biology, the underlying theme of this textbook will be the roles of evolution and diversity in the microbial world. This theme of evolution and biodiversity in the microbial world will be reinforced in a special text box at the end of each chapter.

Questions

Short Answer

1. Identify 10 subdisciplines or fields of microbiology.

2. Who was the first person to describe cells? When?

3. Who was the first person to describe microbes? When?

4. What is the theory of spontaneous generation? When was it developed?

5. Describe Francesco Redi's experiment. What did he conclude?

6. What did critics say about Spallanzani's experiment?

7. What innovative strategy did Pasteur use in his experiments relating to spontaneous generation?

8. What is the germ theory? When was it developed?

9. State Koch's postulates.

10. When is/was the golden age of microbiology? What is special about that time period?

11. What were the first immune cells to be discovered? Who discovered them? When?

12. Who developed the process known as vaccination? When?

13. What two materials were found to constitute viruses?

14. What are restriction endonucleases? Why are they important?

15. Name several diseases that are infectious.

16. Name several diseases that are not infectious.

17. What type of disease is the leading cause of death in the world today?

Critical Thinking

1. Pasteur is credited with disproving the theory of spontaneous generation. Explain why previous experiments by Redi and Spallanzani were not conclusive.

2. Explain the significance of Koch's postulates. Give examples of exceptions to Koch's postulates.

3. Explain the significance of the germ theory of disease.

4. Many early microbiologists (for example, Hooke, Leeuwenhoek, Spallanzani, and Needham) were not scientists. Explain how this was possible. Does this make their work any less significant?

 Supplementary Readings

Aharonowitz, Y., and G. Cohen. 1981. The microbiological production of pharmaceuticals. *Scientific American* 245:140–152. (A discussion of the role of microorganisms in synthesis of antibiotics, vitamins, antiviral drugs, and hormones.)

Beardsley, T. 1994. Big-time biology. *Scientific American* 271:90–97. (A discussion of how a new industry has been generated from the new technology of genetic engineering.)

Brill, W. 1980. Biochemical genetics of nitrogen fixation. *Microbiological Reviews* 44:449–467. (A review of the biochemistry and genetics of nitrogen fixation by bacteria.)

Brock, T., ed. 1961. *Milestones in microbiology.* Englewood Cliffs, N.J.: Prentice-Hall. (A compilation of historical papers written by scientists making significant contributions to the field of microbiology.)

Capecchi, M.R. 1994. Targeted gene replacement. *Scientific American* 270:52–59. (A discussion of how genes cloned and propagated in bacteria can be introduced into living cells to replace defective genes.)

Gilbert, W., and L. Villa-Komaroff. 1980. Useful proteins from recombinant bacteria. *Scientific American* 242:74–94. (A discussion of how recombinant DNA methods can be used to produce insulin, interferon, and other industrially useful compounds.)

Schlessinger, D., ed. 1981. *Genetics and molecular biology of industrial organisms. Microbiology—1981.* Washington, D.C.: American Society for Microbiology. (A series of short research articles describing the use of microorganisms for production of important chemical compounds.)

chapter two

CELL MORPHOLOGY AND MICROSCOPY

Nomarski differential interference
contrast micrograph of diatoms (×500).

Microbes in Motion ——————— PREVIEW LINK

This chapter covers the key topic of classification of bacteria into groups
based on shape and Gram reaction. The following sections of the
Microbes in Motion CD-ROM may be useful as a preview to your reading
or as a supplemental study aid:

Miscellaneous Bacteria: Mycoplasma, 1–6. *Bacterial Structure and
Function:* Cell Wall (Bacterial Shapes) 6–9; Bacterial Groups, 1–4.

Most life-forms that are familiar to us are organisms easily seen with the naked eye. These **macroorganisms** come in all sizes, shapes, and forms. It has been conservatively estimated that over 1 million animal species and 350,000 plant species are known to humans. Beyond the realm of visibility there exists an extensive and diverse group of organisms so small that they normally cannot be seen without the aid of a microscope. These **microorganisms** are ubiquitous and include such widely different types as bacteria, algae, fungi, and protozoa. Most microbes are unicellular and measure, at most, only several micrometers in diameter. A few, such as certain algae and fungi, can form large multicellular structures that rival the sizes of some macroorganisms. Examples include seaweed, which can have lengths approaching 10 m, and mushrooms, with their stalks and prominent umbrella-shaped or cone-shaped caps. Simply because an organism is large, visible, and multicellular does not necessarily exclude its constituent cells from the classification of microorganisms.

There are two kinds of cells: **procaryotic**, from Latin *pro* (before), Greek *karyon* (nucleus), and **eucaryotic**, from Latin *eu* (true). The most notable difference between procaryotic and eucaryotic cells is that procaryotic cells do not have a membrane-enclosed nucleus. Instead of a distinct nucleus, procaryotic cells have a **nucleoid**, a region that contains a single, circular DNA molecule. Eucaryotic cells have, in addition to a well-defined membrane-enclosed nucleus, a variety of specialized membrane-enclosed organelles, including mitochondria and chloroplasts, as well as a high level of internal structural organization not found in procaryotic cells.

Among the five groups of microorganisms, the bacteria are procaryotes,[a] and protozoa, algae, and fungi are eucaryotes. In the past, all procaryotes were considered to be bacteria. It is now recognized that three major groups of organisms (Bacteria, Archaea, and Eucarya) evolved from a universal ancestor. The unique ribosomal RNA structure, plasma membrane lipid composition, cell-wall components, RNA polymerase, and mechanism of protein synthesis in Archaea make them distinct from Bacteria (see Archaea, page 307). In fact, from a phylogenetic perspective, Archaea are more closely related to Eucarya than to Bacteria. Evidence from ribosomal RNA sequencing suggests that the universal phylogenetic tree initially evolved in two directions, Bacteria and Archaea/Eucarya. Archaea, which includes microbes that inhabit extreme environments (high temperature, high salinity, low pH, and so on), are among the most primitive organisms known and may very well represent examples of earth's earliest life-forms.

Viruses are not cellular and therefore are not considered either procaryotes or eucaryotes. A virus is an obligate intracellular parasite composed of nucleic acid (DNA or RNA) within a host cell.

Much of our knowledge of microorganisms as well as macroorganisms comes from studies of procaryotes. Procaryotes are the best-understood microbes. Although procaryotes are diverse in their physical and metabolic properties and include a wide variety of cell forms, they nonetheless have been extensively studied and are well characterized.

Size, Shape, and Arrangement of Procaryotic Cells

Procaryotes come in a variety of sizes, shapes, and arrangements. These characteristics, which frequently are unique to certain groups of procaryotes, help in the identification and classification of these microorganisms. The form and structure, or morphology, of a bacterium usually provides the first clue to its identity.

Size and Scale: Procaryotes Are Small

Procaryotes are the smallest free-living organisms known. They typically cannot be seen without the aid of a microscope; some are so small that specialized microscopes must be used to see them. Even among these minute organisms, however, there is extensive variation in size.

The smallest procaryotes—and probably the smallest organisms capable of autonomous growth—are members of the genus *Mycoplasma*. Mycoplasmas occur as normal inhabitants of the respiratory and genitourinary tracts of humans and other animals. They may cause such diseases as urethritis and primary atypical pneumonia (PAP)—a mild form of pneumonia. Mycoplasmas have diameters of only 125 to 250 nm[b]—5 million of these organisms could be laid side-by-side on the head of a straight pin. These microbes lack the distinctive cell wall that is found in other bacteria and therefore have no specific shape; rather, they have a variety of shapes—a trait known as **pleomorphism** [Greek *pleon*, more, and *morphe*, form]. As a consequence of pleomorphism, *Mycoplasma* cells are capable of passing through membrane filters that would retain larger and more rigid bacteria. The size of a

---

[a]Procaryotes consist of the domain **Bacteria** (from Greek *bakterion* [a small rod]) and the domain **Archaea** (from Greek *archaios* [ancient]). Eucaryotes are taxonomically placed in the domain **Eucarya.** The phylogenetic distinctions within these three domains are explained in Chapter 11. In this chapter and throughout this book, the word *Bacteria* (uppercase "B") refers to organisms in the domain Bacteria, as contrasted phylogenetically to organisms in the domains Archaea and Eucarya. The word *bacteria* (lowercase "b") refers to procaryotes in general, without reference to phylogeny.

[b]Units of linear measurement commonly used in microbiology are:
1 millimeter (mm) = 10^{-3} meter
1 micrometer (μm) = 10^{-6} meter
1 nanometer (nm) = 10^{-9} meter
1 angstrom (Å) = 10^{-10} meter

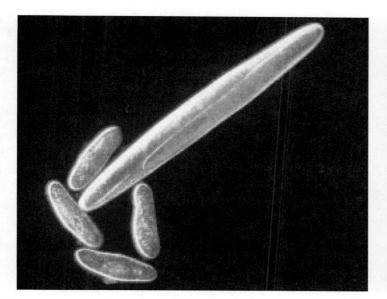

figure 2.1

Photomicrograph of *Epulopiscium fishelsoni*

Epulopiscium, the largest known procaryote, is compared in size with four eucaryotic paramecia (colorized, ×200).

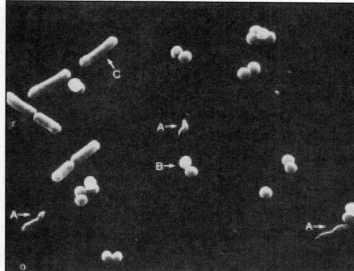

figure 2.2

Scanning Electron Micrograph Comparing Shapes of Procaryotic Cells

Shown are *Campylobacter fetus* (A), spirilla; *Staphylococcus aureus* (B), cocci; and *Bacillus subtilis* (C), rods (×4,200).

Mycoplasma cell approaches the minimum required for a living, independent cell that can still contain the macromolecules and machinery required for self-reproduction.

Miscellaneous Bacteria
Mycoplasma • pp. 1–6

At the other extreme of size among procaryotes are *Spirillum* (1.7 µm × 28 µm) and *Epulopiscium fishelsoni* [Latin *epulatus*, to feast, *piscis*, fish] (80 µm × 600 µm) (Figure 2.1). Members of the genus *Spirillum* are sometimes large enough to be seen without the aid of a microscope. It is believed that some of the first bacteria seen by Leeuwenhoek with his crude microscopes may have been *Spirillum*. In 1993 researchers at Indiana University isolated *E. fishelsoni* from the intestinal tract of the surgeonfish off the Great Barrier Reef in Australia; it is so large that it initially was thought to be a eucaryote. However, analysis of its DNA and cellular features confirms that it is a procaryote.

Procaryotes Have Different Shapes

Procaryotes exist in two basic forms: the **coccus** [Greek *kokkos*, berry], a spherical cell; and the **rod**, or **bacillus** [Latin *baculus*, stick], a cylindrical cell. There are many variations of these two fundamental shapes (Figure 2.2). Some bacteria have shapes that are not exclusively spherical or cylindrical, but a combination of these two forms. These organisms are known as **coccobacilli**. A few bacteria form spirals and are called **spirilla**, [Latin *spira*, coil, twist], or **spirochetes** [Greek *speira*, coil, *chaite*, bristle], depending on their mechanism of motility. A spirillum has a rigid form and moves by flagella (specialized appendages), whereas a spirochete flexes its entire body and moves by axial filaments in an undulating or rotat-

ing motion. Filamentous bacteria form long threads of cellular mass that can branch in several directions up to several hundred micrometers in length. Pleomorphism is a trait of certain types of bacteria that have no definitive shape or have a variety of shapes either because they lack cell walls (*Mycoplasma*), or because their cells divide in unusual manners to produce different forms (*Corynebacterium*) or reproductive buds or appendages (*Hyphomicrobium*).

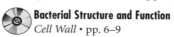

Bacterial Structure and Function
Cell Wall • pp. 6–9

Certain groups of bacteria change forms during the course of their life cycle. For example, *Chlamydia*, a bacterium that causes trachoma and other diseases, alternates between two shapes: (1) a small resistant cell form called an elementary body (0.3 µm in diameter) that is geared for survival in the environment, but is unable to replicate and (2) a much larger reticulate body (1 µm in diameter) that is involved in cellular multiplication within a host. Thus *Chlamydia* can assume two completely different forms, one suited for cellular survival in a harsh environment, and one for intracellular replication and proliferation. *Rhizobium*, a bacterium that converts gaseous nitrogen to ammonium in a process called nitrogen fixation, undergoes a similar type of transformation, changing from rods in a free-living phase to swollen, misshapen forms called bacteroids during infection of plant roots. These bacteroids, incapable of division, carry out nitrogen fixation (see nitrogen fixation, page 418).

Procaryotes Have Different Cell Arrangements

Unlike *Chlamydia* and *Rhizobium*, most bacteria maintain constant, representative shapes that are useful aids in identification. Some bacteria also have cells that remain attached after division,

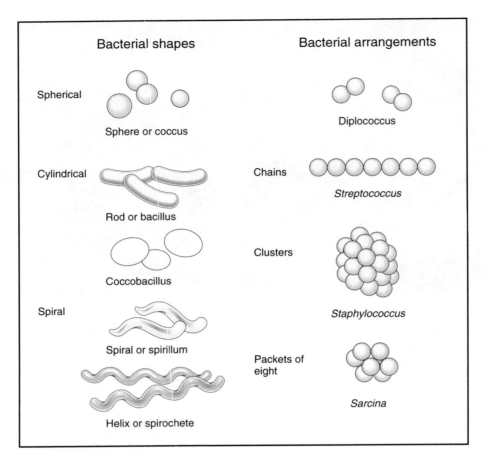

figure 2.3
Representative Cell Shapes and Arrangements of Procaryotes

clumped in distinctive cell arrangements (Figures 2.3 and 2.4). Bacterial names frequently reflect both cell morphologies and cell arrangements, and can be descriptive aids in identification. Thus the genus name *Streptococcus* [Greek *streptos,* winding, twisted] appropriately describes a bacterium that is often found as chains of cocci due to incomplete separation among dividing cells and division in a single plane. Bacteria of the genus *Staphylococcus* [Greek *staphyle,* bunch of grapes] are also cocci but are attached in clusters, which form as the bacteria divide in random planes rather than in a single plane. Other arrangements of bacteria include cubical packets of cells, as in the genus *Sarcina* [Latin *sarcina,* a package, bundle]; angular arrangements of cells, as in *Corynebacterium* [Greek *koryne,* club]; and filaments, as in *Leptothrix* and *Clonothrix* [Greek *trich,* hair].

Cell arrangements may change in response to environmental conditions. The chaining of streptococci is an example (Figure 2.5). Streptococci form chains of cells when they are exposed to nutrient-limiting conditions. Chaining results from incomplete cell division in which new cells remain attached to the original parent cells because of uncleaved cell wall material between adjoining cells (see Perspective at the end of this chapter). Chains also have been found to form in the presence of specific antibodies that inhibit enzymes

responsible for cell separation. Streptococci are generally found in chains when recovered from isolated lesions or grown on laboratory media. When the same bacteria are isolated from an actively spreading lesion in the human body, the cells generally occur as single cocci and diplococci (pairs of cocci).

Microscopy

The light microscope is the workhorse of microbiology. Through the microscope we are not only able to see microorganisms, but also can determine their morphology, arrangements, and structural features. The various morphologies of the bacteria were not appreciated until the development of the microscope, and each new refinement of the microscope has brought enticing new views of the microbial world.

Many different types of microscopes have been developed over the past two centuries. Each has its own characteristics and features that provide it with a specific value in microscopy. Microscopes basically are two kinds: light and electron. The **light microscope** uses light as its source of illumination and may permit four types of microscopy: **bright-field, dark-field, fluorescence,** and **phase-contrast.** The **electron microscope** uses a beam of electrons

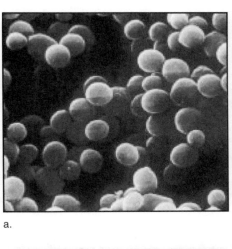
a.

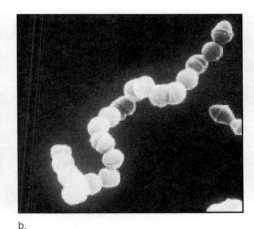
b.

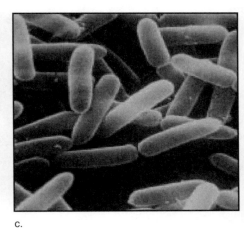
c.

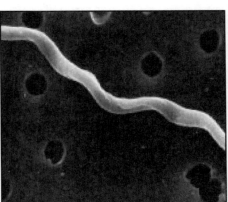
d.

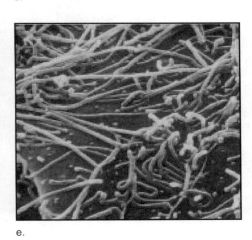
e.

figure 2.4

Scanning Electron Micrographs of Different Bacteria

a. *Staphylococcus aureus*, clusters of cocci (colorized, ×34,000). b. *Streptococcus pyogenes*, chains of cocci (colorized, ×16,000). c. *Bacillus subtilis*, rods (colorized, ×11,000). d. *Cristispira pectinis*, a spirochete (×23,000). e. *Mycoplasma pneumoniae*, pleomorphic cells (colorized, ×18,000).

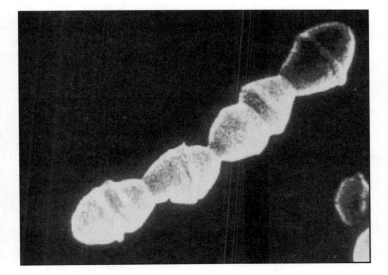

figure 2.5

Chaining of *Streptococcus pyogenes* from Incomplete Cell Division

Under nutrient-limiting conditions, streptococci form chains of cells from incomplete cell division (colorized, ×40,000).

instead of light waves to produce an image. There are two types of electron microscopes: **transmission electron microscopes (TEMs)** and **scanning electron microscopes (SEMs).**

The Compound (Bright-Field) Light Microscope Magnifies Objects Too Small to Be Seen by the Human Eye

The standard instrument used in the laboratory to observe microorganisms is the compound (bright-field) light microscope (Figure 2.6). This instrument is called **compound** because it contains two or more sets of lenses, as compared to a single-lens system such as a magnifying glass or the microscopes of Leeuwenhoek.

A modern compound microscope has a **condenser lens,** which focuses light on the specimen; **objective** lenses that are close to the specimen and magnify it; and **ocular lenses** that are near the eye and further magnify the image. Light rays pass through the specimen in a bright-field microscope. Since objects are seen against a light background, staining of the specimen enhances its contrast against the background. Specimens that are stained and viewed with the bright-field light microscope appear dark against a brightly lit background.

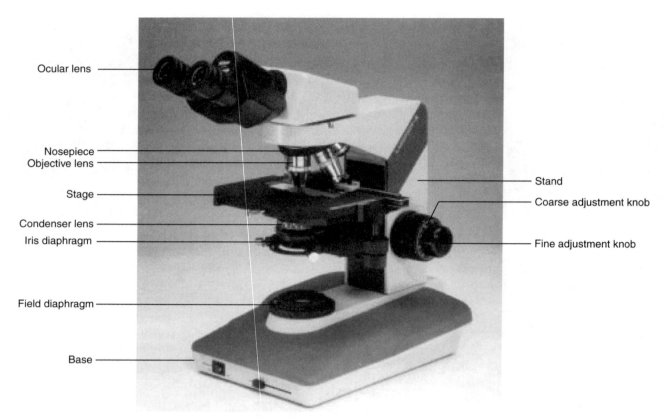

figure 2.6
Basic Elements of the Compound Bright-Field Light Microscope

Objects Are Magnified by the Lenses of a Light Microscope

Most microscopes have several objective lenses, each with a different magnifying power and optical property, located on a revolving nosepiece. The nosepiece is attached to the lower end of a hollow body tube.

Images of a specimen, illuminated by a lamp or by light reflected by a mirror, pass through the objective lens and body tube to the second set of magnifying lenses: the ocular lenses. The ocular lens system, also known as the eyepiece, is located at the upper end of the body tube and is placed next to the observer's eyes. This lens system serves to magnify the primary image formed by the objective lens and renders the image visible.

The total magnification of a specimen seen through a compound microscope is determined by multiplying the magnifications of both the ocular and objective sets of lenses. For example, an objective lens with a magnification of 40× used in combination with an ocular lens having a magnification of 10× would produce a total magnification of 400× (10× times 40×). Most ocular lenses have magnification of 10×, whereas objective lenses have magnifications normally ranging from 4 to 100×.

The objective lenses of a microscope should be free of spherical, chromatic, and other types of aberrations (Figure 2.7). A **spherical aberration** arises when light rays from an object passing through different portions of a curved lens do not meet at a single point for sharp focus. Much like the human eye focuses on an object by adjusting its lens to the path of light rays entering the curved cornea, a microscope lens must minimize spherical aberrations. Light rays must cross at the focal point of the specimen; otherwise the result is a fuzzy and distorted image. Although such aberrations cannot be completely eliminated, they can be minimized by the use of different lens shapes and combinations.

A **chromatic aberration** occurs because white light, not monochromatic light, is typically used for visual observation. White light is composed of a continuum of wavelengths, from 400 to 800 nm. As white light passes through a lens, the light is split into the different colors of the spectrum, ranging from violet to red, because violet has a shorter wavelength and is refracted more than red. As a result, even with a lens corrected for spherical aberration, the image produced by white light is not sharp and is surrounded by colored fringes.

Chromatic aberration can be reduced by using compound lenses of different materials and types. Most widely used objectives are **achromatic,** compensating for red and blue aberrations by combining two types of lenses, a convex and concave, to provide the same focal length for the two colors. There are still minor aberrations with an achromatic lens, but such lenses are popular for student microscopes because of their low cost. The effect of chro-

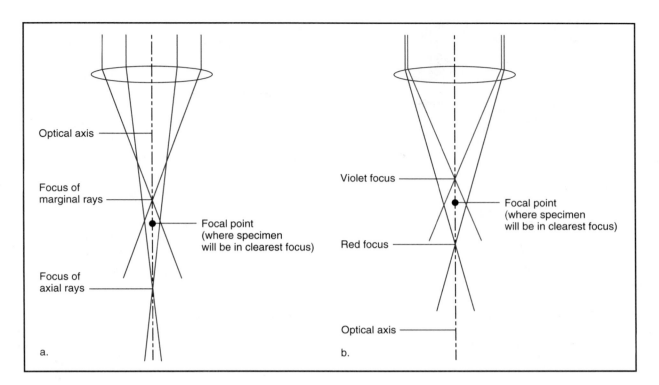

figure 2.7

Aberrations of Lenses

a. Spherical lens aberration. Light rays from the center of a spherical lens (axial rays) focus farther from the lens than the light rays from the margin of the lens, resulting in a distorted image. b. Chromatic lens aberration. Red light has longer wavelengths than violet light; therefore it focuses farther from the lens than violet light.

matic aberrations can also be minimized by using filters to eliminate wavelengths of light for which the lens is uncorrected.

For the detection of faint color or high sensitivity in color photomicrography, **apochromatic** objectives are preferred. Apochromatic objectives combine optical glass with the clear mineral fluorite (crystalline CaF_2) to focus light at three different wavelengths (red, blue, and green) at the same point. Such lenses usually require the use of a compensating eyepiece to make the images of each color the same size in all parts of the field. The images produced by apochromatic lenses are sharp and provide high contrast. Apochromatic systems are expensive and are used primarily for research applications.

A conventional light microscope can produce useful magnifications of approximately 1,000×. Although magnification can be increased beyond 1,000× in a light microscope, this increase is **empty magnification,** because the resolution of the specimen is not increased.

The Light Microscope Can Resolve Objects 0.2 μm Apart

Resolution, or **resolving power,** is defined as the ability of a microscope to distinguish two closely spaced objects as separate and distinct entities. The conventional light microscope can be used to observe specimens that are at least 0.2 μm apart, and therefore is said to have a resolving power of 0.2 μm.

The resolving power of a microscope is determined by three factors: (1) the wavelength of light (λ) used for illumination of the specimen, (2) the numerical aperture of the condenser, and (3) the numerical aperture of the objective lens used. The wavelength of light is a fixed characteristic in most light microscopes, although shorter wavelengths of light (for example, ultraviolet light) can be used in some instruments to achieve greater resolution. The resolving power of a microscope, therefore, depends primarily on the numerical apertures of the objective and condenser lenses. The resolving power of a microscope is mathematically expressed by the formula:

$$\text{Resolving power} = \frac{(0.61)\lambda}{\text{NA objective lens} + \text{NA condenser lens}}$$

The numerical aperture, generally abbreviated N.A., is the light-gathering capability of a lens. Ernst Abbe (1840–1905), a German mathematician and physicist, established a mathematical relationship that correlates the light-gathering ability of a lens with its aperture. This relationship for an objective lens is:

$$\text{N.A.} = n \sin \theta$$

where n is the refractive index of the medium between the objective lens and the specimen, and θ is one-half the angle of light entering the objective lens through the stage (Figure 2.8).

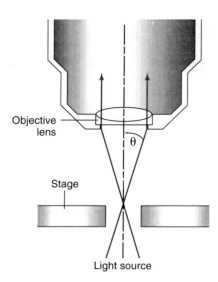

figure 2.8

Determination of Angle θ

The angle θ, which is used to calculate the numerical aperture of a lens, is one-half the cone of light entering the objective lens from the object, at focus.

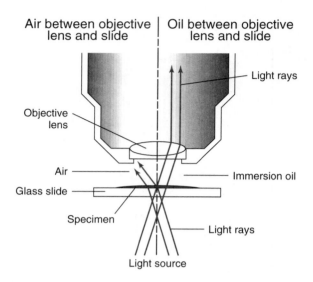

figure 2.9

The Refractive Indices of Oil Versus Air

Comparison of light rays sent through immersion oil and through air. The refractive index of immersion oil is identical to that of the microscope slide (1.52). Consequently, light rays are not bent as much when they pass through the slide and the oil as when they pass through air (refractive index = 1.00). More light from the specimen reaches the objective lens when oil is used.

The refractive index varies with the medium used between the lens and the specimen (Figure 2.9). Air is generally used as the standard surrounding medium. The refractive index of air is assumed to be 1.00. Since the value of sin θ remains constant for any given lens, the numerical aperture of an objective lens can be increased only by inserting a medium with a refractive index higher than 1.00 between the specimen and the lens.

Water has a refractive index of 1.33, whereas immersion oil has a refractive index of 1.52. By changing the medium from air to oil, one thus is able to increase the numerical aperture of the objective lens, thereby improving the resolving power of the microscope. Oil-immersion lenses are objective lenses with high magnifications and high numerical apertures that require oil as an immersion medium to increase resolution. These lenses are used to view bacteria in detail. Dry objective lenses, which use air to occupy the space between the objective and the specimen, are employed for lower magnifications where detail is not as critical. The values of the numerical aperture and magnifying power are generally stamped on the side of objective lenses.

Proper Illumination of a Specimen Is Important in Achieving Optimal Resolution with a Light Microscope

The resolving power of a microscope also is dependent upon the numerical aperture of the **condenser.** The condenser of a light microscope, located below the stage on a focusable mount, gathers light from the light source and concentrates it onto the specimen. Condensers improve resolution by eliminating stray light rays that otherwise would cause glare around the specimen. The uncor-

rected Abbe condenser is the most common type of condenser used in student microscopes. This condenser consists of two or more lenses that are not corrected for spherical or chromatic aberration. Such a condenser is relatively inexpensive and is generally adequate for most routine applications where color correction or precise images of the lamp source are not essential. Other types of condensers (some with as many as six elements) correct for aberrations and provide near-perfect images of the light source.

An adjustable multileaf **iris diaphragm** is located in the condenser. The diaphragm controls the diameter of light leaving the condenser and striking the specimen and therefore functions much like the diaphragm of the eye or in a camera. By adjusting the opening of the diaphragm, one is able to reduce glare and increase clarity of the image. A diaphragm opened too fully results in excessive illumination and glare. One that is too closed decreases resolution of the specimen by effectively reducing the numerical aperture of the objective.

Light intensity in microscopy is not controlled by the condenser or the iris diaphragm. It is determined by adjusting the voltage of the light source or by using filters to block out certain wavelengths of light.

Proper illumination of a specimen is important in achieving optimal resolution with a light microscope. Two basic methods are used to achieve correct illumination in a bright-field light microscope: **critical illumination** and **Köhler illumination** (Figure 2.10). In critical illumination, an image of the light source filament is focused on the specimen with the substage condenser. This method gives bright, but uneven, illumination and is most often used for high-power visual work.

Microscopy

Ocular lens

Specimen image

Objective lens

Specimen

Condenser lens

Iris diaphragm

Light source

Field diaphragm

Lamp condenser lens

Light source

a.

b.

figure 2.10
Critical and Köhler Illuminations

a. In critical illumination, an image of the light source filament is focused on the specimen with the substage condenser to produce bright, but uneven, illumination of the specimen. b. In Köhler illumination, the filament of the light source is focused onto the iris diaphragm by a condenser attached to the microscope lamp. The position of the substage condenser lens is adjusted so as to form an image of the field diaphragm in the plane of the specimen. The field diaphragm is then opened or closed to reduce any spurious light, resulting in even illumination of the specimen.

The Köhler method of illumination uses a separate condenser attached to the microscope lamp to focus an image of the lamp filament onto the iris diaphragm of the substage condenser. The substage condenser is then slowly racked up to focus the image of the lamp condenser in the plane of the specimen. In this procedure the lamp condenser actually becomes the source of illumination. The Köhler method results in a uniform illumination of the specimen without unwanted background glare. Köhler illumination is typically used for general visual work and photomicrography.

Stains Increase the Contrast between a Specimen and Its Background

Bacteria are generally difficult to see, even with the aid of a microscope, because of their transparency. For this reason bacterial cells are often stained with organic dyes to increase the contrast between the specimen and the background. Organic dyes may be separated on the basis of their affinity for specific groups of compounds.

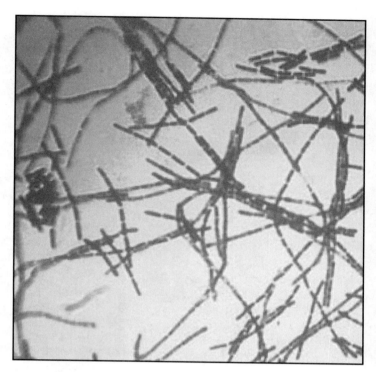

figure 2.11
Example of a Positive Stain
A Gram stain of *Bacillus anthracis*, the cause of anthrax.

Basic dyes are positively charged and combine with negatively charged cell constituents such as nucleic acids and acidic polysaccharides. Examples of basic dyes are crystal violet, methylene blue, and safranin. Acidic dyes have an affinity for positively charged materials such as basic proteins, and include Congo red, eosin, nigrosin, and basic fuchsin.

Bacterial stains are generally one of three types: **simple, differential,** or **special.** Simple stains consist of a single dye that is used to enhance the contrast of the specimen against the background. Such stains are useful in examining cell size, morphology, or arrangement, since the bacterial cell appears as a single, distinct color against an unstained background.

Differential stains use two dyes (the primary dye stains the structure in question and a counterstain is for contrast). They involve several staining and destaining solutions and are used to differentiate cells on the basis of their staining characteristics. The **Gram stain** is a differential stain that is widely used in bacteriology. Most bacteria can be differentiated into two groups based on their Gram stain reaction: **gram positive** (stained violet) and **gram negative** (stained pink or red) (see basis of Gram stain, page 60).

Special stains are used to enhance the features of specific cell constituents such as endospores, nuclear regions, and granules. Dyes used in special stains have an affinity for specific cell structures and highlight these structures (Figure 2.11). All of these staining techniques result in a stained bacterial cell or stained components against an unstained background, and are called **positive stains.**

Thousands of bacterial species are known. How can these organisms be most easily and quickly identified? A Danish physician, Hans Christian Gram

The Gram Stain

(1853–1938), answered this question in part during the period he worked at the morgue of the City Hospital of Berlin. Gram was interested in distinguishing between difficult-to-see bacteria that caused pneumonia and mammalian cell nuclei in infected tissue. Gram was disappointed in the stain he developed, which did not stain all bacteria equally, and this disappointment was evident in his statement in a published paper that he hoped "the method would be useful to other workers." Unknown to Gram at that time, the technique he developed in 1884 would eventually become the most widely used stain in microbiology. The **Gram stain** is used to separate bacteria into two major groups: **gram positive** and **gram negative** (see cell structure basis for differentiation by the Gram stain, page 60). Although this differential stain does not provide definitive identification of bacteria, it is routinely used in clinical and industrial laboratories as one of the first steps in bacterial identification. When the Gram stain is combined with information on cellular morphology and arrangement, as well as biochemical characteristics, a conclusive identification can usually be made.

The Gram stain procedure involves the suspension of freshly grown bacterial cells in a drop of water on a glass slide (Table 2.1). This suspension is gently heated over a low flame to heat-fix the smear onto the slide. The smear is then stained with a primary dye, crystal violet. The smear is washed with water and then covered with iodine. The iodine acts as a mordant (fixative) to form an insoluble complex with crystal violet inside the cell. The smear is then decolorized with alco-hol or acetone-alcohol and counterstained with safranin. After a final wash with water, the material is examined under the microscope. **Gram-positive** bacteria (those that retain the original crystal violet stain even after decolorization) stain a deep violet. **Gram-negative** bacteria (those that are decolorized and are stained with the counterstain safranin) stain pink or red.

Most bacteria are classified as either gram positive or gram negative. Some organisms, however, do not give an obvious Gram stain reaction because of the thickness or composition of their cell walls. These organisms, termed **gram variable,** appear as both gram-positive and gram-negative cells when viewed with a microscope. Other bacteria, which might normally stain gram positive in young cultures, lose their abilities to stain gram positive in older cultures. These older cultures frequently have dying cells with decomposing cell walls that are unable to retain the crystal violet dye during decolorization. Another problem associated with the Gram stain and other similar staining techniques is the distortion of cellular features during heat fixation. This distortion is of minimum consequence with the Gram stain, since one is interested in only the staining characteristics and gross morphology of the cell. Distortions may present problems, however, in other types of stains.

Despite these limitations, the Gram stain is used universally for the preliminary identification of bacteria. It is a simple and rapid technique that can be performed in any laboratory equipped with a microscope and the necessary staining reagents.

Bacterial Structure and Function
Bacterial Groups • pp. 1–4

Gram Stain Procedure

Reagents	Time Applied	Reactions	Appearance
Unstained smear			Cells are colorless and difficult to see.
Crystal violet	1 minute, then rinse with water	Basic dye attaches to negatively charged groups in the cell wall, membrane, and cytoplasm.	Both gram-negative and gram-positive cells are deep violet.
Gram's Iodine (mordant)	1 minute, then rinse with water	Iodine strengthens the attachment of crystal violet to the negatively charged groups.	Both gram-negative and gram-positive cells remain deep violet.
Alcohol or acetone-alcohol mix (decolorizer)	10 to 15 seconds, then rinse with water	Decolorizer leaches the crystal violet and iodine from the cells. The color diffuses out of gram-positive cells more slowly than out of gram-negative cells because of the chemical composition and thickness of the gram-positive cell walls.	Gram-positive cells remain deep violet, but gram-negative cells become colorless and difficult to see.
Safranin (counterstain)	1 minute; then rinse thoroughly, blot dry, and observe under oil immersion	Basic dye attaches to negatively charged groups in both cell types. Few negative groups are free of crystal violet in gram-positive cell, whereas most negative groups are free in gram-negative bacteria. Consequently, gram-positive bacteria remain deep violet, whereas gram-negative bacteria become pink or red.	Gram-positive cells remain deep violet, whereas gram-negative cells are stained pink or red.

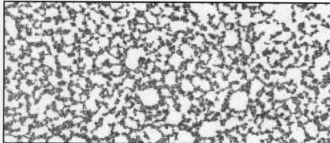

Gram stain of *Staphylococcus aureus*, a gram-positive coccus (×252).

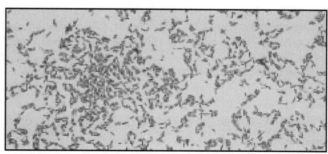

Gram stain of *Escherichia coli*, a gram-negative rod (×252).

Negative stains make cells or other cell materials appear light against a dark background. A negative stain is usually prepared by mixing cells with a substance such as India ink or nigrosin to provide the contrasting, dark background. The mixture is then spread in a thin film across a glass slide and allowed to dry. Negative stains are used to enhance cellular features that are difficult to observe with positive stains, and to do size determinations. An example of a negative stain is the capsule stain. Capsules are coverings surrounding a bacterial cell, composed of polysaccharides or proteins. In the capsule stain, only the background is stained. The stain itself does not penetrate or stain the cell capsule (Figure 2.12). All of these staining techniques provide the microbiologist with tools to enhance certain structures in bacterial cells or to see the cell better.

The Dark-Field Microscope Provides Contrast in Specimens That Normally Lack Sufficient Contrast to Be Seen with the Bright-Field Microscope

Bright-field illumination is used for observation of specimens commonly encountered in the laboratory. Dark-field illumination is useful in situations where high contrast is important. The dark-field method permits minute particles—particularly small and thin line structures such as bacterial flagella, which normally lack sufficient resolution to be seen with bright-field microscopy—to become visible to the eye. In dark-field microscopy, light is focused on the specimen at an oblique angle through a specially constructed dark-field condenser, resulting in the specimen (stained or unstained) appearing light against a dark background (Figure 2.13).

Dark-field illumination is generally achieved by placing an opaque disk, known as a dark-field stop, in the center of the substage condenser. This dark-field stop blocks direct light in the center of the condenser and does not permit it to reach the objective, but allows a hollow cone of light to illuminate the specimen. Thus while no direct light enters the objective, the specimen is seen by scattered or reflected light against a dark background. The effect achieved through dark-field illumination is comparable to seeing dust particles in a darkened room because of the reflection of rays of sunlight coming through a window.

The resolution of specimens by dark-field microscopy is quite good. For this reason, dark-field illumination is frequently used to observe thin or small objects. One use is the examination of *Treponema pallidum,* the very thin (≤0.2 μm in diameter), spiral-shaped bacterium that causes syphilis, in scrapings from syphilitic lesions. An intense, nondiffused light source is essential for good dark-field illumination. Since dirt and other foreign matter on a dirty slide can also scatter light, it is important that clean slides be used in dark-field microscopy.

The Phase-Contrast Microscope Amplifies Small Differences in Refractive Indices to Enhance Specimen Contrast

Unstained microorganisms are transparent and normally do not reflect or refract sufficient light to distinguish them from the background. Specimen contrast can be enhanced with the phase-contrast microscope, which detects small differences in refractive

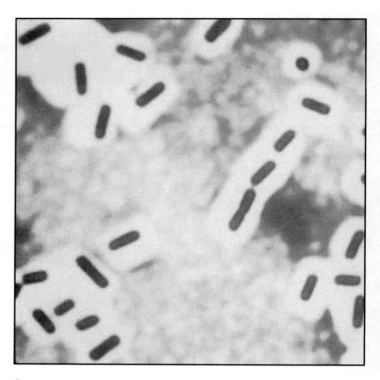

figure 2.12
Example of a Negative Stain
India ink stain of *Clostridium perfringens,* the cause of gas gangrene, showing a thick capsule around each cell (colorized).

indices of the specimen and its surrounding medium. The phase-contrast microscope was first devised by Fritz Zernicke (1888–1966) of the Netherlands in 1932. Zernicke received the Nobel Prize in physics in 1953 for his achievement.

Structures may differ in their refraction of light passing through them. In phase-contrast microscopy, these differences are amplified and converted into variations in light intensity. Phase-contrast microscopy is achieved by mounting an annular aperture diaphragm below the substage condenser so that the specimen is illuminated with a ring of light. Different annular diaphragms are used with objectives of different magnifications to achieve optimum optical results. Light from the lamp source passes around the diaphragm in the substage condenser, illuminating the specimen in a ring of light. Since the specimen and the surrounding medium have different indices of refraction, light waves passing through the specimen and entering the objective lens are somewhat refracted and out of phase compared with those coming from the medium. These differences in refractive indices are converted into variations in light intensity based on the interference of light waves passing through the specimen and the surrounding medium. Light waves that are in phase result in **constructive interference** and increased light intensity. **Destructive interference** occurs when waves are out of phase, resulting in a decrease in light intensity. The naked eye cannot detect these phase differences in light waves. For this reason, the objective lenses of a phase-contrast microscope contain a phase-shifting element (phase ring) that alters light waves passing through the objective by 90°,

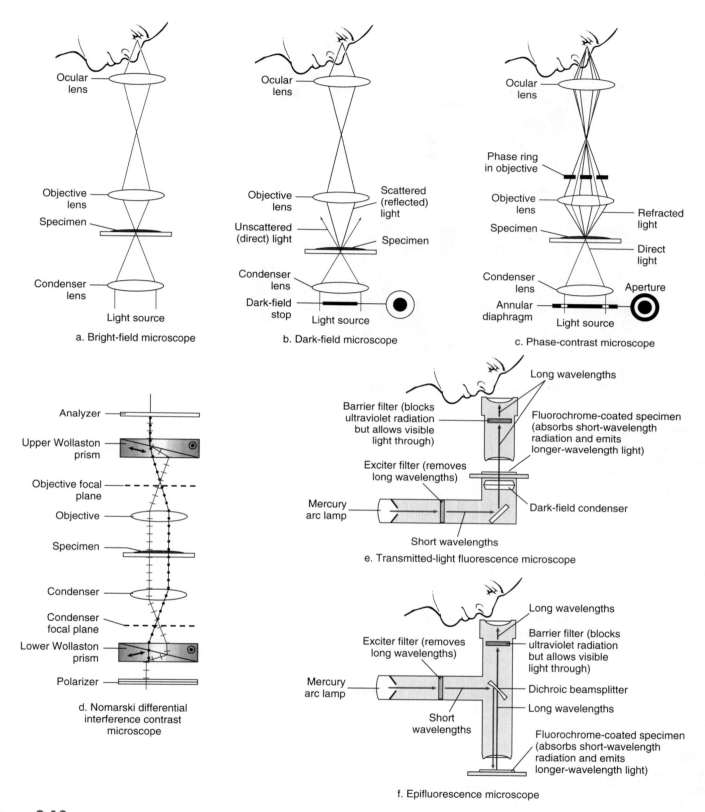

figure 2.13

Schematic Diagrams of Bright-Field, Dark-Field, Phase-Contrast, Nomarski Differential Interference Contrast, Transmitted-Light Flourescence, and Epifluorescence Microscopes

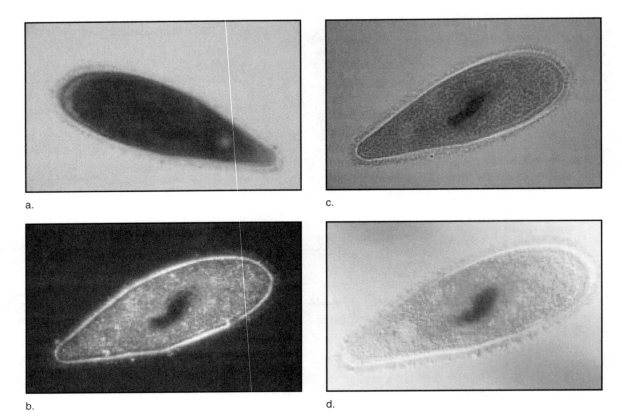

a.   c.

b.   d.

figure 2.14

The Protozoan *Paramecium* as Seen by Different Types of Light Microscopy

a. Bright-field illumination shows the outlines and general features of the specimen. b. Dark-field illumination outlines the edges of the specimen. c. Phase-contrast microscopy details the internal structures of a living specimen. d. Nomarski differential interference contrast microscopy results in a three-dimensional image of the specimen. Magnification is ×240 in all examples (colorized).

or one-quarter of a wavelength. This shift causes an increase in amplitude of the light waves reaching the eyes, resulting in increased brightness and, consequently, contrast of the specimen. Since this contrast depends on proper focusing of light entering the phase-shifting element from the annular diaphragm, precise alignment of the optics in a phase-contrast microscope is critical to achieve optimum results. A special centering telescope, placed on the eyepiece of the microscope, is used to align the adjustable annular diaphragm in the condenser with the phase-shifting element in the objective lens.

The advantage of phase-contrast microscopy is that living microorganisms in their natural state can be studied, since the specimen does not have to be fixed or stained. The specimen appears either in positive contrast (dark against a light background) or in negative contrast (bright against a dark background), depending on the type of wave retardation that occurs. Negative contrast is more commonly used, because it generally gives better resolution and contrast of specimens. The major limitation of phase-contrast microscopy is that it produces a halo, or bright ring, around dark details in a specimen. In spite of this shortcoming, phase-contrast microscopy is valuable in visualizing living cells' minute structures and details that would not be seen by other forms of microscopy.

A variation of the phase-contrast microscope is the **interference contrast microscope.** There are several types of interference contrast microscopes, but one of the more common involves double-beam interference. This method uses a beam of light that is split into two separate beams. The object beam passes through the specimen and is thus retarded in relation to the reference beam, which does not contact the specimen. When two beams reconverge with the assistance of prisms, the phase difference between the two beams provides relieflike, high-contrast images of the specimen.

A different type of double-beam interference contrast is **Nomarski differential interference contrast** microscopy. In the Nomarski microscope, two beams are produced from a single beam of polarized light, and each beam passes through a different part of the specimen. Differences in the refractive index of parts of the specimen alter the phase relationship between the two beams of light so that an interference pattern is produced when the beams are recombined. Interference microscopy does not produce the halos around specimens that are a characteristic drawback of phase-contrast microscopy. Because contrast in interference microscopy depends on differences in refractive indices across a specimen, this type of microscopy gives a relieflike three-dimensional image (Figure 2.14). Structures such as cell walls are sharply defined by interference contrast microscopy.

table 2.2

Summary of the Different Types of Microscopy and Their Applications in Microbiology

Type of Microscopy	Magnification	Specimen Appearance	Applications
Bright field	1,000 to 2,000	Stained or unstained; bacteria are generally stained to enhance contrast against background.	For gross morphological examination of bacteria, yeasts, molds, algae, and protozoa.
Dark field	1,000 to 2,000	Generally unstained; appears bright or "lighted" against a dark background.	For situations where high contrast, particularly of microbial structures, is required.
Fluorescence	1,000 to 2,000	Fluorescent	For diagnostic techniques where the fluorescent dye (antibody) fixed to the organism identifies it.
Phase contrast	1,000 to 2,000	Contrasting degrees of darkness (positive contrast) or brightness (negative contrast).	For examination of minute cellular structures and details in living cells.
Electron	100,000 and higher	Viewed on a screen	For examination of atomic and cell structures and viruses not observable with the light microscope.

The Fluorescence Microscope Detects Fluorescent Objects That Are Illuminated by Ultraviolet or Near-Ultraviolet Light

Many materials naturally fluoresce when examined under ultraviolet or near-ultraviolet radiation. Fluorescence occurs as these materials absorb the short wavelengths of ultraviolet light and then emit, in less than one-millionth of a second, light of longer wavelengths that can be seen by the eye. Fluorescence microscopy was initially developed to detect natural fluorescence of plant and animal structures, but is now extensively used for the observation of specimens that do not fluoresce unless a fluorescent dye (fluorochrome) is added.

Fluorescent dyes such as fluorescein isothiocyanate (FITC), which absorbs blue light and emits green light, are frequently conjugated with antibodies that bind only to specific antigens on a specimen (see immunofluorescence, page 489). The FITC-conjugated antibodies are added to a glass slide with an unknown specimen, and excess conjugate is removed by washing. The specimen can then be observed for fluorescence of the specifically attached dye using a specially constructed microscope. This procedure, known as **immunofluorescence,** is very useful in clinical microbiology for the diagnosis of diseases such as syphilis and rabies and in environmental microbiology for studies of natural microbial populations.

Early systems for observing fluorescence used transmitted light with dark-field illumination. In **transmitted-light fluorescence,** light passes through an excitation filter before it strikes the specimen. The excitation filter permits the passage of only short-wavelength radiation to the specimen. The fluorochrome in the specimen absorbs this radiation and emits longer-wavelength light, which passes through the objective and a barrier filter before it reaches the eye. The barrier filter blocks out ultraviolet radiation from the specimen and permits only visible light to reach the eye. The dark-field condenser removes excessive light from the objective to provide a contrasting black background. Poor image brightness, however, makes transmitted-light fluorescence less than optimal.

Modern systems use a different arrangement in which light is transmitted through the objective lens to the specimen. This method, called **incident-light excitation,** or **epifluorescence,** directs filtered short-wavelength light from the lamp to a chromatic beam splitter. The beam splitter reflects short-wavelength radiation to the specimen and additionally transmits emitted longer-wavelength light from the specimen through the barrier filter to the eye. Epifluorescence both increases the sensitivity of fluorescence, and permits the specimen to be illuminated and visualized with normal substage optics. Figure 2.13 compares transmitted-light fluorescence and epifluorescence.

Objective lenses used in either type of fluorescence microscopy must be made of glass that does not itself fluoresce. The lamps must emit strongly in the excitation range of the fluorochrome. In the case of dyes such as FITC, a mercury arc lamp or a tungsten halogen lamp is used. Shutters are used to limit the ultraviolet exposure times of fluorochromes, which minimizes fading of fluorescence over a period of time. The objective lenses should have the highest possible numerical aperture to collect the faintest fluorescence. As a result of these requirements, objectives used in fluorescence microscopy are generally more expensive than those used in other forms of microscopy. Despite these limitations, fluorescence microscopy is a valuable tool, particularly for fluorochrome-tagged specimens that might not be noticed with ordinary light microscopy.

The Electron Microscope Magnifies Objects Too Small to Be Seen by Light Microscopy

The light microscope can be used to observe specimens with diameters as small as 0.2 μm. For even smaller specimens, observations can be made with the electron microscope, which has a resolution of about 0.001 μm and is capable of magnifying objects 100,000× or more (Table 2.2).

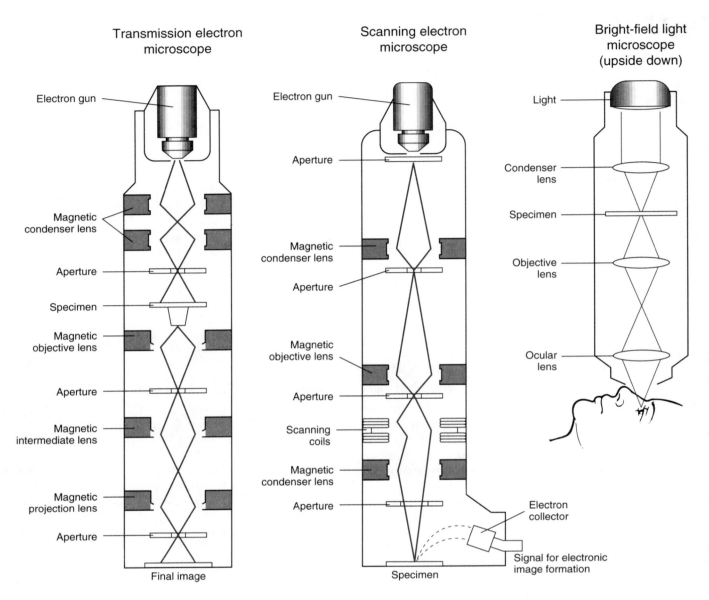

figure 2.15

Transmission and Scanning Electron Microscopes Compared with the Bright-Field Light Microscope

There are two basic types of electron microscopes: the transmission electron microscope (TEM) and the scanning electron microscope (SEM) (Figures 2.15 and 2.16). Both instruments use beams of electrons having wavelengths 100,000 times smaller than the wavelengths of visible light to react with the atomic nuclei of the specimen. The electrons thus substitute for the light in a conventional light microscope and, because of the electrons' extremely short wavelengths, there is increased resolving power.

The Transmission Electron Microscope Focuses a Fine Beam of Electrons Through the Specimen

The beam of electrons in a transmission electron microscope is generated and accelerated by an electron gun. The electrons are emitted in a vacuum and focused by an electromagnetic lens to a

small spot on the specimen. Electrons pass through the specimen; the amount of scattering depends on the electron density of the specimen. Areas that are electron dense—that have large numbers of atoms of high atomic densities within a small region—are not penetrated by electrons and therefore cause their extensive scattering. Since electrons cannot be seen by the human eye, this contrast in electron scattering is visualized by projection of the electrons onto a phosphorus-coated screen that fluoresces when struck with electrons. Electron images can be permanently recorded on a photographic plate.

Biological specimens typically have low electron densities and must generally be treated by negative staining or by shadowing to increase contrast (Figure 2.17). In **negative staining,** electron-dense stains such as phosphotungstic acid are applied to the specimen to provide greater contrast. When the preparation is viewed,

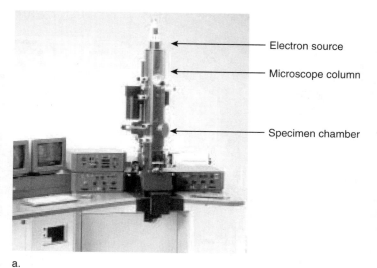

a.

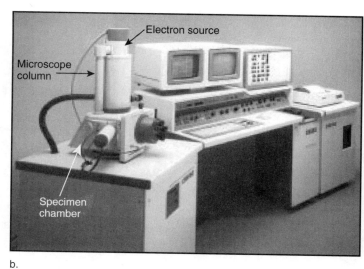

b.

figure 2.16

Transmission Electron Microscope and Scanning Electron Microscope
a. Transmission electron microscope. b. Scanning electron microscope.

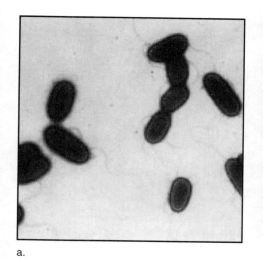

a.

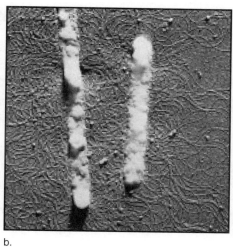

b.

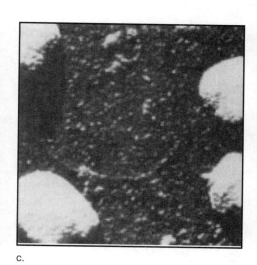

c.

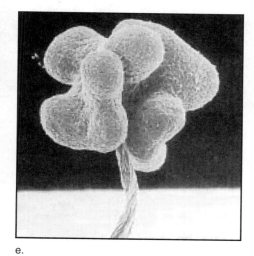

d.

e.

figure 2.17

Microorganisms as Seen by Electron Microscopy

a. *Pseudomonas aeruginosa*, stained with phosphotungstic acid (×6,450).
b. *Clostridium tetani*, metal shadowed, showing flagella (×4,400). c. Vaccinia virus, metal shadowed (×60,000).
d. *Neisseria gonorrhoeae*, freeze-etched (×12,300). e. *Physarum polycephalum*, scanning electron micrograph (×30).

Just as Leeuwenhoek's single-lens microscopes once opened a hitherto unseen world of microorganisms to human observation, a new generation of powerful

The STM can magnify objects up to one hundred millionfold and has already been used to image DNA, protein, and other biological materials (Figure 2.18).

Seeing Atoms Through a New Generation of Microscopes

microscopes developed in recent years has brought images to the atomic scale. These precision instruments—the scanning tunneling microscope (STM), the atomic force microscope (AFM), and the laser-scanning confocal scanning microscope—bring a new and exciting dimension to microscopy, enabling scientists to explore the world of atoms, nucleic acids, and proteins.

The STM, developed only 15 years ago by IBM's Gerd Binnig and Heinrich Rohrer, who shared the 1986 Nobel Prize in physics for their invention, uses a minute probe with a tip that ideally terminates in a single atom to trace the contours of a surface. Unlike a conventional scanning electron microscope, which scans an external beam of electrons across the surface of a specimen, the STM measures the shuttling of electrons between the probe and the specimen's surface, a phenomenon known as the tunneling current. This current is directly related to the distance between the probe and specimen. Changes in probe-to-specimen distance of as little as 0.01 nm can result in exponential tunneling current changes. Consequently, the STM has a resolution well within the subatomic range.

The AFM is a more recent invention derived from the STM. It is similar to the STM except that its probe touches the specimen's surface and traces the outline of atoms on the surface in a manner similar to the way a person reads Braille. The result is a topographical image. The probe in an AFM is mounted on a spring in the form of a cantilever. Minute deflections of the cantilever are recorded as changes in the specimen's topography. The AFM has been used to successfully image viruses, red blood cells, and amino acids (Figure 2.19).

The laser-scanning confocal scanning microscope focuses an illuminating cone of laser light through a pinhole aperture to a specific point within a specimen. As the beam of light is scanned across this area, imaging light from the specimen focuses through a second (confocal) pinhole to a detector. This second pinhole screens out light from all but the focal point, resulting in a crisp and precise two-dimensional image called an optical section. Multiple optical sections can be combined to form three-dimensional images of chromosome arrangements and other

figure 2.18
Scanning Tunneling Microscope Image of the DNA Double Helix (colorized)

cellular structures. The confocal microscope is especially useful in viewing thick specimens, when light otherwise might be diffused by conventional microscopy.

These new developments in microscopy have enabled scientists to visualize what they have theorized for many years. With these sophisticated instruments, scientists will now be able to understand the complexity of atoms and molecules.

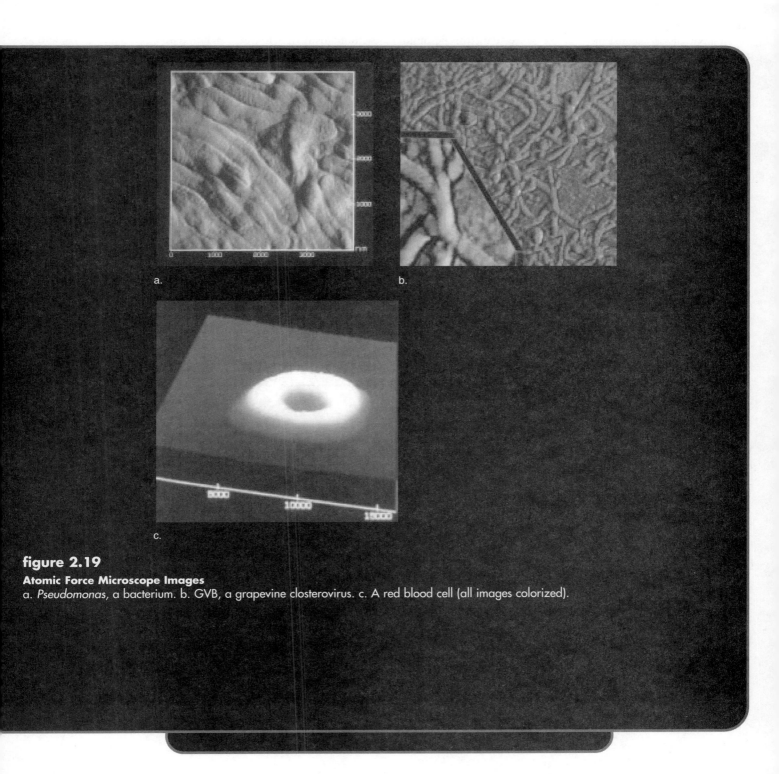

figure 2.19
Atomic Force Microscope Images
a. *Pseudomonas,* a bacterium. b. GVB, a grapevine closterovirus. c. A red blood cell (all images colorized).

regions of the specimen not penetrated by the stain are electron-transparent (light) against an electron-dense (dark) background. In **shadowing,** the specimen is coated at an angle with a thin layer of a heavy metal such as gold, platinum, or chromium. The shadow cast from such a preparation can then be used to visualize the specimen. Addition of an electron-dense stain can result in distortion of the specimen and an artifactual image.

Specimens for examination on transmission electron microscopes are routinely fixed and embedded in a supporting plastic resin to permit slicing of very thin sections of material for observation. Thin sections are made by slicing the embedded specimen with a glass knife or diamond in an instrument called an ultramicrotome. Thin sections are necessary because of the low penetration power of electrons and the large depth of field of the electron microscope. Slicing limits the quantity of material that can be seen, and can result in distortion of the specimen. **Freeze etching** is a process

used to observe structures of cellular organelles and membranes without distortion. In freeze etching, superficial layers are fractured from a frozen specimen, and carbon replicas of the exposed specimen surfaces are made for observation. This method permits examination of the detailed surface or internal structures of cells.

The Scanning Electron Microscope Provides a Three-Dimensional Image

The scanning electron microscope is a recent development in electron microscopy that permits the observations of the surface structure of a specimen. In the scanning electron microscope, a finely focused beam of electrons strikes the specimen. As these electrons are scanned across the surface of the specimen, secondary electrons, as well as other particles such as backscattered electrons and X rays, are released at various angles to produce a

---

PERSPECTIVE · Streptococci and Cell Wall Growth

Streptococci are gram-positive bacteria that form chains of cocci under certain growth conditions. Chaining of streptococci is useful in microscopic identification. Although chain formation has been observed in streptococci and other bacteria for many years, the structural events in cell wall growth that accompany chaining were not known until 1962, when Roger M. Cole and Jerome J. Hahn of the National Institute of Allergy and Infectious Diseases in Bethesda, Maryland, reported on the use of immunofluorescence to demonstrate the process of cell wall growth in *Streptococcus pyogenes*.

Twenty-four-hour cultures of *S. pyogenes* were mixed with fluorescein isothiocyanate-labeled antibodies directed specifically toward bacterial cell wall antigens. The cultures were incubated for growth and, at 15-minute intervals, samples were removed and fluorescent antibody attachment to the cell wall was stopped by one of two methods: (1) acid extraction of the streptococci or their cell wall protein antigens or (2) addition of a nonfluorescent-labeled cell wall antibody. Either technique inhibited further fluorescent labeling of the wall but did not affect the fluorescent label already present on the existing cell wall. The cells then were examined by fluorescence, phase-contrast, and dark-field microscopy.

From these studies it was observed that new segments of cell wall pushed away older segments of the wall (Figures 2P.1 and 2P.2). With cells collected at successively longer incubation periods, the original fluorescent cell wall segment moved farther away from the center of the parent cell. To verify that cell wall formation occurred equatorially along the circumference of the cell and that new wall material was not diffusely intercalated with the old wall, Cole and Hahn conducted a different experi-

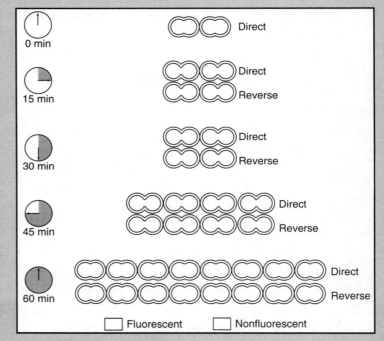

figure 2P.1
Diagrammatic Representation of Stages Shown in Figure 2P.2
In the direct method, the fluorescent label is moved farther from the center of the cell with longer incubation. In the reverse method, older cell wall segments are unlabeled and are seen pushed farther from the center of the cell with increased incubation.

three-dimensional image of the specimen. This image, which is composed of scanner (raster) lines similar to the line patterns seen on a television set, is transferred to a cathode-ray tube (CRT) screen. Images produced by scanning electron microscopy are striking and provide excellent resolution and distinct images of surface structures.

Specimen preparation for scanning electron microscopy differs from preparation for transmission electron microscopy. Since the scanning electron microscope focuses on the surface structure of a specimen, the specimen should be free of surface artifacts such as wrinkles or distortions. Drying and fixation procedures routinely used for transmission electron microscopy are not suitable because they stress the specimen and can result in shrinking or tearing. More delicate methods are used for scanning electron microscopy.

One common procedure used to minimize surface changes during specimen preparation is critical-point drying. This technique is based on the concept that there is a critical temperature and pressure at which conversion of a liquid to its gaseous phase

reaches an equilibrium. When this critical point is reached, no forces are required to convert a liquid to a gas. In critical-point drying, the specimen is first dehydrated in ethanol or acetone to remove water. The specimen is then placed in a critical-point drying chamber with a transitional fluid such as carbon dioxide or Freon 13. As the pressure and temperature of the chamber are raised to the critical point, any remaining liquid in the specimen is converted to its gaseous phase without surface distortion. The chamber is vented, and the dried specimen is transferred to a desiccator to protect it from rehydration.

The dehydrated specimen is next coated with a very thin layer of metal, because the scanning electron microscope uses an electron-emitting surface to produce an image. A common method for metal layering requires the specimen to be coated with carbon to provide an electrically conducting base. A heavy metal such as gold or a gold/palladium alloy, which serves as a source of secondary electrons, is attached to the carbon. The coated specimen can then be mounted and viewed.

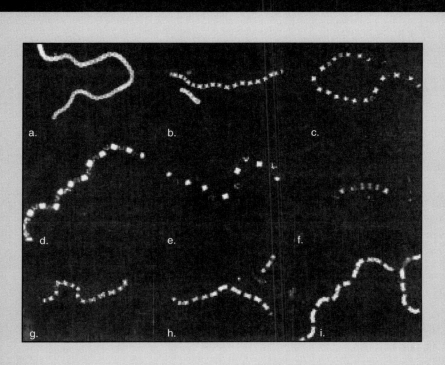

figure 2P.2
Ultraviolet Micrograph of *Streptococcus pyogenes* Showing Cell Wall Growth
a–e. *S. pyogenes* grown in fluorescein-labeled homologous antibody and examined at intervals after the addition of unlabeled homologous antibody (direct method). a. 0 minutes; b. 15 minutes; c. 30 minutes; d. 45 minutes; e. 60 minutes. f–i. *S. pyogenes* grown in unlabeled homologous antibody, removed at intervals after precipitation of the antibody, and stained with fluorescein isothiocyanate-labeled homologous antibody (reverse method). f. 15 minutes; g. 30 minutes; h. 45 minutes; i. 60 minutes.

ment involving **reverse fluorescent labeling.** Streptococci were first incubated in the presence of unlabeled antibody and then at intervals incubated with fluorescein-labeled antibody. As a result of this reverse technique, older cell wall segments were unlabeled and were seen to be pushed away equatorially along the cell circumference by newly fluorescein-labeled cell wall segments.

The results of these experiments were instrumental in showing that cell wall formation in streptococci occurs by

extension of the wall from the cell equator, not by diffuse intercalation of new material within the existing cell wall. The data provided significant insight into the mechanism of cell wall growth and chaining in streptococci.

Source:
Cole, R.M., and J.J. Hahn. 1962. Cell wall replication in *Streptococcus pyogenes. Science* 135:722–724.

Summary

1. There are two kinds of cells: procaryotes and eucaryotes. Procaryotic cells do not have a membrane-enclosed nucleus.

2. There are five groups of microorganisms. Bacteria are procaryotes, whereas protozoa, algae, and fungi are eucaryotes. Viruses are not cellular and therefore are neither procaryotes nor eucaryotes. All living organisms are phylogenetically divided into three domains: Bacteria, Archaea, and Eucarya.

3. Procaryotes come in a variety of sizes, shapes, and arrangements. These morphological characteristics help in the identification and classification of these microorganisms.

4. Microorganisms can be visualized with the aid of a microscope. The light microscope uses light as a source of illumination. There are four types of light microscopy: bright-field, dark-field, fluorescence, and phase-contrast.

5. The conventional microscope is called a compound microscope because it contains two or more sets of lenses. The condenser lens focuses light on the specimen; the objective lenses are close to the specimen and magnify it; and the ocular lenses are near the eye and further magnify the image.

6. Resolution, or resolving power, is the ability of a microscope to distinguish two closely spaced objects as separate and distinct entities. The resolving power of a microscope depends on the wavelength of light used for illumination of the specimen, the numerical aperture of the condenser, and the numerical aperture of the objective lens. The light microscope has a resolving power of 0.2 μm.

7. Stains increase the contrast between a specimen and its background. The Gram stain is an example of a differential stain that separates bacteria into two groups: gram positive (stained violet) and gram negative (stained pink or red).

8. The bright-field light microscope is used for the general observation of microorganisms. The specimen appears against a light background.

9. The dark-field light microscope is used to provide high contrast to specimens. The specimen appears light against a dark background.

10. The phase-contrast light microscope amplifies small differences in refractive indices to enhance specimen contrast. An advantage of phase-contrast microscopy is that the specimen does not have to be fixed or stained and therefore can be observed in its natural state.

11. The fluorescence microscope detects objects that are illuminated by ultraviolet or near-ultraviolet light.

12. Fluorescence microscopy is used to observe fluorochrome-tagged specimens that might not be noticed with ordinary light microscopy.

13. The electron microscope magnifies specimens 100,000× or more by substituting electrons with extremely short wavelengths for the light in a conventional light microscope. Greater magnifications can be obtained by use of a new generation of microscopes: the scanning tunneling microscope, the atomic force microscope, and the laser-scanning confocal scanning microscope. These newer instruments can be used to observe objects as small as atoms.

EVOLUTION *and* BIODIVERSITY

The single cell organization of procaryotes necessitates that these cells function as independent units. Unlike multicellular eucaryotic organisms, which can apportion form and function among specialized cell types like muscle, heart, or nerve cells, a procaryote is autonomous and must perform all functions required for its nutrition, survival, and division. Because they are self-sufficient, procaryotes are considered the ancestral forms of life that existed on earth billions of years ago. An intermediate stage in the evolution of single-celled procaryotes into multicellular eucaryotes may have been the associations that developed in bacterial cells that formed chains or other cell arrangements because of incomplete cell wall formation and, therefore, remained attached after cell division. Today the wide range of size, shape, and arrangements of procaryotes is further evidence of the diversity of these microorganisms and their ability to adapt to changing environments.

Questions

Short Answer

1. Give several examples of macroorganisms. Give several examples of microorganisms.

2. Identify several traits which may help in the identification of bacteria.

3. Identify the two basic shapes of bacteria. What are some variations of these shapes?

4. Identify six types of microscopes.

5. How does a bright-field microscope differ from early microscopes (for example, Leeuwenhoek's)?

6. Identify the major parts of a bright-field microscope.

7. What is the total magnification for a microscope with 10× ocular lenses and a 95× objective lens?

8. When is immersion oil used? Why?

9. What is the smallest size specimen visible with a light microscope? With an electron microscope?

10. Identify several types of staining procedures and their importance.

11. What is the most commonly used bacterial staining procedure?

12. When is dark-field microscopy more beneficial than bright-field?

13. When is phase-contrast microscopy more beneficial than bright-field?

14. When is fluorescence microscopy more beneficial than bright-field?

15. In addition to increased magnification and resolution, what benefits(s) do SEM and TEM offer? Why aren't they routinely used?

16. Why are some bacteria found in chains, while others are clustered or randomly arranged?

Multiple Choice

1. Which of the following does *not* affect the resolving power of a microscope?
   a. the wavelength of the light source
   b. the numerical aperture of the condenser
   c. the numerical aperture of the objective lens
   d. the magnification

2. Positive stains include:
   a. Gram stain
   b. differential stain
   c. simple stain
   d. all of the above

3. Various staining methods can be used to increase the contrast between a specimen and its background; however, staining procedures can kill a specimen. How can a live specimen be viewed through a microscope under high contrast?
   a. Use a bright-field microscope.
   b. Use a phase-contrast microscope.
   c. Use a scanning electron microscope.
   d. Use a transmission electron microscope.

4. The resolving power of an electron microscope is greater than that of a light microscope because:
   a. the magnification can be increased beyond 1,000×.
   b. the wavelength of an electron is 100,000 times smaller than the wavelength of visible light.
   c. there is higher contrast between the specimen and its background.
   d. all of the above.

Critical Thinking

1. Discuss the role of morphology in bacterial identification and explain its limitations.

2. Explain the relationship between magnification and resolution. How can each be improved?

3. Describe how improvements in microscopy led to significant advances in microbiology.

4. Discuss the need for, and benefits of, the various staining procedures described in this chapter.

 Supplementary Readings

Aldrich, H.C., and W.J. Todd, eds. 1986. *Ultrastructure techniques for microorganisms.* New York: Plenum Publishing Corporation. (Individually written chapters dealing with various types of microorganisms and how to prepare them for transmission and scanning electron microscopy. A handbook of techniques.)

Dawes, C.J. 1988. *Introduction to biological electron microscopy: Theory and techniques.* Burlington, Vt.: Ladd Publishing Company. (A general preparation book for both scanning and transmission electron microscopy, with procedures for microorganisms as well as plant and animal tissues. The text includes defined procedures as well as the theory behind each preparation step.)

Gerhardt, P., R.G.E. Murray, W.A. Wood, and N.R. Krieg. 1994. *Methods for general and molecular bacteriology,* pp. 5–103. Washington, D.C.: American Society for Microbiology. (A discussion of various techniques in microbiology, including sections on the principles of light and electron microscopy.)

Hayat, M.A. 1986. *Basic techniques for transmission microscopy.* New York: Academic Press, Inc. (A general preparation handbook that gives fixation and handling procedures for a wide variety of biological samples, including microorganisms.)

Lichtman, J.W. 1994. Confocal microscopy. *Scientific American* 271:40–45. (A discussion of the operation of the confocal scanning microscope and examples of images taken with this type of microscope.)

Perlman, P. 1971. *Basic microscope techniques.* New York: Chemical Publishing Company, Inc. (A primer on the use of light microscopes.)

Rochow, T. G., and E. G. Rochow. 1978. *An introduction to microscopy by means of light, electrons, X rays, or ultrasound.* New York: Plenum Press. (A detailed survey of the types of microscopy.)

Spencer, M. 1982. *Fundamentals of light microscopy.* London, England: Cambridge University Press. (A highly technical description of the principles of light microscopy.)

Wickramasinghe, H.K. 1989. Scanned-probe microscopes. *Scientific American* 261:98–105. (A discussion of the principles of the scanning tunneling microscope.)

chapter three

COMPOSITION AND STRUCTURE OF PROCARYOTIC AND EUCARYOTIC CELLS

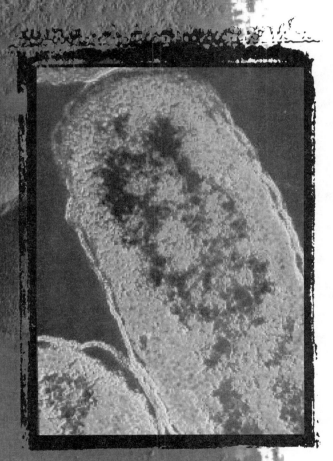

Transmission electron micrograph of the rod-shaped, gram-negative bacterium *Escherichia coli* (colorized, ×38,000).

Microbes in Motion — **PREVIEW LINK**

This chapter covers the key topics of cellular structures for both bacteria (procaryotic cells) and fungi. The following sections of the *Microbes in Motion* CD-ROM may be useful as a preview to your reading or as a supplemental study aid:

Bacteria Structure and Function: Cell Membrane, 1–10; Cell Wall, 1–5 (Antibiotic Sites), 13–15; Gram-Positive Cell, 1–5; Gram-Negative Cell 1–9; External Structures, 1–24; Internal Structures, 1–4 (Protein Synthesis), 12–13. *Fungal Structure and Function:* General Eucaryotic Structures, 1–11; Metabolism and Growth (Reproduction), 8–23.

Billions of years ago, as the earth began to form a hospitable environment for biological molecules, the first forms of life appeared. Although there is no written record of this event, it is believed that the first living organisms were microorganisms, probably Archaea. Archaea, which include organisms that live in extreme environments of high temperature, low pH, and no oxygen—conditions similar to those in the prebiotic soup—have many of the physiological and metabolic characteristics that would be expected of early microbial life. These early organisms were simple in form and structure, but as time passed they evolved structures and characteristics that enabled them to adapt to their changing environments. Today's diverse organisms can trace their origins to these early cells.

The cell is the basic unit of life and is the smallest fundamental unit of all living organisms; it has all of the chemical and physical components necessary for its own maintenance and reproduction. These components of a cell function together to form a dynamic, interactive system capable of carrying on the essential life processes.

Although eucaryotes may generally be larger (see *Epulopiscium,* page 19) and more complex than procaryotes, the macromolecules and structural components of a procaryotic cell are assembled in such a manner as to comprise a functional, living organism. This chapter will examine the chemical composition of living cells and compare procaryotic and eucaryotic microorganisms.

Macromolecules: Building Blocks of the Cell

The chemical composition of a microorganism can easily be determined by analytical chemical techniques. Such analyses reveal that a large portion of the total weight of an average bacterial cell consists of **water.** In a rapidly growing *Escherichia coli* cell, water constitutes 70% or more of the total cell weight. Proteins, nucleic acids, polysaccharides, lipids, an assortment of other organic compounds such as vitamins and metabolic intermediates, and inorganic compounds constitute the remainder.

Proteins Are Composed of Amino Acids

Protein can make up as much as 55% of the dry weight (the cell weight minus its water content) of a cell. Proteins have a variety of important functions in the cell (Table 3.1). One of their most important functions is to act as enzymes. Enzymes catalyze biochemical reactions necessary for cell growth, reproduction, and metabolism. Although not all proteins are enzymes, most enzymes are proteins (catalytic RNAs, called **ribozymes,** have been discovered in procaryotes and eucaryotes and are involved in important biological reactions). Proteins are also found as structural components, transport molecules, and toxins in a cell.

Proteins are polymers of **amino acids.** Twenty different amino acids initially are used to make proteins (Table 3.2). With the exception of proline, all amino acids have an amino group (NH_3^+) and a carboxyl group (COO^-) attached to the same carbon (the α-carbon) and are thus called α-**amino acids.** Proline is similar in structure to the α-amino acids, with the exception that its α-amino nitrogen is in a five-membered ring. Because of this feature, proline is called an α-imino acid. The ring in the α-imino acid structure, which also includes the α-carbon, has a significant effect on protein structure, since it restricts the extent of protein folding.

Also attached to the α-carbon in amino acids are a hydrogen atom and a side chain, or **R group.** The composition of the R group differs in each of the 20 amino acids and is responsible for the structural and charge differences that exist among amino acids.

table 3.1

Some Cellular Functions of Proteins

	Example	
Protein Function	**Procaryotes**	**Eucaryotes**
Catalysis	DNA polymerase—replication and repair of DNA	DNA polymerase—replication and repair of DNA
Transport	Carrier molecules—active transport	Hemoglobin—transport of oxygen in blood
Motion	Flagellin—component of flagella	Tubulin—component of microtubules
Structure	Wall subunits—cell walls of certain Archaea	Collagen—fibrous connective tissue
Toxins	Diphtheria toxin—inactivation of elongation factor 2 in eucaryotic cells	Snake venoms—enzymes that hydrolyze phosphoglycerides
Chemical messengers/receptors	Binding proteins—binding of specific chemicals in chemotaxis	Insulin receptor—specific binding of insulin to modulate glucose metabolism
Ion transport/binding	Bacteriorhodopsin—energy transformation	Transferrin—iron-binding protein in blood

table 3.2

Structural Formulas of the 20 Amino Acids Commonly Occurring in Proteins

Amino Acids with Neutral (uncharged) Polar Side Chains	Amino Acids with Basic (positively charged) Side Chains (cont.)

Amino Acids with Neutral (uncharged) Polar Side Chains

Glycine (Gly)
Molecular weight 75

$$H-\underset{\underset{+}{\overset{|}{N}H_3}}{\overset{\overset{H}{|}}{C}}-COO^-$$

Serine (Ser)
Molecular weight 105

$$HO-CH_2-\underset{\underset{+}{\overset{|}{N}H_3}}{\overset{\overset{H}{|}}{C}}-COO^-$$

Threonine (Thr)
Molecular weight 119

$$CH_3-\underset{\overset{|}{H}}{\overset{\overset{OH}{|}}{C}}-\underset{\underset{+}{\overset{|}{N}H_3}}{\overset{\overset{H}{|}}{C}}-COO^-$$

Cysteine (Cys)
Molecular weight 121

$$HS-CH_2-\underset{\underset{+}{\overset{|}{N}H_3}}{\overset{\overset{H}{|}}{C}}-COO^-$$

Tyrosine (Tyr)
Molecular weight 181

$$HO-\langle ring \rangle-CH_2-\underset{\underset{+}{\overset{|}{N}H_3}}{\overset{\overset{H}{|}}{C}}-COO^-$$

Asparagine (Asn)
Molecular weight 132

$$\underset{O}{\overset{NH_2}{C}}-CH_2-\underset{\underset{+}{\overset{|}{N}H_3}}{\overset{\overset{H}{|}}{C}}-COO^-$$

Glutamine (Gln)
Molecular weight 146

$$\underset{O}{\overset{NH_2}{C}}-CH_2-CH_2-\underset{\underset{+}{\overset{|}{N}H_3}}{\overset{\overset{H}{|}}{C}}-COO^-$$

Amino Acids with Acidic (negatively charged) Side Chains

Aspartic Acid (Asp)
Molecular weight 133

$$\underset{O}{\overset{^-O}{C}}-CH_2-\underset{\underset{+}{\overset{|}{N}H_3}}{\overset{\overset{H}{|}}{C}}-COO^-$$

Glutamic acid (Glu)
Molecular weight 147

$$\underset{O}{\overset{^-O}{C}}-CH_2-CH_2-\underset{\underset{+}{\overset{|}{N}H_3}}{\overset{\overset{H}{|}}{C}}-COO^-$$

Amino Acids with Basic (positively charged) Side Chains

Lysine (Lys)
Molecular weight 146

$$H_3\overset{+}{N}-CH_2-CH_2-CH_2-CH_2-\underset{\underset{+}{\overset{|}{N}H_3}}{\overset{\overset{H}{|}}{C}}-COO^-$$

Amino Acids with Basic (positively charged) Side Chains (cont.)

Arginine (Arg)
Molecular weight 174

$$H_2N-\underset{\underset{+}{\overset{||}{N}H_2}}{C}-NH-CH_2-CH_2-CH_2-\underset{\underset{+}{\overset{|}{N}H_3}}{\overset{\overset{H}{|}}{C}}-COO^-$$

Histidine (at pH 6.0) (His)
Molecular weight 155

$$\begin{array}{c}HC=C-CH_2-\underset{\underset{+}{\overset{|}{N}H_3}}{\overset{\overset{H}{|}}{C}}-COO^- \\ \overset{+}{HN}\quad NH \\ C \\ H\end{array}$$

Amino Acids with Nonpolar (hydrophobic) Side Chains

Alanine (Ala)
Molecular weight 89

$$CH_3-\underset{\underset{+}{\overset{|}{N}H_3}}{\overset{\overset{H}{|}}{C}}-COO^-$$

Valine (Val)
Molecular weight 117

$$\begin{array}{c}CH_3 \\ CH- \\ CH_3\end{array}\underset{\underset{+}{\overset{|}{N}H_3}}{\overset{\overset{H}{|}}{C}}-COO^-$$

Leucine (Leu)
Molecular weight 131

$$\begin{array}{c}CH_3 \\ CH-CH_2- \\ CH_3\end{array}\underset{\underset{+}{\overset{|}{N}H_3}}{\overset{\overset{H}{|}}{C}}-COO^-$$

Isoleucine (Ile)
Molecular weight 131

$$CH_3-CH_2-\underset{\underset{}{\overset{|}{C}H_3}}{CH}-\underset{\underset{+}{\overset{|}{N}H_3}}{\overset{\overset{H}{|}}{C}}-COO^-$$

Proline (Pro)
Molecular weight 115

$$\begin{array}{c}CH_2 \\ CH_2 \quad \overset{H}{\underset{|}{C}}-COO^- \\ CH_2-\overset{+}{N}H_2\end{array}$$

Phenylalanine (Phe)
Molecular weight 165

$$\langle ring \rangle-CH_2-\underset{\underset{+}{\overset{|}{N}H_3}}{\overset{\overset{H}{|}}{C}}-COO^-$$

Tryptophan (Trp)
Molecular weight 204

$$\begin{array}{c}C-CH_2-\underset{\underset{+}{\overset{|}{N}H_3}}{\overset{\overset{H}{|}}{C}}-COO^- \\ CH \\ N \\ H\end{array}$$

Methionine (Met)
Molecular weight 149

$$CH_3-S-CH_2-CH_2-\underset{\underset{+}{\overset{|}{N}H_3}}{\overset{\overset{H}{|}}{C}}-COO^-$$

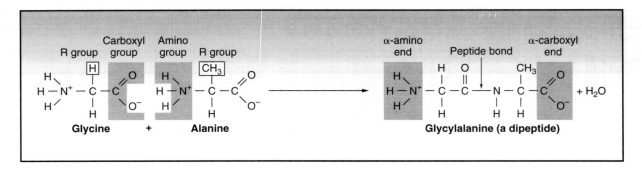

figure 3.1

Formation of a Dipeptide

Two amino acids, glycine and alanine, are joined to form the dipeptide glycylalanine. The free α-amino and α-carboxyl ends are shown.

Amino acids are joined together in proteins by covalent bonds called **peptide bonds** (Figure 3.1). The sequence of amino acids in a protein determines the biological properties of the protein molecule. Peptide bonds are formed by the linking of the α-amino group on one amino acid to the α-carboxyl group on an adjacent amino acid. When two amino acids are joined in this manner, a dipeptide is formed. A tripeptide consists of three amino acids linked by peptide bonds. Short chains of amino acids are called **polypeptides,** and longer chains or combinations of polypeptides are called **proteins.** Since peptides consist of individual amino acids joined by peptide bonds, one end of a peptide (the N-terminal) may have a free, unattached α-amino group, while the opposite end (the C-terminal) may have a free α-carboxyl group. This orderly arrangement of amino acids gives orientation to a protein—a property that is important in biological systems and can be useful in chemical extraction and identification of proteins.

A hierarchy of protein structure has been established by chemists (Figure 3.2). This hierarchy begins with the **primary structure** of a protein, defined as the sequence of amino acids in the protein. Proteins ordinarily do not lie flat or in random coils, but exhibit regular, repeated configurations caused by hydrogen bonding between the atoms within the polypeptide chain. Protein configurations that result from such bonds constitute the **secondary structure** of proteins. There are two regularly occurring types of secondary protein structures. The β-**sheet,** which occurs in silk, consists of extended polypeptide chains folding back and forth while being held together by hydrogen bonds. Wool and collagen have secondary protein structures arranged in an α-**helical** configuration. In such structures the polypeptide backbone is twisted in a helix and held in that manner by hydrogen bonds. The term **tertiary structure** refers to the three-dimensional conformation of a protein molecule. These three-dimensional structures, which can be determined by X-ray diffraction patterns, generally are folded in a particular fashion and represent active forms of proteins. Many proteins, such as DNA-dependent RNA polymerase (the enzyme responsible for synthesis of RNA from DNA) and hemoglobin,

consist of several polypeptide chains that are linked together as a unit. These proteins are said to possess a **quaternary structure.** Quaternary structures of proteins are common. In many cases, each of the polypeptide chains in the quaternary structure has a unique function in the overall activity of the protein.

Environmental effects such as high temperatures or extreme pH can cause tertiary and quaternary protein structures to become disrupted, or **denatured.** When this happens, proteins (especially enzymes) may become biologically inactive. This intolerance of many proteins of environmental extremes is used in microbiology to kill microorganisms by exposure to heat or acid pH.

Nucleic Acids Are Composed of Nucleotides

Nucleic acids are macromolecules composed of individual organic units called **nucleotides** (Figure 3.3). There are two types of nucleic acids: **deoxyribonucleic acid (DNA)** and **ribonucleic acid (RNA).** DNA is the genetic, or hereditary, material in all cells. This genetic information is used for the synthesis of proteins.

Nucleotides are molecules that consist of (1) a pentose (5-carbon) sugar attached to (2) a nitrogenous organic compound called a **base** and (3) one or more phosphates. A **nucleoside** consists of the pentose and the base, without any phosphates. The pentose sugar in DNA is deoxyribose (with a hydrogen atom instead of a hydroxyl at the second carbon position of the sugar), whereas in RNA the sugar is ribose. The bases pyrimidines and purines commonly occur in nucleic acids. Pyrimidines have a single-ring structure, whereas purines consist of two rings. DNA contains the pyrimidines cytosine and thymine and the purines adenine and guanine. RNA contains the same bases, with the exception that thymine is replaced by the pyrimidine uracil. Some RNAs (for example, transfer RNA, which is involved in protein synthesis) have unusual bases such as pseudouridine and dihydrouridine, which contribute to the activity and structure of the RNA molecule.

Most DNA molecules (the exceptions are those in some viruses) consist of two polydeoxynucleotide chains arranged in a

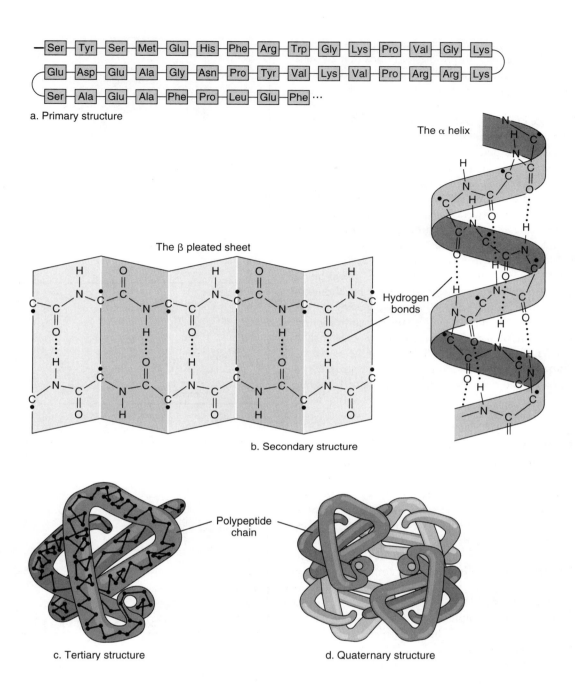

a. Primary structure

The β pleated sheet

Hydrogen bonds

b. Secondary structure

The α helix

Polypeptide chain

c. Tertiary structure

d. Quaternary structure

figure 3.2

Hierarchy of Protein Structure

a. Primary structure, with amino acids connected by peptide bonds.
b. Secondary structure, formed by hydrogen bonds. Dots (●) represent
α-carbons of amino acids. c. Tertiary structure, often formed by

disulfide bonds. Dots (●) represent α-carbons of amino acids.
d. Quaternary structure, consisting of several polypeptides linked to
one another.

double-stranded helix (Figure 3.4). The nucleotides are linked together within each chain by phosphodiester bonds that connect the OH group on the 3′ carbon atom of one deoxyribose to the phosphate on the 5′ carbon atom of the adjoining deoxyribose to give a sugar phosphate backbone. The two strands in the DNA helix are held in place by hydrogen bonds between nucleotide base pairs. This base pairing is not random, but occurs in such a manner that adenine is always paired with thymine by two hydrogen bonds and guanine is always paired with cytosine by three hydrogen bonds.

In contrast to the double-stranded DNA molecule, RNA molecules are usually single-stranded (some viruses have double-stranded RNA molecules). Cells have three types of RNA molecules: messenger RNA (mRNA), ribosomal RNA (rRNA), and transfer RNA (tRNA). All three types of RNA molecules are polyribonucleotide chains consisting of nucleotides linked by 3′, 5′-phosphodiester bonds, giving a sugar phosphate backbone. In cells, RNA is associated with protein synthesis. Messenger RNA carries the genetic information from DNA to the ribosomes, where this information is translated into proteins with the assistance of rRNA and tRNA. The role of DNA and RNA in storage of genetic information and transfer of this information to proteins is discussed in further detail in Chapter 8 (see central dogma, page 212).

Carbohydrates and Lipids Are Organic Macromolecules

Carbohydrates and **lipids** are important classes of organic macromolecules that are found universally in plants, animals, and microorganisms. These molecules are frequently used as carbon and energy sources by these organisms and are also important as major constituents of structures such as cell walls and membranes. For example, two carbohydrate derivatives, *N*-acetylglucosamine and *N*-acetylmuramic acid, form the backbone of the cell wall in the domain Bacteria. Phospholipids (lipids containing one or more phosphate groups) are the principal structural components of biological membranes, which are semipermeable because of the solubility properties of phospholipids.

Carbohydrates are desirable carbon and energy sources for microorganisms because they are often readily available in the environment and can be directly incorporated into metabolic pathways. These organic macromolecules consist of simple sugar units that either exist independently or are joined together as larger polymers (Figure 3.5). Several different levels of classification are used by chemists for carbohydrates: **monosaccharides,** or **simple sugars,** which have the general formula $(CH_2O)_n$, where **n** has a value of three or greater; **disaccharides,** which consist of two similar or dissimilar monosaccharides joined by a glycosidic bond between the aldehyde group of one monosaccharide and an alcohol group of the other monosaccharide; **oligosaccharides** (carbohydrates having up to ten monosaccharide units); and **polysaccharides** (very large carbohydrates, sometimes containing several thousand monosaccharide units). Carbohydrates may also be covalently linked to proteins or lipids to form **glycoproteins** and **lipopolysaccharides.**

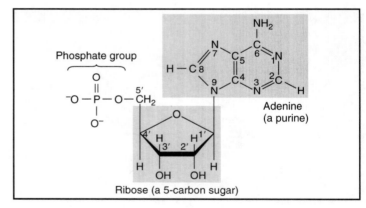

a. Pyrimidines

b. Purines

c. Nucleotide

figure 3.3
Building Blocks of Nucleic Acids
a. The three pyrimidine bases commonly found in nucleotides. b. The two purine bases commonly found in nucleotides. c. A nucleotide (adenosine monophosphate, or AMP).

The 6-carbon (hexose) simple sugar glucose is representative of many monosaccharides and is an important intermediate in carbohydrate metabolism. D-glucose, also known as dextrose, is found in the sap of most plants, in fruit juices, and as a component of animal blood. It is also a constituent of higher carbohydrates such as lactose, sucrose, maltose, starch, and glycogen, and is a major source of energy for both procaryotes and eucaryotes.

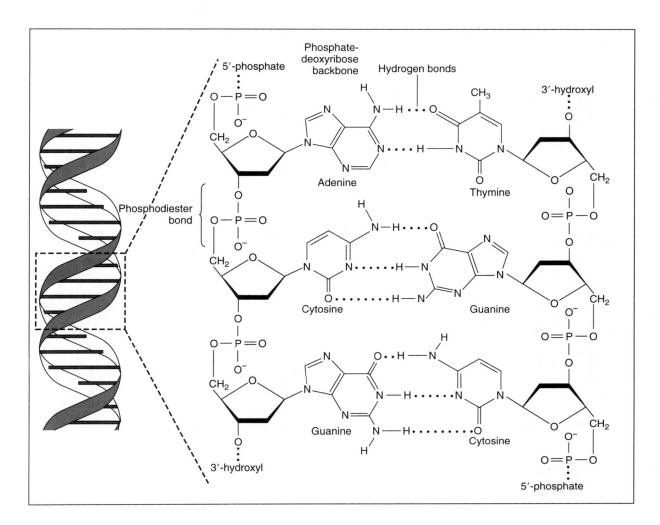

figure 3.4
Structure of a DNA Molecule

Most carbohydrates in nature exist in the form of polysaccharides. The most common polysaccharide is cellulose, the major structural component of plant cell walls and also a component of the cell walls of algae and some fungi. It has been estimated that more than 50% of all organic carbon is cellulose. Cellulose is a straight-chain polymer of glucose units joined by β(1,4) glycosidic bonds. Starch is also a polymer of glucose, but with the glucose units linked by α(1,4) bonds with α(1,6) branching, resulting in a nonlinear molecule. Animals store glucose as polymers, but in the form of glycogen. Starch and glycogen have similar structures, except that glycogen is more highly branched. Microorganisms that use polysaccharides as carbon and energy sources must first hydrolyze these large molecules to smaller monosaccharides and disaccharides, which can then be transported across the plasma membrane into the cell. These microorganisms synthesize enzymes such as cellulases (cellulose) and amylases (starch and glycogen), which hydrolyze the polysaccharides (see polysaccharide hydrolysis, page 190).

The lipids are a class of organic molecules characterized by insolubility in water and solubility in nonpolar solvents such as benzene, chloroform, and acetone. Biologically important lipids can be divided into three major classes: **neutral fats, phospholipids,** and **steroids** (Figure 3.6).

Neutral lipids, so called because they have no charged groups at physiological pH, generally consist of the alcohol glycerol attached by ester linkages to long-chain fatty acids. Such lipids are called mono-, di-, or triglycerides, depending upon whether one, two, or three fatty acids, respectively, are attached to glycerol. Fatty acids are saturated or unsaturated compounds, usually having from 14 to 22 carbon atoms, with a carboxyl group at one end. Saturated fatty acids have only single bonds between carbon atoms, whereas unsaturated fatty acids contain one or more double bonds within the molecule. Fats constitute a major food reserve in animals and, to some extent, in plants. These molecules, because of their bonding characteristics, generally contain more energy than carbohydrates with equivalent numbers of carbon atoms (see lipid metabolism, page 197).

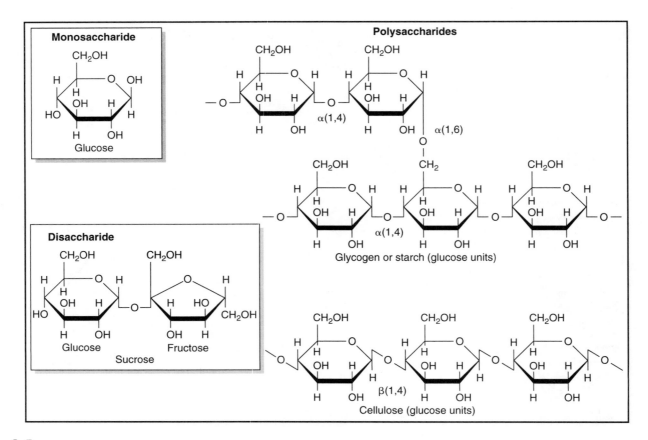

figure 3.5
Structures of Some Common Carbohydrates

Phospholipids, or phosphoglycerides, are fats in which one of the fatty acid chains has been replaced by a phosphate group, frequently with a nitrogen-containing compound attached to it. The resultant molecule is amphipathic—the fatty acid chains are hydrophobic, whereas the ionic phosphate group is hydrophilic.

Steroids, complex organic molecules composed of four interlocking ring structures, do not resemble other lipids. Steroids and the related sterols, which have hydroxyl (OH) groups attached to certain carbons in the structure, are classified as lipids because of their insolubility in water. Steroids and sterols have important biological roles. Cholesterol, a common sterol, is a structural component in eucaryotic plasma membranes and the primary constituent of gallstones, and also forms fatty deposits on the interior walls of arteries. Some vitamins and hormones, including several forms of vitamin D, testosterone, estrogen, progesterone, and cortisone, are steroids. Sterols rarely are found in bacteria except in the membranes of mycoplasmas. Mycoplasmas do not have cell walls, and the sterols appear to be responsible for the increased stability of the plasma membrane necessary to resist osmotic lysis.

The Procaryotic Cell

The electron microscope has made the study of the fine structure of procaryotes possible. Examination of a bacterial cell reveals a variety of structures (Figure 3.7). All bacteria have a plasma membrane, DNA, RNA, and ribosomes. Most bacteria have a cell wall. Other structures such as capsules, flagella, pili, endospores, and inclusion bodies are found only in certain bacteria.

The Cell Envelope Is the Outer Covering of a Procaryote Consisting of the Plasma Membrane, the Cell Wall, and, in Gram-Negative Procaryotes, an Outer Membrane

The cytoplasmic contents of a typical procaryotic cell are encased within an outer covering called the **cell envelope.** This envelope's specific content may vary in different types of procaryotes, but in most procaryotes it consists of a semipermeable **plasma membrane** surrounded by a rigid **cell wall.** In addition

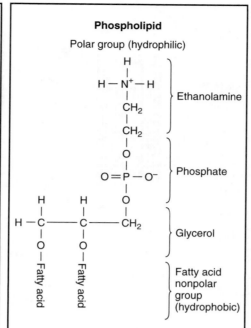

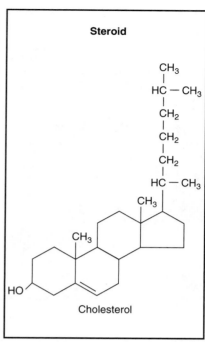

figure 3.6
Some Biologically Important Lipids

to these components, the envelope in gram-negative procaryotes has an extra outer layer known as the **outer membrane** that is part of the cell wall.

The Plasma Membrane Is a Selectively Permeable Barrier

The plasma membrane, also called the cell membrane or cytoplasmic membrane, is a semipermeable barrier that regulates the passage of molecules and ions (Figure 3.8). This discriminant permeability of the membrane is an important property of the cell. If it didn't have this selectivity, the cell would not retain internal (endogenous) pools of metabolites required for its growth and nutrition, nor would the cell prevent entry of undesirable substances from a hostile environment. The plasma membrane also

provides structural integrity to bacteria that lack cell walls (for example, *Mycoplasma*); these microorganisms must rely on this sole outer barrier to withstand environmental osmotic stress. Some microorganisms can exist without a cell wall, but none can survive without a plasma membrane.

The plasma membrane in procaryotes is similar in composition to the basic unit membrane structure found in higher organisms. This procaryotic plasma membrane, as seen by high-resolution electron microscopy, consists of a continuous bimolecular sandwich structure having two thin, dense bands separated by a lighter, less dense middle band. Chemical extraction of membrane fragments isolated from cells reveals that such fragments consist of 60% to 70% protein, and 30% to 40% lipid. The main lipids in the plasma membrane are phospholipids. These

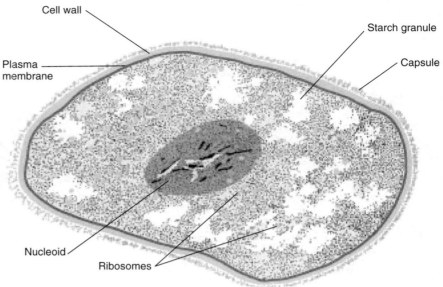

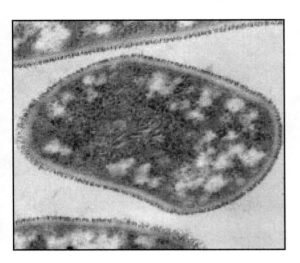

a.

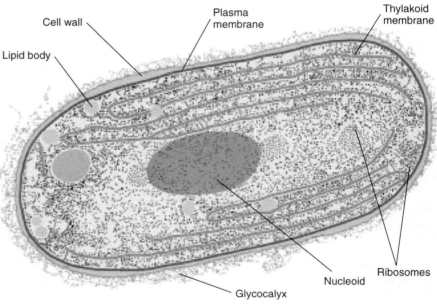

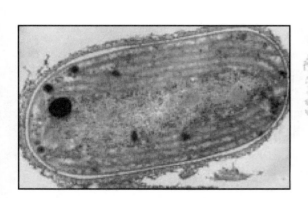

b.

figure 3.7

Structural Organization of a Typical Procaryote

a. Electron micrograph of *Arthrobacter*, a nonphotosynthetic gram-positive bacterium, showing cell structures (×195,000).
b. Electron micrograph of *Agmenellum,* a photosynthetic cyanobacterium, showing cell structures. Not all morphological features shown are necessarily present in a single cell type (×45,000).

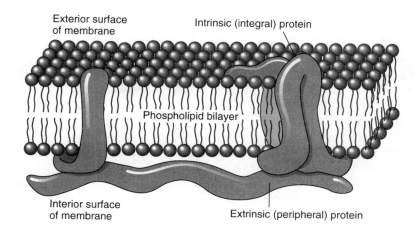

Exterior surface
of membrane

Intrinsic (integral) protein

Phospholipid bilayer

Interior surface
of membrane

Extrinsic (peripheral) protein

figure 3.8

The Plasma Membrane

The bacterial plasma membrane consists of a lipid bilayer and
proteins (intrinsic and extrinsic) that are associated with the bilayer.

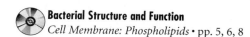

Bacterial Structure and Function
Cell Membrane: Phospholipids • pp. 5, 6, 8

a.

b.

c.

figure 3.9

**Differences Between Membrane Lipids of Bacteria
and Archaea**

a. Membrane lipid of Bacteria with ester linkage between glycerol
and fatty acids. b. Membrane lipid of Archaea with ether linkage

between glycerol and repeating branched aliphatic side chains.
c. Structure of isoprene, the side chain in Archaea membrane lipids.

are amphipathic compounds that have hydrophilic polar groups
attached to hydrophobic nonpolar chains. Membrane lipids of
Bacteria have *ester* linkages between glycerol and the fatty acids,
whereas lipids of Archaea have *ether* linkages between glycerol
and repeating branched aliphatic chains of isoprene (Figure 3.9).
The ether linkage and the substitution of isoprene for fatty acids
in membrane lipids are characteristics that help distinguish
Archaea from Bacteria. The domain Archaea includes the ther-
moacidophilic (high-temperature and acid-loving), halophilic
(sodium chloride-loving), and methanogenic (methane-
producing) procaryotes.

The phospholipids in the procaryotic plasma membrane are
oriented with their polar groups extended outward and the nonpolar chains internalized within the membrane. Although the
membrane exists as a bilayer, it is not symmetrical. The two sides
of the membrane are dissimilar and may contain different proteins
and phospholipids. X-ray diffraction patterns and microscopic

observations show that membrane proteins and lipids are not
fixed, but instead are mobile and freely diffuse within the phospholipid bilayer structure (fluid mosaic model). Fluidity is apparently an important characteristic of the plasma membrane, since
microbes living in extreme temperature environments change the
fatty acid composition of their membranes to maintain their fluidity. The precise role of the mobile lipids within the membrane is
not known, whereas the membrane proteins are involved in molecule transport across the membrane, enzymatic reactions associated with synthesis of membrane and cell wall components, respiration, and energy generation.

Bacterial Structure and Function
Cell Membrane: Phospholipids • pp. 2–8

The proteins that are found in the membrane exist primarily in globular form and are dispersed individually and in aggregates throughout the membrane, giving a mosaic appearance to

this structure. Two classes of proteins have been identified, based on their relative solubility and location in membranes:

1. **Intrinsic (integral) proteins,** embedded in the interior of the lipid bilayer, make up approximately 70% to 80% of all membrane proteins. These intrinsic proteins are bound to the membrane lipids by nonpolar interactions and can be removed only by the use of detergents or nonpolar solvents.

2. **Extrinsic (peripheral) proteins** are found on the lipid bilayer and are removable by relatively mild treatments such as pH adjustments or changes in the ionic strength of the medium surrounding the membrane. The extrinsic proteins are believed to bind to the intrinsic proteins at the surface of the membrane, and possibly to some of the phospholipids.

 **Bacterial Structure and Function**
Cell Membrane: Membrane Proteins • pp. 9–10

Because of the lipid nature of the membrane, lipid-soluble molecules (for example, alcohols) are readily able to enter this barrier. However, such molecules encounter problems when they attempt to exit the plasma membrane and enter into the aqueous cytoplasm; the lipid-soluble molecules must first break their bonds with membrane lipids before they can move into the cytoplasm. Molecule passage through the plasma membrane depends not only on lipid solubility, but also on other parameters. Since the membrane possesses a net negative charge, molecules with similar charges (acidic proteins or acidic polysaccharides) are routinely repelled from entering or leaving the cell. Compounds that are too large to cross the membrane must first be degraded into smaller constituents by extracellular enzymes (amylases, proteases, and lipases) before entry (see polysaccharide, protein, and lipid hydrolysis, pages 190, 194, and 197). Bacteria that synthesize such enzymes often have a selective growth advantage in environments containing these large compounds, which serve as sources of nutrients.

Some procaryotes possess internal membranes formed from invaginations of the plasma membrane. The photosynthetic apparatus of photosynthetic bacteria is found in distinct membranous sacs continuous with the plasma membrane (Figure 3.10). These membranous sacs contain bacteriochlorophylls and accessory light-gathering pigments that are associated with the transfer of light energy in photosynthesis.

Bacteria that oxidize substances such as ammonia, nitrite, and methane have extensive internal membrane systems. The membranes in these bacteria are involved in the formation of hydrogen ion gradients used in the synthesis of ATP.

In certain gram-positive bacteria and a few gram-negative species, the plasma membrane appears to be folded into large convoluted invaginations, which have been called **mesosomes.** Mesosomes were first observed by electron microscopy and were thought to provide additional cell surface area for nutrient absorption, DNA attachment, and septum formation (the cross-wall that is formed in a bacterium during cell division). It is now believed that mesosomes are artifacts of preparations for electron microscopy.

The Cell Wall Maintains Cell Shape and Conformation

The unique shapes of most procaryotes are preserved by a complex, inflexible cell wall, a rigid layer of material external to the plasma membrane. The wall maintains conformation and also enables the cell to survive in hypotonic environments, where the osmotic pressure is higher inside than outside the cell. Under such conditions cells would swell and eventually burst were it not for the rigidity of the wall. Bacteria that lack a cell wall, either naturally or through laboratory manipulations, must in some way compensate for the absence of this structure either with sterol-containing plasma membranes (for example, *Mycoplasma*) or restricted growth in isosmotic habitats.

Cell walls are not unique to procaryotes. Other cells, including those of fungi, algae, and plants, also possess walls. The cell walls of procaryotic and eucaryotic microorganisms have basically similar architecture and function. Cell walls consist of polysaccharides linked by chemical bridges to form a rigid structure. The cell wall of procaryotes, however, is unique in its composition. Most of what is known about procaryotic cell walls has been obtained through electron microscopy, antibiotic studies, and chemical analysis of bacterial walls.

The substance of the bacterial cell wall is **peptidoglycan** (Figure 3.11), which is found only in Bacteria. It is arranged in one to several layers on the cell surface and provides the strength that is necessary for wall integrity. This unique chemical substance consists of repeating units of two carbohydrate derivatives, *N*-acetylglucosamine (NAG) and *N*-acetylmuramic acid (NAM), linked to each other by $\beta(1,4)$ bonds. NAM is found only in peptidoglycan and nowhere else in nature. Four amino acids make up what is known as a tetrapeptide attached to the NAM. The sequence of these amino acids in gram-negative bacteria and certain gram-positive bacteria is generally L-alanine, D-glutamate, *meso*-diaminopimelate, and D-alanine. Most gram-positive cocci have a similar sequence, with the exception that diaminopimelate is replaced by another diamino acid, L-lysine. The amino acid sequence of the tetrapeptide may be further modified in other bacteria. NAM and diaminopimelate are not found in eucaryotic cell walls. NAM is also not found in Archaea. The two amino acids with the D configuration (D-glutamate and D-alanine) are novel to peptidoglycan, since optically active amino acids in proteins are always in the L configuration. The alternating D and L configurations of the amino acids in the tetrapeptide, the $\beta(1,4)$ linkages between NAM and NAG in the repeating carbohydrate structure, and the layered sheet configuration of peptidoglycan contribute to the mechanical strength of this structure in the cell wall.

The major strength of peptidoglycan comes from periodic cross-links between the third and fourth amino acids of adjacent

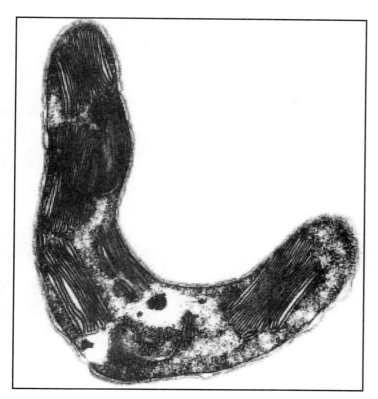

a.

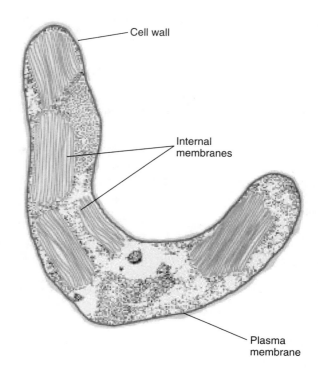

Cell wall

Internal
membranes

Plasma
membrane

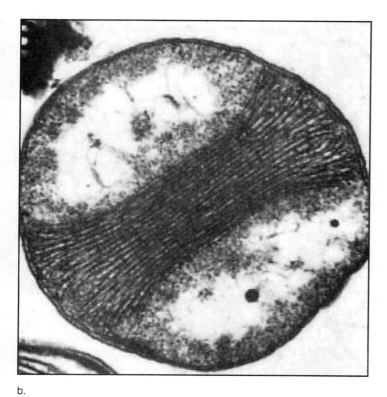

b.

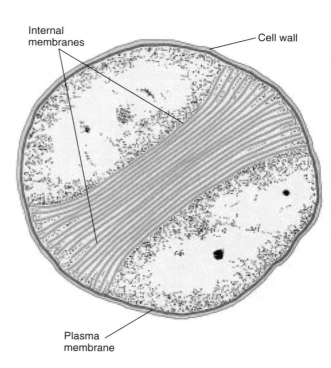

Internal
membranes

Cell wall

Plasma
membrane

figure 3.10

Internal Procaryotic Membranes

Internal membranes in a. *Ectothiorhodospira mobilis,* a photosynthetic bacterium ($\times 53{,}000$); b. *Nitrococcus oceanus,* a nitrifying (ammonia-oxidizing) bacterium ($\times 22{,}500$).

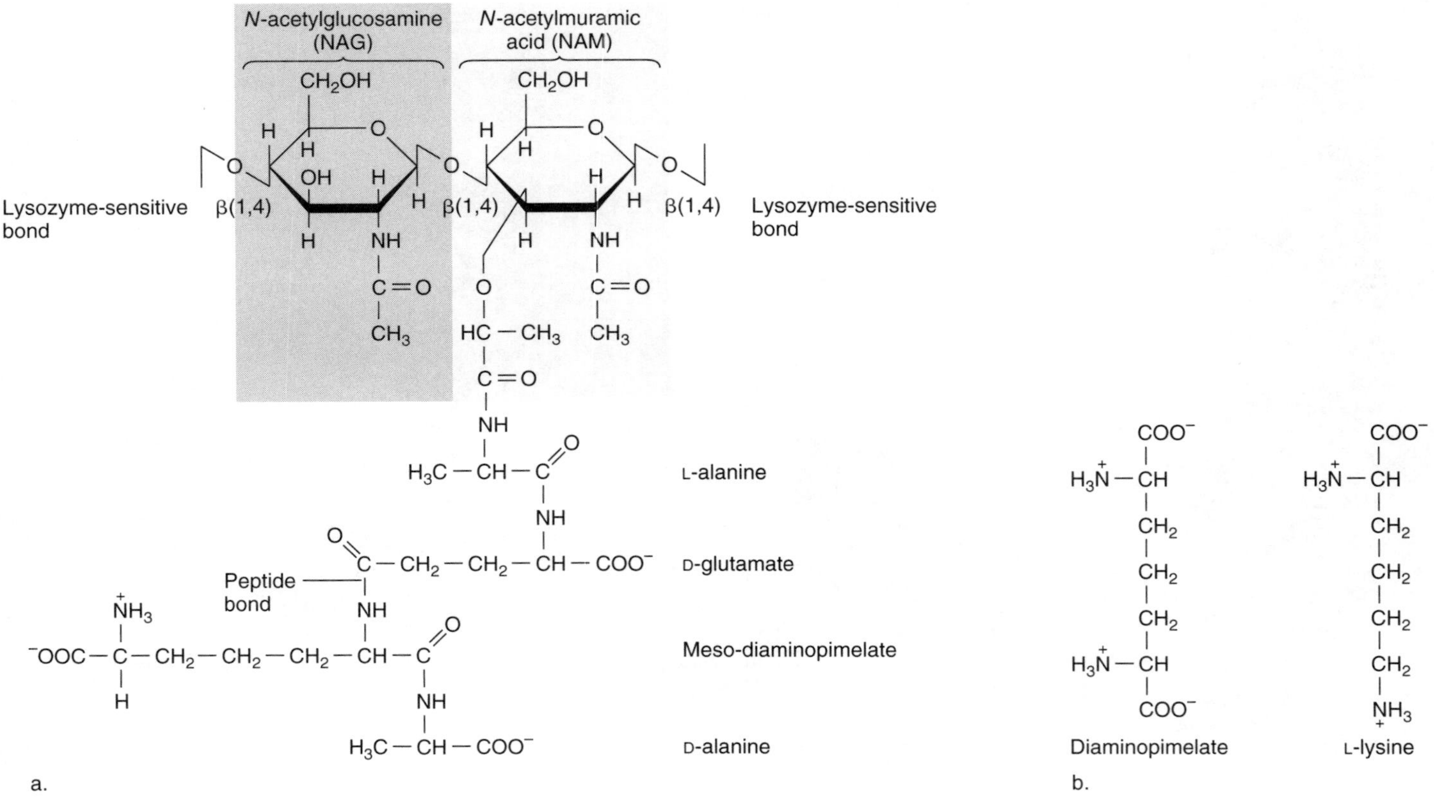

The chemical structure diagram showing a repeating unit in peptidoglycan.

N-acetylglucosamine (NAG)   *N*-acetylmuramic acid (NAM)

CH₂OH   CH₂OH

Lysozyme-sensitive bond   β(1,4)   β(1,4)   β(1,4)   Lysozyme-sensitive bond

L-alanine

D-glutamate

Peptide bond

Meso-diaminopimelate

D-alanine

COO⁻   COO⁻

Diaminopimelate   L-lysine

a.

b.

figure 3.11

Chemical Structure of a Repeating Unit in Peptidoglycan

a. A repeating unit of *N*-acetylglucosamine (NAG) and *N*-acetylmuramic acid (NAM) as found in *Escherichia coli* and other gram-negative bacteria. b. *Staphylococcus aureus* and other gram-positive cocci replace diaminopimelate with L-lysine in the tetrapeptide.

Antimicrobial Action
Cell Wall Inhibitors: Mechanisms • p. 7

tetrapeptides. The frequency, composition, and length of these cross-links vary among different bacteria, thus influencing the rigidity and strength of the wall in these organisms. Cross-linkage may occur either directly between amino acids in neighboring tetrapeptides, as occurs in most gram-negative cells, or alternatively, as in many gram-positive cells, through a peptide bridge (Figure 3.12).

The cell wall of *Staphylococcus aureus,* a gram-positive coccus, has been extensively studied; it is known that in this bacterium, tetrapeptides are linked by a pentaglycine bridge consisting of five molecules of the amino acid glycine. Although not all tetrapeptides may be involved in cross-linking bridges, the frequency of cross-linking in *S. aureus* is considerable and approaches 75%. In contrast, in *Escherichia coli,* like other gram nega-tives, modifications of the peptidoglycan layer cause a significant

portion of the tetrapeptide chains to cleave from the glycan chains. As a result of these losses, *E. coli,* which has peptidoglycan cross-links consisting of a direct bridge between D-alanine and *meso*-diaminopimelate in adjacent tetrapeptides, has a cross-linking fre-quency of only 25%. Cross-linking bridges in bacterial cell walls not only result in a joining of linear polysaccharide chains to form large sheetlike layers of peptidoglycan, but also are responsible for the attachment of these sheets to one another to produce a saclike struc-ture—a single molecule—encircling the cell (Figure 3.13).

Not all procaryotes have peptidoglycan in their cell walls. The Archaea do not have NAM as a constituent of their cell walls, but their walls may be composed of proteins, glycoproteins, and polysaccharides. Another group of procaryotes, the mycoplasmas, lack cell walls and therefore are not inhibited by antibiotics that act on the wall (for example, penicillin).

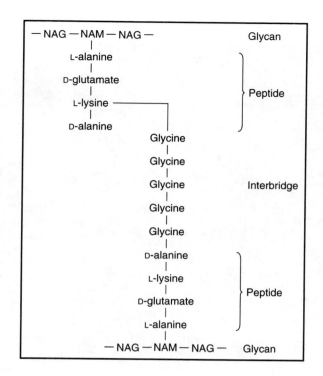

figure 3.12
Glycine Interbridge in the Peptidoglycan of _Staphylococcus aureus_

Antimicrobial Action
Cell Wall Inhibitors: Mechanisms • p. 7

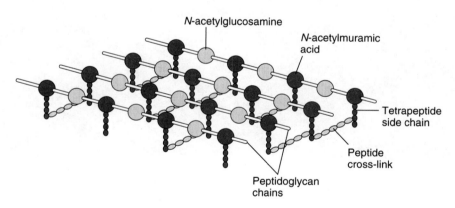

figure 3.13
Structure of Peptidoglycan Layer in Gram-Positive Cells

Antimicrobial Action
Cell Wall Inhibitors: Mechanisms • p. 7

Peptidoglycan Synthesis

The peptidoglycan of the bacterial cell wall is a complex chemical structure. Building blocks for the construction of peptidoglycan form in the cell cytoplasm and then transfer through the plasma membrane to the cell wall, where they link with existing peptidoglycan. The synthesis of these polymers and their incorporation into existing wall material occurs in four distinct stages (Figure 3.14):

1. N-acetylmuramic acid is synthesized in the cytoplasm of the cell from precursor molecules. During its synthesis, NAM attaches to uridine diphosphate (UDP), a carbohydrate carrier, by a high-energy phosphate bond to form uridine diphospho-N-acetylmuramic acid (UDP-NAM). The tetrapeptide portion of peptidoglycan, as well as a fifth amino acid (D-alanine) located at the terminus of the tetrapeptide, is added to the UDP-NAM by the stepwise addition of amino acids requiring energy input from the hydrolysis of ATP. Unlike normal protein synthesis, this peptide synthesis occurs without ribosomes, mRNA, or tRNA.

2. This complex moves to the plasma membrane, where it attaches to a second carrier, bactoprenol, by phosphate ester bonds. The energy for this reaction is derived from cleavage of the high-energy phosphate bond between UDP and NAM. Bactoprenol's role in cell wall synthesis is to make NAM hydrophobic enough for transport across the primarily phospholipid membrane.

3. After attachment to bactoprenol, the NAM-lipid complex is linked to (UDP)-N-acetylglucosamine. The energy requirements for this linkage are met by cleaving the bond between UDP and NAG. The cross-linking peptide bridge (pentaglycine in S. aureus) is added to the pentapeptide at this time. The polymer may be further modified, depending on the bacterium. This entire complex (NAG-NAM-pentapeptide-bactoprenol) now moves across the plasma membrane to the site for incorporation into the existing cell wall.

4. The newly synthesized section of peptidoglycan attaches to the existing wall by transglycosylation. During transglycosylation, the bactoprenol lipid carrier is released from the NAG-NAM disaccharide and moves back across the plasma membrane to the cytoplasm, where it is regenerated and reused. The NAG-NAM is linked by β(1,4) bond to the existing cell wall peptidoglycan backbone. The terminal D-alanine on NAM is cleaved at this time. The energy released from the cleavage of this peptide bond is used to form the peptide bond that attaches the cross-linking peptide to the existing wall (transpeptidation). Since cross-links are not always formed between adjacent tetrapeptides, in those instances where cross-links are absent, the terminal D-alanine is cleaved by the enzyme D-alanine carboxypeptidase.

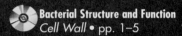

Bacterial Structure and Function
Cell Wall • pp. 1–5

The antibiotic penicillin specifically inhibits the transpeptidation step in cell wall synthesis. This explains why penicillin is ineffective in nongrowing cells that are not synthesizing new wall material. In the presence of penicillin, growing cells are unable to synthesize an intact cell wall. As a result, the cells lyse. Cells that do not have cell walls or walls containing peptidoglycan, such as mycoplasmas, animal cells, and fungi, are not affected by penicillin. Gram-negative bacteria are relatively resistant to penicillin because the antibiotic must pass through the outer membrane to reach the peptidoglycan of the cell wall, and it cannot easily do so.

Bacterial Structure and Function
Cell Wall: Antibiotic Sites • pp. 13–15

The peptidoglycan layer is frequently associated with other components in the cell wall. In gram-positive bacteria, peptidoglycan constitutes approximately 90% of the cell wall and can be up to 40 layers thick (Figure 3.15). The remainder of the wall in these organisms consists of acidic polysaccharides. These polysaccharides, the **teichoic acids,** are repeating units of glycerol or ribitol joined by phosphodiester linkages, and are located throughout the wall. In some gram-positive organisms (most notably *Bacillus* and *Staphylococcus*), up to 50% of the peptidoglycan can be complexed through the 6-OH group of NAM to teichoic acids. Teichoic acids, which can be as long as 30 units, are also found in the plasma membrane. Because they are negatively charged, teichoic acids are believed to bind and regulate cation levels at the cell surface.

Bacterial Structure and Function
Gram-Positive Cell • pp. 1–5

Gram-negative bacteria have a considerably thinner peptidoglycan layer that constitutes only about 5% to 20% of the total cell envelope. Chemical analyses of the wall in gram-negative bacteria such as *E. coli* suggest that there may only be one layer of peptidoglycan in these organisms.

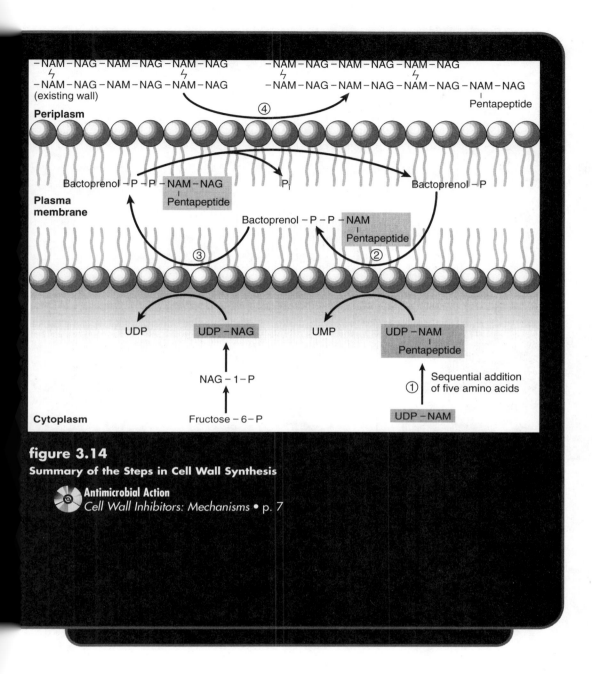

figure 3.14
Summary of the Steps in Cell Wall Synthesis

Antimicrobial Action
Cell Wall Inhibitors: Mechanisms • p. 7

The Outer Membrane Is the Exterior Portion of the Cell Envelope in Gram-Negative Procaryotes

An outer membrane is part of the cell wall in gram-negative procaryotes. The outer membrane, when examined in transverse sections by electron microscopy, resembles the trilaminar fine structure characteristic of most other biological membranes. This outer covering consists of a phospholipid bilayer interspersed with proteins and lipoproteins. The proteins and lipoproteins are firmly embedded in the matrix of the outer membrane, with the lipoproteins anchoring the outer membrane to the underlying peptidoglycan layer. The matrix proteins may also be responsible for the permeability of the outer membrane to small molecules having molecular weights of up to 800 daltons. The pores responsible for this permeability are formed through specific arrangements of membrane proteins that form part of the lipid bilayer. Rearrangements of these proteins after gene mutation and subsequent protein modification can cause changes in membrane permeability.

Lipopolysaccharide (LPS) molecules are arranged within the external phospholipid layer of the outer membrane and account for approximately 40% of the total cell surface in gram-negative bacteria

Gram-Positive Cell Envelope

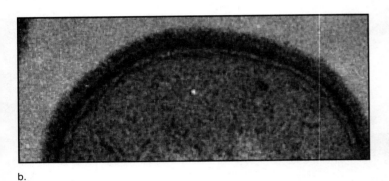

Cell wall consists of thick peptidoglycan layers

Tetrapeptide side chain

Plasma membrane

Phospholipid

Protein

a.

Gram-Negative Cell Envelope

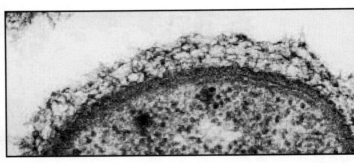

Protein

Pore

O antigen

Lipopolysaccharide (LPS)

Lipid A

Outer membrane

Lipoprotein

Periplasm

Peptidoglycan

Plasma membrane

d.

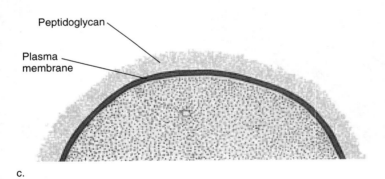

b.

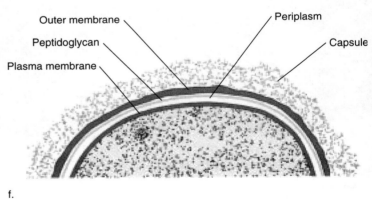

e.

Peptidoglycan

Plasma membrane

c.

Outer membrane

Periplasm

Peptidoglycan

Capsule

Plasma membrane

f.

figure 3.15

Cell Envelopes of Gram-Positive and Gram-Negative Bacteria

a and c. Schematic diagrams of a gram-positive cell envelope.
b. Transmission electron micrograph of the cell envelope of the gram-positive bacterium *Bacillus fastidiosus* (×90,000). d and f. Schematic diagrams of a gram-negative cell envelope. e. Transmission electron micrograph of the cell envelope of the gram-negative bacterium *Pseudomonas aeruginosa* (×120,000).

Bacteria Without Walls

Although most bacteria possess distinct cell walls, some exist without this outer covering (Figure 3.16). As might be expected, such bacteria are shapeless and have greater exposure to the surrounding environment. The cell walls of certain bacteria can be removed in the laboratory by treatment with the enzyme lysozyme. Lysozyme is commonly found in body secretions such as tears and saliva and is an important first line of defense for the body in repelling bacterial invasion. This enzyme hydrolyzes peptidoglycan β(1,4) linkages in which the number 1 carbon of *N*-acetylmuramic acid is joined to the number 4 carbon of *N*-acetylglucosamine, resulting in lysis (cell disruption) and release of cellular contents into the environment. Cell lysis can be prevented by incubation of lysozyme-treated cells in an isotonic environment. Under such conditions the intact cell (without the cell wall) is called a **protoplast.** Cells that retain portions of the wall on their surfaces even after such treatment are called **spheroplasts.**

Bacteria exposed to penicillin often, but not always, develop into forms without walls, called **L-phase variants,** or **L-forms** (the *L* stands for the Lister Institute in London, where these unique organisms were first observed). L-forms also sometimes arise spontaneously when bacteria are grown in hypertonic media. The role of these unusual bacteria in human disease is not well-defined. They may be associated with persistent diseases (for example, pulmonary infections, nephritis, and endocarditis).

Bacteria of the genus *Mycoplasma*, which causes primary atypical pneumonia, are naturally occurring microbes that do not have cell walls. Since they lack walls that provide shape and rigidity, mycoplasmas have no definitive forms and are pleomorphic. To compensate for the lack of cell walls, mycoplasmas have sterol-strengthened plasma membranes. As one might expect, mycoplasmas are not affected by penicillin or other antibiotics that act solely on the cell wall, but they are sensitive to antibiotics that have targets other than the wall.

Bacterial Structure and Function
Gram-Negative Cell: Cell Wall Exceptions • p. 17

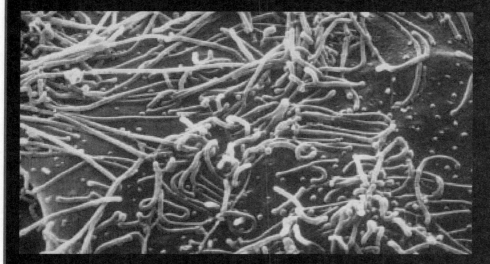

figure 3.16
Scanning Electron Micrograph of *Mycoplasma pneumoniae*
The irregular morphology is due to the lack of a cell wall (colorized, ×18,000).

(Figure 3.17). The lipopolysaccharide molecule consists of three components (listed in order from the outside to the inside of the cell):

1. An O-specific side chain (O antigen) composed of polysaccharides of varying types and proportions, depending on the bacterium

2. A core polysaccharide of relatively constant composition

3. A Lipid A portion, composed of glycophospholipid, which is associated with toxic activity in gram-negative bacteria

The LPS is more than a simple structural component of the cell wall. The O-specific side chain is responsible for surface antigenicity, which induces antibody formation in vertebrates. This region of the LPS consists of repeating oligosaccharide sequences containing up to 40 monosaccharides. The types and arrangement of the monosaccharides in the O-specific side chain determine the antigenicity of the LPS.

The Lipid A portion of the LPS is responsible for toxicity. Fever, shock, and other general physiological symptoms associated with diseases caused by *Salmonella, Escherichia,* and other gram-negative bacteria are caused by the endotoxic activity of the LPS (see endotoxins, page 450). Lipid A is usually attached to the core polysaccharide of LPS by three units of ketose-linked ketodeoxyoctonate (KDO), a molecule that is unique to bacteria.

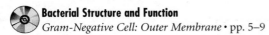 **Bacterial Structure and Function**
Gram-Negative Cell: Outer Membrane • pp. 5–9

The differences in wall composition between gram-positive and gram-negative bacteria explain in part why these bacteria stain differently in the Gram stain procedure. During decolorization with alcohol, the thick peptidoglycan layer in gram-positive bacteria becomes dehydrated. This dehydration causes the crystal violet-iodine complex, formed during the initial steps of the Gram stain, to remain trapped within the cell. The result is a violet-stained cell. Gram-negative bacteria, in contrast, have a thinner peptidoglycan layer and do not retain the crystal violet-iodine complex during destaining as effectively. The large proportion of lipids in the cell wall of gram-negative bacteria may also explain the response of these organisms to the Gram stain. It has been suggested that these lipids are extracted during the decolorization step, resulting in increased wall permeability. In either case, the gram-negative cell, which has not retained the primary stain, is subsequently counterstained with the red safranin. The wall composition of bacteria, however, is only partially responsible for the Gram stain reaction. Cyanobacteria, which have a wall almost identical in composition to the wall of gram-negative bacteria, stain gram positive. The reason for this difference is not known, but it suggests that more than simple wall composition is involved in the Gram stain reaction.

The Periplasm Separates the Plasma Membrane from the Outer Membrane in Gram-Negative Procaryotes

The plasma membrane is separated from the outer membrane in gram-negative procaryotes by a gap known as the **periplasm.** Within this periplasm are the peptidoglycan and approximately 50 different kinds of proteins, many of which are hydrolytic

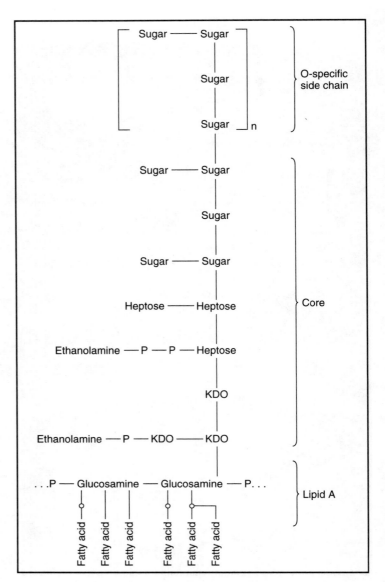

figure 3.17
The Lipopolysaccharide of the Gram-Negative Cell Envelope

enzymes and binding proteins. Examples of enzymes found in the periplasm are those that bind sugar molecules, amino acids, and inorganic ions. Specialized mechanisms are postulated for the translocation of many of these periplasmic proteins from the cell cytoplasm (where they are initially synthesized) across the plasma membrane and into the periplasm. One of the main functions of the periplasm may be to sequester enzymes in this space and prevent them from leaving the cell. Gram-positive procaryotes, which have no outer membrane, apparently do not have a periplasm.

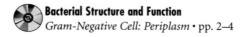 **Bacterial Structure and Function**
Gram-Negative Cell: Periplasm • pp. 2–4

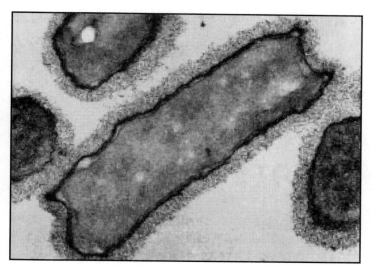

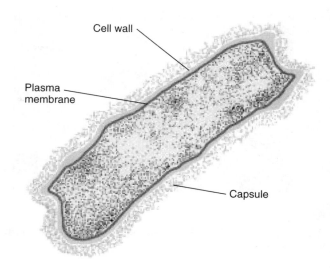

Cell wall

Plasma membrane

Capsule

figure 3.18

Electron Micrograph Showing the Thick Capsule of _Klebsiella pneumoniae_ (×22,536)

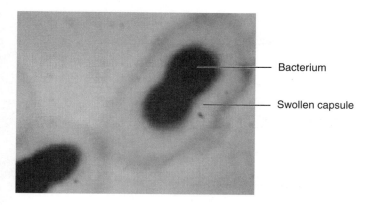

Bacterium

Swollen capsule

figure 3.19

Light Micrograph Showing the Quellung Reaction
Cells of _Streptococcus pneumoniae_ are surrounded by apparently swollen capsules from the quellung reaction.

A Variety of Specialized Structures Are Located Outside the Cell Envelope

Some bacteria have specialized structures external to the cell envelope. These structures are involved in the protection of the bacteria from phagocytes (host cells that ingest particulate matter), adhesion of the bacteria to solid surfaces, and motility.

Capsules Protect the Cell from Phagocytosis, Desiccation, and Nutrient Loss

Certain bacteria have an additional layer of material, called a capsule, that is external to the cell wall (Figure 3.18). Capsules are found on many pathogenic bacteria and protect the bacteria from ingestion by phagocytes (see phagocytosis, page 460). Removal of the capsule from bacteria by chemical treatment or genetic manip-

ulation results in an unprotected cell that is easily phagocytized and is far less virulent for the host organism.

External layers also protect microbial cells from desiccation and nutrient loss. Carboxyl groups found in these layers bind cations and may function in cation absorption. In some instances, capsular polysaccharides act as receptors for bacterial viruses, enabling the virus to attach to the cell.

Bacterial capsules are composed of polysaccharide, protein, or a combination of the two (glycoprotein). The thickness of the capsule is not fixed, and varies depending on the growth medium and growth conditions. Bacteria with particularly thick capsules often form mucoid colonies on solid media. Capsules on bacterial cells can be demonstrated by a simple capsule stain, in which cells are suspended in India ink and examined under a microscope. The colloidal particles of the India ink are displaced by the capsule, which appears as an unstained halo around the cell. An alternative procedure for visualizing capsules is the **quellung** reaction [German _quellen,_ to swell]. In the quellung reaction, encapsulated cells are mixed with antibodies directed specifically against capsular components. The antibodies increase the refractivity (light deflection) of the capsule, giving the appearance of a swollen capsule (Figure 3.19). This can easily be seen with a light microscope using the oil-immersion lens and reduced illumination. Some bacteria have surface macromolecules that promote adherence to solid surfaces. The **glycocalyx** is a fibrous matrix of polysaccharides that binds cells together in an aggregate mass and attaches the cell to solid surfaces. In the oral cavity, bacteria of the genus _Streptococcus,_ responsible for dental plaque, produce an exopolysaccharide called dextran that binds these organisms to the tooth surface. Dextran is a glucose polymer synthesized from the hydrolysis products of sucrose, a sugar that is well-known for its role in cariogenicity. The dental plaque that forms on tooth surfaces is a matrix composed of bacteria intermixed with epithelial cells, leukocytes (white blood cells), dextran, and other polymers. As the

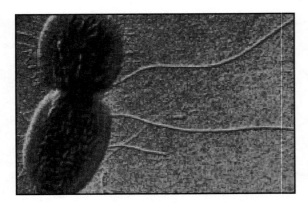

figure 3.20
Electron Micrograph of Pili (Short Appendages) Extending from *Proteus vulgaris*
The longer appendages are flagella (colorized, ×52,000).

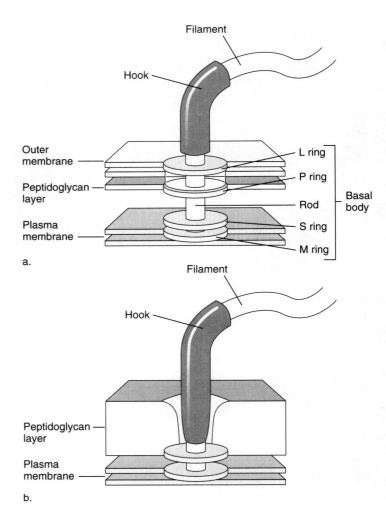

figure 3.21
Structure of the Bacterial Flagellum
The flagellum of bacteria consists of three parts: a basal body attached to the plasma membrane, a hook, and a filament. a. Gram-negative bacterial flagellum. b. Gram-positive bacterial flagellum.

bacteria grow and metabolize, they secrete lactic acid and other organic acids that are believed to be responsible for the demineralization of tooth enamel, leading to dental caries.

Bacterial Structure and Function
External Structures • pp. 1–11

Pili Are Involved in Conjugation and Attachment

Pili (singular, **pilus**) [Latin *pilus,* hair] are short, thin, straight appendages (10 nm × 300 to 1,000 nm) found in large quantity on the surfaces of some bacteria, notably Gram-negative cells (Figure 3.20). There are 10 to 250 pili, also called **fimbriae,** per cell. Pili known as **type I pili** are involved in attachment of bacteria to cell surfaces, particularly those of eucaryotic cells. Some pathogenic bacteria, such as *Neisseria gonorrhoeae,* the etiologic agent of gonorrhea, use pili for attachment to epithelial cells during infection. One specialized type of pilus (the **F,** or **sex pilus**) is associated with the transfer of genetic material between bacterial cells (a process called *conjugation*) (see conjugation, page 263). Although the exact function of the sex pilus in genetic transfer is not known, it apparently is involved in stabilizing the association between two mating bacterial cells while DNA is transferred.

Pili originate from the plasma membrane and are composed almost entirely of a protein called **pilin.** Pili are too small to be seen under a light microscope and can only be observed with an electron microscope.

Bacterial Structure and Function
External Structures: Pili • pp. 15–17

Flagella Are Used for Cellular Locomotion

Flagella (singular, **flagellum**) [Latin *flagellum,* whip] are appendages on bacteria that are involved in locomotion. These appendages are long, thin (average 10 to 20 nm × 1 to 70 μm) helical filaments.

The bacterial flagellum is composed of three parts: a **basal body** attached to the plasma membrane, a **hook,** and a **filament** (Figure 3.21). The basal body is a thin structure composed of protein and

constitutes a relatively small proportion (approximately 1%) of the total mass of the flagellum. In gram-negative bacteria the basal body is surrounded by four collars, or rings. The S and M rings are attached to the plasma membrane. The P ring is anchored to the peptidoglycan; the fourth ring, the L ring, is associated with the outer membrane. Basal bodies of gram-positive bacteria have only two rings. One ring is attached to the plasma membrane, and the other is associated with the cell wall. The rings around the basal body probably aid in anchoring the flagellum to the membrane and wall.

The filament is linked to the basal body by a thick, curved hook. Filaments are composed of protein subunits called **flagellin.** Flagellin has a unique amino acid composition (some flagellins contain the unusual amino acid ε-*N*-methyllysine) and is different from the other proteins that make up the basal body and hook.

Flagella on a bacterium are less numerous than pili and may be arranged in different patterns on the cell surface (Figure 3.22). Bacteria that possess only one flagellum are termed **monotrichous** [Greek *trichos,* hair], whereas those with more than one flagellum

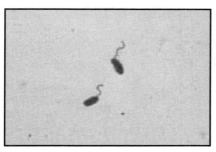

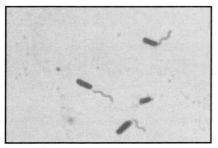

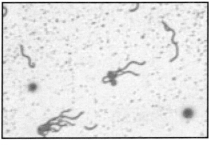

figure 3.22
Flagellation Patterns in Bacteria
a. Light micrograph of *Vibrio parahaemolyticus*, showing a single polar flagellum. b. Light micrograph of *Pseudomonas aeruginosa*, showing a single polar flagellum. c. Light micrograph of *Bacillus megaterium*, showing peritrichous flagellation.

are **multitrichous. Polar** flagellated organisms have flagella on one or both ends of the cell. The term **lophotrichous** is used to describe bacteria with a tuft of flagella. **Peritrichous** flagellation refers to the presence of flagella throughout the cell surface. Flagellar arrangement can sometimes be used to differentiate between different types of bacteria. For example, *Escherichia coli* and *Pseudomonas aeruginosa* are both gram-negative rods. However, *E. coli* has peritrichous flagellation, whereas *P. aeruginosa* is polarly flagellated.

The cell moves by the rotation of its flagella. For many years it was thought that flagella propelled bacteria by a whiplike motion. It is now known that flagella rotate around their bases in a counterclockwise direction with the expenditure of energy. This rotational movement was demonstrated in 1974 by Michael Silverman and Melvin Simon of the University of California at San Diego, who anchored monotrichously flagellated bacteria by their flagella to a slide. Antibodies on the slide attached to the flagella,

and the tethered cells were observed to rotate around the immobilized flagella.

Flagellar movement propels the cell at velocities of approximately 20 to 200 μm/sec. This speed may not appear to be very fast, but it is 10 to 100 cell lengths per second. A dog with a length of 1 meter would have to move at a speed of 30 to 300 km/hr to reach an equivalent velocity.

The type of flagellation also influences the way bacteria move through an environment. Polar flagellated bacteria dart around rapidly, whereas those that are peritrichously flagellated move in a directional manner, followed by a tumble and roll.

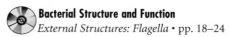

Bacterial Structure and Function
External Structures: Flagella • pp. 18–24

Chemotaxis Is the Movement of Procaryotes Toward or Away from Chemical Substances

Some bacteria have the ability to move toward or away from chemical substances. This movement, called **chemotaxis,** occurs in response to chemicals (for example, carbohydrates or amino acids) that either attract them (attractants) or repel them (repellents).

The movement of a bacterium can be followed by a tracking microscope, a special microscope with a moving stage that follows the movement of an individual cell. Using such an instrument, it has been observed that in the absence of a chemical gradient *E. coli,* a peritrichously flagellated bacterium, moves randomly. The bacterium travels in one direction with steady counterclockwise rotation of its flagella in a motion called a *run,* followed by an abrupt reversal of flagellar rotation, resulting in a *tumble* (Figure 3.23). When the bacterium is exposed to a chemical gradient, the runs are longer and the general movement is toward the higher concentration of an attractant or away from a repellent.

The responses of microbes to specific chemical substances are mediated by chemoreceptors located in the plasma membrane or in the periplasm. These receptors consist of binding proteins that tightly and specifically bind the chemical and signal the bacterium to move. The binding of chemoreceptors to specific chemicals activates a series of events, including the methylation or demethylation of certain bacterial proteins called **methyl-accepting chemotaxis proteins (MCPs),** or **transducers,** that signals flagellar movement.

MCPs sense the presence of and directly bind attractants and repellents or indirectly interact with these chemicals after they have bound to the chemoreceptors. If the concentration of the attractant remains constant or decreases, the enzyme CheB, a methylesterase, demethylates the MCP. The result is a tumble by the cell. As the concentration of an attractant increases, MCP is methylated by the enzyme CheR, a methyltransferase, with the methyl group coming from the donor S-adenosylmethionine. This methylation of the MCP results in a straight run by the cell.

A cascading series of events occurs that transfers the signal from the MCP to the bacterial flagellum (Figure 3.24). Demethylation of the MCP (under constant or decreased concentrations of attractant) causes a cytoplasmic protein called CheW to couple the receptor-generated signal to autophosphorylation of the protein kinase CheA, which in turn transfers its phosphate to CheB and

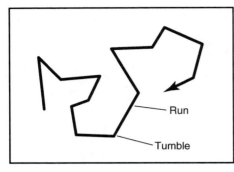
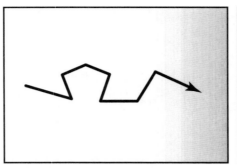
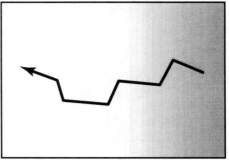

a. No chemical gradient

b. Gradient of chemical attractant

c. Gradient of chemical repellent

figure 3.23

Movement of Bacteria as Seen by a Tracking Microscope

a. Random movement of a bacterium in an area without a chemical gradient. Straight runs are followed by tumbles. b. Directed movement in a gradient of a chemical attractant. Runs are longer and the general movement is toward the higher concentration of the attractant. c. Directed movement in a gradient of a chemical repellent. The

general movement is away from the higher concentration of the repellent.

Bacterial Structure and Function
External Structures: Flagella • p. 24

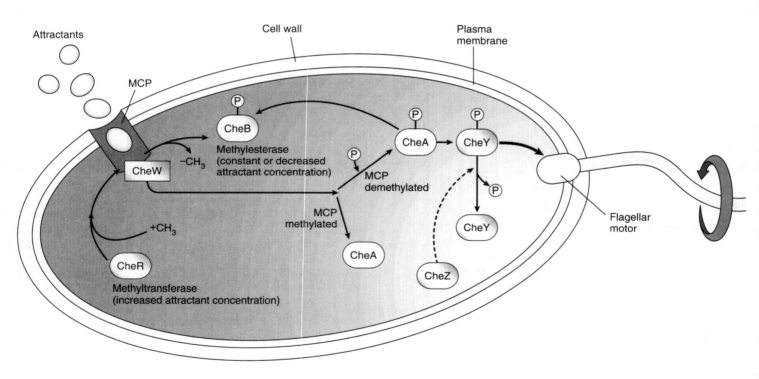

figure 3.24

Role of Methyl-Accepting Chemotaxis Proteins (MCPs) in Chemotaxis

Demethylation of MCPs when attractant concentration is constant or decreases results in a cascade phosphorylation of CheA and CheY. The CheY interacts with the bacterial flagellum, causing it to rotate clockwise and resulting in a tumble by the cell. When attractant

concentration increases, methylation of MCP results in dephosphorylation of CheY by CheZ. Under these conditions, the flagellum rotates counterclockwise and the cell makes a straight run.

CheY, a protein that interacts with the flagellum. ATP is the initial source of the phosphate for phosphorylation of CheA. Phosphorylation stimulates CheB methylesterase activity and contributes to adaptation by the cell to attractant concentrations. When CheY is phosphorylated, the flagellum rotates clockwise, resulting in a tumble. When MCP is methylated (under high concentrations of attractant), CheY is dephosphorylated by the phosphatase CheZ and the flagellum switches to a counterclockwise rotation, resulting in a straight run by the cell.

Bacterial cells may have several different kinds of chemoreceptors. For example, *Escherichia coli* has approximately 20 attractant receptors and 10 repellent receptors. Some of these receptors, such as those for galactose, ribose, and maltose, are present in substantial concentrations (10,000 or more receptors per cell). With such receptors, the cell is able to migrate toward areas containing higher concentrations of these nutrients.

Chemotaxis is not unique to bacteria. It also occurs in other types of organisms, such as the amoeba *Dictyostelium* and the protozoan *Paramecium*. The phenomenon, however, has been most extensively studied in bacteria. Responses of microbes to attractants or repellents depend on the species of microorganism involved, the type of chemical, and the concentration of the substance. Chemotaxis is of obvious advantage to microorganisms that live in environments containing harmful chemicals or limited supplies of nutrients, and is an example of microbial adaptation to changes in the environment.

Bacteria are also able to respond to other environmental stimuli. Photosynthetic bacteria move toward areas of high light intensity (**phototaxis**). Movements of bacteria can be affected by oxygen concentrations (**aerotaxis**). Bacteria requiring oxygen will move toward oxygen, whereas those inhibited by oxygen will be repelled by it.

One of the more unique responses is to the earth's magnetic fields (**magnetotaxis**). Certain aquatic bacteria such as *Aquaspirillum magnetotacticum* have intracellular crystal particles of the iron oxide magnetite (Fe_3O_4) called **magnetosomes** that act as tiny magnets (Figure 3.25). The magnetosomes help the bacteria orient their movements along magnetic fields and move primarily in northward and southward directions, as well as downward toward nutrient-rich sediments. Magnetosomes are also found in eucaryotes such as some algae.

Procaryotes Do Not Have Membrane-Enclosed Organelles, but Do Have Specialized Internal Cell Structures

Although procaryotic cells generally do not have internal membrane-enclosed organelles like those found in eucaryotic cells, they do have certain specialized structures. These structures are involved in the storage of genetic information, protein synthesis, and other cell activities.

The Nucleoid Is the Chromosome-Containing Region of the Cell

The **nucleoid** is the nuclear region of the bacterial cell that contains the bacterial chromosome (Figure 3.26). Most of the genetic information of the cell is contained within the chromosome; some may be in extrachromosomal structures called **plasmids** (see plasmid, page 258). Plasmids are small, circular pieces of double-stranded DNA that replicate autonomously and may be transferred between closely related bacteria. Plasmids contain genes that are generally not crucial for cell growth and reproduction; not all bacteria have them. Plasmids can carry a variety of genes, including those for resistance to antibiotics, tolerance to toxic metals, and pili-mediated DNA transfer.

Bacteria do not possess the membrane-enclosed nucleus that is characteristic of eucaryotic cells. The DNA of bacteria, however, can be visualized by electron microscopy as thin, fibrillar material confined within the nucleoid. Bacterial DNA occurs as a double-stranded helix arranged in a covalently closed circle near or associated with the plasma membrane. In *E. coli*, the DNA has a molecular weight of approximately 2.5×10^9 daltons and constitutes only about 2% to 3% of the dry weight of the cell. Yet, when stretched linearly, the DNA measures 1,100 μm long, or 550 times the length of the *E. coli* cell. The length of DNA is such that it must be tightly folded in a twisted supercoil to fit within the cell. Negative charges of DNA, resulting from the sugar phosphate backbone, are neutralized with divalent cations such as Mg^{2+} or Ca^{2+} that prevent electrostatic repulsions between the DNA strands. Recently a histonelike protein (labeled HU) was discovered in *E. coli* that may neutralize the negative charges of bacterial DNA in the same manner as histones do in eucaryotic cells.

Bacterial Structure and Function
Internal Structures • pp. 1–4

Ribosomes Are RNA-Rich Particles That Are the Sites of Protein Synthesis

Ribosomes are the sites of protein synthesis. It is not unusual to find 30,000 or more in a rapidly growing bacterium. Ribosomes have characteristic sizes that are usually described by the rate of movement during ultracentrifugation. The Svedberg (S) is a unit of measure for the sedimentation rate of molecules in a gravitational field. Bacterial ribosomes have a sedimentation constant of 70S and consist of two subunits, 30S and 50S. (Since sedimentation behavior of molecules is affected by shape as well as mass, the individual subunit values add up to a higher value than that of the intact ribosome.) Eucaryotic ribosomes are larger and have a sedimentation constant of 80S, with subunits of 40S and 60S.

Bacterial ribosomes, composed of 40% protein and 60% rRNA, are often found on mRNA as polyribosomes. The 30S subunit consists of about 21 proteins and a 16S rRNA molecule. Two rRNA molecules (a 23S rRNA and a 5S rRNA) and about 34 proteins make up the 50S ribosome subunit. Both subunits come together at one end of a mRNA to form an intact 70S ribosome during protein synthesis.

Bacterial Structure and Function
Internal Structures • pp. 12–13

Inclusion Bodies Are Storage Depots for Lipids, Polysaccharides, and Inorganic Compounds

Bacteria frequently are found in adverse environments where nutrients are scarce. They can survive in these environments by drawing on reserve materials that have accumulated in **inclusion**, or **storage**,

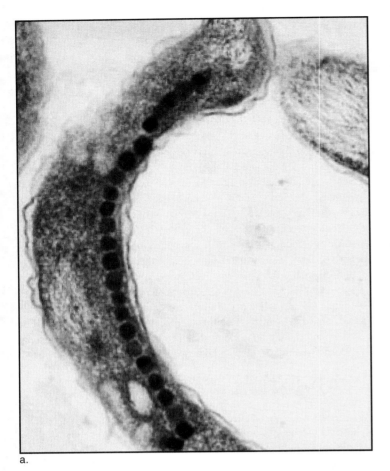

a.

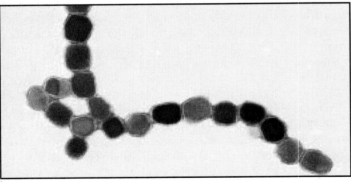

b.

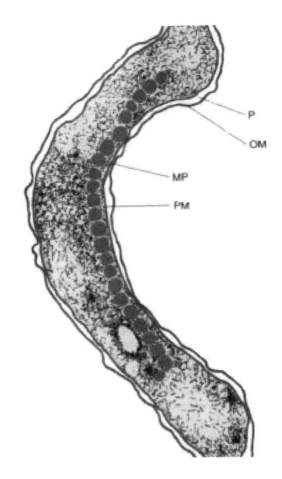

figure 3.25

Magnetotactic Bacteria

a. Transmission electron micrograph of the magnetotactic bacterium, *Aquaspirillum magnetotacticum,* showing intracellular crystal particles of magnetite (MP). PM, plasma membrane; OM, outer membrane; P, periplasm (×123,000). b. Isolated magnetosomes (×140,000).

bodies. These electron-dense structures range from 20 to 100 nm in diameter. Among the substances that are stored in inclusion bodies are lipids, polysaccharides, and inorganic compounds. A bacterial cell usually produces only one kind of inclusion body. The storage compounds found in these bodies often are negatively charged and can be preferentially stained with basic dyes. For example, *Corynebacterium* stores the inorganic compound polymetaphosphate in inclusion bodies. The inclusion bodies, containing the anionic phosphates, are readily stained with the basic dye methylene blue. The stained bodies are referred to as **metachromatic granules** (because of their staining characteristics) or **Babès-Ernst bodies** (named after their discoverers). The staining technique is called the **granule stain** and is useful in identifying metachromatic granules not only in *Corynebacterium,*

but also in other bacteria (Figure 3.27). Poly-β-hydroxybutyrate, a lipidlike storage molecule for carbon and energy, is commonly found in *Bacillus* and *Pseudomonas* and is preferentially stained with a fat-soluble dye such as Sudan black. Poly-β-hydroxybutyrates form long polymers that have plasticlike properties. These microbial plastics are becoming increasingly popular as a source of raw materials for the manufacture of biodegradable plastic products.

Gas Vacuoles Retain Gases and Provide Buoyancy to the Cell

Some procaryotes (photosynthetic bacteria and cyanobacteria) control their buoyancy in water by using hollow protein cylinders called **gas vacuoles** that retain gases (Figure 3.28). A vacuole measures

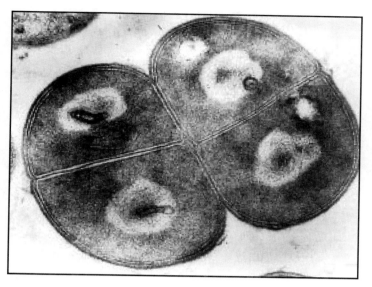

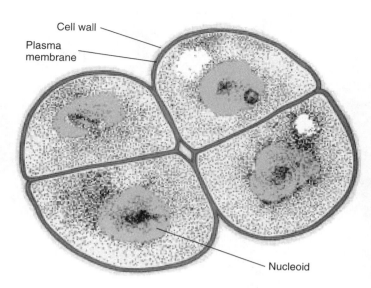

Cell wall

Plasma membrane

Nucleoid

figure 3.26
Nucleoids Within Dividing *Sporosarcina ureae*
The nucleoids are the light areas within each of the four cells.

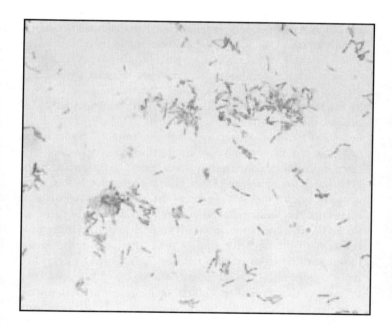

figure 3.27
Granules Inside Cells of *Corynebacterium diphtheriae*
Dark blue metachromatic granules are shown inside *C. diphtheriae* cells.

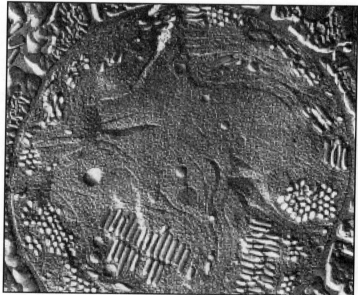

figure 3.28
Gas Vacuoles Within a Freeze-Etched *Microcystis aeruginosa* Cell
The gas vacuoles are the cylinders inside the cell (×21,000).

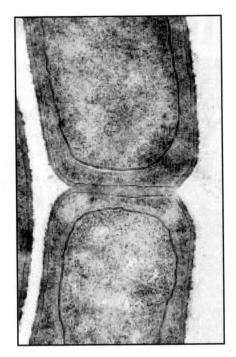

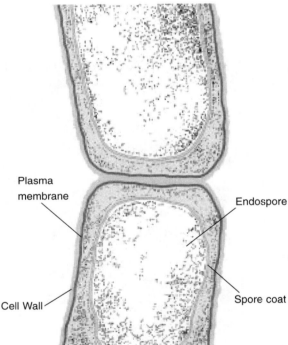

Plasma
membrane

Endospore

Cell Wall

Spore coat

figure 3.29
Developing Endospores in *Bacillus*

Transmission electron micrograph showing endospores in *Bacillus cereus* (×49,500).

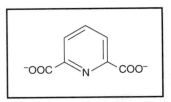

figure 3.30
Chemical Structure of Dipicolinate

75 nm in diameter and 200 to 1,000 nm in length. It is bounded by a rigid layer of a proteinaceous membrane 2 nm thick that is impermeable to water and solutes, but is freely permeable to gases. The buoyancy of the cell can be controlled through the uptake of gases into, or release of gases from, the vacuoles. The outer protein layer provides the strength and rigidity necessary for the vacuole to withstand the pressure extremes encountered in aquatic environments. By controlling their buoyancy in water, bacteria with gas vacuoles are able to maintain a depth that is optimal for nutrient levels, oxygen concentration, and light intensity.

Endospores Enable the Cell to Survive Adverse Environmental Conditions

The bacterial cells that have been described are referred to as **vegetative cells.** Vegetative cells of bacteria are associated with growth, metabolism, and reproduction. These cells are not exceptionally resistant to environmental stress and therefore are susceptible to lysis and destruction when such conditions prevail. Under nutrient-limiting conditions, certain types of bacteria (mainly in the genera *Bacillus* and *Clostridium*) have the unusual ability to form a resistant, dormant cell type called an **endospore** (so called because the spore is formed within the cell) (Figure 3.29).

The bacterial endospore is a highly refractile multilayered cell that can survive adverse environmental conditions. Bacterial endospores contain only 15% water, compared with the 70% water found in vegetative cells. Because of this low water content, endospores are dormant and do not metabolize or reproduce. Bacterial endospores can withstand drying and are up to 10,000 times more resistant to heat and 100 times more resistant to ultraviolet radiation than vegetative cells. Spores have been known to survive for hundreds of years under dormant conditions. Although many theories have been postulated to explain the unusual resistance of spores, none has proved completely satisfactory. The most attractive theory proposes that high levels in spores of the chemical compound dipicolinate, in combination with calcium ions, may be responsible for their heat resistance (Figure 3.30). Calcium dipicolinate forms a gel-like polymer that extrudes water from the spore; hence structures and macromolecules are not subject to denaturation or breakdown by water molecules upon exposure to high temperatures. Calcium dipicolinate comprises as much as 15% of the dry weight of a spore. Another theory suggests that expansion of the peptidoglycan in the spore cortex in the absence of divalent cations may play a role in heat resistance. Whatever the mechanism involved in spore resistance, spores clearly pro-

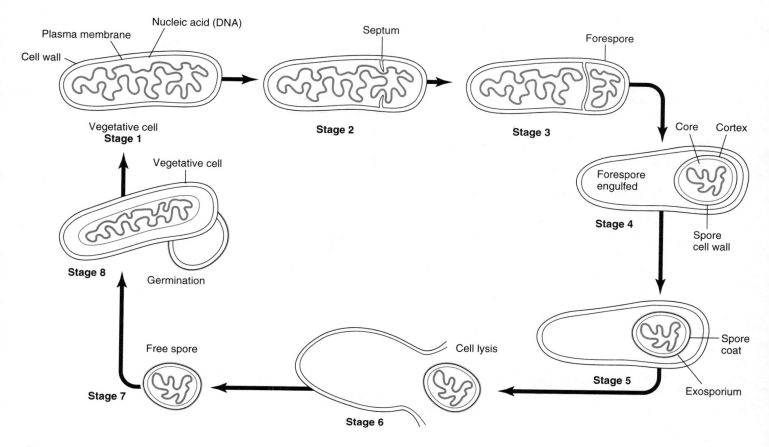

figure 3.31

Stages in Endospore Formation and Germination
Stage 1. Replication of nucleic acid in vegetative cell to form two complete sets of DNA. **Stage 2.** Invagination of the plasma membrane to form a spore septum separating the two sets of DNA. **Stage 3.** Development of a forespore. **Stage 4.** Forespore is engulfed and the core is surrounded by the spore cell wall and the cortex. **Stage 5.** Completion of endospore formation with the formation of the spore coat and, in some cases, an exosporium around the spore. **Stage 6.** Release of the endospore through lysis of the sporangium. **Stage 7.** Free spore. **Stage 8.** Germination.

vide bacteria with a specialized structure to withstand environmental stress and nutrient deprivation.

Bacterial endospore formation is a complex process that involves several distinct morphological stages (Figure 3.31):

Stage 1. In the first stage the vegetative cell replicates its nucleic acid to form two complete copies of DNA. The nucleic acid extends as a continuous filament along the entire length of the cell.

Stage 2. The second stage of endospore differentiation begins with an invagination of the plasma membrane to form a spore septum. The two copies of DNA separate and compartmentalize in two membrane-enclosed areas of the cell. Only one of these two areas will eventually differentiate into the endospore.

Stage 3. During the next stage of spore formation, a recognizable **forespore** develops from one of the compartments.

Stage 4. Next, the forespore is engulfed by the mother cell and a thick cortical layer (the **cortex**), composed of peptidoglycan, is formed. A highly cross-linked peptidoglycan layer, the **spore cell wall,** is found between the cortex and the **core,** or interior of the spore (plasma membrane, protoplasm, DNA, ribosomes, and so forth). At this stage the forespore becomes increasingly refractile. Calcium dipicolinate is synthesized and apparently incorporated into the core.

Stage 5. The fifth stage of spore formation begins with the formation of a **spore coat** around the spore. The proteinaceous spore coat is exceptionally rich in the amino acid cysteine. The proteins of the coat are different from those synthesized by vegetative cells and probably contribute to the coat's hydrophobic nature. The completed endospore consists of the spore coat, cortex, spore wall, and core in association with calcium dipicolinate. In some endospore-forming bacteria, such as *Bacillus cereus,* a loose outer envelope surrounds the spore. This envelope, called the **exosporium,** is composed mainly of protein, carbohydrate, and lipid.

Following maturation, the intact spore is released from the cell through lysis of the sporangium. The sporangium is the cell that contains the endospore. This **free spore** is a highly resistant structure, able to withstand desiccation and environmental stress (Figure 3.32). The entire spore differentiation process is commonly called **sporogenesis.**

Certain characteristics of sporogenesis have recently been defined. It is known that spore formation in bacteria is triggered by nutrient deprivation, environmental stress, or both. Under such conditions, genes that are normally repressed in vegetative cells are activated. These genes code for enzymes that catalyze the synthesis of proteins that are incorporated into the surrounding layers of the developing spore.

Spores convert back to vegetative cells again by a process called **germination.** Although some spores will germinate spontaneously in a favorable growth medium, most must first be activated. Activation occurs when spores are exposed for short periods of time to a nutrient-rich environment, to certain types of traumatic conditions such as heat or low pH, or to reducing agents like mercaptoethanol. The activated spore goes through a series of germination steps in which up to 30% of the dry weight of the spore (primarily its cortical layer and calcium dipicolinate) is excreted into the surrounding medium. Degradation of the protective spore layers is followed by a period of **outgrowth,** during which DNA, RNA, and proteins are actively synthesized. Outgrowth continues until the vegetative cell matures and divides. The complete process of germination usually takes less than 90 minutes.

Endospores are impermeable to dyes used in normal staining procedures. In Gram-stained preparations, the refractile endospores appear as unstained structures against the remaining stained cell material. A special technique called the **spore stain** is used to selectively stain endospores. In the spore stain, a dye such as carbolfuchsin is driven into the spore by steaming the smear. The cells are stained with a secondary dye and spores are seen as red. Endospores can be found in different areas of the cell (Figure 3.33). Some are located at the end of the cell (**terminal spores**), whereas others are found in the middle (**central spores**). Still others are situated between the end and the middle portion of the cell (**subterminal spores**). The location of the endospore is characteristic for some species of bacteria and can be used in identification.

Endospore-forming bacteria represent a unique group of organisms with the ability to differentiate and develop into a specialized form adapted for survival in a hostile environment. The mechanisms involved in sporogenesis and germination have only recently begun to be understood and should provide scientists with an insight into the differentiation process not only of spores, but also of other cell types.

The Eucaryotic Cell

Many of the structures in procaryotic cells are also found in eucaryotic cells. However, eucaryotic cells possess certain structures that are different from, or do not occur, in procaryotic cells.

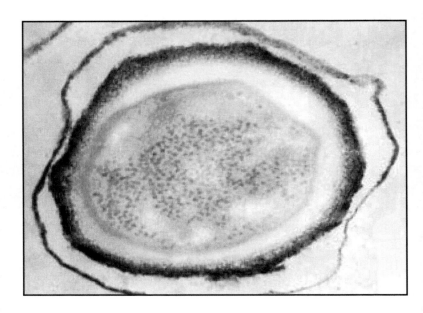

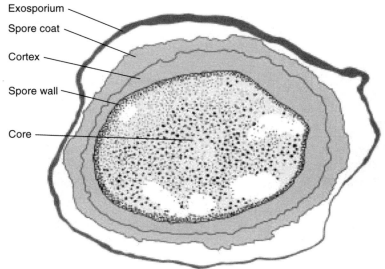

figure 3.32
Endospore Structure
Bacillus anthracis endospore, showing the core, surrounded by the spore wall, cortex, the spore coat, and the exosporium (×151,000).

The Eucaryotic Cell Wall and Plasma Membrane Are Chemically Different from, but Function Similarly as, Their Procaryotic Counterparts

Eucaryotic cells, like procaryotic cells, are surrounded by a plasma membrane and, in some cases, a cell wall (Figure 3.34). The cell wall in eucaryotes is found only in algae, plants, and fungi, and is one of the principal distinctions between these organisms and animals. The eucaryotic cell wall functions much like its counterpart in the procaryotic cell. It maintains shape and rigidity, and protects the cell from osmotic stress. Eucaryotic walls, however, do not possess peptidoglycan. Instead they typically contain cellulose and 6-carbon sugars known as hexuronic acids. In some instances, as in certain fungi, the cellulose in

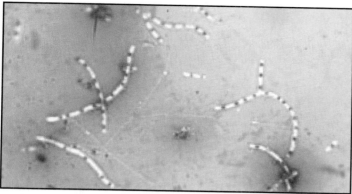

a.

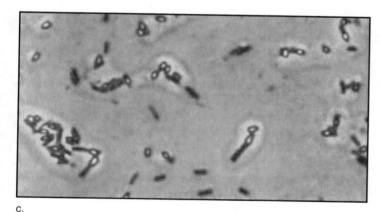

b.

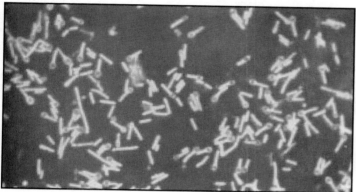

c.

figure 3.33
Endospore-Forming Bacteria
a. *Bacillus subtilis* endospore stain showing red endospores (×500).
b. *Clostridium tetani*, terminal endospores with characteristic
"drumstick" appearance (×500). c. *Clostridium botulinum*, subterminal
endospores (phase contrast, ×600).

figure 3.34
**Organization of a Procaryotic Cell Compared with a
Eucaryotic Cell**
a. A typical procaryotic cell. b. A typical eucaryotic plant cell. c. A
typical eucaryotic animal cell. Illustrated structures are not found in all cells.

Procaryotic cell

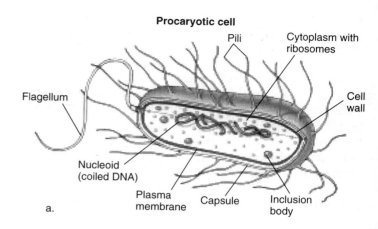

a.

Eucaryotic cells
A typical plant cell

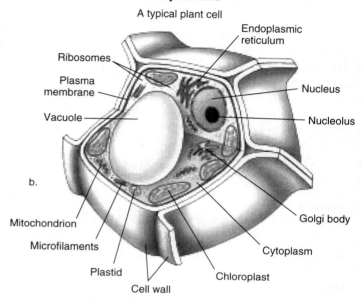

b.

A typical animal cell

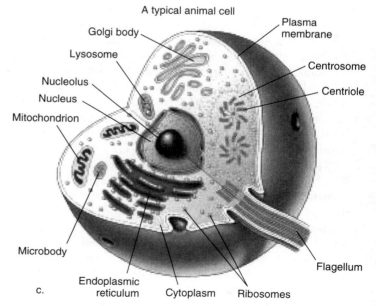

c.

the wall is replaced in part by glucans, chitin (the same tough, resistant polysaccharide that is found in the exoskeletons of arthropods), and other substances. Structural polysaccharides in the wall are interwoven into strands called microfibrils that are cross-linked with a matrix of other sugars. The wall is located external to the plasma membrane and, in some mature plant cells, a nonflexible secondary wall may form underneath the primary wall. This secondary wall contains cellulose and the polyphenol lignin, molecules that do not occur in the primary wall and that impart strength to older, nongrowing cells. Cells that are adjacent to one another often have an additional layer between them called the middle lamella, composed of pectin (the same organic substance that forms the basis of jellies), which holds these cells together.

Fungal Structure and Function
General Eucaryotic Structures: Cell Wall • pp. 2–3

Eucaryotic plasma membranes are similar in structure to procaryotic membranes, with the exception that sterols are present. The sterols in the eucaryotic membrane impart strength to it, important because many eucaryotic cells lack a rigid wall. Both eucaryotic and procaryotic membranes perform similar functions. They act as semipermeable barriers for the movement of substances into and out of the cell.

Fungal Structure and Function
General Eucaryotic Structures: Cell Membrane • pp. 4–5

Eucaryotic Cells Contain Membrane-Enclosed Organelles

A fundamental difference between eucaryotes and procaryotes is the presence of certain membrane-enclosed organelles in the eucaryotic cell cytoplasm. These organelles include mitochondria, chloroplasts, the nucleus, and other specialized structures.

Eucaryotic DNA is contained within a membrane-enclosed **nucleus.** Inside the nucleus is the nucleolus, a small body that is the site of ribosomal RNA synthesis. The nucleus is surrounded by a nuclear envelope consisting of two separate unit membranes. Each membrane is approximately 75 Å thick; the two membranes are separated by a space of 400 to 700 Å. The outer membrane is connected at different points to a structure called the **endoplasmic reticulum,** an extensive network of internal membranes that is often associated with ribosomes and is involved in protein synthesis. Small pores (30 to 100 nm in diameter) in the nuclear envelope serve to connect the nucleoplasm with the cell cytoplasm.

The nucleus contains the genetic information of the cell, which is complexed with **histones** (positive-charged proteins) and **nonhistone proteins** (Figure 3.35). The DNA and its associated proteins form structures called chromosomes. These chromosomes are linear, longer, and more numerous than the circular chromosomes found in bacteria. Eucaryotic cells are **diploid** (have two sets of chromosomes), in comparison with procaryotes, which usually are **haploid** (have one set of chromosomes). However, at some point in their life cycles, eucaryotic cells that sexually reproduce form haploid sex cells called **gametes.** When gametes fuse during mating, the diploid state is reestablished. Although multicellular

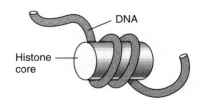

figure 3.35
Association of Histones with DNA
Eucaryotic DNA is complexed with positive-charged proteins called histones.

eucaryotes usually exist in the diploid phase, the haploid growth phase generally predominates in eucaryotic microorganisms.

Located near the nucleus in many eucaryotic cells is a dense area of cytoplasm called the **centrosome.** Within the centrosome are two small (about 0.2 μm in diameter) cylindrical structures, the **centrioles,** which are involved in chromosomal movements during cell division. Each centriole consists of nine groups of triplet microtubules (hollow protein cylinders, each approximately 18 to 25 nm in diameter) that are spaced around the circumference of the centriole.

Two other membrane-enclosed organelles found in eucaryotic cells are the **mitochondrion** (plural, **mitochondria**) and the **chloroplast** (Figure 3.36). Both structures, like the nucleus, have two sets of membranes. The mitochondrion, the site of cellular respiration and ATP production, is considered the energy factory of the cell. Cells with high energy requirements contain many more mitochondria than cells that have more modest energy requirements. The two membranes found in mitochondria are the external membrane, which lacks sterols and is not as rigid as the plasma membrane, and the inner membrane. The inner membrane is folded into convoluted structures called **cristae** that form internal compartments. The **matrix,** a semifluid material that contains many of the enzymes involved in respiration and energy production, is found within these compartments.

Chloroplasts are part of a larger group of membrane-enclosed organelles called **plastids,** which are found only in algae and plants. Plastids are surrounded by double membranes and are of three different types: **leucoplasts** (nonpigmented organelles found in root and underground stem cells, and associated with the synthesis and storage of starch, proteins, and oils), **chromoplasts** (pigmented plastids responsible for the bright colors seen in flowers, fruits, and fall leaves), and **chloroplasts.**

Chloroplasts are the sites of photosynthesis in algae and plants. The disk-shaped organelles have an extensive internal structure, with parallel saclike internal membranes known as thylakoids or lamellae that are stacked neatly in layers called grana (singular, granum). The interior compartment of the chloroplast, the stroma, contains the enzymes involved in the dark reactions of photosynthesis and carbon dioxide fixation (see chloroplast, page 180). Chlorophylls and carotenoids are pigments associated with photosynthesis and the thylakoid membranes. Both chloroplasts and mitochondria contain DNA and RNA, numerous proteins, and 70S ribosomes like those of bacteria. Because of their similarity to bacteria, chloroplasts and mitochondria are believed by some scientists

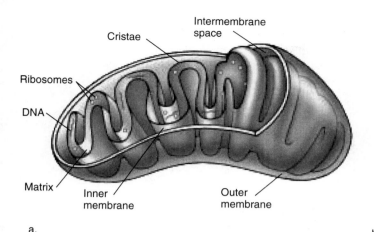
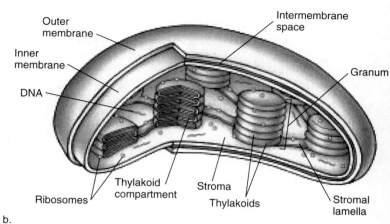

figure 3.36
Structures of the Mitochondrion and the Chloroplast
a. Mitochondrion. b. Chloroplast.

to have been procaryotes that developed into eucaryotic organelles (see endosymbiotic hypothesis, page 206).

Other types of membrane-enclosed organelles are found in some eucaryotic cells. **Microbodies** are spherical organelles, bounded by a single membrane, that are depositories for enzymes involved in cellular metabolism. **Vacuoles** are organelles filled with fluid and found more often in plant cells than animal cells. Plant vacuoles contain a fluid mixture of organic compounds known as the cell sap. These vacuoles occupy most of the volume in mature cells, exert pressure on the cell wall, and maintain the turgidity typical of plant cells. Animal cells often have organelles called **lysosomes,** which store enzymes that are involved in intracellular digestion of macromolecules and particles taken into the cell. The segregation of these enzymes within the lysosomes prevents them from attacking the cell's own macromolecules. Lysosomes fuse with vacuoles containing foreign particles and food materials and release hydrolytic enzymes into the vacuoles for the digestion of these materials. Lysosomes arise from membrane-enclosed structures called the **Golgi complex,** or **Golgi apparatus,** located near the nuclear envelope. The Golgi complex, first described by the Italian cytologist Camillo Golgi (1844–1926) in 1899, consists of flattened sacs called **cisternae.** The complex is involved in secretion of chemical substances from the interior of the cell and through the plasma membrane to the exterior; it also may be responsible for inserting proteins into the plasma membrane.

 **Fungal Structure and Function**
General Eucaryotic Structures: Internal Structures • pp. 6–11

Eucaryotic Cells Use Flagella, Cilia, and Cytoplasmic Streaming for Locomotion

Locomotion is achieved in eucaryotic cells by the use of specialized structures (flagella and cilia) or by cytoplasmic streaming. Eucaryotic flagella are more complex than procaryotic flagella. The eucary-

otic flagellum is organized with nine pairs of microtubules surrounding two separate microtubules in the center of the flagellum (Figure 3.37a). This "nine-plus-two" arrangement is surrounded by an extension of the plasma membrane. The flagellum is connected to the cell surface by a basal body (an extension of the flagellum containing nine triplets of microtubules but no central microtubules). Flagellar movement occurs by a sliding motion of the microtubules in relationship to one another, driven by ATP hydrolysis and resulting in flagellar bending. Cilia are similar in structure to flagella but are more numerous and shorter (Figure 3.37b).

Some eucaryotic cells move across surfaces by a process known as **cytoplasmic streaming.** This type of locomotion is most evident in amoebae, which form **pseudopodia** (extensions of the cell cytoplasm) in the direction of movement. An analogous type of motility is seen in plasmodial slime molds. These organisms are thin streaming protoplasmic masses that creep along surfaces. Composed of the protein actin, microfilaments within the cytoskeleton of eucaryotic cells are associated with cytoplasmic streaming.

Eucaryotes Reproduce Asexually by Fission, Fragmentation, or Spore or Bud Formation, or Sexually by Union of Haploid Gametes

Eucaryotic cells reproduce either by asexual methods similar to those seen in procaryotes (fission, fragmentation, spore or bud formation) or by sexual exchange of genetic material and division. Sexual reproduction occurs through the union of haploid gametes (which are either similar or dissimilar in morphology and composition) to form a diploid zygote. Both the individual haploid gametes and their nuclei fuse during this process. The result is a doubling of the chromosome number (diploidy) in the nucleus of the newly formed zygote. If chromosomal doubling were to occur repeatedly in subsequent generations, the nucleus would eventually be filled with genetic material. This is prevented

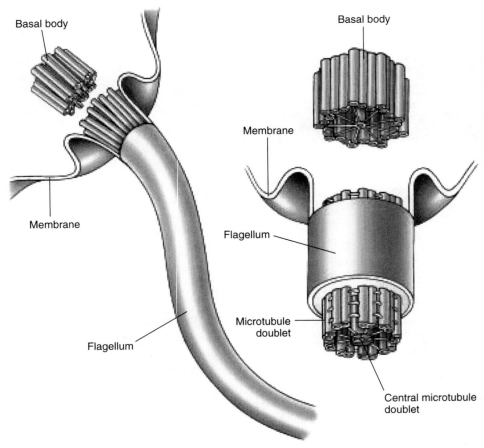

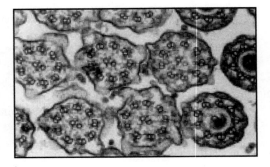

a.

b.

figure 3.37
The Eucaryotic Flagellum and Cilium
a. Diagram of a flagellum, showing its microtubules and underlying basal body. b. Electron micrograph of the cilia of the protozoan *Tetrahymena*, showing its structure in cross section. The distinctive "nine-plus-two" arrangement of the microtubules can be seen (×66,200).

by a halving or reduction of the chromosome number at some stage in the life cycle. This halving of chromosome number, called **meiosis** or reduction division, typically accompanies sexual reproduction. The process of meiosis and its location in the life cycle may vary from organism to organism, but the result is always the same: the formation of haploid cells.

As eucaryotic cells grow, they eventually reach a stage and size at which they divide into daughter cells. Eucaryotic cell division, termed **mitosis,** consists of two distinct steps: **karyokinesis** (nuclear division) and **cytokinesis** (cytoplasmic division). Chro-

mosomes divide and migrate to opposite sides of the cell during karyokinesis. Cytokinesis takes place during the later stages of karyokinesis. The result is the formation of two indistinguishable daughter cells, each identical to the original parent cell. In certain eucaryotes, such as some algae and fungi, cytokinesis does not necessarily follow karyokinesis; a multinucleated (coenocytic) organism is then produced.

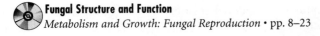

Fungal Structure and Function
Metabolism and Growth: Fungal Reproduction • pp. 8–23

Calcium Dipicolinate and Heat Resistance of Endospores

The heat resistance of bacterial endospores is an important characteristic to the survival of *Bacillus* and *Clostridium* in harsh, unfavorable environments. It currently is believed that large quantities of calcium dipicolinate probably confer heat resistance to endospores. Evidence for this association came from a series of studies performed by Joan F. Powell and R. E. Strange in 1953.

Powell and Strange examined products excreted by *Bacillus subtilis* and *Bacillus megaterium* during spore germination. Cultures of each bacterium were grown and then harvested by centrifugation. It was observed that centrifuged bacterial spores washed three to five times with water were deprived of glucose and did not germinate, even when exposed to heat shock (60°C). However, unwashed or incompletely washed spores apparently retained endogenous (internal) pools of glucose and, when exposed to heat shock, germinated spontaneously. These germinated spores lost their heat resistance because they were not vegetative cells, but remained viable.

Using this principle, Powell and Strange measured decreases in dry weight of *Bacillus* spores during germination and found a loss of 27 to 30 mg per 100 mg cell dry weight. At the same time, the surrounding culture medium increased by approximately an equivalent amount, indicating that material lost from the spore during germination had been excreted to the surrounding medium (Table 3P.1).

The material released by germinating spores was chemically analyzed and found to consist primarily of amino acids, peptides, glucosamine, and a substance having an absorption spectrum in the ultraviolet range, with maxima at 263, 270, and 278 nm (Figure 3P.1). This ultraviolet-absorbing substance was also recovered from resting spores of *Bacillus* that were mechanically disrupted in a tissue disintegrator. The substance occurred as a sparingly soluble calcium salt and upon crystallization was found to contain 36.3% carbon, 2.7% hydrogen, 5.7% nitrogen, and 15.8% calcium. Further chemical analyses revealed this substance to be calcium dipicolinate. Calcium

dipicolinate was found to constitute 50% of the solids excreted by germinating spores of *B. megaterium*, and to make up approximately 15% of the spore dry weight. Powell and Strange were the first to report on the isolation of calcium dipicolinate and its association with endospores.

Sources:

Powell, J.F. 1953. Isolation of dipicolinic acid (pyridine-2:6-dicarboxylic acid) from spores of *Bacillus megaterium*. *Biochemical Journal* 54:210–211.

Powell, J.F., and R.E. Strange. 1953. Biochemical changes occurring during the germination of bacterial endospores. *Biochemical Journal* 54:205–209.

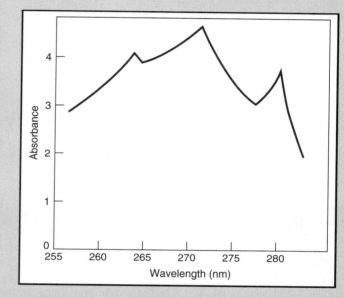

figure 3P.1

Ultraviolet Absorption of Calcium Dipicolinate Recovered from Germinating Spores of *Bacillus subtilis* and *Bacillus megaterium*

table 3P.1

Decrease in Dry Weight of *Bacillus megaterium* Spores During Germination

Medium	Number of Spores	Spore Dry Weight (mg)	Germination (%)	Change in Dry Weight for Complete Germination (mg/100mg)	
				Cells	Surrounding Medium
Nutrient tryptic digest broth	1.08×10^{11}	105	90	−30	+33
Nutrient tryptic digest broth	1.15×10^{11}	108	73	−27	+36
5 mM Glucose, 30 mM phosphate, pH 7.3	1.08×10^{11}	105	69	−29	+33

Summary

1. Macromolecules are the building blocks of the cell and consist of proteins, nucleic acids, carbohydrates, and lipids.

2. The cell envelope is the outer covering of a bacterium, and consists of the plasma membrane, cell wall, and in gram-negative bacteria, an outer membrane.

3. The plasma membrane is a semipermeable barrier that regulates the passage of molecules and ions. The procaryotic plasma membrane is similar in composition to the basic unit membrane structure found in eucaryotes. Membrane lipids of Bacteria have ester linkages between glycerol and the fatty acids, whereas membrane lipids of Archaea have ether linkages between glycerol and isoprene.

4. The cell wall is a rigid layer comprised of peptidoglycan in most Bacteria and of proteins, glycoproteins, and polysaccharides in the Archaea. The cell wall maintains conformation and also enables the cell to survive in hypotonic environments.

5. Gram-negative bacteria have an outer membrane containing lipopolysaccharide molecules. The periplasm, which contains the peptidoglycan, enzymes, and binding proteins, separates the outer membrane from the plasma membrane.

6. Some bacteria have capsules, which protect the cell from phagocytosis, desiccation, and nutrient loss; pili, which are involved in attachment and the transfer of genetic information between bacterial cells; and/or flagella, which are involved in cell motility.

7. Various structures can be found inside the bacterial cell, including inclusion bodies, which are used as storage depots for lipids, polysaccharides, and inorganic compounds; and gas vacuoles, which retain gases and provide buoyancy to the cell.

8. *Bacillus* and *Clostridium* are examples of bacteria that form endospores. Endospores are resistant, dormant cell types that protect the cell from heat, desiccation, and other adverse environmental conditions. The unusual heat resistance of endospores is believed to be associated with high levels of calcium dipicolinate.

9. Eucaryotic cells have membrane-bound organelles such as mitochondria, chloroplasts, and nuclei that are not found in procaryotes. A summary of the principal differences between procaryotes and eucaryotes is shown in Table 3.3.

table	3.3

Summary of Differences Between Procaryotes and Eucaryotes

Characteristic	Procaryote	Eucaryote
Genetic material	Circular DNA molecule in nucleoid; no discrete nucleus; plasmids	Linear DNA arranged in chromosomes within a membrane-enclosed nucleus; chromosomes complexed with histones
Membrane-enclosed organelles	Absent	Present; examples include lysosome, Golgi complex, endoplasmic reticulum, mitochondrion, and chloroplast
Ribosomes	Small size (70S)	Large size (80S), except for small size (70S) in mitochondrion and chloroplast
Vacuoles	Rare	Common
Plasma membrane	Sterols generally lacking	Sterols present
Cell wall	Present in most procaryotes and usually contains peptidoglycan in Bacteria and proteins, glycoproteins, and polysaccharides in Archaea	Present in algae, plants, and fungi; usually contains polysaccharide
Capsule	Present in some procaryotes	Absent
Locomotion	Submicroscopic flagella of simple composition; some move by gliding motility	Microscopic flagella and cilia of complex composition; cytoplasmic streaming; gliding motility
Cell division	Usually by binary fission	By mitosis (usually accompanied by meiosis)

EVOLUTION and BIODIVERSITY

Although there are significant structural differences between procaryotes and eucaryotes, many similarities exist between the two groups of organisms. Both types of organisms have nucleic acids, proteins, carbohydrates, and lipids as the building blocks for their cell structures and constituents. Procaryotes and eucaryotes have closely similar plasma membranes consisting of a basic unit membrane structure. Genetic information is carried on DNA and proteins are synthesized from an mRNA template in association with ribosomes. Differences between these two groups of organisms have slowly evolved over the years and have led to the diversity that exists today between procaryotes and eucaryotes. Even with this divergence, there remains evidence of the common ancestry of these organisms. Eucaryotic mitochondria and chloroplasts contain DNA and RNA, numerous proteins, and 70S ribosomes like those of procaryotes. Both organelles function somewhat independently of the cell in the generation of ATP by processes (aerobic respiration and photosynthesis) found in procaryotes. Mitochondria are similar to procaryotes in size. Although procaryotes do not have membrane-bound organelles like those found in eucaryotic cells, photosynthetic bacteria have invaginations of the plasma membrane that function in photosynthesis, and some bacteria have extensive specialized internal membranes that are associated with ammonia, nitrite, and methane oxidation. The plasma membrane of the cell wall-less *Mycoplasma* is strengthened by sterol, a lipid that is found in the membranes of all eucaryotes. It is evident that over time procaryotes and eucaryotes have evolved distinctive structures and characteristics, but yet retain many similar properties that suggest a common thread that is woven through all living organisms.

Questions

Short Answer

1. Which microorganisms are procaryotic cells? Which microorganisms are eucaryotic cells?

2. Why are viruses considered to be neither eucaryotic nor procaryotic?

3. What is the major difference between eucaryotic and procaryotic cells?

4. Identify four major groups of macromolecules which are components of all cells and identify their building blocks.

5. Other than the four groups referred to in question 4, what compounds are major constituents of cells?

6. Identify the structural components found in all procaryotic cells. What structures are not found in procaryotes?

7. Identify at least six organelles.

8. Explain some of the basic differences between Archaea and Bacteria.

9. How do the membranes of the Bacteria, Archaea, and eucaryotes differ?

10. How do procaryotic cell walls differ from those of eucaryotic cells?

11. How do the cell walls of gram-positive and gram-negative bacteria differ?

12. How can you distinguish gram-positive from gram-negative bacteria?

13. What is a capsule? What is (are) its function(s)?

14. What is a pilus? What is its function?

15. Describe the bacterial flagellum. How does it differ in structure from eucaryotic flagella or cilia?

16. What is a nucleoid? How does it differ from a nucleus?

17. What is a plasmid? How does it differ from a chromosome?

18. What is a ribosome? How do procaryotic ribosomes differ from eucaryotic ribosomes?

Multiple Choice

1. The group of microorganisms classified as Archaea:
   a. are among the most primitive organisms.
   b. can inhabit extreme environments.
   c. do not have a membrane-enclosed nucleus.
   d. all of the above.

2. Which of the following statements about proteins is always true?
   a. All proteins are enzymes.
   b. All proteins have a quaternary structure.
   c. All proteins have a primary structure.
   d. All of the above statements are true.

3. The outer membrane is present in:
   a. gram-positive cells.
   b. gram-negative cells.
   c. eucaryotic cells.
   d. all of the above.

4. The arrangement of flagella on the cell surface can sometimes help in the identification of an organism. For example, *E. coli* has flagella throughout the cell surface that is referred to as:
   a. lophotrichous flagellation.
   b. monotrichous flagellation.
   c. peritrichous flagellation.
   d. none of the above.

5. The movement of an organism toward or away from a chemical substance in its environment is called:
   a. tracking.
   b. chemotaxis.
   c. tumbling.
   d. none of the above.

Critical Thinking

1. Compare and contrast procaryotic and eucaryotic cells.

2. Compare and contrast gram-positive and gram-negative cells.

3. Compare and contrast the phospholipid membrane and the LPS outer membrane.

4. Explain how to fight bacterial infections targeting the bacterial cell wall and membrane structures.

5. Present evidence of procaryotic and organelle structures that supports the endosymbiont hypothesis of eucaryotic evolution.

Supplementary Readings

Alberts, B., D. Bray, J. Lewis, M. Raff, K. Roberts, and J.D. Watson. 1994. *Molecular biology of the cell*, 3d ed., New York: Garland Publishing, Inc. (An in-depth textbook on cell structure and function.)

Armitage, J.P., and J.M. Lackie, eds. 1990. *Biology of the chemotactic response*. London, England: Cambridge University Press. (A series of papers on the structure of bacterial flagellum and the mechanisms involved in chemotaxis.)

Berg, H.C. 1975. How bacteria swim. *Scientific American* 234:40–47. (A discussion of the role of flagella in bacterial motility.)

Beveridge, T.J., and L.L. Graham. 1991. Surface layers of bacteria. *Microbiological Reviews* 55:684–705. (A review of the surface layers of bacteria, as seen by electron microscopy.)

Errington, J. 1993. *Bacillus subtilis* sporulation: regulation of gene expression and control of morphogenesis. *Microbiological Reviews* 57:1–33. (A review of the genetics of sporogenesis in *B. subtilis*.)

Hoch, J.A., and P. Setlow. 1985. *Molecular biology of microbial differentiation*. Washington, DC: American Society for Microbiology. (Symposium presentations on molecular biology of sporulation in *Bacillus subtilis* and differentiation in other procaryotes.)

Lake, J. 1981. The ribosome. *Scientific American* 245:84–97. (A discussion of the structure and function of the ribosome.)

Rogers, H.J. 1978. Biogenesis of the wall in bacterial morphogenesis. *Advances in Microbial Physiology* 19:1–62. (A review of bacterial cell wall synthesis.)

Rogers, H.J., H.R. Perkins, and J.B. Ward. 1981. *Microbial cell walls and membranes*. New York: Chapman & Hall/Mehuen. (A review of cell wall and membrane structure and function.)

Rose, A.H. 1976. *Chemical microbiology: An introduction to microbial physiology*. New York: Plenum Publishing Corporation. (A detailed discussion of bacterial structure and metabolism.)

Salton, M.R.J., and P. Owen. 1976. Bacterial membrane structure. *Annual Review of Microbiology* 30:451–482. (A review of membrane structure in bacteria.)

Walsby, A.E. 1994. Gas vesicles. *Microbiological Reviews* 58:94–144. (A review of the structure and function of gas vesicles.)

Young, M., and J. Mandelstam. 1979. Early events during bacterial endospore formation. *Advances in Microbial Physiology* 20:103–162. (A discussion of the biochemical events that occur during endospore formation in bacteria.)

chapter five

GROWTH AND CONTROL OF GROWTH

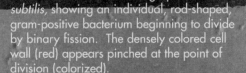

Transmission electron micrograph of *Bacillus subtilis*, showing an individual, rod-shaped, gram-positive bacterium beginning to divide by binary fission. The densely colored cell wall (red) appears pinched at the point of division (colorized).

Microbes in Motion — **PREVIEW LINK**

This chapter covers the key topics of growth curves and control of microbial growth. The following sections in the *Microbes in Motion* CD-ROM may be useful as a preview to your reading or as a supplemental study aid:

Microbial Metabolism and Growth: Growth (Growth Curves), 26–35. *Control—Physical and Chemical:* Physical Control, 1–22; Chemical Control, 1–38. *Antimicrobial Action:* Cell Wall Inhibitors, 1–19; Protein Synthesis Inhibitors, 1–9; Agents Affecting Nucleic Acid, 1–8; Agents Affecting Enzymes, 1–9; Antibiotic Susceptibility Testing (Terminology), 7–8, (Disk Diffusion), 11–16. *Antimicrobial Resistance:* Acquisition and Expression of Resistance Genes, 1–9.

onsider a few cubic centimeters of soil on your campus lawn. Within this small amount of soil is a diverse and extensive population of microorganisms, growing on the decaying organic matter, minerals, and other chemicals in the ground.

Bacterial growth occurs all around us—in food, water, and soil, and in plants, animals, and humans. Because bacteria are so small, we seldom consider the implications of the rapid growth of many of them. It may easily be calculated that a single bacterium growing under optimal conditions for 27 hours would produce a population that would cover the world in a layer of bacteria 6 feet high! This is particularly amazing because a single bacterium is only a few micrometers long.

Fortunately, optimal growth conditions do not exist indefinitely, and growth and reproduction of living organisms cannot continue long at maximum rates. Organisms grow and die, and growth is self-limited by availability of nutrients and the buildup of toxic, metabolic end products. Nonetheless, the growth rates of bacteria and similar types of microorganisms are impressive. This chapter will discuss bacterial growth and methods to measure it.

Bacterial Growth

Growth is defined as the orderly increase in all major constituents of an organism. Growth involves the synthesis of cellular structures, nucleic acids, proteins, and other cell components from nutrients obtained outside the cell. All living organisms must take up nutrients and be able to excrete waste products. This exchange of materials occurs via the outer surface of the organism. Smaller organisms tend to have larger ratios of surface to internal volume than do larger organisms. This large surface-to-volume ratio allows rapid entry of nutrients and permits more rapid metabolic and growth rates.

The Typical Bacterium Reproduces by Binary Fission

Bacteria generally reproduce by a process known as **binary fission.** In binary fission, a single cell grows progressively larger until at some stage in growth it divides into two separate and equal daughter cells. The time required for the cell to divide (or for a population of organisms to double in number) is referred to as the **generation time** or the **doubling time.**

The generation time depends on the bacterial species and its growth conditions (Table 5.1). Under specified growth conditions, the generation time is constant and characteristic for a particular bacterium.

Microbial Metabolism and Growth
Growth: Growth Curves • p. 27

Binary fission in bacteria differs from mitosis in higher organisms; in binary fission there is continuous DNA synthesis during the replication cycle of bacteria. Replication of the entire bacterial chromosome takes approximately 40 minutes at 37°C in *Escherichia coli* cells. The doubling time for *E. coli* under ideal growth conditions, however, is much shorter (about 20 minutes or less) than the DNA replication time. In order to maintain con-

table 5.1

Generation Times of Selected Bacteria

Bacterium	Growth Medium	Temperature (°C)	Generation Time (min)
Bacillus subtilis	Complex medium	36	35
Clostridium botulinum	Glucose broth	37	35
Escherichia coli	Broth	37	17
Lactobacillus acidophilus	Milk	37	66
Mycobacterium tuberculosis	Synthetic medium	37	792
Pseudomonas aeruginosa	Glucose broth	37	31
Pseudomonas aeruginosa	Lactose broth	37	34
Pseudomonas aeruginosa	Tryptic meat broth	35	32
Salmonella typhimurium	Trypticase soy broth	37	24
Shigella dysenteriae	Milk	37	23
Staphylococcus aureus	Glucose broth	37	32
Streptococcus lactis	Lactose broth	30	48
Streptococcus lactis	Glucose milk	37	26
Streptococcus lactis	Peptone milk	37	37
Streptococcus pneumoniae	Glucose broth	37	30
Xanthomonas campestris	Glucose broth	25	74

From Philip L. Altman and David S. Dittmer, *Biology Data Book*, Volume 1. Copyright © 1972 Federation of American Societies for Experimental Biology. Reprinted by permisiion.

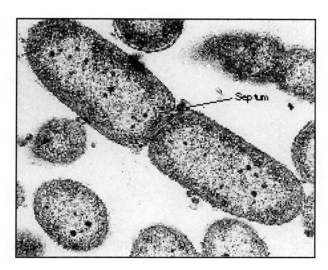

figure 5.1

Electron Micrograph of Dividing *Pseudomonas aeruginosa*, a Gram-Negative Bacterium

Two rod-shaped cells are formed from binary fission of the parent cell. A septum is shown at the point of cell division between the two cells (×34,200).

 **Microbial Metabolism and Growth**
Growth: Growth Curves • p. 26

tinuity between cell division and DNA replication, the bacterial cell initiates a new round of DNA replication approximately every 20 minutes. By doing this, the bacterium has completed copies of its chromosome ready for each daughter cell at the time of division.

Not all aspects of bacterial DNA replication are known. During replication, DNA appears to migrate and attach to a portion of the plasma membrane. As DNA replicates in this area of the membrane, there is concomitant synthesis of new membrane material. The formation and partition of new membrane probably aids in separation of the DNA to opposite ends of the dividing cell.

After the DNA replication and separation, the cell forms a transverse septum of membranous material (Figure 5.1). New cell wall is synthesized, and two separate and equal daughter cells form. Incomplete cleavage of the septum sometimes can result in formation of such cellular arrangements as chains, clusters, or filaments. Some bacterial cells have multiple copies of DNA; such a condition is encouraged, particularly if the cells are grown in a nutritionally rich environment in which cell division lags behind DNA synthesis.

Bacterial Populations Increase in Cell Mass and Numbers over Time

Growth is typically considered as an increase in cell mass, but it may also be defined as an increase in cell numbers within a population. Both growth parameters are interrelated, since increases in cell mass eventually result in cell division and an increase in cell numbers. Under optimal conditions, the growth of bacteria

is **balanced**— there is an orderly increase in the DNA, RNA, and protein of the cell population. Growth of bacteria and other microorganisms is usually expressed as population growth because of the small size of microbes. This expression is valid since bacterial populations consist of millions of cells that are identical products of binary fission.

Quantitative Relationships of Population Growth Can Be Expressed Mathematically

Bacterial reproduction by binary fission results in a doubling of the population for each generation. Consequently, since the population is in balanced growth, there is also a doubling of the DNA, RNA, and protein of the cell population. The generation time of a bacterial population can be expressed mathematically as follows:

$$g = t - t_0/(\log_2 N - \log_2 N_0)$$

where g is the generation time, and N and N_0 represent cell concentrations at times t and t_0, respectively.

In microbiology, populations are usually plotted on graph paper as the logarithm to the base 10. Conversion of the equation to logarithms to the base 10 results in the following equation:

$$g = 0.301 (t - t_0)/(\log_{10} N - \log_{10} N_0)$$

Using this equation, the generation time of a culture can be determined if the cell concentration of the culture is known at two different incubation times. For example, the generation time of a culture containing 10^3 cells/ml at time t_0 and 10^7 cells/ml 7 hours later would be calculated as follows:

$$g = 0.301 (t - t_0)/(\log_{10} N - \log_{10} N_0)$$

$$g = 0.301 (7 - 0)/(\log_{10} 10^7 - \log_{10} 10^3)$$

$$g = 0.301 (7)/(7 - 3)$$

$$g = 2.107/(7 - 3)$$

$$g = 2.107/4$$

$$g = 0.527 \text{ hour, or } 31.6 \text{ minutes}$$

Because bacteria grow exponentially (at least for a portion of their growth), bacterial growth curves are plotted on a semilogarithmic scale (logarithm of number or mass of bacteria versus time) instead of an arithmetic (linear) scale (Figure 5.2). A semilogarithmic graph provides a linear relationship of the logarithm of cell concentration against time and can be used directly to determine population doubling time from the slope of the line.

Measurement of Growth

A zoologist can easily enumerate elephants in a herd and record increases in their numbers, although such monitoring may take decades. An ornithologist monitors changes in bird populations through field studies. Even ant behavior and development can be observed in the field or in the laboratory under controlled conditions. But how does a bacteriologist follow growth of billions of microorganisms that cannot be seen without the aid of a microscope? Are there limitations to the study of bacterial population growth?

Bacterial populations are easy to monitor. Bacteria grow rapidly and may produce several generations of identical progeny within a few hours. Their propagation does not require acres of pasture. A bacterial population with 10 billion members can easily be grown in a few milliliters of broth in a small Erlenmeyer flask.

Because bacteria grow in so little space in such a short time, it is simple to alter growth parameters to determine the effects on growth rate and cellular metabolism. Temperature, atmospheric conditions, rate of aeration, and composition of the medium can be changed to customize an experiment.

Bacterial growth can be measured in a number of different ways. Each type of measurement has advantages and disadvantages in terms of ease, accuracy, and sensitivity. The primary methods used to monitor bacterial growth involve following changes in cell numbers, cell mass, or cell activity.

Bacterial Growth Can Be Followed by Increases in Cell Numbers

The size of a bacterial population can be determined by counting the individual cells in a measured volume. These cells can be counted directly by using a microscope or indirectly by counting colonies on a plate of agar.

The Total Number of Cells in a Population Can Be Counted Using a Microscope

The most direct way to measure population growth is to count the number of cells in a suspension under a microscope (**direct microscopic count**). Since the field of vision in a slide preparation is limited, particularly at high magnifications, only a small volume of cell suspension can be enumerated by microscopy at any one time. Counting by microscopy is performed with special chambers (hemocytometer chambers or Petroff-Hausser counting chambers) that are divided into squares of known areas. The Petroff-Hausser counting chamber, which is designed specifically for bacterial cell enumeration, consists of a whole grid containing 25 large squares for a total area of 1 mm^2 and a total volume of 0.02 mm^3 (Figure 5.3). A small volume of cell suspension is added to the counting chamber. A special coverslip is then placed over the chamber so that each square is filled with suspension to a depth of 0.02 mm, and thus has a constant volume. By counting the number of cells in designated squares, one can extrapolate and estimate the total cell count in the original cell suspension.

Microbial Metabolism and Growth
Growth: Growth Curves • p. 30

Although the direct microscopic count method is rapid and performed with just a counting chamber and a light microscope, the technique is not very sensitive. A dense culture (10^6 or more per ml of suspension) is required to make the count statistically

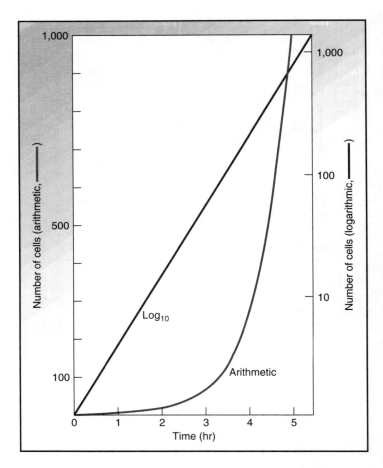

figure 5.2
Bacterial Growth Plotted on Arithmetic and Semilogarithmic Scales

accurate. Furthermore, the count obtained by microscopic observation includes both viable cells and nonviable cells; visual inspection cannot differentiate between living and dead cells.

The Number of Viable Cells in a Population Can Be Determined by Growing the Cells on Plates of Agar Media

Direct microscopic counts provide the bacteriologist with the total number of cells (viable and nonviable) in a population. In most instances, however, it is desirable to know the number of viable bacteria in a suspension. This is particularly true if one is interested in the infectious capability of live organisms. In these cases, the **viable count** is an alternative to a microscopic cell count (Figure 5.4).

The viable count technique involves growth of bacteria from a suspension on plates of agar media. When a single bacterium grows and divides on an agar medium, it forms a colony of cells, which is usually easily seen with the naked eye. Colonies that appear on the medium are enumerated to determine the original number of cells in the suspension. Problems are often encountered with bacteria that grow in chains or filaments, such as many of the bacilli. When these cells fail to separate on plating, the formation of fewer colonies than the actual number of cells plated results. Because of this effect,

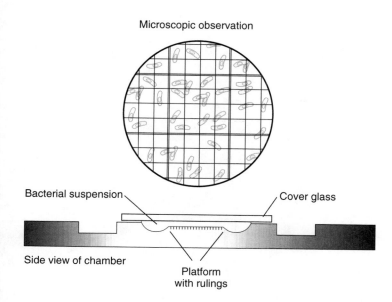

figure 5.3

Direct Microscopic Count with the Petroff-Hausser Counting Chamber

The Petroff-Hausser counting chamber consists of 400 small squares (0.0025 mm² each) and 25 large squares (0.04 mm² each). The number of cells is counted in several large squares and averaged. In the example given, 12 cells are counted in the large square. If this count is consistent with the counts obtained from several other large squares, then the number of cells per milliliter in the original cell suspension is determined in the following manner:

12 cells × 25 large squares (0.04 mm² each) = 300 cells/mm²

300 cells/mm² × 50/mm (each square has a depth of 0.02 mm; 0.02 × 50 = 1 mm) = 1.5×10^4 cells/mm³

1.5×10^4 cells/mm³ × 1,000 (1,000 mm³ = 1 cm³) = 1.5×10^7 cells/cm³, or 1.5×10^7 cells/ml

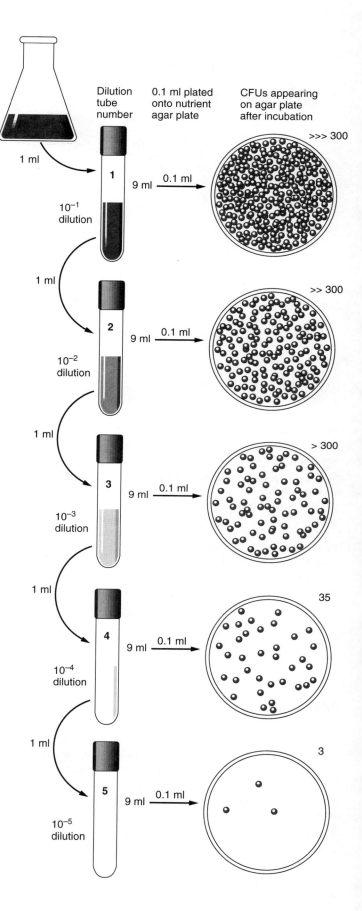

figure 5.4

Dilution of Bacteria for a Viable Count

In the example shown, bacteria from a cell suspension are diluted in 9-ml water blanks, and 0.1 ml of each dilution is plated onto a nutrient agar plate. After incubation, only the agar plate prepared from dilution tube 4 has between 30 and 300 colonies. The 35 colonies on the agar plate represent the number of bacteria in 0.1 ml from this dilution tube. Thus tube 4 contains 350 colony-forming units (CFU)/ml (35 CFU/0.1 ml × 10 = 350 CFU/ml). Tube 3 contains ten times this quantity, (3,500 CFU/ml), tube 2 contains 35,000 CFU/ml, and tube 1 contains 350,000 CFU/ml (3.5×10^5 CFU/ml). Since tube 1 has 10 ml and contains 1 ml of the original suspension, the original suspension has 3.5×10^6 CFU/ml.

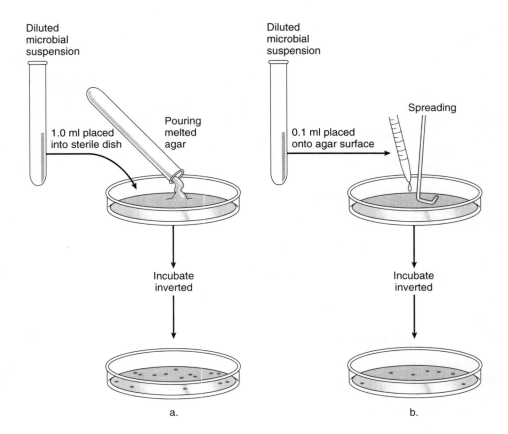

Spreading

Diluted microbial suspension

1.0 ml placed into sterile dish

Pouring melted agar

Diluted microbial suspension

0.1 ml placed onto agar surface

Incubate inverted

Incubate inverted

a.

b.

figure 5.5
Pour and Spread Plate Techniques for Enumerating Microorganisms

a. In the pour plate technique, a known volume of a diluted microbial suspension is placed into a sterile dish and melted agar is poured into the dish. After incubation, the number of colonies in the agar is counted, and the concentration of microorganisms in the original suspension is calculated. b. In the spread plate technique, a known volume of diluted microbial suspension is placed onto a nutrient agar medium. The suspension is spread evenly on the agar surface with a bent glass rod that has been sterilized by dipping in alcohol and flaming. The agar medium is incubated, and the number of colonies that develop on the agar is counted to determine the concentration of microorganisms in the original suspension.

 **Microbial Metabolism and Growth**
Growth: Growth Curves • p. 31

viable count results are usually expressed as colony-forming units (cfu) per milliliter of suspension rather than as cells per milliliter.

Since the number of bacteria in a heavy suspension easily approaches 10^9 cells/ml, dilution of the original cell suspension prior to placing the bacteria on agar media is often necessary to reduce sufficiently the number of cells per milliliter in order that growth on the plate will not be too sparse or too crowded. Ideally, plated dilutions of the culture result in 30 to 300 colonies on an agar plate. The growth of fewer than 30 colonies on a plate results in a statistically invalid count, and more than 300 colonies on a plate can cause interference among cells and colonies during growth. The dilution of bacteria from a suspension is performed aseptically, using diluents of water, saline, or buffered saline (dilution blanks). Buffered saline is sometimes required as a diluent because some bacteria (for example, *Neisseria gonorrhoeae*) lyse in the absence of a buffered solution. By counting the number of colonies appearing on the agar plate after a period of incubation, the researcher can extrapolate and determine the number of living cells in the original suspension.

There are two versions of the viable count: the **spread plate** and the **pour plate** (Figure 5.5). A spread plate is prepared by spreading a small volume of diluted cell suspension onto the surface of an agar plate with a glass rod bent into the shape of an L. The plate is then inverted (to prevent condensation on the agar surface, which would result in confluent growth) and incubated, after which colonies are counted. A pour plate is prepared by mixing diluted bacteria into a sterile Petri dish. Melted agar (at a tem-

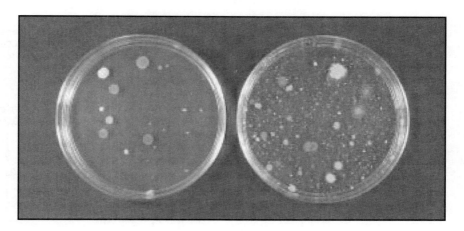

figure 5.6
Examples of Pour Plates, Showing Distinct Colony Morphologies

perature of 45°C to 50°C) is added and the mixture is allowed to solidify at room temperature. The plate is inverted and incubated for 24 to 48 hours; then colonies are counted.

There are advantages and disadvantages to each of these techniques for viable counts. Pour plates can be used to count larger volumes of bacteria (1 milliliter or more), particularly those in viscous samples such as food suspensions or milk. However, some microorganisms (for example, psychrophiles and many mesophiles) are killed at the temperature of melted agar. The pour plate is also more time-consuming than the spread plate, since tubes of melted agar must be prepared and maintained at a constant temperature of 45°C to 50°C, usually in a water bath, before being poured into Petri dishes. Spread plates have the disadvantage that bacteria that are unable to tolerate large amounts of oxygen grow poorly on their surfaces. Although spread plates could be incubated anaerobically, this is not practical.

The viable count technique is accurate because each colony theoretically is derived from one viable cell in the suspension. Nonviable cells do not form colonies on the agar medium and are therefore not included in the count. The technique is more sensitive than direct microscopic counts, since suspensions containing small quantities of bacteria can be counted. Furthermore, because each colony on the agar plate is derived from a single cell, mixed populations of bacteria in the original suspension are often discernible through differences in colony morphology and pigmentation (Figure 5.6). Single isolated colonies from these plates can also be used to obtain a pure culture of a bacterium.

 **Microbial Metabolism and Growth**
Growth: Growth Curves • pp. 29, 31

Are there any disadvantages to the viable count procedure? The technique is more time-consuming than direct microscopic counts. Agar plates and dilution blanks must be prepared prior to examining a suspension for bacteria. Since bacteria growth is a necessary prerequisite for colony formation, the viable count enumerates only those microorganisms capable of reproduction in the growth medium and under the environmental incubation conditions. Some bacteria such as *Mycobacterium* grow slowly on agar

media, even under optimal conditions. Other bacteria such as *Treponema* and *Chlamydia* cannot be propagated on artificial media. Despite these limitations, the viable count remains as one of the most important techniques for the enumeration of bacteria.

The Number of Viable Cells in a Population Can Be Determined by Filtration

The viable count technique is not feasible for the enumeration of bacteria in samples that contain very low concentrations of cells (for example, water or air samples). In these situations, bacteria are concentrated by filtration onto a gridded nitrocellulose filter (Figure 5.7). The filter, with minute pores (0.22 or 0.45 μm in diameter), traps the bacteria and is then placed onto agar in a Petri dish and incubated. Colonies appearing on the filter are counted (see filtration of water samples, page 591).

The Most Probable Number Method Can Be Used to Estimate the Number of Viable Cells in a Population

Some microorganisms do not grow well on solid media or are more easily identified by growth in liquid media. The **most probable number (MPN)** method for liquid media provides an alternative to the viable count for enumeration of microbes (Figure 5.8). The MPN technique is based on the statistical distribution of organisms in a suspension. When samples of fixed volume are taken from a cell suspension, some may have more cells than others. Repeated samples from the suspension, however, will yield an average number of organisms, termed the *most probable number*.

For example, consider a 100-ml suspension with a total of 100 cells. Ten 10-ml aliquots from such a suspension will yield an average of ten organisms per sample (some aliquots will contain more organisms and others will have fewer). If each of these 10-ml aliquots is inoculated into broth, all of the broth tubes would be expected to show growth after incubation. In a similar manner, each 1-ml sample from the same suspension is expected to average one organism per sample. Many of these samples will contain one organism or more and will yield growth when inoculated into broth.

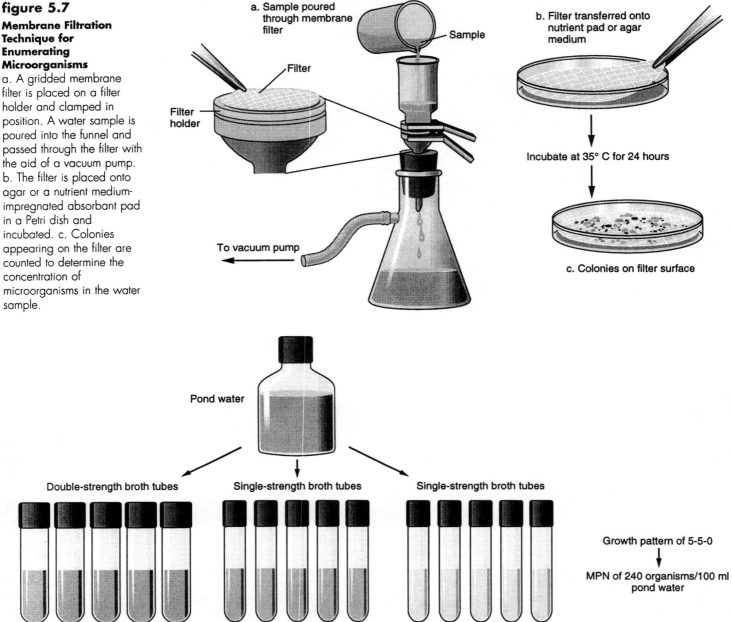

figure 5.7
Membrane Filtration Technique for Enumerating Microorganisms
a. A gridded membrane filter is placed on a filter holder and clamped in position. A water sample is poured into the funnel and passed through the filter with the aid of a vacuum pump. b. The filter is placed onto agar or a nutrient medium-impregnated absorbant pad in a Petri dish and incubated. c. Colonies appearing on the filter are counted to determine the concentration of microorganisms in the water sample.

a. Sample poured through membrane filter

Sample

Filter

Filter holder

To vacuum pump

b. Filter transferred onto nutrient pad or agar medium

Incubate at 35° C for 24 hours

c. Colonies on filter surface

Pond water

Double-strength broth tubes

Single-strength broth tubes

Single-strength broth tubes

Growth pattern of 5-5-0

MPN of 240 organisms/100 ml pond water

10 ml samples

1 ml samples

0.1 ml samples

figure 5.8
Most Probable Number Technique for Estimating Numbers of Microorganisms

A sample of pond water is examined for bacterial density by the most probable number (MPN) technique. Five tubes of double-strength broth (10 ml per tube) are inoculated with 10-ml samples of the water. Five tubes of single-strength broth (10 ml per tube) are inoculated with 1-ml samples of the water, and five more tubes of single-strength broth (10 ml per tube) are inoculated with 0.1-ml samples. The broth tubes are incubated and examined for growth. The growth pattern is compared with a standard MPN table, and the "most probable number" of bacteria in the original pond water sample is determined. As an example, if the pattern growth were 5-5-0 (all of the broth tubes inoculated with 10 ml and 1 ml of pond water were turbid and indicated growth, and none of the broth tubes inoculated with 0.1 ml

of the pond water were turbid), then the MPN for the sample would be 240 organisms/100 ml pond water.

Other volumes of sample can be used for the MPN determination. For example, if the pond water were believed to contain very few bacteria, samples of 100, 10, and 1 ml would be used for inoculation of broth tubes or bottles. In this case, the MPN table would be used to estimate cell numbers in the original pond water, but all MPN index values would be multiplied by a factor of 0.1 (to compensate for the difference in sample volumes).

The table shown on page 113 is based on the inoculation of five tubes of broth with each dilution of sample, but other MPN tables are available for three-tube series of inoculations.

Five-Tube MPN Table

a	b	c	MPN Index per 100 ml	a	b	c	MPN Index per 100 ml
0	0	0	<2	4	2	1	26
0	0	1	2	4	3	0	27
0	1	0	2	4	3	1	33
0	2	0	4	4	4	0	34
1	0	0	2	5	0	0	23
1	0	1	4	5	0	1	30
1	1	0	4	5	0	2	40
1	1	1	6	5	1	0	30
1	2	0	6	5	1	1	50
				5	1	2	60
2	0	0	4				
2	0	1	7	5	2	0	50
2	1	0	7	5	2	1	70
2	1	1	9	5	2	2	90
2	2	0	9	5	3	0	80
2	3	0	12	5	3	1	110
				5	3	2	140
3	0	0	8				
3	0	1	11	5	3	3	170
3	1	0	11	5	4	0	130
3	1	1	14	5	4	1	170
3	2	0	14	5	4	2	220
3	2	1	17	5	4	3	280
				5	4	4	350
4	0	0	13	5	5	0	240
4	0	1	17	5	5	1	300
4	1	0	17	5	5	2	500
4	1	1	21	5	5	3	900
4	1	2	26	5	5	4	1,600
4	2	0	22	5	5	5	≥1,600

Note: a = Number of broth tubes showing growth after inoculation with 10-ml samples.

b = Number of broth tubes showing growth after inoculation with 1-ml samples.

c = Number of broth tubes showing growth after inoculation with 0.1-ml samples.

From *Standard Methods for the Examination of Water and Wastewater,* 19th edition. Copyright 1995 by the American Public Health Association, the American Water Works Association, and the Water Environment Federation. Reprinted with permission.

figure 5.8 (continued)
Most Probable Number Technique for Estimating Numbers of Microorganisms

However, a few samples will have no organisms and, when inoculated into broth, will yield no growth. Now if several 0.1-ml samples are removed from the original 100-ml suspension, there will be an average of one organism per every ten samples (the majority of the samples will contain no organisms and will result in no growth when inoculated into broth). On the basis of this principle, the number of organisms in a cell suspension can be estimated by the pattern of growth in broth culture of several different dilutions of the sample.

The MPN technique, based on successive dilutions of the original cell suspension until there are no bacteria in the final dilution used to inoculate into broth, is not as accurate as the viable count method. It is used most often to estimate the number of coliform bacteria in water samples (see processing of water samples, page 590). Coliform bacteria are gram-negative aerobic or facultatively anaerobic non-spore-forming rods that ferment lactose with gas production within 48 hours at 35°C. The technique allows not only bacterial enumeration, but also presumptive identification of the bacteria by their growth in liquid media. Only certain types of bacteria will grow in the media used for the MPN technique, which depends on the biochemical activities of the bacteria. In addition, the MPN technique is used in the enumeration of algae, which do not form distinct colonies on solid media.

Turbidimetric Measurements Detect Bacteria in a Solution by Light Scattering

Although measurements of bacterial numbers in populations provide useful information, these measurements are often time-consuming. Turbidimetric measurements are based on the principle that particles such as bacteria in a solution scatter light when a beam of light is transmitted through the solution. The number of bacteria in the solution is directly proportional to the amount of light scattered (and inversely proportional to the amount of unscattered light transmitted through the solution).

Turbidity is measured by absorbance—or, as it is often called, optical density (OD)—using a spectrophotometer or photometer (Figure 5.9). A spectrophotometer measures the amount of light absorbed by a specimen. Absorbance (A) is the logarithm of the ratio of the light intensity striking the suspension (I_0) to that passing through the specimen (I):

$$A = \log(I_0 / I)$$

where absorbance is directly proportional to the concentration of the suspension.

Measurements of turbidity are rapid and easy to perform, and provide an estimate of cell numbers and cell mass. If several similar aliquots are removed from a culture at the same time, then turbidimetric measurements, total viable cell counts, and cell mass can be determined simultaneously. By plotting the values obtained for these growth parameters on a semilogarithmic graph, a standard curve can be generated. This standard curve, which remains the same under identical conditions of growth, can be used to derive cell counts or cell mass indirectly from turbidimetric data (Figure 5.10).

There are limitations to turbidity measurements. Particles other than cells in the suspension can scatter or absorb light and

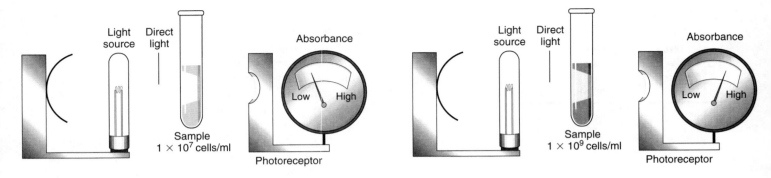

figure 5.9
Turbidity Measurements with a Spectrophotometer
The turbidity of a cell suspension is measured by light transmission through it. Light transmission is detected by a photoreceptor and is read on a meter as absorbance.

may therefore mask bacterial turbidity. Turbidimetric measurements do not differentiate between viable cells and nonviable cells. A large number (greater than 10^6 cells/ml) of bacteria must be present in the sample to provide enough turbidity for measurement. When interpreted with a standard curve, however, turbidimetric measurements provide a rapid and simple method to estimate bacterial population densities.

Microbial Metabolism and Growth
Growth: Growth Curves • p. 32

Cell Mass Can Be Determined by Weighing Cells

Cell mass can be measured directly by determining the dry weight of a cell suspension. Moisture content varies in any given cell, and dry weight (the weight of cells minus any moisture) is preferred over wet weight in measurements of cell mass. Dry weight is determined with a known volume of cell suspension that is washed to free the cells of extraneous materials (for example, media components), dried in an oven, and then weighed. If the number of cells in the original volume is known (by total cell count), the average mass of an individual cell can be calculated.

Cell Growth Can Be Measured by Changes in Cell Activity

Sophisticated methods have been developed in recent years to measure bacterial growth through changes in cell activity. All living cells must synthesize macromolecules (DNA, RNA, and proteins) during growth. Increases in amounts of these molecules as a function of growth can be monitored. Changes in nucleic acid and protein quantities are determined by measuring the actual amounts of these macromolecules through chemical analyses. Alternatively, the incorporation of radiolabeled precursors into newly formed nucleic acids or proteins can be used to follow cellular growth (Figure 5.11).

Most bacteria take up oxygen and release carbon dioxide during growth. Changes in the levels of these gases can be measured with an oxygen meter and electrode to measure cellular growth (Figure 5.12). However, these measurements are subject to changes in environmental barometric pressures and furthermore cannot be performed with anaerobic organisms, which do not require oxygen for growth.

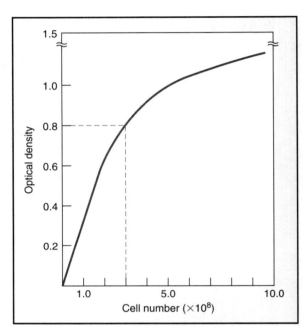

figure 5.10
Derivation of Cell Count from Turbidity Measurements
Optical density readings can be converted to cell numbers by using a standard curve in which optical density units are plotted against the viable cell count. In the example shown, an optical density reading of 0.8 corresponds to a cell count of 3×10^8.

Which of these many different procedures is the procedure of choice to measure bacterial population growth? Each method has advantages and disadvantages (Table 5.2). Measurements of environmental samples normally involve viable cells (viable counts, membrane filter counts, and MPN), since the primary interest is in the number of viable bacteria present in the environment. In many industrial applications, where optimal product development is of primary concern, cell mass or synthesis of certain products is used to monitor growth. Laboratory research experiments often use macromolecular synthesis as a measurement of growth, particularly when there is interest in the effects of chemical or inhibitory agents on growth and metabolism.

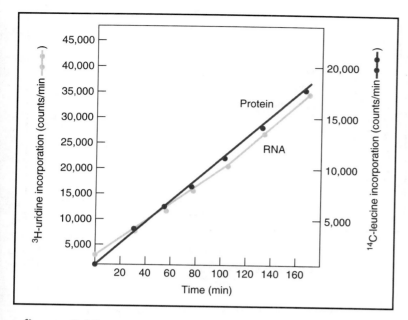

figure 5.11

RNA and Protein Synthesis During Microbial Growth
The growth of microorganisms can be measured by RNA synthesis (determined by the incorporation of radiolabeled uridine into newly synthesized RNA) or by protein synthesis (determined by the incorporation of a radiolabeled amino acid, such as leucine, into newly synthesized protein). As growth occurs, increased amounts of radioactive uridine and leucine appear in the newly synthesized RNA and protein.

Growth Curve

Bacterial population growth occurs in a series of distinct steps referred to as a **population growth curve.** A bacterial population growth curve is used to characterize changes in a cell population during growth. There are four distinct phases in a closed system, or **batch culture:** lag phase, exponential (sometimes called logarithmic) phase, stationary phase, and death (or decline) phase (Figure 5.13). The growth curve is plotted with cell mass, numbers, or content against time. Under identical conditions of incubation, media, and inoculum, a specific bacterium will always generate the same growth curve. Although not all cells in a culture divide at the same time, the rapid growth rate of most bacterial populations in combination with the vast number of cells in the population result in a common growth curve for the entire population.

There Is No Increase in Cell Numbers During the Lag Phase of Growth

Growth usually does not commence immediately when bacteria are inoculated into a new growth medium. In many cases, the bacteria must first synthesize enzymes required for growth under the new conditions. This period is called the **lag phase** of growth. During this phase, there is no increase in cell numbers. However, this is not

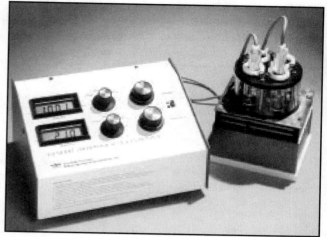

a.

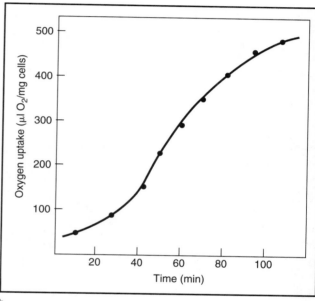

b.

figure 5.12

Determination of Dissolved Oxygen Concentration in a Solution
The concentration of oxygen in a solution can be determined with an oxygen electrode coated with an oxygen-permeable membrane. As oxygen diffuses across the membrane, it alters the conductivity. Changes in oxygen concentration are indicated on the monitor, which reads from 0% to 100% oxygen saturation. The quantity of oxygen consumed (or evolved) by microorganisms in the solution can be determined by standard conversions and is expressed as $\mu l\ O_2$/hour or $\mu l\ O_2$/mg cells. a. Oxygen monitor and electrode. b. Oxygen uptake curve.

table 5.2

Summary of Methods for Measurement of Microbial Growth

Method	Use	Limitations
Direct microscopic count	Rapid laboratory enumeration of cell suspension	Requires large number ($\geq 10^6$ cells/ml) of cells for accuracy
Viable count	Enumeration of viable cells in water, milk, and other products	Time-consuming, requires proper medium for growth
Membrane filtration	Enumeration of bacteria from water, milk, and other products, especially when numbers are low	Time-consuming, requires proper medium for growth
Most probable number (MPN)	Enumeration of bacteria from water, milk, and other products	Time-consuming, requires proper medium for growth, provides indirect estimate of numbers
Turbidimetric measurement	Rapid estimation of cell density in a suspension	Does not differentiate between viable and nonviable cells, provides only estimate of cell density, requires $>10^6$ cells/ml
Dry weight determination	Determination of cell mass for industrial or laboratory applications	Time-consuming, does not differentiate between viable and nonviable cells
Cell activity measurement	Research applications to follow cell metabolism	Involves extensive preparatory time

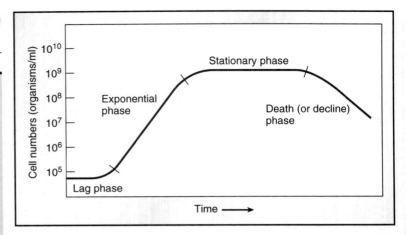

figure 5.13

Population Growth Curve

A population growth curve consists of four distinct growth phases: lag phase, exponential phase, stationary phase, and death, or decline, phase. Each growth phase reflects changes in the environment and metabolism of the cells.

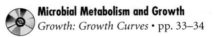 **Microbial Metabolism and Growth**
Growth: Growth Curves • pp. 33–34

increase the synthesis of certain enzymes to produce the precursors needed for biosynthesis.

Not all bacterial populations exhibit a lag phase. This phase is absent when an exponentially growing culture is transferred to a medium of the same chemical composition and incubation conditions. Under such conditions, the transferred cells have all of the requisite enzymes and metabolic pathways to begin exponential growth in the fresh medium immediately.

The Population Grows at a Constant Rate During the Exponential Phase of Growth

The **exponential,** or **logarithmic, phase** of the growth curve is that period in which the population is actively growing at a constant rate. This growth results in a doubling of the population per generation time. A semilogarithmic plot, against time, of growth during the exponential phase yields a straight line from which the generation time can easily be derived. The exponential phase of growth cannot continue indefinitely.

Growth Slows and a Steady State in Cell Numbers Is Reached in the Stationary Phase of Growth

As nutrient supplies are depleted and toxic waste products accumulate, growth begins to slow, and soon thereafter the bacteria enter the **stationary phase.** Here, although growth and cell division may still occur, a steady state in cell numbers is reached—there is neither an increase nor a decrease in cell numbers. The net result is a plateau of the growth curve that represents the maximum population dividing under the defined growth conditions for a bacterial species.

a dormant period; the bacteria are actively synthesizing enzymes in preparation for the next, exponential phase of growth (Figure 5.14).

The length of the lag phase depends on many factors, including environmental conditions (temperature, pH, and presence or absence of oxygen) and growth medium constituents. For example, a shift of cells from a nutrient-rich growth medium to one that is deficient in a number of nutrients may result in an extended lag phase as the bacteria adapt to the new environment and synthesize enzymes necessary for metabolic pathways. In environments that lack nutrients present in the former environment, the cell must

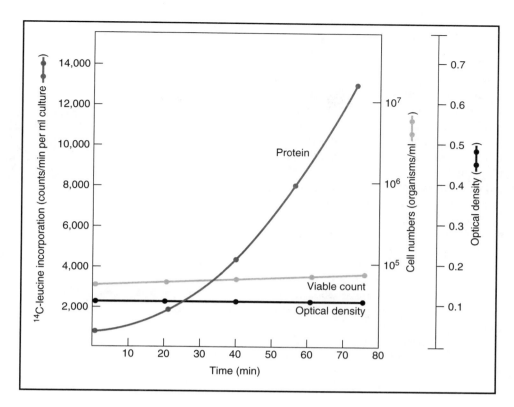

figure 5.14

Protein Synthesis and Viable Count During the Lag Phase of Growth

There is a continuous increase in protein synthesis (measured by the incorporation of radiolabeled leucine into newly synthesized protein) but no increase in cell numbers or optical density during the lag phase of growth. The example here is *Escherichia coli.*

There Is a Net Decrease in Viable Cell Numbers in the Death Phase of Growth

In many populations the steady state is eventually replaced by a **death phase,** or **decline phase.** Here, more cells die than are replaced by new cells, and there is a net decrease in certain parameters, especially viable cell numbers, used to measure cell growth.

There are several explanations for the death phase of the growth curve. Some bacteria (for example, *Streptococcus* and *Lactobacillus*) produce acidic compounds as by-products of cellular metabolism. These acids lower the pH of the medium, resulting in cell death. Growth of such bacteria in media may be extended by buffering the medium to maintain a neutral pH. Some bacteria synthesize autolytic enzymes as they age. These enzymes cause cell lysis. *Streptococcus pneumoniae,* for example, produces an autolytic enzyme, *N*-acetylmuramyl-L-alanine amidase, during the latter stages of growth. The enzyme cleaves the linkage between *N*-acetylmuramic acid and L-alanine in the cell wall peptidoglycan, resulting in lysis of the cell. *N*-acetylmuramyl-L-alanine amidase is also activated by surface-active agents (for example, bile salts and sodium deoxycholate). This characteristic is used in a test, the bile solubility test, commonly used to identify *S. pneumoniae*. In the bile solubility test, addition of sodium deoxycholate to a growing culture of *S. pneumoniae* results in a decrease in the turbidity of the culture with time.

Regardless of the manner of cell death, the population growth curve is directly affected by environmental conditions and composition of the medium. Although conditions in the microenvironment of a bacterium may mimic a batch culture, nature is not a closed system. Growth of bacteria in nature is limited by nutrient availability and accumulation of toxic waste products.

 **Microbial Metabolism and Growth**
Growth: Growth Curves • pp. 33–35

Special Techniques for Culture

Up to this point we have talked about batch cultures. In batch cultures, exponential growth continues for relatively few generations until nutrients are exhausted or toxic products accumulate. However, it is desirable in some instances to maintain exponential, or balanced, growth for a longer period of time. This is especially true if we wish to examine the effects of environmental factors on bacterial growth.

Exponential Growth Can Be Prolonged Through Continuous Culture

Bacteria can be maintained in the exponential phase in a growth curve through the use of **continuous cultures.** In continuous culture, the culture volume and the growth rate are maintained at a constant level by the addition of fresh medium and the removal of an equal amount of used medium and old cells. In a continuous culture system, fresh medium is supplied to a fixed-volume culture vessel, and spent medium is removed through an overflow tube. The culture is said to be in **steady state** when the system reaches an equilibrium point where cell numbers and nutrient levels in the culture vessel become constant.

There are two types of continuous culture systems that are commonly used in microbiology. A **chemostat** is a system in which growth is controlled by the flow rate of the system and the concentration of a limiting nutrient (Figure 5.15). In such a system, the growth rate is controlled by the rate at which nutrients are added to the growth vessel, and the population density is controlled by nutrient limitation. The investigator adjusts both parameters to meet the requirements for the system. A **turbidostat,** in contrast, contains a light-sensing device that measures the turbidity of the culture. The flow rate of fresh medium is automatically adjusted to maintain the desired turbidity level.

The chemostat and turbidostat have similar operating principles. As fresh medium is added to the culture vessel and spent medium and excess cells are removed through the overflow tube, the bacteria in the culture vessel are maintained at a constant growth rate. This is because bacteria in the culture vessel grow at a rate just fast enough to replace the cells that are removed through the overflow tube. If the flow rate is increased, there is a concomitant increase in removal of spent medium and cells. As a consequence, the population grows at a fast rate (up until a point at which it cannot keep up with the flow rate and the culture is "washed out" of the vessel). If the flow rate is decreased, the growth rate of the culture also decreases. In instances where the limiting nutrient is the energy source for the culture, there is a minimum amount of energy (maintenance energy) that must exist in the culture vessel for cells to carry out nongrowth functions such as regulation of ion balance, motility, and accumulation of substrates against a concentration gradient. The cell density in a chemostat is controlled by regulating the concentration of a limiting nutrient in the culture medium. The fresh growth medium used in a chemostat contains an excess of all but one nutrient. As this nutrient is depleted by the bacteria and is replenished at a constant rate, cell density stabilizes.

Continuous culture systems have widespread applications in microbiology. They are used to examine the effects of substrates and environmental factors (the limiting nutrient in the system) on population growth. These systems also are used in industry, providing information on optimal growth conditions for microorganisms in the synthesis of commercial products. Geneticists use continuous cultures to select mutant strains of bacteria. It is possible to select for a population of cells that can outgrow all other cell

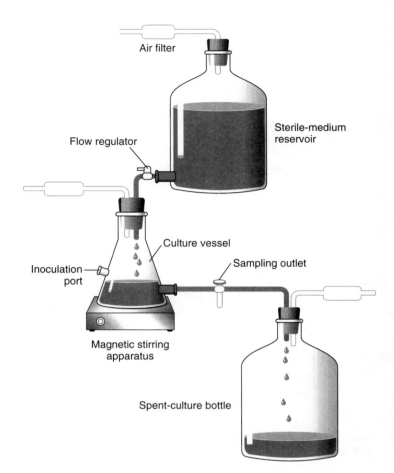

figure 5.15

A Chemostat Used for Continuous Culture of Bacteria
A chemostat is used to maintain microbial populations in continuous culture. It consists of a reservoir of sterile culture medium, a flow regulator to control the rate at which fresh medium is added to the culture vessel, the culture vessel, and a spent-culture container to collect the used culture medium.

types under certain conditions simply by varying the growth conditions in a chemostat. Continuous culture has proven to be a valuable tool in the study of microbes.

Synchronous Cultures Are Cell Populations That Are All in the Same Stage of Growth

The typical population growth curve, with its distinct phases, represents the combined growth pattern of a large number of individual cells, each one of which is growing and dividing without regard to the others. Some experimental work requires information on the growth behavior of individual cells. This information can be obtained through **synchronous cultures.** These cultures consist of populations of cells that are all in the same stage of growth—virtually every cell in the population grows and divides at the same time. This synchrony results in a steplike growth curve that plateaus each time the population divides (Figure 5.16). Synchronous populations rapidly lose their synchrony, because cells of

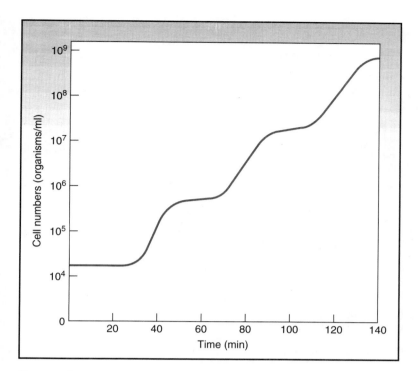

figure 5.16

Synchronous Growth Curve
Synchrony can be maintained for only a few generations. Eventually cells divide at different times, and synchrony is lost.

a population do not all age at the same rate, eventually resulting in different division times.

Synchronous growth may be achieved by altering the environment (temperature or nutrient supply) so that all cells in the population complete cellular growth and begin division simultaneously. For example, cells can be shifted to a low temperature at which they grow to full size, but do not divide. Upon a return to their optimal growth temperature, the cells will undergo a synchronized division. Synchronous growth may also be obtained by the filtration of a cell population so that organisms of the same size, and thus of the same stage of growth, are collected on the filter. These bacteria then can be inoculated into a medium to obtain a synchronized culture.

The value of synchronous culture is obvious. Bacteria are too small to study as individual cells, so a synchronous population of bacteria that are all in the same phase of growth, differentiation, or cellular organization can serve as a model of a single cell.

Control of Microbial Growth

Growth of microorganisms is influenced by environmental factors such as temperature, pH, water availability, and the presence or absence of oxygen (see physical and gaseous requirements of microorganisms, page 89). These factors not only affect growth of microbes in their natural environment, but also can be used to control or eliminate growth in the laboratory. For example, removal of oxygen in an environment can control growth of an aerobic bacterium such as *Mycobacterium tuberculosis*. Prior to the

discovery of antibiotics, treatment of tuberculosis included artificial collapse of the lung to limit the amount of oxygen available to the bacterium.

Sterilization is the killing or removal of all living organisms, a necessary prerequisite for culture media. Unsterilized media are not suitable for cultivation of microorganisms, because the media may contain unwanted organisms that mask the growth of the desired microbe.

High Temperature Can Be Used to Remove All or Most Microorganisms

Different methods are used for sterilization. The most common is **autoclaving.** An autoclave is, in essence, a large pressure cooker (Figure 5.17). Unlike boiling, which kills vegetative cells but not endospores, an autoclave kills all living organisms by a combination of high temperature and moist heat, or steam. A sterilization temperature of 121°C is obtained by increasing the pressure within the instrument to 15 lb/sq inch at sea level (higher pressures are required at higher altitudes, where barometric pressures are lower, to reach the temperature of 121°C). The air within the autoclave chamber must be replaced with saturated, flowing steam during the sterilization process to achieve a temperature of 121°C. This temperature reached during autoclaving is sufficient to kill even bacterial endospores, given an adequate time of exposure. The time required for sterilization by autoclaving depends on the volume of media and materials being processed. Large volumes require longer sterilization periods to allow heat penetration. Small volumes of media (test tube volumes and small flask volumes) are autoclaved routinely for 15 minutes.

An alternative to the autoclave is fractional sterilization **(tyndallization),** developed by the British physicist John Tyndall (1820–1893) in 1877. In tyndallization, the solution to be sterilized is heated to 100°C for 30 minutes in the presence of flowing steam on three successive days. After each cycle of heating, the material is incubated, usually at 37°C, until the next day. In the first heating cycle, all vegetative cells are destroyed. Bacterial endospores are not killed, but they germinate into vegetative cells as a result of the heat shock. These cells are subsequently killed during the second day of heating. The material is heated a third time as a precautionary measure. Tyndallization is a more tedious process than autoclaving but uses less expensive equipment and can be used for liquids that are degraded at the higher autoclave temperature. It is rarely used today, but was used in the past as an alternative to the autoclave.

Pasteurization is the process of treating liquids with heat below the boiling point to kill most pathogenic and spoilage microorganisms. Pasteurization was devised by Louis Pasteur (1822–1895) as a method to control microbial contamination of wine. It is commonly used to kill pathogenic bacteria such as *Mycobacterium tuberculosis, Brucella abortus, Salmonella,* and *Streptococcus* in milk and other beverages. Pasteurization also reduces the total bacterial population in these products and extends shelf life. The dairy industry uses two methods to pasteurize milk: the low-temperature holding (LTH) method, in which

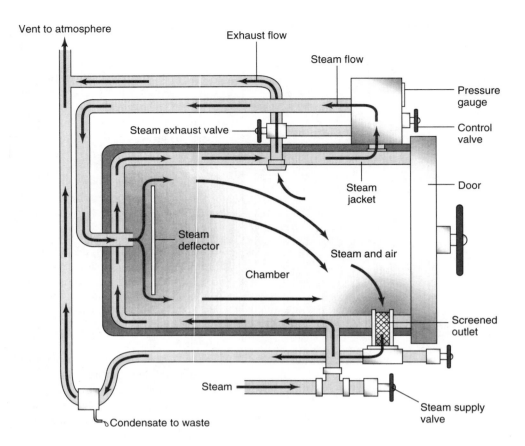

figure 5.17
An Autoclave

During autoclaving, air is forced out of the chamber by incoming steam. The steam pressure increases to 15 lb/sq in, and the temperature rises to 121°C. When sterilization is completed, the steam exhaust valve opens and steam flows out of the chamber. Liquids are autoclaved with slow steam exhaust to prevent their evaporation and boiling over.

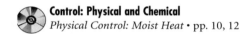
Control: Physical and Chemical
Physical Control: Moist Heat • pp. 10, 12

milk is heated to 62.8°C for 30 minutes, and the high-temperature short-time (HTST), or flash pasteurization, method which exposes milk to a temperature of 71.7°C for 15 seconds (see pasteurization of milk, page 608) .

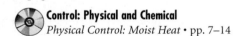
Control: Physical and Chemical
Physical Control: Moist Heat • pp. 7–14

Other Methods Are Effective in Killing or Removing Microorganisms

Some chemical compounds (for example, amino acids, vitamins, and enzymes) are sensitive even to moderate levels of heat and cannot be sterilized by high temperatures. These substances are sterilized by **filtration** through membrane filters with pore sizes of 0.22 or 0.45 µm. The pores in the filters are small enough to retain most bacteria (bacteria without cell walls, such as *Mycoplasma,* are pliable and may squeeze through these filters), but they do not retain the smaller viruses. Because viruses are unable to grow without suitable

hosts, they seldom present problems in sterilization of bacteriological media by filtration. However, these viruses can be a major problem in filter-sterilized media used for tissue culture (culture of human, animal, or plant cells for the propagation of viruses).

Air is commonly filtered to remove microorganisms. **High-efficiency particulate air (HEPA) filters** capable of removing 99.97% of particles 0.3 µm and larger are placed in laminar flow biological safety cabinets to provide a curtain of sterile air within the cabinet. This prevents contamination of the work space from outside the cabinet and also protects the laboratory worker from any escape of dangerous microorganisms inside the cabinet. Laminar flow biological safety cabinets are used when one is working with infectious agents such as tumor viruses (see tumor viruses, page 408), *Mycobacterium tuberculosis* (see tuberculosis, page 510), and *Legionella pneumophila* (see legionellosis, page 505), and recombinant DNA (see recombinant DNA, page 272).

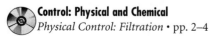
Control: Physical and Chemical
Physical Control: Filtration • pp. 2–4

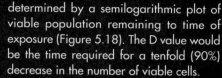

Measurement of Heat-Killing Efficiency

Heat is a useful sterilizing procedure, but its effectiveness can vary depending on the procedure used. One method for measuring the effectiveness of heat steril-ization is the **thermal death time (TDT),** the shortest time required to kill all of the microorganisms in a suspension at a specific temperature. The TDT is determined by heating aliquots of a microbial suspension for different periods of time and mixing the heated suspen-sions with a culture medium to determine the absence or presence of growth from any surviving cells.

Another method for measuring heat inactivation is to determine the **decimal reduction time (DRT),** or **D value,** the time required to kill 90% of the microor-ganisms in a suspension at a specific tem-perature. The DRT of a bacterium can be determined by a semilogarithmic plot of viable population remaining to time of exposure (Figure 5.18). The D value would be the time required for a tenfold (90%) decrease in the number of viable cells.

The effectiveness of heat sterilization depends on several factors, including the types and initial concentrations of microor-ganisms in the population, the nature of material to be treated, pH, and the pres-ence of organic matter. Endospore-forming bacteria such as *Clostridium botulinum* are more resistant to heat sterilization than vegetative cells of *Staphylococcus aureus* and *Salmonella enteritidis.* Sterilization of a powder may require a different temper-ature and time of exposure than steriliza-tion of a liquid. High-acid foods (for example, sauerkraut, pickles, and straw-berry preserves) can be heat sterilized at lower temperatures than low-acid foods (for example, carrots, peas, and beans), partially because most microorganisms do not survive in high-acid environments and those that do have lower thermal resis-tance. Materials heavily covered with organic matter may be partially protected from the effects of heat sterilization.

The D value is used extensively by the canning industry to determine the shortest time required for effective heat sterilization in canning operations. Be-cause excessive exposure to heat can alter the texture and flavor of foods, it is impor-tant to know the shortest time and lowest temperature necessary to kill food-borne pathogens.

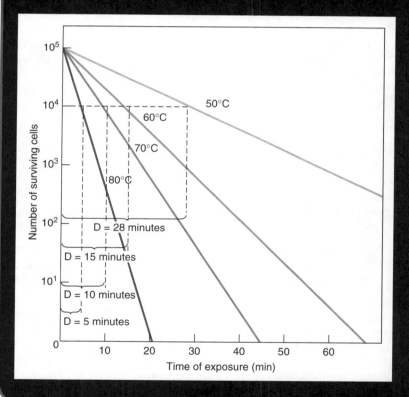

figure 5.18
Effect of Temperature on the D Values for a Bacterium
The D values are shown for a bacterium at four different temperatures. Note that the D values decrease as the temperature increases.

Dry heat is frequently used for the sterilization of glassware and laboratory equipment. Microbial cells are apparently killed by oxidation of their constituents and protein denaturation in dry heat sterilization. The process requires a longer period of time than autoclaving, since flowing steam is not used. Incineration is one form of dry heat sterilization. Inoculating loops are sterilized by incineration in the flame of a Bunsen burner or in an electric heating coil. Animal carcasses, hospital and laboratory infectious wastes, and disposable gowns, bedding, bandages, syringes, and needles are incinerated. Glassware and other similar objects can be sterilized by placing them in an oven at 160°C to 170°C for two to three hours. Although dry heat sterilization is a slower process than autoclaving, it has the advantages of not corroding metal instruments and not introducing moisture into powders and oils. A disadvantage of dry heat sterilization is that it cannot be used to sterilize objects or materials that would be affected by high temperatures.

Control: Physical and Chemical
Physical Control: Dry Heat • pp. 5–6

Ionizing radiation with gamma rays is used for the sterilization of pharmaceuticals and disposable medical supplies such as plastic syringes and surgical gloves. Gamma rays from cobalt 60 have high penetration for solids and liquids and destroy microorganisms by the formation of hydroxyl free radicals and peroxides from water and other substances (see hydroxyl free radicals and peroxides, page 93). Ionizing irradiation has been used to reduce bacterial populations in foods such as strawberries, apples, poultry, and fish, thereby increasing their shelf lives.

Nonionizing radiation, or **ultraviolet radiation,** is not as penetrating as ionizing radiation and is only effective on microorganisms that are fully exposed such as those on a surface or in a thin layer of water or other liquid. This type of radiation does not penetrate glass, paper, or solids. At a wavelength of 260 nm, ultraviolet radiation damages DNA by the formation of pyrimidine dimers that distort the structure of DNA and interfere with replication and transcription (see pyrimidine dimers, page 246). Ultraviolet lamps are sometimes used in laboratories, hospital rooms, operating rooms, and biological safety cabinets to sterilize the air and any exposed surfaces, and in aquariums to reduce microbial populations in circulating water. Because prolonged exposure to ultraviolet radiation can damage the eyes and burn the skin, its use is carefully monitored.

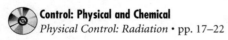

Control: Physical and Chemical
Physical Control: Radiation • pp. 17–22

Other methods for control of microbial growth include refrigeration, deep freezing, dehydration, osmotic pressure, and the use of chemicals such as sodium benzoate, calcium propionate, boric acid, and sorbic acid for food preservation. These methods used to preserve foods and reduce spoilage are further discussed in Chapter 20 (see food preservation, page 614).

Antimicrobial Agents

Antimicrobial agents are chemicals that inhibit or destroy microbial growth. Some of these agents are **cidal** (**algicidal, bactericidal,** and **fungicidal**) and kill the microbe (but not necessarily their

table	5.3	
Common Disinfectants and Antiseptics		
Class	**Examples**	**Mode of Action**
Phenol and phenolic compounds	Carbolic acid, hexachlorophene, cresol, phenol, orthophenylphenol	Disruption of plasma membrane through protein denaturation
Alcohols	Ethanol, isopropanol (50%–70% aqueous solution)	Lipid solvents and protein denaturants
Surfactants	Quaternary ammonuim compounds	Disruption of plasma membrane through charge interactions with phospholipids
	Soaps, detergents	Disruption of plasma membrane through charge interactions with lipoproteins
Halogens	Iodine (tincture of iodine, povidone-iodine)	Reaction with tyrosine to inactivate proteins
	Chlorine	Oxidizing agent
Alkylating agents	Formaldehyde, glutaraldehyde, ethylene oxide	Denaturation of proteins and nucleic acids through attachment of methyl or ethyl groups to these molecules
Heavy metals	Mercury (merbromin, nitromersol, thimerosal), silver (1% silver nitrate), copper (copper sulfate)	Protein denaturant

spores). The term **germicide** often is used to collectively describe cidal agents. Other antimicrobial agents are **static** (**algistatic, bacteriostatic,** and **fungistatic**) and reversibly inhibit growth. A bacteriostatic agent is effective only as long as it is in the immediate vicinity of the susceptible bacterium. If the bacteriostatic agent is removed, the bacterium may resume growth. Some bacteriocidal agents are also **bacteriolytic** and kill cells by cell lysis. Agents that inhibit cell wall synthesis (for example, penicillin) or damage the plasma membrane (for example, polymyxin) are bacteriolytic.

Disinfectants Are Used on Inanimate Objects, Whereas Antiseptics Are Used on External Body Surfaces

Antimicrobial agents may be divided into four distinct categories: **disinfectants, antiseptics, antibiotics,** and **synthetic drugs.** Disinfectants are chemical compounds that destroy disease-causing

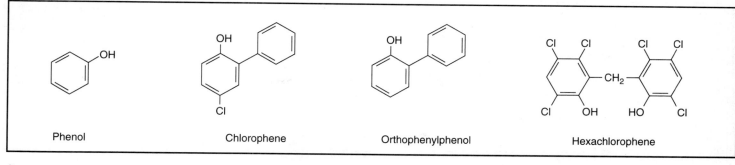

figure 5.19
Structures of Some Phenolic Disinfectants

microorganisms and their products on inanimate objects; they are distinguished from antiseptics, which are used on external body surfaces (Table 5.3). Antiseptics are less toxic than disinfectants and usually inhibit, but do not always kill, microorganisms.

A convenient way to measure the germicidal action of a chemical is to compare its killing action to a known standard. The **phenol coefficient** of a compound is the ratio of its effectiveness to that of phenol (the standard) against a test organism. For example, if a standard suspension of *Staphylococcus aureus* is killed by a 1:2,500 dilution of hexachlorophene but requires a 1:20 dilution of phenol to cause the same results, the phenol coefficient of hexachlorophene is 2,500/20 or 125.0. This phenol coefficient means that hexochlorophene is 125 times more effective than phenol as a germicide in killing *S. aureus* in vitro. The phenol coefficient provides a reasonable index of germicidal activity, but it is more accurate for phenolic compounds (which have chemical properties and modes of action similar to phenol) than for other agents.

Phenolic compounds, alcohols, surface-active agents (**surfactants),** halogens, alkylating agents, and heavy metals are examples of disinfectants and antiseptics. Some of the more important chemicals are described in the following sections.

Phenol Causes Membrane Damage and Leakage of Cell Cytoplasmic Contents

Phenols are compounds that have a hydroxyl group attached directly to an aromatic ring (Figure 5.19). Phenols have long been recognized as effective disinfectants—since 1865, when Joseph Lister (1827–1912) used phenol to disinfect surgical instruments and dressings. Lister discovered that phenol applications dramatically reduced the incidence of postsurgical infections. A 5% phenol solution effectively kills all vegetative bacteria and many spores by causing membrane damage and leakage of cell cytoplasmic contents. Cresol, a methylphenol that is a distillation product of coal tar, is used as a preservative and in some soaps and detergents. In the past, one of the most widely used phenolic derivatives was hexachlorophene, which consists of two phenol groups. Hexachlorophene is usually mixed with soaps and is particularly effective against gram-positive bacteria such as *S. aureus*, a common source of infections in newborn infants. It has been discovered, however, that hexachlorophene penetrates

the skin and can cause neurological damage; therefore its use is more restricted today.

Control: Physical and Chemical
Chemical Control: Phenols • pp. 26–31

Alcohols Are Lipid Solvents that Disrupt Plasma Membrane Lipids and Denature Proteins

Alcohols are lipid solvents that kill cells by disrupting the lipids in the plasma membranes and also by denaturing proteins. Ethanol and isopropanol are widely used disinfectants that are most effective at a concentration of approximately 70%. Isopropanol alcohol is slightly more effective as a germicidal agent than ethanol, is less expensive, and is not subject to legal regulations. For these reasons, isopropanol is used for such purposes as the disinfection of thermometers.

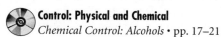
Control: Physical and Chemical
Chemical Control: Alcohols • pp. 17–21

Surfactants Disrupt the Plasma Membrane by Reacting with Membrane Lipids

Surface-active substances (surfactants) are compounds that have both hydrophilic (water-attracting) and hydrophobic (water-repelling) groups that reduce surface tension and the miscibility of molecules. Surfactants have widespread applications as emulsifiers, soaps, detergents, and cleansing agents. The most important surface-active agents are quaternary ammonium compounds, cationic (positively charged) compounds with positively charged groups that react with the negatively charged phosphate groups of the membrane phospholipids to disrupt the plasma membrane (Figure 5.20). Cationic detergents are frequently used to disinfect food and beverage utensils in restaurants, equipment in food-processing plants, and floors and walls in hospitals and nursing homes. Anionic (negatively charged) organic molecules affect the lipoprotein portion of the plasma membrane, are milder than cationic agents (because they are repelled by the net negative charge of the bacterial surface), and therefore are often used as soaps and detergents. The cleansing action of soaps and detergents in everyday use, particularly by restaurant workers and food handlers, plays an important role in reducing potential food-poisoning outbreaks.

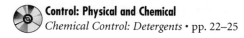
Control: Physical and Chemical
Chemical Control: Detergents • pp. 22–25

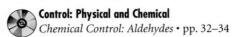

Benzethonium chloride   Benzalkonium chloride   Cetylpyridinium chloride

figure 5.20
Structures of Some Surfactants

Halogens Are Strong Oxidizing Agents

The halogens (chlorine, fluorine, bromine, and iodine) are strong oxidizing agents that react with enzymes, proteins, fats, or other cellular molecules to disrupt cell function. Iodine and chlorine are among the most widely used disinfectants. A 2% solution of iodine in sodium iodide and dilute alcohol (tincture of iodine) is commonly used as an antiseptic for treating minor cuts, abrasions, and wounds. Povidone-iodine (Betadine) is an iodine-detergent mixture (iodophore) that is frequently used as an alternative to tincture of iodine, especially for children because it does not irritate the skin or sting as much when applied to open wounds. Iodine inactivates many proteins by altering their structure through iodination of the amino acid tyrosine.

Chlorine compounds are potent disinfectants for swimming pools, water supplies, and hot tubs. When elemental chlorine or a chlorine compound is added to water, the chlorine reacts with the water to form hypochlorous acid, a powerful oxidizing agent. Because chlorine's activity is reduced by the presence of organic matter, which combines with chlorine, it is customary to add sufficient amounts of chlorine to water so that the free chlorine concentration is 0.5 to 1.0 parts per million (ppm); this ensures effective disinfection.

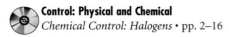
Control: Physical and Chemical
Chemical Control: Halogens • pp. 2–16

Alkylating Agents Generally Attach Methyl or Ethyl Groups to Cellular Molecules Such as Proteins and DNA, Making Them Nonfunctional

Formaldehyde, glutaraldehyde, ethylene oxide, and β-propiolactone are alkylating agents that often are used as preservatives and disinfectants. Alkylating agents generally attach methyl or ethyl groups to proteins and DNA, rendering these molecules nonfunctional and causing death of the microorganism. Formaldehyde is used primarily as a preservative in embalming. Formalin, a 37% solution of formaldehyde gas, is used for the preservation and fixation of tissue. It is also used in the preparation of vaccines, because it destroys microorganisms but does not affect their anti-

genic properties. Glutaraldehyde is more effective and less toxic than formaldehyde as a disinfectant and has been used increasingly for sterilizing surgical instruments.

Control: Physical and Chemical
Chemical Control: Aldehydes • pp. 32–34

Ethylene oxide (EtO) readily penetrates paper, cloth, and certain types of plastics and is used to sterilize disposable plastic Petri dishes, syringes, catheters, and sutures. Ethylene oxide has wide applications in the food industry as a preservative for spices, dried fruit, and nuts. It also has been used by hospitals to sterilize instruments and surgical equipment and by NASA to decontaminate spacecraft components. The gas is released into a tightly sealed chamber containing the items to be sterilized for three to four hours in a temperature-controlled and humidity-controlled environment. Because EtO is toxic if inhaled, and explosive, it is normally mixed with an inert gas (Freon or carbon dioxide) to reduce the danger of its use. After sterilization, the chamber is extensively flushed with an inert gas to remove any residual EtO.

Control: Physical and Chemical
Chemical Control: Gases • pp. 35–38

β-propiolactone (BPL) is occasionally used as an alternative to EtO. BPL is less explosive and destroys microorganisms more readily than EtO, but has poor penetration capabilities and may be carcinogenic. Therefore it is not used as a sterilizing agent as often as EtO.

Heavy Metals Bind to the Sulfhydryl Groups of Proteins, Resulting in Protein Denaturation

Heavy metal ions of mercury, silver, and copper are toxic to microorganisms because they bind to the sulfhydryl groups of proteins and denature them. Organic mercuric compounds such as merbromin (Mercurochrome), nitromersol (Metaphen), and thimerosal (Merthiolate) are often used for sterilization of instruments, skin antisepsis, and irrigation of the urethra. An eyedrop solution containing 1% silver nitrate ($AgNO_3$) is sometimes used to prevent an eye disease called ophthalmia neonatorum, which is often caused by *Neisseria gonorrhoeae* and occurs in infants deliv-

table 5.4

Major Categories of Chemotherapeutic Agents

Mode of Action	Examples
Inhibition of cell wall synthesis	Penicillins, cephalosporins, vancomycin, bacitracin, oxacillin, nafcillin
Damage to plasma membrane	Polymyxin, nystatin, amphotericin B
Inhibition of protein synthesis	Streptomycin, kanamycin, gentamicin, amikacin, neomycin, chloramphenicol, erythromycin, tetracyclines
Inhibition of nucleic acid synthesis	Rifamycins, actinomycin D, nalidixic acid, ciprofloxacin, norfloxacin
Structure analogs	Sulfonamides

ered through an infected birth canal. Copper sulfate ($CuSO_4$) is useful as an algicide. A 1-ppm concentration of copper sulfate is usually sufficient to control the obnoxious and odoriferous algal blooms that often occur in lakes and reservoirs.

Antibiotics and Synthetic Drugs Are Used in Chemotherapy to Selectively Inhibit or Kill Microorganisms Without Harming Host Tissue

Unlike disinfectants and antiseptics, which are applied on nonliving materials or on external tissue, antibiotics and synthetic drugs can be taken internally. The term *antibiotic* was originally used by Selman Waksman (1888–1973) to describe any antimicrobial chemical substance produced by microorganisms. Waksman, who received the Nobel Prize in physiology and medicine in 1952 for his discovery of streptomycin, was a microbiologist who searched for antimicrobial agents in bacteria. Today many antimicrobial agents are produced synthetically or semisynthetically. These synthetic chemicals are called synthetic drugs to distinguish them from the naturally produced antibiotics.

To be useful, antimicrobial agents must have **selective toxicity.** The agent must inhibit or kill the microorganism without damaging the cells of the animal host. Although many natural and synthetic chemicals kill microorganisms, only a much smaller group has selective toxicity and can be used as **chemotherapeutic agents.** Chemotherapeutic agents vary in their range of activity. **Narrow-spectrum** agents are effective against only specific microorganisms or groups of microorganisms. Bacitracin and gentamicin are examples of narrow-spectrum drugs that are targeted specifically at gram-positive bacteria and gram-negative bacteria, respectively. **Broad-spectrum** agents such as chloramphenicol, streptomycin, and tetracycline are effective against a relatively wide range of microorganisms. Physicians sometimes prescribe

broad-spectrum drugs when time is of the essence in initiating chemotherapy for a potentially lethal infectious disease in which the etiologic agent has not yet been identified. With the emergence of drug-resistant bacteria in recent years, concern has been raised about the overuse of antimicrobial agents and the initiation of treatment before diagnosis of the disease. It is now recommended that cultures be performed and antimicrobial susceptibilities be determined before the use of antimicrobial agents.

Chemotherapeutic agents may be classified by their mechanism of action. These mechanisms include: (1) the inhibition of cell wall synthesis, (2) damage to the plasma membrane, (3) the inhibition of protein and nucleic acid synthesis, and (4) the inhibition of cell metabolism (Table 5.4). Some examples of chemotherapeutic agents in each category are given in the following sections.

Penicillins Inhibit Biosynthesis of the Cell Wall Peptidoglycan

Some of the more common antibiotics used today are those that inhibit the biosynthesis of the cell wall peptidoglycan structure. The peptidoglycan gives strength and rigidity to the cell wall, and antibiotics such as the penicillins, cephalosporins, vancomycin, bacitracin, oxacillin, and nafcillin interfere with the synthesis of this important structure (Figure 5.21).

The penicillins are among the most widely used class of antibiotics in the world. They inhibit the transpeptidation step of peptidoglycan synthesis (see peptidoglycan synthesis, page 56) and are effective only on microorganisms actively synthesizing peptidoglycan. All of the penicillins have a common basic structure: a thiazolidine ring joined to β-lactam ring. Different forms of penicillin have different side groups attached to the basic structure. One of the original natural penicillins isolated from microorganisms is benzylpenicillin (penicillin G). Penicillin G is effective against gram-positive organisms and gram-negative cocci, but can cause hypersensitive reactions. Penicillin G is usually administered intramuscularly because it is readily inactivated by gastric acids. Phenoxymethyl penicillin (penicillin V) is more resistant to acids and therefore, unlike penicillin G, can be given orally.

Many of the natural and synthetic penicillins are sensitive to the action of β-**lactamase (penicillinase),** a plasmid-coded enzyme produced by many clinically significant bacteria, including *Staphylococcus aureus* and *Neisseria gonorrhoeae* (see β-lactamase, pages 527 and 534). β-lactamase hydrolyzes the β-lactam ring of penicillin and renders the antibiotic ineffective. Because penicillinase is an extracellular enzyme, its production by certain bacteria in an area of the body may destroy penicillin that is designated for use against other, non-penicillinase-producing bacteria in the general vicinity. For this reason, penicillinase-producing microorganisms can represent significant problems in the clinical management of a disease. Some of the semisynthetic penicillins (for example, oxicillin or nafcillin) that have bulky side groups next to the β-lactam ring are resistant to the action of penicillinase and are effective against penicillinase-producing bacteria.

 **Antimicrobial Action**
Cell Wall Inhibitors • pp. 1–19

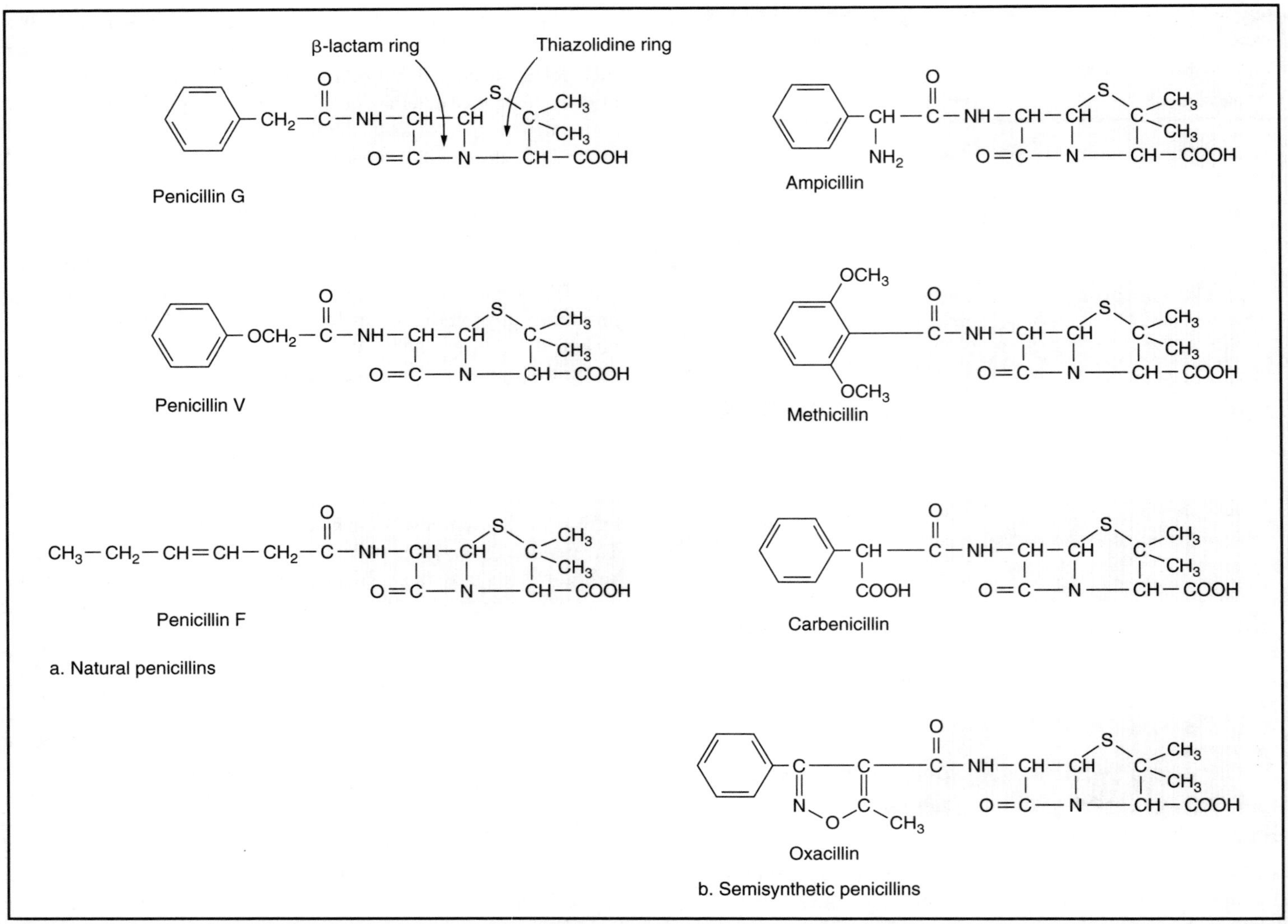

figure 5.21

Structures of Some Common Penicillins

The shaded areas represent the common nucleus; the unshaded areas are the side chains that are specific for each type of penicillin.

Damage to the Plasma Membrane Results in Leakage of Metabolites and Other Cytoplasmic Constituents

The plasma membrane is an important microbial structure that regulates the transport of substances into and out of the cell and is also the site of respiratory electron transport and other cellular activities. Antibiotics that damage or impair the function of the plasma membrane are toxic for microorganisms. Polymyxin, nystatin, and amphotericin B are examples of these antibiotics (Figure 5.22).

Polymyxin is a natural polypeptide synthesized by *Bacillus polymyxa*. It binds to the outer surface of plasma membranes to disrupt membrane structure, causing leakage of metabolites. However, because polymyxin is toxic to tissue, its use is reserved for serious infections caused by *Pseudomonas aeruginosa,* a bacterium

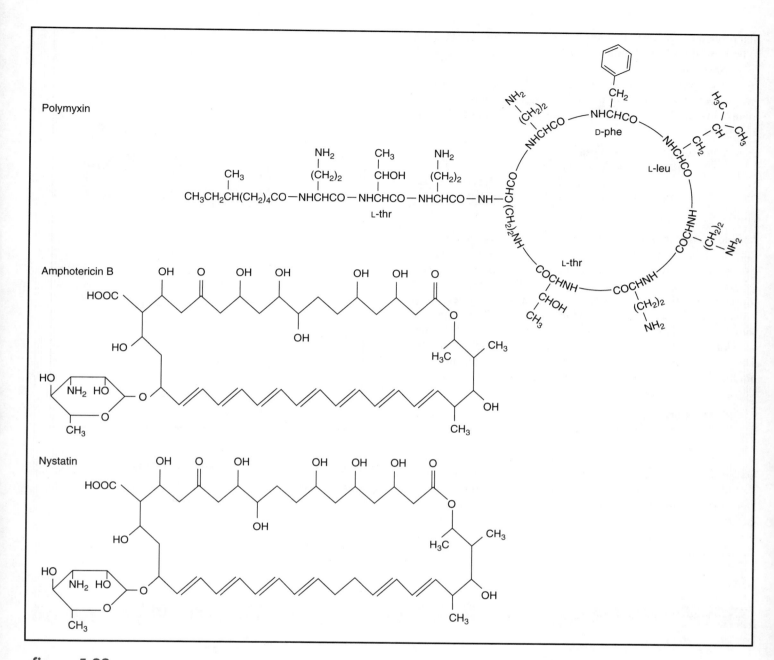

figure 5.22
Polymyxin, Amphotericin B, and Nystatin

that is resistant to most other antibiotics, or for topical application to prevent minor skin wound infections.

Nystatin and amphotericin B are polyene antibiotics that have large ring structures with many double bonds. The polyenes selectively inhibit organisms containing sterols in their membranes and therefore are used for the treatment of fungal infections.

Fungal Structure and Function
Diseases: Antifungal Therapy • pp. 51–52

Inhibitors of Protein and Nucleic Acid Synthesis Disrupt Cell Function

Antibiotics that inhibit protein and nucleic acid synthesis seriously impair cell function. The aminoglycosides (streptomycin, kanamycin, gentamicin, tobramycin, amikacin, and neomycin) are a large class of antibiotics that have an aminocyclitol ring and one or more amino sugars (Figure 5.23). The aminoglycosides impair procaryotic ribosome function by interacting with the 30S ribosomal subunit and causing, in many cases, misreading of the messenger RNA (Table 5.5). These antibiotics are bactericidal and have a broad spectrum, but they are not effective against obligate anaerobes. Apparently, anaerobiosis affects assimilation of aminoglycoside antibiotics into the cell.

Antimicrobial Action
Protein Synthesis Inhibitors: Mechanisms • pp. 4–5

The tetracyclines are antibiotics that inhibit bacterial growth by binding to the small (30S) ribosomal subunit and interfering with the attachment of aminoacyl-transfer RNA to the ribosome. Unlike the aminoglycosides, tetracyclines bind to procaryotic and eucaryotic ribosomes, but they are more selective for procaryotes because eucaryotic membranes are less permeable to the antibiotic.

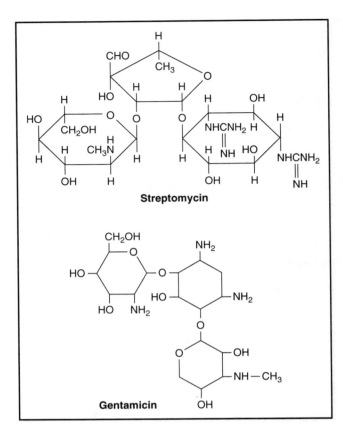

figure 5.23
Structures of Representative Aminoglycosides

Antimicrobial Action
Protein Synthesis Inhibitors: Protein Inhibition Mechanisms • pp. 4–5

table	5.5

Inhibitors of Protein Synthesis

Antimicrobial Agent	Ribosome Subunit Affected		Protein Function Inhibited			
	30S	50S	Initiation	Codon Recognition	Peptide Bond Formation	Translocation
Streptomycin	+		+	+		
Kanamycin	+					+
Gentamicin	+					+
Amikacin	+					+
Neomycin	+			+		
Chloramphenicol		+			+	
Erythromycin		+			+	+
Tetracycline	+			+		

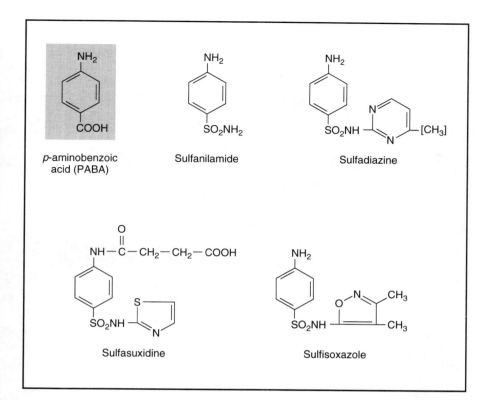

figure 5.24
Sulfonamides
The sulfonamides are structurally similar to *p*-aminobenzoic acid (PABA), a precursor of folic acid.

Chloramphenicol is an antibiotic that binds to the 23S rRNA on the 50S ribosomal subunit and inhibits peptidyl transferase, thereby preventing peptide bond formation. Because chloramphenicol can be neurotoxic, it is used sparingly and generally in situations when no other antibiotic is effective. Both chloramphenicol and the tetracyclines are broad-spectrum bacteriostatic agents that are effective against many gram-positive and gram-negative bacteria.

Erythromycin, an antibiotic that binds to the 50S ribosomal subunit, blocks peptide bond formation and translocation. Erythromycin is generally bacteriostatic and is effective against gram-positive bacteria and some gram-negative bacteria. It is frequently used as an alternative to penicillin in patients who are allergic to penicillin or who are infected with penicillin-resistant organisms.

 **Antimicrobial Action**
Protein Synthesis Inhibitors • pp. 1–9

Erythromycin belongs to a class of antibiotics called macrolides, in which a lactone ring is attached to one or more sugars. Erythromycin is produced by a strain of the bacterium *Streptomyces erythraeus* that was originally isolated from soil in the Philippines. It is the preferred drug for treating legionellosis, mycoplasma pneumonia, and whooping cough. Although erythromycin is the most widely used macrolide, newer semisynthetic macrolides such as clarithromycin and azithromycin have been developed.

The rifamycins are antibiotics that inhibit bacterial DNA-dependent RNA polymerase of bacteria. Rifampicin, a synthetic

derivative of the naturally occurring rifamycin B, binds to the β subunit of RNA polymerase and inhibits the initiation of RNA synthesis. Rifampicin is a broad-spectrum drug that is especially effective against mycobacterial infections.

Actinomycin D, an antibiotic produced by *Streptomyces antibioticus*, binds between guanine-cytosine base pairs on DNA and blocks RNA chain elongation in both procaryotes and eucaryotes. Nalidixic acid, ciprofloxacin, and norfloxacin are synthetic drugs called quinolones, which act by binding to DNA gyrase (topoisomerase), the enzyme involved in the unwinding of DNA. Gyrase activity is affected by the binding, and DNA replication is inhibited.

 **Antimicrobial Action**
Protein Synthesis Inhibitors • p. 8

Sulfonamides Are Structure Analogs That Structurally Resemble and Compete with Metabolites in Cellular Enzymatic Reactions

Some of the first antimicrobial agents used in chemotherapy were the sulfonamides. There are numerous sulfonamides, but all are derivatives of *p*-aminobenzenesulfonamide (Figure 5.24). Sulfonamides are **structure analogs**—chemical compounds that structurally resemble cellular metabolites and compete with these metabolites in cellular enzymatic reactions. Sulfonamides are structurally similar to *p*-aminobenzoic acid (PABA), a precursor of folic acid. Folic acid is a vitamin that is synthesized by most bacteria. Sulfonamide competes with folic acid synthesis, thereby blocking formation of this vitamin, which is involved in purine and pyrimidine synthesis. Sulfonamides are selectively toxic for certain bacteria for two reasons: (1) Some bacteria are impermeable to folic acid, and therefore exogenous folic acid cannot enter and (2) mammals cannot synthesize folic acid and must be provided with preformed folic acid as a vitamin in their diets. Therefore mammalian cells can survive sulfonamide because they receive preformed folic acid into their cells, whereas folic acid-impermeable bacteria, in the presence of sulfonamide, cannot make the folic acid they need.

Antifungal and Antiprotozoan Chemotherapy Represents Special Challenges

Treatment of human fungal and protozoan infections with antimicrobial agents represents a special challenge because the infecting eucaryotic pathogens share structural, metabolic, and molecular characteristics with human cells. Fewer drugs are available to treat fungal and protozoan diseases than are available for procaryotic diseases, and some of the drugs that are used are potentially toxic to human tissue.

Amphotericin B and nystatin, produced by *Streptomyces,* are polyene antibiotics that are among the most effective antifungal

The War Against Antibiotic-Resistant Microbes

The discovery of penicillin and other antibiotics in the early 1900s established a new era of miracle drugs that appeared to give humans a marked edge over bacteria in their seemingly endless host-parasite war. Infectious diseases such as pneumonia, tuberculosis, and gonorrhea that once were the scourge of humanity and affected millions of people could now be effectively controlled by magic bullets bearing names like penicillin, tetracycline, and rifamycin. By the 1970s, it appeared that complete victory over many once deadly diseases was just a matter of time.

However, in the early 1970s, this scenario began to dramatically change. In 1976, penicillin-resistant *Neisseria gonorrhoeae* harboring β-lactamase genes appeared in the United States. Since then, the percentage of these resistant strains has increased in some years to more than 10% of all gonorrhea cases reported, making treatment more difficult and expensive (Figure 5.25). Tetracycline-resistant strains of *N. gonorrhoeae* also began to appear in 1986. Other bacterial pathogens have become more resistant to antibiotics as well (Figure 5.26). *Enterococcus*, which causes bladder infections, endocarditis, and septicemia, has developed resistance to many antibiotics including vancomycin. Most strains of *Staphylococcus aureus*, which causes a wide variety of diseases ranging from pyoderma to toxic shock syndrome, are now penicillin resistant; an increasing number are also methicillin and gentamicin resistant. In fact, methicillin-resistant *S. aureus* (MRSA) have become a major problem in nosocomial, or hospital-acquired, infections and have become resistant to most other antibiotics. The potential nightmare, which may become reality in a few years, is a supermicrobe resistant to all known antibiotics.

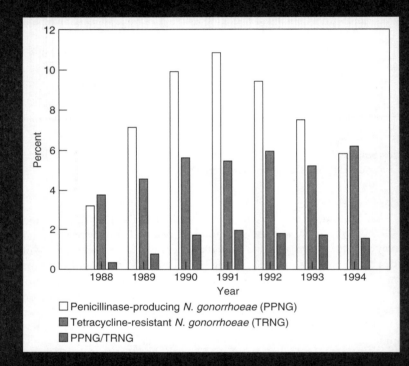

figure 5.25
Percentage of *Neisseria gonorrhoeae* Strains Resistant to Penicillin and/or Tetracycline

What has caused this recent emergence of antibiotic-resistant strains? The indiscriminate use of antibiotics in the 1950s and 1960s to treat upper respiratory tract infections before diagnosis (most upper respiratory tract infections are caused by viruses, not by bacteria) has contributed to selection of drug-resistant strains. Patients who do not complete their entire regimen of prescribed antibiotics add to the problem. When antibiotic therapy is ended early, drug-resistant strains can develop. The widespread use of antibiotics in animal feed to increase weight gain in cattle, pigs, and chickens is a contributing factor. In recent years, it has been discovered that some bacteria can transfer plasmid-borne antibiotic-resistant genes to other bacteria. There is evidence of the transfer of the β-lactamase gene between *S. aureus* and other bacteria.

Fortunately, new drugs developed by pharmaceutical companies help shift the balance of scales in this seesaw biological battle on the side of humanity. However, as bacteria continue to evolve new mechanisms to evade drugs, it becomes increasingly important for physicians and scientists to maintain their vigilance against antibiotic-resistant microbes.

Antimicrobial Resistance
Acquisition and Expression of Resistance Genes • pp. 1–9

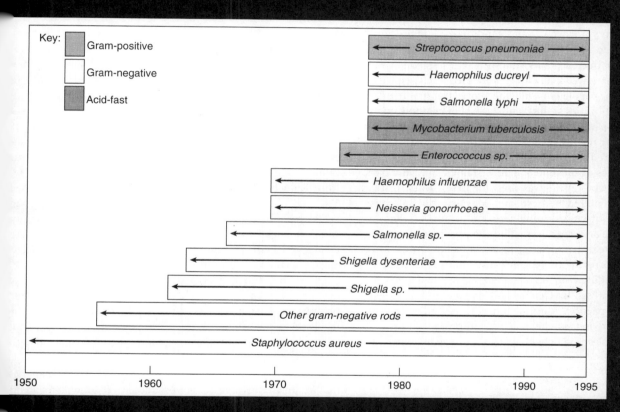

Figure 5.26
Emergence of Antibiotic Resistance in Bacterial Pathogens Since the Beginning of Antibiotic Therapy

medicines. Both drugs bind to sterols in fungal membranes, causing alterations in membrane permeability and leakage of cell constituents. Amphotericin is given intravenously for the treatment of cryptococcosis, histoplasmosis, coccidioidomycosis, and candidiasis (see fungal respiratory tract diseases, page 512; and fungal oral diseases, page 515), but frequently causes toxic side effects including kidney damage and anemia, and therefore its use is closely monitored. Nystatin is applied as a topical ointment or suppository and is useful in the treatment of candidiasis.

Griseofulvin, produced by *Penicillium,* is an antimicrobial agent that is used for ringworm, athlete's foot, and other fungal infections of the skin, nails, and hair (see fungal skin diseases, page 530). Griseofulvin is taken orally and is absorbed from the intestinal tract into the bloodstream, where it is carried to the deep skin layers and accumulates in keratinous tissue (epidermis, nails, and hair). The antibiotic is thought to disrupt the mitotic spindle and to inhibit fungal cell division.

Flucytosine is a synthetic derivative of cytosine that is useful in the treatment of cryptococcosis and candidiasis. Fungi deaminate the compound to yield fluorouracil, a highly toxic substance that prevents normal nucleic acid synthesis.

Many protozoa have several stages in their life cycles (see protozoan life cycle, page 377) and, therefore, treatment often requires different antibiotics at different stages. For example, treatment of malaria, which is caused by *Plasmodium,* involves the use of primaquine during the liver phase of infection and chloroquine during infection of red blood cells. Primaquine and chloroquine are synthetic derivates of quinine, a drug obtained from the bark of the chinchona tree. Quinine was used for many years to treat malaria until it was replaced by these less toxic derivatives. Because of the development of chloroquine-resistant strains of *Plasmodium,* quinine and a newer drug, mefloquine, have been used in recent years for the treatment of drug-resistant malarial infections.

The synthetic drug metronidazole is used to treat several protozoan diseases, including amoebic dysentery, caused by *Entamoeba histolytica;* diarrhea caused by *Giardia lamblia* (see protozoan gastrointestinal diseases, page 523); and vaginitis caused by *Trichomonas vaginalis.* Pentamidine isethionate, another antiprotozoan drug, is used to treat African sleeping sickness, caused by *Trypanosoma.*

Antiviral Drugs Take Advantage of the Unique Properties of Viruses

Viruses are unable to reproduce independently and replicate only within a living host cell (see virus replication, page 395). Since viruses use the host metabolic machinery during replication, treatment of viral diseases is difficult without affecting the host cell. There are few antiviral drugs and those that have been approved in the United States take advantage of the unique properties of viruses (Table 5.6).

Most antiviral agents are synthetic nucleosides that mimic the structures of purines and pyrmidines. These analogs block viral DNA or RNA synthesis either by inhibiting the viral polymerase or by becoming incorporated into the growing viral DNA or RNA molecule, resulting in a nonfunctional viral nucleic acid. Acyclovir (Zovirax), a structure analog of guanosine, is used in the

table	5.6	
Some Examples of Antiviral Drugs		
Pathogen	**Disease**	**Drugs of Choice**
Herpesvirus	Genital herpes, shingles, chickenpox keratoconjunctivitis	Acyclovir (Zovirax), idoxuridine (IudR), trifluridine, vidarabine (ara-A)
Human immunodeficiency virus	AIDS	Azidothymidine (AZT), didanosine (ddI), dideoxycytosine (ddC)
Influenza A virus	Influenza	Amantadine

treatment of genital herpes, shingles, chickenpox, and other infections caused by herpesviruses. The drug, which is administered as an ointment, orally, or by injection, is phosphorylated by herpesvirus kinase and inhibits viral DNA polymerase, thus blocking viral DNA replication. Because acyclovir is activated specifically by herpesvirus kinase, the drug has selective antiviral activity, making it useful in chemotherapy. Idoxuridine (IUdR) and trifluridine, analogs of thymidine, and vidarabine (ara-A), an analog of adenine, are also used in the treatment of herpesvirus infections.

Azidothymidine (AZT), also called zidovudine, is an analog of thymidine that is used for treatment of acquired immune deficiency syndrome (AIDS) patients. AIDS is caused by human immunodeficiency virus (HIV), a retrovirus that synthesizes DNA from RNA by the enzyme reverse transcriptase (see AIDS, page 536). AZT inhibits reverse transcriptase, thereby blocking further DNA synthesis and viral replication. Although AZT does not cure AIDS, it does slow the course of the disease in many instances. Didanosine (ddI) and dideoxycytosine (ddC) are other nucleoside analogs that are used to inhibit reverse transcriptase.

Amantadine is a drug that specifically inhibits the replication of influenza A viruses. Because the drug blocks the penetration and uncoating of virus particles, it is usually given prophylactically to prevent disease. Use of this drug can reduce the incidence of influenza by 50% to 80%. Amantadine has some side effects, including dizziness, confusion, and insomnia.

Interferons are glycoproteins that inhibit the translation of viral mRNA. Interferons are naturally produced by mammalian cells during viral infection and may be useful in the treament of hepatitis, genital herpes, influenza, and the common cold (see interferon, page 406).

Antimicrobial Susceptibility Tests Are Used to Determine the Type and Quantity of Antimicrobial Agents Used in Chemotherapy

One of the most important functions of a hospital laboratory is to determine the antimicrobial susceptibilities of pathogens causing disease in patients. This information is used by the physician to determine the type and quantity of antimicrobial agent to use in chemotherapy. There are two methods that can be used to determine the susceptibility of a bacterium to antimicrobial agents: the **tube dilution method** and the **disk diffusion method**.

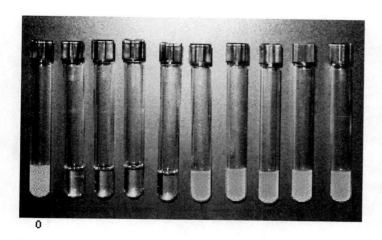

figure 5.27

Tube Dilution Method for Determining Antimicrobial Susceptibility
This series shows the growth of *Staphylococcus aureus* in tubes containing up to 8 µg/ml of the antibiotic ampicillin. There is no growth in tubes containing 16 µg/ml or more of ampicillin. The minimal inhibitory concentration (MIC) of ampicillin for *S. aureus* is thus 16 µg/ml.

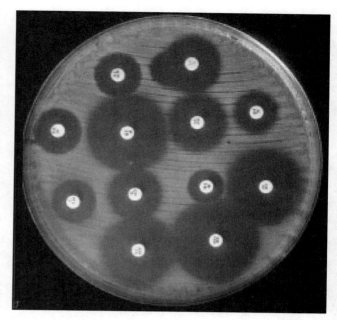

figure 5.28

Disk Diffusion Method for Determining Antimicrobial Susceptibility
Disks containing different antibiotics are placed on an agar plate inoculated with *Staphylococcus aureus*. Clear zones appear around disks with antibiotics that are inhibitory for the bacterium.

 Antimicrobial Action
Antibiotic Susceptibility Testing: Terminology • pp. 7–8

The Tube Dilution Method Is Used to Determine Susceptibility to Precise Quantities of an Antimicrobial Agent

In the tube dilution method, the test bacterium is inoculated into broth tubes containing serial dilutions of the antimicrobial agent (Figure 5.27). The inoculated cultures are incubated for a suitable period of time (usually 24 hours), and the presence or absence of growth is determined by the turbidity in each tube. Tubes containing moderate to high concentrations of the antimicrobial agent would normally be expected to have no growth. The **minimal inhibitory concentration (MIC)** of the antimicrobial agent for the test bacterium can be determined by the lowest concentration of the agent that produces no observable growth.

At the MIC end point, bacterial growth is inhibited, but there may still be viable bacteria in the tube. To check for viable cells, an aliquot of tubes showing no growth can be inoculated onto agar plates. The plates are incubated and then observed for growth. The **minimal bactericidal concentration (MBC)** is the concentration of antimicrobial agent in the tube that has produced no growth.

The tube dilution method is considered accurate for determining susceptibility to precise quantities of an antimicrobial agent. However, the method is time-consuming, expensive, and not practical for use in most hospital laboratories for routine susceptibility testing.

 **Antimicrobial Action**
Antibiotic Susceptibility Testing: Broth Dilution • pp. 14–16

The Disk Diffusion Method Uses Filter Paper Disks Containing Known Concentrations of Antimicrobial Agents to Determine Antimicrobial Susceptibility

A more common procedure used for susceptibility testing in hospitals is the disk diffusion method. Filter paper disks containing known concentrations of antimicrobial agents are placed onto the surface of an agar plate inoculated with the test bacterium. The plate is incubated for 16 to 18 hours, and the zones of inhibition are read around each paper disk (Figure 5.28).

During the incubation period, the antimicrobial agent diffuses through the agar, and a concentration gradient of the agent is established. At some point in this gradient, growth of the susceptible bacteria is suppressed, and no growth is observed within a circular zone around the disk. The size of the zone of inhibition is determined by the type of agar medium used, the incubation conditions, the type of antimicrobial agent used, and the susceptibility of the test organism to the diffusing agent. In 1966, William Kirby and Alfred Bauer first introduced the principle of measuring zones of inhibition around disks to determine antimicrobial agent susceptibilities, so this test is often called the **Kirby-Bauer test.** The Kirby-Bauer test is a rapid, convenient method to determine the susceptibilities of microorganisms to antimicrobial agents.

 **Antimicrobial Action**
Susceptibility Testing: Disk Diffusion • pp. 11–13

Antimicrobial susceptibility tests are important for the clinical management of infectious diseases. Without rapid methods to determine the susceptibility of microbial has significantly impacted the microbiology laboratory. Most automated instruments for susceptibility testing use one of two basic principles: (1) microbial growth to detect microbial growth (Figure 5.29). A microorganism in pure culture is inoculated into several broth tubes containing different antimicrobial agents. Growth is then monitored turbidimetrically over a short time period (usually three to eight hours). Antimicrobial susceptibility is determined by the

Automated Methods for Antimicrobial Susceptibility Testing

pathogens to antibiotics, disease can run rampant in a host and possibly cause death.

In the past, susceptibility tests using the tube dilution or disk diffusion method required several days to perform. Today automation has decreased the processing time of antimicrobial susceptibility tests and is measured by turbidity or (2) microbial growth is measured by the detection of metabolites.

Instruments such as the MS-2 of Abbott Laboratories, the AutoMicrobic System (AMS) of Vitek Systems, and the Autobac IDX of General Diagnostics use turbidity absence of growth in broth tubes containing the effective antimicrobial agents.

An alternative to turbidity measurements is the detection of carbon dioxide released during microbial growth and metabolism in a closed system. The BACTEC System (Becton Dickinson Diagnostic Instrument Systems) measures carbon dioxide as a product of microbial metabolic activity by infrared spectrophotometry. Any level of carbon dioxide above a preset baseline indicates microbial growth (Figure 5.30).

Both the turbidimetric and metabolic activity systems have been automated. Following inoculation of the microorganism into broths, the systems automatically read and analyze all results and provide a printout of the results within a few hours. These systems have significantly improved the ability of the microbiology laboratory to provide antimicrobial susceptibility test results to the physician within a short time.

figure 5.29
The AutoMicrobic System
Disposable test cards containing broths with different antimicrobial agents are inoculated with the microorganism. The test cards are loaded into the AutoMicrobic System Reader/Incubator (second chamber from the left). After incubation, the test cards are read and analyzed automatically, and a computer printout is produced.

figure 5.30
The BACTEC System
Vials containing metabolic substrates (for example, glucose), antimicrobial agents, and the microorganism are monitored for CO_2 production by infrared spectrophotometry.

The Carbon Dioxide Requirement of Neisseria meningitidis

Many bacteria, fungi, and protozoa require carbon dioxide (CO_2) for growth, but for many years it was not known why. One of the first studies to show the role of CO_2 in cell growth and metabolism was performed by Dorothy M. Tuttle and Henry W. Scherp in 1952. They examined the effects of different nutrients on the CO_2 requirement for the bacterium *Neisseria meningitidis*.

Cells of *N. meningitidis* were serially diluted and inoculated into parallel series of defined media containing different growth factors (yeast extract, purines and pyrimidines, casein hydrolysate, and vitamins) and incubated in the presence or absence of added CO_2. The incubation of bacteria under added CO_2 was achieved by placing cultures in sealed jars in an atmosphere of 3% CO_2 added from a commercial tank. Cultures were incubated at 37.5°C and then examined for the presence or absence of turbidity after 24 and 48 hours.

The results showed that larger inocula of bacteria were required to obtain growth without CO_2 than with 3% CO_2 (Table 5P.1). Furthermore, it was observed that 0.01% yeast extract or a combination of 0.03% guanine/uracil/cytosine + 0.5% casein hydrolysate + B vitamins could effectively substitute for the CO_2 requirement. Other combinations of growth factors were not as effective in promoting bacterial growth with no added CO_2.

Previous studies by G.P. Gladstone, P. Fildes, and G.M. Richardson had suggested that the CO_2 requirement of bacteria was related to cell growth; CO_2 reduced the length of the lag phase of the growth curve. Based on this information, Tuttle and Scherp surmised that the function of the growth factors in their experiments was to stimulate the production of CO_2, thereby reducing the length of the lag phase for growth of *N. meningitidis* and stimulating the growth of these bacteria. Subsequent experiments by other investigators have shown that growth factors such as those used by Tuttle and Scherp probably supply CO_2 that is necessary for CO_2-fixing reactions in the cell. The experiments of Tuttle and Scherp were instrumental in first showing that these growth factors could replace atmospheric CO_2 for the growth of bacteria.

Source:

Tuttle, D.M., and H.W. Scherp. 1952. Studies on the carbon dioxide requirement of *Neisseria meningitidis*. *Journal of Bacteriology* 64:171–181.

References

Gladstone, G.P., P. Fildes, and G.M. Richardson. 1935. Carbon dioxide as an essential factor in the growth of bacteria. *British Journal of Experimental Pathology* 16:335–348.

Griffin, P.J., and S.V. Rieder. 1957. A study on the growth requirements of *Neisseria gonorrhoeae* and its clinical application. *Yale Journal of Biology and Medicine* 29:613–621.

Wimpenny, J.W.T. 1969. Oxygen and carbon dioxide as regulators of microbial growth and metabolism. In *19th Symposium of the Society for General Microbiology, volume 19, Microbial growth*, pp. 161–197. Cambridge: Cambridge University Press.

table 5P.1

Substitutes for Supplemental CO_2 in the Growth of *Neisseria meningitidis*

Supplement	Number of Organisms Inoculated per 5 ml ($\times 2.0$)[a]							
	10^7	10^6	10^5	10^4	10^3	10^2	10^1	10^0
None	+	+	−	−	−	−	−	−
3% CO_2	+	+	+	+	+	+	+	+
0.01% yeast extract	+	+	+	+	+	+	+	+
0.03% GUC (total)[b]	+	+	+	+	c	−	−	−
0.5% casein hydrolysate	+	+	+	+	c	−	−	−
B vitamins[d]	+	+	−	−	−	−	−	−
0.03% GUC + 0.5% casein hydrolysate	+	+	+	+	c	c	c	−
0.03% GUC + B vitamins	+	+	+	+	c	c	−	−
0.5% casein hydrolysate + B vitamins	+	+	+	+	+	+	c	−
0.03% GUC + 0.5% casein hydrolysate + B vitamins	+	+	+	+	+	+	+	+

[a]+ = growth in 24 hr; − = nongrowth in 48 hr.
[b]GUC = 0.004% guanine, 0.013% uracil, and 0.013% cytosine.
[c]growth in 48 hr, but not in 24 hr.
[d]B vitamins = thiamine, pantothenic acid, pyridoxine, and nicotinic acid, 1 µg/ml; riboflavin, 0.5 µg/ml; biotin, 0.001 µg/ml; and folic acid concentrate, 0.01 µg/ml.

Summary

1. Growth is the orderly increase in all major constituents of an organism. Growth of microorganisms is usually expressed as population growth because of the small size of microbes.

2. Bacteria generally divide by binary fission. The generation time, or the doubling time, is the time required for a population of bacteria to double in number.

3. Bacterial population growth can be followed by increases in cell numbers and cell mass, turbidimetric measurements, and changes in cell activity.

4. A common procedure to monitor bacterial population growth is the viable count. The viable count technique involves diluting bacteria from the sample population and placing the diluted suspensions on an agar medium by the spread plate or pour plate procedure.

5. The most probable number (MPN) procedure estimates the number of viable cells in a sample population by successive dilutions of the sample until no bacteria are left.

6. A bacterial population growth curve in a closed system, or batch culture, consists of four phases: lag, exponential, stationary, and death, or decline. Bacteria synthesize enzymes for growth during the lag phase, but cell numbers do not increase. Bacteria actively grow at a constant rate during the exponential phase, and then enter the stationary phase as nutrient supplies are depleted and toxic waste products accumulate. The death phase occurs when more cells die than are replaced by new cells.

7. Continuous cultures are established when a culture reaches an equilibrium point wherein cell numbers and nutrient levels in the culture vessel become constant. A chemostat is an example of a continuous culture system in which growth is controlled by the flow rate of the system and the concentration of a limiting nutrient. Synchronous cultures consist of populations of cells that are all in the same stage of growth.

8. Sterilization is the killing or removing of all living organisms. An autoclave sterilizes materials by a combination of high temperature (121°C) and moist heat (steam). Pasteurization is the treatment of liquids with heat at 62.8°C for 30 minutes (low-temperature holding method) or 71.7°C for 15 seconds (high-temperature short-time method) to kill most pathogenic and spoilage microorganisms.

9. Antimicrobial agents are chemicals that inhibit or destroy microbial growth. These agents can be divided into four categories: disinfectants, antiseptics, antibiotics, and synthetic drugs. Disinfectants are used on inanimate objects, whereas antiseptics are less toxic and are used on external body surfaces. Antibiotics are naturally produced antimicrobial agents, whereas synthetic drugs are synthetic chemicals developed by the pharmaceutical industry.

10. Chemotherapeutic agents are antimicrobial agents that are selectively toxic for microorganisms and do not damage the animal host. Narrow-spectrum agents are effective against only specific microorganisms or groups of microorganisms. Broad-spectrum agents are effective against a wide range of microorganisms. Chemotherapeutic agents can inhibit peptidoglycan synthesis, protein synthesis, and nucleic acid synthesis; damage the plasma membrane; or act as structure analogs to compete with cellular metabolites in enzymatic reactions.

11. Antimicrobial susceptibility tests are useful in determining the proper antimicrobial agent to use in chemotherapy. Use of these tests on a routine basis prior to treatment can help reduce the development of antibiotic-resistant microorganisms.

EVOLUTION *and* BIODIVERSITY

The emergence of antimicrobial drug resistance in recent years has brought renewed concerns that microbial pathogens that were once thought to be nearly eradicated by successful chemotherapy may now be reappearing as more highly resistant forms. Increased microbial drug resistance has resulted in higher death rates, increased health care costs, and often more toxic drugs or drug combinations used in chemotherapy. When the first antibiotics were introduced for general use in the 1940s, it was thought that these "miracle drugs" might eradicate infectious disease. Yet today, drugs that at one time were used successfully to treat tuberculosis, gonorrhea, pneumonia, and hospital-acquired staphylococcal infections have lost their effectiveness. What has happened to cause this increased resistance? As antimicrobial agents became widely used, they were overprescribed in many instances. Physicians would administer antibiotics before identifying the disease agent, which in the case of respiratory tract infections was often a virus not affected by antibiotics. Patients would take only part of the prescribed dosage of antibiotics, not realizing that this partial treatment would only help microbes develop resistance. Antibiotics were incorporated into livestock feeds to prevent disease and promote growth of animals. As a consequence of these practices, microorganisms adapted to increasingly higher levels of antibiotics and became more resistant to these drugs. This evolution of microbes has resulted in the highly resistant strains that now present so many problems in chemotherapy and are an indication of the remarkably rapid ability of microorganisms to adapt to changes in their environments.

Short Answer

1. How do bacterial cells divide?

2. What is meant by bacterial "growth"?

3. Given g = 30 minutes, how long would it take for a cell to yield a population of 1,024?

4. List several methods for counting bacteria.

5. Which method of viable count determination is best for cultures that are anaerobic? Which is best for heat-sensitive cultures?

6. What method of enumeration would you use if you wanted:
   a. to determine the utilization of various carbon sources?
   b. to count bacteria in a relatively clean water supply?
   c. a quick answer?

7. Identify, in sequence, the phases of a bacterial growth curve. During which phase(s) is (are) there no cell division?

8. How do we know bacteria are not dormant during the lag phase?

9. Why doesn't the constant rate of growth observed during the exponential phase continue indefinitely?

10. Could exponential growth be extended artificially? Explain.

11. Which method of microbial control would you use to sterilize:
    a. surgical instruments or glassware?
    b. surfaces (for example, operating or transfer room)?
    c. culture media?

12. List several antiseptics. List several disinfectants.

13. Identify the mechanisms of action for chemotherapeutic antimicrobial agents.

14. Identify several factors which have led to the development of drug-resistant bacteria.

15. The term "antibiotic" is generally used for any drug given to control microbial growth. Why is this a misnomer?

16. Describe the Kirby-Bauer test. Explain its significance.

Multiple Choice

1. Which of the following methods of control does *not* sterilize?
   a. autoclave
   b. ionizing radiation
   c. pasteurization
   d. tyndallization
   e. All of the above sterilize.

2. Which of the following bind sulfhydryl groups to denature proteins?
   a. phenols, alcohols
   b. surfactants
   c. halogens (for example, iodine and chlorine)
   d. formalin, glutaraldehyde, ethylene oxide
   e. heavy metals (for example, copper and mercury)

3. Which of the following inhibit cellular metabolism?
   a. penicillins
   b. polymyxin, nystatin, amphotericin B
   c. aminoglycosides
   d. sulfonamides

4. Which of the following is (are) narrow-spectrum agents?
   a. chloramphenicol
   b. gentamicin
   c. streptomycin
   d. tetracycline

Critical Thinking

1. Explain why we would employ methods (for example, pasteurization and disinfection) that do *not* kill 100 percent of the organisms.

2. Compare and contrast antiseptics and disinfectants.

3. Describe the characteristics of bacteria that are exploited by antimicrobial therapy.

4. Discuss (pros and cons) the use of antimicrobial agents.

Supplementary Readings

Baron, E.J., L.R. Peterson, and S.M. Finegold. 1994. *Bailey & Scott's diagnostic microbiology*, 9th ed. St. Louis: Mosby. (A textbook of diagnostic microbiology with chapters on antimicrobial susceptibility testing.)

Davies, J. 1994. Inactivation of antibiotics and the dissemination of resistance genes. *Science* 264:375–382. (A research article describing common mechanisms of antibiotic resistance in bacteria.)

Garrod, L.P., H.P. Lambert, and F. O'Grady, eds. 1981. *Antibiotics and chemotherapy*, 5th ed. Edinburgh: Churchill Livingstone. (Detailed discussion of modes of action of chemotherapeutic agents and their uses in treatment of diseases.)

Mandelstam, J., K. McQuillen, and I.W. Dawes. 1973. *Biochemistry of bacterial growth*, 2d ed. New York: Blackwell Scientific Publications, Ltd. (A discussion of physiological and chemical changes during bacterial growth.)

Murray, P.R., E.J. Baron, M.A. Pfaller, F.C. Tenover, and R.H. Yolken, eds. 1995. *Manual of clinical microbiology*, 6th ed. Washington, D.C.: American Society for Microbiology. (An extensive clinical laboratory manual with chapters on antimicrobial susceptibility testing.)

Neidhardt, F.C., J.L. Ingraham, and M. Schaechter. 1990. *Physiology of the bacterial cell: A molecular approach*. Sunderland, Mass.: Sinauer Associates. (A well-written textbook of bacterial physiology and genetics.)

Norris, J. A., and D.W. Robbins, eds. 1969. *Methods in microbiology, volume 1*. New York: Academic Press. (A description of methods for culture of microorganisms and the various techniques used for measurement of microbial growth.)

Norris, J. A., and D.W. Robbins, eds. 1970. *Methods in microbiology, volume 2*. New York: Academic Press. (A description of continuous culture techniques, methods to optimize microbial growth, and the effects of temperature and pH on growth.)

Pirt, S. J. 1975. *Principles of microbe and cell cultivation*. New York: John Wiley & Sons. (An in-depth discussion of the effects of environmental and chemical parameters on growth and the chemistry of microbial growth.)

ENERGY AND METABOLISM

EVOLUTION AND BIODIVERSITY

Computer-generated graphic of the high-energy compound, adenosine triphosphate (ATP). The positions of the component atoms are represented by different colors: carbon (green), nitrogen (blue), oxygen (red), phosphorus (white), and hydrogen (white).

 Microbes in Motion ———————— PREVIEW LINK

This chapter covers the key topics of microbial energy mechanisms—aerobic and anaerobic. The following sections in the *Microbes in Motion* CD-ROM may be useful as a preview to your reading or as a supplemental study aid:

Bacterial Structure and Function: Cell Membrane (Energy Production), 12–21. *Microbial Metabolism and Growth:* Metabolism, 1–20.

ne of the most fascinating aspects of life is the ability of a living cell to oxidize simple chemical substances and release **energy** that can be used to drive all of life's processes. Even more amazing is the fact that these minute, microscopic cells can perform this transformation more rapidly and efficiently than any machine or artificial device. Like a steam engine or electric generator, the cell performs its job continuously. But unlike these manufactured devices, a cell can use energy to reproduce itself, generate other similar cells, and convert disordered chemicals from the environment into highly organized cellular constituents.

However, to do this, cells must have a constant source of energy. Energy, defined as the capacity to do work, is rarely available to the cell in the proper form to perform chemical work. Living organisms have devised a variety of ways to extract energy from their surroundings and convert it to useful forms.

Concepts of Energy

Microorganisms are dynamic, self-propagating entities that perform different types of work: mechanical, electrical, and chemical. Mechanical work is physical, such as the movement of flagella or cilia or the streaming cytoplasm of amoebae. The movement of chemical compounds or ions against a concentration gradient, such as the active transport of glucose by a bacterium, is also considered work. When the transported substance is a charged molecule, the concentration gradient is also a potential gradient, and electrical work is involved. Organisms are constantly synthesizing complex organic molecules that function as the chemical building blocks of cells; this biosynthesis is an example of chemical work.

To perform work, microbes and other living organisms must have a source of energy. Energy exists in different forms (mechanical, thermal or heat, electrical, and chemical) and can be converted, though not with perfect efficiency, from one form to another. Several units may be used to measure energy; the most frequently used unit in biological systems is the **kilocalorie (kcal)**. A kilocalorie is the quantity of heat energy required to raise the temperature of 1 kg of water 1°C.

Other than phototrophs, which derive energy from light, all other organisms obtain their energy ultimately from chemical substances. Chemical energy resides in the bonds of chemical molecules, but not all molecules have the same number of bonds or the same amount of energy.

For example, the equation

$$C_6H_{12}O_6 + 6 O_2 \rightarrow 6 CO_2 + 6 H_2O$$

is balanced and has the same number and types of atoms on both sides of the equation, but the number and types of bonds differ. Consequently, the energy contained in the molecules differs. When

molecules are rearranged in a chemical reaction, energy is either liberated or required. Energy-liberating processes (**exergonic reactions**) provide the cell with the energy required to perform work, which is an energy-requiring process (**endergonic reaction**). For example, ATP hydrolysis (an exergonic reaction) can be coupled with phosphorylation of glucose (an endergonic reaction):

$$ATP + H_2O \rightarrow ADP + PO_4 \qquad \Delta G = -7.3 \text{ kcal/mole}$$

$$Glucose + PO_4 \rightarrow glucose\text{-}6\text{-}PO_4 + H_2O \qquad \Delta G = +3 \text{ kcal/mole}$$

This **coupling** of exergonic and endergonic reactions is fundamentally important to all cellular processes.

Energy, in addition to its different forms, can also assume two different states: **potential energy** and **kinetic energy.** Potential energy is defined as stored energy or energy of position. Kinetic energy is energy of work or motion. The energy contained within any given substance or object is initially all in the state of potential energy. This potential energy, however, is gradually converted to kinetic energy as the condition or position of the substance or object changes. An example of such change is the conversion of potential energy (energy of position) in a stationary rock at the top of a hill to kinetic energy (energy of motion) as the rock moves and rolls down the hill. Chemical molecules represent storehouses of potential energy. As these molecules are oxidized by living organisms, the potential energy stored within the chemical bonds is liberated and made available for performing work.

Thermodynamics Is the Study of Energy Transformations

Energy not only exists in different forms, but also has the ability to change from one form to another. During fuel combustion, chemical energy is converted into heat (thermal energy) and light (electromagnetic energy). Electromagnetic energy from the sun is transformed by phototrophs into chemical energy in the form of organic compounds through the process of photosynthesis. The chemical energy that is released when molecules are broken down into simpler compounds is used by living organisms for movement, metabolism, and growth. Each of these examples represents transformation of energy.

The study of energy transformations forms a branch of science known as **thermodynamics.** In thermodynamics, energy exchanges are considered within the framework of a defined system and its surroundings. A thermodynamic system is defined by such variables as temperature, volume, pressure, and chemical content.

Bioenergetics refers specifically to the study of energy transformations in living systems (Figure 6.1). Energy exchanges are especially important to living organisms, since energy is usually available to these organisms only in the form of chemical or electromagnetic energy and must first be converted to perform work. Because energy is not always readily available in a usable form, organisms must be able to store energy in forms such as chemical energy for later use.

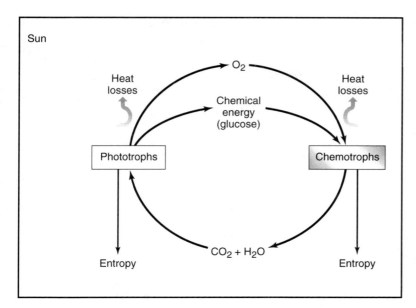

figure 6.1
Energy Transformations in the Biosphere
Energy from sunlight is transformed to chemical energy (for example, glucose) by phototrophs. These chemical compounds (for example, glucose) are then used by chemotrophs during respiration or fermentation to produce ATP for cellular activity. Carbon dioxide and water are produced during respiration and fermentation, completing the cycle.

Energy Can Be Neither Created Nor Destroyed

Although energy is convertible from one form to another, it can be neither created nor destroyed. This principle of energy conservation, known as the **first law of thermodynamics,** states that in any transformation of energy, whether the transformation is a chemical reaction in a laboratory beaker or photosynthesis by a living cell, energy cannot be created or destroyed; it is conserved. The total amount of energy present after the reaction must equal the initial amount of energy.

The energy contained within the products is less than the energy of the reactants in spontaneous reactions. The difference in energy content between the initial and final states of a reaction (the total amount of energy released during the reaction) is called **enthalpy** and is designated by ΔH. Not all energy released during a reaction, however, is available for doing work. That portion of released energy that can potentially be used for work is known as **free energy.** Changes in free energy of a reaction are designated by ΔG ($\Delta G°$ if determined under standard conditions of one atmosphere pressure and one molar concentration; $\Delta G°'$ if determined under standard conditions at pH 7.0, which approximates biological conditions). Free energy changes are expressed in units of kilocalories per mole. Reactions that occur spontaneously have a decrease in free energy level from reactants to products (negative $\Delta G°'$) and are exergonic. Endergonic

reactions have a positive $\Delta G°'$ and require the input of energy to proceed.

The term *free energy* includes not only energy that is actually used for work, but also energy that has the potential for work. Heat or thermal energy, although seldom used for work in biological systems, is thus included as part of free energy. In most reactions, however, heat does not perform work and is simply lost to the surroundings. When heat is lost to the surroundings during energy transformations, as in the combustion or oxidation of glucose, the reaction is termed **exothermic. Endothermic** reactions are those in which heat is absorbed from the surroundings. An example of an endothermic reaction is the addition of ammonium sulfate to water. As the salt dissolves in water, heat is absorbed, resulting in cooling of the solution.

All Natural Processes Proceed in Such a Manner That There Is an Increase in Entropy

Free energy constitutes the portion of liberated energy that can be used for work. The other portion of energy released during a reaction cannot under any condition be used for work and is considered to be unrecoverable energy. This unrecoverable energy is termed **entropy** and is designated by the letter **S.** Entropy is a measurement of the disorder of a system. Spontaneous reactions always proceed with an increase in entropy, a characteristic embodied in the **second law of thermodynamics.**

The second law of thermodynamics states that all processes in the universe occur in such a manner that there is an increase in total entropy. As a consequence of this law, the universe constantly moves toward maximum disorder, or entropic doom. Fortunately there is enough usable energy in the universe to make entropic doom a distant and remote possibility. The increase in entropy under the second law explains why a rock that has rolled down a hill cannot return up the hill on its own; additional energy from some other source must be made available to push it. The additional energy is necessary because a part of the original energy in the rock has been lost to entropy and cannot be recovered.

Chemical reactions also occur in such a manner that there is an increase in entropy. These reactions move in the direction of the products, have a negative $\Delta G°'$, and cannot be reversed without an input of energy. The oxidation of glucose to carbon dioxide and water is an example; it is accompanied by a $\Delta G°'$ of -673 kcal/mole and increased entropy:

$$C_6H_{12}O_6 + 6\,O_2 \rightarrow 6\,CO_2 + 6\,H_2O \qquad \Delta G°' = -673 \text{ kcal/mole}$$

The concept of increased randomness in chemical reactions can be compared to differences in order observed with an assembled automobile engine and a disassembled engine. A completely assembled engine is more ordered than one that is disassembled.

The possibilities for disorder are greater with several hundred parts than with one large entity. In a similar sense, a large chemical molecule is considered more ordered than a rearrangement of the molecule and its bonds into several smaller molecules. Glucose is a more ordered molecule than the products of its oxidation, carbon dioxide and water. Thus when glucose is oxidized to its products, there is an increase in entropy.

The relationships among the terms free energy, enthalpy, and entropy are brought together in the equation

$$\Delta G^{o\prime} = \Delta H - T\Delta S$$

where $\Delta G^{o\prime}$ represents the free energy change, ΔH is the total energy change, T is the absolute temperature (degrees Kelvin) of the system, and ΔS represents the change in entropy. This equation not only provides information on the quantity of energy that is available for work ($\Delta G^{o\prime}$) as a result of a reaction; it also indicates whether a reaction is exergonic ($\Delta G^{o\prime} < 0$) or endergonic ($\Delta G^{o\prime} > 0$). The equation also takes into consideration entropy changes during a reaction.

Reactions that release free energy and have a negative $\Delta G^{o\prime}$ move in the direction of the products. In contrast, reactions that have a positive $\Delta G^{o\prime}$ value cannot proceed without an input of energy.

Reversible Chemical Reactions Proceed to an Equilibrium Point

Reversible chemical reactions continue until they reach an **equilibrium point,** at which there is a balance between reactants and products. At the equilibrium point, the amounts of reactants associating into products equal the amounts of products dissociating into reactants. For reactions that occur at given temperatures, the ratio of the concentrations of reactants and products at the equilibrium point takes on a specific value called the **equilibrium constant** (K_{eq}). In the reaction $A + B \rightleftarrows C + D$, the equilibrium constant is represented by the equation

$$K_{eq} = \frac{[C][D]}{[A][B]}$$

where the square brackets denote concentrations in moles per liter.

The free energy of the reaction will be at a minimum at equilibrium, with no further change in free energy (that is, $\Delta G^{o\prime} = 0$). It is therefore possible to calculate the standard free energy change of a reaction from its equilibrium constant using the equation

$$\Delta G^{o\prime} = -RT \ln K_{eq}$$

where R is the gas constant (1.99 cal/mole/degree), T is the absolute temperature, and ln is the natural logarithm (2.3 times the logarithm to the base 10) of the equilibrium constant.

If the K_{eq} of a reaction is known, we can calculate the $\Delta G^{o\prime}$ and the direction of the reaction under standard conditions and 1 molar concentrations of substrate and products. The standard free energy change value is useful because it provides a way to compare different reactions and the quantity of energy released or required by the reactions.

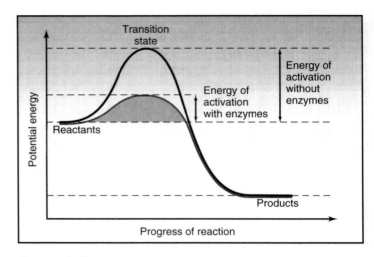

figure 6.2
Energy Requirements of a Chemical Reaction
Activation energy is required for all chemical reactions. Enzymes lower the amount of activation energy required.

Enzymes Accelerate Reaction Rates Without Themselves Being Changed

Not all spontaneous (exergonic) reactions occur at fast rates or velocities. The velocity or speed of a reaction at a given temperature and concentration is determined by the **activation energy** (E_a), the difference between the free energy of the reactants and the highest free energy state of the reactants during their transition to product (Figure 6.2).

The activation energy barrier can be significant, and depends on the types of molecules. The rate at which chemical reactions occur can be increased by increasing the rate at which reactants move and collide. Increases in temperature or reactant concentrations result in increased reaction rates. An example of this is the mixing of hydrogen and oxygen gases. The reaction $H_2 + 1/2\ O_2 \rightarrow H_2O$ has a $\Delta G^{o\prime}$ of -57 kcal/mole; yet when the two gases are mixed at room temperature, no discernible reaction occurs. If, however, the mixture is ignited with an electrical spark, water forms immediately. The spark—or rise in temperature—provides the E_a required for the reaction to proceed. After the initial spark, the ΔG continues the reaction.

Reaction rates may also be increased by the action of **catalysts,** chemical agents that increase reaction rates without themselves being changed. In the reaction of H_2 and O_2, instead of using a spark, we could have used a catalyst; a palladium catalyst lowers the E_a sufficiently to allow the reaction to occur at room temperature. This principle is illustrated by the GasPak system, in which an enclosed chamber is used to grow anaerobic bacteria (see GasPak system, page 93). Oxygen, which is toxic to anaerobic bacteria, is removed from the chamber's atmosphere by the palladium-catalyzed reaction of oxygen with hydrogen to form water.

Enzymes are protein (or, in the case of ribozymes, RNA) catalysts that occur in living organisms. The molecule (or molecules)

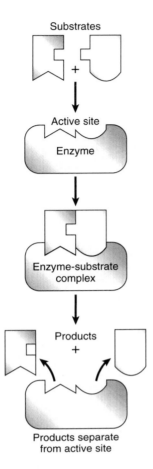

Substrates

Active site

Enzyme

Enzyme-substrate
complex

Products
+

Products separate
from active site

figure 6.3
Enzyme-Substrate Interaction
The lock-and-key mechanism is one model for enzyme action. The substrate fits into the active site, much as a key fits a lock, to form an enzyme-substrate complex. The enzyme catalyzes the reaction and releases the product. Note that the enzyme is not changed by the reaction and is now free to interact with another substrate molecule.

on which an enzyme acts is called its **substrate.** An average bacterial cell has thousands of different enzymes, each catalyzing specific chemical reactions. The kinds of enzymes present or absent in an organism determine the types of chemical pathways active in that particular organism. Enzymes do not change the equilibrium and the ΔG of the chemical reaction, but they do lower the activation energy level and permit the reaction to proceed at sufficient speed at lower temperatures to meet the cell's needs. As a consequence of this reduced activation energy, cellular reactions proceed at a faster rate.

Enzyme-substrate interactions are very specific. This specificity allows for fine control of enzymatic reactions and prevents unnecessary and energy-wasting reactions from operating continuously in the cell. Substrates bind with the enzyme at a site called the **active site** to form temporary enzyme-substrate complexes resulting in lower activation energy requirements for the reaction (Figure 6.3). After the activated transition state is reached, the enzyme-substrate complex disso-

ciates into reaction products and enzyme. The enzyme has not changed during the reaction and is now free to react with another substrate. The entire enzyme-catalyzed reaction is summarized as

$$E + S \rightleftarrows ES \rightleftarrows E + P$$

where E is enzyme, S is substrate, and P is product.

Enzymes not only are specific in their ability to react with substrates; their activity is also influenced by environmental factors such as pH and temperature. The pH of a reaction mixture affects the charge characteristics of amino acids comprising the structure of the enzyme and its active site or sites. Temperature affects enzyme activity in the same manner that it affects other chemical reactions. As temperature decreases, molecules move at slower rates and the reaction proceeds more slowly. However, since enzymes are proteins, an increase in temperature can lead to denaturation of the enzyme and a dramatic decrease in reaction rate. At higher temperatures the reaction rate increases until the point at which the enzyme becomes denatured and inactivated.

Certain chemical substances called **inhibitors** prevent or slow down enzyme reactions by binding to the enzyme and preventing substrate attachment. The inhibition of enzyme activity by such inhibitors includes two categories: reversible and irreversible. Reversible inhibition can be either competitive or noncompetitive. Competitive inhibitors structurally resemble the normal substrate of the enzyme and compete with the substrate for binding at the enzyme active site. Competitive inhibition can thus be reversed by increasing substrate concentration. An example of a competitive inhibitor is malonate, which has a structure that closely resembles the structure of succinate (Figure 6.4). Malonate competes with succinate for the active site on succinate dehydrogenase, an enzyme involved in cellular metabolism. By increasing the concentration of the substrate succinate, the inhibitory effects of the competitive inhibitor can be decreased.

Noncompetitive inhibitors are not structurally related to the enzyme substrate. Increasing the proportion of substrate to inhibitor therefore does not reverse the effects of noncompetitive inhibition. Substances such as cyanide, mercury, and arsenic are noncompetitive inhibitors that bind to enzymes at sites other than the substrate-binding site and thus reduce the catalytic activity of the enzyme. The effects of such inhibition depend on the relative concentrations of enzyme and inhibitor.

Allosteric inhibition is a special type of noncompetitive inhibition important in regulation of metabolic pathways. **Allosteric enzymes** are enzymes that have two types of specific binding sites: an active site, where substrate binds, and an allosteric site, where small molecules called **effectors** specifically bind. The binding of an effector at the allosteric site changes the conformation of the enzyme at the active site and results in a corresponding inhibition (or activation, in the case of allosteric activation) of enzyme activity (Figure 6.5a). **Feedback inhibition** is a mechanism regulated by allostery. In feedback inhibition, the effector is an end product of a biosynthetic pathway; it interacts with and inhibits the activity of a key enzyme (usually the first) early in the pathway (Figure 6.5b). End-product accumulation

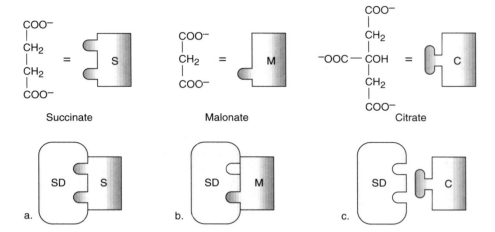

figure 6.4

Competitive Inhibition

Malonate competes with succinate for the active site on succinate dehydrogenase. a. Proper fit between succinate (S) and succinate dehydrogenase (SD). b. Competitive inhibition by malonate (M). Malonate binds, but not as well, to succinate dehydrogenase and prevents the binding of succinate. c. Citrate (C), which is not recognized by the succinate dehydrogenase active site, does not bind to the enzyme.

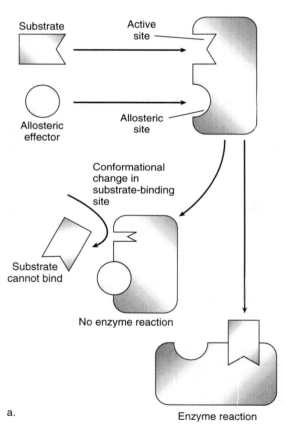

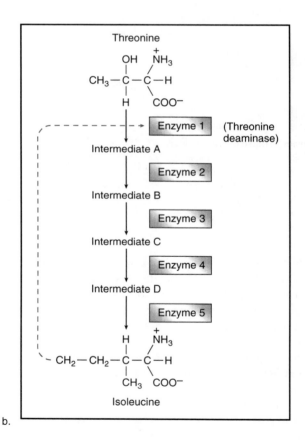

figure 6.5

Allosteric Enzymes and Feedback Inhibition

a. The mechanism of enzyme inhibition by an allosteric effector. The effector combines with the allosteric site, changing the conformation of the enzyme so that the substrate can no longer bind to the active site.

b. Feedback inhibition in a biosynthetic pathway. Five enzymes catalyze the biosynthesis of isoleucine from threonine. If the product of the pathway (isoleucine) accumulates, it allosterically inhibits threonine deaminase.

table 6.1

Some Important Coenzymes and Their Functions in the Cell

Coenzyme	Vitamin Source	Function
Biotin	Biotin	Carboxylation
Coenzyme A	Pantothenic acid	Activation of acetyl groups during pyruvate and fatty acid catabolism
Flavin adenine dinucleotide (FAD)	Riboflavin (B_2)	Electron transport and dehydrogenations
Flavin mononucleotide (FMN)	Riboflavin (B_2)	Electron transport and dehydrogenations
Nicotinamide adenine dinucleotide (NAD)	Niacin	Electron transport and dehydrogenations
Nicotinamide adenine dinucleotide phosphate (NADP)	Niacin	Electron transport and dehydrogenations
Pyridoxal phosphate	Pyridoxine (B_6)	Transamination, decarboxylation, and racemization of amino acids
Tetrahydrofolic acid	Folic acid	Transfer of one-carbon units
Thiamine pyrophosphate	Thiamine (B_1)	Group transfers; oxidation and decarboxylation of keto acids

results in feedback inhibition of enzyme activity. If the end product is used up, enzyme activity resumes. Feedback inhibition is an important mechanism by which microorganisms and other cells regulate the synthesis of amino acids and other low molecular weight compounds without accumulation of unwanted metabolic intermediates. Synthesis of glycogen, a cellular storage product, is regulated by allosteric activation. When intermediates of pathways such as glycolysis (see the Embden-Meyerhof pathway, page 150) accumulate, allosteric enzymes associated with glycogen synthesis are activated.

Enzymes can also be inhibited noncompetitively in a permanent, or irreversible, manner. Irreversible inhibition may be complete or partial and generally involves the denaturation or alteration of enzyme structure. This type of inhibition is caused by chemical or physical treatment of enzymes.

A special class of compounds called **cofactors** often binds tightly to enzyme surfaces and is required for enzymatic activity. Cofactors are nonprotein and can be either organic or inorganic. The inorganic cofactors are often metallic ions (for example, Mg^{2+} or Na^+), whereas the organic cofactors are vitamin derivatives. Organic cofactors, generally called **coenzymes,** are involved in numerous important cellular reactions (Table 6.1). Coenzymes frequently are carriers of electrons, chemical groups, or atoms and can move these substances from one substrate to another during chemical reactions.

Coupled Reactions

Biosynthetic reactions in living systems are endergonic reactions that cannot proceed without an input of energy. Endergonic reactions generally obtain this requisite energy by linking, or **coupling,** with exergonic reactions. For coupling reactions to be successful, the free energy released by the exergonic portion of the reaction (ΔG) must be greater than the energy required by the endergonic portion (that is, the overall ΔG of the coupled reaction must be negative).

Cells Obtain Energy by the Oxidation of Molecules

The coupled reactions most common in biological systems are those involving oxidation and reduction (**oxidation-reduction,** or **redox,** reactions). These reactions involve the transfer of electrons from one molecule to another.

Oxidation describes any reaction in which electrons are lost from a substance. The substance losing the electrons is called the electron donor (or reducing agent) and is said to be oxidized upon loss of the electrons. Electrons do not remain unassociated; those that are released from a substance must be accepted by another compound or element in a reaction known as **reduction.** The substance receiving electrons is called an electron acceptor (or oxidizing agent) and is reduced upon accepting these electrons. The two substances involved in an oxidation-reduction reaction are referred to as the **redox pair.** Redox pairs are written with the oxidized form listed first, such as SO_4^{2-}/H_2S, Fe^{3+}/Fe^{2+}, and NO_3^-/NO_2^-.

Oxidations in biological systems frequently involve dehydrogenation reactions, the removal of hydrogen ions (protons) along with electrons from a substance. Addition of hydrogen ($H^+ + e^-$) to substances during reduction occurs in reactions called hydrogenations. Such reductions accompany oxidations, and the oxidation and reduction reactions are therefore said to be coupled. Substances that become oxidized upon loss of electrons are subsequently able to act as electron acceptors, and thus become reduced again. In a similar manner, substances that gain electrons through reduction are subsequently able to serve as electron donors.

Substances Differ in Their Oxidation-Reduction Potentials

Substances differ in their abilities to donate or accept electrons. Those that serve as electron acceptors must have greater affinities for electrons than the electron donors. The ability of a substance to donate or accept electrons is described by a measurable physical parameter called the **oxidation-reduction potential,** or **redox potential** (E_0). The redox potential for a redox pair is electrically measured relative to the standard hydrogen electrode: $1/2\ H_2 \rightleftarrows H^+ + e^-$. At a pH equal to 0 and standard conditions, the redox potential of the hydrogen electrode is 0.00 V. At pH 7.0, which is more meaningful for biological systems, the redox potential is expressed as E'_0 and for the hydrogen electrode is -0.42 V. The potential of all other redox pairs can be determined electrically and placed on a scale relative to the redox potential of the $2\ H^+/H_2$ redox pair (Figure 6.6).

From this redox potential gradient, the relative affinity of different substances for electrons may be obtained. Two general rules should be remembered with respect to oxidation-reduction reactions. The first rule is that the reduced substance of the redox pair, which has the more negative E'_0, donates electrons to the oxidized substance of the pair, which has the more positive redox value. For example, the oxidation reaction

$$Fe^{2+} \rightleftharpoons Fe^{3+} + e^- \quad (+0.77 \text{ V})$$

can be coupled with any reduction reaction having a less negative (more positive) redox potential, including the reaction

$$1/2\ O_2 + 2\ H^+ + 2\ e^- \rightleftharpoons H_2O \quad (+0.82 \text{ V})$$

The oxidation of ferrous ion (Fe^{2+}), however, cannot be coupled with the reaction

$$Fumarate + 2\ H^+ + 2\ e^- \rightleftharpoons succinate \quad (+0.03 \text{ V})$$

which has a more negative (less positive) redox potential than the oxidation half of the coupled reaction.

The second rule is that the greater the difference (ΔE) in redox potential between the redox pair serving as the electron donor and the pair serving as an electron acceptor, the greater the energy available via the oxidation-reduction reaction. The standard free energy that is made available through electron transfer in oxidation-reduction reactions is expressed by the equation

$$G = -nF\Delta E$$

where n is the number of electrons and F is a constant (Faraday's constant) equal to 23 kcal/volt/mole.

Compounds or elements that have high redox potentials and are very reduced (for example, glucose) generally liberate large amounts of energy as their electrons are released and donated to electron acceptors. This occurs only if the electron acceptor available to the cell has a sufficiently more positive redox potential. Other substances lower on the redox potential gradient are less reduced and consequently do not release as much energy during their oxidation. Some compounds are completely oxidized (for example, CO_2); these cannot serve as sources of energy, although they can accept electrons.

Oxidation-reduction reactions, like any other type of chemical reaction, are accompanied by changes in free energy. Part of the energy that is liberated during the exergonic oxidative portions of these reactions is conserved in the bonds of the reduced products when the released electrons are accepted in endergonic reduction reactions. The remaining portion of the energy, which is not conserved, is used for work or lost as heat or to entropy.

Electron Carriers Transfer Electrons from Electron Donors to Electron Acceptors

Electrons released by a chemical compound during a biological oxidation often are not directly accepted by the ultimate electron acceptor. Instead, these electrons are transferred through a series of **electron carriers** before reaching the final electron acceptor. Electron carriers act as relays to transfer electrons from the initial donor to the final acceptor. As these transfers occur, the electron

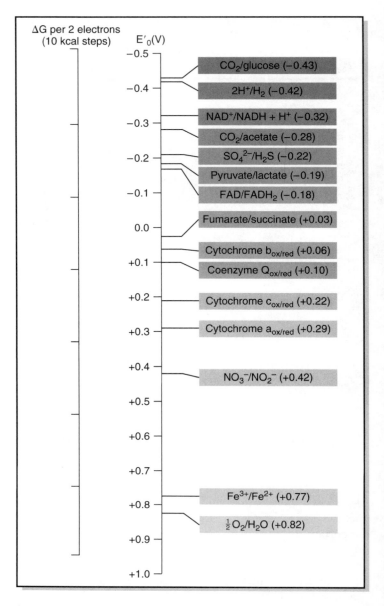

figure 6.6
Gradient of Redox Potentials
The susceptibility of a substance to oxidation or reduction is measured quantitatively as its oxidation-reduction (redox) potential relative to the voltage required to remove or add an electron to H_2. Thus the standard hydrogen electrode is assigned an arbitrary redox potential (E'_0) of 0.00 V under standard conditions (all reactants and products at 1 molar or 1 atm). At pH 7.0 (biological conditions), the redox potential (E'_0) for the hydrogen electrode is -0.42 V. The more reduced components have more negative voltages.

carriers themselves are oxidized and reduced. These oxidation-reduction reactions are accompanied by free energy changes and a liberation of energy. During electron transport, electrical potential may be converted to chemical energy that is stored in the high-energy phosphate bonds of ATP.

Among the more important electron carriers are those that transfer not only electrons but also hydrogen atoms (Figure 6.7).

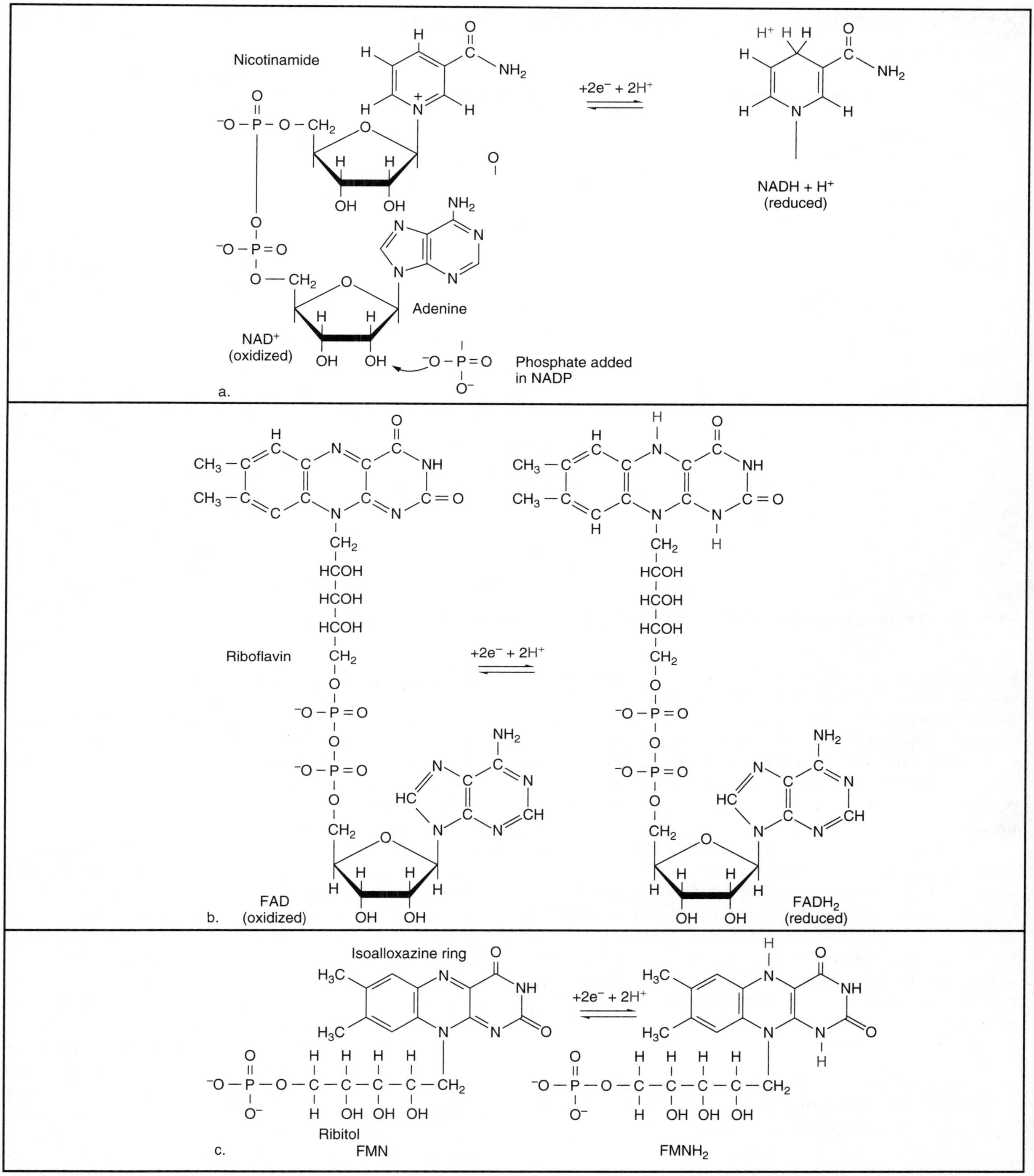

figure 6.7

Examples of Electron Carriers

a. Nicotinamide adenine dinucleotide (NAD reduced to NADH + H$^+$). b. Flavin adenine dinucleotide (FAD reduced to FADH$_2$). c. Flavin mononucleotide (FMN reduced to FMNH$_2$).

table 6.2

Examples of High-Energy Compounds

Compound	Reaction (hydrolysis)	ΔG (kcal/mole)
Adenosine triphosphate	adenosine—P~P~P $\rightleftarrows$ adenosine—P~P + P_i	−7.3
Adenosine diphosphate	adenosine—P~P $\rightleftarrows$ adenosine—P + P_i	−7.3
Creatine phosphate	(see structure)	−8.0
Acetyl-CoA	$CH_3C(=O)$~CoA $\rightleftarrows$ $CH_3COH(=O)$ + CoA	−8.0
1,3-diphosphoglycerate	(see structure)	−11.8
Phosphoenolpyruvate	$CH_2=C(—O~P)—COO^-$ $\rightleftarrows$ $CH_3—C(=O)—COO^-$ + P_i	−14.8

These carriers include (1) the pyridine nucleotides NAD (nicotinamide adenine dinucleotide) and NADP (NAD phosphate) and (2) the flavoproteins FAD (flavin adenine dinucleotide) and FMN (flavin mononucleotide). As a result of the association of these carriers with specific biochemical pathways in the cell, released energy is conserved in the form of high-energy compounds such as ATP. ATP can then be used by the cell at its discretion to supply the energy needs for work.

Electron carriers such as NAD^+ undergo reversible oxidations and reductions. In the oxidized state, NAD^+ has a positive charge on the nitrogen atom in the pyridine ring and one less hydrogen atom than in the reduced form. Upon reduction, two electrons and two hydrogen ions are picked up by NAD^+. One of the hydrogen atoms is added to the carrier molecule while the proton from the second hydrogen atom remains in solution as a hydrogen ion, H^+. The reversible oxidation-reduction reaction is expressed as

$$NAD^+ + 2\ e^- + 2\ H^+ \rightleftarrows NADH + H^+$$

NAD^+ and other similar compounds serve only as intermediate proton and electron carriers. The electrons and hydrogen atoms they carry are transferred to other acceptors in the cell, which subsequently become reduced.

Bacterial Structure and Function
Cell Membrane: Energy Production • pp. 12–16

High-Energy Compounds

Energy obtained from chemical compounds can be converted to high-energy compounds that can be used by the cell to perform work (Table 6.2). Molecules are typically considered to be high-energy if their hydrolysis is characterized by a large negative free-energy change (greater than −7 kcal/mole). Without high-energy compounds, energy that is released during normal oxidations would be wasted as heat. High-energy compounds are like organic batteries that provide the organism with stored energy for work and other cellular functions. Like batteries, these energy storehouses can be recharged after they have discharged their energy.

Many high-energy compounds have one or more high-energy phosphate bonds. These phosphate bonds occur in such organic substances as ATP, PEP (phosphoenolpyruvate), acetyl phosphate, and 1,3-diphosphoglycerate. Energy stored and later liberated by bond hydrolysis can be used for cellular work.

The most common of these high-energy compounds is ATP (Figure 6.8). Only the outer two phosphate linkages (γ- and β-linkages, generally called the pyrophosphate) of ATP are considered to be high-energy bonds. Cleavage of the bonds is accompanied by energy release. Hydrolysis of each of the two phosphate bonds results in a $\Delta G^{o\prime}$ of −7.3 kcal/mole.

The high negative $\Delta G^{o\prime}$ that results from hydrolysis of the high-energy bonds of ATP is a consequence of the charge relationships in

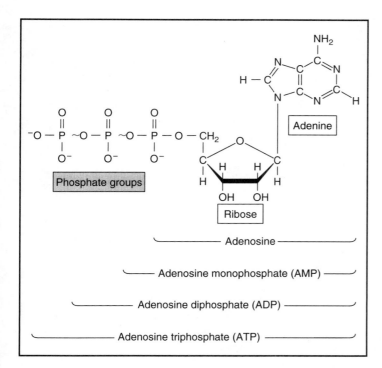

figure 6.8
Structure of ATP Showing Location of High-Energy Phosphate Bonds
High-energy bonds are designated by a ~.

the pyrophosphate linkages. The P—O bonds in pyrophosphate are actually small dipoles, with the phosphorus atoms having partial positive charges and the oxygen atoms surrounding each phosphorus having partial negative charges. As a result, there are repulsive positive charges within the anhydride linkages and repulsive negative charges among the peripheral oxygen atoms. Hydrolysis of the anhydride linkages not only dissipates these charge repulsions, but also results in a more stable structure and a negative free-energy change. The innermost ester linkage (α-phosphate) between phosphorus and carbon (P—O—C) lacks such charge repulsions. As a consequence its cleavage does not result in as large a free-energy change (–3 kcal/mole), and this bond is not considered to be a high-energy linkage.

Concepts of Metabolism

Most microorganisms obtain their energy by the oxidation of chemical compounds. This breakdown of chemical compounds, or **catabolism,** is one of the two general classes of reactions that occur within a cell. **Anabolism,** the processes associated with the biosynthesis of chemical compounds, is the other class of cell reactions. **Metabolism** is the total of the reactions (catabolic and anabolic) carried out by the cell.

Catabolic reactions serve two purposes in living cells. They are an important source of chemical energy for the cell, because such reactions are accompanied by the release (exergonic reaction) of free energy (the net ΔG is negative). Part of

this released energy is conserved in the form of ATP and other high-energy compounds. Catabolism is also the process by which the cell is able to degrade low molecular weight compounds such as glucose, as well as large polymeric substances, into smaller, simpler constituents. These smaller molecules are the carbon skeletons used as precursors for synthesis of the subunits needed for growth.

In comparison to the exergonic catabolic reactions, anabolic reactions often are endergonic and require an input of energy (the net ΔG is positive). The necessary energy is made available through catabolic pathways. Both catabolic and anabolic reactions constitute cellular metabolism and are coupled through energy exchanges usually involving ATP and other high-energy compounds. Certain biochemical pathways have dual roles, functioning in both catabolism and anabolism. Key metabolites in these **amphibolic pathways** serve as substrates for catabolism and as precursors for anabolism. The tricarboxylic acid cycle, which is discussed in this chapter, is an example of an amphibolic pathway.

Mechanisms of ATP Synthesis

Microorganisms use three mechanisms to generate ATP: **oxidative phosphorylation, photophosphorylation,** and **substrate-level phosphorylation.** In oxidative phosphorylation and photophosphorylation, ATP is synthesized during the transfer of electrons through an electron transport chain to some final electron acceptor. Electron transport chains are sequences of oxidation-reduction reactions. As electrons are transferred through a series of carriers having sequentially lower redox potentials, a portion of the free energy that is liberated is conserved in the form of ATP. Oxidative phosphorylation and photophosphorylation are similar to each other; they differ primarily in the original source of electrons. Electrons are supplied by reduced chemicals in oxidative phosphorylation and by reduced chlorophyll molecules, which have recently absorbed light energy, in photophosphorylation.

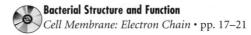
Bacterial Structure and Function
Cell Membrane: Electron Chain • pp. 17–21

In substrate-level phosphorylation, phosphate is added to an organic compound. ATP is synthesized when a phosphorylated metabolic intermediate transfers its phosphate to ADP. The energy used to drive substrate-level phosphorylation is provided by the oxidation of a reduced chemical compound. An example of substrate-level phosphorylation is the oxidation of glyceraldehyde-3-phosphate to 1,3-diphosphoglycerate (Figure 6.9). Some of the energy from this oxidation reaction is used to phosphorylate the glyceraldehyde-3-phosphate in the first carbon position of the molecule. The phosphate bond formed is a high-energy bond. The 1,3-diphosphoglycerate may transfer this high-energy phosphate bond to adenosine diphosphate (ADP) to form the energy-rich storage compound ATP and 3-phosphoglycerate.

This chapter discusses some of the major pathways by which microorganisms generate ATP via substrate-level phosphorylation and oxidative phosphorylation. Photophosphorylation will be discussed in Chapter 7.

Pathways Involving Substrate-Level Phosphorylation

Carbohydrates are the most common energy sources for microorganisms. However, proteins, lipids, and even nucleic acids also can be used as sources of energy. Carbohydrates are useful energy sources because they are compounds with large quantities of electrons to donate during oxidation. These organic substances are universally available to plants, animals, and microorganisms and are central in the metabolism of these organisms.

Chemoheterotrophic Microorganisms Obtain Energy by Fermentation and/or Respiration

Chemoheterotrophic microorganisms obtain energy from carbohydrates by two basic processes: **fermentation** and **respiration.** In fermentation, an organic substrate serves as the electron donor; an oxidized intermediate of the substrate acts as the final electron acceptor and subsequently becomes reduced. Because fermentation does not require the presence of oxygen, microorganisms that ferment carbohydrates may do so in the absence of oxygen.

In contrast to fermentation, respiration requires an external electron acceptor for substrate oxidation. When molecular oxygen is the terminal electron acceptor, it is reduced to H_2O; this process is called **aerobic respiration.** In **anaerobic respiration,** another inorganic molecule such as nitrate (NO_3^-) or sulfate (SO_4^{2-}) serves as the terminal external electron acceptor and becomes reduced to nitrite (NO_2^-), nitrous oxide (N_2O), and nitrogen (N_2), or to hydrogen sulfide (H_2S), respectively. Although different in their mechanisms for electron transfer, both fermentation and respiration use substrate oxidation to channel energy from chemical compounds into energy-rich molecules such as ATP.

Glucose Is Oxidized to Pyruvate in the Embden-Meyerhof Pathway

The oxidation of glucose is an important example in nature of carbohydrate oxidation by chemoheterotrophic microorganisms. Glucose may be oxidized by several different pathways, but in many organisms glucose oxidation begins by the **Embden-Meyerhof pathway.** This pathway, named after two of its discoverers, employs substrate-level phosphorylation to generate ATP. The Embden-Meyerhof scheme is an example of a **glycolytic pathway**—a catabolic pathway that literally lyses (splits) sugars. In the Embden-Meyerhof pathway, a molecule of glucose is oxidized to two molecules of pyruvate with the net production of two molecules of ATP and two molecules of NADH + H^+.

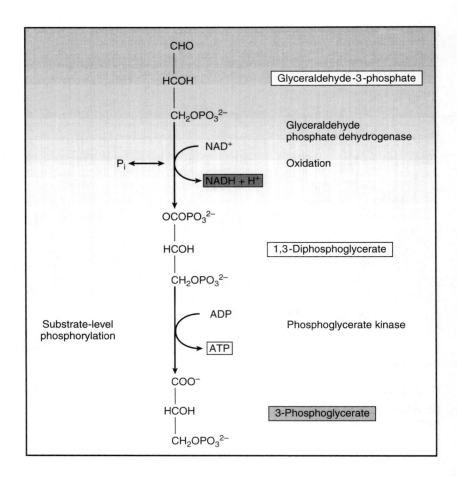

figure 6.9
Substrate-Level Phosphorylation
Glyceraldehyde-3-phosphate is phosphorylated and oxidized to 1,3-diphosphoglycerate. This high-energy compound donates its C-1 phosphate to ADP to produce ATP, an example of substrate-level phosphorylation.

The Embden-Meyerhof pathway consists of ten distinct reactions, each of which is catalyzed by a different enzyme. Figure 6.10 provides a schematic overview of the Embden-Meyerhof pathway. A detailed discussion of the pathway follows.

The first reaction of the Embden-Meyerhof pathway is the phosphorylation of glucose to glucose-6-phosphate by hexokinase (EM-1). Glucose-6-phosphate is important not only as a metabolic intermediate in this pathway, but also as an intermediate in other pathways of carbohydrate metabolism. It therefore is an important link between the Embden-Meyerhof scheme and other metabolic pathways.

The second reaction of the Embden-Meyerhof pathway is the isomerization of glucose-6-phosphate to fructose-6-phosphate by the enzyme phosphoglucoisomerase (EM-2). Third, fructose-6-phosphate is phosphorylated by phosphofructokinase (EM-3), which transfers a phosphate group from ATP to fructose-6-phosphate to form fructose-1,6-diphosphate. Phosphofructokinase is a key

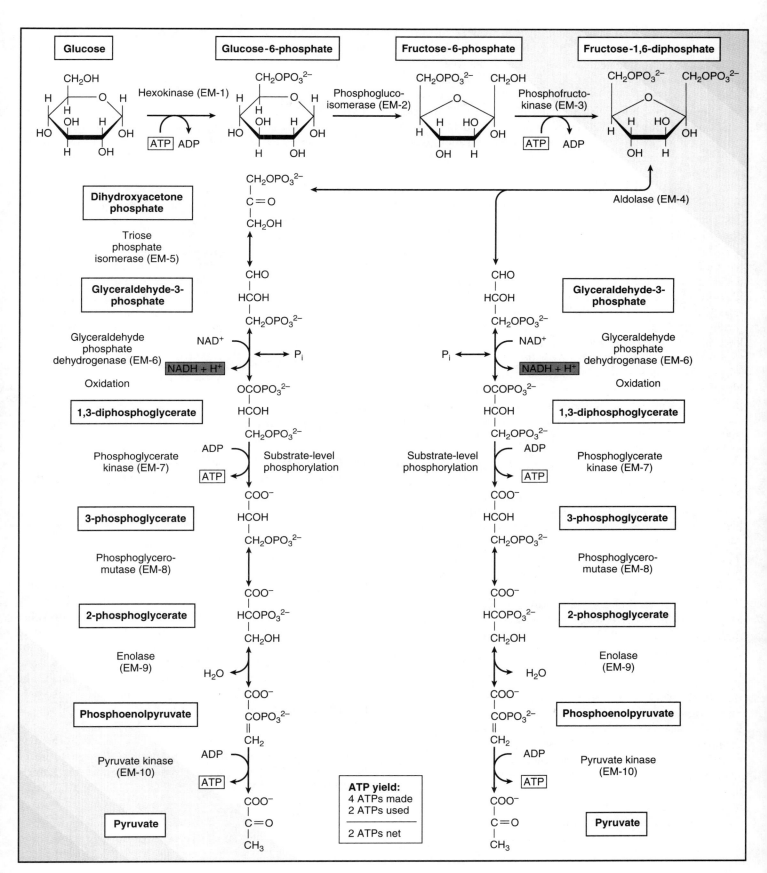

figure 6.10
The Embden-Meyerhof Pathway for Glucose Metabolism

Microbial Metabolism and Growth
Metabolism: Catabolism • pp. 2–4

regulatory enzyme that is activated by high concentrations of ADP and AMP and conversely inhibited by high concentrations of ATP. This regulation, linked to the ATP supply, allows the cell to determine if additional quantities of ATP are required for cell processes. If ATP supply is low—resulting in high cellular levels of ADP and AMP—phosphofructokinase is activated. Under such conditions of low ATP levels in the cell, the Embden-Meyerhof pathway is "turned on" for synthesis of additional molecules of ATP. As ATP concentrations increase in the cell, the pathway is "turned off."

This inhibition of phosphofructokinase by ATP is an example of allosteric inhibition. ATP is an allosteric effector that has a negative effect on phosphofructokinase activity. When phosphofructokinase is present in large quantities, ATP binds to it and stabilizes the enzyme in an inactive state, thereby effectively blocking the further oxidation of glucose in glycolysis. In his experiments with fermenting yeast, Louis Pasteur observed that yeasts grown in the presence of oxygen use glucose less rapidly than those grown in the absence of oxygen. This decrease in the rate of glucose consumption during aerobic respiration, known as the **Pasteur effect,** is explained by the allosteric inhibition of phosphofructokinase by ATP. When oxygen is available, more ATP is produced through the complete oxidation of a glucose molecule via glycolysis and respiration than is produced per glucose molecule metabolized by fermentation. The ATP that is generated inhibits phosphofructokinase, thereby reducing the quantity of substrate that is sent through the Embden-Meyerhof pathway.

The fourth step in the Embden-Meyerhof pathway is cleavage of fructose-1,6-diphosphate by the enzyme fructose-1, 6-diphosphate aldolase (EM-4) into two triose phosphate molcules: dihydroxyacetone phosphate and glyceraldehyde-3-phosphate. The two trioses are isomers of each other and are interconvertible by the enzyme triose phosphate isomerase (EM-5). Since glyceraldehyde-3-phosphate and dihydroxyacetone phosphate are interconvertible, two triose molecules from each glucose actually participate in the remaining reactions.

The sixth reaction is the only oxidation step of the Embden-Meyerhof pathway. Glyceraldehyde-3-phosphate is oxidized to 1,3-diphosphoglycerate by the enzyme glyceraldehyde-3-phosphate dehydrogenase (EM-6) in the presence of inorganic phosphate (P_i). The pair of electrons and accompanying hydrogen atoms that are released during this oxidation are accepted by the electron carrier NAD^+, which is reduced to $NADH + H^+$. Part of the energy made available from the oxidation of glyceraldehyde-3-phosphate is used to make the high-energy bond of the phosphate group on the number 1 carbon of 1,3-diphosphoglycerate. The energy contained within each 1,3-diphosphoglycerate is subsequently used to synthesize two molecules of ATP. The first molecule of ATP is synthesized as each 1,3-diphosphoglycerate is converted to a molecule of 3-phosphoglycerate. The energy released by the bond cleavage ($\Delta G^{o'} = -11.8$ kcal/mole) is sufficient to transfer the phosphate group on the number 1 carbon of 1,3-diphosphoglycerate to ADP

to generate ATP ($\Delta G^{o'} = +7.3$ kcal/mole) by substrate-level phosphorylation. This reaction is catalyzed by the enzyme phosphoglycerate kinase (EM-7).

The second ATP molecule generated by substrate-level phosphorylation is synthesized when the remaining phosphate on 3-phosphoglycerate is eventually transferred to ADP. 3-phosphoglycerate is first converted to 2-phosphoglycerate by phosphoglyceromutase (EM-8) and then to 2-phosphoenolpyruvate by enolase (EM-9). Phosphoenolpyruvate, unlike its precursor 2-phosphoglycerate, is an energy-rich substance with a high-energy phosphate bond ($\Delta G^{o'} = -14.8$ kcal/mole). ATP is produced as phosphoenolpyruvate transfers its phosphate group to ADP. This reaction, catalyzed by pyruvate kinase (EM-10), results in the formation of pyruvate.

The ultimate result of the Embden-Meyerhof pathway is the gross formation of four ATP molecules by substrate-level phosphorylation. However, because two molecules of ATP are expended in the initial reactions of the pathway, the net gain is two molecules of ATP from the oxidation of one molecule of glucose to two molecules of pyruvate and two molecules of $NADH + H^+$.

Microbial Metabolism and Growth
Metabolism: Catabolism • pp. 2–5

Microorganisms Have Other Glycolytic Pathways for the Oxidation of Glucose

The Embden-Meyerhof scheme is only one of several glycolytic pathways by which glucose is converted to pyruvate. At least three other glycolytic pathways occur in bacteria.

6-phosphogluconate Dehydratase and 2-keto-3-deoxy-6-phosphogluconate Aldolase Are Key Enzymes in the Entner-Doudoroff Pathway

One alternative glycolytic pathway was reported in *Pseudomonas saccharophila* by Nathan Entner and Michael Doudoroff in 1952 (Figure 6.11). This pathway, the **Entner-Doudoroff pathway,** has since been found in other species of *Pseudomonas* and in certain other gram-negative procaryotes, but not in eucaryotes. In the Entner-Doudoroff pathway, glucose is phosphorylated to glucose-6-phosphate, which is then oxidized to 6-phosphogluconate. The 6-phosphogluconate is dehydrated to yield 2-keto-3-deoxy-6-phosphogluconate, which is cleaved by an aldolase to produce one molecule of pyruvate and one molecule of glyceraldehyde-3-phosphate. The glyceraldehyde-3-phosphate is transformed to pyruvate via reactions identical to reactions 6 through 10 in the Embden-Meyerhof pathway. The overall reaction for the Entner-Doudoroff pathway follows:

$$\text{Glucose} + NADP^+ + NAD^+ + ADP + P_i \rightarrow$$

$$2 \text{ pyruvate} + NADPH + H^+ + NADH + H^+ + ATP$$

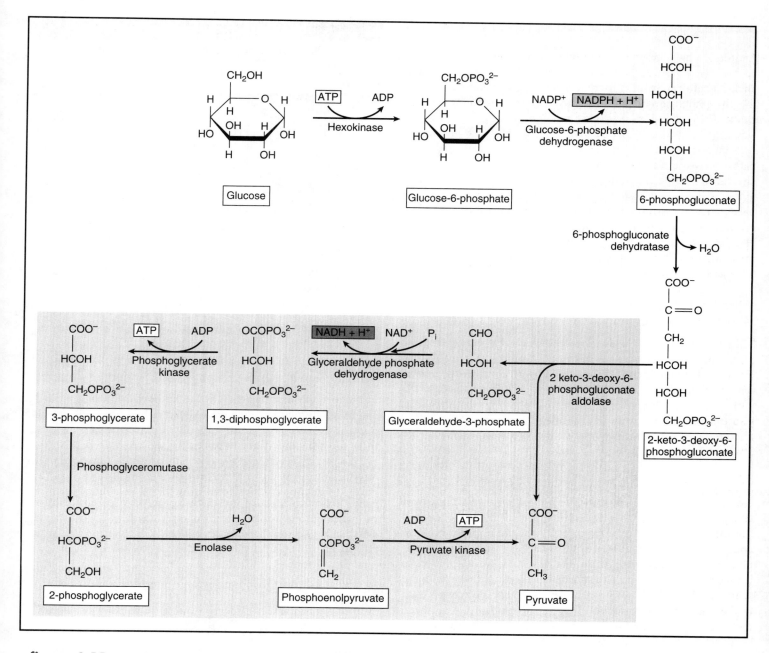

figure 6.11

The Entner-Doudoroff Pathway for Glucose Metabolism

The shaded area is identical to the last portion of the Embden-Meyerhof pathway.

The key enzymes of the Entner-Doudoroff pathway are 6-phosphogluconate dehydratase and 2-keto-3-deoxy-6-phosphogluconate aldolase. The Entner-Doudoroff pathway can be distinguished from the Embden-Meyerhof pathway by assaying for these unique enzymes.

Both pathways result in formation of NADH + H⁺ during the oxidation of glyceraldehyde-3-phosphate. One net molecule of ATP is produced by substrate-level phosphorylation for each molecule of glucose oxidized in the Entner-Doudoroff pathway (compared with two net ATP molecules in the Embden-Meyerhof pathway). Despite the lower yield of ATP, the Entner-Doudoroff pathway is useful because it generates NADPH + H⁺ from the oxidation of glucose-6-phosphate to 6-phosphogluconate. The generation of NADPH + H⁺ is very important, since this reduced coenzyme is required as the immediate electron donor in many biosynthetic reactions. The Entner-Doudoroff pathway is used more frequently by aerobes than anaerobes, which can obtain more energy from the Embden-Meyerhof pathway.

The Pentose Phosphate Pathway Is a Shunt of Glycolysis

Another pathway of glucose utilization is the **pentose phosphate pathway** (Figure 6.12). This pathway is also known as the **Warburg-Dickens pathway** (named after Otto Warburg and Frank Dickens), the **phosphogluconate pathway,** and the **hexose monophosphate shunt.** The pathway involves some reactions of the glycolytic pathway and therefore is frequently called a shunt of glycolysis. Although energy can be generated from the pentose phosphate pathway by the transfer of liberated electrons to the respiratory electron transport chain, the pathway generally is not considered to be a major energy-yielding pathway in microorganisms. Certain bacteria use the pentose phosphate pathway as yet another way to produce biosynthetic reducing power in the form of NADPH + H$^+$. The pathway is also a principal source of pentoses used in nucleotide synthesis and is important in the interconversion of hexoses and pentoses.

Phosphoketolase Is a Key Enzyme in the Phosphoketolase Pathway

The enzyme phosphoketolase, which cleaves acetyl phosphate from phosphorylated pentoses and hexoses, is found in some bacteria, including heterofermentative lactic acid bacteria such as *Leuconostoc mesenteroides* and *Bifidobacterium bifidus;* it forms the basis for pathways that are branches of the pentose phosphate pathway. The **phosphoketolase pathway** was originally discovered in *L. mesenteroides* and is summarized by the following overall reaction:

$$\text{Glucose} + \text{ADP} + P_i \rightarrow \text{pyruvate} + \text{ethanol} + CO_2 + \text{ATP}$$

Although the products of this reaction give the appearance of glucose oxidation via the Embden-Meyerhof pathway, a different set of enzymes and intermediates is used (Figure 6.13). Phosphoketolase, the key enzyme in the pathway, catalyzes the phosphorylation and breakdown of xylulose-5-phosphate to glyceraldehyde-3-phosphate and acetyl phosphate. The glyceraldehyde-3-phosphate is converted to pyruvate via the normal glycolytic pathway, with the synthesis of two ATP molecules. Since one ATP molecule was used in the initial phosphorylation of glucose to glucose-6-phosphate, the net yield of the pathway is one molecule of ATP produced by substrate-level phosphorylation per molecule of glucose. The pathway also generates NADPH + H$^+$, which is used in biosynthetic reactions, and the key intermediate xylulose-5-phosphate, which serves as an entry point for the metabolism of pentoses.

These pathways of glucose metabolism are not universally found in all organisms (Table 6.3). The Embden-Meyerhof and pentose phosphate pathways occur in both procaryotes and eucaryotes. The Entner-Doudoroff and phosphoketolase pathways are found only in certain procaryotes; they have not been found in other organisms. In many cases, alternative pathways for glucose oxidation are less energy efficient than a primary pathway such as the Embden-Meyerhof pathway. Nonetheless, these alternative pathways make it possible for microorganisms to utilize a wide variety of substrates (an evolutionary consideration) and also to produce NADPH + H$^+$ and metabolic intermediates that may be important precursors for synthesis of other compounds involved in cell function.

From G. Gottschalk, *Bacterial Metabolism,* 2nd edition. Copyright © 1986 Springer-Verlag, New York. Reprinted by permission.

table	6.3		
Distribution of Major Pathways of Glucose Metabolism among Procaryotes			
Organism		**Embden-Meyerhof**	**Entner-Doudoroff**
Alcaligenes eutrophus		−	+
Arthrobacter sp.		+	−
Azotobacter chroococcum		+	−
Bacillus sp.		+	−
Escherichia coli and other enteric bacteria		+	−
Pseudomonas sp.		−	+
Rhizobium sp.		−	+
Thiobacillus sp.		−	+
Xanthomonas sp.		−	+

Pyruvate Can Be Further Degraded to a Variety of Products

In the formation of pyruvate by the Embden-Meyerhof pathway and other glycolytic pathways, NAD$^+$ is reduced to NADH + H$^+$. Because the cell has a limited supply of oxidized NAD (NAD$^+$), there must be a mechanism to regenerate NAD$^+$ from NADH + H$^+$ if these glycolytic pathways are to continue functioning. In fermentation, electrons and hydrogens from NADH + H$^+$ are passed to organic compounds during the processing of pyruvate. This transfer of electrons to an internal electron acceptor (that is, to a product of the pathway) is a requisite of fermentation. Some of the resulting metabolic end products formed during fermentations are discussed in this section (Figure 6.14). The end products that accumulate depend on the particular enzymes of the fermenting organism and the organic intermediates used as electron acceptors.

Lactic Acid Bacteria Reduce Pyruvate to Lactate

A number of bacteria regenerate NAD$^+$ by reducing pyruvate to lactate (lactic acid) using the enzyme lactate dehydrogenase. Many, though not all, of the bacteria that carry out this reaction are called **lactic acid bacteria** and include members of the genera *Lactococcus, Lactobacillus, Leuconostoc,* and *Pediococcus.* Lactic acid bacteria are important in the dairy industry, where they are used in the preparation of fermented milk products including yogurt, kefir, acidophilus milk, and Bulgarian milk (see milk and dairy products, page 609). The acids synthesized during growth of lactic acid bacteria reduce the pH of the surrounding environment and eventually inhibit bacterial growth. Synthetic media used for growth of lactic-acid-producing microorganisms are often buffered to neutralize these acids and prolong growth.

 **Microbial Metabolism and Growth**
Metabolism: Catabolism • pp. 6–8

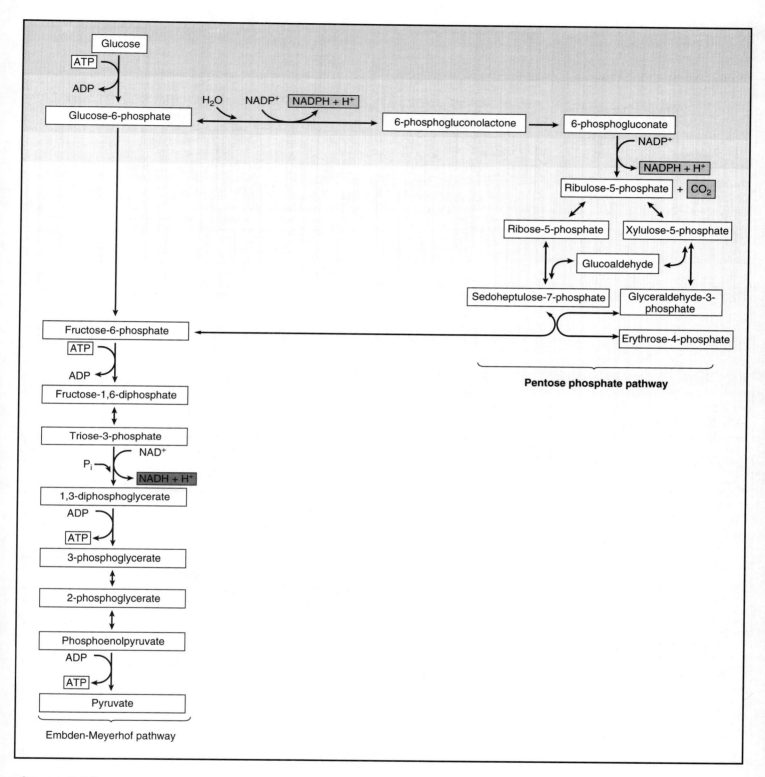

figure 6.12
The Pentose Phosphate Pathway in Relationship to the Embden-Meyerhof Pathway

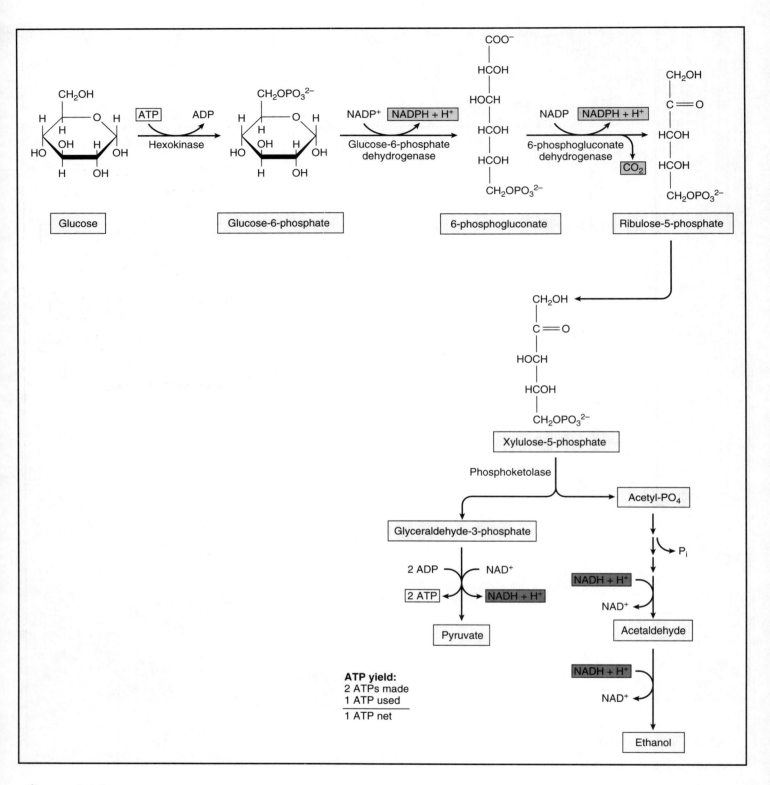

figure 6.13
The Phosphoketolase Pathway

Yeasts Produce Ethanol and Carbon Dioxide from Pyruvate

Fermenting yeasts decarboxylate pyruvate to acetaldehyde. The CO_2 released during decarboxylation causes bread dough to rise (leavening); the carbohydrates in the dough are fermented by the yeast. Acetaldehyde is subsequently reduced to ethanol, which is driven off during baking. The electrons for this reduction are provided by NADH + H$^+$, which is thus reoxidized to NAD$^+$. Ethanol is an important product of fermentation in the chemical, beverage, and baking industries. Alcohol is formed during the fermentation of the carbohydrates present in grains by yeasts, particularly those of the genus *Saccharomyces*.

Propionic Acid Bacteria Form Propionate, Acetate, and Carbon Dioxide from Lactate

Propionic acid bacteria (genus *Propionibacterium*) ferment lactate (the end product of fermentation of many bacteria) to propionate (propionic acid), acetate (acetic acid), and CO_2. These bacteria are thus able to extract some of the bond energy from lactate. Pyruvate, derived from oxidation of lactate, is carboxylated to oxaloacetate; this is subsequently reduced to succinate, resulting in the reoxidation of NADH + H$^+$ to NAD$^+$. The succinate is then decarboxylated to yield propionate as an end product. The conversion of pyruvate to propionate involves a cyclic series of reactions that can be summarized as follows:

Pyruvate + methylmalonyl-CoA → oxaloacetate + propionyl-CoA

Oxaloacetate + NADH + H$^+$ → succinate + NAD$^+$

Succinate + propionyl-CoA → succinyl-CoA + propionate

Succinyl-CoA → methylmalonyl-CoA

Such bacteria are used in the production of Swiss cheese (see cheese production, page 611). The propionate is responsible for the flavor of the cheese, and the CO_2 released during the decarboxylation of succinate contributes to the natural characteristic holes (eyes) of the cheese.

Butyrate, Butanol, Acetone, Isopropanol, and Carbon Dioxide Are Produced in Butyrate Fermentation

Organisms in the genus *Clostridium* actively ferment a variety of compounds (including amino acids and carbohydrates) to obtain energy. Many clostridia metabolize carbohydrates to pyruvate, which is then converted to a number of different products, including

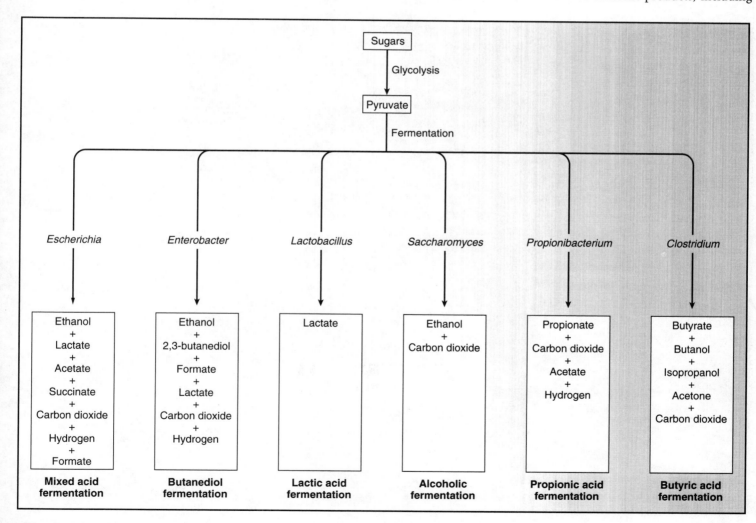

figure 6.14

Major Fermentation Pathways and Fate of Pyruvate in Bacteria

Homofermentative and Heterofermentative Microorganisms

Lactic-acid-producing microorganisms fall into two categories: **homofermentative** bacteria and **heterofermentative** bacteria. These two groups are distinguished by the types of products synthesized from carbohydrate fermentation (Figure 6.15).

Homofermentative bacteria synthesize a single product, lactate (lactic acid). These organisms include *Lactococcus, Pediococcus,* and some species of *Lactobacillus.*

Heterofermenters, in contrast, produce equal quantities of lactate, ethanol, and carbon dioxide as well as minor quantities of other products (acetate, formate, and so forth) from fermentation of glucose. Examples of heterofermentative organisms are *Leuconostoc* and certain species of *Lactobacillus.*

The difference in the fermentation products formed by these two groups of organisms is explained by the presence or absence of the enzyme **fructose-1,6-diphosphate aldolase,** which cleaves fructose-1,6-diphosphate to dihydroxyacetone phosphate and glyceraldehyde-3-phosphate in the Embden-Meyerhof pathway. This enzyme is found in homofermentative bacteria but not in heterofermentative bacteria. As a result, heterofermentative bacteria cannot ferment glucose by the Embden-Meyerhof pathway; they use the phosphoketolase pathway. Heterofermentative organisms phosphorylate glucose to glucose-6-phosphate, and convert it to 6-phosphogluconate. The 6-phosphogluconate is decarboxylated to pentose phosphate and is cleaved to form glyceraldehyde-3-phosphate and acetyl phosphate by the enzyme phosphoketolase. The glyceraldehyde-3-phosphate goes through an oxidation step and a reduction step, and eventually forms lactate. The acetyl phosphate is converted to ethanol through two consecutive reductions. Because of the initial oxidations and the formation of one instead of two triose phosphates in this pathway, only one net ATP is gained by substrate-level phosphorylation from each glucose fermented in heterofermentative organisms. Two net ATP molecules are generated from glycolysis in homofermenters. This difference in ATP yield is evident in the greater cell yield of homofermenters as compared to heterofermenters that are provided the same quantity of glucose. The two groups of organisms can be distinguished either by assaying fructose-1,6-diphosphate aldolase (which is absent in heterofermenters) or by inspecting for the production of CO_2 (produced by heterofermenters, but not homofermenters).

figure 6.15
Pathways for Glucose Fermentation in Homofermentative and Heterofermentative Bacteria

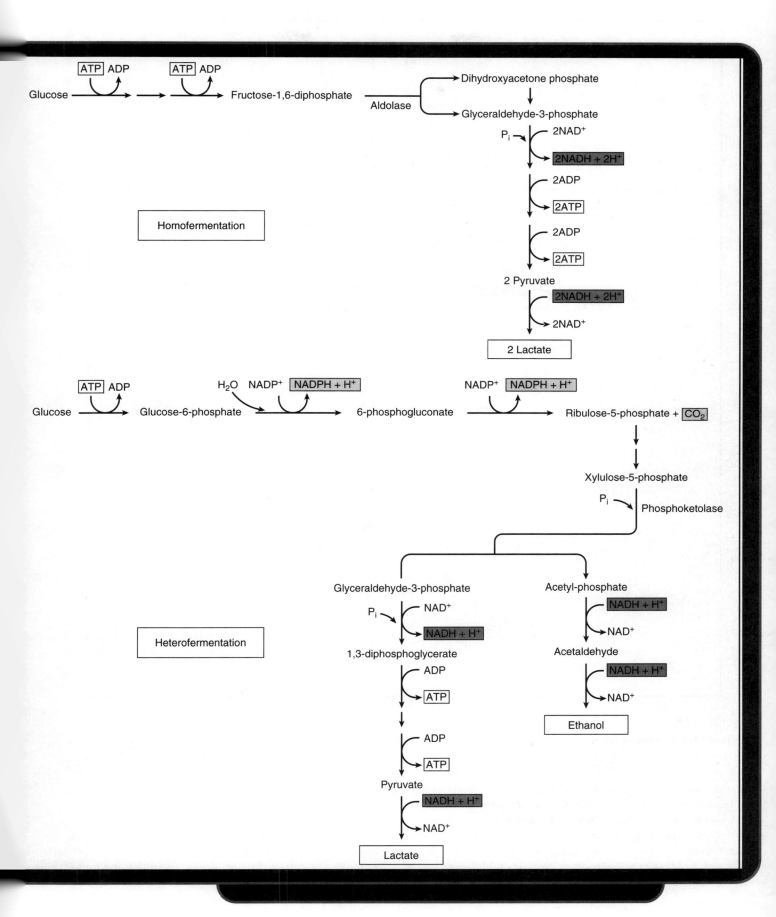

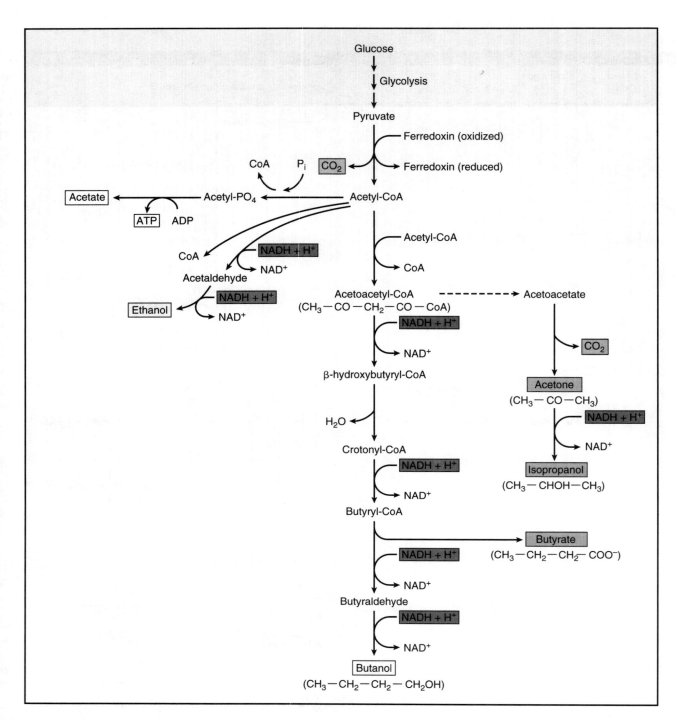

figure 6.16

Pathway for Butyrate Formation in *Clostridia*

butyrate (butyric acid), butanol, acetone, isopropanol, and CO_2. The key reaction in butyrate fermentation is the formation of acetoacetyl-CoA by the condensation of two molecules of acetyl-CoA derived from pyruvate or acetate (Figure 6.16). The acetoacetyl-CoA subsequently is reduced by two molecules of NADH + H⁺, and butyrate is formed. In addition to *Clostridium*, bacteria of the genera *Butyrivibrio, Eubacterium,* and *Fusobacterium* also produce butyrate.

Mixed Acid Fermentation and Butanediol Fermentation Are Distinguished by the Quantity of Acid Produced

Pyruvate that is produced from glucose metabolism in gram-negative enteric bacilli such as *Escherichia, Salmonella,* and *Enterobacter* can be further degraded under anaerobic conditions into different products, depending on the species and their

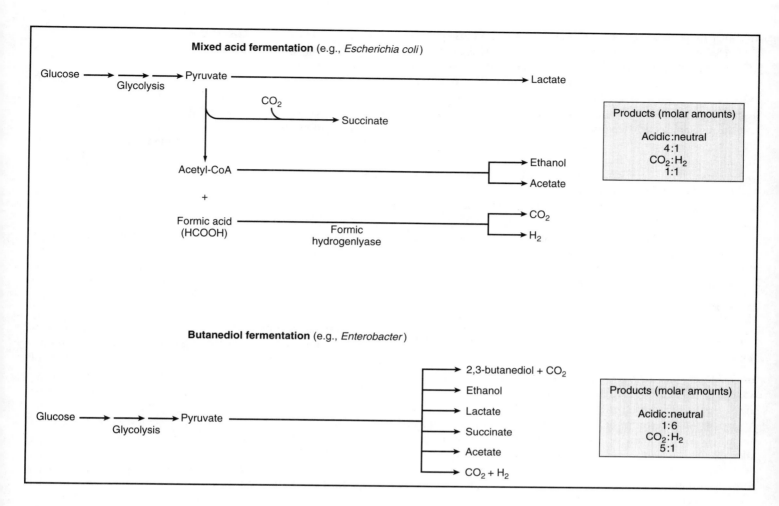

figure 6.17
Mixed Acid versus Butanediol Fermentation

enzyme complement. This degradation of pyruvate occurs by one of two distinct fermentative pathways: **mixed acid fermentation** and **butanediol fermentation** (Figure 6.17). Mixed acid fermentation produces (1) three major acids: lactate (lactic acid), succinate (succinic acid), and acetate (acetic acid), (2) ethanol, (3) and either formate or CO_2 and H_2, depending on the absence or presence of the enzyme formic hydrogenlyase. Butanediol fermentation also produces lactate, succinate, and acetate, but in smaller quantities. Other products of butanediol fermentation are butanediol, ethanol, CO_2, and H_2.

The two pathways may be easily distinguished by the quantity of acid produced. More acid is produced during mixed acid fermentation than in butanediol fermentation. The ratio of CO_2 to H_2 produced in the two pathways is also different: it is equimolar (1:1) in mixed acid fermentation and 5 (CO_2):1 (H_2) in butanediol fermentation. The difference in acid production in these two types of fermentations can be detected by the **methyl red test**. This test is performed by growing bacteria in glucose broth and quantitatively measuring the amount of acid produced after 48 hours of growth, using the pH indicator methyl red. When added to the growth medium, the indicator remains red at low pHs (<5) and turns yellow-

orange at higher pHs (>5.5). A red color is indicative of a positive test for mixed acid fermentation, whereas a yellow-orange color indicates a negative test. The 48-hour incubation period prior to the methyl red test is necessary, since all enterics will initially produce some acid from glucose fermentation. With prolonged incubation, mixed acid fermenters continue to excrete large amounts of acid in comparison to butanediol fermenters. However, the 48-hour incubation period for the methyl red test can be reduced to 18 to 24 hours if smaller substrate volumes and larger inocula are used.

Another test, the **Voges-Proskauer test**, may be used to identify the butanediol fermenters such as *Enterobacter*. The reagents used in the test detect acetylmethylcarbinol (acetoin), an intermediate in butanediol production. This intermediate is not produced by *E. coli*, *Salmonella*, and the other enteric mixed acid producers.

Oxidative Phosphorylation

One or two net ATP molecules are synthesized by substrate-level phosphorylation through the metabolism of glucose to two molecules of pyruvate. This ATP yield can be increased to as many as 38 ATP molecules in bacteria if these pyruvates are subsequently channeled into the tricarboxylic acid (TCA) cycle, with accompanying electron transport and oxidative phosphorylation. This increased ATP yield is possible because the complete oxidation of pyruvate is realized through the TCA cycle. The electrons released from these oxidations and the earlier oxidations in glycolysis are sent through an electron transport chain to a final acceptor, resulting in the generation of additional molecules of ATP. Oxygen or inorganic molecules such as ions of nitrate (NO_3^-) or sulfate (SO_4^{2-}) may be the terminal electron acceptor of these electrons. The energy available during the transport of electrons to the final acceptor (an acceptor with a highly positive redox potential) is conserved in ATP by a process known as oxidative phosphorylation. Up to three ATP molecules are formed by the energy change realized from the difference in the reduction potential of the NAD^+/$NADH + H^+$ pair ($E'_0 = -0.32$ V) and the $1/2$ O_2/H_2O pair ($E'_0 = +0.82$ V) when oxygen is the final electron acceptor.

The Tricarboxylic Acid Cycle Generates Intermediates for Other Pathways and Cellular Activities and Is Central to Cell Metabolism

The **TCA cycle** (also known as the **Krebs cycle** or the **citric acid cycle**) was elucidated by Sir Hans Krebs, an English biochemist who received the Nobel Prize in physiology and medicine in 1953 jointly with Fritz A. Lipman for their studies on intermediary metabolism. This major pathway generates intermediates required for other pathways and cellular activities and is the center of cell metabolism. Activation of the TCA cycle can therefore lead to increased activity of other metabolic pathways. Inhibition of the TCA cycle has deleterious effects on overall cellular metabolism. Figure 6.18 provides a schematic overview of the TCA cycle. A detailed discussion of the cycle follows.

The pyruvate generated by glycolysis or other pathways can feed into the TCA cycle by first being oxidatively decarboxylated in a reaction requiring coenzyme A (CoA) to form acetyl-CoA, with the release of CO_2 and the reduction of NAD^+. The acetyl group of acetyl-CoA then enters the TCA cycle by combining with oxaloacetate to form citrate. The enzyme responsible for this reaction, citrate synthase, is a key enzyme in the TCA cycle. Citrate synthase is an allosteric enzyme with activity regulated by $NADH + H^+$, α-ketoglutarate, and/or ATP concentrations, depending on the type of bacterium. Citrate synthase activity in gram-negative bacteria is inhibited by high concentrations of $NADH + H^+$ and/or α-ketoglutarate. The activity of the same enzyme in gram-positive bacteria is controlled by ATP levels.

In the next series of reactions following formation of citrate, citrate is converted first to isocitrate (*cis*-aconitate is an unstable intermediate of this reaction) and then to α-ketoglutarate. The conversion of isocitrate to α-ketoglutarate is an oxidative decarboxylation reaction catalyzed by the enzyme isocitrate dehydrogenase. The immediate product of the oxidation is oxalosuccinate, but this product is rapidly decarboxylated to yield α-ketoglutarate. NAD^+ is reduced to $NADH + H^+$, and a molecule of CO_2 is released during these reactions.

α-ketoglutarate becomes the substrate for a second oxidative decarboxylation reaction, which produces succinyl-CoA. This reaction is catalyzed by α-ketoglutarate dehydrogenase and is accompanied by the release of one molecule of CO_2 and the reduction of NAD^+ to $NADH + H^+$.

The next reaction in the TCA cycle is the conversion of succinyl-CoA to succinate. This is the only exergonic reaction in the TCA cycle directly coupled with the generation of a high-energy compound—either ATP, as in bacteria and higher plants, or guanosine triphosphate (GTP), as in mammals—via substrate-level phosphorylation. GTP can be used directly by the cell or converted to ATP by the following reaction:

$$GTP + ADP \xrightarrow{\text{nucleoside diphosphate kinase}} ATP + GDP$$

The TCA cycle continues with the oxidation of succinate to fumarate by the enzyme succinate dehydrogenase. The electrons and hydrogen atoms released during this oxidation are accepted by flavin adenine dinucleotide (FAD), not NAD. FAD is a coenzyme similar to NAD in its action. In this particular instance FAD serves as the specific coenzyme and is covalently bound to succinate dehydrogenase.

Fumarate is converted to malate. Malate is subsequently oxidized to oxaloacetate, with NAD accepting the electrons and protons of this oxidation. This final oxidation completes one turn of the TCA cycle. The cycle can now repeat with the condensation of oxaloacetate with a new molecule of acetyl-CoA entering the pathway from pyruvate.

The result of one turn of the TCA cycle, starting from acetyl-CoA, is the production of two CO_2 molecules, one ATP (GTP) molecule, three molecules of $NADH + H^+$, and one molecule of $FADH + H^+$. An additional CO_2 molecule and $NADH + H^+$ are generated in the preliminary step to the cycle, in which pyruvate is oxidized to acetyl-CoA and CO_2. Since two molecules of pyruvate are formed from each molecule of glucose sent through the Embden-Meyerhof pathway, it takes two complete turns of the TCA cycle to process these pyruvates.

Most of the energy that is liberated from the oxidation of pyruvate through the TCA cycle is conserved in reduced cofactors and then in ATP molecules synthesized by oxidative phosphorylation. These ATP molecules are produced as electrons released during oxidation, transferred by such carriers as $NADH + H^+$ and $FADH_2$ to an electron transport chain, and accepted ultimately by the terminal acceptor, oxygen, or some other molecule.

Energy That Is Liberated While Electrons Are Transported in an Electron Transport Chain Can Be Coupled to the Formation of ATP

The **electron transport chain** is an alternating oxidation-reduction chain of electron carriers located in the plasma membrane in procaryotes and in the inner mitochondrial membrane in eucaryotes. Electrons from $NADH + H^+$ or $FADH_2$ are transported in the chain through a set of electron carriers. The number and types of electron carriers vary from bacterial species to species. The most common carriers in bacterial electron transport chains are pyridine nucleotides, flavoproteins, quinones, iron-sulfur proteins, and cytochromes. Pyridine nucleotides, flavoproteins, and quinones are carriers of protons and electrons; iron-sulfur proteins and cytochromes are electron carriers.

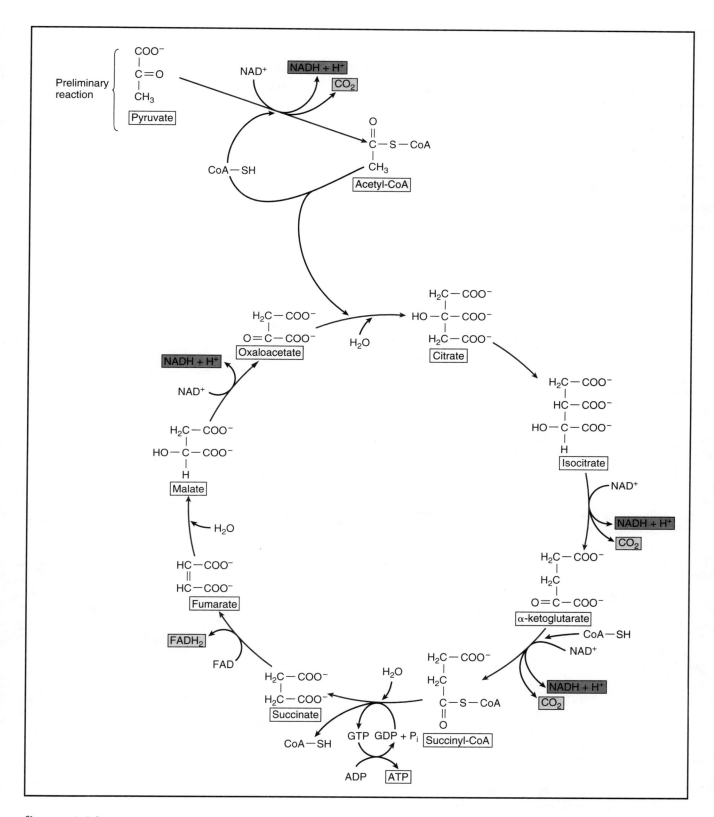

figure 6.18
The Tricarboxylic Acid Cycle

Microbial Metabolism and Growth
Metabolism: Catabolism • pp. 10–13

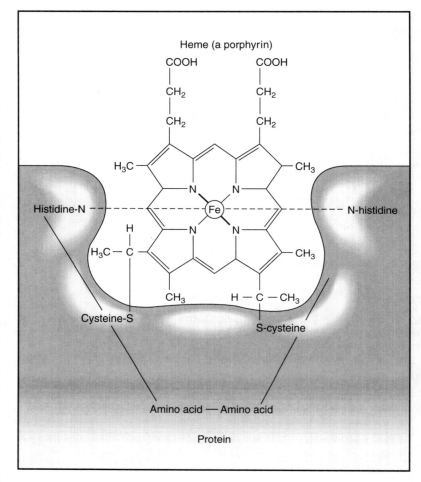

$$+2e^- + 2H^+ \longrightarrow$$

Oxidized   Reduced

Coenzyme Q

figure 6.19
Coenzyme Q

Electrons usually enter the electron transport chain through the pyridine nucleotide NADH + H⁺. Occasionally flavoproteins accept electrons in the oxidation reactions of metabolism. Flavoproteins are proteins containing a prosthetic group derived from riboflavin (see Figure 6.7). The prosthetic group, which may be either FAD or flavin mononucleotide (FMN), is reduced as it accepts electrons (and protons) or oxidized as the electrons (and protons) are passed on. The flavoprotein FMN has a more positive redox potential than NAD and therefore serves as an intermediate acceptor for electrons passed from NADH + H⁺ in electron transport.

Quinones are lipid-soluble substances of low molecular weight. One of the more common quinones, coenzyme Q, or ubiquinone (so named because it is ubiquitous and is found in all organisms), is a dual electron-proton carrier (Figure 6.19).

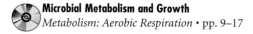

Microbial Metabolism and Growth
Metabolism: Aerobic Respiration • pp. 9–17

Iron-sulfur proteins are proteins containing iron and sulfur atoms complexed with four cysteine residues of the protein. The iron atoms in these proteins are the actual electron carriers and can be in either the oxidized (Fe³⁺) or the reduced (Fe²⁺) state. Ferredoxin is an iron-sulfur protein present in the electron transport chain of some bacteria.

Cytochromes are heme proteins, with an iron-containing porphyrin ring attached to proteins. The iron ligand of the cytochrome serves as the electron carrier by becoming alternately reduced and oxidized from the ferrous (Fe²⁺) form to the ferric (Fe³⁺) form. Cytochromes carry only electrons, not protons. Each cytochrome can carry only one electron at a time. The cytochromes were first discovered in 1886 by C.A. McMunn. They were divided into three major classes by D. Keilin in 1930 on the basis of their absorption spectra. Cytochrome a absorbs at

figure 6.20
Cytochrome c
The iron-porphyrin group of cytochrome c, showing the manner in which the porphyrin is attached to the protein.

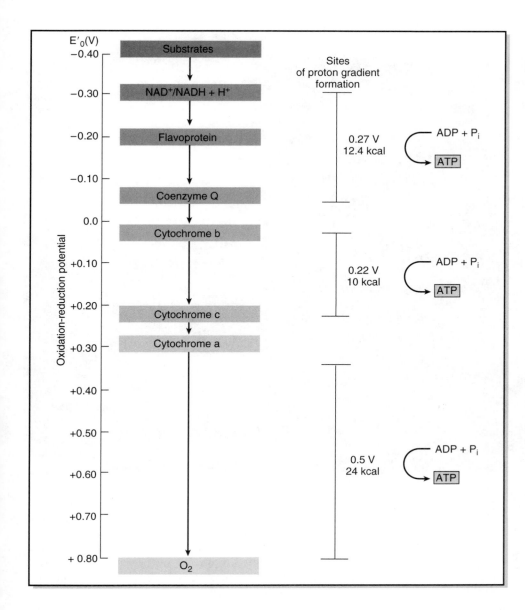

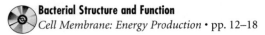

E'$_0$(V)

Oxidation-reduction potential

-0.40
-0.30
-0.20
-0.10
0.0
+0.10
+0.20
+0.30
+0.40
+0.50
+0.60
+0.70
+0.80

Substrates

NAD$^+$/NADH + H$^+$

Flavoprotein

Coenzyme Q

Cytochrome b

Cytochrome c

Cytochrome a

O$_2$

Sites
of proton gradient
formation

0.27 V
12.4 kcal

ADP + P$_i$

ATP

0.22 V
10 kcal

ADP + P$_i$

ATP

0.5 V
24 kcal

ADP + P$_i$

ATP

figure 6.21
The Electron Transport Chain
Electrons during glucose oxidation enter the electron transport chain through NADH + H$^+$ or FADH$_2$. The electrons are transported via a series of carriers with progressively more positive redox potentials, and eventually reach oxygen. The energy liberated during this process is partially conserved in the synthesis of ATP + P$_i$ at discrete coupling sites. There are three coupling sites for ATP generation between NADH + H$^+$ and oxygen.

Bacterial Structure and Function
Cell Membrane: Electron Transport Chain • pp. 18–19

the longest wavelength; cytochrome b, at an intermediate wavelength; and cytochrome c, at the shortest wavelength (Figure 6.20). Additional cytochromes have since been discovered and are designated by subclasses (a$_1$, a$_2$, a$_3$, and so forth).

Each of the different electron carriers has a different redox potential and is arranged in the electron transport chain in a specific location (Figure 6.21). Electrons are passed from carriers having more negative redox potentials to carriers having more positive redox potentials; eventually electrons reach the terminal electron acceptor. The energy liberated while electrons move through this gradient is partially conserved in the synthesis of ATP from ADP + P$_i$. Although enough free energy is liberated during electron transport to form approximately seven ATP molecules from ADP and P$_i$, at most three ATP molecules are actually made because there are only three discrete coupling sites of ATP generation between NADH + H$^+$ and the terminal electron acceptor. ATP generation is associated with the three main enzyme

complexes of electron transport: NADH + H$^+$ dehydrogenase (site I), cytochrome c reductase (site II), and cytochrome c oxidase (site III). FADH$_2$, which has a more positive redox potential than NADH + H$^+$, feeds electrons into the transport chain via coenzyme Q, bypassing one of the three ATP coupling sites. As a consequence, only two ATP molecules at most are formed for each electron pair entering the electron transport chain through FADH$_2$ instead of NADH + H$^+$.

Bacterial Structure and Function
Cell Membrane: Energy Production • pp. 12–18

Chemiosmosis Explains How Electron Transport Is Used to Generate ATP

Chemiosmosis, or **proton motive force,** first proposed in 1961 by Peter Mitchell, explains how ATP is synthesized during electron transport. Mitchell, who received a Nobel Prize in chemistry in

The types of cytochromes and associated enzymes located in the electron transport chain vary from organism to organism. Some bacteria, specifically facultatively

Oxidase Test

anaerobic organisms such as the enterics, lack cytochrome c oxidase. The absence or presence of cytochrome c oxidase can be detected in a diagnostically useful test, the **oxidase test,** which is used to distinguish enteric bacteria from bacteria that have cytochrome c oxidase (for example, *Pseudomonas* and *Neisseria*).

The oxidase test is performed by mixing a drop of N,N-dimethyl-*p*-phenylenediamine on a piece of filter paper with a young culture of bacteria, or by adding a drop of the reagent to bacteria on an agar plate. The

dye serves as an electron donor and is oxidized to a purple-blue product (indophenol) by organisms that have cytochrome c oxidase (Figure 6.22). Cytochrome c oxidase oxidizes cytochrome c, which in turn oxidizes N,N-dimethyl-*p*-phenylenediamine to indophenol. The dye is not oxidized and remains colorless when reacted with oxidase-negative organisms.

The oxidase test provides a simple, rapid technique to distinguish oxidase-positive bacteria, particularly pathogens such as *Neisseria gonorrhoeae* and *Neisseria meningitidis*, from those that are oxidase negative. It is commonly used in clinical laboratories as a diagnostic aid in the preliminary identification of these bacteria.

figure 6.22
Oxidase Test for the Presence of Cytochrome c Oxidase
The oxidase test is performed by mixing a drop of N,N-dimethyl-*p*-phenylenediamine on filter paper with a young culture of bacteria. Oxidase-positive bacteria produce cytochrome c oxidase, which indirectly oxidizes the colorless N,N-dimethyl-*p*-phenylenediamine to a purple-blue product (indophenol).

1978 in recognition of his work, hypothesized that electron transport is accompanied by the translocation of protons from the inside to the outside of the plasma membrane to establish an electrochemical gradient that is the driving force (proton motive force) for ATP synthesis (Figure 6.23). This proton gradient represents an electrical potential, similar to the potential in a battery between the positive and negative poles. As the gradient dissipates, its energy may be transferred in part to the synthesis of ATP.

The proton gradient is established during electron transport, a process that occurs in the membrane (the plasma membrane in procaryotes and the mitochondrial membrane in eucaryotes). The electron carriers are oriented in the membrane in such a way that there is a separation of electrons and hydrogen ions (protons) during transport. Between NADH + H$^+$ (or FADH$_2$) and the cytochromes, carriers that transport both electrons and protons (flavoproteins and quinones) alternate with carriers that transport only electrons (the iron-sulfur proteins and cytochromes); consequently protons are translocated across and to the outside of the membrane during electron transport.

As each pair of electrons is sent through the transport chain, protons are released to the outside of the membrane. This translocation results in an excess of protons on the exterior side of the membrane and the establishment of a proton gradient. The gradient does not automatically dissipate, since the membrane is impermeable to protons. However, protons are able to traverse the membrane via enzyme complexes (ATPases) spanning the mem-

brane at certain sites. These enzyme complexes act as proton channels across the membrane. The inward movement of protons across the membrane is coupled with ATP synthesis.

This proton pump mechanism for ATP synthesis is reversible. When the pump operates in the reverse reaction, ATP hydrolysis drives protons across the membrane to the cell exterior, resulting in an energized membrane. This reverse reaction is important in active transport (see transport mechanisms, page 86).

The establishment of a proton gradient, not electron transport, is responsible for ATP synthesis. Evidence for this role of the proton motive force came from studies with bacteriorhodopsin, a protein in the purple plasma membrane fraction of *Halobacterium* (domain Archaea). Bacteriorhodopsin, which is responsible for the patches of purple membrane on the cell surface of *Halobacterium*, has a chemical structure similar to the sensory pigment rhodopsin of the vertebrate retina. Covalently bound to bacteriorhodopsin is the carotenoid derivative retinal, a chromophore that normally exists in the *trans* configuration. Bacteriorhodopsin strongly absorbs light at 570 nm and functions as a light-driven proton pump. When the pigment is illuminated, the retinal chromophore absorbs the light and temporarily changes to a *cis* configuration. This transformation results in deprotonation and the transfer of protons across the plasma membrane to the periplasm. The retinal molecule then slowly takes up a proton from the cytoplasm and isomerizes back to the *trans* form. The proton gradient generated across the plasma membrane is used to

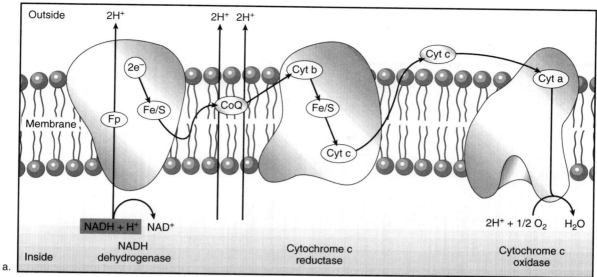

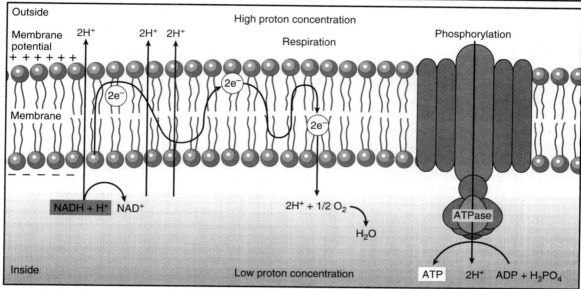

figure 6.23

The Chemiosmotic Theory of ATP Synthesis and Proton Translocation

a. Electron carriers in the electron transport chain pump protons (H^+) to the outside of the cell, establishing a proton gradient across the membrane.
b. As the protons reenter the cell via ATPases, the gradient dissipates, and the released energy is coupled to the synthesis of ATP. Fp, flavoprotein; Fe/S, iron-sulfur protein; CoQ, coenzyme Q; Cyt, cytochrome.

Bacterial Structure and Function
Cell Membrane: Electron Transport Chain • p. 20

drive ATP synthesis via an ATPase complex, as in oxidative phosphorylation, but in the absence of electron transport. Halobacteria benefit from such an oxygen-independent proton pump mechanism, since they are commonly found in salt-saturated environments where oxygen solubility is low and there is ample light. In such environments, these bacteria have an alternative light-mediated system for ATP production.

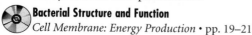

Bacterial Structure and Function
Cell Membrane: Energy Production • pp. 19–21

Uncouplers Inhibit ATP Synthesis Without Inhibiting Electron Transport

Some of the strongest evidence for ATP synthesis by a proton pump comes from the use of chemical agents that specifically inhibit electron transport, oxidative phosphorylation, or both (Table 6.4). One group of chemical agents, called uncouplers, causes membranes to be leaky to protons. These uncouplers are lipid-soluble substances that combine with protons on the exterior

table 6.4

Inhibitors of Electron Transport

Inhibitor	Result
Uncouplers:	
2,4-dinitrophenol	Uncoupling of oxidative phosphorylation from electron transport
Dicumarol	
Salicylanilide	
Inhibitors of electron transport:	
Amobarbital (Amytal)	Blockage of electron transport between FAD and quinone
Antimycin A	Blockage of electron transport between cytochrome b and cytochrome c
Cyanide	Blockage of electron transport at cytochrome a
Inhibitors of phosphorylation:	
Oligomycin	Inhibition of ATPase
Atractyloside	Inhibition of membrane carrier for adenine nucleotides in plants

table 6.5

Examples of Electron Acceptors in Anaerobic Respiration

Electron Acceptor	Reduced Product	Genus
NO_3^-	NO_2^-, N_2O, N_2	Alcaligenes Bacillus
NO_2^-	N_2O, N_2	Paracoccus Pseudomonas Spirillum
SO_4^{2-}	H_2S	Desulfococcus Desulfomonas Desulfovibrio
Fumarate	Succinate	Desulfovibrio Vibrio

of the cell and carry them across the membrane to the cell interior, bypassing the ATPase in the membrane. Although electron transport still occurs in the presence of uncouplers, no proton gradient is established. The result is an uncoupling of oxidative phosphorylation from electron transport—energy released during electron transport is lost as heat and not conserved in the form of ATP. Examples of uncouplers are 2,4-dinitrophenol (DNP), dicumarol, and salicylanilide. For example, when *E. coli* cells are incubated in the presence of 2,4-dinitrophenol, glucose is oxidized, but ATP is not formed during electron transport. Uncouplers provide evidence that although electron transport and oxidative phosphorylation usually are coupled, each is able to operate separately.

Other chemical agents directly affect electron transport by combining with carriers of the chain. Cyanide, an irreversibly bound noncompetitive inhibitor, binds with cytochrome a to block electron transport at that step. Antimycin A inhibits electron transport between cytochrome b and cytochrome c. These chemical agents have proven useful in establishing the precise locations of carriers in the electron transport chain.

Aerobic Respiration Is More Efficient Than Fermentation in Coupling Liberated Energy to ATP Formation

The majority of the ATP molecules formed during respiration is provided by oxidative phosphorylation. The $NADH + H^+$ and $FADH_2$ formed in the TCA cycle, as well as the $NADH + H^+$ produced during glycolysis, can be shunted into the electron transport chain when oxygen is available. As many as 3 ATP molecules are synthesized for each $NADH + H^+$, and 2 ATP molecules may be synthesized for each $FADH_2$ sent through the chain. Thus in addition to the 2 net ATP molecules formed during glycolysis and the 2 ATP molecules formed from GTP in the TCA cycle as a result of glucose oxidation, 34 additional ATP molecules (30 ATP molecules

from ten molecules of $NADH + H^+$ and 4 ATP molecules from two molecules of $FADH_2$) are made available through oxidative phosphorylation under optimal conditions.

Most microorganisms obtain energy from chemical compounds by fermentation and aerobic respiration. The total amount of free energy available from the oxidation of glucose to carbon dioxide and water is −688 kcal/mole. Theoretically as many as 38 net ATP molecules are generated by bacteria in aerobic respiration from the oxidation of one molecule of glucose. If it is assumed that each ATP formed has −7.3 kcal/mole of free energy available in its terminal phosphate bond, approximately 40% of the available energy released as a result of glucose oxidation (38 ATP molecules × −7.3 kcal/mole) is conserved in the form of ATP.

The fermentation of glucose to ethanol and carbon dioxide, in comparison, releases 57 kcal/mole of free energy, of which only 14.6 kcal/mole (26%) is conserved in the 2 ATP molecules that are formed. Aerobic respiration is thus more efficient than fermentation in the conservation of released energy. The greater yield of ATP and the higher efficiency of aerobic respiration is evident when the growth of facultatively anaerobic organisms is compared under anaerobic and aerobic conditions (that is, the Pasteur effect) (see Pasteur effect, page 152). When grown aerobically with the same quantities of carbohydrates, the same microorganism reaches a greater cell mass (fourfold greater) than when grown under anaerobic conditions.

Anaerobic Respiration Is a Process Unique to Procaryotes

Fermentation and aerobic respiration occur in procaryotes and eucaryotes. Additionally, some procaryotes have a variation of aerobic respiration called anaerobic respiration, by which they synthesize ATP. This process, which is unique to procaryotes, is similar to aerobic respiration; the major exception is that the terminal electron acceptor in the electron transport chain is a chemical compound other than molecular oxygen. A wide variety of substances can serve as alternate electron acceptors to oxygen (Table 6.5).

Nitrate (NO_3^-) is an example of a terminal electron acceptor used by some microbes in anaerobic respiration. Organisms such as *Pseudomonas* and *Bacillus* that can respire aerobically generally uti-

Oxidative phosphorylation is similar in eucaryotes and procaryotes, with certain exceptions. Glycolysis in eucaryotes takes place in the cytoplasm, whereas the TCA cycle

example of such a system is the transfer of electrons from NADH + H⁺ to glycerol-3-phosphate, which is synthesized from dihydroxyacetone phosphate by the cyto-

acetone phosphate exits the mitochondrion to be reduced at the expense of NADH + H⁺ again to continue the cycle. Since the electrons transported into the mitochondrion by

Oxidative Phosphorylation in Eucaryotes

and oxidative phosphorylation operate in the mitochondrion. The proton gradient in oxidative phosphorylation is established across the inner mitochondrion membrane. The outer mitochondrion membrane, however, is impermeable to NADH + H⁺. Consequently the two molecules of NADH + H⁺ formed from the glycolytic pathway are unable to enter the mitochondrion through the membrane.

The electrons of NADH + H⁺ enter the mitochondrion via shuttle systems. One

plasmic enzyme glycerol phosphate dehydrogenase (dihydroxyacetone phosphate/glycerol-3-phosphate shuttle); (Figure 6.24). Glycerol-3-phosphate is able to penetrate the mitochondrion membrane. Once inside the mitochondrion, glycerol-3-phosphate is oxidized back to dihydroxyacetone phosphate by an FAD-linked glycerol phosphate dehydrogenase, which passes the electrons to coenzyme Q in the electron transport chain. The dihydroxy-

the dihydroxyacetone phosphate/glycerol-3-phosphate shuttle are transferred to coenzyme Q, they bypass the first ATP coupling site of the transport chain and yield only two ATP molecules per electron pair. As a consequence, since glycolysis contributes two molecules of cytoplasm-derived NADH + H⁺ for each molecule of glucose oxidized, only 36 ATP molecules are theoretically produced from complete oxidation of glucose.

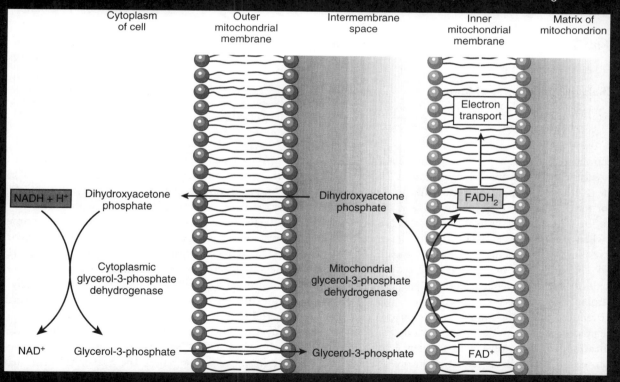

figure 6.24

The Dihydroxyacetone Phosphate/Glycerol-3-Phosphate Shuttle

This shuttle transports electrons from cytoplasmic NADH + H⁺ into the electron transport chain of the inner mitochondrial membrane. Electrons move inward via glycerol-3-phosphate, which can be oxidized to dihydroxyacetone phosphate by an FAD-linked dehydrogenase in the inner membrane.

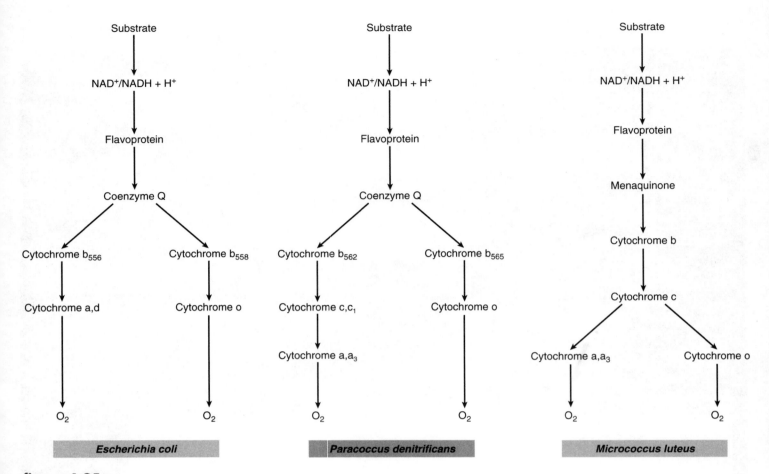

figure 6.25
Electron Transport Chains of Three Types of Bacteria
Escherichia coli, Paracoccus denitrificans, and *Micrococcus luteus* have electron transport chains that branch in two directions before reaching the terminal electron acceptor. Branch points occur at the coenzyme Q level and at the cytochrome c level.

lize oxygen as an electron acceptor. However, if oxygen is absent, some species of these genera may shift to anaerobic respiration. They reduce nitrate to nitrite (NO_2^-) by the enzyme nitrate reductase. The reduction potential for the NO_3^-/NO_2^- pair is only +0.42 V, compared with +0.82 V for the $1/2\ O_2/H_2O$ pair used in aerobic respiration. Consequently, when nitrate is used as a terminal electron acceptor in anaerobic respiration, less energy is released during electron transport, an ATP coupling site is lost, and at most only two instead of three molecules of ATP are generated. Since the nitrite that is formed during anaerobic respiration is toxic to many procaryotes, it frequently is further reduced to nontoxic nitrous oxide (N_2O) or nitrogen gas (N_2). The process of nitrate reduction to gaseous nitrogen is called **denitrification,** which is considered a **dissimilatory** process. In comparison, **assimilatory nitrate reduction** involves the uptake of nitrate as a source of cell nitrogen and its reduction to organic nitrogen. Most organisms that carry out denitrification are soil inhabitants and use the nitrate in soil in a dissimilatory fashion. Reduction of nitrate to gaseous products is detrimental to plants, since it results in loss of fixed nitrogen from the soil. The antithesis of this process is nitrogen fixation by cyanobacteria and certain other procaryotes, symbiotically or nonsymbiotically.

Other procaryotes (for example, *Desulfovibrio*) use sulfate (SO_4^{2-}) as the electron transport system terminal external electron acceptor, and reduce sulfate to hydrogen sulfide (H_2S) by **dissimilatory sulfate reduction.** Sulfate-reducing bacteria typically are obligate anaerobes that exist in aquatic environments and anaerobic soils. They are economically important in corrosion of metals such as iron and copper, both of which react with sulfides to form insoluble sulfide precipitates. Some organisms accumulate sulfate and reduce it intracellularly for incorporation into organic sulfur in a process called **assimilatory sulfate reduction.**

A number of other chemical compounds, including fumarate ($^-OOC—CH=CH—COO^-$) and carbon dioxide, are used as electron acceptors in anaerobic respiration. The yield of ATP generated by anaerobic respiration depends on the difference in reduction potential of the electron donor and acceptor pairs, but it is typically less in anaerobic respiration than in aerobic respiration. Nonetheless, this alternative for electron transport gives procaryotes the flexibility that enables them to grow and survive in a wide range of environments.

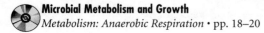 **Microbial Metabolism and Growth**
Metabolism: Anaerobic Respiration • pp. 18–20

table 6.6

Examples of Chemolithotrophs

Group		Oxidizable Substrate	Oxidized Product	Genus
Sulfur oxidizers		H_2S, S^0 $S_2O_3^{2-}$	SO_4^{2-}	*Sulfolobus* *Thiobacillus*
Iron bacteria		Fe^{2+}	Fe^{3+}	*Gallionella* *Sphaerotilus* *Thiobacillus*
Nitrifying bacteria	Ammonia oxidizers	NH_3	NO_2^-	*Nitrosococcus* *Nitrosolobus* *Nitrosomonas* *Nitrosospira*
	Nitrite oxidizers	NO_2^-	NO_3^-	*Nitrobacter* *Nitrococcus* *Nitrospina*
Hydrogen bacteria		H_2	H_2O	*Alcaligenes* *Nocardia* *Pseudomonas*

ATP Yield from Glucose Oxidation Is Not the Same in All Microorganisms

The possession of an electron transport chain undoubtedly increases the ATP yield from oxidation of chemical compounds. The examples given in this chapter indicate a theoretical maximum yield of 38 molecules of ATP from the complete aerobic oxidation of one molecule of glucose. This ATP yield assumes the synthesis of three ATP molecules from the transport of electrons from $NADH + H^+$ to oxygen in the electron transport chain.

However, this ATP yield is only theoretical and may be much lower among bacterial species, depending on the nature of their electron transport chains and the reduction potential of the terminal electron acceptor in these chains. For example, the electron transport chains of *Escherichia coli*, *Paracoccus denitrificans*, and *Micrococcus luteus* differ in their components (Figure 6.25). The chain of *E. coli* lacks cytochrome c, but has a cytochrome d that is not found in *P. denitrificans* and *M. luteus*. *M. luteus* has menaquinone instead of coenzyme Q as an intermediate electron carrier in its chain. These differences in electron carriers affect ATP generation during electron transport in these chains. Experimental evidence indicates that the electron transport chain of *E. coli* has two ATP coupling sites, but the chains of *P. denitrificans* and *M. luteus* (at least the branch via cytochrome a, a$_3$) have three ATP coupling sites. These differences would suggest that the ATP yield from complete aerobic oxidation of one mole of glucose in *E. coli* is significantly less than in the other two types of bacteria with different electron transport chains.

A similar situation occurs in bacteria that generate ATP by anaerobic respiration. The basic mechanism of electron transport is the same as in aerobic respiration. The terminal electron acceptors in the transport chain of anaerobically respiring bacteria, however, frequently have less-positive reduction potentials than the $1/2$ O_2/H_2O pair. For example, *P. denitrificans* forms three molecules of ATP per atom of oxygen when grown aerobically. Under anaerobic conditions, this same bacterium uses nitrate as the terminal external electron acceptor and generates at most two molecules of ATP per molecule of nitrate because of the loss of the third ATP coupling site in electron transport.

As may be seen from these examples, there are variations in electron transport chains in different bacteria. One must consider these differences when estimating the efficiency of ATP yield from oxidative phosphorylation.

Chemolithotrophs

Chemolithotrophs are procaryotes that oxidize reduced inorganic compounds for energy (Table 6.6). Most of these organisms can also obtain all of their carbon from carbon dioxide and therefore are autotrophs. Chemolithotrophs generate ATP by the oxidation of inorganic compounds and electron transport phosphorylation. Inorganic compounds commonly used as energy sources by chemolithotrophs include reduced sulfur compounds, ferrous compounds, reduced nitrogenous compounds, and H_2.

Hydrogen Sulfide Is Oxidized to Elemental Sulfur and Eventually to Sulfate

Microbes that oxidize reduced sulfur compounds are found in such sulfide-rich environments as sulfur springs, acid mine waters, sewage, and marine mud. The procaryotes *Thiobacillus* (domain Bacteria) and *Sulfolobus* (domain Archaea) are among those that oxidize hydrogen sulfide (H_2S) to elemental sulfur and eventually to sulfate (SO_4^{2-}). The elemental sulfur formed in the first oxidation step is highly insoluble and is deposited in or outside the procaryotic cell as sulfur granules. Production of sulfate in a subsequent oxidation step results in acidic conditions. Many of the sulfur-oxidizing procaryotes are able to tolerate low pH environments and, in fact, maintain the acidity of these environments through their metabolic products.

Ferrous Iron Is Oxidized to Ferric Iron

Ferrous iron (Fe^{2+}) is aerobically oxidized to ferric iron (Fe^{3+}) by bacteria that are typically encrusted with coats of iron oxide and inhabit aquatic environments containing large quantities of reduced iron salts. Among these organisms are *Sphaerotilus*, *Gallionella*, and *Thiobacillus ferrooxidans*. Many of these iron-oxidizing bacteria also oxidize sulfur to sulfuric acid and are therefore acidophiles. The acidic environment generated by these bacteria results in a proton gradient across the bacterial plasma membrane, which is used to drive ATP synthesis by a classical chemiosmotic ATPase reaction.

T. ferrooxidans is able to oxidize ferrous or sulfur compounds and is often found in drainage water from mines. This organism oxidizes ferrous iron in the following manner:

$$4\ FeSO_4 + O_2 + 2\ H_2SO_4 \rightarrow 2\ Fe_2(SO_4)_3 + 2\ H_2O$$

When the ferric sulfate that is produced from this oxidation comes in contact with water, it is hydrated:

$$2\ Fe_2(SO_4)_3 + 12\ H_2O \rightarrow 4\ Fe(OH)_3 + 6\ H_2SO_4$$

As a result of these reactions, mine waters are very acidic and are often uninhabitable for other forms of life (Figure 6.26) (see leaching of metals from ores, page 582).

Ammonia Is Oxidized to Nitrite, Which Then Can Be Further Oxidized to Nitrate

The oxidation of reduced nitrogen compounds is a two-step process. The first step of the series—the oxidation of ammonia (NH_3) to nitrite (NO_2^-)—is carried out by *Nitrosomonas*, *Nitrosospira*, *Nitrosococcus*, and *Nitrosolobus*. Oxidation of nitrite to nitrate (NO_3^-) is accomplished by *Nitrobacter*, *Nitrospina*, and *Nitrococcus*. The complete oxidation of ammonia to nitrate is called **nitrification**, and the bacteria that carry out this process in sequence are known as nitrifying bacteria. These bacteria are typically found in the soil where they play an important role in the nitrogen cycle (see nitrogen cycle, page 576).

figure 6.26
Acid Mine Drainage from a Coal Strip Mine
Iron-oxidizing bacteria oxidize ferrous compounds associated with the coal, resulting in the formation of insoluble ferric hydroxide deposits. Since the pH of these acidic mine waters is very low, damage to the environment is common.

Oxygen Is Reduced to Water During the Oxidation of Hydrogen Gas

Bacteria using hydrogen gas as an energy source oxidize it by this simple reaction:

$$H_2 \xrightarrow{\text{hydrogenase}} 2\ H^+ + 2\ e^-$$

The electrons released from the oxidation of H_2 typically go through an electron transport chain, resulting in ATP synthesis and reduction of oxygen to water. Most of the hydrogen-oxidizing bacteria were formerly classified in the genus *Hydrogenomonas*. This genus has been eliminated, and the hydrogen-oxidizing bacteria are now placed in several genera, including *Pseudomonas*, *Alcaligenes*, and *Nocardia*. In contrast to other groups of chemolithotrophs, hydrogen-oxidizing bacteria are **facultative** chemolithotrophs; most can utilize a wide variety of organic substrates as carbon and energy sources.

One of the most remarkable characteristics of some bacteria is their ability to emit light. These luminescent bacteria, which include *Photobacterium* and *Lucibacterium*, frequently live as symbionts of fish, and their light emission may serve to assist their hosts in predation, in avoiding predators, and in communication with other members of the host species. The bacterial enzyme responsible for the light-emitting reaction is **luciferase.**

Bacterial luciferase catalyzes the bioluminescent oxidation of $FMNH_2$ and a long-chained aliphatic aldehyde (RCHO) by molecular oxygen:

$$FMNH_2 + RCHO + O_2 \xrightarrow{\text{luciferase}}$$
$$0.1\ h\nu\ + FMN + H_2O + RCOOH$$

Oxidized FMN, water, acid (RCOOH), and light are produced as a result of this reaction. The bioluminescent pathway is hypothesized to be a branch of electron transport in luminescent bacteria, where electrons may either be sent through a conventional electron transport chain to the terminal electron acceptor oxygen or be shunted to oxygen via the luciferase system (Figure 6P.1). Because oxygen is required for bioluminescence, luminescent bacteria provide a sensitive assay for oxygen.

The chemiluminescent quantum yield of bacterial luciferase is quite significant; it was measured in a series of experiments reported by J.W. Hastings, W.H. Riley, and J. Massa in 1965. In these experiments, the luminescent bacterium *Photobacterium fischeri* was grown in a 50-gallon fermenter. Cells were harvested at the time of maximum light emission, and luciferase was extracted from the cell paste. Luciferase activity was then measured by incubating purified enzyme with aldehyde, $FMNH_2$, and other chemicals (Table 6P.1). Light intensity was measured with a photomultiplier photometer and calcu-

lated as units of quanta per second, using [3]H- or ^{14}C-labeled hexadecane as a liquid light standard. It was determined that pure luciferase gave a chemiluminescent quantum yield of 0.27 per enzyme molecule.

Hastings and his colleagues not only were able to calculate the quantum yield of luciferase from *P. fischeri*, but also observed that there were large amounts of luciferase (approximately 5% of the total cell protein) in the cell and that luminescence accounted for as much as 20% of the total oxygen consumption of the cell. These data suggest that luciferase synthesis represents a significant proportion of the cell's biosynthetic activities.

Sources

Hastings, J.W., and K.H. Nealson. 1977. Bacterial bioluminescence. *Annual Reviews of Microbiology* 31:549–595.

Hastings, J.W., W.H. Riley, and J. Massa. 1965. The purification, properties, and chemiluminescent quantum yield of bacterial luciferase. *The Journal of Biological Chemistry* 240:1473–1481.

table 6P.1

Reaction Mixture for Assay of Luciferase

Reaction Mixture	Volume (ml)
2-mercaptoethanol (5×10^{-3} M)	0.95
Phosphate buffer (1.25 M, pH 7.0)	0.20
Bovine serum albumin (1%)	0.20
Enzyme preparation	0.05
n-decyl aldehyde (10^{-2} M)	0.10
$FMNH_2$ (5×10^{-5} M), to initiate reaction	1.00

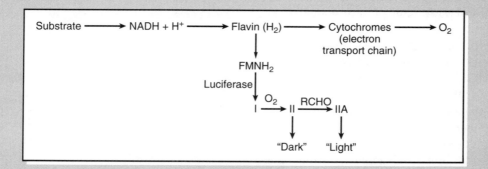

figure 6P.1
Possible Pathways for Electron Transport in Luminescent Bacteria

⬤ Summary

1. All living organisms must have a source of energy to perform work. Most organisms obtain their energy ultimately from chemical substances (phototrophs obtain their energy from light). Energy-liberating processes (exergonic reactions) provide the cell with the energy to carry out energy-requiring processes (endergonic reactions). The coupling of exergonic and endergonic reactions is fundamentally important to all cellular processes.

2. Thermodynamics is the study of energy transformations; bioenergetics is the study of energy transformations in living systems. The first law of thermodynamics states that energy can be neither created nor destroyed during its transformation. The second law of thermodynamics states that spontaneous reactions always proceed with an increase in entropy.

3. Enzymes are protein catalysts that occur in living cells and accelerate reaction rates without themselves being changed. Inhibitors are chemical substances that prevent or slow down enzyme reactions by binding to the enzyme. Allosteric inhibition occurs when a small molecule called an effector binds to an allosteric site on the enzyme, resulting in a change in conformation of the active site and inhibition of enzyme activity.

4. Oxidation-reduction, or redox, reactions involve the transfer of electrons from one molecule to another. Oxidation describes any reaction in which electrons are lost from a substance, whereas reduction describes a reaction in which electrons are accepted by a substance.

5. The ability of a substance to donate or accept electrons is determined by its oxidation-reduction, or redox, potential. The reduced substance of a redox pair can donate electrons to the oxidized substance of the pair, which has the more positive redox potential. The greater the difference in redox potential between the redox pair serving as the electron donor and the pair serving as an electron acceptor, the greater the energy available as a result of the oxidation-reduction reaction.

6. Electron carriers are oxidized and reduced as they transfer electrons from a donor to an acceptor molecule. Some electron carriers such as NAD and FAD transfer hydrogen atoms as well as electrons.

7. Energy liberated as a result of oxidation-reduction reactions can be stored in high-energy compounds. ATP, phosphoenolpyruvate, acetyl phosphate, and 1,3-diphosphoglycerate are examples of high-energy compounds.

8. Chemical compounds are broken down by exergonic catabolic pathways and synthesized by endergonic anabolic pathways. Both types of pathways constitute the metabolic pathways of a cell (Figure 6.27).

9. Microorganisms use three mechanisms to generate ATP: oxidative phosphorylation, photophosphorylation, and substrate-level phosphorylation. ATP is synthesized during the transfer of electrons via an electron transport chain to a final electron acceptor in oxidative phosphorylation and photophosphorylation. In substrate-level phosphorylation, ATP is synthesized when a phosphorylated metabolic intermediate transfers its phosphate to ADP.

10. An organic substrate serves as the electron donor, and an oxidized intermediate of the substrate acts as the final electron acceptor and subsequently becomes reduced in fermentation. An external terminal electron acceptor receives electrons and is reduced in respiration. Molecular oxygen is the terminal electron acceptor in aerobic respiration, whereas some other molecule such as nitrate or sulfate is the electron acceptor in anaerobic respiration.

11. The Embden-Meyerhof pathway, an example of glycolysis, consists of ten distinct reactions in which glucose is oxidized to pyruvate. ATP is synthesized in the Embden-Meyerhof pathway by substrate-level phosphorylation. The pyruvate that is formed in glycolysis is further degraded to a variety of products during fermentation.

12. The tricarboxylic acid (TCA) cycle is a central pathway of cellular metabolism. Electrons from NADH + H$^+$ and FADH$_2$ generated by the TCA cycle are sent through an electron transport chain to generate ATP by chemiosmosis.

13. Chemolithotrophs are procaryotes that oxidize reduced inorganic compounds such as hydrogen sulfide, ferrous iron, ammonia, and hydrogen for energy. Many chemolithotrophs also obtain their carbon from carbon dioxide and therefore are autotrophs. Chemolithotrophs generate ATP by the oxidation of inorganic compounds and electron transport phosphorylation.

EVOLUTION *and* BIODIVERSITY

Although procaryotes are the smallest of all living cells, as a group they show the most metabolic diversity. Procaryotes can use sunlight, organic compounds, and inorganic compounds as sources of energy. They use a variety of substrates, and some—the autotrophs—can even produce their own organic compounds from carbon dioxide. They are able to live in anaerobic environments and in locales that would be inhospitable to other forms of life. This wide diversity of procaryotes is made possible by their myriad of enzymes and metabolic pathways. Some of the first living organisms were probably heterotrophic procaryotes capable of fermenting organic substances on a primitive earth lacking atmospheric oxygen. As organic compounds were used, heterotrophs may have evolved into autotrophs, which replenished the supply of organic molecules. With the evolution of cyanobacteria, algae, and plants came photosynthesis and oxygen. Despite the diversity of metabolism among organisms today, common metabolic threads run through the various forms of life. ATP is synthesized during electron transport; fundamental pathways such as the TCA cycle are found in a wide variety of organisms; and certain molecules such as ATP, NAD, and cytochromes are remarkably similar in all organisms. This biochemical unity among even the most diverse of organisms suggests that all organisms evolved from a common ancestral stock.

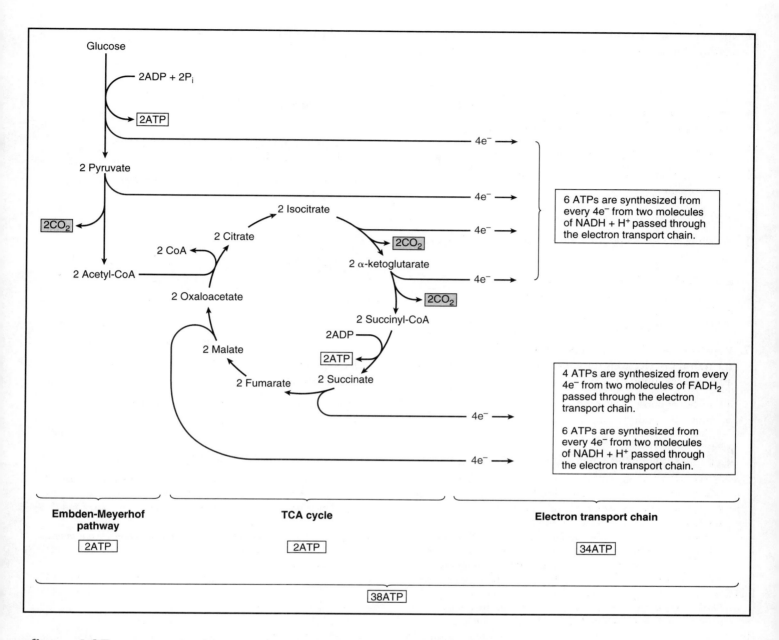

figure 6.27 Summary of Pathways of Energy Generation in Chemotrophic Bacteria

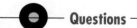 Questions

Short Answer

1. State the first and second laws of thermodynamics.

2. Explain what enzymes are and why they are important.

3. Identify several factors that will decrease the rate of enzymatic reactions.

4. Compare and contrast competitive and noncompetitive inhibitors.

5. Explain feedback inhibition and its importance.

6. Compare and contrast oxidation and reduction reactions.

7. Identify several common electron carriers. Explain their importance.

8. Identify several high-energy compounds.

9. Compare and contrast anabolism and catabolism.

10. Identify three methods of ATP generation.

11. Compare and contrast fermentation and respiration.

12. Identify several pathways for glycolysis. Which is the major pathway for bacteria? Why does more than one pathway exist?

13. Are all fermentation products acidic?

14. Briefly describe by equations or sentences the fate of glucose when it is completely catabolized by aerobic respiration.

15. Compare and contrast aerobic and anaerobic respiration.

16. Explain how chemolithotrophs differ from chemoorganotrophs.

Multiple Choice

1. Which of the following reactions represents an endergonic reaction?

   a. $C_6H_{12}O_6 + 6\ O_2 \rightarrow 6\ CO_2 + 6\ H_2O$
   b. Glucose-6-PO_4 + H_2O → Glucose + PO_4
   c. ADP + PO_4 → ATP + H_2O
   d. All of the above are endergonic.

2. Which of the following methods of ATP generation involves the transfer of electrons through an electron transport chain and requires sunlight?

   a. oxidative phosphorylation
   b. photophosphorylation

   c. substrate-level phosphorylation
   d. None of the above.

3. Pyruvate may be used to make:

   a. lactate, proprionate, butyrate
   b. ethanol and CO_2
   c. glucose
   d. All of the above can be formed from pyruvate.
   e. Both a and b, but not c.

4. Which of the following represents a final electron acceptor reaction?

   a. $H_2S \rightarrow SO_4^{2-}$
   b. $NO_3^- \rightarrow NO_2^-$
   c. $FeSO_4 \rightarrow Fe_2(SO_4)_3$
   d. $NH_3 \rightarrow NO_2^-$

Critical Thinking

1. Explain how, and why, protons (not electrons) are responsible for ATP synthesis by oxidative phosphorylation.

2. Explain how bacteria could continue to grow if their carbohydrate supply were depleted.

3. Discuss the role of fermentation for bacteria in an aerobic environment.

● — **Supplementary Readings** —

Caldwell, D.R. 1995. *Microbial physiology & metabolism*. Dubuque, Iowa: Wm. C. Brown Publishers. (A microbial physiology textbook with discussions of metabolism, fermentation, and genetics.)

Gerhardt, P., R.G.E. Murray, W.A. Wood, and N.R. Krieg. 1994. *Methods for general and molecular bacteriology*, pp. 463–599. Washington, D.C.: American Society for Microbiology. (A discussion of various techniques in microbiology, including sections on microbial metabolism and assays for metabolic and enzymatic activities.)

Haddock, B. A., and C. W. Jones. 1977. Bacterial respiration. *Bacteriological Reviews* 41:47–99. (A comprehensive discussion of bacterial electron transport chains and ATPase complexes.)

Hinckle, P.C., and R.E. McCarthy. 1978. How cells make ATP. *Scientific American* 238:104–123. (A review article on ATP synthesis.)

Hobbs, A.S., and R.W. Albers. 1980. The structure of proteins involved in active membrane transport. *Annual Reviews of Biophysics and Bioengineering* 9:259–291. (A review of transport mechanisms in procaryotes and eucaryotes.)

Ingledew, W.J., and R.K. Poole. 1984. The respiratory chains of *Escherichia coli*. *Microbiological Reviews* 48:222–271. (An in-depth discussion of electron transport and respiration in *E. coli*.)

Neidhardt, F.C., J.L. Ingraham, and M. Schaechter. 1990. *Physiology of the bacterial cell: A molecular approach*. Sunderland, Mass.: Sinauer Associates. (A textbook of bacterial physiology and genetics.)

Nichols, D.G. 1982. *Bioenergetics: An introduction to the chemiosmotic theory*. New York: Academic Press. (An excellent discussion of chemiosmosis.)

Stryer, L. 1988. *Biochemistry,* 3d ed. San Francisco: W. H. Freeman. (A detailed review of biochemistry, with discussions of chemical reactions and structures.)

Wood, W.B., J.H. Wilson, R.B. Benbow, and L.E. Hood. 1981. *Biochemistry: A problems approach,* 2d ed. Menlo Park, Calif.: Benjamin/Cummings Publishing Company. (A concise review of major topics in biochemistry, with extensive and thought-provoking problems.)

Zubay, G. 1993. *Biochemistry,* 3d ed. Dubuque, Iowa: Wm. C. Brown Publishers. (A general textbook of biochemistry.)

chapter seven

PHOTOSYNTHESIS AND OTHER METABOLIC PATHWAYS

Tapering filaments of the heterocystous cyanobacterium *Gloeotrichia echinulata* (×**63**).

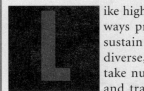

ike highways of life, a cell's metabolic pathways provide the essential ingredients to sustain life and support growth. These diverse, interconnected chemical arteries take nutrients found in the surroundings and transform them into the energy and building blocks necessary to construct the myriad of chemicals and structures needed for a functional organism. Energy released through the catabolism of nutrients is used by the cell to drive anabolic reactions for the synthesis of cellular constituents.

Among metabolic pathways, none are more important to life than those that participate in photosynthesis. Without photosynthesis, the cycling of carbon into glucose (the basic energy source and fundamental building block of carbohydrates for all organisms) would be incomplete. Oxygen, which is important in aerobic respiration, would not be available. Photosynthesis is considered the ultimate source of life for all plants and animals because it provides the fundamental necessary ingredients.

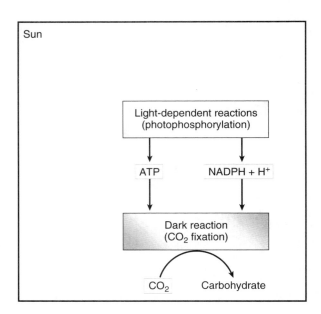

figure 7.1
Schematic Diagram of Photosynthesis

Photosynthesis

Photosynthesis, a process known for many years, occurs in green plants and algae. It was not until the 1880s—when Sergei Winogradsky found that purple and green bacteria oxidized H_2S to SO_4^{2-} with transient accumulation of sulfur granules in their cells—that these photosynthetic microorganisms were studied in greater detail. Winogradsky, however, thought that these microbes were ordinary autotrophic sulfur bacteria and not photosynthetic. At about the same time, Theodor Wilhelm Engelmann (1843–1909), a German microbiologist, discovered that these bacteria were phototactic and grew better when exposed to certain wavelengths of the light spectrum. Although he was unable to show that these organisms produced oxygen in the presence of light, Engelmann nonetheless proposed that they might be photosynthetic. Unfortunately, it was widely believed at the time that oxygen production was an indispensable part of the photosynthetic process, and Engelmann's proposal received little support. Not until the 1930s was it discovered that not all photosynthetic organisms formed oxygen.

Photosynthesis is now known to occur in algae, plants, and several groups of procaryotes. Photosynthesis consists of two major sets of reactions: **photophosphorylation** and **carbon dioxide fixation** (Figure 7.1). Photophosphorylation, or the **light-dependent reactions** of photosynthesis, occurs only in the presence of light and generates ATP and reducing power in the form of $NADPH + H^+$. The ATP and reducing power are used to drive carbon dioxide fixation, or the **dark (light-independent) reactions** of photosynthesis, which can occur without light. Although photophosphorylation and carbon dioxide fixation are both part of photosynthesis, they are autonomous sets of reactions able to function independently.

Chlorophylls Are the Principal Photosynthetic Pigments in Phototrophic Eucaryotes and Cyanobacteria

Photosynthesis is carried out in specialized membranes found only in phototrophs. These structures contain pigments that trap light (electromagnetic) energy and transform it to chemical energy in the form of ATP. The principal light-trapping pigment molecule in phototrophic plants, algae, and cyanobacteria is **chlorophyll.** Chlorophylls and cytochromes both contain porphyrins, but they differ in two ways. First, chlorophylls have magnesium, not iron, as the central atom in the porphyrin ring. Second, a long-chain hydrophobic alcohol (phytol) is attached to one of the four pyrrole groups in the chlorophyll porphyrin ring structure. The solubility of phytol in lipids determines the orientation of the chlorophyll molecules in the internal membranes of chloroplasts.

At least three major types of chlorophylls are found in phototrophic plants, algae, and cyanobacteria: a, b, and c. These three types of chlorophylls are distinguished by slight differences in their chemical structures and absorption spectra. The absorption spectrum is a plot of the absorption of a substance over a continuous spectrum of wavelength of light. The absorption spectra of chlorophylls depends not only on the chemical structure of the pigment molecules, but also on the chlorophylls' interactions with binding proteins in photosynthetic membranes or, in the case of purified chlorophylls, the solution in which they are suspended.

Chlorophyll a is the most common and extensively studied chlorophyll (Figure 7.2). When suspended in acetone, chlorophyll a shows strong absorption of red light and blue light at wavelengths of 675 nm and 420 nm, respectively. Chlorophyll b, which occurs in green algae and higher plants, also absorbs red and blue light but at different wavelengths—645 nm and 470 nm. Chlorophyll c replaces chlorophyll b in brown algae, diatoms, and dinoflagellates.

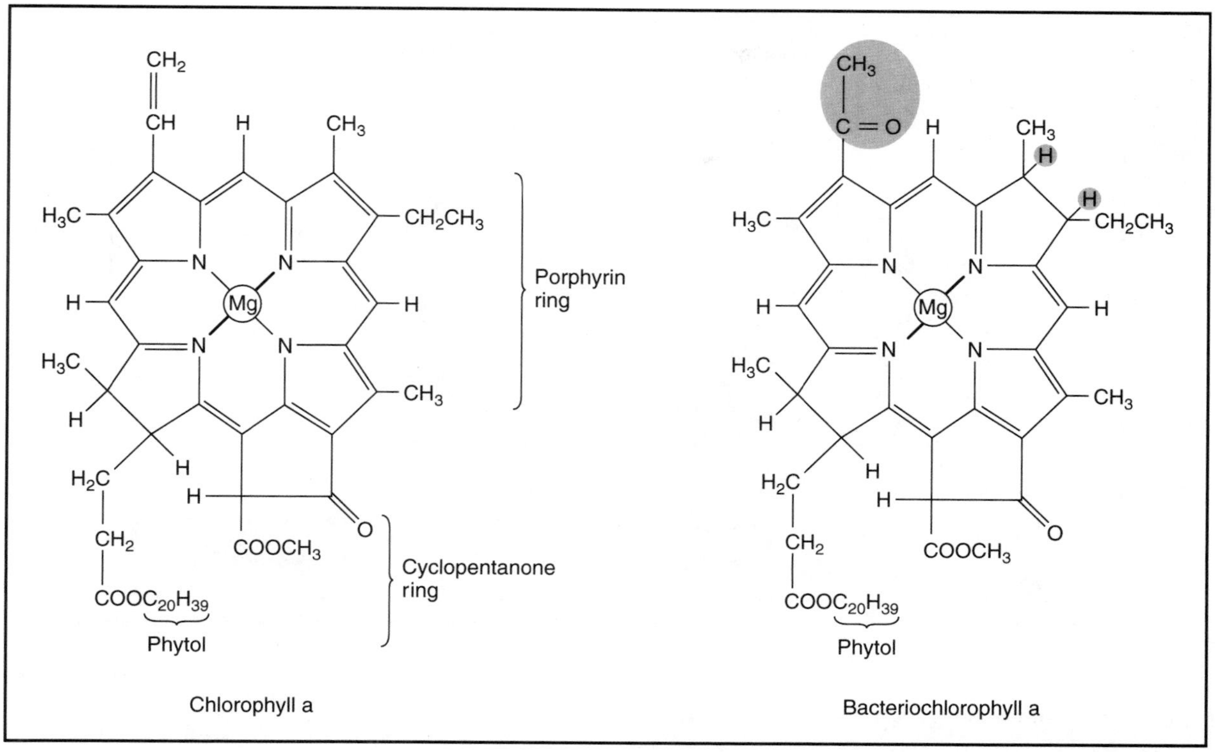

figure 7.2
Structures of Chlorophyll a and Bacteriochlorophyll a
The two structures are identical except for the atoms circled and shaded on the bacteriochlorophyll a structure.

Bacteriochlorophylls Are the Principal Photosynthetic Pigments in Bacteria

The photosynthetic pigments of phototrophic procaryotes other than cyanobacteria are similar in structure to chlorophylls, with slight differences in certain side groups. They are called **bacteriochlorophylls** because they are found in bacteria (Figure 7.2). There are five major types of bacteriochlorophylls: a, b, c, d, and e. The absorption peaks of bacteriochlorophylls c, d, and e approximate those of chlorophylls a, b, and c, with wavelengths ranging from approximately 400 to 650 nm (Figure 7.3).

Bacteriochlorophylls a and b have an extra double bond in one of the pyrrole groups and are able to absorb light further toward the infrared portion of the spectrum (near 750 nm). The purple phototrophic bacteria (*Chromatiaceae* and *Rhodospirillaceae*) have either bacteriochlorophyll a or b. In comparison, the green phototrophic bacteria (*Chlorobiaceae* and *Chloroflexaceae*) contain large quantities of one major bacteriochlorophyll (bacteriochlorophyll c, d, or e) and smaller amounts of bacteriochlorophyll a as a minor pigment.

Although chlorophylls and bacteriochlorophylls are found in phototrophic organisms, what proof do we have that these pigments are directly responsible for photosynthesis? Several major lines of evidence indicate a clear association with photosynthesis.

1. Only those organisms that possess these pigments photosynthesize.

2. Light provided at wavelengths that match the absorption spectra of chlorophylls or bacteriochlorophylls in an organism is most effective for photosynthesis.

3. Organisms do not photosynthesize if cultured under conditions in which chlorophylls or bacteriochlorophylls are not produced.

4. Mutant organisms that no longer synthesize chlorophylls or bacteriochlorophylls lose their ability to photosynthesize.

Accessory Pigments Harvest Light from Other Portions of the Spectrum for Photosynthesis

Chlorophylls and bacteriochlorophylls absorb light from only a small portion of the spectrum. Were it not for a special group of pigments called **accessory pigments,** which harvest light from other portions of the spectrum, much of the sun's light would be lost as heat. The accessory pigments fall into two classes: **carotenoids** and **biliproteins** (or **phycobilins**).

Carotenoids are lipid-soluble, long-chain, conjugated (having alternating single and double bonds) hydrocarbons found in photosynthetic eucaryotes and procaryotes. As a rule, carotenoids

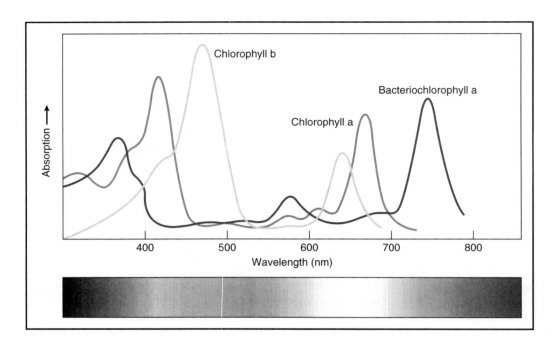

figure 7.3

Absorption Spectra of Common Chlorophylls and Bacteriochlorophylls
The absorption spectra of chlorophylls a and b and bacteriochlorophyll a in ether are shown. Note that chlorophyll a has different absorption peaks than bacteriochlorophyll a.

are yellow or orange and absorb light in the blue range of the spectrum (400 to 550 nm). These accessory pigments usually are associated with chlorophylls, to which they transfer absorbed light energy (Figure 7.4). Two major types of carotenoids occur in photosynthetic organisms. The carotenes (for example, β-carotene) are pure hydrocarbons. Carotenols (for example, xanthophyll) have hydroxyl (–OH) groups on both ends of the hydrocarbon chain.

The second class of accessory pigments, the biliproteins, occurs only in red algae and cyanobacteria. Biliproteins are water-soluble, linear tetrapyrroles coupled to proteins. Phycoerythrin (a red pigment that absorbs light at a wavelength of 550 nm) and phycocyanin (a blue pigment that absorbs light at 620 to 640 nm) are examples of biliproteins.

The accessory pigments not only assist chlorophylls in capturing light energy; they also protect the photosynthetic apparatus from a destructive process known as **photooxidation.** Phototrophs are especially sensitive to bright light because chlorophylls and bacteriochlorophylls act as photosensitizers. As these pigment molecules are exposed to light, they become oxidized and the excited molecule combines with oxygen. This light-dependent oxidation is termed photooxidation. Carotenoids protect chlorophylls and bacteriochlorophylls from photooxidation with their more readily oxidizable double bonds. These accessory pigments absorb most of the harmful light and thus act as shields for the light-sensitive chlorophylls. The role of carotenoids as photoprotective agents is evident, since bacteriochlorophylls in photosynthetic bacterial mutants that no longer synthesize carotenoids are sensitive to photooxidation.

Chlorophylls Are Contained Within Chloroplasts in Eucaryotes

The pigments that harvest light energy in eucaryotic photosynthesis occur in specialized organelles called **chloroplasts** (Figure 7.5). Chloroplasts vary in number from a few in algal cells to several hundred in cells of higher plants.

In chloroplasts, chlorophylls and carotenoids are located in flattened disklike membranous sacs known as **thylakoids,** which form part of the elaborate internal membranes. Biliproteins are found in granules called **phycobilisomes,** which are located on the surfaces of thylakoids. The thylakoids in most algal and plant cells are arranged in stacks called **grana** [singular, granum]. Thylakoids of adjacent grana are periodically connected by stromal lamellae, which are extensions of the thylakoid membranes. Most chloroplasts contain from 40 to 60 grana, each consisting of anywhere from a few to a hundred or more thylakoids. The structures found within the chloroplast are separated from the cell cytoplasm by two sets of membranes, an inner and outer membrane. These components are embedded in a chloroplastic ground substance called the **stroma.** All three sets of chloroplast membranes (thylakoids, inner membrane, and outer membrane) consist of lipids and proteins. Eighty percent of the membrane lipids are glycolipids, whereas most of the proteins are involved in electron transport and photophosphorylation.

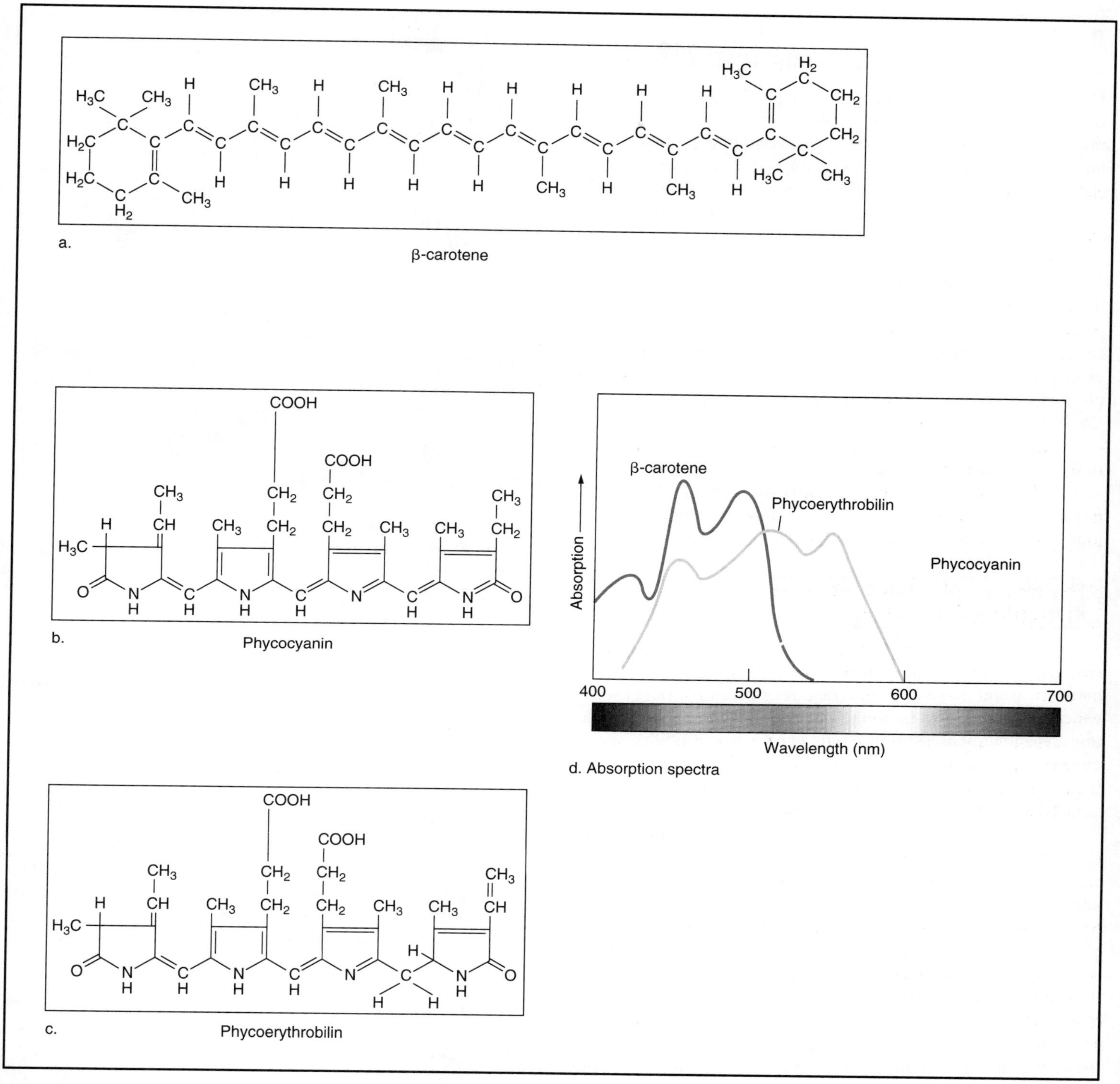

figure 7.4

Accessory Pigments and Their Absorption Spectra

The structures of β-carotene, phycocyanin, and phycoerythrobilin (the chromophore of phycoerythrin) and their absorption spectra in aqueous solution are shown. The accessory pigments and the chlorophylls or bacteriochlorophylls together absorb light at wavelengths spanning the spectrum. a. β-carotene. b. Phycocyanin. c. Phycoerythrobilin. d. Absorption spectra.

The Photosynthetic Apparatus of Procaryotes Is Contained Within Specialized Membranes or Chlorobium Vesicles

Unlike eucaryotic phototrophs, photosynthetic procaryotes do not carry out photosynthesis in chloroplasts. The photosynthetic apparatus of cyanobacteria is found in thylakoids, but these are not contained within chloroplasts. Cyanobacterial thylakoids are found in elaborate invaginated membranes dispersed throughout the cell.

Phototrophic bacteria have specialized membranes or vesicles to carry out photosynthesis (Figure 7.6). The photosynthetic membranes of *Rhodospirillaceae* and *Chromatiaceae* are infolded portions of the plasma membrane. The extent of these membranes depends on the quantity of pigment and degree of photosynthesis in the organism. Bacteria that are actively photosynthetic have large quantities of photosynthetic pigments and more extensive membrane systems than those that are not as active in photosynthesis. Phototrophic bacteria belonging to the families *Chlorobiaceae* and *Chloroflexaceae* have specialized structures called **chlorosomes** or **chlorobium vesicles,** which are adjacent to the plasma membrane but remain as distinct structures. These vesicles have dimensions of approximately 50 nm by 100 to 150 nm and are enclosed by a nonunit membrane. Photosynthetic pigments are present within the chlorobium vesicles.

The Nature of Photosynthesis: Photophosphorylation

Although photophosphorylation and carbon dioxide fixation are separate sets of reactions in photosynthesis, they are coupled because carbon dioxide fixation requires ATP and NADPH + H$^+$, which are provided by photophosphorylation. Photophosphorylation depends upon electromagnetic energy, which occurs in discrete packets (quanta) called **photons** or **Einsteins.** A photon of light contains an amount of energy equal to the frequency of the light (velocity in centimeters per second/wavelength in nanometers) times Planck's constant (1.58×10^{-34} cal-sec). Since Planck's constant and the velocity of light are constant values, the energy of a photon increases as the wavelength of light decreases. Thus the energy content of a quantum of red light at a wavelength of 650 nm (43 kcal/Einstein) is considerably less than that of a quantum of blue light at a wavelength of 490 nm (58 kcal/Einstein).

When light interacts with matter, photons are annihilated. According to the first law of thermodynamics, energy can be neither created nor destroyed (see first law of thermodynamics, page 141). However, it can be transformed. Several things can happen to the energy that is contained within photons striking a molecule (Figure 7.7).

1. The energy can be dissipated as heat.

2. The energy can be reemitted as a new photon of light at a longer wavelength, with a portion of the initial energy lost as heat. This change commonly occurs in fluorescence.

3. The energy contained within the photons can cause a chemical change in the compound that absorbs them.

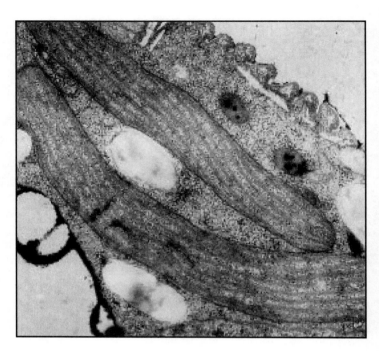

figure 7.5

Electron Micrograph Showing Chloroplasts from the Alga *Euglena gracilis*

Note the parallel thylakoid membranes within each chloroplast (×15,000).

This last possibility occurs in photosynthesis when a molecule of chlorophyll is struck by a photon of light. When the quantum of energy in the photon is absorbed by an electron in the chlorophyll, the electron moves to an orbital having a higher energy level. The electron has gone from an unexcited state known as the ground state to an excited state. The excited electron in its new orbital is extremely unstable and, if located adjacent to an acceptor molecule, is transferred to that acceptor. Electron carriers associated with photosynthesis accept these ejected electrons. The chlorophyll molecules become stronger reducing agents (that is, have lower redox potentials) after absorbing light energy. The electrons are shuttled through carriers that have more positive redox potentials. In plants, algae, and cyanobacteria, these electrons eventually reduce NADP$^+$ to NADPH + H$^+$. During this electron transport, energy is liberated and used to synthesize ATP through the process known as photophosphorylation, similar to oxidative phosphorylation.

The overall sequence of events that occurs in the light-dependent reactions of photosynthesis (that is, photophosphorylation) is summarized by the following equation:

$$12 \text{ H}_2\text{O} + 12 \text{ NADP}^+ + 18 \text{ ADP} + 18 \text{ P}_i \xrightarrow{\text{light}}$$

$$6 \text{ O}_2 + 12 \text{ NADPH} + 12 \text{ H}^+ + 18 \text{ ATP}$$

The ATP and NADPH + H$^+$ produced by photophosphorylation can subsequently be used in the dark reactions of photosynthesis

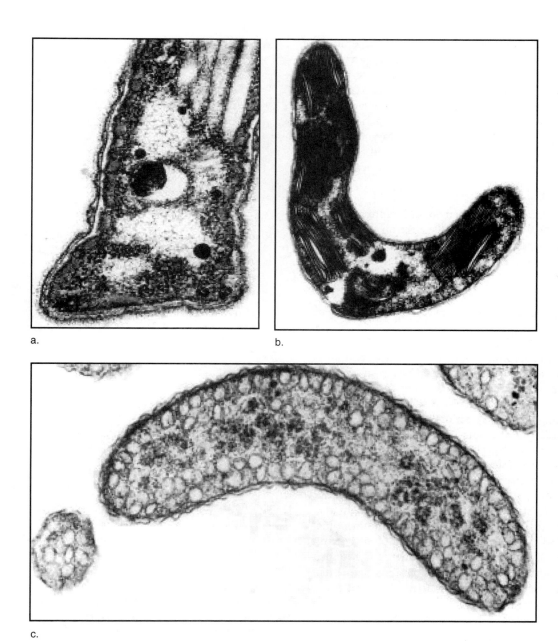

figure 7.6

Electron Micrographs of Bacterial Photosynthetic Vesicles and Membranes

a. Chlorobium vesicles in *Pelodictyon clathratiforme*. Chlorobium vesicles (dark gray) are shown underlying and attached to the plasma membrane. Gas vacuoles (light gray with pointed ends) are in the upper portion of the cell (×72,000). b. Intracytoplasmic photosynthetic membranes in *Ectothiorhodospira mobilis* (×30,000). c. Intracytoplasmic photosynthetic membranes (vesicles) in *Rhodospirillum rubrum* (×51,000).

to fix carbon dioxide into organic compounds. Carbon dioxide fixation is summarized by this equation:

$$12 \ NADPH + 12 \ H^+ + 18 \ ATP + 6 \ CO_2 \longrightarrow$$

$$C_6H_{12}O_6 + 12 \ NADP^+ + 18 \ ADP + 18 \ P_i + 6 \ H_2O$$

These two equations can be combined to obtain an overall equation for photosynthesis:

$$6 \ CO_2 + 6 \ H_2O \ \xrightarrow{\text{light}} \ C_6H_{12}O_6 + 6 \ O_2$$

In this equation, six molecules of carbon dioxide are fixed into one molecule of hexose ($C_6H_{12}O_6$). Water serves as the electron and hydrogen donor in this series of reactions. Oxygen is released as the water is lysed to replace electrons ejected from chlorophylls during light-dependent electron transport and photophosphorylation.

Although this formula may be representative of photophosphorylation in plants, algae, and cyanobacteria, which carry out **oxygenic** photosynthesis, it does not reflect photophosphorylation in phototrophic bacteria, in which photosynthesis is **anoxygenic** (without production of oxygen). Phototrophic bacteria carry out photophosphorylation using electron and hydrogen donors other than water. Cornelius B. van Niel, who studied photosynthesis in bacteria, realized this; in 1935 he proposed a generalized equation that applies to photosynthesis in both eucaryotes and procaryotes:

$$6\ CO_2 + 6\ H_2A \xrightarrow{\text{light}} C_6H_{12}O_6 + H_2O + 6\ A$$

In this equation the electron and hydrogen donor is represented by H_2A rather than by H_2O. Whereas H_2O is the electron and hydrogen donor in plants, algae, and cyanobacteria, other reduced compounds such as H_2S and even H_2 are used in the same capacity by photosynthetic bacteria.

Photophosphorylation Occurs in Assemblages of Electron Carriers Called Photosystems

Photophosphorylation in all phototrophs (plants, algae, and procaryotes) takes place in **photosystems,** assemblages of chlorophylls and accessory pigments in groups of 250 to 400 molecules. As individual pigment molecules are struck by photons, they become excited. Through electron ejection, these light-absorbing molecules (chlorophylls and accessory pigments) transfer a portion of the absorbed energy to molecules having longer wavelength absorption maxima. Energy transfer continues until the light energy eventually reaches a chlorophyll molecule in the photosystem having the longest wavelength absorption maximum. This special chlorophyll acts as an "energy sink," absorbs light at a wavelength of approximately 700 nm (870 nm in phototrophic bacteria), and is called the **reaction center** of the photosystem. The chlorophylls and accessory pigments that attract and funnel light energy to this reaction center are called **antenna pigments.** These function as the first step in light energy transfer to the reaction center.

The Mechanism of Photophosphorylation Is Similar in Plants, Algae, and Cyanobacteria

Plants, algae, and cyanobacteria have similar mechanisms for the generation of ATP by photophosphorylation. ATP is generated from the flow of electrons through a series of electron carriers.

ATP and NADPH + H+ Are Generated during Noncyclic Photophosphorylation

Present evidence indicates that there are two separate photosystems that operate in plants, algae, and cyanobacteria. The reaction center in both photosystems is a chlorophyll a molecule. In photosystem I the chlorophyll a that is the reaction center is called **P700**—a Pigment that absorbs light at a wavelength of *700* nm. The reaction center in photosystem II is chlorophyll **P680,** which absorbs light at *680* nm.

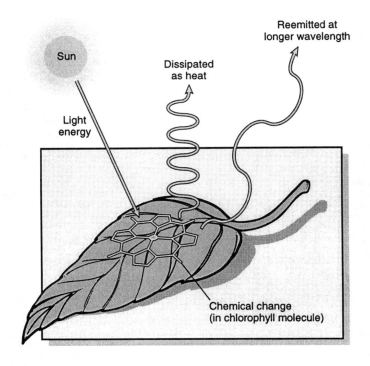

figure 7.7
Fate of Light Striking an Object
The light can be (1) dissipated as heat, (2) reemitted as a new photon at a longer wavelength, or (3) used to cause a chemical change in the object absorbing it.

The two photosystems are coupled by an electron transport system. As carriers transport electrons from one photosystem to the next, energy is released and conserved in the form of ATP. The electrons also function to reduce $NADP^+$ to $NADPH + H^+$.

The sequence of events in photophosphorylation was first outlined by Robin Hill and Fay Bendall in 1960. The Hill-Bendall scheme, often called the Z-pathway because of its resemblance to the letter Z, postulates that one electron is raised from the ground state to an activated state and released from chlorophyll P680 in photosystem II for every quantum of light energy reaching that reaction center (Figure 7.8). The electron is replaced in the reaction center chlorophyll by electrons released from the splitting of a water molecule. This light-dependent splitting of water is termed **photolysis.** Since two electrons are made available from the splitting of one water molecule, electrons are believed to move in pairs in the Hill-Bendall model for the light-dependent reactions. The oxygen evolved during photosynthesis also is derived from photolysis, whereas the hydrogen made available through the splitting of water is used for the eventual reduction of $NADP^+$ to $NADPH + H^+$.

High-energy electrons released from chlorophyll P680 are passed to an unidentified primary electron acceptor. Electrons pass from the primary electron acceptor through a series of electron carriers, which have sequentially more positive redox potentials, until they arrive at reaction center chlorophyll P700 in photosystem I. The electron carriers in this transport chain between chloro-

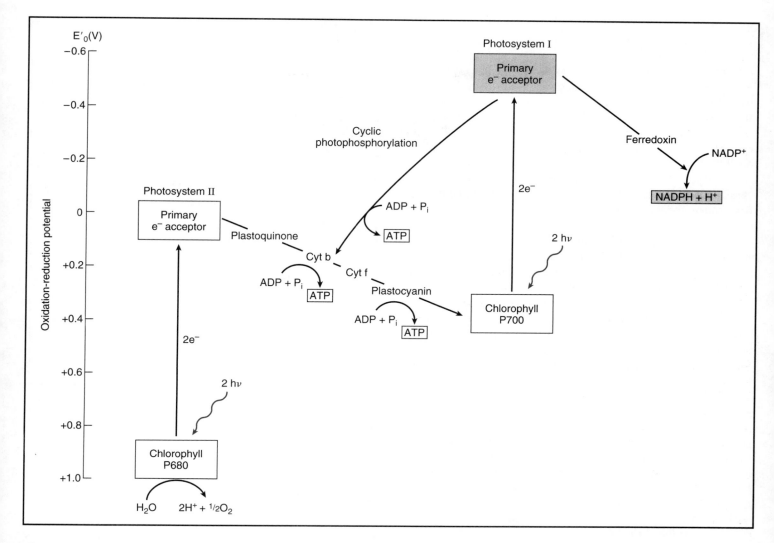

figure 7.8

The Hill-Bendall Scheme for Photophosphorylation

Two photosystems (I and II) are involved in photophosphorylation in plants, algae, and cyanobacteria. Electrons released from chlorophyll P680 are sent to a primary electron acceptor in photosystem II. The electrons are then passed through a series of electron carriers to chlorophyll P700 in photosystem I. Electrons from chlorophyll P700 are sent to an electron acceptor and eventually through ferredoxin to NADP+, which becomes reduced to NADPH + H+. ATP is synthesized during the movement of electrons from photosystem II to photosystem I. The electrons lost from chlorophyll P680 are replaced by the splitting of H_2O (photolysis).

phylls P680 and P700 include plastoquinone, cytochrome b, cytochrome f, and plastocyanin. As each pair of electrons is passed to lower energy level acceptors (that is, electron carriers with more-positive redox potentials), the released energy is conserved in the formation of one—possibly two—molecules of ATP from $ADP + P_i$. This light-dependent synthesis of ATP is known as **photophosphorylation.**

The electrons reaching chlorophyll P700 are energized once more as the reaction center chlorophyll absorbs light energy. The energized electrons are passed from chlorophyll P700 to an iron-sulfur protein (FeS) and eventually through ferredoxin and flavoprotein to NADP+. The NADP+ is reduced to NADPH + H+.

As a result of electrons passing through the Z-pathway, NADP+ is reduced and ATP is synthesized. One molecule of NADPH + H+ and one to two molecules of ATP are formed for every four quanta of light. Two quanta of light strike chlorophyll P680 in photosystem II, releasing a pair of electrons. These electrons reach chlorophyll P700 in photosystem I, where two additional quanta of light are required for the ejection of a pair of electrons from this reaction center chlorophyll. The electrons lost from chlorophyll P680 are replaced by the splitting of a molecule of H_2O, resulting in liberation of $1/2 \; O_2$. This process, in which electrons ejected from chlorophyll P680 move through the Z-pathway and eventually are accepted by NADP+, is known as **noncyclic photophosphorylation.**

Electrons Are Cycled Continuously in Cyclic Photophosphorylation

Electrons are not always passed through the entire Z-pathway. They alternatively can be cycled continuously through a small portion of the pathway. This recycling of electrons is accomplished by shunting electrons reaching the FeS protein in photosystem I through cytochrome b in the electron transport chain. From cytochrome b, the electrons continue in the Z-pathway to chlorophyll P700 and then back to the FeS protein in a continuous cycle. As each pair of electrons is passed from the FeS protein to cytochrome b, which has a more-positive redox potential than the FeS protein, there is a drop in energy level. The result is the synthesis of at least one molecule of ATP.

This **cyclic photophosphorylation** provides the cell with ATP in the absence of $NADP^+$ reduction and photolysis-induced O_2 evolution. Cells probably carry out cyclic photophosphorylation when there is insufficient total light or light at the wavelengths needed for photosystem I (only reaction center chlorophyll P700 is activated in a cyclic scheme). Alternatively, if there is enough $NADPH + H^+$ in the cell, but additional ATP is required, there may be a shift from noncyclic photophosphorylation to cyclic photophosphorylation. The synthesis of ATP by cyclic photophosphorylation is believed to be more primitive than noncyclic photophosphorylation and in many ways resembles the process of photophosphorylation in bacteria.

There are several pieces of evidence that support the Hill-Bendall scheme of two photosystems in the light reactions of oxygenic photosynthesis. Monochromatic (single wavelength) light activates only one of these two photosystems in plants. Far-red light at a wavelength of 700 nm is inefficient in bringing about oxygen evolution. However, if this light is combined with light of a shorter wavelength (680 nm), oxygen is evolved—evidence that noncyclic photophosphorylation with both photosystems I and II is required for photolysis and the release of oxygen.

Further evidence for the existence of two distinct photosystems comes from the effect of the plant herbicide 3-(3,4-dichlorophenyl)-1,1-dimethylurea (DCMU) on photosynthesis. DCMU specifically inhibits photosystem II by blocking electron flow to plastoquinone. As a result of this inhibition, only cyclic electron flow occurs. This specific inhibition of only one photosystem by DCMU while a second photosystem is still operative indicates that two separate photosystems exist in phototrophic eucaryotes. DCMU has no effect on bacterial photosynthesis, since only one photosystem is present in these microbes.

Procaryotic (Other Than Cyanobacterial) Photophosphorylation Is Cyclic

Photosynthetic bacteria are anoxygenic; that is, unlike plants, algae, and cyanobacteria, they do not produce O_2 during photosynthesis. In fact, photosynthetic bacteria can carry out the light reactions only under anaerobic conditions, although they may grow aerobically without photosynthesis. In bacterial photosynthesis, ATP is synthesized by cyclic photophosphorylation, only

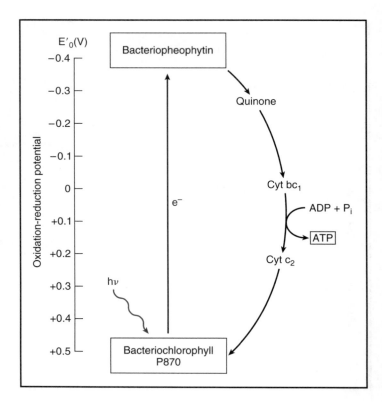

figure 7.9
Bacterial Cyclic Photophosphorylation
Photosystem I is involved in bacterial cyclic photophosphorylation. Electrons released from bacteriochlorophyll P870 are sent to bacteriopheophytin. The electrons are then cycled back through electron carriers to bacteriochlorophyll P870, resulting in the synthesis of ATP.

using a single photosystem containing bacteriochlorophyll P870 as the reaction center (Figure 7.9). As light strikes bacteriochlorophyll P870, an electron is passed to bacteriopheophytin within the reaction center. The electron is then cycled through a quinone molecule, a cytochrome bc_1 complex, cytochrome c_2, and back to the reaction center. One or more molecules of ATP are synthesized as electrons are transferred down to electron carriers of more-positive redox potentials in this cyclic pathway.

In ATP synthesis via cyclic photophosphorylation in bacteria, electrons ejected from bacteriochlorophyll P870 eventually cycle back to it. In bacterial photosynthesis, photolysis of water and the evolution of oxygen do not occur because oxidized bacteriochlorophyll P870 is not sufficiently oxidized to receive electrons from water. The synthesis of ATP fulfills one of the requirements for carbon dioxide fixation. But where does the bacterium obtain the reducing power also required for carbon dioxide fixation?

This reducing power comes from reduced substances in the environment. Photosynthetic bacteria are typically found in such anaerobic environments as sulfur springs or at the bottom of stratified lakes and ponds. Reduced compounds in these environments transfer their reducing power directly or indirectly to $NADP^+$ (Figure 7.10). Molecules such as hydrogen gas (H_2), which has a more nega-

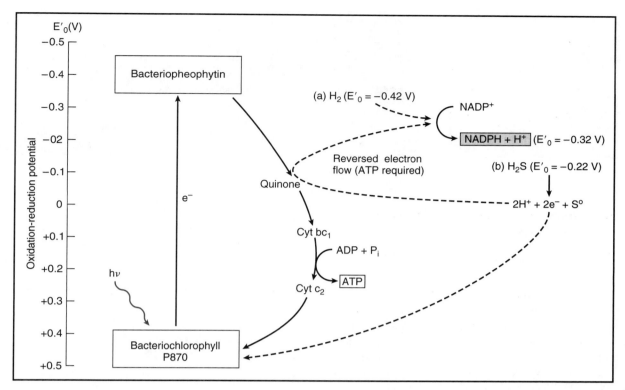

figure 7.10

Generation of Reduced NADP (NADPH + H⁺) by Photosynthetic Bacteria

Photosynthetic bacteria generate NADPH + H⁺ by one of two possible mechanisms: a. Directly, by the transfer of reducing power from reducing compounds having a more negative redox potential than NADP⁺. b. Indirectly, by the transfer of reducing power to NADP⁺ via an ATP-requiring reversal of the electron transport chain used in oxidative phosphorylation. Reversed electron flow occurs when reduced compunds have a more positive redox potential than NADP⁺ and cannot transfer their reducing power directly to NADP⁺.

tive redox potential ($E'_0 = -0.42$ V) than NADP⁺ ($E'_0 = -0.32$ V), transfer their electrons directly to NADP⁺. Other reduced compounds, such as hydrogen sulfide (H_2S), which has a more positive redox potential ($E'_0 = -0.22$ V) than NADP⁺, cannot directly transfer their reducing power to NADP⁺ but are still able to be used as reductants by photosynthetic bacteria. It is postulated that the reducing power of these compounds is transferred to NADP⁺, probably by an ATP-requiring reversal of the electron transport chain used in oxidative phosphorylation. Reversed electron flow has been demonstrated in chemolithotrophic procaryotes, and therefore it is reasonable to assume that such a mechanism may also exist in other procaryotes.

As H_2S is oxidized by photosynthetic bacteria, elemental sulfur accumulates either inside the cell, as in many purple sulfur bacteria, or outside the cell, as in green sulfur bacteria (Figure 7.11). These sulfur granules, although not unique to photosynthetic bacteria (they are also produced by sulfur-oxidizing bacteria such as *Thiobacillus*), are useful morphological traits in the identification of these organisms. Under certain conditions, some cyanobacteria and algae carry out anoxygenic photosynthesis using reduced substances as electron donors. When this occurs, the cyanobacteria can accumulate sulfur granules outside their cells if H_2S is used as a reducing agent.

Chemiosmosis Explains the Mechanism of Photophosphorylation

The mechanism for ATP generation during photosynthesis is explained by chemiosmosis (see chemiosmosis, page 165). Components of the electron transport chain in the light reaction are oriented across the thylakoid or photosynthetic membranes in such a manner that protons are extruded to one side of the membrane during photosynthesis. In plants, algae, and cyanobacteria, the protons move from the stroma to the interior of the thylakoid during electron transport. In photosynthetic bacteria, electrons are believed to move to the exterior of membrane vesicles, or infoldings. This movement in both cases results in the establishment of a pH or proton gradient across the membrane. Although the membrane is impermeable to protons, protons are able to reenter it by linking with ATPases spanning the membrane. The energy released from dissipation of the proton gradient as these protons are brought back across the membrane by the ATPases is conserved in the formation of ATP from ADP + P_i.

Chemiosmosis for photophosphorylation is thus essentially the same as it is for oxidative phosphorylation. Such a model's validity is supported by numerous experimental observations. Intact impermeable photosynthetic membranes are necessary for

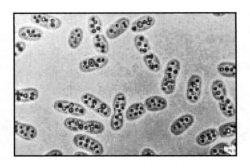
a.

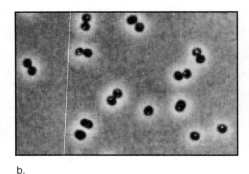
b.

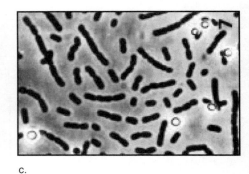
c.

figure 7.11

Sulfur Granules Produced by Photosynthetic Bacteria

a. *Chromatium vinosum*, a purple sulfur bacterium, bright field. Note the intracellular sulfur granules. b. *Thiocapsa roseopersicina*, a purple sulfur bacterium, phase contrast. Note the intracellular sulfur granules.

c. *Chlorobium limicola*, a green sulfur bacterium, phase contrast. Note the extracellular sulfur granules.

the establishment of a proton gradient and ATP synthesis. The formation of an artificial proton gradient across photosynthetic membranes results in a burst of ATP synthesis. It has been repeatedly observed that electron transport results in an accumulation of protons on one side of these membranes. The system can also be made to run in reverse by placing photosynthetic membranes in a solution of excess ATP. Under such conditions, the ATPase is forced to run in reverse, leading to the formation of a proton gradient of opposite orientation across the membrane.

The Nature of Photosynthesis: Carbon Dioxide Fixation

The light-dependent reactions of photosynthesis are used to capture light energy in the form of ATP and—in plants, algae, and cyanobacteria—also to produce NADPH + H⁺. The term *photosynthesis,* however, is most often associated with the synthesis of glucose from carbon dioxide and water. Because the fixation of carbon dioxide into organic compounds can occur in the absence of light—as long as sufficient quantities of ATP and NADPH + H⁺ are available—it is known as the dark reactions of photosynthesis. Organisms that fix carbon dioxide are called autotrophs and may be either phototrophic (generating ATP from light as an energy source) or chemotrophic (generating ATP from the oxidation of chemical compounds)(see carbon and energy requirements of procaryotes, page 80).

Carbon Dioxide Fixation Is Catalyzed by Ribulose Diphosphate Carboxylase

The incorporation of carbon dioxide into organic compounds was first observed by chemist Melvin Calvin of the University of California at Berkeley during the 1940s and 1950s. Calvin, who received the Nobel Prize in chemistry in 1961 for his work on carbon dioxide fixation, followed the uptake of radioactively labeled carbon dioxide ($^{14}CO_2$) in the eucaryotic alga *Chlorella*. He noted from algal extracts that the ^{14}C label first appeared in the 3-carbon compound 3-phosphoglycerate. By limiting the quantity of carbon

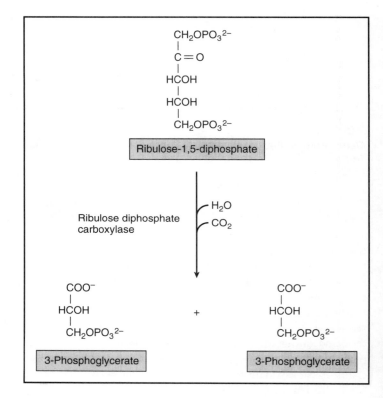

figure 7.12

Carboxylation of Ribulose-1,5-Diphosphate to Two Molecules of 3-Phosphoglycerate

dioxide made available to the algae, Calvin further found that a nonradioactive 5-carbon sugar, ribulose-1,5-diphosphate (RuDP) accumulated in the chloroplasts as 3-phosphoglycerate quantities decreased. This observation suggested that RuDP is the carbon dioxide acceptor in carboxylation and must be regenerated for carbon dioxide fixation to continue (Figure 7.12).

The regeneration of RuDP is fundamental to carbon dioxide fixation. The pathway responsible for RuDP regeneration after

chapter nine

MICROBIAL GENETICS

Mutation
Base Substitution
Deletion and Insertion
Reversible Effects
Mutagenic Agents
DNA Repair Mechanisms in Bacteria
Replica Plating

Transfer of Genetic Material
Transformation
Transduction
Plasmids
Conjugation

PERSPECTIVE
Lysogenic Conversion of *Corynebacterium diphtheriae*

EVOLUTION AND BIODIVERSITY

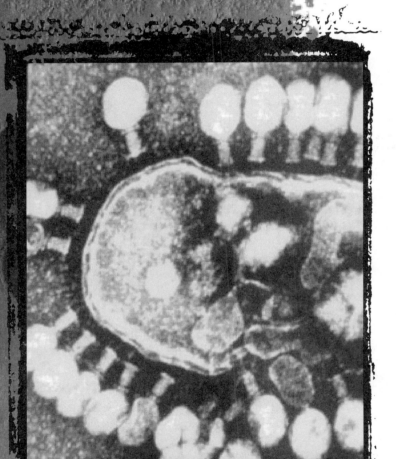

Electron micrograph of *Escherichia coli* infected with bacteriophage T4 (colorized).

 Microbes in Motion ——————— **PREVIEW LINK**

This chapter covers the key topics of transfer of genetic material between microorganisms and the effect this has on development of antibiotic resistance. The following sections in the *Microbes in Motion* CD-ROM may be useful as a preview to your reading or as a supplemental study aid:

Microbial Metabolism and Growth: Genetics (Mutation), 4–8, (Recombination) 11–24. *Antimicrobial Resistance:* Transfer and Spread of Resistance (Conjugation), 4–5.

T he most impressive feature of DNA is its accuracy in replication. The precision of DNA replication is such that errors occur in approximately 1 out of every 10^9 bases copied. This faithful copying of DNA is important; otherwise many genes would be changed during replication, causing extensive alterations in genotype and phenotype with each cell division. Nonetheless, there is a strong advantage to small and limited modifications in the genome of a microorganism. These genetic changes enable a microbial species to adapt to constantly changing physical and biological environments; therefore they are important in microbial evolution.

DNA in microorganisms may be altered by two methods: mutation, and transfer of genetic material.

Mutation

A **mutation** is defined as an inheritable change in the sequence of DNA. Organisms that have undergone mutations are termed **mutants.** The result of a mutation is usually a phenotypic change in an organism. This new phenotype can be used to differentiate the mutant from its original **wild-type** form.

Mutations may be either **spontaneous** or **induced.** Spontaneous mutations occur naturally, usually as a result of errors in DNA replication. Induced mutations arise as a result of chemical or radiation effects on genes. Mutagenic agents increase the mutation rate (the average number of mutations per cell per generation) in comparison with that of spontaneous mutations and also can be used to cause more specific classes of mutations in the genome.

Bases Can Be Substituted by Other Bases

The simplest type of mutation is one in which there is a **substitution** of one or more bases in the DNA (Figure 9.1). Most substitutions are **point mutations** involving a single base change. There are different consequences of such a mutation. If the change occurs in the third position of the codon, which is degenerate, the event is known as a **silent mutation** because there is no effect on the amino acid coded by the affected area of the DNA. For example, any base can be inserted in the third position of the codon for serine (UC_) with no alteration in the reading of the codon. Substitutions in either the first or second bases of a codon, however, generally have a more serious effect because they will code for an entirely different amino acid. Such changes are known as **missense mutations.** If the amino acid occupies an indispensable position in the protein, there will be a significant alteration in the protein, possibly resulting in a change in protein structure or—in the case of enzymes—inactivation of protein function. Sometimes there may be no change in function. A serious consequence of a substitution occurs in **nonsense mutation,** where the mutation results in the formation of a nonsense codon. With such an event, premature termination of protein synthesis often results in a nonfunctional protein or a lack of expression of downstream genes (genes further along the 3' end of the ribonucleic acid) in polycistronic messages.

Bases Can Be Deleted or Inserted

Mutations in which segments of the genome are removed are termed **deletions.** When one or more bases are added to the DNA, they are called **insertions.** These changes can involve one or many bases. Single-base deletions and insertions can cause a **reading frame shift,** which completely changes the amino acid sequence of the protein starting from the point of the mutation. The effects of such mutations may be minimized if another frame shift mutation occurs downstream of the affected region. A single-base deletion may offset the effects of a single-base insertion if it occurs near the site of the first mutation. Larger deletions and insertions, however, generally have irreversible effects and typically produce unusable proteins.

The Effects of Some Mutations Are Reversible

Mutation effects can sometimes be reversed. The consequences of a second deletion or insertion in reversing the effects of a reading frame shift have already been mentioned. The simplest type of reversion is a **back mutation** in which, for example, a mutated base is changed back to its original form. In other cases biosynthetic pathways turned off by a mutation that affects synthesis of a particular enzyme can be made functional again by an alternative pathway that bypasses the affected enzyme.

Suppressor mutations overcome or suppress the effects of the initial mutation without any alteration in the original gene. For example, a suppressor mutation might alter a tRNA anticodon. Suppose a single-base substitution causes the codon GCU to be changed to ACU. The new codon codes for threonine instead of alanine. If, however, the anticodon on the alanine-tRNA is also changed by a suppressor mutation so that it now recognizes ACU instead of GCU, the effects of the original mutation will have been suppressed. Because there are multiple genes for alanine-tRNA, the cell will now have alanine-tRNA that recognizes the codon GCU as well as alanine-tRNA modified by the suppressor mutation that recognizes the codon ACU.

The Rate of Mutations Can Be Increased by Mutagenic Agents

Different mutagenic agents can be used to increase the rate of mutations (Table 9.1). Unfortunately, mutagenic agents are found in the environment and undoubtedly affect the mutation rates not only of microorganisms, but also of higher organisms, including humans. Since many mutagens are also carcinogens, increased exposure to these mutagens may lead to higher incidences of cancer in humans.

Ultraviolet radiation causes formation of pyrimidine dimers in the chromosomes. Examples of such dimers, formed between adjacent pyrimidines on a DNA strand, are thymine-thymine, thymine-cytosine, and cytosine-cytosine. The dimers, which consist of adjacent pyrimidines joined by covalent linkages on the same DNA strand, distort the DNA structure and interfere with replication and transcription.

Base analogs are chemical compounds that resemble DNA bases but cause faulty base pairing. Examples of base analogs are 5-bromouracil and 2-aminopurine. The analog 5-bromouracil substitutes for thymine, but unlike thymine, it occasionally pairs with

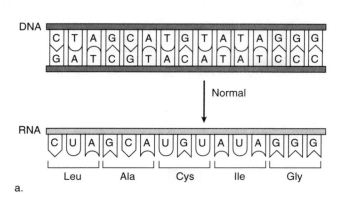

a.

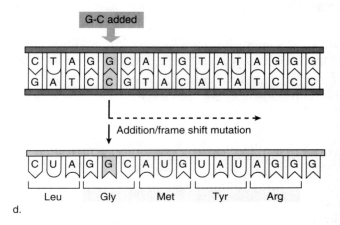

b.

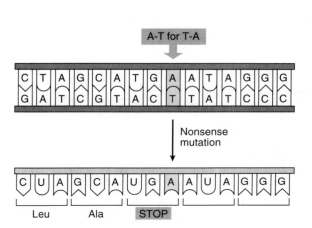

c.

d.

figure 9.1
Different Types of Mutations

a. Normal gene segment. b. Missense mutation: The substitution of adenine for guanine in the DNA leads to an A-T instead of a G-C base pair and the substitution of tyrosine for cysteine in the peptide. c. Nonsense mutation: The substitution of adenine for thymine leads to an A-T instead of a T-A base pair. The result is coding for a nonsense

codon and termination of protein synthesis. d. Addition/frame shift mutation: The addition of an extra guanine (G-C base pair) in the DNA leads to a shift in the reading frame. The result is a completely different peptide starting with the second codon.

guanine instead of adenine. This incorrect pairing leads to errors in replication, with a G-C base pair replacing the original A-T base pair. Instead of thymine, which normally would pair with adenine to form a final A-T base pair in the replicated DNA, the analog 5-bromouracil pairs with guanine to form a final G-C base pair after DNA replication. A similar result occurs with 2-aminopurine, which substitutes for adenine but pairs with cytosine instead of thymine.

Microbial Metabolism and Growth
Genetics: Mutation • p. 7

Other mutagens cause specific chemical changes in bases, resulting in transitions (replacement of a purine by a different purine or replacement of a pyrimidine by a different pyrimidine) or transversions (replacement of a purine by a pyrimidine or replacement of a pyrimidine by a purine). Nitrous acid deaminates adenine and cytosine, forming hypoxanthine (which pairs with cytosine) and uracil (which pairs with adenine), respectively. Hydroxylamine converts cytosine to a compound that pairs with adenine instead of guanine. Monofunctional alkylating agents (ethyl methanesulfonate and methyl methanesulfonate) alkylate guanine

table 9.1

Common Mutagens and Their Modes of Action

Mutagen	Basis of Action	Mutagenic Effect
Chemical mutagens		
Ethyl methanesulfonate, methyl methanesulfonate	Alkylation of purines followed by depurination	G-C $\rightleftarrows$ A-T transitions; transversions
Hydroxylamine	Conversion of cytosine to hydroxylaminocytosine	G-C $\rightleftarrows$ A-T transitions
N-methyl-*N'*-nitro-*N*-nitrosoguanidine	Alkylation of guanine	G-C $\rightleftarrows$ A-T transitions
Nitrous acid	Deamination; conversion of cytosine to uracil and of adenine to hypoxanthine	G-C $\rightleftarrows$ A-T transitions
Base analogs		
2-aminopurine	Adenine analog; causes mispairing with cytosine	G-C $\rightleftarrows$ A-T transitions
5-bromouracil	Thymine analog; causes mispairing with guanine	G-C $\rightleftarrows$ A-T transitions
Others		
Ultraviolet radiation	Formation of pyrimidine-pyrimidine dimers	G-C $\rightleftarrows$ A-T transitions, frame shifts
Acridine, ethidium bromide	Intercalation	Frame shifts

so that it pairs with thymine and not cytosine. *N*-methyl-*N'*-nitro-*N*-nitrosoguanidine, a bifunctional alkylating agent, acts specifically at the DNA replication fork and causes crosslinking of the DNA strands and errors in replication. Other agents such as acridine and ethidium bromide are mutagenic because they are intercalated directly into DNA between successive bases and distort the structure of the double helix. The result of their action is the addition or removal of a single base, causing a shift in the reading frame.

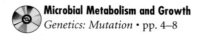
Microbial Metabolism and Growth
Genetics: Mutation • pp. 4–8

Bacteria Have Different DNA Repair Mechanisms

Damage to DNA can have serious consequences for a bacterium. Bacteria have developed several different mechanisms for repair and replacement of damaged DNA.

Excision repair corrects damage that causes distortion in the DNA helix such as what occurs with pyrimidine dimers that are formed as a result of exposure to ultraviolet radiation (Figure 9.2). A UvrABC endonuclease (Uvr means *Uv repair*) encoded by three genes (*uvrA*, *uvrB*, and *uvrC*) makes cuts on both sides of the damaged area. This excision results in release of a 12-nucleotide single-stranded DNA segment containing the damaged bases. The single-stranded gap left in the DNA is filled by DNA polymerase I, and DNA ligase joins the fragments.

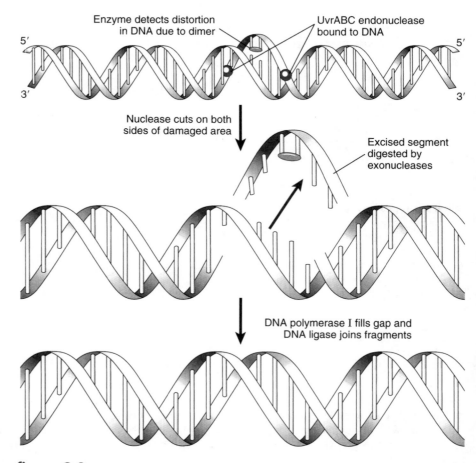

figure 9.2
Excision Repair of Distortion-Related Damage to DNA
A UvrABC endonuclease excises the damaged DNA segment. DNA polymerase I fills the resultant gap and DNA ligase joins the fragments.

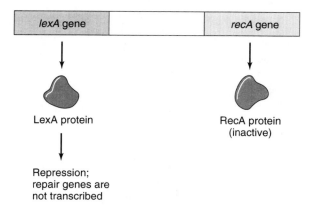

a. Uninduced state

LexA protein

Repression;
repair genes are
not transcribed

**RecA protein
(inactive)**

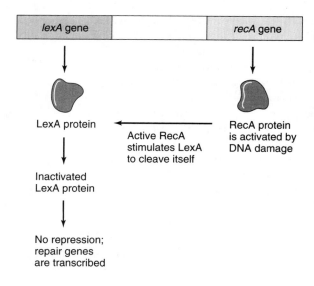

b. Induced state

LexA protein

Inactivated
LexA protein

No repression;
repair genes
are transcribed

Active RecA
stimulates LexA
to cleave itself

**RecA protein
is activated by
DNA damage**

figure 9.3

The SOS Response

a. The SOS system is normally repressed by a *lexA*-encoded protein, LexA. b. When there is DNA damage, a *recA*-encoded protein, RecA, stimulates LexA to cleave itself and become inactivated. As a result of LexA inactivation, the SOS system is derepressed.

Correction of pyrimidine dimers can occur also by **photoreactivation.** In photoreactivation, a light-activated enzyme, photolyase, cleaves the covalent linkages between the damaged pyrimidines. This type of repair does not require the removal and replacement of bases as in excision repair.

Damaged bases can be removed by enzymes called **glycosylases** that detect and remove an unnatural base. The resultant hole is called an AP site (for *apyrimidinic* or *apurinic,* depending on what type of base has been removed). DNA polymerase I removes a few additional bases in this region and fills in the gap. DNA ligase then joins the fragments.

In instances where DNA damage is so serious that it affects DNA replication, such as leaving gaps in the helix, a distress signal is sent to the cell to induce a complex repair system called the **SOS response** (Figure 9.3). In *E. coli,* the SOS system consists of about 17 genes involved in the excision and repair of various types of DNA damage. Expression of these genes is controlled by a *lexA* gene and a *recA* gene. The SOS system is normally repressed by a *lexA*-encoded protein, LexA. When there is DNA damage, a *recA*-encoded protein, RecA (which also is involved in homologous recombination, as described on p. 252), stimulates LexA to cleave itself and become inactivated. As a result, the DNA repair genes in the SOS system are derepressed. The repair genes are transcribed and the DNA is repaired.

Replica Plating Differentiates Mutants from Wild Types by Their Growth Differences

Mutagenic agents are typically used in quantities that will kill most of the cells in a population. The small number of surviving cells have a greater chance of having undergone a mutagenic event. Even under such optimal conditions, the mutation rate is quite low, usually 10^{-3} to 10^{-5} mutation per bacterium per generation (that is, one bacterium in 10^3 to 10^5 is likely to undergo a mutational event each generation). This rate is much higher than the spontaneous mutation rate of 10^{-6} to 10^{-12}. Nonetheless, the rate of induced mutations is small enough to make detection of mutants difficult unless a selection technique is used.

Mutagenesis results in a genotypic and, frequently, a phenotypic change from the **wild type** (the unaltered original genotype). These differences in characteristics can be used to separate mutants from wild types. Antibiotic-resistant mutants can be separated from wild-type susceptible strains by growing both types of bacteria on a medium containing the antibiotic; only the mutant will grow. Mutants that have undergone changes in cell or colony morphology, such as pigmentation, encapsulation, or motility, are usually distinguished by their readily observable differences in colony morphologies from wild-type organisms. **Auxotrophic** mutants (strains that require one or more growth factors because of a genetic mutation) can be distinguished from **prototrophs** (the wild-type strain that does not have this growth factor requirement) by the inability of the auxotroph to grow on a medium lacking the required growth factor(s). The change in genotype of an auxotrophic mutant is usually symbolized by a minus sign after the compound that is required for growth. Thus an auxotroph of *Escherichia coli* having growth requirements for arginine, histidine, and leucine is indicated by the notation: *E. coli* (arg^-, his^-, leu^-). The genotypes of prototrophs are sometimes symbolized by a plus sign to emphasize their differences from auxotrophs: *E. coli* (arg^+, his^+, leu^+).

A technique that is commonly used to identify mutants is **replica plating** (Figure 9.4). Mutated and wild-type bacteria are grown on an enriched medium. Each cell develops into an individual colony. The colonies of both types are then transferred either to several different media, each of which lacks a certain type of nutrient, or to the same medium incubated under different environmental conditions. Transfer from the original plate (called the master plate) to the new plates is performed by carefully placing a pad of sterile velvet onto the surface of the master plate. The velvet picks up some cells from each colony. If this inoculated velvet pad is removed from the master plate and placed consecutively onto one or more uninoculated plates of different test media, a replica of the master plate is made on these subsequent plates. Since theoretically only one cell is required to initiate growth and form a colony per plate of medium, several replica plates can be made from one inoculated velvet pad. The inoculated plates are incubated, and the patterns of growth are then compared to determine the nutritional or environmental requirements of the bacteria. For example, in screening for arginine-requiring auxotrophs by replica plating, colonies would grow on a replicate plate with arginine, but would not grow on a plate lacking this amino acid.

Microbial Metabolism and Growth
Genetics: Mutation • p. 8

Transfer of Genetic Material

Mutation is important in changing the genetic information in a cell, but it is not the only process that causes genetic modifications. Procaryotes and eucaryotes can produce new genotypes from the transfer of genetic material from one cell to another cell. In eucaryotes genetic transfer occurs after two haploid gametes fuse to form a diploid zygote. Procaryotes do not produce male and female gametes and do not exchange DNA by this sexual method. However, procaryotes can occasionally transfer genetic material from a **donor cell** to a **recipient cell.** The recipient becomes a partial diploid for the genetic material transferred; such partial zygotes are called **merozygotes.** The genetic material introduced into the recipient cell is called the **exogenote.** The exogenote may recombine with the recipient genome, the **endogenote;** may persist as a self-replicating plasmid; or may eventually be lost through dilution during cell division.

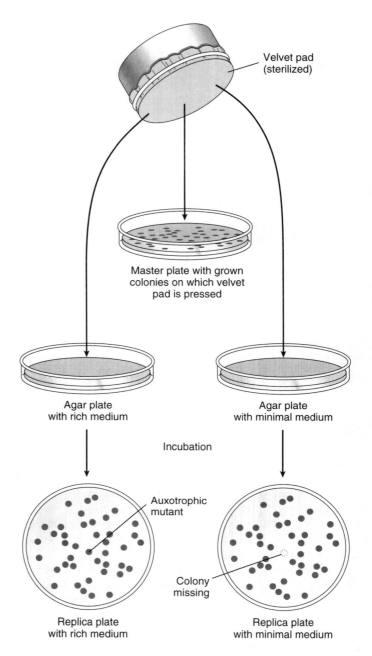

figure 9.4
Replica Plating
Colonies from a master plate are transferred to replica plates with a sterile velvet pad. The replica plates are incubated and the patterns of growth are then compared to determine the presence of mutants.

Carcinogens are substances that produce cancer. Many mutagens are also carcinogens because they cause changes in the organism that can eventually lead to cell transformation.

typhimurium to nonmutant, histidine-synthesizing prototrophs in the presence and absence of the substance being tested. The test is performed with strains of *S. typhimurium* that rarely revert spontaneously to prototrophy, and that contain either a base substitution or a frame shift mutation. Furthermore, the test strains are devoid of DNA repair enzymes, so they are more sensitive to DNA alterations, and they are mutated so that their envelopes are more permeable to chemical agents.

carcinogenic unless they are first converted to other metabolites; this conversion in animals usually takes place in the liver. A small amount of the mixture is spread onto a solid growth medium that lacks histidine. The test chemical is then added to the medium. If the chemical is mutagenic, some histidine mutants (*his⁻*) will revert to the wild type (*his⁺*) and produce visible colonies on the medium. Chemicals that result in large numbers of revertants are considered highly mutagenic and thus also highly carcinogenic. The Ames test can be performed inexpensively and rapidly with bacterial populations, unlike other tests for carcinogens that require laboratory animals. The test takes advantage of the short generation times and selection techniques of bacteria. The Ames test is used extensively to screen for carcinogens that are mutagens, and is comparable to animal testing in its detection abilities.

The Ames Test for Carcinogenesis

Several years ago Bruce Ames, a scientist at the University of California at Berkeley, developed a bacterial test to screen carcinogens. This test, called the **Ames test,** is based on the assumption that carcinogens either are or can generate mutagens. If this assumption is true, the potency of a carcinogen can be determined by its ability to cause mutations.

The Ames test measures the reversion of histidine auxotrophs of *Salmonella*

The Ames test is carried out by mixing the bacteria with a rat liver extract (Figure 9.5). The rat liver extract is used because many chemicals do not become

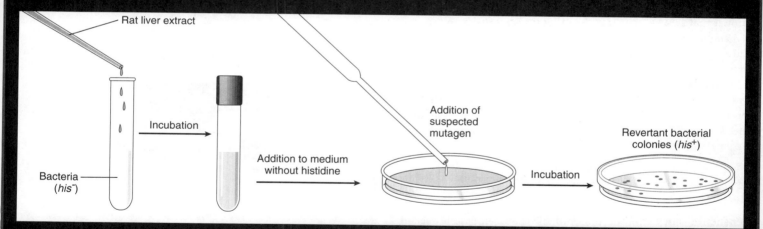

figure 9.5

The Ames Test

His⁻ mutants of *Salmonella typhimurium* are mixed with rat liver extract. This mixture is spread onto an agar plate lacking histidine, and the suspected mutagen is added to the agar. The greater the mutagenicity of the chemical, the more revertant (*his⁺*) colonies will develop on the medium.

At the molecular level, the reciprocal exchange between two homologous (identical or nearly identical sequences) DNA molecules is called **general,** or **homologous, recombination** (Figure 9.6). This recombination between homologous DNA molecules begins with the nicking of a single strand of one of the DNA molecules by an endonuclease. Next, a RecA protein binds to the single-stranded fragment and forms a complex between the nicked single-stranded region and the complementary sequence in the homologous DNA duplex. Following this strand invasion of the DNA duplex, there is cross-strand exchange and ligation. This breakage and reunion of homologous DNA molecules results in **recombinant molecules,** which consist of DNA from each of the two original DNA molecules.

There are three methods of genetic transfer in bacteria. The first method, **transformation,** involves the insertion of naked DNA from a donor cell into a recipient cell. If a bacteriophage (bacterial virus) is the intermediary vector for the genetic material, the process is termed **transduction.** The third method of bacterial gene transfer, **conjugation,** requires contact between donor and recipient cells for DNA transfer. Regardless of the DNA transfer mechanism, natural genetic exchange in procaryotes is a rare event. Nonetheless, genetic exchange is an important event that leads to genetic diversity and evolution.

DNA Is the Transforming Principle

Fred Griffith's discovery of bacterial transformation in 1928 was a historic milestone in microbiology (see transformation of *Streptococcus pneumoniae,* page 215). As a result of these early studies on transformation in *Streptococcus pneumoniae,* it is now known that DNA—the "transforming principle"—is the source of genetic information for all living cells. Natural transformation occurs in only certain bacteria, including *Haemophilus, Neisseria, Staphylococcus, Bacillus, Pseudomonas,* and *Rhizobium,* but it has been most extensively investigated in the bacterium *S. pneumoniae.* Studies of transformation in these and other bacteria have provided us with an insight into the physiological and molecular mechanisms associated with this gene transfer process.

Only Competent Cells Can Receive DNA During Transformation

Genetic transformation occurs optimally between closely related bacteria in the late logarithmic phase of growth. Even under such ideal conditions, only a small portion of the total DNA from a donor cell is transferred to the recipient cell. Not all bacteria are transformable. Even among those organisms that can be transformed, transformation appears to depend on the physiological state of the recipient cell. A bacterium that is able to receive DNA from a closely related donor cell and be transformed by it is said to be **competent.**

Competence is determined by the presence of a **competence factor** on the cell surface. This factor is found on the surfaces of competent *S. pneumoniae* cells and is released into the medium by the cells. The competence factor has been partially characterized

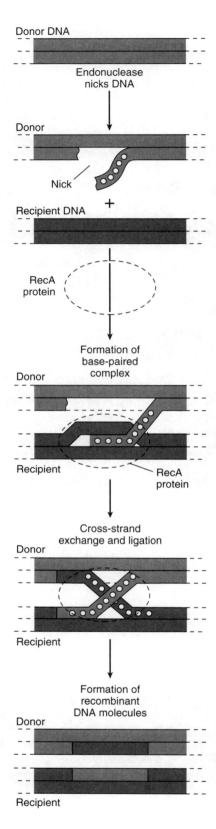

figure 9.6

Homologous Recombination

The breakage and reunion of homologous (identical or nearly identical) DNA molecules results in recombinant molecules.

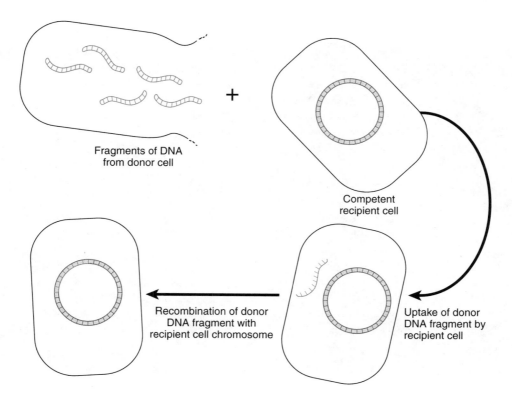

figure 9.7
Transformation
Donor DNA is taken up by a competent recipient cell and recombines with the recipient cell's chromosome in transformation.

and appears to be a protein of low molecular weight. When competence factor is added to noncompetent cells, it binds to their surfaces and changes them into competent cells. Competency depends on several conditions, including composition of the growth medium and growth stage of the culture.

Naked DNA Enters a Competent Recipient Cell During Transformation

Transformation begins with the release or removal of DNA from a donor cell (Figure 9.7). In natural transformation, DNA is released into the surrounding environment when a cell lyses. These DNA fragments may be taken up by competent cells and transformed. In artificial transformation carried out in the laboratory, DNA is extracted from donor bacteria by chemical or enzymatic lysis of the donor cells. The nucleic acid is sheared into short pieces during its extraction, purified from contaminating proteins through phenol treatment, and then is precipitated with ethanol. This relatively pure DNA preparation can now be added to a suspension of competent bacteria treated with calcium chloride to permeabilize their plasma membranes to DNA.

The naked double-stranded donor DNA binds to receptor sites on the cell surface of a competent bacterium. These receptor sites are exposed only when the bacterium is in a competent stage. There is evidence that the competence factor may play a role in

unmasking receptor sites during periods of competence. The externally bound DNA remains on the cell surface only long enough for it to be cleaved by a membrane-associated endonuclease into fragments of 7,000 to 10,000 base pairs in length.

Bacteria differ in their uptake of DNA fragments. In *Streptococcus pneumoniae, Bacillus subtilis,* and other gram-positive bacteria, the double-stranded DNA bound to the cell surface is degraded to yield single-stranded DNA. These single-stranded DNA fragments are transported into the cell. In *Haemophilus influenzae,* a gram-negative bacterium, double-stranded DNA fragments are transported into the cell, but only single-stranded fragments are incorporated into the chromosome through recombination.

A single-stranded DNA fragment incorporated into the bacterial chromosome displaces a portion of one strand of the chromosome. The two strands comprising this heteroduplex region of the cell genome may not be identical, and there may be areas in which mismatched bases are not held together by hydrogen bonds. Under these circumstances, the integrity of the chromosome may be restored by replacement of the mismatched bases on one strand with complementary matched bases. This correction mechanism shows a preference for removing mismatched bases on the donor DNA. Alternatively, if replication occurs first, the two strands including the heteroduplex region are copied, and the exogenote is maintained in intact form through the progeny.

Transduction was first observed in 1952 by Joshua Lederberg and his graduate student Norton Zinder, who actually were looking for conjugation in *Salmonella typhimurium*.

U separated by a sintered glass filter impervious to bacteria (Figure 9.8). Bacteria incubated in the same culture medium in either arm of the U-tube thus are unable

exchange was not affected by the addition of DNase to the bacterial cultures, a procedure that would normally degrade naked DNA in transforming populations.

The Discovery of Transduction

In the course of their experiments, Lederberg and Zinder found that the transfer of genetic characteristics from donor to recipient cells did not require the cell-to-cell contact characteristic of bacterial conjugation. The two scientists made this discovery while utilizing a U-tube first devised by Bernard D. Davis in 1950 in his studies of conjugation.

The Davis U-tube consists of a U-shaped glass tube with the two sides of the

to come in contact with each other.

Davis originally used the U-tube to show that such contact was necessary for bacterial conjugation. Lederberg and Zinder also used the Davis U-tube in their experiments and hoped to show that conjugation was possible in *Salmonella*. However, much to their surprise, transfer of genes occurred between donor and recipient bacteria in the U-tube. The genetic

Further investigation revealed that the genes had been transferred not directly via cell-to-cell contact, but with an intermediate agent, a bacteriophage (*Salmonella* phage P22) that could pass through the glass filter in the tube. These studies provided the first evidence that bacteriophages are important in bacterial genetic exchange.

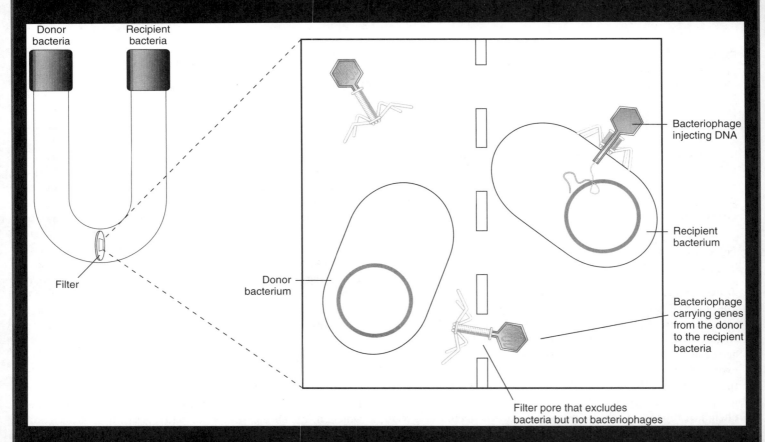

figure 9.8
The Davis U-tube
A sintered glass filter separates bacteria in the two arms of the U-tube. Bacteriophages and naked DNA can pass through the pores of the filter, whereas the larger bacteria cannot.

Although many DNA fragments may be available for uptake by the recipient cell, only a few such fragments (generally ten or less) are actually incorporated into it. The recipient is unable in principle to distinguish one fragment from another and therefore cannot selectively bind and incorporate fragments that contain specific genetic markers. As a consequence of this random uptake of DNA, the possibilities are slight that any given gene will be in the DNA fragments entering the cell. The frequency of transformation of a specific genetic marker therefore is very low (usually less than 1%).

Microbial Metabolism and Growth
Genetics: Recombination • pp. 15–18

Naked Bacteriophage DNA Enters the Competent Recipient Cell During Transfection

Transfection, which involves the introduction of bacteriophage DNA into a cell, is a special case of transformation in *Escherichia coli.* The most common technique for transfection is the treatment of bacteria with cold calcium chloride to make their membranes permeable to DNA. Following this treatment, the bacteria can be infected with phage DNA that has been isolated from a suspension of phage.

The process of transfection is a valuable tool in genetic engineering, where the phage genome can be used as a vehicle to carry foreign genetic material into a competent host bacterium. Transfection is also useful in identifying DNA isolated from an infected bacterium as phage DNA. The isolated DNA is separated into different fractions and transfected to other bacteria. The fraction containing the phage DNA causes phage production in the transfected bacteria.

DNA Is Transferred by a Bacteriophage from One Bacterium to Another During Transduction

A bacteriophage serves as a vehicle for the transfer of bacterial DNA from one bacterium to another in transduction. Transduction was first described by Norton Zinder and Joshua Lederberg in 1952 for *Salmonella* and the bacteriophage P22. This phage-mediated method of genetic transfer has since been found to occur in many other bacteria and to involve many different types of DNA-containing bacteriophages.

Transduction of host genes by viruses happens in two ways. Random fragments of DNA are transferred in **generalized transduction,** resulting in a low transduction frequency of a specific genetic marker. **Specialized,** or **restricted, transduction** occurs only with **temperate bacteriophages** (those able to incorporate their DNA into the host chromosome without cell lysis). Specific portions of the host genome are excised with the prophage during induction. The phage injects this attached host DNA into a recipient cell, where it recombines with the recipient genome. No successful infection takes place because the virus is incomplete. The result is highly efficient transduc-

tion of specific donor genes. Not all bacteriophages transduce, but the variety and number that do is significant enough to make transduction an important phenomenon for microbial genetic exchange.

Random Portions of the Bacterial Chromosome Are Transferred During Generalized Transduction

Generalized transduction can occur in any population of bacterial cells susceptible to infection by bacteriophages (Figure 9.9). Following infection of a host, bacteriophages often initiate a **lytic cycle** in which the phage nucleic acid is replicated and packaged into phage particles (see bacteriophage replication, page 398). Under normal conditions, these phage particles are released upon lysis of the host cell. Occasionally, however, the host chromosome is fragmented into small portions (fragments that contain only 1% to 2% of the total bacterial DNA) during the lytic cycle, and these DNA fragments are mistakenly packaged into some of the progeny phage particles and released upon cell lysis. Other progeny phages contain only phage DNA. The lysate produced by generalized transduction thus consists of a mixture of both phages that contain random fragments of the bacterial chromosome and those that contain only phage nucleic acid.

Transducing phage particles containing host DNA have very little additional room within their available space for phage DNA and are considered **defective.** Defective phages, although able to infect susceptible bacteria, do not have a full complement of phage genes. Such phages are unable to carry through a complete lytic cycle in the infected bacterium. However, they are able to infect the recipient cell and insert the donor bacterial DNA. This donor DNA subsequently is incorporated into the recipient chromosome in much the same manner as in transformation.

Bacterial lysates of transducing phage also have large quantities of normal, nontransducing phage. Since each transducing phage particle in the lysate contains only a small portion of the entire donor chromosome, the probability that any given donor gene is transferred to a recipient bacterium is quite low—usually only one out of every 10^5 to 10^8 recipient cells infected with such a lysate is transduced for a specific gene.

Microbial Metabolism and Growth
Genetics: Recombination • pp. 19–20

Specific Genes Are Transferred During Specialized Transduction

The probability that a given gene is transferred to a recipient cell is considerably increased in specialized transduction, which occurs only with temperate phages. In specialized transduction the phage DNA integrates at a specific attachment site in the bacterial chromosome (Figure 9.10). The phage DNA in the chromosome is called a **prophage,** and a bacterium carrying such a prophage is

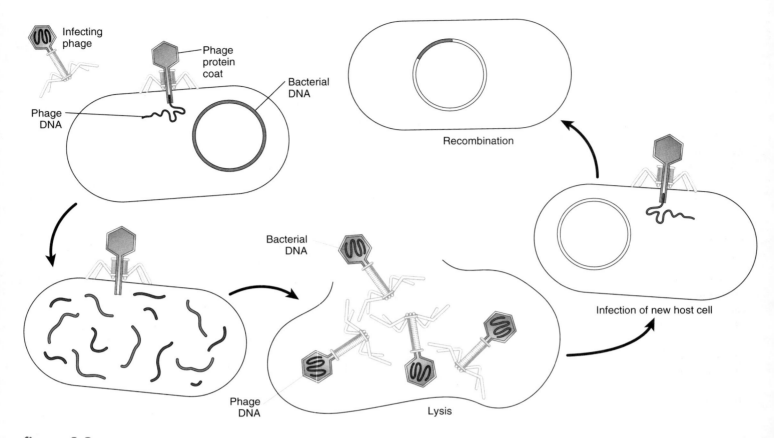

figure 9.9

Generalized Transduction

In generalized transduction, a bacteriophage infects a bacterium. A lytic cycle begins, but portions of the bacterial chromosome are incorporated inside phage particles. Upon lysis of the host cell, phages containing these host DNA fragments can infect other bacteria, resulting in the insertion of the DNA into the chromosome of the newly infected cell.

Microbial Metabolism and Growth
Genetics: Recombination • p. 19

said to be **lysogenic** (see lysogeny, page 410). A prophage—for example lambda (λ)—always inserts at the same location in the DNA of a specific host bacterium. Different prophages may be integrated at specific sites in the host DNA, and a host cell may be lysogenized for more than one prophage at the same time. Upon induction with ultraviolet radiation or other inducing agents, a portion of the bacterial genome is removed with some of the phage DNA. This material is replicated and packaged into maturing phage particles, which are released from the lysed cell. Since the size of the DNA molecule incorporated into phage particles remains relatively constant, an equal amount of phage DNA is lost for the host DNA that is inserted into the phage. These progeny

bacteriophages lack a complete phage genome and are considered defective. Defective phage particles can still inject their genetic material into recipient cells, where genetic exchange occurs between donor and recipient DNA. The efficiency of gene transfer for specific genes is very high in specialized transduction, because bacteriophages carry only those bacterial genes adjacent to the prophage at the time of excision.

The most widely used and best understood example of specialized transduction is the bacteriophage-mediated transfer of the galactose (*gal*) genes, which control galactose fermentation in *E. coli*. Lambda (λ) phage particles infecting a culture of *E. coli* have their DNA inserted specifically into the host chromosome at a site

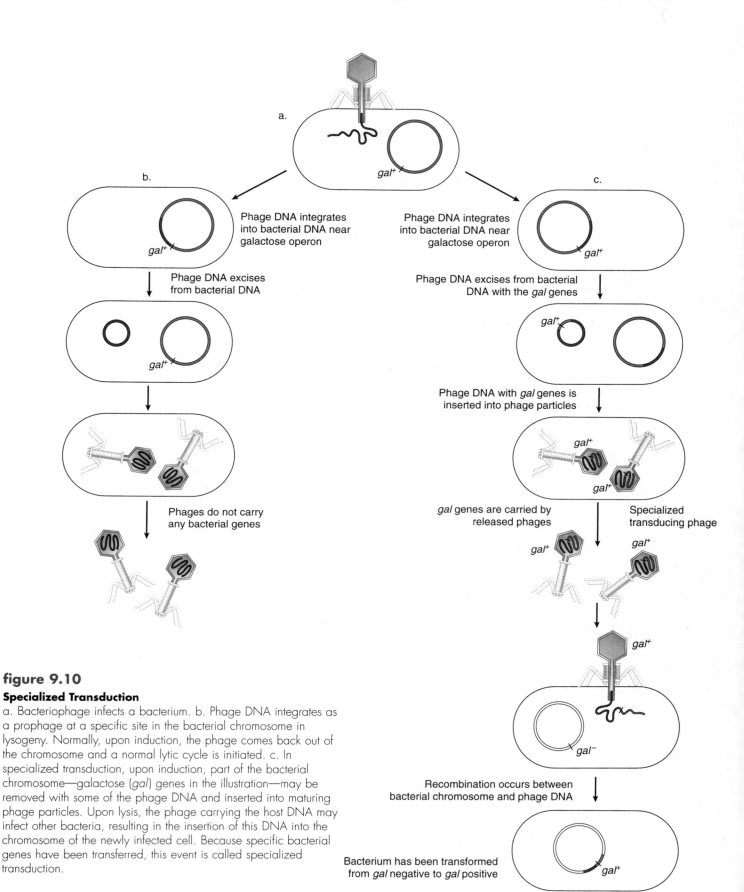

figure 9.10

Specialized Transduction

a. Bacteriophage infects a bacterium. b. Phage DNA integrates as a prophage at a specific site in the bacterial chromosome in lysogeny. Normally, upon induction, the phage comes back out of the chromosome and a normal lytic cycle is initiated. c. In specialized transduction, upon induction, part of the bacterial chromosome—galactose (*gal*) genes in the illustration—may be removed with some of the phage DNA and inserted into maturing phage particles. Upon lysis, the phage carrying the host DNA may infect other bacteria, resulting in the insertion of this DNA into the chromosome of the newly infected cell. Because specific bacterial genes have been transferred, this event is called specialized transduction.

Within the figure:

a.

b.

gal⁺

Phage DNA integrates into bacterial DNA near galactose operon

Phage DNA excises from bacterial DNA

gal⁺

Phages do not carry any bacterial genes

c.

Phage DNA integrates into bacterial DNA near galactose operon

gal⁺

Phage DNA excises from bacterial DNA with the *gal* genes

gal⁺

Phage DNA with *gal* genes is inserted into phage particles

gal⁺
gal⁺

gal genes are carried by released phages

gal⁺   *gal⁺*

Specialized transducing phage

gal⁺

gal⁻

Recombination occurs between bacterial chromosome and phage DNA

Bacterium has been transformed from *gal* negative to *gal* positive

gal⁺

between the loci for *gal* and *bio* (the *bio* locus contains genes that control the synthesis of the vitamin biotin).

One of two events occurs when the bacterial culture is induced. The prophage may come out of the bacterial chromosome with its entire complement of phage genes and initiate a normal lytic cycle. Alternatively, only a portion of the prophage may detach from the genome, carrying with it either the *gal* genes or the *bio* genes, and enter a lytic cycle. This latter possibility occurs in specialized transduction and results in progeny phage containing only a portion of their normal phage genetic complement and part of the host DNA. Since a given prophage is always inserted at the same sites in a specific bacterium, only those host genes on either side of the prophage insertion site can be transduced in specialized transduction.

As a consequence of this specificity, transducing λ phage particles are either λdg (defective and carrying the *gal* genes) or λdbio (defective and carrying the *bio* genes). These progeny phages, although defective and unable to carry out a complete lytic cycle, can still infect *E. coli* cells and insert the donor genes into the recipient chromosome. Such defective λ phage particles can replicate if normal nondefective λ phages, termed **helpers,** also infect the bacterial cell and supply the phage genes missing in the defective particle. Although specific genes are transferred in specialized transduction, the frequency of transduction in a population of bacteria is low. Because not every bacterium in a culture produces transducing phage, a typical lysate contains only about 1 λdg or λdbio phage particle per every 10^5 normal nondefective particles.

The frequency of specialized transduction can be significantly increased through a phenomenon known as **high-frequency transduction.** A lysate containing, for example, λdg and normal phages is used to infect *gal⁻ E. coli* at high multiplicity. A high multiplicity of infection is achieved by infecting a culture with defective transducing phage particles and a large number of normal helper phage particles. Under such conditions, bacteria infected by a λdg phage are also infected with a normal λ phage and are thus considered to be double lysogens. If such a culture is now induced, each infected bacterium in the population will produce both normal and λdg phage particles. The lysate contains a one-to-one ratio of these bacteriophages. When this lysate is used to infect a culture of *gal⁻ E. coli* cells, roughly 50% of the infected cells will be transduced by the λdg phages—a high frequency of transduction for the *gal* genes.

Donor DNA Is Not Incorporated into the Recipient Chromosome During Abortive Transduction

In certain instances of transduction, the transducing phage DNA is not incorporated into the host chromosome. The exogenote neither replicates nor is destroyed; it remains separate from the endogenote and is transmitted unilinearly to only one of two daughter cells formed at cell division (Figure 9.11). Such **abortive transduction** is very common and is easily recognized by expression of exogenote genes in bacteria carrying this genetic material.

For example, if a bacterium lacking the gene for proline synthesis (*pro⁻*) is infected with a transducing phage carrying the proline gene (*pro⁺*) and an abortive transduction occurs, the *pro⁺* gene is initially expressed in the infected bacterium. This bacterium synthesizes proline and therefore is able to grow on a plate medium containing no proline. As this originally infected bacterium grows and divides, the exogenote is passed to only one of the two daughter cells. The daughter cell receiving the *pro⁺* gene continues to synthesize proline and grows like the parent. The daughter cell without the exogenote, however, grows only until the endogenous pool of proline carried over from the parent is depleted. This pattern of unilinear transmission of the exogenotes continues in subsequent cell divisions. The result is the formation of slow-growing microcolonies of daughter cells lacking exogenotes that are detectable with magnification. Abortive transduction is quite common among transducing bacteriophages and, in some phage suspensions, accounts for 90% of all transductions.

Properties of a Bacterium Can Be Influenced by the Expression of Bacteriophage Genes in the Bacterial Chromosome

The properties of some bacteria depend upon the expression of phage genes in the bacterial chromosome, a phenomenon known as **lysogenic conversion** (see lysogenic conversion, page 411). Lysogenic conversion occurs when a normal (nondefective) temperate bacteriophage lysogenizes a cell and one or more of the prophage genes are expressed. For example, *Corynebacterium diphtheriae* produces toxin only when it is lysogenized with the phage β. The phage clearly contains the structural gene for toxin production, since lysogenization with a mutated β phage lacking this gene results in a non-toxin-producing strain of *C. diphtheriae*. A second example of phage conversion is the change in the lipopolysaccharide structure of *Salmonella anatum* when this bacterium is lysogenized by the phage ε[15]. In both of these examples, phage genes are expressed in the lysogenic state.

Microbial Metabolism and Growth
Genetics: Recombination • pp. 19–20

Plasmids Are Extrachromosomal Circular Pieces of DNA

Bacteria have a genetic exchange process called conjugation that involves cell-to-cell contact. It is during this association that DNA is transferred from either the bacterial chromosome or extrachromosomal genetic material (**plasmid**). The DNA entering the recipient cell from the donor cell may recombine with the recipient chromosome, altering the genotype of that bacterium. Whether or not a bacterium conjugates depends upon genes that are found on a plasmid.

Microbial Metabolism and Growth
Genetics: Recombination • pp. 21–24

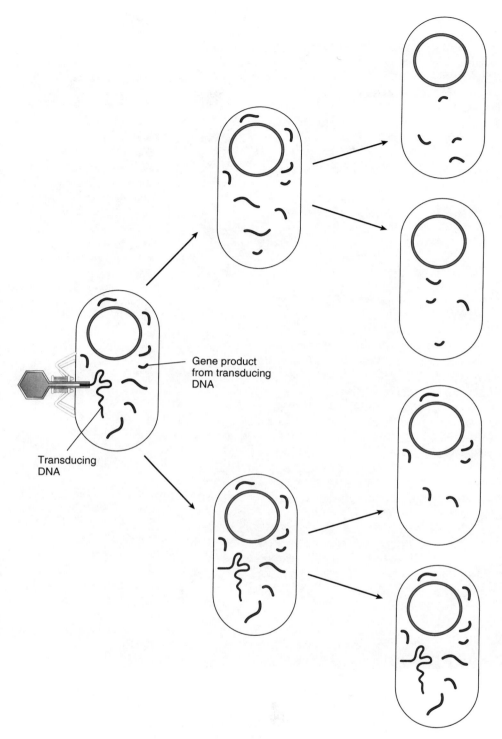

figure 9.11

Abortive Transduction

In abortive transduction, the transducing DNA is not integrated into the bacterial chromosome. The exogenote neither replicates nor is destroyed; it is transmitted unilinearly to only one of the two daughter cells formed at cell division. Gene products from the transducing DNA are transmitted to both daughter cells. However, in those cells that do not receive the exogenote, the gene products are progressively diluted as cell multiplication proceeds.

Gene product from transducing DNA

Transducing DNA

Transposable Genetic Elements

Transfer of genetic material between two organisms requires not only similarity between the organisms involved, but also a homology between the donor and host DNA. Fragments of donor DNA injected into a bacterium are incorporated into the recipient chromosome only at those sites having complementary base sequences. The low frequency of natural DNA transfer results from this specificity of genetic exchange.

Mutation and transfer of DNA were long considered to be the only mechanisms for modification and evolution of genetic sequences in living organisms. In the 1940s, however, Barbara McClintock discovered a new mechanism for chromosomal modification. McClintock, in her studies on pigmentation in the corn plant *Zea mays*, noted a variegation that was caused not by mutation, but by the movement of discrete genetic elements among chromosomes. These genetic elements appeared to control the expression of genes adjacent to their insertion sites on the chromosomes. It was not until two decades later, in the 1960s, that similar controlling genetic elements were discovered and characterized in *Escherichia coli*. Additional DNA sequences were found inserted into portions of the bacterial chromosome. Like the genetic elements first observed by McClintock, these **transposable elements,** or **transposons,** move blocks of genetic material from one location to another on the bacterial chromosome or to plasmids or bacteriophages.

Transposons are now recognized to be common constituents of bacterial chromosomes, plasmids, and bacteriophages. They contain genes coding for antibiotic resistance, carbohydrate utilization, toxin production, amino acid synthesis, and hydrocarbon degradation. Electron micrographs have revealed that the ends of transposons contain inverted repeating base sequences of 9 to 40 bases. It is believed that these inverted repeating ends recognize regions in the DNA for insertion—possibly those DNA regions that have base sequences complementary to the repeat sequence.

One type of mobile genetic element is the **insertion sequence (IS).** An insertion sequence is a short piece of DNA less than 2,000 base pairs long that can be inserted at a specific site in a chromosome or plasmid. Unlike transposons, which are longer and contain genes that are unrelated to insertion as well as insertion genes, ISs contain only insertion genes. ISs can be instrumental in regulating the expression of certain phenotypes. For example, the gram-negative flagellated bacterium *Salmonella* can synthesize two distinct types of flagellin (Figure 9.12). The genes coding for the flagellins (*H1* and *H2*) are located in operons residing at different chromosomal locations. The *H2* gene is closely linked to another gene (*RH1*) that codes for a repressor of the *H1* operon. Thus when the *H2* operon is turned on, the repressor is synthesized and represses the *H1* operon. The promoter for the *H2* operon is located within an IS. This IS contains a gene, *hin,* with a product that is a protein mediating the inversion of the entire IS and its site-specific recombination with the DNA. When the IS is in the normal orientation, the *H2* gene is transcribed and the *H1* operon is repressed. However, if the IS is inverted with the promoter facing in the opposite direction of the *H2* operon, the *H2* gene (including the *RH1* gene for the repressor) is not transcribed. The absence of repressor results in transcription of the *H1* gene. Thus the orientation of the IS determines the type of flagellin synthesized by *Salmonella.*

The discovery of transposons indicates that cells do not have to rely on only mutation and genetic exchange for chromosome modification and the regulation of gene expression. Transposons represent nature's way of genetically engineering DNA sequences in evolution.

Plasmids are small, circular pieces of DNA that exist independently of the bacterial chromosome (Figure 9.13). These extrachromosomal elements replicate autonomously in the cytoplasm and have been found to carry different types of genetic markers, including those for antibiotic resistance and production of toxins, virulence factors, and metabolic enzymes (Table 9.2). The amount of plasmid DNA may constitute as much as 1% to 2% of the total cellular DNA in a bacterium. A bacterium may contain several plasmids.

Plasmids Are Both Conjugative and Nonconjugative

Plasmids, like bacterial chromosomes, are circular, double-stranded DNA molecules. Unlike larger chromosomes, plasmids carry only a few genes and these genes are not essential for cell growth. These extrachromosomal elements are divided into two major classes: **conjugative plasmids,** which are associated with conjugation, and **nonconjugative plasmids.** Conjugative plasmids carry a sequence of genes called the *tra* (for *transfer)* **genes**

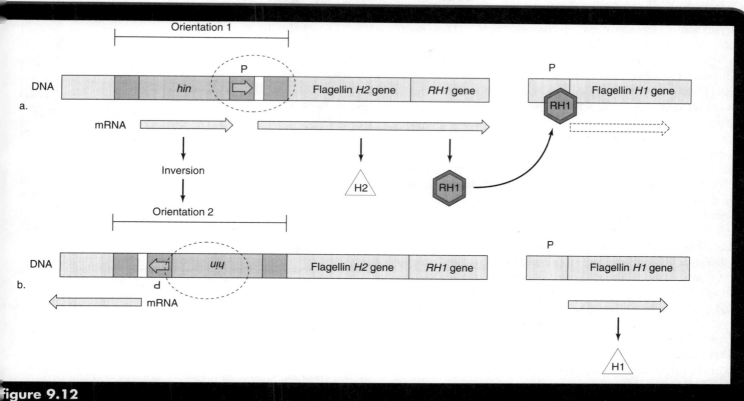

Figure 9.12

Regulation of Flagellin Synthesis in *Salmonella* by an Insertion Sequence (IS)

a. The IS, containing the *hin* gene, is oriented so that the flagellin *H2* gene and the *RH1* gene are transcribed. The *RH1* gene codes for a repressor that represses the *H1* operon. b. The IS is inverted, with the promoter (P) facing in the opposite direction of the *H2* operon. Under such conditions, the flagellin *H2* gene and the *RH1* gene are not transcribed, resulting in transcription of the flagellin *H1* gene.

that are associated with conjugative transfer. Genes in the *tra* region are associated with cell attachment and plasmid transfer between bacteria during conjugation. An example of a conjugative plasmid is the **F** (for *fertility*) **plasmid** of *E. coli*, which has been extensively studied. The F plasmid is 94.5 kilobase pairs long. Because the *tra* region, which consists of about 20 genes, occupies one-third of the plasmid genome, conjugative plasmids are much larger than nonconjugative plasmids. Nonconjugative plasmids (for example, many Col plasmids) do not have *tra*

genes, but can have *mob* (**mobilization**) **genes** that allow them to take advantage of the *tra* function of a conjugative plasmid for transfer between bacteria.

Resistance Plasmids Carry Genes for Antibiotic Resistance

Bacteria can become resistant to antibiotics by mutating existing chromosomal genes or by transferring antibiotic-resistant genes. Although transformation and transduction of antibiotic-resistant genes can occur between bacteria of the same species, transfer of resistance genes across genus and species lines is more likely to occur by conjugation. Plasmids that carry genes for antibiotic resistance are found in strains of many pathogenic bacteria. These **resistance plasmids (R plasmids)** spread by conjugative transfer through bacterial populations and confer resistance to a number of antibiotics. Classical R plasmids have two functionally distinct parts: (1) *tra* **genes,** which are associated with conjugative transfer, and (2) **resistance genes (R determinant),** which code for antibiotic resistance and may consist of as many as seven or eight genes for resistance to multiple antibiotics. R plasmids generally acquire resistance genes by transposons, which can move between plasmids. Multiple resistance plasmids were first discovered in Japan in the 1950s during a period when there was a rapid increase in multiple drug resistance in clinical isolates of *Shigella,* which causes dysentery. When cultures of *Shigella* were exposed to chloramphenicol, streptomycin, tetracycline, or sulfonamide, the bacteria exhibited resistance to more than one of the antimicrobial agents. Furthermore, this multiple resistance could be transmitted to other nonresistant strains of *Shigella* as well as to other intestinal bacteria such as *E. coli.* Since then, multiple resistance plasmids have been found in other clinically significant bacteria, including *Staphylococcus aureus, Pseudomonas aeruginosa, Klebsiella pneumoniae,* and *Enterococcus faecalis.* The emergence of these multiple-drug-resistant bacteria has presented major problems in chemotherapy as fewer and fewer antimicrobial agents are effective in treatment of microbial diseases (see antibiotic resistance, page 130).

One hypothesis for the origin of antibiotic resistance genes is that these genes may have evolved in antibiotic-producing bacteria such as *Streptomyces* as a mechanism by which the bacterium could protect itself from its own antimicrobial products. This theory is supported by the observation that genes coding for antibiotic resistance and antibiotic production often occur in the same gene cluster and that antibiotic resistance genes are found in low frequency in bacterial strains stored before the widespread use of antibiotics in chemotherapy.

Antimicrobial Resistance
Transfer and Spread: Conjugation • pp. 4–5

Plasmids Can Carry Genes That Code for Bacteriocins, Toxins, Resistance to Heavy Metals, and Metabolic Processes

Bacteriocinogenic plasmids carry genes for the synthesis of **bacteriocins,** proteins that inhibit or kill other bacteria. Bacteriocins are distinguished from antibiotics, which have a broader antimicrobial spectrum and are less potent. One molecule of a bacteriocin is often sufficient to kill a bacterium. **Colicins,** bacteriocins produced by *E. coli* and carried by **Col plasmids,** have been the most extensively studied, and the mode of action of some colicins is known in detail. Colicin E2 causes single-stranded nicks in DNA and interferes with DNA replication. Colicin E3 inactivates 30S ribosomes by cleaving the 16S rRNA, thereby stopping protein synthesis.

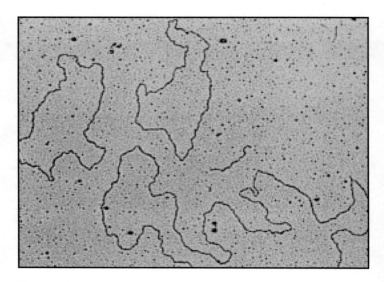

figure 9.13
Electron Micrograph Showing Two Different Plasmids
The large molecule is plasmid pBF4 (containing genes for resistance to clindamycin and erythromycin) from *Bacteriodes fragilis;* the small molecules are plasmid pSC101 (containing the gene for resistance to tetracycline) from *Escherichia coli* (colorized).

Other bacterial plasmids contain genes that code for toxins, resistance to heavy metals, and special types of metabolism. Plasmid-coded enterotoxins in enteropathogenic *E. coli* enable the bacteria to cause disease. Some bacteria, such as *Staphylococcus aureus* and species of *Pseudomonas,* have plasmids that confer resistance to certain heavy metals such as cadmium, lead, and mercury. Many species of *Pseudomonas* are able to utilize an extraordinarily large number of organic compounds as energy sources. In many instances, genes for utilization of these organic compounds are carried on plasmids.

Plasmids Can Be Integrated into the Chromosome

Most kinds of plasmids entering a cell remain separate from the chromosome, but some can be integrated into the chromosome. The term **episome** is used to describe a plasmid that is capable of existing either extrachromosomally or as part of the chromosome. Since plasmids carry genetic markers, they influence the genotype of an organism.

Although a bacterial cell may contain more than one type of plasmid, plasmids tend to prevent any other plasmids of the same or closely related type from establishing themselves in the same cell. This **plasmid incompatibility** is determined by plasmid genes that regulate their DNA replication. Plasmids can be separated, therefore, into incompatibility groups. Plasmids of the same incompatibility group are closely related and interfere with each other.

Plasmids, like prophages in lysogenic bacteria (see curing of lysogenic bacteria, page 411), can be removed from bacterial cells

table 9.2

Examples of Major Types of Plasmids

Type	Representatives	Hosts	Copy Number (Copies/ Chromosome)	Approximate Size (kb)	Phenotypic Features[a]
Fertility Factor[b]	F factor	E. coli, Salmonella, Citrobacter	1–3	95–100	Sex pilus, conjugation
Col Plasmids	ColE1	E. coli	10–30	9	Colicin E1 production
	ColE2	Shigella	10–15		Colicin E2
	CloDF13	Enterobacter cloacae			Cloacin DF13
R Plasmids	RP4	Pseudomonas and many other gram-negative bacteria	1–3	54	Sex pilus, conjugation, resistance to Ap, Km, Nm, Tc
	R1	Gram-negative bacteria	1–3	80	Resistance to Ap, Km, Su, Cm, Sm
	R6	E. coli, Proteus mirabilis	1–3	98	Su, Sm, Cm, Tc, Km, Nm
	R100	E. coli, Shigella, Salmonella, Proteus	1–3	90	Cm, Sm, Su, Tc, Hg
	pSH6	Staphylococcus aureus		21	Gm, Tm, Km
	pSJ23a	S. aureus		36	Pn, Asa, Hg, Gm, Km, Nm, Em
	pAD2	Enterococcus faecalis		25	Em, Km, Sm
Metabolic Plasmids	CAM	Pseudomonas		230	Camphor degradation
	SAL	Pseudomonas		56	Salicylate degradation
	TOL	Pseudomonas putida		75	Toluene degradation
	pJP4	Pseudomonas			2,4-dichlorophenoxyacetic acid degradation
		E. coli, Klebsiella, Salmonella			Lactose degradation
		Providencia			Urease
	sym	Rhizobium			Nitrogen fixation and symbiosis
Virulence Plasmids	Ent (P307)	E. coli		83	Enterotoxin production
	K88 plasmid	E. coli			Adherence antigens
	ColV-K30	E. coli		2	Siderophore for iron uptake; resistance to immune mechanisms
	pZA10	S. aureus		56	Enterotoxin B

[a]Abbreviations used for resistance to antibiotics and metals: Ap, ampicillin; Asa, arsenate; Cm, chloramphenicol; Em, erythromycin; Gm, gentamycin; Hg, mercury; Km, kanamycin; Nm, neomycin; Pn, penicillin; Sm, streptomycin; Su, sulfonamides; Tc, tetracycline.
[b]Many R plasmids, metabolic plasmids, and others are also conjugative.
Source: Data from Lansing M. Prescott et al., *Microbiology,* 3rd edition, Times Mirror Higher Education Group, 1996.

by **curing.** Plasmid curing either occurs spontaneously or is induced by treatment of the host cell with chemical agents such as ethidium bromide or acridine, or with ultraviolet irradiation. The curing process apparently inhibits the replication of plasmids without affecting chromosomal replication.

Plasmids share many features that are similar to viruses and, in fact, are believed by some scientists to be the ancestors of viruses. It is possible that plasmids originated from pieces of chromosome that were excised and were not necessary for cell growth and replication. With the passage of time, portions of this extrachromosomal material evolved viral coats and became modern-day viruses.

Cell-to-Cell Contact Is Required for DNA Transfer During Conjugation

Conjugation occurs between two closely related but different bacterial cells—a donor and a recipient. In *E. coli,* the donor cell contains a conjugative F plasmid. The recipient cell does not contain this plasmid. As a result of this difference, the donor cell is often called an **F⁺ cell,** and the recipient cell is termed an **F⁻ cell.** Like other plasmids, the F plasmid can be lost from the cell through curing. F⁺ cells incubated in the stationary phase of growth for prolonged periods are cured of the F plasmid and changed into F⁻ cells.

F⁺ cells contain not only the F plasmid, but also have a special, elongated pilus known as the **sex pilus,** the production of which is determined by genes in the *tra* region of the F plasmid. If F⁺ cells are mixed in culture with F⁻ cells, the two cell types come in contact with each other through the aid of the sex pilus. One strand of the F plasmid is nicked at a site called *oriT* (origin of transfer), and the 5′ end of the cut strand is transferred into the recipient cell (Figure 9.14). During transfer, the plasmid DNA is replicated via a rolling circle mechanism of replication. Inside the recipient cell, the single strand of donor plasmid is replicated and recircularized (a complete copy of the plasmid remains in the donor). Because the recipient cell now contains an F plasmid, it becomes an F⁺ cell like the donor. Genetic markers other than the sex factor located on the F plasmid are also transferred to the recipient cell. However, the chromosomal genes of the donor bacterium are not transferred in mating between F⁺ and F⁻ cells.

Donor Genes Can Be Transferred at High Frequencies During High-Frequency Recombination

Under certain conditions the F plasmid is integrated into the donor chromosome. Although this event rarely happens—approximately once per every 10⁵ cells—when it does occur, the result is a **high-frequency recombination (Hfr)** cell. The F plasmid in Hfr cells is integrated at one of several specific sites and orientations in the chromosome. When an Hfr cell donates genes to an F⁻ cell, the Hfr cell chromosome opens internally at the *oriT* where the F plasmid is located. Part of the F plasmid moves into the recipient cell, followed by the transfer of chromosomal genes in a sequential manner. Only if and when all of the chromosomal genes are transferred to the recipient cell is the remainder of the F plasmid transferred. Thus during conjugation between an Hfr cell and an F⁻ cell, the F⁻ cell rarely receives the entire F plasmid. Although the recipient cell remains F⁻, it does receive donor genes at high frequencies—this is the reason why such genetic exchange is termed high-frequency recombination. The distal end of the F plasmid is transferred to the recipient cell only if mating remains uninterrupted long enough for the entire donor chromosome, including the F plasmid, to be transferred. In the case of *E. coli*, this time is between 90 to 100 minutes, an extremely long period

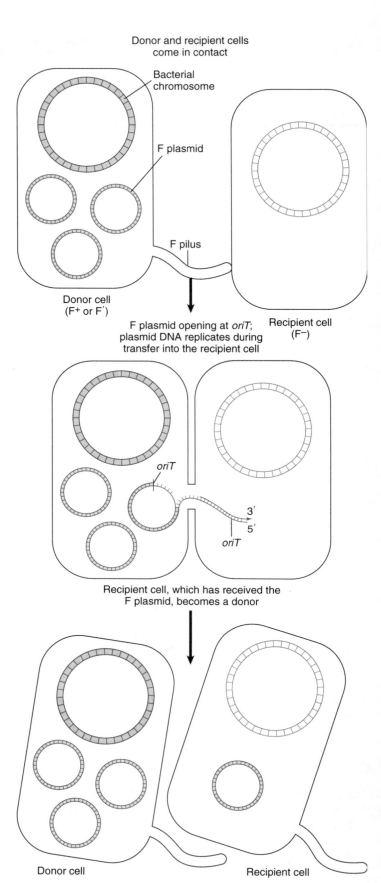

Donor and recipient cells come in contact

Bacterial chromosome

F plasmid

F pilus

Donor cell (F⁺ or F′)

Recipient cell (F⁻)

F plasmid opening at *oriT*; plasmid DNA replicates during transfer into the recipient cell

oriT

3′
5′
oriT

Recipient cell, which has received the F plasmid, becomes a donor

Donor cell

Recipient cell

figure 9.14

Transfer of DNA During Conjugation

In conjugation, donor and recipient cells come in contact. One strand of the F plasmid in the donor cell is cut at the *oriT* site and enters the recipient cell. During transfer, the plasmid DNA is replicated via the rolling circle model. Inside the recipient cell, the donor plasmid is recircularized. The recipient cell, which now contains an F plasmid, becomes a donor (F⁺ or F′) cell.

Microbial Metabolism and Growth
Genetics: Recombination • p. 11

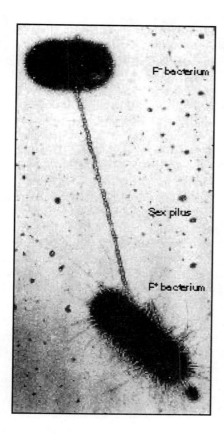

Conjugation between F' cells and F⁻ cells results in the transfer of not only the F plasmid, but also the donor cell genes that are now part of the F' plasmid. Donor genes are transferred at high frequencies in matings between F' and F⁻ cells. Under these conditions, the recipient cell is changed to an F' cell and receives the donor cell genes that are part of the F' plasmid. Since the bacterial genes in the F' plasmid may also be present in the recipient cell chromosome, the recipient, in effect, can become a partial diploid as a result of such transfer.

Donor Cells Have a Sex Pilus Associated with Conjugation

The sex pilus in donor cells is a hollow structure consisting of subunits of a phosphoprotein, **pilin** (see pilin structure, page 62). Although the sex pilus is large enough to allow transfer of DNA between the donor and recipient cells, there is no evidence that this occurs. The sex pilus does appear to form a bridge between the two cells and may be involved in the recognition of the recipient cell during conjugation (Figure 9.15).

An alternative hypothesis is that DNA transfer occurs between cells as a result of wall-to-wall contact. This hypothesis is supported by the observation that the sex pilus immediately retracts upon cell-to-cell contact. This retraction may in fact promote formation of wall-to-wall contact during conjugation.

Microbial Metabolism and Growth
Genetics: Recombination • pp. 11–14

The Sequential Transfer of Chromosomal Genes During Conjugation Can Be Used to Map Genes

Conjugation between Hfr cells and F⁻ cells has been used to map bacterial chromosomes. In such mapping, Hfr cells are mixed with F⁻ cells. Mating is allowed to proceed for a given period of time and then is deliberately interrupted by disrupting the cell mixture, usually by vigorous agitation in a mixer or blender. The recipient cell is phenotypically examined for the markers it has received from the Hfr donor. Since in any specific Hfr strain, the F factor is always inserted at the same site in the chromosome, and the order of gene transfer is the same from Hfr cell to F⁻ cell, the order of genes on the chromosome can be determined by allowing mating to proceed for set periods of time before interruption. It has been discovered that the *E. coli* chromosome takes 90 to 100 minutes to completely transfer over to the recipient cell during mating. The *E. coli* chromosome is thus considered to have a 90- to 100-minute genetic map. The genes on that map are now well-known and precisely located through interrupted mating experiments and other techniques. These interrupted mating experiments also provided the first evidence for the circular nature of the bacterial chromosome.

figure 9.15
Cell-to-Cell Contact During Bacterial Conjugation
Two bacteria (a donor F⁺ bacterium and a recipient F⁻ bacterium) are shown connected by the sex pilus.

Antimicrobial Resistance
Transfer and Spread of Resistance: Conjugation • pp. 4–5

of time for bacterial mating. Under precise laboratory conditions in which mating cells are undisturbed, such long mating periods are possible.

F' Cells Have F' Plasmids Carrying Chromosome Genes

F plasmids that have integrated into the donor chromosome in Hfr cells occasionally are excised from the chromosome. When such an event occurs, the excised F plasmid may carry with it a part of the bacterial chromosome. Such a plasmid is called an **F' plasmid.** If the genes now on the F' plasmid are indispensable to the bacterium, loss of the plasmid through curing will result in cell death.

Lysogenic conversion is a characteristic known to be responsible for the toxigenic properties of some medically important bacteria, including *Corynebacterium diphtheriae* (diphtheria toxin), *Streptococcus pyogenes* (erythrogenic toxin), and some strains of *Clostridium botulinum* (botulinum toxin). The ability of a temperate bacteriophage to carry genes that determine bacterial properties was discovered by Victor Freeman in 1951.

Freeman examined lysogenic conversion in *Corynebacterium diphtheriae* by combining diphtheria bacteria known to be avirulent by guinea pig inoculation with bacteriophages from filtrates of lysed virulent cultures of *C. diphtheriae*. Five avirulent strains (numbers 411, 444, 770, 1174, and 1180) of *C. diphtheriae* and two bacteriophages (A and B) were used in Freeman's studies. Bacteria and phage were mixed in two different ways. In the first method, heart infusion agar was inoculated with 0.5 ml of an 18-hour broth suspension of bacteria, dried for half an hour, and then inoculated with 0.5 ml of filtered bacteriophage lysate. In the second method, 3 ml of heart infusion broth was inoculated with 0.15 ml of an 18-hour culture of bacteria, incubated for one hour until growth was visible, and then inoculated with 0.15 ml of filtered bacteriophage lysate. Table 9P.1 shows the susceptibility of the five *C. diphtheriae* strains to bacteriophages A and B. Only *C. diphtheriae* strain 411 was resistant to phage infection. Phage A failed to show any visible lysis of diphtheria bacteria growing in broth.

Freeman then injected suspensions of each culture's lysates into guinea pigs (0.1 ml intradermally or 1.0 ml subcutaneously) for in vivo toxigenicity tests. Suspensions of agar plate lysates were prepared by washing the surface growths of the plates with 0.85% NaCl and using the washes as material for injection. Broth lysates were injected directly into guinea pigs. A naturally virulent strain of *C. diphtheriae* was used as a positive control for virulence tests. In addition, diphtheria antitoxin was injected with lysates in a separate series of experiments to confirm the specificity of toxicity. The results of the in vivo toxigenicity tests are summarized in Table 9P.2. Phage B lysates contained a dermal necrotic factor that phage A lysates lacked. The virulence factor in the phage B lysates appeared to be diphtheria toxin, since diphtheria antitoxin prevented necrosis from occurring. Furthermore, the absence of toxicity by strain 411 provided two important controls. First, it indicated that extracellular phage was not toxic. Second, this result ruled out any possibility that carryover toxin from the original phage suspensions (those used to infect diphtheria bacteria) was responsible for the necrotic reactions. Similar results were obtained from subcutaneous injections of culture lysates into guinea pigs, except that the animals died (Table 9P.3).

These studies by Freeman were important because they were the first evidence that bacteriophage-infected strains of *C. diphtheriae* were toxigenic. We now know that a prophage can carry toxin genes not only for *C. diphtheriae*, but also for other bacteria.

Source

Freeman, V.J. 1951. Studies on the virulence of bacteriophage-infected strains of *Corynebacterium diphtheriae*. *Journal of Bacteriology* 61:675–688.

table 9P.1

Bacteriophage Susceptibility of Avirulent Strains of *Corynebacterium diphtheriae*

Strain Number	Degree of Clearing on Agar Medium		Degree of Clearing in Broth	
	Phage A[a]	Phage B[a]	Phage A	Phage B
444	2+[b]	4+	0	1–2+
1174	2+	4+	0	1–2+
1180	2+	4+	0	1–2+
770	2+	4+	0	1–2+
411	0	0	0	0

[a]Material spotted on plate previously inoculated with the culture indicated in the first column.
[b]Degree of clearing: 0 = none; 1+ = slight; 2+ = moderate; 3+ = marked; 4+ = complete.

Intradermal Tests of Bacteriophage Lysates in Guinea Pigs

| Strain Number | Avirulent Culture Grown on Agar | | | | | | Avirulent Culture Grown in Broth | | | | | |
| | Control[a] | | Phage A Filtrate[a] | | Phage B Filtrate[a] | | Control | | Phage B Added | | Filtrate of Incubated Culture Phage B Mixture | |
	T	C	T	C	T	C	T	C	T	C	T	C
444	O	O	O	O	4+[b]	O	O	O	4+	O	2+	O
1174	O	O	O	O	4+	O	O	O	4+	O	2+	O
1180	O	O	O	O	4+	O	O	O	4+	O	2+	O
770	O	O	O	O	4+	O	O	O	4+	O	2+	O
411	O	O	O	O	O	O	O	O	O	O	—	—

Note: The intradermal method used involves a second inoculation of the test substances 4 hours after the initial injections and immediately following an intraperitoneal injection of 1,000 units of diphtheria antitoxin. The test results are recorded under "T" and the control antitoxin results, under "C."
[a]Material used for the second inoculation of the plates; saline was used in the control cultures.
[b]The symbol 4+ indicates the presence of both erythema and necrosis involving an area greater than 1 cm^2, 2+ indicates a similar reaction, except for the absence of necrosis.

Subcutaneous Tests of Bacteriophage Lysates in Guinea Pigs

Strain Number	Culture plus Saline	Culture plus Phage A	Culture plus Phage B	Culture plus Phage B and Antitoxin
444	0/3[a]	0/1	4/4	0/2
1174	0/1	0/1	2/2	0/1
1180	0/1	0/1	2/2	0/1
770	0/1	0/1	2/2	0/1
411	0/1	0/1	0/1	0/1
Total	0/7	0/5	10/11	0/6

Note: All cultures and culture lysates were washed off the agar media with 0.85% saline and inoculated in 1.0-ml doses.
[a]The numerator represents the number of guinea pigs that died; the denominator, the total number tested.

1. A mutation is an inheritable change in the sequence of DNA. The rate of mutation can be increased by mutagenic agents.

2. Bacteria have several different mechanisms for repair and replacement of damaged DNA. Excision repair excises and replaces damaged DNA. Photoreactivation uses the enzyme photolyase and light to cleave the covalent linkages within pyrimidine dimers. Glycosylases are enzymes that detect and remove unnatural bases. The SOS system is normally repressed by LexA, but when there is DNA damage, RecA stimulates LexA to cleave itself and become inactivated, resulting in expression of the SOS system genes for repair of the DNA damage.

3. A technique commonly used to identify mutants is replica plating, which involves the transfer of colonies from a master plate to one or more uninoculated plates of different test media. Autotrophic mutants can be identified by their absence of growth on replicated plates that lack the required growth factor for the mutant.

4. Bacteria can transfer genetic material between cells by three methods: transformation, transduction, and conjugation.

5. Transformation involves the entry of free, naked DNA from a donor cell into a competent recipient cell and recombination into the chromosome. Transfection, a type of transformation, involves the insertion of bacteriophage DNA into a cell.

6. Transduction involves the transfer of DNA from one cell to another cell via a bacteriophage. In generalized transduction, a fragment of the host cell genome may be packaged into a phage particle during a lytic cycle. In specialized transduction, a specific portion of a host cell genome is packaged into the phage particle following lysogeny.

7. Cell-to-cell contact is required for conjugation between a donor cell containing a conjugative F plasmid and a recipient cell lacking this plasmid. A high-frequency recombination (Hfr) cell is one in which the F plasmid is integrated into a specific region of the bacterial chromosome, resulting in transfer of the chromosomal genes in a sequential manner to the recipient cell during conjugation.

8. A plasmid is a small, circular piece of DNA that exists independently of the chromosome. Conjugative plasmids carry a sequence of genes called the *tra* genes associated with conjugation and plasmid transfer. Nonconjugative plasmids do not have *tra* genes. Plasmids can carry genes for antibiotic resistance, the synthesis of bacteriocins and toxins, resistance to heavy metals, and metabolic activity.

EVOLUTION *and* BIODIVERSITY

With the thousands of genes and millions of base pairs in an average bacterial chromosome, one would think that mutations would be common during DNA replication. Surprisingly, the rate of mutation during DNA replication is extremely low. Mistakes occur in only 1 out of every 10^9 bases copied. This accuracy of DNA replication is important because it enables the stable inheritance of genetic traits from generation to generation. In those rare instances when mutations do occur, they arise not only from errors in replication but also from the action of mutagenic agents such as ultraviolet light and chemicals in the environment. Not all mutations are harmful. Some are neutral or beneficial. Occasionally mutations confer a selective advantage to a microorganism and enhance its competitiveness in nature. For example, a mutation resulting in increased resistance to an antibiotic might enable the affected microbe to survive in environments where it might normally be inhibited or killed by the antibiotic. Over evolutionary time, the cumulative effects of mutations can play an important role in the gradual selection of certain phenotypic traits. In this sense, mutations can serve as a molecular clock for measuring the divergence of species.

Questions

Short Answer

1. Explain why procaryotes are dependent on mutation or genetic exchange for evolution.

2. How do spontaneous mutations occur? What factors will increase the rate of mutation?

3. Explain how it is possible that a mutation could have no effect on the cell.

4. Explain why it is likely that the deletion or insertion of a single nucleotide will have a major impact on a cell.

5. Can the substitution, addition, or deletion of a single nucleotide be lethal to a cell? Can a mutation be helpful?

6. Identify several mutagens and explain how they affect a cell.

7. Explain why many mutations are not permanent.

8. If auxotrophic mutants cannot grow without the necessary growth factor, how do you identify them?

9. Without extensive biochemical or genetic tests, how might you identify a bacterial mutant?

10. Identify three mechanisms of genetic exchange used by bacteria.

11. Why is general or homologous recombination necessary, after genetic exchange, for the permanent acquisition of new traits?

12. How does transfection differ from transduction?

13. How does generalized transduction differ from specialized transduction?

14. What are plasmids?

15. Why are plasmids helpful to a cell?

16. What role do plasmids play in conjugation?

Multiple Choice

1. Which of the following types of mutations will result in the premature termination of protein synthesis?
   a. missense mutations
   b. nonsense mutations
   c. silent mutations

2. Which of the following requires the assistance of a virus?
   a. conjugation
   b. transformation
   c. transduction
   d. None of the above.

3. Griffith's classic experiment (discussed in chapter 8) is an example of:
   a. conjugation
   b. transformation
   c. transduction
   d. All of the above.

4. Which of the following would be associated with the highest rate of conjugation and recombination?
   a. F plasmid
   b. R plasmid

   c. Col plasmids
   d. episomes

5. After conjugation with a(n) _____, the F^- cell will become F^+.
   a. F^-
   b. F^+
   c. Hfr

Critical Thinking

1. Many mutagens are also carcinogens. Describe how a change in a cell's hereditary information may result in carcinogenesis.

2. You have been given a culture of *Serratia marcescens* grown at room temperature and notice the colonies are pink. After transferring the culture and incubating at 37°C, your culture has produced white colonies. What hypothesis can you form? Design an experiment to test your hypothesis.

3. Genetic exchange among procaryotes is a rare occurrence. Even so, which process would you expect to be most common? Why?

4. Describe several factors (both internal and external) which prevent genetic exchanges between procaryotes. How are the mechanisms which prevent genetic exchange advantageous to procaryotes?

5. After decades of abuse, the medical profession has called for restraint in the use of antimicrobial agents. Discuss why and present guidelines for the appropriate use of antimicrobial agents.

Dale, J.W. 1989. *Molecular genetics of bacteria*. New York: John Wiley & Sons. (A textbook of microbial genetics.)

Miller, J.H. 1992. A *short course in bacterial genetics: A laboratory manual and handbook for* Escherichia coli *and related bacteria*. Cold Spring Harbor, NY: Cold Spring Harbor Laboratory Press. (An in-depth laboratory manual describing techniques used in molecular biology and microbial genetics.)

Neidhardt, F.C., J.L. Ingraham, and M. Schaechter. 1990. *Physiology of the bacterial cell: A molecular approach*. Sunderland, Mass.: Sinauer Associates, Inc. (A textbook of microbial physiology and genetics.)

Russell, P.J. 1996. *Genetics*, 4th ed. New York: HarperCollins. (A fundamental textbook of genetics, with sections on DNA replication, transcription, translation, genetic exchange in bacteria, transposable elements, and recombinant DNA technology.)

Streips, U.N., and R.E. Yasbin, eds. 1991. *Modern microbial genetics*. New York: Wiley-Liss. (An advanced textbook on the genetics of *Escherichia coli* and other bacteria.)

Watson, J.D., N.H. Hopkins, J.W. Roberts, J.A. Seitz, and A.M. Weiner. 1987. *Molecular biology of the gene,* 4th ed. Menlo Park, Calif.: The Benjamin/Cummings Publishing Company. (An in-depth textbook on macromolecular synthesis, gene function, and molecular genetics.)

chapter eleven

PROCARYOTES: THE BACTERIA AND THE ARCHAEA

Classification of Microorganisms

Ribosomal RNA and Phylogeny

Classification of Procaryotes

Gram-Negative Bacteria of General, Medical, or Industrial Importance

Gram-Positive Bacteria Other Than the Actinomycetes

The Archaea, Cyanobacteria, and Remaining Gram-Negative Bacteria

The Actinomycetes

PERSPECTIVE
Symbiotic Association of Chemoautotrophic Bacteria with a Marine Invertebrate

EVOLUTION AND BIODIVERSITY

Colorized scanning electron micrograph of the spirochete *Leptospira interrogans*, showing a periplasmic flagellum wrapped around the flexible helical cell (×22,000).

🔵 **Microbes in Motion** ──────── [PREVIEW LINK]

Among the key topics in this chapter is characteristics of certain groups of bacteria: Yersinia, Vibrio, Chlamydia, and Mycoplasma. The following sections in the *Microbes in Motion* CD-ROM may be useful as a preview to your reading or as a supplemental study aid:

Miscellaneous Bacteria: Zoonoses (Yersinia), 57–67. *Gram-Negative Organisms:* Bacilli—Facultative Anaerobes (Vibrionaceae), 30–38. *Miscellaneous Bacteria:* Chlamydiae, 1–6: Mycoplasma, 1–6.

imagine a university library, with its many thousands of volumes, without a logical method for arranging these books. Such a disordered library would be practically useless. Books could not be easily found, and once found, could not be replaced in locations where they could be found again. There would be no method for the systematic addition of new publications to the collection. Books on a similar subject would be randomly dispersed throughout the building.

Now consider a living library that contains as many as 5 million different kinds of organisms. The sheer numbers and diversity of organisms, including microorganisms, make it necessary to have an organized system for classification. Clearly the identification of microorganisms becomes a formidable, if not impossible, task without such a system. The systematic categorization of organisms into a coherent scheme is known as **taxonomy.** Taxonomy serves not only to organize plants, animals, and microbes into categories, but also can be useful in showing possible evolutionary relationships among similar types of organisms. Taxonomy provides order; organisms with common characteristics are recognized as such, and assigned to the same taxon (group or rank).

Classification of Microorganisms

Microorganisms occupy a unique position among living organisms because they are able to exist as independent, self-sufficient cells. Microbes may be either procaryotes (lacking a nucleus) or eucaryotes (possessing a true nucleus). Unlike animals or plants, which have distinctive organs, tissues, or structures for specialized functions, microbes are autonomous units of living matter. Each microbial cell is a dynamic system, able to grow, metabolize, and reproduce without the assistance of sister cells. In contrast, cells in an animal or a plant work together for the benefit of the entire organism. They act collectively to gather food and energy from the environment for the growth and reproduction of the whole organism. Even in instances where several thousand microbial cells aggregate to form a large structure, such as in the case of algae, fungi, or the fruiting bodies of myxobacteria, each cell within the structure maintains its independence and autonomy. It is this characteristic of independence and autonomy that distinguishes microbial cells from cells of other forms of life.

Microorganisms are named by the traditional binomial system first used by the Swedish physician and naturalist Carolus Linnaeus (1707–1778). This method of **nomenclature** (the systematic naming of organisms), widely used for the classification of plants and animals, assigns a species name and a genus name to each organism. Microbial taxonomists refer to a species as a group of microorganisms that have similar **phenotypic** (observable) characteristics. Organisms of the same species often have similar, although not necessarily identical, **genotypic** (genetically derived) characteristics. Similar species are placed into a higher taxon called

table 11.1

Nomenclature of the Bacterium _Treponema pallidum_

Taxonomic Rank	Example
Domain	Bacteria
Division	Gracilicutes
Class	Scotobacteria
Order	_Spirochaetales_
Family	_Spirochaetaceae_
Genus	_Treponema_
Species	_pallidum_
Strain	Nichols

a genus. Similar genera (plural of genus), in turn, are grouped into families, and families are part of orders (Table 11.1). An additional classification category used in bacteriology is the **strain.** A species can consist of several different strains; cells of a strain are all derived from the same ancestor and retain the characteristics of the ancestor. Thus a bacterium such as _Escherichia coli_ (genus and species name) may consist of several thousand different strains, each of which shares the defining set of phenotypic traits.

Classification Schemes for Microorganisms Have Evolved over the Years

Many different classification schemes have been proposed for microorganisms (Table 11.2). Early classification systems established before the discovery of microbes divided all living organisms into either plants (kingdom **Plantae**) or animals (kingdom **Animalia**) on the basis of characteristics such as photosynthetic capabilities, motility, and structural features. Plants were photosynthetic, stationary, and had rigid cell walls. Animals were generally motile, nonphotosynthetic, and lacked cell walls. This two-kingdom system was used without major difficulty for many years. As microorganisms were discovered, however, many problems arose. Microbes had unusual characteristics, neither plantlike nor animal-like. Some microorganisms were photosynthetic and motile, whereas other, nonphotosynthetic microbes were stationary. Still others had the ability to change their metabolic characteristics under different environmental conditions. As a result of such traits, taxonomists began to search for classification schemes that would take into consideration these newly discovered forms of life.

An expanded three-kingdom classification system to accommodate microorganisms was proposed in 1866 by the German zoologist Ernst H. Haeckel (1834–1919). Haeckel proposed that those organisms that were basically unicellular and simple in organization be placed into a third distinctive kingdom, designated the **Protista.** The protists consisted of bacteria, algae, fungi, and protozoa. Haeckel's proposal never gained complete acceptance, but his use of the word _Protista_ to denote microorganisms was incorporated into subsequent classification schemes.

table 11.2

Some Classification Systems for Living Organisms

System's Original Proposer	Classification by Kingdom or Domain and Major Groups of Organisms

Linnaeus (1753)	Animalia
	  Animals, protozoa
	Plantae
	  Plants, algae, bacteria, fungi

Haeckel (1866)	Animalia
	  Animals
	Plantae
	  Plants, multicellular algae
	Protista
	  Unicellular algae, bacteria, fungi, protozoa

Whittaker (1969)	Animalia
	  Animals
	Plantae
	  Plants
	Protista
	  Algae, protozoa
	Fungi
	  Fungi
	Monera (Procaryotae)
	  Procaryotes

Woese (1981)	Archaea Bacteria } Domains Eucarya

As additional traits of microorganisms became known through improvements in microscopy and the development of biochemical techniques, more detailed and scientific classification schemes were proposed. One of the most widely accepted systems is the five-kingdom system suggested in 1969 by Robert H. Whittaker. Whittaker's system recognizes five kingdoms of living organisms based on cell structure and modes by which organisms obtain their nutrients (*photosynthesis, absorption* of dissolved nutrients, and *ingestion* of undissolved food particles): **Monera** (also called **Procaryotae), Fungi, Protista, Plantae,** and **Animalia.** Other classification systems separate microorganisms—bacteria (including the cyanobacteria, or blue-green bacteria), algae, fungi, and protozoa—into two groups: the **procaryotes** and the **eucaryotes.** This distinction is determined by cellular structure. In such classifications, bacteria, which do not have membrane-enclosed nuclei, are defined as procaryotes and placed in the kingdom Monera.

Unlike procaryotes, eucaryotic cells undergo mitotic division and have well-defined chromosomes with associated histones (basic proteins that neutralize the negative charges of the DNA) and membrane-enclosed organelles such as mitochondria, chloro-

plasts, lysosomes, and the endoplasmic reticulum. Eucaryotes are generally physically larger than procaryotes and have more complex mechanisms of locomotion. In Whittaker's classification system, the various eucaryotic microbes are assigned to the kingdoms Fungi (fungi) and Protista (protozoa and algae). Whittaker's system is based to a large extent on evolutionary divergence. In this evolutionary scheme, Monera is regarded as the most primitive kingdom. A few organisms in this kingdom are believed to have evolved into the Protista, some members of which in turn developed into the other three kingdoms. The orderly arrangement and evolution-oriented progression of Whittaker's system makes it one of the more widely accepted classification schemes today.

A different system was proposed in 1981 by Carl R. Woese. Woese argued that the division of organisms into procaryotes and eucaryotes was insufficient and that the procaryotes could be further separated based on their 16S rRNA sequences. He therefore split the procaryotes into two groups based on the nucleotide sequences of their 16S rRNA sequences: **Archaea** [Greek *archaios*, ancient, as in the Archaean era 3.9 to 2.6 billion years ago], and **Bacteria.** The two groups of procaryotes also had other distinguishing differences. The Archaea are procaryotes, because they do not have a membrane-enclosed nucleus, and morphologically resemble the Bacteria. Archaea have several different kinds of cell walls or no cell wall, but no true peptidoglycan, which is always found in the cell walls of Bacteria. Archaea, furthermore, possess plasma membrane lipids and ribosomal ribonucleic acids that are different from those found in Bacteria and eucaryotes (see Archaea and Bacteria membrane lipids, page 51). These dissimilarities are significant enough, in the opinion of Woese and other scientists, to warrant a separate taxonomic classification for the Archaea based on genetic content, specifically the sequence of nucleotides in 16S ribosomal RNA. Under this classification the Archaea include procaryotes currently divided into three main categories: the methanogens, the extreme halophiles, and the extreme thermophiles. Woese's classification system groups all living organisms into one of three domains: Bacteria, Archaea, and Eucarya.

Despite the variety and complexity of classification schemes that have been proposed, no one scheme is completely satisfactory. Living organisms, particularly microbes, which grow and reproduce at rapid rates, undergo constant modifications in structure, physiology, and genetic composition. As a consequence of these evolutionary changes, the characteristics of organisms change. Such changes, although not easily incorporated into most classification systems, are readily adaptable to schemes that take evolutionary divergence into consideration.

Three Major Approaches Have Been Used to Identify and Place Microorganisms in Classification Systems

Regardless of the system used to classify microorganisms, varied methods have been used to identify and place these microbes in their appropriate places in classification schemes. These methods are: the classical approach, numerical taxonomy, and molecular approaches.

table 11.3

Criteria Used in the Classical Approach to Procaryotic Taxonomy

Category	Examples of Criteria
Structure/morphology	Shape
	Size
	Arrangement
	Capsules
	Sheaths
	Flagella and their arrangement
	Endospores
	Inclusion bodies
	Gram stain
Biochemical/physiological	Range of carbohydrates used as carbon and energy sources
	Optimum temperature for growth
	Range of temperature for growth
	Optimum pH for growth
	Range of pH for growth
	Growth factor requirements
	Aerobic, anaerobic, facultatively anaerobic
	End products of respiration and fermentation
	Antibiotic sensitivities

The Classical Approach Orders Procaryotes on the Basis of Morphology and Physiology

The **classical approach** to procaryotic taxonomy is one in which procaryotes are grouped into **species** and **genera** primarily on the basis of their structural and morphological characteristics and, secondarily, on the basis of biochemical and physiological traits (Table 11.3). Organisms with similar cell shapes or structures are thus in the same group. Other physical attributes used in the classical approach to taxonomy include the presence and type of flagella, staining properties, and the presence of external coverings such as capsules. Examples of secondary characteristics used in taxonomy are nutritional or atmospheric growth requirements and by-products of cellular metabolism.

Numerical Taxonomy Groups Microorganisms into Phenoms Based on Their Similarities

Although the classical approach is used by many taxonomists, it has the disadvantage of an inherent bias. The taxonomist must determine which characteristics among the many in an organism are the most important. This bias led to the establishment in the eighteenth century of an alternate system for classification known as **numerical,** or **Adansonian, taxonomy,** named after its inventor, the French botanist Michael Adanson (1727–1806). In numerical taxonomy, all observable characteristics of an organism carry equal weight and therefore are considered equally in determining similarities among organisms (Figure 11.1).

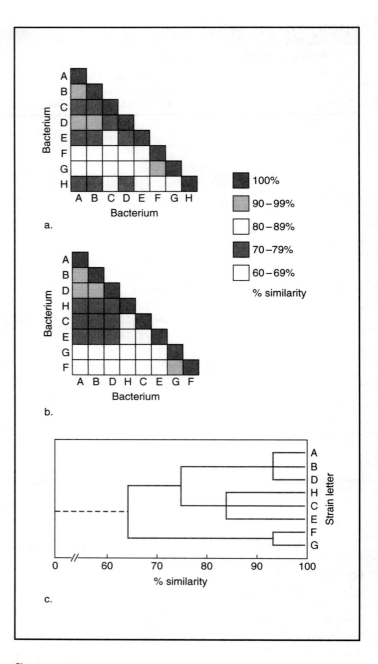

figure 11.1

Numerical Taxonomy
Eight different bacterial strains (A through H) are compared with one another by similarity coefficients. a. Matrix of strains before rearrangement. b. Matrix of strains after rearrangement by percent similarity. Strains with similar characteristics are clustered. c. Dendrogram constructed from similarity values. Vertical lines define the percent similarity between different strains or groups of strains. For example, strains A, B, and D are 90% to 99% similar, as are strains F and G. Strains H, C, and E are 80% to 89% similar. However, when strains A, B, and D are compared to strains F and G, there is only a 60% to 70% similarity.

table 11.4

Determination of Similarity Coefficient and Matching Coefficient by Numerical Taxonomy for Two Procaryotes

Number of characteristics present in both organisms: a

Number of characteristics present in organism #1 and absent in organism #2: b

Number of characteristics absent in organism #1 and present in organism #2: c

Number of characteristics absent in both organisms: d

Matching coefficient $(S_S) = \dfrac{a + d}{a + b + c + d}$

Similarity coefficient $(S_J) = \dfrac{a}{a + b + c}$

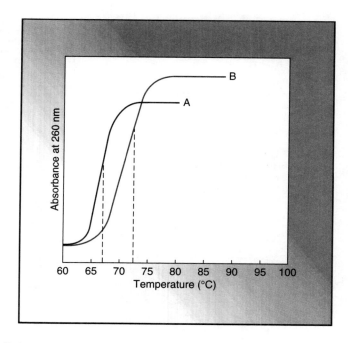

figure 11.2

DNA Melting Curve

Double-stranded DNA is heated, and the extent of hydrogen bonding between the two strands is determined by the melting temperature (T_m, the temperature at the midpoint of the absorbancy increase). In the example, the T_m of curve A is 67°C and of curve B, 72.5°C.

Similarities between two or more organisms are determined using one of two methods (Table 11.4). Both methods compare the number of identical characteristics to the total number of characteristics observed in the organisms. The **matching coefficient (S_S) method** is based on the percentage of characteristics that are common to two organisms when compared (that is, characteristics present in both organisms or absent in both organisms). The **similarity coefficient (S_J) method** determines the percentage of characteristics that are present in both organisms and does not consider characteristics absent in the two organisms. Both types of comparisons cluster similar organisms into groups called **phenoms** (categories comparable to species or genera in classical taxonomy), with boundaries established by predetermining matching or similarity coefficient values. In instances where several organisms and many characteristics are compared, a diagrammatic matrix called a **dendrogram** is used to illustrate similarity levels (Figure 11.1c).

Numerical taxonomy eliminates the biases common to other taxonomic approaches and provides an objective comparison among organisms. Comparisons become statistically more significant as larger numbers of characteristics are compared. Such analyses of many organisms and their similarities clearly cannot be performed without the aid of computers.

Molecular Approaches Group Microorganisms Based on Nucleic Acid Comparisons

Development of modern techniques for genetic analysis in microorganisms has led to more refined methods for microbial classification. **Molecular approaches** to taxonomy involve comparisons of nucleic acids among organisms. Such comparisons include determinations of DNA or RNA sequences and studies of hybridization among nucleic acids from different organisms.

DNA contains four different bases (adenine, thymine, guanine, and cytosine). Their structures and bonding arrangements are such that in double-stranded DNA (the usual form of bacterial DNA), guanine and cytosine are always paired, as are adenine and thymine. The proportion of guanine-cytosine base pairs in the DNA of the genome (commonly expressed as the mole percent of guanine plus cytosine content or **mole% G + C**) will vary in different organisms. Two different species of organisms usually will not have identical mole% G + C. Among procaryotes, the mole% G + C ranges from 25 to 75. By determining the proportion of G + C in isolated chromosomal DNA, limits on the genetic relatedness of two organisms can be established. Organisms that have vastly different mole% G + C contents are assumed to be genetically dissimilar and therefore not related. However, the corollary to this statement—procaryotes with similar mole% G + C are closely related—is not always valid because the mole% G + C values do not take into consideration the sequence of bases in the DNA.

Mole% G + C values can be determined by a procedure known as the thermal denaturation method (Figure 11.2). In this method, a solution of double-stranded DNA is slowly heated, and its strand separation, or denaturation, is followed by an increase in absorbance as detected by a spectrophotometer. Single-stranded DNA has approximately 40% greater absorbance than double-stranded DNA when measured at a wavelength of 260 nm. The temperature at which strand separation occurs depends on the extent of hydrogen bonding between the two DNA strands and can be plotted on a melting curve of temperature versus absorbance. Since guanine and cytosine base pairs are joined by three hydrogen bonds, whereas adenine and thymine base pairs are joined by only two hydrogen bonds, the melting temperature (T_m, the temperature at the midpoint of this curve) indicates the extent of hydrogen bonding in double-stranded DNA. As the mole% G + C value increases, the T_m also increases.

A more precise approach to molecular taxonomy is a comparison of genetic relatedness by nucleic acid hybridization (Figure 11.3). In this procedure, nucleic acids from two different organisms are isolated and combined together as either DNA-DNA or DNA-mRNA double strands—a process known as hybridization. Many different methods have been developed to determine DNA homology between two organisms. In one method, one of the organisms is grown in the presence of radio-labeled thymine, which is incorporated into newly synthesized DNA of the organism. The second organism is grown in a medium containing nonradiolabeled thymine; its newly synthesized DNA is nonradioactive. The DNAs from both organisms are isolated and denatured with high temperature (100°C) or high pH (pH ≥ 13). The resultant single strands are allowed to hybridize on a nitrocellulose filter. After hybridization, any remaining single-stranded DNA is digested with a nuclease, such as S1 nuclease from *Aspergillus*, that digests single-stranded but not double-stranded DNA. The extent of hybridization is determined by measuring the amount of radioactivity remaining in the hybrid molecules.

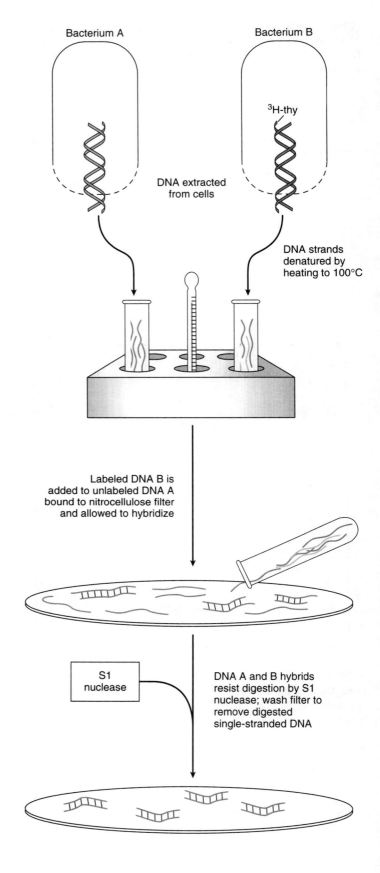

figure 11.3
Nucleic Acid Hybridization
DNA is extracted from two organisms (bacterium A and bacterium B), one of which has been grown in the presence of tritiated thymine (^{3}H-thy) to label radioactively its DNA. Each DNA suspension is heated to 100°C to denature the double-stranded nucleic acids. The nucleic acids are allowed to hybridize by adding the labeled single-stranded DNA to unlabeled single-stranded DNA immobilized on a nitrocellulose filter. After hybridization, any remaining single-stranded DNA is digested by a nuclease such as S1 nuclease from *Aspergillus* (double-stranded DNA is not attacked by nucleases) and the filter is washed. The amount of radioactivity remaining in the double-stranded hybrid molecules is a measure of the genetic relatedness of the two organisms.

Organisms that are closely related would be expected to have a higher degree of DNA homology than organisms that are not as closely related.

Other methods used for comparisons of genetic relatedness among organisms are determinations of nucleic acid (DNA and RNA) base sequences and the extent of genetic exchange between organisms (see exchange of genetic material, page 250). A popular method recently developed for clinical diagnosis of microorganisms involves the use of DNA probes—small pieces of DNA that recognize specific genes—to identify gene sequences in an organism (see nucleic probes, page 295). This procedure, which is based on DNA:DNA hybridization, is a powerful diagnostic aid because of its high degree of specificity in rapidly identifying microorganisms. Such genetic tools provide what many believe may be the most accurate approaches to taxonomy, since relatedness is ultimately traced to the genetic composition of organisms.

Ribosomal RNA and Phylogeny

The advent of molecular techniques made possible not only genetic analysis of microorganisms, but also the study of evolutionary relationships among living organisms, or **phylogeny.** Although there are many ways to study phylogenetic relationships (for example, amino acid sequences of proteins, nucleotide sequences of nucleic acids found in organisms, or presence or absence of essential enzymes), it is now recognized that ribosomal RNA (rRNA) sequences are important indices of phylogeny, particularly among procaryotes. Ribosomal RNAs have characteristics that are important in studying evolutionary divergences among organisms. These universal characteristics have identical functions in all living organisms. This functional constancy makes rRNAs ideal molecular chronometers to measure evolutionary change over the billions of years that procaryotes have existed. Because rRNA is a small molecule that cannot tolerate much structural change and still retain its function, its sequence is moderately well **conserved,** or constant, across phylogenetic lines. Consequently, small differences in rRNA sequences can be used to determine evolutionary distances between organisms. Among the three rRNA molecules (5S, 16S, and 23S) in procaryotes, 16S rRNA is used most commonly as a phylogenetic tool. The small size (125 nucleotides) of the 5S rRNA limits the amount of information that can be generated from this molecule, whereas the large size (2,900 nucleotides) of the 23S rRNA makes this molecule more difficult to experimentally analyze than the 16S rRNA (about 1,500 nucleotides). Carl R. Woese and Norman R. Pace revolutionized microbial systematics in the 1970s and 1980s by using 16S rRNA as a molecular chronometer to follow evolutionary divergence among procaryotes.

Sequencing of Ribosomal RNA Is Relatively Simple

The sequencing of ribosomal RNA is relatively simple. After cell lysis and phenol extraction of the total RNA, the RNA is precipitated with alcohol and salt. A small DNA primer that has a complementary base sequence to a highly conserved region of the 16S rRNA is added to the mixture. Reverse transcriptase and deoxyribonucleotides are then added to generate cDNA from the 16S rRNA template. The cDNA is sequenced and this information can be used to deduce the sequence of the 16S rRNA. The polymerase chain reaction (PCR) can also be used to amplify the rRNA genes (the cDNA). PCR amplification requires far fewer cells than direct rRNA sequencing and is more rapid and convenient when processing many samples.

Phylogenetic Trees Can Be Developed from Ribosomal RNA Sequences

Because 16S rRNA has several regions containing highly conserved sequences, slight differences in the 16S rRNA sequences from different organisms can be used to determine their phylogenetic relationships. The 16S rRNA sequences from organisms are compared and phylogenetic trees showing evolutionary distances and relationships among these organisms are constructed from differences in RNA alignment. The concept behind this type of comparison is that procaryotes branching off from other procaryotes a long time ago will have had time to diversify, and their 16S rRNA sequences will be less similar than those of procaryotes that have branched off more recently.

As a result of such analyses, phylogenetic trees have been developed for different groups of procaryotes. **Signature sequences,** or short nucleotide sequences unique to certain groups of procaryotes, have been useful in defining three specific domains (Bacteria, Eucarya, and Archaea) of a **universal phylogenetic tree** (Figure 11.4). Organisms within each of these three domains are distinctly separated from each other by large sequence distances in their 16S rRNA (18S rRNA in eucaryotes). The root of the universal tree represents the common ancestor from which all living organisms evolved.

Interestingly, this universal tree shows the Archaea to be more closely related phylogenetically to Eucarya than to Bacteria. It is clear from rRNA sequence analyses that the universal ancestor branched in two directions: the Bacteria and the Archaea/Eucarya. With the passage of time, the Archaea and the Eucarya diverged from one another.

These phylogenetic relationships were further confirmed in 1996 when the 1.66 million base pair genome of the Archaeon *Methanococcus jannaschii* (named after Holger Jannasch, leader of an expedition that discovered this methane-producing microorganism in a deep-sea hydrothermal vent beneath the Pacific Ocean

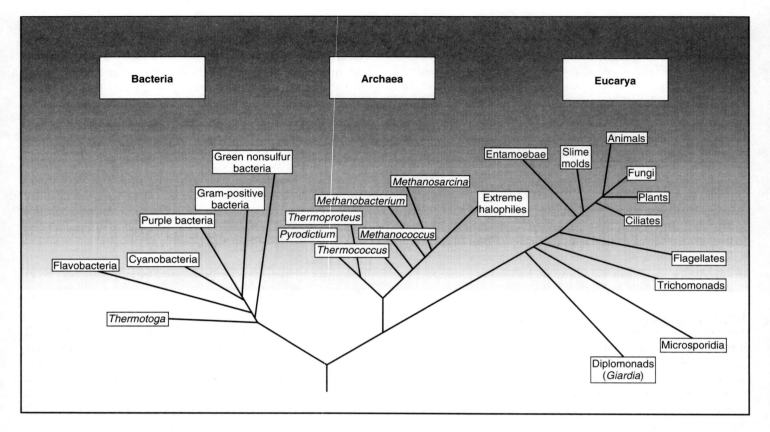

figure 11.4

The Universal Phylogenetic Tree as Determined by Ribosomal RNA Sequencing

Phylogenetic relationships among organisms in the three domains are shown.

in 1982) was sequenced. The genome of *M. jannaschii* (domain Archaea) could now be compared to the genomes of organisms from the other two branches of the universal tree: *Haemophilus influenzae* (domain Bacteria), *Mycoplasma genitalium* (domain Bacteria), and *Saccharomyces cerevisiae* (domain Eucarya). When such a comparison was made, it was discovered that 56% of the 1,738 genes identified in *M. jannaschii* were unique and had not previously been detected in Bacteria and eucaryotes. Of the remaining genes, those involved in cell division, metabolism, and energy production were similar to genes found in Bacteria, whereas most of the genes associated with transcription, translation, and replication were more similar to those found in eucaryotes.

The universal tree has Archaea branching off the root earlier than Bacteria and Eucarya, suggesting that the Archaea are the most primitive among the three domains (Figure 11.5). This placement of the Archaea near the universal ancestor is reasonable considering that many of these organisms inhabit extreme environments (for example, high temperature and low pH) that resemble conditions on a primitive planet. It appears that the ancestral procaryote was

an anaerobic, thermophilic, sulfur-metabolizing organism (domain Archaea). This ancestor eventually gave rise to two major branches that are phylogenetically and phenotypically distinct: the extreme thermophile branch and the methanogen/extreme halophile branch. Eucaryotes eventually arose from the Archaea and over time diverged into the various branches associated with this domain. Although the Archaea are procaryotes and share many common characteristics with the Bacteria, they also share characteristics with the phylogenetically related Eucarya, (Table 11.5). Unlike the single RNA polymerase of Bacteria, Archaeal and Eucaryal RNA polymerases are of several types and, in the case of the extreme thermophiles, are structurally more complex (Figure 11.6). Translation in Bacteria generally begins with an initiator tRNA carrying a modified methionine, *N*-formylmethionine (see initiation of translation, page 229), whereas the initiator tRNA in Archaea and Eucarya contains an unmodified methionine. Some antimicrobial agents such as chloramphenicol, erythromycin, and streptomycin, which affect protein synthesis in Bacteria, do not affect protein synthesis in Archaea or Eucarya.

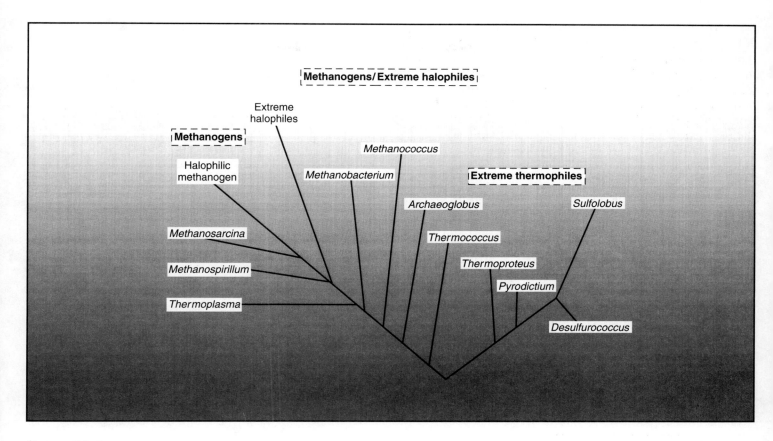

figure 11.5
The Archaea Phylogenetic Tree
The relationships among the Archaea are based on 16S rRNA comparisons.

table 11.5

Distinguishing Characteristics of Bacteria, Archaea, and Eucarya

Characteristic	Bacteria	Archaea	Eucarya
Cell wall	Contains muramic acid	Lacks muramic acid	Lacks muramic acid
Membrane lipids	Ester-linked straight hydrocarbon chains	Ether-linked branched aliphatic hydrocarbon chains	Ester-linked straight hydrocarbon chains
Membrane-bound nucleus	Absent	Absent	Present
Chromosome	Single circular chromosome	Single circular chromosome	Linear chromosomes
RNA polymerase	One type, with 6 different subunits	Several types, each with 8 to 12 different subunits	Several types, each with 12 to 14 different subunits
Ribosomes	70S	70S	80S (70S in mitochondria and chloroplasts)
Amino acid carried by initiator tRNA	N-formylmethionine	Methionine	Methionine
tRNA	Thymine and dihydrouridine usually present	Thymine absent and dihydrouridine usually absent	Thymine and dihydrouridine usually present
Cellular organelles	Absent	Absent	Present
Sensitivity to chloramphenicol erythromycin, and streptomycin	Sensitive	Resistant	Resistant

The Bacteria are divided phylogenetically into at least eleven different phyla (Figure 11.7). With the exception of the *Thermotoga* phylum, the remaining ten phyla of Bacteria originate from a common root. *Thermotoga* and *Thermosipho*, the two known genera of the *Thermotoga* phylum, are extreme thermophiles with cell walls containing peptidoglycan (a signature characteristic of Bacteria). Members of this phylum are clearly Bacteria, although they appear to represent a phylogenetic position between the Archaea (which include many extreme thermophiles) and the Bacteria.

The advent of molecular biology, along with its tools to determine phylogenetic relationships among living organisms, has brought profound changes in how we view procaryotes and eucaryotes. Previously, procaryotes were considered distinct and unique from eucaryotes. Through RNA sequencing, we now know that procaryotes can be divided into two domains, the Bacteria and the Archaea, and that the Archaea are more closely related to the Eucarya than to the Bacteria. Although the Bacteria and Archaea are both irrefutably procaryotes, they occupy different ecological niches and appear to have evolved in separate directions. As rRNAs from additional species are sequenced, it should be possible to further delineate the phylogenetic relationships among living organisms.

Classification of Procaryotes

Procaryotes represent a heterogeneous group of microorganisms with a vast range of characteristics. The most widely accepted organization of this diversity is found in **Bergey's Manual of Determinative Bacteriology,** an extensive reference manual used for bacterial classification. The concept for this manual, considered by many to be the bible of bacteriology, was first conceived by David H. Bergey with the assistance of a special committee of the Society of American Bacteriologists (organized in 1899 and now known as the American Society for Microbiology), chaired by Francis C. Harrison. The first edition of *Bergey's Manual* was published in 1923, with subsequent editions published as procaryotes were reclassified.

Prior to the first edition of *Bergey's Manual,* a number of scientists had attempted to organize bacteria systematically in concise publications. In the late 1800s, Ferdinand Cohn (1828–1898), a botanist, drew comparisons between bacteria and the cyanobacteria. K. B. Lehmann and R. E. Neumann of Germany organized procaryotes into distinct groups in their *Bakteriologische Diagnostik.* The Society of American Bacteriologists assisted Frederick D. Chester in the publication of a *Manual of Determinative Bacteriology* in 1901. By the early 1920s, *Chester's Manual* had become outdated, and it was at this point

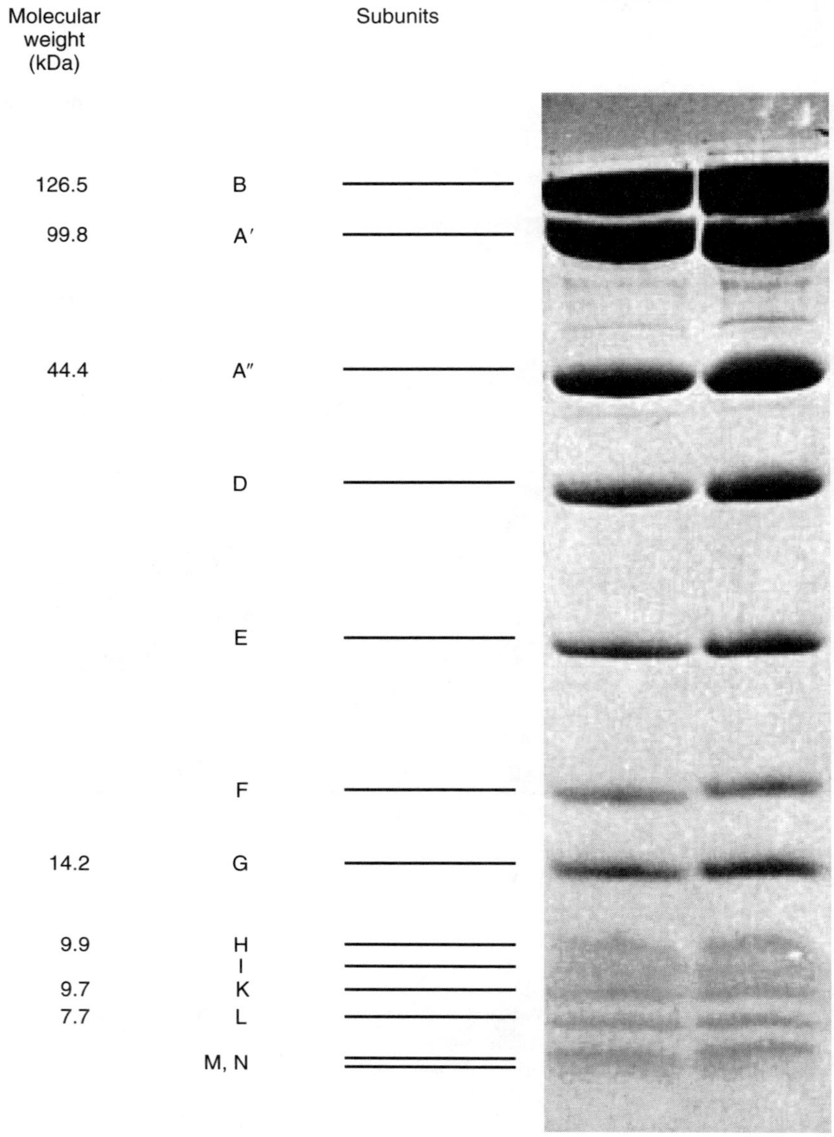

figure 11.6

Subunit Composition of RNA Polymerase of *Sulfolobus acidocaldarius,* Domain Archaea

S. acidocaldarius, an extremely thermophilic elemental sulfur metabolizer, has a structurally complex RNA polymerase consisting of 13 different subunits named A', A", B, D, E, F, G, H, I, K, L, M, and N. The purified RNA polymerase protein subunits are denatured and separated by polyacrylamide gel electrophoresis.

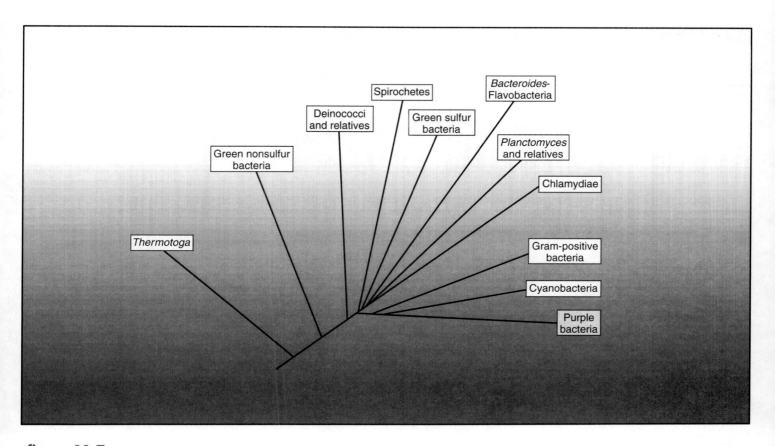

figure 11.7
The Bacterial Phylogenetic Tree
The relationships among the Bacteria are based on 16S rRNA comparisons.

that Bergey and Harrison decided to revise the publication into what has since been known as *Bergey's Manual of Determinative Bacteriology.* The ninth edition of *Bergey's Manual,* published in 1994, separated procaryotes into 35 groups. Since 1936 the *Manual* has been compiled by a group of bacteriologists under the auspices of the Bergey's Manual Trust, which was established with accumulated royalties by Bergey prior to his death in 1937.

The rapid evolution of procaryotic nomenclature combined with the constant discovery of new microorganisms, however, has made it necessary for the Bergey's Manual Trust to reexamine its approach to publication of *Bergey's Manual.* Members of the Trust began to realize in the late 1970s and early 1980s that a new approach was needed to minimize the manual's obsolescence upon publication. The Trust decided on a plan to publish *Bergey's Manual* not as a single volume, but as a series of four subvolumes. It was further decided that the new format would include a greater amount of information on the ecology, enrichment and isolation, and general characteristics of procaryotes as they relate to taxonomy. The new format, which has an expanded scope and examines relationships between organisms (systematics), is called ***Bergey's Manual of Systematic Bacteriology.***

Work on the first volume in the four-volume sequence began in 1980 and was completed in 1982, with subsequent publication in 1984. *Bergey's Manual of Systematic Bacteriology* groups procaryotes into four categories: gram-negative Bacteria of general, medical, or industrial importance (Volume 1); gram-positive Bacteria other than the actinomycetes (Volume 2); the Archaea, cyanobacteria, and remaining gram-negative Bacteria (Volume 3); and the actinomycetes (Volume 4). Members of the Bergey's Manual Trust believe that the division of procaryotes into four groups for treatment in separate volumes will permit the timely revision and publication of material.

The classical approach to classification in *Bergey's Manual of Systematic Bacteriology* will be used to organize the description of representative groups of procaryotes in the rest of this chapter. This description of procaryotes is intended not to be an exhaustive coverage of *Bergey's Manual,* but to acquaint the student with the diverse forms and metabolic types that make up the procaryotes. Although the phylogenetic approach is becoming more defined and will be used in the next edition of *Bergey's Manual of Systematic Bacteriology,* the classical approach is traditionally used by most laboratories today to identify and classify procaryotes.

table 11.6

Gram-Negative Bacteria of General, Medical, or Industrial Importance

Section	Major Characteristics
The Spirochetes	Slender, winding, or helically coiled cells; outer sheath surrounds protoplasmic cylinder and periplasmic flagella
Aerobic/microaerophilic, motile, helical/vibrioid, gram-negative bacteria	Rigid, helical to vibrioid cells with polar flagella; aerobic or microaerophilic
Nonmotile (or rarely motile), gram-negative, curved bacteria	Curved, vibrioid, or helical cells; nonmotile
Gram-negative aerobic rods and cocci	Straight or curved rods and cocci; respiratory modes of metabolism
Facultative anaerobic, gram-negative rods	Straight or curved rods; respiratory and fermentative modes of metabolism; includes many human parasites
Anaerobic, gram-negative, straight, curved, and helical rods	Obligate anaerobes; form wide variety of fermentation products
Dissimilatory sulfate- or sulfur-reducing bacteria	Obligate anaerobes; use sulfur, sulfate, or other oxidized sulfur compounds as electron acceptors in anaerobic respiration
Anaerobic, gram-negative cocci	Obligate anaerobes; nonmotile
The Rickettsias and Chlamydias	Small, obligate intracellular parasites of humans, other animals, and arthropods
The Mycoplasmas	Small free-living organisms; lack cell walls
Endosymbionts	Microorganisms that exist intracellularly as endosymbionts of fungi, protozoa, insects, and other invertebrates

Gram-Negative Bacteria of General, Medical, or Industrial Importance

The first volume of *Bergey's Manual* includes gram-negative Bacteria of general, medical, or industrial importance and divides them into 11 separate sections (Table 11.6). These Bacteria are further separated into orders, families, genera, and species.

The Spirochetes

The first section of Volume 1 of *Bergey's Manual,* on the spirochetes, contains five genera of bacteria (**Spirochaeta, Christispira, Treponema, Borrelia,** and **Leptospira**) that are *flexuous,* slender, and helically coiled. The cytoplasm and nuclear region of a spirochete are contained within a plasma membrane–cell wall complex and form what is known as a protoplasmic cylinder. Wrapped around the protoplasmic cylinder are periplasmic flagella (also called axial fibrils or axial filaments) that are attached to one end of the cell and extend along most of the cell length (Figure 11.8). The number of periplasmic flagella in a cell ranges from 2 to more than 100. The flagella and their arrangement around the protoplasmic cylinder are responsible for the unique rotating, screwlike motility of these bacteria. Spirochetes also move by flexing their bodies as well as by creeping or crawling across solid surfaces. Both the protoplasmic cylinder and the periplasmic flagella are surrounded by a trilaminar outer sheath. The entire cell, which may be up to 250 μm

long, is typically only 0.1 to 0.75 μm in diameter (some members of the genus *Christispira* have diameters up to 5 μm). It is difficult to see spirochetes by bright-field light microscopy because of their typically very small diameter. However, they can be seen by dark-field microscopy, and by fluorescence microscopy when tagged with the appropriate fluorescent antibodies.

Many types of human disease are associated with the spirochetes. Bacteria of the genus **Treponema** [Greek *trepo*, turn, *nema*, thread] cause such diseases as syphilis (**T. pallidum**)(see syphilis, page 534), yaws—a non-sexually-transmitted tropical disease characterized by painful, debilitating lesions on the soles of the feet and the palms of the hand—(**T. pertenue**), and pinta—a non-sexually-transmitted tropical disease characterized by hyperpigmentation followed by depigmentation of the skin (**T. carateum**) (Figure 11.9). **Borrelia burgdorferi** and **Leptospira interrogans** are responsible for Lyme disease and leptospirosis, respectively. Lyme disease was first discovered in 1975 during an investigation of several hundred people with a mysterious illness in the town of Old Lyme, Connecticut. Since 1975, Lyme disease has been reported in over 40 states in the United States and in other countries. *B. burgdorferi*, the etiologic agent of Lyme disease, is generally transmitted to humans by the deer tick, *Ixodes scapularis*, which is found in association with animals such as white-tailed deer and white-footed mice. The disease begins as a rash with concentric red rings resembling a "bull's eye" at the site of the tick bite, followed by fatigue, fever, headache, and arthritis. Over 7,000 cases

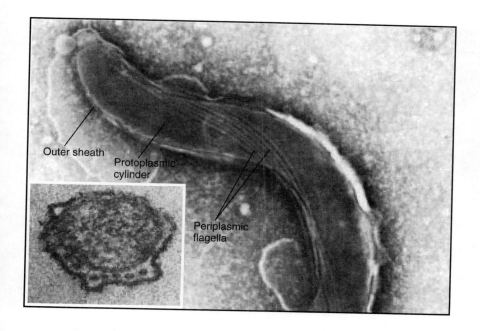

Outer sheath

Protoplasmic cylinder

Periplasmic flagella

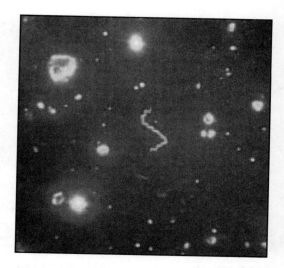

figure 11.9

Fluorescent Micrograph of the Spirochete *Treponema carateum*

Fluorescent antibodies bound to the bacterium illuminate it against the dark background.

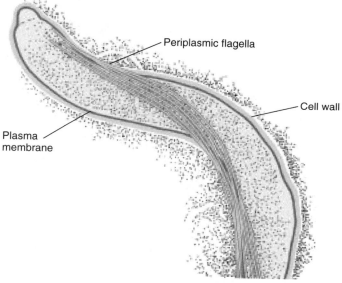

Periplasmic flagella

Cell wall

Plasma membrane

figure 11.8

Electron Micrograph and Schematic Diagram of *Treponema pallidum* Showing Periplasmic Flagella

Several periplasmic flagella can be seen extending from one end of the cell (×50,000). Cross section inset shows the outer sheath, periplasmic flagella, and central protoplasmic cylinder (×120,000).

Bacterial Structure and Function
External Structures: Flagella • p. 25

of Lyme disease are reported annually in the United States. Leptospirosis is characterized by influenza-like symptoms and jaundice. *L. interrogans,* a thin (6 to 20 µm in length by 0.1 µm in diameter) spirochete with a characteristic hook on one or both ends of the cell, is transmitted to humans by contact with water contaminated with urine from infected animals (Figure 11.10).

Other spirochetes do not cause disease, but can be found in symbioses with insects such as wood-eating cockroaches and termites. *Pillotina* (host: wood-eating cockroaches and termites), *Diplocalyx* (host: termites), *Hollandina* (host: termites), and *Clevelandina* (host: termites) are genus names that have been proposed for these bacteria that live in the anaerobic or microaerophilic hindguts of the insects but have not yet been cultivated in the laboratory.

Many of the spirochetes are difficult to identify in the laboratory, not only because of their small size, but also because many of these bacteria are anaerobic and have not been successfully cultivated on artificial media. The spirochetes are distinguished by characteristics such as size, morphology, relationship to oxygen, habitat, and pathogenicity (Table 11.7).

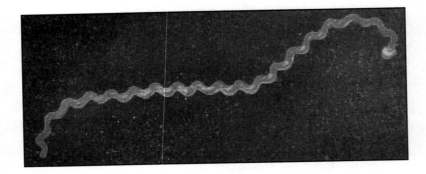

figure 11.10
Electron Micrograph of _Leptospira interrogans_
Note the hook at one end of the cell, characteristic of this bacterium (colorized).

table 11.7

Characteristics of Spirochetes (family: _Spirochaetaceae_)

Genus	Morphology	Oxygen Requirement	Diseases
Spirochaeta	Helical cells, 0.2–0.75 µm in diameter and 5–250 µm in length	Obligately anaerobic or facultatively anaerobic	None known to be pathogenic
Cristispira	Helical cells, 0.5–3.0 µm in diameter and 30–180 µm in length; generally contain 2 to 10 complete helical turns	Unknown (have not been grown in pure culture)	Widely distributed among marine and freshwater mollusks (clams, mussels, and oysters), but not believed to be pathogenic to these hosts
Treponema	Helical rods, 0.1–0.4 µm in diameter and 5–20 µm in length; cells have tight regular or irregular spirals	Obligately anaerobic or microaerophilic	Pinta, syphilis, yaws
Borrelia	Helical cells, 0.2–0.5 µm in diameter and 3–20 µm in length; composed of 3 to 10 loose coils	Microaerophilic	Tick-borne and louse-borne relapsing fever

Aerobic/Microaerophilic, Motile, Helical/Vibrioid Gram-Negative Bacteria

In the second section of Volume 1 of _Bergey's Manual,_ the bacteria, unlike the spirochetes, are _rigid,_ helical to vibrioid (comma-shaped) cells that move by conventional polar flagella. These bacteria, 0.2 to 1.7 µm in diameter and up to 60 µm in length, are larger than the spirochetes and thus can be seen with a bright-field light microscope. Members of the genus **Spirillum** are considered to be among the largest bacteria discovered (Figure 11.11).

Spirillum and bacteria of two other related genera, **Aquaspirillum** and **Oceanospirillum,** are aerobic to microaerophilic organisms frequently found in freshwater and marine habitats. It has been hypothesized that these bacteria may be important in the recycling of organic matter from decomposing plants in such habitats.

Campylobacter [Greek _campylo,_ curved, _bacter,_ rod], another member of this group, is found in the reproductive organs, gastrointestinal tract, and oral cavity of humans and ani-

mals (see _Campylobacter_ infections, page 520). **Campylobacter fetus,** first isolated as _Vibrio fetus_ in 1909 and given its current name in 1973, causes a sexually transmitted disease of animals that results in abortions and infertility in infected cattle and sheep. Since the bacterium is carried asymptomatically for long periods of time in the genitourinary and intestinal tracts of these animals, it can persist undetected in herds. _Campylobacter_ infections can lead to serious economic losses and are of great concern to ranchers. In humans, _C. fetus_ is responsible for opportunistic infections—typically fever and blood infections—primarily in people who have debilitating conditions. A sister species, **Campylobacter jejuni,** is an important human intestinal pathogen that causes gastroenteritis.

The bacterium **Bdellovibrio** [Greek _bdella,_ leech] a small, curved, motile rod, has the unique ability to parasitize other bacteria (see _Bdellovibrio_ parasitism, page 429). Parasitic strains of this bacterium attack gram-negative organisms, inserting themselves into the periplasm between the cell wall and membrane. Within this narrow space, the bacterium utilizes the host cell as a substrate

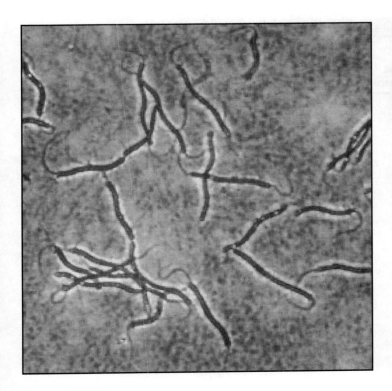

figure 11.11
Phase-Contrast Micrograph of *Spirillum volutans*
S. volutans is a helical, polar-flagellated bacterium found in aquatic environments.

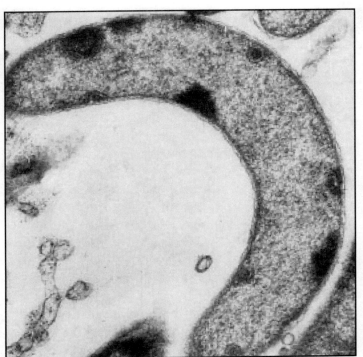

figure 11.12
Electron Micrograph of *Microcyclus aquaticus*, a Curved Rod (×31,400)

for development and replication. The growing *Bdellovibrio* elongates into a snakelike form, which eventually fragments into smaller, highly motile progeny that leave the host, thereby reinitiating the life cycle. The predilection of bdellovibrios for gram-negative prey is due to the absence of a periplasm in gram-positive bacteria. Evidence suggests that components of the lipopolysaccharide in the gram-negative cell envelope may serve as receptor sites for the predator. Bdellovibrios are found in diverse habitats, including soil, oceans, rivers, streams, estuaries, and sewage systems. High concentrations of these bacteria are found in polluted environments, an observation that has led some scientists to infer that prey densities may have an influence on the levels of bdellovibrios in such areas.

Nonmotile (or Rarely Motile), Gram-Negative, Curved Bacteria

The third section of Volume 1 of *Bergey's Manual* consists of gram-negative curved, vibrioid, or helical cells that are nonmotile. These bacteria are nonpathogenic and are generally found in soil, freshwater, and marine environments. An example of a bacterium in this section is *Microcyclus*, a curved rod that has a tendency to form rings after division and prior to cell separation (Figure 11.12). Some species of *Microcyclus* produce gas vacuoles, which make these bacteria buoyant in their aquatic habitat.

Gram-Negative Aerobic Rods and Cocci

A large number of bacteria with diverse properties are found in the fourth section of Volume 1 (Table 11.8). These gram-negative bacteria all possess the common characteristic of having a respiratory mechanism of metabolism, although some can use electron acceptors other than oxygen.

The ***Pseudomonadaceae*** are polar-flagellated straight or curved rods. Most of these bacteria use a wide variety of chemical compounds as energy sources and are useful in the degradation of hydrocarbons in oil spills (see *Pseudomonas putida* and hydrocarbon degradation, pages 11 and 584) and grease in restaurant grease traps (see grease degradation, page 95). Because they are so nutritionally diverse, members of this family are widespread in nature and cause many different diseases in plants, humans, and animals.

Pseudomonas aeruginosa is a common inhabitant of soil and water and is an opportunistic pathogen, causing wound, burn, and urinary tract infections in humans (see *Pseudomonas* infections, page 528). The bacterium is especially a problem in hospital environments, where it is a frequent contaminant of nonsterile wet surgical instruments and respiratory apparatus. Infections by *P. aeruginosa* are a great risk for burn victims, where these bacteria are the single greatest cause of death. Hospitals are particularly concerned about pseudomonad infections, since most strains of *Pseudomonas* are unusually resistant to antibiotic therapy.

table 11.8

Characteristics of the Gram-Negative Aerobic Rods and Cocci

Family	Morphology	Flagellar Arrangement	Distinctive Characteristics
Pseudomonadaceae	Rods	Polar (most)	Use a wide variety of chemical compounds as energy sources: are common inhabitants of soil and water; some are human, animal, or plant pathogens
Azotobacteraceae	Rods	Peritrichous, polar, or nonmotile	Are capable of fixing nitrogen nonsymbiotically; are common inhabitants of soil and water
Rhizobiaceae	Rods	Peritrichous or polar	Are capable of fixing nitrogen symbiotically; are common soil inhabitants
Methylococcaceae	Rods or cocci	Polar or nonmotile	Use 1-carbon compounds (methane, methanol, and formaldehyde) as sole carbon and energy sources
Halobacteriaceae	Rods or other forms (bent and swollen rods, clubs, ovoids, spheres, spindles, and other irregular forms)	Polar or nonmotile	Most require at least 2.5 M NaCl for growth
Acetobacteraceae	Rods	Peritrichous, polar, or nonmotile	Oxidize ethanol to acetic acid
Legionellaceae	Rods or filaments, 20 μm or more in length	Peritrichous, polar, or nonmotile	Are capable of causing pneumonia-like illness; are commonly found in streams, lakes, air-conditioning cooling towers, and evaporative condensers
Neisseriaceae	Cocci or Rods	Nonmotile	Cause gonorrhea (Neisseria gonorrhoeae), cerebrospinal meningitis, (Neisseria meningitidis), and other diseases of humans and animals

A few species of *Pseudomonas*, including *P. aeruginosa,* produce pigments that assist in identification. *P. aeruginosa* synthesizes two such pigments: pyoverdin and pyocyanin. Pyoverdin, a siderophore (see siderophore, page 88), is an unstable pigment that fluoresces upon excitation by ultraviolet irradiation. Pyocyanin is a blue phenazine pigment that diffuses freely into the surrounding medium. These two pigments give cultures of *P. aeruginosa* a characteristic blue-green fluorescent appearance.

Xanthomonas, another genus of the family *Pseumonadaceae,* is a common plant pathogen. The 1974 edition of *Bergey's Manual* condenses more than 100 of these plant pathogens into five species, including the species **Xanthomonas campestris.** Although this condensation may have been a rational taxonomic decision, it caused considerable confusion among plant pathologists who no longer could identify specific diseases with a specific bacterium. *Bergey's Manual of Systematic Bacteriology* corrects this problem by listing specific strains of *X. campestris* and their characteristics by the term **pathovar.** Among these is **X. campestris** pathovar **citri,** a highly infectious bacterium that causes citrus canker, a disease of citrus trees that is characterized by lesions on leaves and unsightly scabs on the fruit. *X. campestris* pathovar *citri* is not common in the United States, but causes endemic (habitually present within a geographical area) citrus disease in South America and the Far East. In 1984 citrus in Florida was affected by citrus bacterial leaf spot disease. This disease is similar to citrus canker, but is caused by a different pathovar of *X. campestris* (Figure 11.13).

Azotobacter and **Rhizobium** are gram-negative rods capable of fixing nitrogen nonsymbiotically or symbiotically, respectively. Rhizobia enter into symbiotic associations with leguminous plants (peas, beans, alfalfa, clover), causing characteristic root nodules to form during nitrogen fixation. Although azotobacters and rhizobia are aerobic organisms, their nitrogen-fixing enzymes are oxygen sensitive. These enzymes, called nitrogenases, remain active, apparently because the bacterial cells are able to reduce oxygen tensions in areas of the cytoplasm where the enzymes are located. An oxygen-binding protein called leghemoglobin is produced when rhizobia enter a symbiotic relationship with leguminous plants. This hemoglobinlike protein binds oxygen and removes it from the vicinity of nitrogenases (see nitrogen fixation, page 418). Azotobacters are large ovoid cells that probably have the highest respiration rate of any living organism. This high respiration rate undoubtedly contributes to the rapid removal of oxygen from the cytoplasm. Biological nitrogen fixation contributes significantly to the total quantity of fixed nitrogen added to the soil each year.

figure 11.13

Grapefruit Leaf Showing Distinctive Lesions of Citrus Bacterial Leaf Spot Disease Caused by *Xanthomonas campestris*

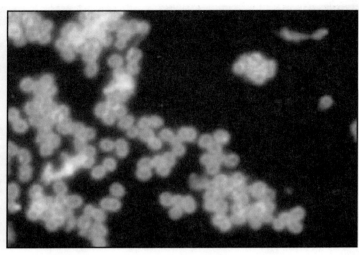

figure 11.14

Fluorescent Antibody Stain of *Neisseria gonorrhoeae,* Cause of Gonorrhea
Fluorescent antibodies bound to the gram-negative diplococci illuminate them against the dark background.

The family ***Methylomonadaceae*** consists of two genera of bacteria, ***Methylomonas*** and ***Methylococcus,*** which use 1-carbon compounds such as methane, methanol, and formaldehyde as sole carbon and energy sources. These bacteria are found in aerobic environments adjacent to areas where these compounds are located, such as natural gas deposits, coal formations, and anaerobic muds.

In the family ***Neisseriaceae*** is the bacterium ***Neisseria gonorrhoeae,*** which causes gonorrhea (Figure 11.14) (see gonorrhea, page 533). This sexually transmitted disease occurs in an estimated 1 million people in the United States annually. Gonorrhea affects all races and socioeconomic classes, male and female, and is so prevalent that it is considered endemic in the United States and many other countries. ***N. gonorrhoeae*** is a gram-negative aerobic coccus that is extremely fastidious and requires a moist environment for growth. Such environments are generally found in such areas of the human body as the conjunctiva, the nasopharynx, and the urogenital area. Thus it is not surprising that the transmission of *N. gonorrhoeae* occurs by sexual contact involving these areas. ***Neisseria meningitidis,*** another bacterium in this family, causes meningitis, particularly in children. Both pathogens are identified in the clinical laboratory as gram-negative, kidney bean–shaped pairs of cocci (diplococci). These organisms contain the enzyme cytochrome c oxidase, which is not present in many other bacteria (see oxidase test, page 166). The bacteria require increased levels of carbon dioxide (3% to 5%) and specialized media containing hemoglobin, vitamins, amino acids, and other nutrients for their growth and subsequent isolation.

Several other genera, in addition to genera of the eight recognized families, are found in this section of *Bergey's Manual* under the category "Other Genera." These bacteria have the common characteristics of this section (they are aerobic gram-negative rods or cocci) but are not easily classified under any of the eight recognized families. Such designations of bacteria are not uncommon in *Bergey's Manual;* in fact, they are used quite often to place certain bacteria in specific sections. Among the genera in this section are ***Brucella*** (the cause of infectious abortion in cattle), ***Bordetella*** (the causative agent of whooping cough), and ***Francisella*** (responsible for tularemia, an infectious disease of rabbits that is transmissible to humans who come in close contact with diseased animals).

table 11.9

Characteristics of Facultatively Anaerobic Gram-Negative Rods

Family	Representative Genera	Diseases or Characteristics
Enterobacteriaceae	Escherichia	Gastroenteritis, urinary tract infections
	Shigella	Bacillary dysentery
	Salmonella	Typhoid fever, gastroenteritis
	Klebsiella	Pneumonia, urinary tract infections
	Serratia	Opportunistic pathogen[a]
	Proteus	Urinary tract infections, opportunistic pathogen[a]
	Yersinia	Bubonic plague, diarrhea
Vibrionaceae	Vibrio	Cholera, gastroenteritis
	Aeromonas	Wound infections, meningitis, septicemia[b]
	Plesiomonas	Diarrhea
Pasteurellaceae	Pasteurella	Septicemia[b] (mice and rabbits)
	Haemophilus	Meningitis (especially in children)

[a]An organism that normally is nonpathogenic, but is capable of causing disease in a compromised host.
[b]An infection of the blood.

Facultatively Anaerobic Gram-Negative Rods

The organisms in the fifth section of Volume 1 of *Bergey's Manual* are called facultative anaerobes because they can respire or ferment carbohydrates and therefore can exist and grow in the presence or absence of oxygen. These gram-negative rods are divided into three families, **Enterobacteriaceae, Vibrionaceae,** and **Pasteurellaceae** (Table 11.9).

The family *Enterobacteriaceae* includes a number of significant human parasites, including **Escherichia, Salmonella, Shigella,** and **Yersinia. Escherichia coli,** a common inhabitant of the gastrointestinal tract and an organism frequently found in soil and water, is the most studied microbe in the scientific world. *E. coli* is frequently chosen for study because it is easily cultivated and grows rapidly in the laboratory, and much is already known about its genetics, physiology, and structure. It is considered by many to be the darling of molecular biology.

E. coli is the predominant facultative anaerobe in the large intestine. Normally *E. coli* is not a problem in the gastrointestinal tract and actually is beneficial to the human host, since it synthesizes some important vitamins (for example, vitamin K) and prevents growth of some potentially harmful bacteria by competing with them for nutrients and oxygen. However, under certain conditions, *E. coli* can cause disease—most notably gastroenteritis and urinary tract infections (see gastrointestinal diseases by *E. coli,* page 521). Some strains of *E. coli* that are enteroinvasive (invade the gastrointestinal tract) or enterotoxigenic (produce toxins that affect the intestines) cause short-term diarrheal illnesses. Such ill-nesses are especially common in infants in newborn nurseries and in travelers in countries having poor sanitary conditions, where contaminated drinking water or food cause what is often known as traveler's diarrhea. Enterohemorrhagic *E. coli* produces a toxin that causes hemolytic-uremic syndrome, which is characterized by lysis of erythrocytes and kidney failure. A 1993 oubreak of enterohemorrhagic *E. coli* infections affecting more than 400 people was traced to inadequately cooked hamburgers served by a fast-food restaurant chain.

E. coli is the most common cause of urinary tract infections in females (in males, the number one cause is *Proteus mirabilis*). Such infections generally affect elderly people with structural abnormalities in their urinary tract and women having gynecologic problems. Urinary tract infections persist until the obstruction is removed or the physical abnormality is corrected. *E. coli* and similar bacteria that ferment lactose are routinely used as indices of fecal contamination of water (see coliform, page 591). The presence of these bacteria in water suggests that other intestinal microbes, including pathogenic organisms, may also be present in the water.

Many other bacteria in the family *Enterobacteriaceae* are capable of causing human disease. **Shigella dysenteriae,** a non-motile gram-negative rod, invades the mucous membrane, causing bacillary dysentery. The genus **Salmonella** consists of a large group of bacteria divided into more than 1,700 serotypes, or serovars, on the basis of their antigenic characteristics. These bacteria have undergone several changes in taxonomic classification. *Bergey's Manual of Systematic Bacteriology* divides the sal-

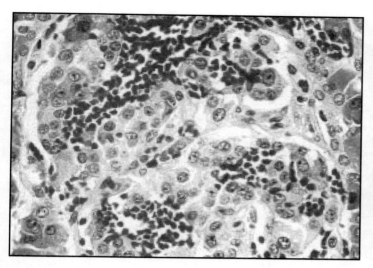

figure 11.15

Gram Stain of *Yersinia pestis* in the Pancreas of a Fatal Human Case of Plague

Gram-negative cells are seen throughout the tissue specimen.

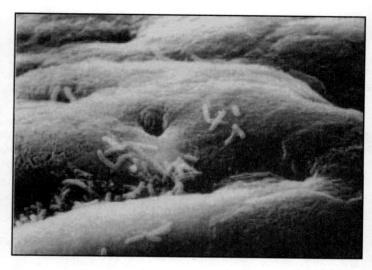

figure 11.16

Scanning Electron Micrograph of *Vibrio cholerae* Adhering to Intestinal Mucosa

Numerous curved cells of *V. cholerae* are visible on the intestinal surface (×4,260).

monellae into five subgenera, under which are listed the different serovars. Among the serovars of salmonellae are ***Salmonella typhi,*** which causes typhoid fever, and ***Salmonella typhimurium,*** the most common cause of *Salmonella*-induced gastroenteritis in humans.

Yersinia pestis, the agent responsible for the dreaded disease bubonic plague, is also a member of the family *Enterobacteriaceae* (Figure 11.15). This bacterium is named after the French bacteriologist Alexandre J.E. Yersin (1863–1943), who first isolated it from plague victims in Hong Kong in 1894. Plague is not as prevalent today as it was in the sixth century A.D., when it killed more than 100 million people during a 50-year period, and in the fourteenth century when it killed one-quarter of Europe's population and was known as the Black Death because of the many deaths and the black patchy hemorrhaging that quickly developed under the skin. Sporadic outbreaks still occur, however, especially in the Far East, and sporadic cases are reported in other areas of the world. In the western and southwestern United States, prairie dogs, rock squirrels, and wild rodents are the main reservoirs for *Y. pestis* and occasionally transmit the bacterium to a human host through bites or infected rat fleas.

 **Miscellaneous Bacteria**
Zoonoses: Yersinia • pp. 57–67

The family ***Vibrionaceae*** contains several human pathogens, most notably ***Vibrio cholerae.*** This gram-negative curved rod was first associated with cholera in 1883 by Robert Koch (1843–1910),

the German bacteriologist who isolated the bacterium from cholera patients during epidemics in Egypt and India (Figure 11.16). Unlike *Enterobacteriaceae* and many other bacteria, vibrios grow well in media of highly alkaline pH (pH 9.0). This characteristic is frequently used to isolate vibrios selectively from other microorganisms present in clinical specimens. *V. cholerae* is generally endemic in countries having poor sanitary conditions, but the bacterium has also been isolated in the United States, especially in waters along the Gulf coast. In recent years several cases have been documented of human illness and deaths in states along the Gulf coast from the ingestion of shellfish such as raw oysters contaminated with *V. cholerae* (see cholera, page 518). The extent of shellfish contamination and the public health relevance of such contamination with *V. cholerae* remains to be determined. *V. cholerae* is presently considered to be authochthonous (indigenous) to water. ***Vibrio vulnificus,*** a halophilic bacterium that is also associated with the ingestion of raw oysters, can cause septicemia (infection of the blood), wound infections, and gastroenteritis in people with compromised immune systems and liver disease. ***Vibrio parahaemolyticus,*** another halophilic bacterium, is a major cause of gastroenteritis in Japan and other countries where raw seafood is widely consumed. Other marine species of *Vibrio* are nonpathogenic and occur as normal flora in the gastrointestinal tracts of fish and other aquatic organisms.

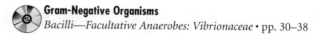 **Gram-Negative Organisms**
Bacilli—Facultative Anaerobes: Vibrionaceae • pp. 30–38

Using Flowcharts to Identify Bacteria

With the tens of thousands of bacteria found in *Bergey's Manual of Systematic Bacteriology*, all with their own traits, it may seem impossible for a person to identify bacteria in a patient specimen or an environmental sample. However, bacterial identification is not difficult if a logical scheme is followed to recognize species by their biochemical characteristics.

Such a scheme, or **flowchart,** is frequently used in diagnostic microbiology as a road map to differentiate bacteria and other microorganisms on the basis of a few key biochemical reactions. By using a few classical biochemical tests, the genus or, in some cases, the species of a bacterium can be determined.

An example of a flowchart that might be used to differentiate genera in the family *Enterobacteriaceae* is illustrated in Figure 11.17. Seven basic biochemical tests (phenylalanine deaminase, urease, citrate utilization, lysine decarboxylase, sucrose fermentation, H$_2$S production, and acetoin production as detected by the Voges-Proskauer test) are used for initial identification of *Enterobacteriaceae*. On the basis of the results from one or more of these tests, a preliminary identification of the suspect bacterium can be made. Additional tests can then be performed to speciate the microorganism.

Flowcharts do not replace the need for morphological observations or the performance of more specific tests, but they do simplify the identification of bacteria, particularly when the suspect bacterium is part of a large family such as the *Enterobacteriaceae*.

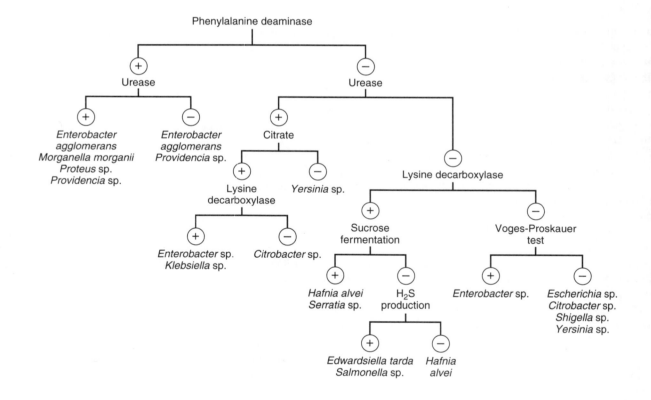

figure 11.17

Flowchart for Initial Identification of *Enterobacteriaceae* Based on a Few Key Biochemical Tests

table 11.10

Characteristics of Anaerobic, Gram-Negative Straight, Curved, and Helical Rods

Genus	Morphology	Major End Products of Fermentation
Bacteroides	Rods; nonmotile or motile by peritrichous flagella	Mixture of succinic, acetic, formic, lactic, and propionic acids
Fusobacterium	Rods; nonmotile	Butyric acid (major product); smaller amounts of acetic, propionic, formic, or lactic acid possible
Leptotrichia	Straight or slightly curved rods, with one or both ends pointed or rounded; nonmotile	Lactic acid (major product); small amounts of formic, acetic, or succinic acid possible
Butyrivibrio	Curved rods; polar or subpolar flagella	Butyric acid
Succinimonas	Short rods or coccobacilli; single polar flagellum	Succinic and acetic acids
Succinivibrio	Helical or spiral-shaped cells; single polar flagellum	Succinic and acetic acids
Anaerobiospirillum	Helical or spiral-shaped cells; bipolar tufts of flagella	Succinic and acetic acids
Wolinella	Helical, curved, or straight rods; single polar flagellum	Carbohydrates not fermented (hydrogen and formic acid used as energy sources)
Selenomonas	Crescent-shaped cells; tuft of flagella on side of cell	Propionic and acetic acids
Anaerovibrio	Slightly curved rods; single polar flagellum	Propionic and acetic acids
Pectinatus	Slightly curved rods; lateral flagella on only one side of cell	Propionic and acetic acids
Acetivibrio	Straight to slightly curved rods; single flagellum or multiple flagella on side of cell	Acetic acid
Lachnospira	Straight to slightly curved rods; single lateral to subpolar flagellum	Ethanol; carbon dioxide; hydrogen; formic, lactic, and acetic acids

Anaerobic, Gram-Negative Straight, Curved, and Helical Rods

Three sections of *Bergey's Manual* are devoted exclusively to anaerobic bacteria (bacteria that do not tolerate oxygen well and exist and grow best in its absence). The bacteria in the section on anaerobic gram-negative straight, curved, and helical rods form different fermentation products. The types of products formed and the morphology and flagellation of these organisms are characteristics used in their classification and identification (Table 11.10).

Many of these anaerobic organisms are found in the gastrointestinal tract or oral cavity of humans and other animals. How are anaerobic bacteria able to exist in body locations that are usually considered to be aerobic? Facultatively anaerobic bacteria in the gastrointestinal tract use up the available oxygen during cellular metabolism, leaving an oxygen-free environment. Anaerobic bacteria in the oral cavity are found primarily in areas of plaque and dense pockets of bacteria along the gingiva and periodontal membrane—sites in which anaerobic conditions prevail.

Contrary to popular opinion, *E. coli* is not the most common bacterium in normal human feces. **Bacteroides,** an anaerobic bacterium, and other obligately anaerobic bacteria outnumber facultative anaerobic bacteria in the colon by a ratio of 100 to 1 (Figure 11.18a). **Fusobacterium,** also an obligate anaerobe, is a common inhabitant of the mouth, where it may constitute a large proportion of the microbial population and may be involved in periodontal disease (Figure 11.18b).

Anaerobic bacteria are important agents of disease, particularly in patients with abscesses or puncture wounds. These provide the anaerobic conditions necessary for growth and multiplication. Foul-smelling discharges, gas formation in tissues, and tissue discoloration are clinical signs frequently associated with anaerobic infections. Many hospitals now recognize the clinical significance and prevalence of anaerobic infections and have bacteriology laboratories specifically equipped for the identification of these microbes.

Dissimilatory Sulfate- or Sulfur-Reducing Bacteria

The diverse group of anaerobic bacteria in the section of *Bergey's Manual* on dissimilatory sulfate- or sulfur-reducing bacteria use sulfur, sulfate, or other oxidized sulfur compounds as electron acceptors in anaerobic respiration (see anaerobic respiration, page 168). These bacteria live in anaerobic muds and sediments of freshwater, brackish water, and marine environments, as well as in the gastrointestinal tracts of animals and humans. The best-known genus in this group is **Desulfovibrio,** which can be found in polluted waters showing blackening and sulfide production. *Desulfovibrio* is a major problem in the oil industry, because it can corrode iron pipes. This bacterium is environmentally important, however, because it neutralizes acidic sulfur compounds such as sulfur dioxide, and thus mitigates the effects of pollution and has been used to help reduce acid mine wastes (see acid mine drainage, pages 580 and 583).

Anaerobic, Gram-Negative Cocci

The section in *Bergey's Manual* on anaerobic, gram-negative cocci is small and contains only three genera. These bacteria are all anaerobic, nonmotile, and found in the alimentary tract of humans and animals. **Veillonella,** a representative genus, has been isolated from dental abscesses and urinary tract infections. However, because it is always isolated along with other bacterial pathogens, its role in disease, if any, is unknown. Another bacterium in this group, **Acidaminococcus,** is able to use amino acids as sole energy sources for growth; most strains require several amino acids. The acidaminococci are frequently found in the intestinal tract of humans and animals, but are apparently not pathogenic.

The Rickettsias and Chlamydias

The organisms described in the rickettsiae and chlamydiae section of *Bergey's Manual* were for many years thought to be viruses rather than bacteria. They were mistakenly identified as viruses because they are small (most are 0.2 to 0.5 μm in diameter) and are obligate intracellular parasites. These organisms are now known to be bacteria. Rickettsiae and chlamydiae possess both DNA and RNA (viruses have only one type of nucleic acid), have cell walls similar to those found in gram-negative bacteria (viruses have a protein coat, but no cell wall), divide by binary fission (viruses assemble within a host after infection, but do not divide by binary fission), and are susceptible to antibiotics that affect bacteria (bacterial antibiotics are ineffective against viruses).

The genus **Rickettsia** contains several species that cause such diseases as Rocky Mountain spotted fever and different forms of typhus (Table 11.11). These diseases are transmitted by arthropod vectors and are characterized by body rashes and fever (see rickettsial diseases, page 529).

A second genus in this group, **Chlamydia,** is responsible for trachoma, the leading cause of blindness in the world. *Chlamydia* also causes the sexually transmitted disease lymphogranuloma

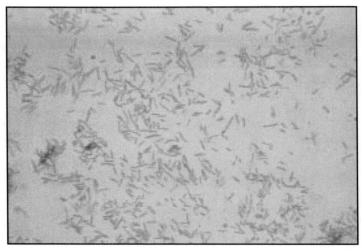

a.

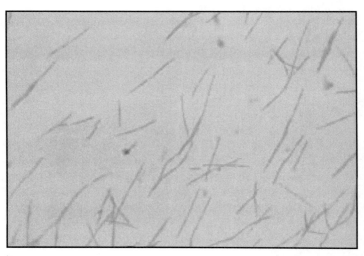

b.

figure 11.18
Gram-Negative Anaerobes
a. *Bacteroides.* b. *Fusobacterium.*

venereum (LGV) and is one of the agents responsible for nongonococcal urethritis (NGU), a generalized type of urethritis that is not associated with *Neisseria gonorrhoeae* (see nongonococcal urethritis, page 536). *Chlamydia* has a unique developmental cycle in which it alternates between a noninfectious form that reproduces by binary fission inside the cell and a smaller, dense-centered infectious form that is released upon cell death and lysis (see *Chlamydia* developmental cycle, page 430).

Diseases caused by rickettsiae and chlamydiae are difficult to diagnose in a bacteriology laboratory because these obligate intracellular parasites cannot be grown on artificial bacteriological media. Diagnosis is usually based on clinical symptoms and serological tests.

Miscellaneous Bacteria
Chlamydia • pp. 1–6

table	11.11

Diseases Caused by Rickettsiae and Chlamydiae

Family	Organism	Diseases	Vector or Mode of Transmission
Rickettsiaceae	*Rickettsia prowazekii*	Epidemic typhus	Human body louse
	Rickettsia typhi	Endemic typhus	Rat flea
	Rickettsia rickettsii	Rocky Mountain spotted fever	Tick
	Rickettsia tsutsugamushi	Scrub typhus	Mite
	Rochalimaea quintana	Trench fever	Human body louse
	Coxiella burnetii	Q fever	No known arthropod vector (transmitted by dust and food)
Chlamydiaceae	*Chlamydia trachomatis*	Trachoma	Use of common washing utensils
		Lymphogranuloma venereum (LGV)	Sexual intercourse
		Nongonococcal urethritis (NGU)	Sexual intercourse
	Chlamydia psittaci	Psittacosis	Contact with infected birds (parrots and parakeets)

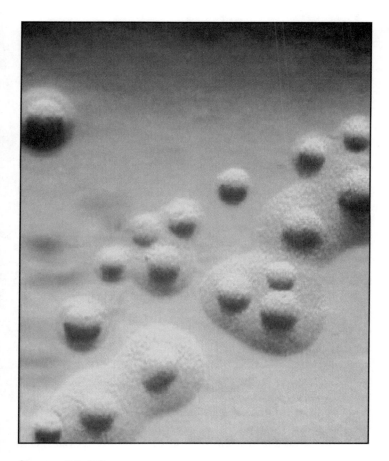

figure 11.19

Typical Fried Egg Appearance of *Mycoplasma pneumoniae* Colonies on Agar

Mycoplasmas from colonies 10 to 600 μm in diameter on solid media (×100).

The Mycoplasmas

The smallest free-living organisms known to humans are those of the genus **Mycoplasma.** Most rickettsiae, although smaller than *Mycoplasmas,* are obligate parasites and are not free-living. The mycoplasmas are not only small in size (125 to 250 nm in diameter), they also are the only bacteria that normally exist without a cell wall (see bacteria without cell walls, page 59). Unlike other bacteria, some mycoplasmas have sterols in their plasma membranes. These sterols provide the strength needed in the membranes to maintain cellular integrity without a wall. Mycoplasmas are unable to synthesize sterols and therefore must be provided with them in their growth media, a requirement usually met by growing mycoplasmas on media containing animal serum. On solid media, most mycoplasmas form very small colonies (10 to 600 μm in diameter) that have a fried egg appearance; an opaque, granular central area; and a flat, translucent peripheral zone (Figure 11.19).

Mycoplasma pneumoniae causes a disease known as primary atypical pneumonia (PAP), a mild form of pneumonia confined to the lower respiratory tract. Because mycoplasmas do not have cell walls, penicillin is ineffective in chemotherapy. Tetracycline, which inhibits protein synthesis, is recommended as the preferred antibiotic for treatment of PAP.

Miscellaneous Bacteria
Mycoplasma • pp. 1–6

Endosymbionts

A large number of microorganisms have been found to exist intracellularly as endosymbionts (microorganisms growing within the host cell) of other, larger organisms (see endosymbiosis, page 425). Many of these symbionts are bacteria; these have their own section of *Bergey's Manual* and include bacteria symbiotic with fungi, protozoa, insects, and other invertebrates.

Not much is known about these endosymbionts. Their growth requirements are difficult to duplicate in the laboratory, and only a few have been cultured. All of the endosymbionts seem to adapt well to the host environment, and many appear to benefit the host by providing it with necessary vitamins and other nutrients. Such symbiotic relationships lend support to the endosymbiont hypothesis, which describes the origin of mitochondria and chloroplasts in eucaryotes (see endosymbiont hypothesis, page 206). An example of an endosymbiont is *Lyticum flagellatum,* which is symbiotic for the ciliate protozoan *Paramecium tetraurelia*.

Gram-Positive Bacteria Other Than the Actinomycetes

The second volume of *Bergey's Manual of Systematic Bacteriology* describes the gram-positive Bacteria other than the actinomycetes. A diverse group of Bacteria is listed in this volume, including cocci, endospore-forming bacteria, filamentous forms, and irregularly shaped bacteria (Table 11.12).

Gram-Positive Cocci

The gram-positive cocci include bacteria that innocuously inhabit the human body as well as those that cause many different types of diseases.

Bacteria of the genus *Staphylococcus* are found in many parts of the human body. The external areas of our body are colonized with the nonpathogenic species, *Staphylococcus epidermidis.* This species does not cause any major problems to the host but is a nuisance when it contaminates clinical cultures taken from other areas of the body. *Staphylococcus aureus,* another species in the same genus, is pathogenic, causing such human diseases as impetigo, osteomyelitis, and toxic shock syndrome (see staphylococcal diseases, page 526). It is also one of the most common causes of food poisoning in the United States (see staphylococcal food intoxication, page 518). Staphylococci are gram-positive bacteria typically arranged as clusters of cocci and can be distinguished from the chain-forming streptococci (Figure 11.20). Staphylococci also produce the enzyme catalase, whereas streptococci do not.

Members of the genus *Streptococcus* are responsible for a number of different diseases, including streptococcal pharyngitis (strep throat), bacterial pneumonia, rheumatic fever, scarlet fever, endocarditis, and necrotizing fasciitis (the so-called flesh-eating disease) (see streptococcal diseases, page 498). Both staphylococcal and streptococcal diseases are frequently characterized by pus for-

table 11.12

Gram-Positive Bacteria Other Than the Actinomycetes

Section	Major Characteristics
Gram-positive cocci	Chemoorganotrophic, mesophilic, non-spore-forming cocci
Endospore-forming gram-positive rods and cocci	Mostly gram-positive motile rods; many commonly found in the soil; all form endospores
Regular, nonsporing gram-positive rods	Chemoorganotrophic, mesophilic, non-spore-forming rods
Irregular, nonsporing gram-positive rods	Bacteria that may exhibit club-shaped forms, rod/coccus cycles, filamentous forms, or other unusual cell morphologies
The Mycobacteria	Rod-shaped to filamentous bacteria with unusually large quantities of lipids in cell envelopes; stain acid fast
Nocardioforms	Aerobic bacteria that form mycelia; frequently have large amounts of lipids in cell envelopes and stain acid fast

mation, so these bacteria are often described as *pyogenic cocci.* *Neisseria* are also pyogenic cocci, causing pus-forming diseases such as gonorrhea and meningitis. Staphylococci and streptococci are distinguished from organisms of the genus *Micrococcus,* which are frequently present on normal skin. Micrococci utilize glucose by respiration, whereas staphylococci and streptococci ferment glucose. Staphylococci and streptococci produce a variety of enzymes and toxins that aid in invasion and infection of the host (see staphylococcal and streptococcal enzymes and toxins, pages 448 and 498).

Ruminococcus, another gram-positive coccus, is a normal inhabitant of animal rumens, where it is important in cellulose digestion. Without this bacterium, ruminants would not be able to use hay and grass as food (see ruminants, page 427).

Endospore-Forming Gram-Positive Rods and Cocci

The bacteria in the next section of *Bergey's Manual* all are gram-positive and form endospores (Figure 11.21). The genus *Bacillus* consists of organisms that are frequently found in the soil. *Bacillus anthracis* causes anthrax in animals and humans. Other species of *Bacillus* are producers of important antibiotics such as polymyxin and bacitracin (see antibiotics, page 126), biological pesticides (see biological pesticides, page 585), and industrial enzymes (see industrial microbial enzymes, page 623).

The genus *Clostridium* consists of anaerobic sporeformers that are responsible for a number of human diseases, including botulism (see botulism, page 517), gas gangrene, and tetanus. Clostridia are inhabitants of the intestinal tracts of animals, sewage, and soil. These bacteria ferment a wide variety of organic compounds such as proteins, purines, alcohols, and many different types of polysaccharides (see cellulose and chitin degradation, page 575).

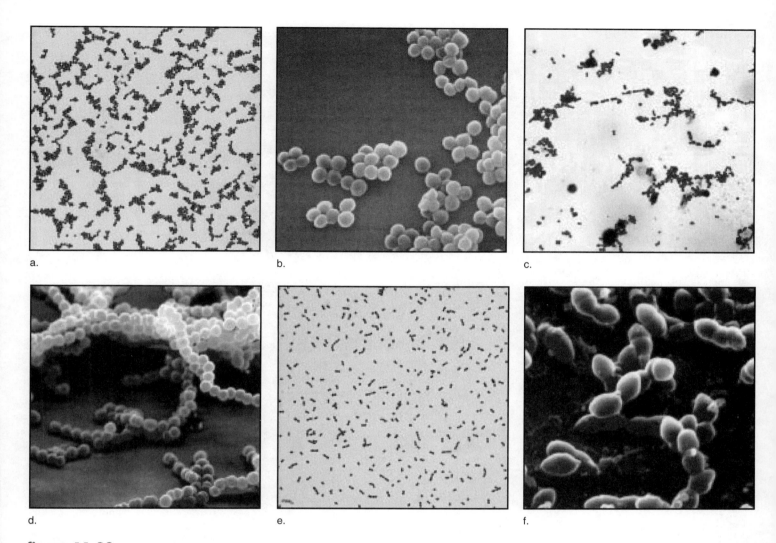

figure 11.20

Representative Gram-Positive Cocci

a. *Staphylococcus aureus,* Gram-stained smear (×400). b. Clusters of staphylococci, scanning electron micrograph (colorized, ×10,000). c. *Streptococcus lactis,* carbolfuchsin stain (×400). d. Chains of strep-tococci, scanning electron micrograph (colorized, ×6,500). e. *Streptococcus pneumoniae,* Gram-stained smear (×322). f. *Streptococcus pneumoniae,* scanning electron micrograph (colorized, ×17,000).

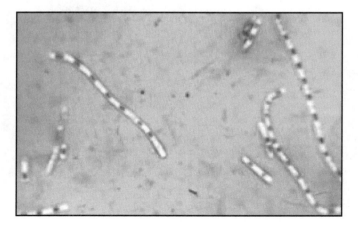

figure 11.21

Spore Stain of *Bacillus subtilis,* Showing Central Endospores Stained Red (×1,000)

Bacillus spores are hardy and have been known to survive dormant in the soil for many years. In 1995 an extraordinary discovery was reported by the microbiologist Raúl Cano and graduate student Monica Borucki at California Polytechnic State University at San Luis Obispo. These two scientists claimed that they had successfully revived bacillus spores from the digestive tract of an amber-encased stingless Dominican bee, *Proplebeia dominicana*, that existed 25 to 40 million years ago (Figure 11.22). Abdominal tissue from the fossil bee was aseptically removed and inoculated into trypticase soy broth. Within two weeks the bacillus spores germinated

Revival of 25-Million-Year-Old Procaryotes?

and produced viable vegetative cells. After extensive analysis of the microbe's DNA and comparison of its ribosomal gene sequences with the sequences of genes from other procaryotes, including about 50 different bacillus species, Cano and Borucki concluded that this ancient procaryote most closely resembled the modern *Bacillus sphaericus*.

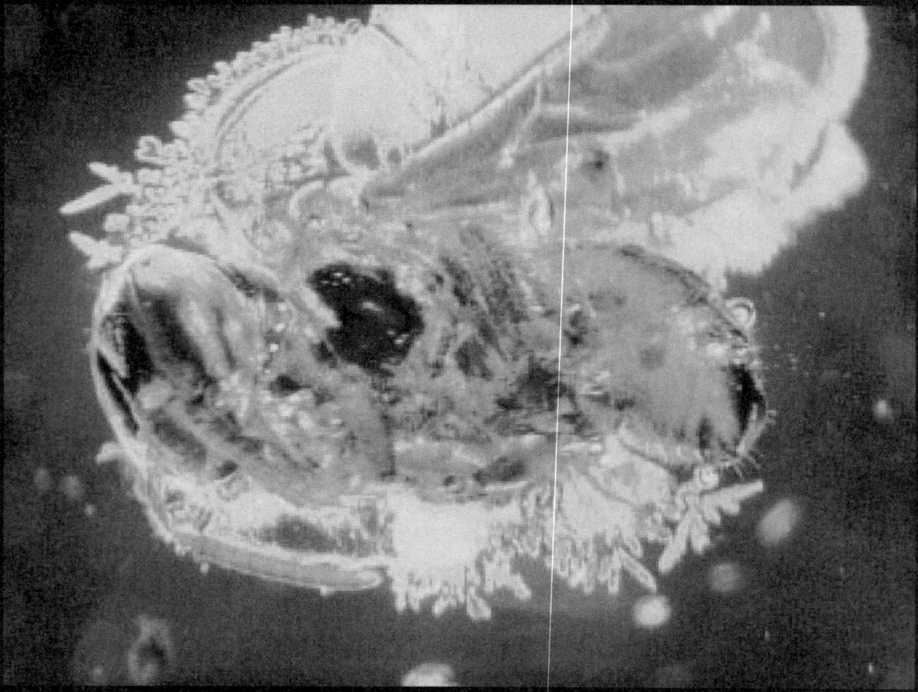

Skeptics questioned whether this isolated microorganism may actually have been a present-day bacillus introduced into the bee by laboratory contamination. Although Cano and Borucki used careful techniques to avoid contamination, including working in a clean laboratory hood and checking for contamination by trying to grow microbes from other pieces of the amber, some scientists feel that contamination is difficult to avoid.

If Cano and Borucki's finding is proven to be true, it would eclipse the previous documented record for longest spore survival—70 years for spores stored in ampules by Louis Pasteur and revived in 1956. Amber—the sticky, honey-colored, translucent tree resin that encases fossil lifeforms—may be the reason for this long-term survival of spores. As amber hardens, it becomes waterproof and virtually airtight. Together with the ability of bacterial spores to survive adverse conditions (see endospores, page 68), the amber provides a hardened crypt for the entombed microbe. The recovery of viable ancient procaryotes has potential scientific and industrial value for unique drugs, natural pesticides, and microbial enzymes that are not produced by present-day microbes. Furthermore, nucleic acid analysis of such organisms may provide useful information on the rates of evolutionary change in genes.

figure 11.22
Amber-Encased Stingless Dominican Bee
Viable spores resembling *Bacillus sphaericus* were revived from the digestive tract of a bee similar to the one illustrated.

table 11.13

Roles of *Lactobacillus* in the Food Industry

Organism	Product That Bacterium Is Used To Prepare
L. acidophilus	Acidophilus milk
L. brevis	Green olives, pickles
L. bulgaricus	Bulgarian milk, kefir, mozzarella cheese, Parmesan cheese, Swiss cheese, yogurt
L. casei	Cheddar cheese
L. helveticus	Swiss cheese
L. lactis	Swiss cheese
L. plantarum	Cheddar cheese, green olives, pickles, sauerkraut

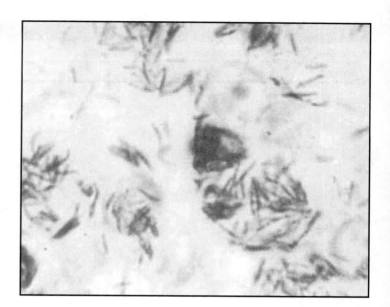

figure 11.23

Acid-Fast Stain of *Mycobacterium leprae*, Showing Retention of the Carbolfuchsin Dye by the Acid-Fast Bacteria

Regular, Nonsporing Gram-Positive Rods

Lactobacillus is the primary genus in the section of *Bergey's Manual* on non-spore-forming, gram-positive rods of regular shape. Lactobacilli are frequently associated with cattle and are found in dairy products. As their name implies, lactobacilli form lactic acid (and other products) from carbohydrate metabolism, and consequently tolerate pHs as low as 5. This resistance to acid is useful in the selective isolation of these bacteria from among other less-acid-resistant bacteria on media of low pH. *Lactobacillus* is normally part of the human vaginal flora, where it competes with and inhibits other members of the flora such as yeasts (*Candida albicans*). This competition reduces the chances for vaginal yeast infections (see microbial antagonism, page 440). Lactobacilli are used extensively in the food industry for the preparation of yogurt, cheeses, sauerkraut, and pickles (Table 11.13) (see food microbiology, page 610). In the past, streptococci, which also produce lactic acid, were included with the lactobacilli in a group called lactic acid bacteria. The streptococci and lactobacilli are now distinguished from each other on the basis of their cell morphologies.

Irregular, Nonsporing Gram-Positive Rods

The next section of *Bergey's Manual* includes non-spore-forming, gram-positive rods of irregular shape, ranging from straight rods to club-shaped forms. Included in this group are some human pathogens and industrially important bacteria.

The childhood disease diphtheria, characterized by the formation of a pseudomembrane in the throat, is caused by the bacterium ***Corynebacterium diphtheriae*** (see diphtheria, page 507). Corynebacteria [Greek *coryne*, club] are easily identified by their distinctive club-shaped morphology and grouping of cells to form arrangements resembling Chinese letters. This unusual arrangement is caused by a snapping cell division in which cells do not completely separate after binary fission. Cells of *Corynebacterium* also contain stainable polyphosphate granules, which can

be an aid in identification. Most corynebacteria are not pathogenic and are found as part of the normal flora in the nasopharynx and on the skin. The term **diphtheroid** (coryneform) is used to describe gram-positive pleomorphic bacteria that resemble *C. diphtheriae* in morphology but are less virulent (see diphtheroids, page 498).

The genus ***Arthrobacter***, which is widely distributed in soils, is included in this group. *Arthrobacter* cells have an unusual life cycle in which there is a change from rod-shaped cells to coccoid cells. The coccoid cells appear during the stationary growth phase and are referred to as arthrospores.

Propionibacterium, another bacterium in this section, produces propionic acid and carbon dioxide during cellular metabolism. The acid and the gas are responsible for the unique flavor and holes seen in Swiss cheese (see cheese production, page 611). Propionibacteria have morphologies ranging from rods to club-shaped forms.

The Mycobacteria

The mycobacteria section of *Bergey's Manual* contains only one genus: ***Mycobacterium***. Mycobacteria are rod-shaped to filamentous bacteria that have unusually large quantities of lipids in their cell envelopes; up to 60% of the envelope's dry weight consists of lipids as compared with only 2% normally in other bacteria. This characteristic makes mycobacteria extremely resistant to destaining by acid-alcohol and easily identifiable by this acid-fast trait (Figure 11.23). The high lipid content of the envelope is responsible for the slow growth rate of mycobacteria and their resistance to most ordinary bactericides. Mycobacteria are found in soil, water, animals, and humans. In humans they cause a wide variety of diseases, including leprosy (see leprosy, page 527), tuberculosis (see tuberculosis, page 510), and respiratory ailments.

table 11.14

The Archaea, Cyanobacteria, and Remaining Gram-Negative Bacteria

Section	Major Characteristics
Anoxygenic phototrophic bacteria	Bacteria that contain bacteriochlorophyll, do not produce oxygen during photosynthesis, have only one photosystem, and can use light as an energy source
Oxygenic photosynthetic bacteria	Bacteria that contain chlorophylls, produce oxygen during photosynthesis, have two photosystems, and can use light as an energy source
Aerobic chemolithotrophic bacteria and associated organisms	Bacteria that utilize inorganic compounds as an energy source or that oxidize metals or deposit metals on their cell surfaces
Budding and/or appendaged bacteria	Bacteria that reproduce by budding, by the production of appendages, or by a combination of the two
Sheathed bacteria	Bacteria that form an external sheath around chains of cells
Nonphotosynthetic, nonfruiting gliding bacteria	Nonfruiting gliding bacteria that may exist as rods or filaments
Fruiting gliding bacteria: the myxobacteria	Fruiting gliding bacteria that may have a complex developmental cycle in which cells aggregate to form fruiting bodies
Archaea	Procaryotes that are phylogenetically distinct from Bacteria and are distinguished from them by their unusual rRNA structure, different RNA polymerase, membrane lipid composition, mechanism of protein synthesis, and lack of muramic acid in the cell wall

The Archaea, Cyanobacteria, and Remaining Gram-Negative Bacteria

The procaryotes in Volume 3 of *Bergey's Manual* have diverse types of metabolism and unusual structures (Table 11.14). They include the Archaea, cyanobacteria, and remaining gram-negative Bacteria. Some of these procaryotes use light as a source of energy (phototrophic), whereas others obtain their energy from inorganic compounds (chemolithotrophic). There are gliding, budding, stalked, and sheathed bacteria. The Archaea include procaryotes that live in extreme environments and are phylogenetically distinct from other procaryotes.

Anoxygenic Phototrophic Bacteria

Bacteria that use light as an energy source are called phototrophs [Greek *phot,* light, *trephein,* to nourish]. Anoxygenic phototrophic bacteria differ from photosyntheic plants and the oxygenic photosynthetic bacteria (the cyanobacteria) because they: (1) have bacteriochlorophylls instead of chlorophylls as their photosynthetic pigments; (2) do not produce oxygen during photosynthesis; and (3) possess only one photosystem in comparison to the two photosystems (photosystems I and II) that are found in the cyanobacteria (see photosynthesis, page 186). Many of the phototrophic bacteria are also autotrophs (able to use CO_2 as a sole source of carbon).

The anoxygenic phototrophic bacteria stain gram negative and are divided into two major groups on the basis of their pigmentation: purple bacteria and green bacteria (Table 11.15). The green bacteria have an array of photosynthetic pigments (bacteriochlorophylls c, d, e, and some a) different from that of the purple bacteria (bacteriochlorophylls a and b). The photosynthetic apparatus of the green bacteria is located in specialized cylindrical vesicles called chlorosomes, which underlie and are attached to the plasma membrane. The photosynthetic machinery of the purple bacteria, in comparison, is contained within elaborate internal membranes found in the cell cytoplasm. In addition to their major pigments, the purple and green bacteria may be pigmented in shades of brown, orange, and yellow.

table 11.15

Anoxygenic Phototrophic Bacteria

Group	Family/Subgroup	Genera
Purple bacteria	Chromatiaceae	Chromatium
		Thiocystis
		Thiospirillum
		Thiocapsa
		Lamprobacter
		Lamprocystis
		Thiodictyon
		Amoebobacter
		Thiopedia
	Ectothiorhodospiraceae	Ectothiorhodospira
	Purple nonsulfur bacteria	Rhodospirillum
		Rhodopila
		Rhodobacter
		Rhodopseudomonas
		Rhodomicrobium
		Rhodocyclus
Green bacteria	Green sulfur bacteria	Chlorobium
		Prosthecochloris
		Pelodictyon
		Ancalochloris
		Chloroherpeton
	Multicellular, filamentous, green bacteria	Chloroflexus
		Heliothrix
		Oscillochloris
		Chloronema
Genera incertae sedis		Heliobacterium
		Erythrobacter

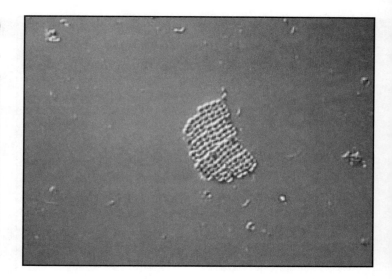

figure 11.24

Nomarski Differential Interference Contrast Micrograph of *Thiopedia rosea*, a Photosynthetic Purple Sulfur Bacterium that Grows in Sheets

Both the purple and green bacteria are further subdivided on the basis of their metabolism. Purple sulfur bacteria (***Chromatiaceae*** and ***Ectothiorhodospiraceae***) use sulfur compounds such as H_2S as electron donors in photosynthesis (Figure 11.24). As H_2S is oxidized, sulfur granules accumulate as globules inside the bacterial cell (*Chromatiaceae*) or outside the cell (*Ectothiorhodospiraceae*). In the past the purple sulfur bacteria were distinguished from the purple nonsulfur bacteria (for example, ***Rhodospirillum***) because of this sulfur metabolism. Recent studies, however, have shown that the purple nonsulfur bacteria, although not able to utilize elemental sulfur, do use sulfide at low concentrations. The purple nonsulfur bacteria also oxidize organic acids, alcohols, and other organic molecules.

The green bacteria are divided into two groups: green sulfur bacteria and multicellular, filamentous, green bacteria. Most green sulfur bacteria can oxidize simple organic molecules for phototrophic growth, provided that a reduced sulfur compound is also available as a sulfur source. ***Chloroflexus***, a multicellular, filamentous, green bacterium, is versatile and able to grow heterotrophically in the dark under aerobic conditions, as well as phototrophically in the light.

Phototrophic bacteria are generally found in anaerobic aquatic environments, where reduced compounds (compounds that contain extra electrons and are normally more stable in environments without oxygen) are readily available as sources of electrons for photosynthesis. These bacteria must reside in habitats close enough to the water surface to allow light penetration for photosynthesis. In contrast, the cyanobacteria and algae photosynthesize aerobically. Electrons for these photosyntheses are derived from the photolysis of water, resulting in the release of oxygen.

Oxygenic Photosynthetic Bacteria

The oxygenic photosynthetic bacteria include the **cyanobacteria** [Greek *kyanos*, blue] and the **prochlorophytes.** Members of this group became part of the chloroplasts in photosynthetic eucaryotic cells, according to the endosymbiont hypothesis. These microbes fit phylogenetically into the Bacteria tree, and molecular analysis indicates that chloroplasts, cyanobacteria, and the prochlorophytes shared a common ancestor.

Cells of cyanobacteria resemble the cells of other bacteria because they have a cytoplasm surrounded by a plasma membrane and cell wall, but no membrane-enclosed nucleus (Figure 11.25).

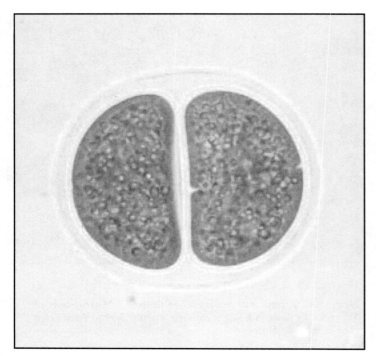

a.

figure 11.25

Cyanobacteria

a. Bright-field micrograph of *Chroococcus turgidus*, showing cells remaining together with a surrounding sheath following cell division (×300). b. Phase-contrast micrograph of *Spirulina*, showing the helical structure of this oscillatorian cyanobacterium (×300).

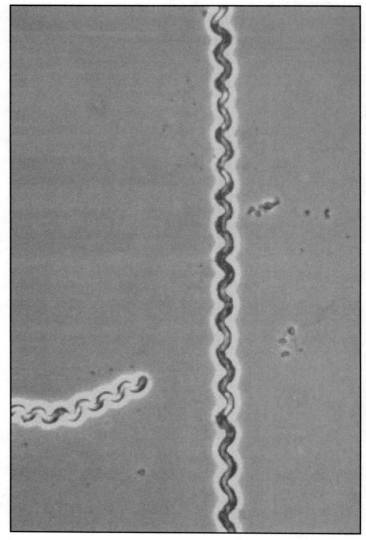

b.

The cyanobacterial cell wall is composed of murein (peptidoglycan) and several additional amino acids. External to the wall is a sheath of slimy material that the organism uses for gliding motility along solid surfaces. The cyanobacteria have photosynthetic saclike membranes (thylakoids) resembling those of eucaryotic plants and algae, but the thylakoids are not segregated from the cytoplasm by a membrane. The cyanobacteria do have chlorophylls and a light-gathering photosystem that parallel similar pigments and systems in photosynthetic eucaryotes. However, all the other characteristics of these organisms strongly indicate that they are procaryotes, not eucaryotes.

The cyanobacteria are a large heterogeneous group of microorganisms (approximately 150 genera with 1,500 species). Like other bacterial groups, they are found in many habitats. The Red Sea is so named because of the red color imparted by occasional blooms of **Oscillatoria,** a cyanobacterium. Some cyanobacteria exist in thick mats in water beneath the ice in Antarctica, and they even grow in the fur of polar bears, giving the fur a green tint. Other cyanobacteria are found in hot springs and desert soils. Thick mats of dome-shaped, layered chalk deposits called stromatolites, consisting of cyanobacteria bound to calcium carbonate, occur in a few places such as shallow pools of water in hot, dry climates (Figure 11.26). Fossilized stromatolites, dated at over 3 bil-

lion years old, contain the remains of ancient cyanobacteria and indicate that these microbes played an important evolutionary role in the introduction of oxygen to the atmosphere of the earth.

Although sometimes called blue-green bacteria, the cyanobacteria display a variety of colors, including red, brown, yellow, dark purple, and even black. This color range results from the presence of different photosynthetic pigments, including chlorophyll a, carotenoids, and phycobilins. Even though cyanobacteria are phototrophic, a few are able to grow slowly in darkness by using carbohydrates as sources of energy and carbon.

Many of the cyanobacteria are able to fix nitrogen to ammonia. Consequently these microbes are often found in symbiosis with other organisms in such areas as bare rock and soil. The genus *Oscillatoria,* containing organisms that are common inhabitants of seas, contributes extensively to fixation of atmospheric nitrogen. Nitrogen fixation by cyanobacteria generally occurs within heterocysts, enlarged cells usually found along the filament. The thick-

figure 11.26
Stromatolites
Stromatolites consist of cyanobacteria bound to calcium carbonate to form domed structures like the ones illustrated.

table	11.16

Classification of Cyanobacteria

Family	Major Characteristics
Chroococcaceae	Unicellular rods or cocci; reproduction by binary fission or budding
Pleurocapsaceae	Single cells enclosed in a fibrous layer; reproduction by multiple fission
Oscillatoriaceae	Vegetative cells in trichomes[a]; reproduction by trichome fragmentation
Nostocaceae	Vegetative cells or heterocysts in nonbranching trichomes; reproduction by trichome fragmentation; can form akinetes[b]
Stigonemataceae	Vegetative cells or heterocysts in branching trichomes; reproduction by trichome fragmentation; can form akinetes

[a] a strand or chain of cells
[b] a vegetative cell that is transformed into a resistant spore

walled heterocysts appear to be resting stages of vegetative cells and lack photosystem II, which is associated with oxygen evolution. Consequently the oxygen-labile nitrogenase enzyme is stable and active, and nitrogen fixation is possible within the heterocysts.

The cyanobacteria have three different types of cellular organization: unicellular, colonial, and filamentous. Unicellular forms exist as single cells that are either free-living or attached to rocks, walls, and other organisms. Colonial forms arise when dividing cells adhere to one another. Filaments are formed when cell division occurs in only one direction (unbranched) or in several directions (branched). These filaments form large masses that sometimes exceed 1 m in length. The individual cells of cyanobacteria, however, are typically 0.5 to 60 μm in diameter. Reproduction occurs by cell division in unicellular forms and by fragmentation in colonial and filamentous forms. Some species form resistant resting cells (akinetes) for protection against environmental extremes such as low temperatures or desiccation.

Classification of the cyanobacteria is relatively simple. There are five families: *Chroococcaceae, Pleurocapsaceae, Oscillatoriaceae, Nostocaceae,* and *Stigonemataceae* (Table 11.16). The *Chroococcaceae* are unicellular rods or cocci that reproduce by binary fission or budding. The *Pleurocapsaceae* consist of single cells enclosed in a fibrous layer. Unlike the *Chroococcaceae,* these cyanobacteria reproduce by multiple fission. Numerous small coccoid daughter cells, called baeocytes, form as a result of this division. Oscillatorian cyanobacteria form long filamentous strands, called trichomes, containing vegetative cells. Reproduction is by fragmentation of the trichomes. Cyanobacteria of the families *Nostocaceae* and *Stigonemataceae* form trichomes containing vegetative cells and also heterocysts. In some instances, heterocysts can differentiate into akinetes (Figure 11.27).

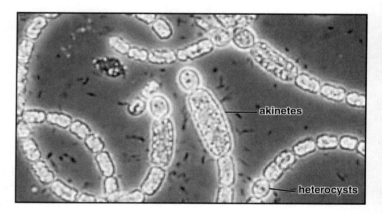

figure 11.27
Phase-Contrast Micrograph of the Cyanobacterium *Nostoc,* Showing Akinetes and Heterocysts

The prochlorophyta are similar to the cyanobacteria, except for three distinguishing characteristics: (1) The prochlorophyta contain chlorophyll b in addition to chlorophyll a, (2) they do not have phycobilins and therefore appear bright green instead of blue-green, and (3) they have thylakoids with double membranes (unlike the single membranes in cyanobacterial thylakoids). There are two recognized genera of prochlorophytes. One is *Prochloron,* a spherical, single-celled organism that lives as an extracellular symbiont of marine vertebrates; it has not yet been cultured. The other is *Prochlorothrix,* a free-living cylindrical organism that forms filaments; it has been grown in pure culture and is found in Dutch lakes. There are also prochlorophytes that

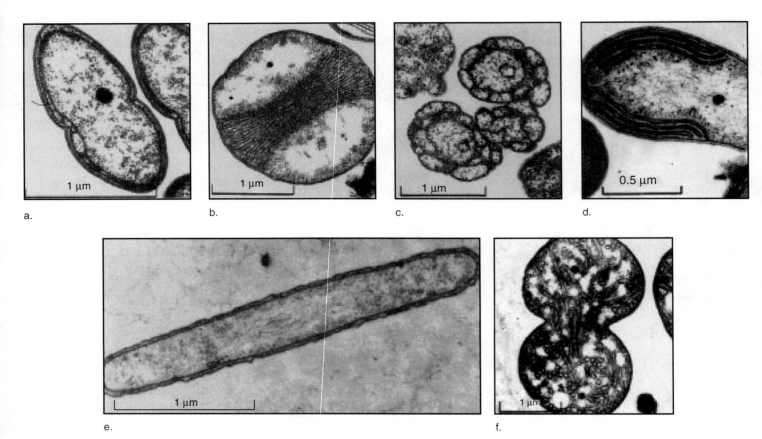

figure 11.28
Nitrifiers

a. Electron micrograph of *Nitrosomonas europaea*, showing peripheral cytomembranes (×32,000). b. Electron micrograph of *Nitrosococcus oceanus*, showing cytomembranes arranged as flattened lamellae in the center of the cell (×22,500). c. Electron micrograph of *Nitrosolobus multiformis*, showing its lobular shape and cytomembranes that partially compartmentalize the cell (×22,500). d. Electron micrograph of *Nitrobacter winogradskyi*, showing polar cap of peripheral cytomembranes (×41,000). e. Electron micrograph of *Nitrospina gracilis*, showing the absence of extensive cytomembranes found in other nitrifiers but the presence of small bleb-like intrusion of the plasma membrane (×37,500). f. Electron micrograph of *Nitrococcus mobilis*, showing tubular type of cytomembranes extending throughout the cytoplasm (×16,000).

are found free-living in open ocean waters and are referred to as picoplankton. These organisms are thought to be important ecologically as the primary producers in these waters.

Aerobic Chemolithotrophic Bacteria and Associated Organisms

Chemolithotrophic organisms utilize inorganic compounds as an energy source, an activity that is unique to bacteria (see chemolithotrophy, page 171). *Bergey's Manual* divides the chemolithotrophs into five groups: (1) nitrifiers, (2) colorless sulfur bacteria, (3) obligate hydrogen oxidizers, (4) iron and manganese oxidizing and/or depositing bacteria, and (5) magnetotactic bacteria.

The nitrifiers are bacteria that oxidize ammonia to nitrite and nitrite to nitrate in two separate stages. Nitrosofying bacteria such as **Nitrosomonas, Nitrosospira, Nitrosococcus,** and **Nitrosolobus** oxidize ammonia to nitrite. The nitrite can then be oxidized to nitrate by the true nitrifying bacteria (**Nitrobacter, Nitrospina,** and **Nitrococcus**). Both types of bacteria are required for the complete oxidation of ammonia to nitrate. Many of the nitrifiers have complex and distinctive internal membrane systems that are involved in ammonia or nitrite oxidation (Figure 11.28). Nitrifiers are found in soil, freshwater, and marine environments that are rich in ammonia, nitrite, and other inorganic salts.

Microorganisms that oxidize reduced sulfur compounds to sulfate are frequently found in acid environments, where the pH of

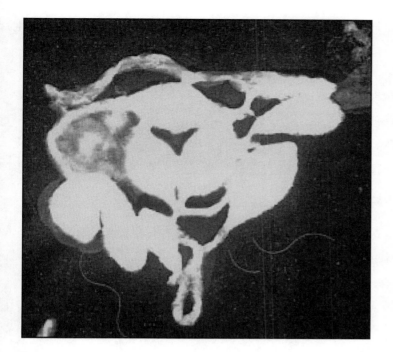

figure 11.29
Hyphomicrobium
Electron micrograph of *Hyphomicrobium*, showing hyphae and terminal buds (colorized, ×9,000).

the environment is lowered by the sulfuric acid that is produced by the oxidation. An example of a sulfur-oxidizing bacterium is *Thiobacillus ferrooxidans,* which is used in mining operations to recover valuable metals from sulfur-containing ores (see leaching of metals, page 582). *Hydrogenobacter,* an example of an obligate hydrogen oxidizer, uses H_2 as an electron donor and O_2 as an electron acceptor to produce H_2O from the reduction of O_2 with H_2.

Bacteria that oxidize metals or deposit metals on their cell surfaces use organic compounds as a source of energy and are not chemolithotrophs. Nonetheless, they are included with the chemolithotrophs because they are not easily placed in any other section of *Bergey's Manual.* This group includes such bacteria as *Siderocapsa* [Greek *sidero,* iron] *Siderococcus,* and *Naumanniella.* These bacteria are found in iron-bearing waters, where their cells are encrusted with iron, manganese oxides, or both.

Magnetotactic bacteria (for example, *Aquaspirillum*) demonstrate directed movement in a magnetic field, a phenomenon called **magnetotaxis** (see magnetotaxis, page 65). These bacteria synthesize intracellular crystals of magnetite (Fe_3O_4) arranged as chains along the long axis of the cell. These chains of magnetite serve as internal magnets to orient the cell along a specific magnetic line. Although the function of magnetotaxis is

unknown, it has been suggested that such behavior may direct these microaerophilic, aquatic bacteria downward along magnetic lines, away from oxygen-enriched surface waters and toward the more anaerobic sediments.

Budding and/or Appendaged Bacteria

Although most bacteria reproduce by binary fission, some do not. The bacteria in the section of *Bergey's Manual* on budding and/or appendaged bacteria reproduce by budding, by the production of appendages, or by a combination of the two. Unlike the nonliving stalks of the myxobacteria (see gliding, fruiting bacteria, page 338), the buds and appendages formed by these bacteria are usually direct cytoplasmic extrusions of the cell, called **prosthecae.** The prosthecae provide the bacterium with a greater surface area for the absorption of nutrients from the surrounding environment.

An example of a budding bacterium is **Hyphomicrobium** [Greek *hyphe,* thread], which forms buds at the tips of filamentous outgrowths (hyphae) of the cell (Figure 11.29). As each bud matures, it synthesizes a flagellum and breaks away from the parent cell. This daughter cell eventually loses its flagellum, forms its own hyphae, and repeats the budding process.

Bacteria of the genus **Caulobacter** [Latin *caulis,* stalk] reproduce in a different manner. These microbes attach themselves to a solid surface by a stalk that is an extension of the cell, with a wall, membrane, and cytoplasm. Not infrequently, several cells may adhere to each other by the bases of their stalks to form rosettes. Cell division in *Caulobacter* commences with the elongation of the cell at the end opposite the point of surface attachment. As the cell elongates, the newly formed portion develops a flagellum and the flagellated cell is released into the environment. This flagellated swarmer cell eventually loses its flagellum and replaces it with a stalk that anchors the bacterium to the solid surface. The life cycle is then repeated. *Caulobacters* are generally found in aquatic environments that have low levels of organic matter. In these environments, the stalk serves not only as an anchor, but also as additional surface area for the absorption of limited nutrients. In fact, the length of the stalk increases dramatically when nutrient supply (especially phosphorus) is limited.

Sheathed Bacteria

The sheathed bacteria are gram-negative cells, often arranged as chains within filaments surrounded by outer sheaths composed of proteins, polysaccharides, and lipids (Figure 11.30). These organisms are usually found in aquatic environments, particularly slow-running, fresh water contaminated with sewage or wastewater, where the organisms' sheaths may become encrusted with iron or manganese oxides. In some instances the sheaths have an adhesive holdfast that is used for attachment to solid surfaces.

Members of the genus **Sphaerotilus,** an example of the sheathed bacteria, are nutritionally versatile and widespread in nature. These bacteria use a variety of organic acids and sugars as sources of carbon and energy. They frequently are found in activated sludge (a product of sewage treatment), where they can cause a detrimental condition called bulking. In this phenomenon, tangled filaments of bacteria increase the bulk of the sludge so that it does not properly settle during wastewater treatment.

The sheathed bacteria reproduce by binary fission, with the release of motile daughter cells called **swarmer cells** from one end of the sheath. Swarmer cells migrate and eventually form their own filaments.

Nonphotosynthetic, Nonfruiting Gliding Bacteria

The nonphotosynthetic, nonfruiting gliding bacteria have no flagella, but they exhibit gliding motility. Gliding bacteria include those that form fruiting bodies (see the next section) and those that do not form fruiting bodies (this section). They move across solid surfaces either on a slime layer deposited by the cell or on small rotating protein particles, acting like ball bearings, which lie between the plasma membrane and the outer envelope of these gram-negative bacteria.

Nonfruiting gliding bacteria of the genus *Cytophaga* have the unusual ability to digest such compounds as cellulose, chitin, and agar, using extracellular enzymes synthesized by the bacteria. Some *Cytophaga* are pathogens of fish, causing such diseases as fin rot, tail rot, and bacterial gill disease.

Beggiatoa, Thiothrix, and *Leucothrix* are examples of gliding bacteria having long filaments. These organisms live in aquatic environments rich in H_2S (sulfur springs, decaying seaweed beds, and waters heavily polluted with sewage). For energy, the H_2S is oxidized to elemental sulfur, which is deposited as granules inside the filaments (Figure 11.31).

Fruiting Gliding Bacteria: The Myxobacteria

The fruiting gliding bacteria move by gliding and often produce colorful fruiting bodies. This section consists of only one order of bacteria: *Myxobacterales.*

The *Myxobacterales* have complex developmental cycles. Under certain environmental conditions that are not well-defined but generally associated with nutrient limitation, the rod-shaped vegetative cells of these bacteria aggregate to form a colorful structure visible to the naked eye, called the **fruiting body** (Figure 11.32). This represents the resistant, or resting, stage of the bacterium, and either lies on the surface of the ground or is raised above it on a stalk of slime. Contained within the fruiting body are resistant cells called **myxospores.** As the fruiting body matures, it ruptures and releases the myxospores into the environment. The mature myxospores germinate and give rise to vegetative cells.

Myxobacteria are soil organisms found in abundant numbers in environments containing rich organic matter. Their distinctive and strikingly colorful fruiting bodies are frequently seen on tree barks, decomposing plant material, and manure.

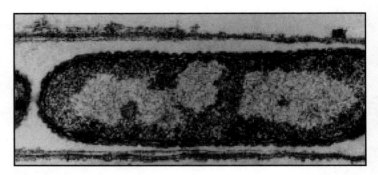

figure 11.30
Sheathed Bacteria
Electron micrograph of *Sphaerotilus natans,* showing cell enclosed by a sheath. The sheath is composed of a lipoprotein-lipopolysaccharide complex external to the cell wall (×36,000).

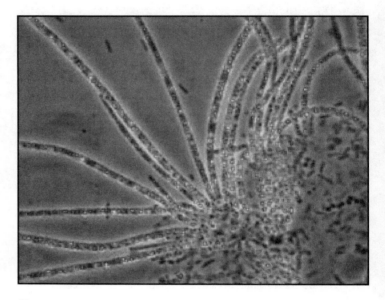

figure 11.31
Gliding Bacteria
Phase-contrast micrograph of *Thiothrix,* showing long filaments and bright sulfur granules inside the cells (×1,000).

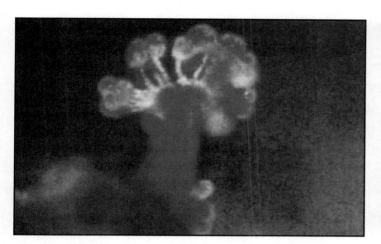

figure 11.32
Colorful Fruiting Body of the Myxobacterium *Stigmatella aurantiaca*

Archaea

The Archaea are a group of organisms distinguished from other procaryotes by their unusual rRNA structure, different RNA polymerase, plasma membrane lipid composition, mechanism of protein synthesis, and absence of peptidoglycan in the cell wall. The phylogenetic relationship of these unique procaryotes to the Bacteria and the Eucarya was described earlier in this chapter.

The Archaea Are Diverse in Their Morphology and Physiology

The Archaea are a diverse group of procaryotes, ranging morphologically from cocci to rods to spiral-shaped cells. They consist of gram-positive and gram-negative cells, with diameters ranging from 0.1 to over 15 μm. The Archaea can be aerobic, facultatively anaerobic, or anaerobic. Some are organotrophs, while others are autotrophs. Their habitats extend from deep sea, geothermally heated vents and hot sulfur springs (the extreme thermophiles) to the rumens and intestinal systems of animals, and the anaerobic sediments of lakes, swamps, and bogs (the methanogens) to marine salterns and salt lakes like the Great Salt Lake in Utah and the Dead Sea between Israel and Jordan (the extreme halophiles) (Figure 11.33).

None of the Archaea have muramic acid or D-amino acids in their cell walls, chemical molecules that are characteristic of the peptidoglycan in the Bacteria. Consequently penicillin, which inhibits the transpeptidation step in peptidoglycan synthesis (see peptidoglycan synthesis, page 56), is ineffective against these procaryotes. A pseudopeptidoglycan is formed in some Archaea, notably *Methanobacterium, Methanothermus,* and *Methanobrevibacter,* but consists of alternating repeats of *N*-acetylglucosamine and *N*-acetyltalosaminuronic acids and L-amino acids (not the D-amino acids found in traditional peptidoglycan). The *N*-acetylglucosamine and *N*-acetyltalosaminuronic acids are linked by lysozyme-resistant β(1,3) bonds instead of the lysozyme-sensitive β(1,4) bonds found in peptidoglycan of the Bacteria.

a.

b.

c.

figure 11.33
Habitats of Archaea

a. Hot sulfur spring, a common habitat for the thermoacidophile *Sulfolobus.* b. Boiling springs and geysers in Yellowstone National Park. c. Great Salt Lake, Utah, a habitat for *Halobacterium* and other extreme halophiles.

table 11.17

The Archaea

Group	Representative Genera	Major Characteristics
Methanogenic Archaea	Methanobacterium Methanobrevibacter Methanococcus Methanolobus Methanomicrobium Methanosarcina Methanospirillum Methanothermus	Strictly anaerobic; chemoautotrophic or chemoheterotrophic, with methane always the product of metabolism; produce coenzyme F_{420} and methanopterin
Sulfate reducers	Archaeoglobus	Strictly anaerobic; chemolithotrophic or chemoorganotrophic growth; autotrophic growth occurs with thiosulfate and H_2; produce coenzyme F_{420} and methanopterin
Extremely halophilic Archaea	Halobacterium Halococcus Haloferax Natronobacterium Natronococcus	Aerobic, although some can grow anaerobically in the presence of nitrate; chemoheterotrophic; require at least 1.5 M NaCl for growth; some members are alkalophilic, growing only at pH>8.5
Cell wall-less Archaea	Thermoplasma	Obligately thermophilic; obligately acidophilic; facultatively anaerobic; chemoorganotrophic
Extremely thermophilic S^0-metabolizers	Desulfurolobus Pyrococcus Pyrodictium Sulfolobus Thermococcus Thermoproteus	Obligately thermophilic; acidophilic or neutrophilic; chemoautotrophic or chemoheterotrophic; most are sulfur metabolizers

Halobacterium, some methanogens (for example, *Methanolobus*), and several extreme thermophiles (for example, *Sulfolobus, Pyrodictium*, and *Thermoproteus*) have cell walls made of glycoprotein, whereas certain methanogens (for example, *Methanococcus* and *Methanomicrobium*) have cell walls composed exclusively of protein.

The plasma membranes of the Archaea are chemically unique. They lack fatty acids and have the branched chain hydrocarbon isoprene attached to glycerol by ether (instead of ester) linkages. However, their membranes have polar and nonpolar orientations and form lipid bilayers similar to the membranes of the Bacteria and the Eucarya. The difference in membrane lipids of the Archaea may be associated with the extreme environments of these procaryotes. Branched chain hydrocarbons may impart greater mechanical strength and chemical resistance to the membranes of such Archaea as *Sulfolobus* (an extreme thermophile that grows in sulfur-rich hot acid springs) and *Halobacterium* (an extreme halophile).

The Archaea Are Separated into Five Groups in Bergey's Manual

The Archaea are divided into five groups in *Bergey's Manual*: the methanogenic Archaea, the sulfate reducers, the extremely halophilic Archaea, the Archaea lacking cell walls, and

the extremely thermophilic elemental sulfur metabolizers (Table 11.17).

The methanogenic Archaea are strict anaerobes that oxidize compounds such as H_2 or formate for energy and use carbon dioxide as an electron acceptor to produce methane (CH_4). Methanogens are found in anaerobic environments such as swamps, marshes, and the intestinal tract of animals. **Methanobacterium** and **Methanosarcina** are examples (Figure 11.34). It is generally believed that methanogenic procaryotes were the predominant organisms on a primitive earth that contained a large amount of carbon dioxide and little or no oxygen.

Only one genus, **Archaeoglobus**, is currently recognized as a sulfate reducer. This organism, isolated from marine hydrothermal vents, is unique among the Archaea in its ability to use sulfate as an electron acceptor. Cells of *Archaeoglobus* grow at temperatures as high as 92°C with an optimum of 83°C. Interestingly, *Archaeoglobus* produces coenzyme F_{420} and methanopterin, two coenzymes found in methanogenic Archaea and associated with methane production. Phylogenetically, *Archaeoglobus* lies between the methanogens and the extremely thermophilic elemental sulfur metabolizers, and may be an intermediate link between these two groups.

The extremely halophilic Archaea require high concentrations of NaCl for survival. These organisms, which include **Halobacterium** and **Halococcus**, are generally found in high-salt

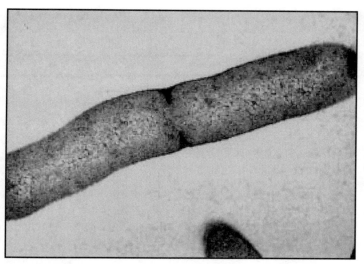

a.

b.

figure 11.34

Methanogenic Archaea

a. Electron micrograph of *Methanobacterium thermoautotrophicum,* a thermophile, in the process of division (×30,000). b. Electron micrograph of *Methanosarcina barkeri.* Cells of the organism remain attached in sarcinoid colonies, reaching 2 to 3 mm in diameter. Dark spots are polyphosphate granules inside the cells (×10,000).

habitats such as the Dead Sea, the Great Salt Lake, and salt-drying beds formed by the evaporation of seawater in shallow ponds. Halophilic procaryotes are able to tolerate the high-salt content of these environments because their enzymes have adapted to require a high-salt concentration for activity. In fact, the ribosomes, cell wall proteins, and other cell constituents of these bacteria require high-salt environments for stability.

Thermoplasma is a cell wall-less procaryote that grows in coal refuse piles. These piles contain iron pyrite (FeS), coal fragments, and organic by-products of coal mining operations that become very hot and acidic through spontaneous combustion and leaching of the organic compounds. *Thermoplasma,* a thermoacidophile that grows optimally at 55°C and pH 2, thrives in this environment where it apparently uses the organic compounds leached from the coal. The plasma membrane of *Thermoplasma* contains a chemically unique lipopolysaccharide composed of a tetraether lipoglycan containing glucose and mannose units. Together with membrane glycoproteins, this and other membrane molecules enable *Thermoplasma,* without a cell wall, to withstand the low pH and high temperature of its environment. Phylogenetically, *Thermoplasma* more closely resembles the methanogen/extreme halophile branch of the Archaea phylogenetic tree than the extremely thermophilic sulfur metabolizer branch.

The extremely thermophilic Archaea include three orders (***Thermococcales, Thermoproteales,*** and ***Sulfolobales***) and at least nine genera. Many of the microorganisms in this group are acidophilic and sulfur metabolizers. ***Thermococcus*** and ***Pyrococcus,*** members of the order *Thermococcales,* are obligate anaerobes that grow near deep-sea hydrothermal vents. Both are chemoorganotrophs that grow on proteins, starch, and other organic matter and use elemental sulfur (S⁰) as an electron acceptor, reducing it to H_2S during anaerobic respiration. ***Thermoproteus*** has similar metabolic properties as *Thermococcus* and *Pyrococcus.* It is an anaerobic chemoorganotroph that can use S⁰ as an electron acceptor, but it can also grow chemolithotrophically on H_2. *Thermoproteus* grows at temperatures ranging from 60°C to 96°C and at pH values between 1.7 and 6.5, and is found in sulfur-rich, hot, aquatic environments such as hot springs. ***Sulfolobus,*** a member of the order *Sulfolobales,* is a thermoacidophile that grows best at temperatures of 75°C to 85°C and pH values between 2 and 3. *Sulfolobus* is an obligate aerobe capable of oxidizing S⁰ or H_2S to H_2SO_4, and of fixing CO_2 to organic forms of carbon. *Sulfolobus* is also able to grow chemoorganotrophically. It is generally found in hot sulfur springs and similar habitats.

The Actinomycetes

The fourth volume of *Bergey's Manual* contains Bacteria called the actinomycetes—a category with an extremely large number of organisms, as is evident because they make up an entire volume. This volume is divided into eight sections, including a section on nocardioform actinomycetes that is repeated, with two additional genera, from Volume 2 (Table 11.18). The actinomycetes [Greek *aktis,* a ray, beam, *mykes,* fungus] are gram-positive bacteria that are rod-shaped or form branching filaments that in some genera develop into a mycelium. A common property of the actinomycetes is the high G + C content (≥52 mole%) of their DNA, which separates these organisms from other procaryotes containing DNA with lower G + C contents. For a long time, these microbes, because of their similarities to both the bacteria and the fungi, were considered

table 11.18

The Actinomycetes

Section	Genera	Major Characteristics
Nocardioform actinomycetes	Nocardia Rhodococcus Nocardioides Pseudonocardia Oerskovia Saccharopolyspora Faenia (Micropolyspora) Promicromonospora Intrasporangium Actinopolyspora Saccharomonospora	Aerobic bacteria that form mycelia; frequently have large amounts of lipids in their cell envelopes; stain acid fast
Actinomycetes with multilocular sporangia	Geodermatophilus Dermatophilus Frankia	Bacteria that produce branching filaments that divide by longitudinal and transverse septa, giving rise to coccoid-like elements
Actinoplanetes	Actinoplanes Ampullariella Pilimelia Dactylosporangium Micromonospora	Bacteria in which spores are produced within spore vesicles or sporangia
Streptomyces and related genera	Streptomyces Streptoverticillium Kineosporia Sporichthya	Aerobic bacteria that are highly oxidative and form extensive branching substrate and aerial mycelia
Maduromycetes	Actinomadura Microbispora Microtetraspora Planobispora Planomonospora Spirillospora Streptosporangium	Bacteria that contain the sugar madurose in their cell walls
Thermomonospora and related genera	Thermomonospora Actinosynnema Nocardiopsis Streptoalloteichus	Mesophilic and thermophilic bacteria with cell walls containing *meso*-diaminopimelate and no other characteristic sugars or amino acids; produce spores (not endospores) that may be borne on substrate and aerial hyphae
Thermoactinomycetes	Thermoactinomyces	Thermophilic bacteria with cell walls containing *meso*-diaminopimelate and no other characteristic sugars or amino acids; single spores are borne on hyphae and have the typical structure of endospores
Other genera	Glycomyces Kibdelosporangium Kitasatosporia Saccharothrix Pasteuria	

to be intermediates of the two groups. They are now considered to be bacteria because of their procaryotic properties.

Actinomycetes systematics has undergone many changes in the last 20 years. The current division of the actinomycetes in *Bergey's Manual* separates these bacteria on the basis of such characteristics as cell wall structure and composition, spore production, and temperature resistance. Representative examples of actinomycetes are described here.

Nocardia is a nocardioform actinomycete that is widely distributed in water and soil, but can also cause pulmonary and tissue infections in animals and humans. The nocardioform actinomycetes are aerobic bacteria that form mycelia, or masses of hyphae (see hyphae, page 361). In most instances, the hyphae fragment to form rod-shaped or coccoid cells. Like mycobacteria, nocardioforms frequently have large amounts of lipids in their cell envelopes and therefore are also acid fast.

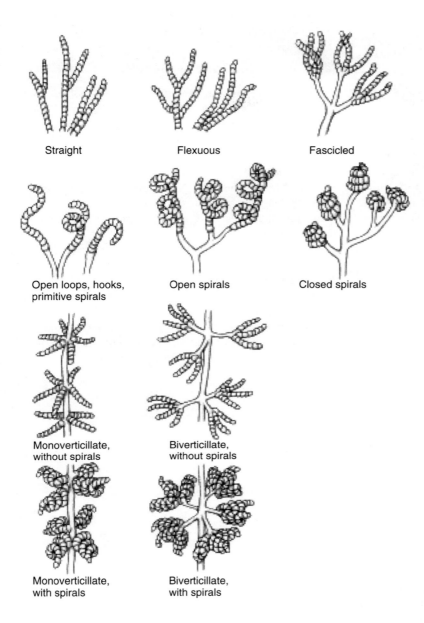

Straight

Flexuous

Fascicled

Open loops, hooks, primitive spirals

Open spirals

Closed spirals

Monoverticillate, without spirals

Biverticillate, without spirals

Monoverticillate, with spirals

Biverticillate, with spirals

figure 11.35

Conidia Arrangements of Aerial Mycelia in the Streptomyces

Dermatophilus is a pathogen that causes skin infections, usually in the hooves of cattle, sheep, and similar animals. The lesions result in a pustular dermatitis that eventually becomes crusty. Human infection is rare. Dermatophili are short, branched, and filamentous, with the filaments dividing by longitudinal and transverse septa. Filament septation leads to the formation of coccoid-like bodies that mature into zoospores.

Frankia is a nitrogen-fixing symbiont of plants such as the alder, Australian pine, bayberry, sweet fern, and autumn olive. These organisms produce nodules on the roots of these plants and fix nitrogen by a mechanism similar to that used by *Rhizobium*. Like *Dermatophilus*, *Frankia* forms branching filaments with transverse and longitudinal septation.

Actinoplanes is a bacterium that forms extensive mycelia, with spores contained within sporangia. The spores are flagellated and may be spherical, ovoid, club-shaped, or cylindrical. Actinoplanes are present in most soils and are especially abundant in soils with a neutral pH. These organisms are capable of producing secondary metabolites (see secondary metabolites, pages 204 and 629), and in recent years some species have been used in the production of new antibiotics (see antibiotics, page 125).

Streptomyces comprises a large group of bacteria that are important in antibiotic production and as soil organisms. More than 300 species of *Streptomyces* have been characterized, and many of these produce antibiotics such as streptomycin, tetracycline, chloramphenicol, and erythromycin. In the soil, streptomyces produce exoenzymes that degrade polysaccharides (starch, cellulose, pectin, and chitin), proteins, fats, and other large molecules. Metabolites (geosmins) of streptomyces are responsible for the distinctive aroma of soil. Streptomyces form aerial mycelia that give rise to asexual reproductive spores called conidia (Figure 11.35). The aerial mycelia allow airborne dispersion of these spores.

The maduromycetes are actinomycetes that contain the sugar madurose (3-O-methyl-D-galactose) in their cell walls. *Streptosporangium,* a genus in this group, forms single or clustered sporangia on aerial mycelia. Nonmotile spores are released as the sporangia rupture. Streptosporangia are a significant component of the actinomycete population in soil.

Mesophilic and thermophilic actinomycetes with cell walls containing *meso*-diaminopimelate and no other characteristic sugars or amino acids are placed into two groups: (1) thermomonospora and related genera and (2) thermoactinomycetes. Members of both groups form spores on aerial hyphae. However, spores produced by *Thermoactinomyces* contain calcium dipicolinate and have the typical structure of endospores. Most *Thermoactinomyces* species have a growth temperature range of 30°C to 60°C, with an optimum growth temperature of 50°C. *Thermoactinomyces* organisms are commonly found in natural high-temperature habitats such as leaf and compost heaps and overheated stores of hay, grain, and other plant materials.

One of the most intriguing discoveries in recent years has been the detection of sulfur-oxidizing chemoautotrophic bacteria living in apparent symbiosis with marine invertebrates in deep-sea hydrothermal vents (Figure 11P.1). These vents are located at depths of 2,500 m and lower and are fed with H_2S-rich waters having temperatures as high as 350°C. Similar symbioses have been postulated for bacteria and invertebrates living in marine muds and salt marsh sediments. In 1983 Collen Cavanaugh of Harvard University and the Marine Biology Laboratory at Woods Hole reported on the symbiotic association of chemoautotrophic bacteria with a marine bivalve, *Solemya velum* Say (phylum Mollusca), collected from eelgrass beds near Woods Hole, Massachusetts.

Cavanaugh analyzed *S. velum* and another bivalve, *Geukensia demissa* (Dillwyn) obtained from creek banks in Little Sippewussett Salt Marsh, Falmouth, Massachusetts, for the presence and activity of chemoautotrophic bacteria by five parameters: (1) ribulose-1,5-diphosphate (RuDP) carboxylase activity, (2) transmission electron microscopy, (3) epifluorescence microscopy, (4) lipopolysaccharide assays, and (5) sulfide and thiosulfate enhancement of CO_2 fixation. The two bivalves were used in the study because both had access to the materials required for sulfur-based chemoautotrophic metabolism: CO_2, O_2, and reduced inorganic sulfur compounds.

RuDP carboxylase activity was detected only in the gill tissue of *S. velum* (Figure 11P.2). Because RuDP carboxylase is a key enzyme in CO_2 fixation, its absence in *G. demissa* gill tissue indicated that RuDP carboxylase activity in *S. velum* was not due to contamination by phytoplankton or free-living chemoautotrophic bacteria.

Transmission electron microscopy of *S. velum* gill tissue sections showed the presence of intracellular rod-shaped bacteria (Figure 11P.3). These were also seen by epifluorescence microscopy of gill tissue homogenates of *S. velum* stained with acridine orange, a nucleic-acid–specific stain. Approximately 1.2×10^9 bacteria per gram wet weight were present in gill tissue, as determined by direct counts of fluorescent-stained cells. The bacteria were not seen in gill tissue preparations of *G. demissa*.

S. velum gills were found to contain 1,000 times more lipopolysaccharide (2 µg/g wet weight) than *G. demissa*. Because lipopolysaccharide occurs in the outer membrane of gram-negative bacteria, its presence in large quantities in *S. velum* gills was indicative of bacteria.

^{14}C-labeled CO_2 incorporation in *S. velum* gill tissue was enhanced in the presence of Na_2S and $Na_2S_2O_3$, whereas little or no enhancement occurred in *G. demissa* tissue (Table 11P.1). These data suggested the presence of chemoautotrophic bacteria in *S. velum* tissue.

These observations by Cavanaugh indicated that chemoautotrophic bacteria existed in symbiosis with the marine bivalve *S. velum* and may be important in the nutrition of this invertebrate. Furthermore, the data suggest that such associations are possible and may also occur around sulfide-rich deep-sea hydrothermal vents (Figure 11P.4). It is now known that sulfur-oxidizing chemoautotrophs such as *Thiobacillus* and *Thiovulum* are the bacteria observed by Cavanaugh. The presence of these bacteria in such unusual environments is indicative of the diversity of procaryotes.

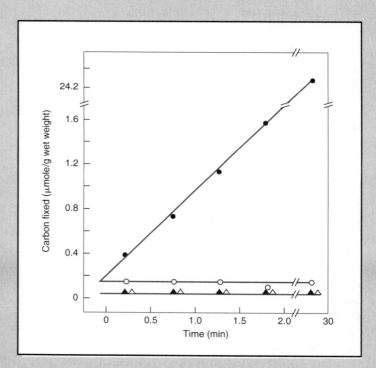

figure 11P.2

Time Course of RuDP-dependent CO_2 Fixation in Cell-free Extracts of the Gill Tissues of *Solemya velum* and *Geukensia demissa*

RuDP-dependent CO_2 fixation is an indication of RuDP carboxylase activity. ● = *S. velum* gill tissue with RuDP added; ○ = *S. velum* gill tissue with no added RuDP; ▲ = *G. demissa* gill tissue with RuDP added; △ = *G. demissa* gill tissue with no added RuDP.

figure 11P.1

Mussel Bed in the Vicinity of a Hydrothermal Vent

Chemoautotrophic bacteria live in close association with the mussels and other marine invertebrates in this community.

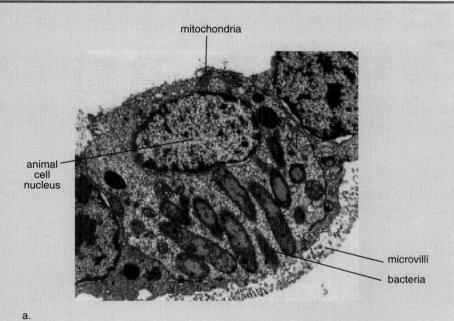

mitochondria

animal cell nucleus

microvilli

bacteria

a.

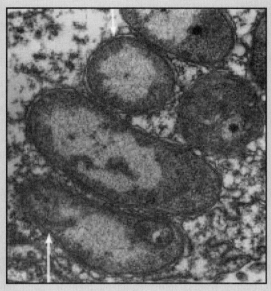

b.

figure 11P.3

Transmission Electron Micrographs Showing Bacteria in Gill Tissue Cells of *Solemya velum*

a. Transverse section of gill filament showing rod-shaped bacteria within an animal cell (×4,600). b. Higher magnification showing oblique and transverse sections of rod-shaped bacteria. Arrows point to an outer unit membrane, possibly that of the host animal cell, surrounding the bacteria (×28,500).

table 11P.1

Rates of Carbon Dioxide Fixation in Gill Tissue of *Solemya velum* and *Geukensia demissa*

Organism	Sulfur Compound	+ Sulfur	− Sulfur
Solemya velum	0.2 mM Na₂S	4.50	0.70
		4.60	0.49
	1.0 mM Na₂S₂O₃	6.50	0.57
		8.30	0.43
		9.10	0.35
Geukensia demissa	0.2 mM Na₂S	0.13	0.08
		0.18	0.09
	1.0 mM Na₂S₂O₃	0.10	0.08
		0.10	0.09

Note: Data are expressed as micromoles of CO_2 fixed per gram wet weight per hour. Whole gills (*S. velum*) or pieces of gill (*G. demissa*) were incubated in filtered seawater containing radiolabeled $NaH^{14}CO_3$. After 3 hrs of incubation, gill tissues were solubilized and radioactivity determined. Values are given for each of several experiments.

Source

Cavanaugh, C.M. 1983. Symbiotic chemoautotrophic bacteria in marine invertebrates from sulphide-rich habitats. *Nature* 302:58–61. Reprinted by permission from *Nature*, Vol. 302, No. 5903, pp. 58–61, ©1983 Macmillan Journals Limited.

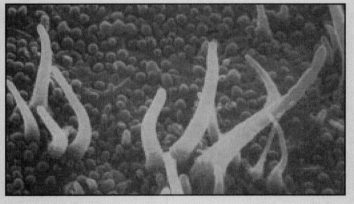

figure 11P.4

Microbial Mats of Deep-Sea Vent Bacteria

A variety of different forms are shown, including cocci, rods, and filaments, in this scanning electron micrograph of a mixed population of chemoautotrophic bacteria from the Galápagos Rift vents (colorized, ×6,000).

References

Grassle, J.F. 1985. Hydrothermal vent animals: Distribution and biology. *Science* 229:713–725.

Ruby, E.G., and H.W. Jannasch. 1982. Physiological characteristics of *Thiomicrospira* sp. L-12 isolated from deep-sea hydrothermal vents. *Journal of Bacteriology* 149:161–165.

Ruby, E.G., C.O. Wirsen, and H.W. Jannasch. 1981. Chemolithotrophic sulfur-oxidizing bacteria from the Galápagos Rift hydrothermal vents. *Applied and Environmental Microbiology* 42:317–324.

1. Phylogeny is the study of evolutionary relationships among organisms. All living organisms can be separated into one of three domains on the basis of their 16S rRNA sequence: Bacteria, Archaea, and Eucarya.

2. Three major approaches are used to identify and place microorganisms in classification systems. The classical approach is based primarily on structural and morphological characteristics and secondarily on biochemical and physiological traits. Numerical taxonomy groups microorganisms based on their similarities. Molecular approaches compare nucleic acid sequences among organisms.

3. *Bergey's Manual of Systematic Bacteriology* provides bacteriologists with a guide to the classification and identification of most bacteria. It groups procaryotes into four categories: gram-negative Bacteria of general, medical, or industrial importance (Volume 1); gram-positive Bacteria other than the actinomycetes (Volume 2); the Archaea, cyanobacteria, and remaining gram-negative Bacteria (Volume 3); and the actinomycetes (Volume 4).

4. The spirochetes are slender, winding, or helically coiled bacteria that are motile by periplasmic flagella (also called axial fibrils or axial filaments) wrapped around the cell.

5. The bacteria in the second section of Volume 1 of *Bergey's Manual* are rigid, helical to vibrioid cells that move by conventional polar flagella.

6. The third section of Volume 1 of *Bergey's Manual* consists of gram-negative curved, vibrioid, or helical cells that are nonmotile.

7. *Pseudomonas* and *Xanthomonas* are examples of aerobic, gram-negative rods that are polar flagellated.

8. *Escherichia, Salmonella, Shigella,* and *Yersinia* are facultatively anaerobic, gram-negative rods that are often found associated with the human body, and that may cause disease.

9. *Bacteroides,* an anaerobic, gram-negative bacterium, is the most common bacterium in the human intestine.

10. *Desulfovibrio* is an example of a dissimilatory sulfate-reducing or sulfur-reducing bacterium that uses oxidized sulfur compounds as electron acceptors in anaerobic respiration.

11. *Veillonella* and *Acidaminococcus* are anaerobic, gram-negative cocci found in the alimentary tract of humans and animals.

12. *Rickettsia* and *Chlamydia* are obligate intracellular parasites that are responsible for diseases such as Rocky Mountain spotted fever, typhus, and trachoma.

13. *Mycoplasma* is a cell wall-less bacterium that has sterols in its plasma membrane.

14. *Staphylococcus* and *Streptococcus* are gram-positive cocci that cause diseases such as impetigo, toxic shock syndrome, streptococcal pharyngitis (strep throat), rheumatic fever, and necrotizing fasciitis (flesh-eating disease).

15. *Bacillus* and *Clostridium* are examples of endospore-forming, gram-positive bacteria.

16. *Lactobacillus* is a non-spore-forming, gram-positive rod that is used extensively in the food industry for the preparation of yogurt, cheeses, sauerkraut, and pickles.

17. *Corynebacterium* is a club-shaped, gram-positive bacterium that has stainable polyphosphate granules and is the etiologic agent of diphtheria.

18. *Mycobacterium* is a rod-shaped to filamentous bacterium that has unusually large quantities of lipid in its cell envelope, is acid-fast, and causes diseases such as tuberculosis and leprosy.

19. Nocardioforms such as *Nocardia* are aerobic bacteria that form mycelia, or masses of hyphae.

20. The anoxygenic phototrophic bacteria have bacteriochlorophylls, do not produce oxygen during photosynthesis, have only one photosystem, and can use light as an energy source.

21. The oxygenic photosynthetic bacteria have chlorophylls, produce oxygen during photosynthesis, have two photosystems, and can use light as an energy source.

22. Chemolithotrophic bacteria use inorganic compounds as a source of energy. *Nitrosomonas* oxidizes ammonia to nitrite; *Nitrobacter* oxidizes nitrite to nitrate; *Thiobacillus* oxidizes sulfur to sulfate.

23. *Hyphomicrobium* is a budding bacterium that forms buds at the tips of filamentous outgrowths (hyphae) of the cell. *Caulobacter* attaches itself to solid surfaces by a stalk that is an extension of the cell.

24. *Sphaerotilus* is an example of a sheathed bacterium that forms an external sheath around its cells.

25. Fruiting gliding bacteria move by gliding and often produce colorful fruiting bodies that represent the resting stage.

26. The Archaea are distinguished from other procaryotes by their unusual rRNA structure, different RNA polymerase, plasma membrane lipid composition, mechanism of protein synthesis, and lack of muramic acid in the cell wall. They are divided into five groups: the methanogenic Archaea, the

sulfate reducers, the extremely halophilic Archaea, the Archaea lacking cell walls, and the extremely thermophilic elemental sulfur Archaea.

27. The actinomycetes are gram-positive bacteria that are rod-shaped or form branching filaments that in some genera develop into a mycelium. Actinomycetes have a high G + C content (≥52 mole%) of their DNA, which separates them from other procaryotes containing DNA with lower G + C contents.

EVOLUTION and BIODIVERSITY

One of the most spectacular concepts that has emerged in science has been the development of phylogenetic relationships among microorganisms. This molecular revolution in microbiology has enabled us to see microorganisms in a new light—not simply as culturable organisms that are to be characterized and identified by artificial laboratory conditions for growth and enrichment, but as organisms that can be identified directly in their natural environments through nucleic acid analysis. Limitations associated with the traditional approach of identifying and classifying microorganisms through their morphological and physiological characteristics have become apparent with the discovery of nonculturable microbes that cannot be cultivated in the laboratory. Nucleic acid analysis not only makes possible identification of these nonculturable microbes, but also provides an understanding of the natural and evolutionary relationships among organisms. The direct extraction and analysis of nucleic acids from microorganisms in a natural niche permit identification of these organisms and studies of phylogenetic relationships. Through phylogeny, sense and order can now be made of the diversity of the microbial world and the role of the Archaea in linking procaryotes and eucaryotes.

● Questions

Short Answer

1. Compare and contrast nomenclature and taxonomy.

2. Identify the kingdoms of living organisms according to Whittaker's system. Identify the domains according to Woese's system.

3. Which system of classification is phylogenetic?

4. Identify three approaches to identifying and classifying microorganisms.

5. Explain how and why flowcharts are commonly used to identify bacteria. Discuss their advantages and disadvantages.

6. Compare and contrast Archaea and Bacteria phenotypically.

7. Identify the major groups of procaryotes as described in *Bergey's Manual of Systematic Bacteriology*.

8. Identify and describe the 11 sections of gram-negative Bacteria described in Volume 1 of *Bergey's Manual*.

9. Identify and describe the six sections of gram-positive Bacteria other than actinomycetes described in Volume 2 of *Bergey's Manual*.

10. Identify and describe the eight sections of Archaea, cyanobacteria, and the remaining gram-negative Bacteria described in Volume 3 of *Bergey's Manual*.

11. Identify and describe the eight sections of actinomycetes described in Volume 4 of *Bergey's Manual*.

12. Compare and contrast mycoplasmas and other bacteria.

13. Compare and contrast *Rickettsia* and *Chlamydia*. How do these organisms differ from other bacteria?

14. Compare and contrast actinomycetes and fungi.

Multiple Choice

1. Which of the following is a spirochete?
   a. *Escherichia*
   b. *Pseudomonas*
   c. *Treponema*
   d. *Streptomyces*

2. Which of the following is most similar to *Rickettsia* and *Chlamydia*?
   a. *Bdellovibrio*
   b. *Clostridium*
   c. *Mycobacterium*
   d. *Mycoplasma*

3. How could you distinguish *Pseudomonas* species from *E. coli*?
   a. Gram stain reaction
   b. morphology
   c. glucose fermentation vs. respiration
   d. All of the above.

4. How could you distinguish staphylococci from streptococci?
   a. Gram stain reaction
   b. morphology
   c. glucose fermentation vs. respiration
   d. All of the above.

5. Which of the following produce endospores?
   a. *Bacillus* and *Clostridium*
   b. *Neisseria* and *Treponema*
   c. *Rickettsia* and *Chlamydia*
   d. *Salmonella* and *Shigella*

Critical Thinking

1. Several classification schemes have been proposed over the years. Both Whittaker's and Woese's systems are widely accepted today. Discuss the advantages and disadvantages of each system. Which is correct? Explain.

2. Examine a copy of *Bergey's Manual* and, if possible, compare it with a botany or zoology taxonomy reference. How is it similar? How does it differ? Why haven't Whittaker and Woese produced references to rival *Bergey's Manual?*

3. Considering the rate of advances in phylogenetics, outline or describe a possible organization of *Bergey's Manual* for the year 2010.

4. As a clinician striving to diagnose and treat disease, which of the three approaches to identification and classification would you use? Why?

Supplementary Readings

Amann, R.I., W. Ludwig, and K-H. Schleifer. 1995. Phylogenetic identification and in situ detection of individual microbial cells without cultivation. *Microbiological Reviews* 59:143–169. (A discussion of the procedures and applications of identifying bacteria in their natural environments without cultivation.)

Buchanan, R.E., and N.E. Gibbons, eds. 1994. *Bergey's manual of determinative bacteriology.* 9th ed. Baltimore: Williams & Wilkins. (An extensive reference guide to all of the procaryotes known through 1994. Each species is characterized with respect to morphological and biochemical traits.)

Bult, C.J., et al. 1996. Complete genome sequence of the methanogenic Archaeon, *Methanococcus jannaschii. Science* 273:1058–1073. (A scientific article reporting the genome sequence of *M. jannaschii* and comparing the genes of this Archaeon with the genes of Bacteria and eucaryotes.)

Goodfellow, M., M. Mordarski, and S.T. Williams, eds. 1983. *The biology of the actinomycetes.* London: Academic Press. (A comprehensive, authoritative survey of the current knowledge of actinomycete biology. There are detailed reviews of systematics, morphology, cell wall composition, genetics, and ecology of the actinomycetes.)

Holt, J.G., editor-in-chief. *Bergey's manual of systematic bacteriology.* Vol. 1, 1982 (Krieg, N.R., ed.). Vol. 2, 1986 (Sneath, P.H.A., ed.). Vol. 3, 1988 (Staley, J.T., ed.). Vol. 4, 1988 (Williams, S.T., ed.). Baltimore: Williams & Wilkins. (The new format of procaryotic taxonomy in four volumes. This reference contains extensive, up-to-date descriptions of each major group of procaryote.)

Olsen, G.J., C.R. Woese, and R. Overbeek. 1994. The winds of (evolutionary) change: Breathing new life into microbiology. *Journal of Bacteriology* 176:1–6. (A mini-review summarizing the advances in phylogenetics and including a comprehensive figure of the procaryotic phylogenetic tree.)

Starr, M.P., H. Stolp, H.G. Truper, A. Balows, and H.G. Schlegel, eds. 1981. *The prokaryotes.* New York: Springer-Verlag. (An extensive, detailed survey of procaryotes, with discussions on laboratory methods for the growth and isolation of these microorganisms and their clinical significance.)

Woese, C.R. 1987. Bacterial evolution. *Microbiological Reviews* 51:221–271. (An extensive review of phylogenetics and the universal phylogenetic tree.)

Woese, C.R. 1994. There must be a prokaryote somewhere: Microbiology's search for itself. *Microbiological Reviews* 58:1–9. (A treatise on the scientific search for phylogenetic relationships among the Archaea, the Bacteria, and the Eucarya.)

Woese, C.R., and R.S. Wolfe, eds. 1985. *The bacteria: A treatise on structure and function.* Vol. 8, *Archaebacteria.* London: Academic Press. (A comprehensive review of the Archaea, including their distinctive biological and molecular properties.)

chapter thirteen

THE VIRUSES

Electron micrograph of tobacco mosaic
virus (TMV) (colorized, ×103,000).

EVOLUTION AND BIODIVERSITY

Microbes in Motion — **PREVIEW LINK**

Among the key topics in this chapter are viral pathogenesis and disease,
and the structure and infection cycle (invasion, replication, assembly) of
viruses. The following sections in the *Microbes in Motion* CD-ROM may be
useful as a preview to your reading or as a supplemental study aid:

Viral Structure and Function: Structure, 1–9; Invasion, 1–8; Replication,
1–24; Assembly, 1–6; Pathogenesis (Host Cell Damage), 7–13,
(Persistent/Latent), 21–23; Diseases (Enveloped DNA Virus), 6–8, (Viral
Therapy), 19–27.

ach winter a serious infectious disease stalks young infants in nurseries throughout the United States. Children between the ages of three or four weeks and one year appear to be most susceptible to serious disease, whereas younger or older children are more resistant. The disease begins as a mild infection of the upper respiratory tract and then rapidly spreads into the lower respiratory tract, where it causes bronchitis (an infection of the small airways entering the lungs) and pneumonia.

Unlike most other infectious agents, which invade a body once and then are blocked in subsequent attacks by antibodies of the body's immune system, the agent responsible for this respiratory disease may return and strike the same person again and again. Furthermore, this is one of the few respiratory pathogens that consistently causes a major disease outbreak year after year. After each outbreak, the agent mysteriously disappears, only to reappear in the winter of the following year.

This "Houdini" pathogen is a virus called **respiratory syncytial virus (RSV),** named after the respiratory disease it produces and the characteristic syncytial (cell-fusing) masses it forms in infected cell cultures. RSV is a major cause of respiratory disease in young children. Infections are especially severe in infants with congenital heart disease; RSV infections in these infants can lead to mortality rates as high as 37%. Unfortunately there is no method to prevent RSV infection effectively. It appears to be transmitted in the hospital environment by unsuspecting doctors and nurses who spread the virus from one infant to another. Exposed infants do not seem able to effectively mount a defense against the viral invasion and vaccines do not help in preventing this disease.

As strange and unorthodox as RSV disease may seem, it is typical of many viral diseases. **Viruses** are obligate intracellular parasites that rely upon a host for metabolism and reproduction. Viruses that use bacteria as their host are called **bacteriophages** (or simply **phages**). Bacteria such as rickettsiae and chlamydiae are also obligate parasites (see rickettsiae and chlamydiae, page 326), but viruses (1) possess a single type of nucleic acid, either DNA or RNA (not both) and (2) possess a protein coat that surrounds the nucleic acid. Unlike most bacteria, algae, and fungi, viruses are metabolically inert and lack the metabolic machinery to generate energy or synthesize macromolecules. Although viruses contain genetic information encoded in their nucleic acid, they do not have ribosomes or any of the enzymes required to fully process this information. Consequently, viruses are no more alive outside a host than fragments of DNA. However, inside a suitable host the inert virus particle comes "alive" as it takes over the host biosynthetic machinery to synthesize the viral nucleic acids and proteins necessary for replication. Viruses therefore are unlike any other form of microorganism. These distinctive acellular forms are neither procaryotic nor eucaryotic and thus are usually considered separately from other types of microorganisms (Table 13.1).

table 13.1

Comparison of Viruses with Other Microorganisms

Characteristic	Viruses	Other Microorganisms
Size	Generally ≪200 nm	Generally ≥200 nm
Nucleic acid	DNA or RNA	DNA and RNA
Outer covering	Usually simple protein coat	Complex membrane, wall, or both
Reproduction	Requires host	Generally self-reproducing
Metabolism	Utilizes host metabolic machinery	Macromolecular or synthetic machinery; has own metabolic machinery
Cultivation	Cannot be cultivated on cell-free media	Usually can be cultivated on cell-free media

Properties of Viruses

Regardless of the type of host they infect, all viruses have the same general structure: genetic material in the form of either DNA or RNA surrounded by a protein coat and, in some cases, an outer membrane. The complete virus particle with its nucleic acid and its outer covering is called a **virion.**

Viruses Are Extremely Small

Most viruses are smaller than bacteria (≪200 nm) and can only be seen with an electron microscope (Figure 13.1). A few viruses, such as the poxviruses, have diameters exceeding 300 nm and are within the theoretical limit of resolution of the light microscope. All viruses, however, are so small that the quantity of genetic material they carry is limited. As a consequence, most viral genomes code for only the minimum amount of information required for structural integrity. This characteristic is reflected in the simple composition of a virus.

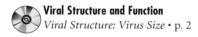

Viral Structure and Function
Viral Structure: Virus Size • p. 2

Viruses Consist of DNA or RNA Surrounded by a Protein Coat

Viruses consist of a single type of nucleic acid, either single- or double-stranded DNA or RNA, enclosed within a protein coat (Figure 13.2). The size of the nucleic acid in viruses ranges from only a few thousand bases in the case of **picornavirus** to several hundred thousand bases for the **poxvirus.** An average gene is estimated to contain approximately 1,000 bases (1 kilobase). Most viruses are able to fit only a few genes into their limited genomes.

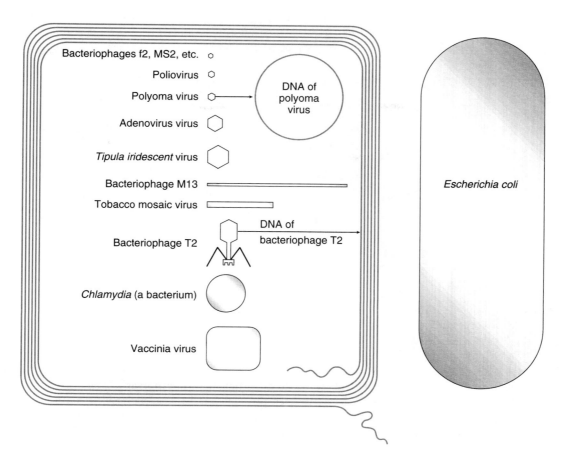

figure 13.1

Comparative Sizes of Some Common Viruses and Bacteria

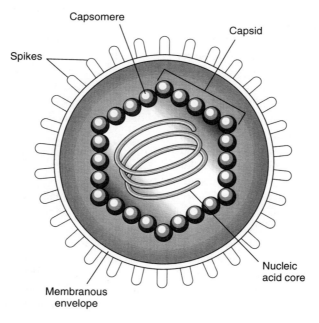

figure 13.2

Structure of an Enveloped Animal Virus

This drawing shows the major components that may be part of an enveloped animal virus. The nucleic acid core surrounded by a capsid, composed of capsomeres, constitutes the nucleocapsid. Some animal viruses may also have a membranous envelope surrounding the capsid, and glycoprotein spikes with either hemagglutinin or neuraminidase activity.

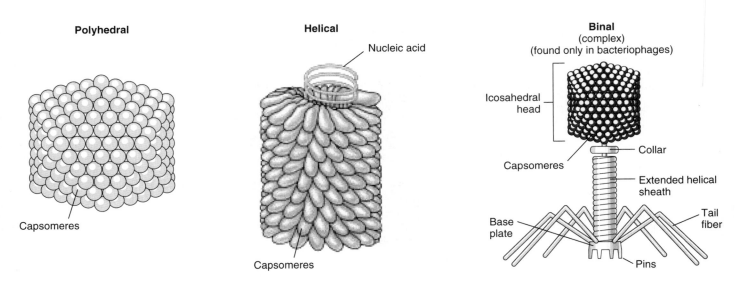

Polyhedral

Capsomeres

Helical

Nucleic acid

Capsomeres

Binal
(complex)
(found only in bacteriophages)

Icosahedral head

Capsomeres

Collar

Extended helical sheath

Base plate

Tail fiber

Pins

figure 13.3

Basic Nucleocapsid Forms

There are three basic categories of capsid architecture: polyhedral, helical, and binal.

For example, the **adenovirus,** which causes acute respiratory and ocular infections, has a double-stranded DNA genome with about 35 kilobases. These bases code for only a few genes. Even the largest and most complex viruses have genomes coding for fewer than 200 to 300 different proteins. In comparison, the genome of *Escherichia coli* is estimated to contain anywhere from 2,000 to 4,000 genes.

Naked nucleic acids are highly susceptible to degradation by the nucleases that often are found in the environment. To protect their nucleic acids from these enzymes, viruses are constructed with a protein coat surrounding their genome. This protective coat, called a **capsid,** is made up of repeating protein subunits called **capsomeres.** Because some viruses do not devote much of their limited genes for the coding of capsomere proteins, capsomeres in the smaller, more elementary viruses generally are composed of only one type of protein. In the more complex viruses, capsomeres can consist of several different types of proteins. The capsid, in combination with the nucleic acid, is commonly referred to as the **nucleocapsid.**

Some animal viruses (viruses with animal hosts) have a membranous envelope surrounding the capsid. **Matrix proteins** are located in the space between the envelope and the nucleocapsid. They strengthen the envelope and connect it to the nucleocapsid. The envelope is composed of **glycoproteins,** embedded within a **lipid bilayer** that is derived from the host cell's plasma membrane as the virus is released by an extrusion process following virus replication. Glycoproteins are complexes of carbohydrates and proteins. They are located on the outer envelope surface and often take the form of spikes called **peplomers. Influenza viruses** (orthomyxoviruses), for example, have glycoprotein spikes with either hemagglutinin or neuraminidase activity. The hemagglu-

tinin spikes on these viruses can bridge red blood cells in clusters to cause **hemagglutination;** as will be discussed later in this chapter, this characteristic can be used to assay for the presence and quantity of virus in a solution. Neuraminidase is an enzyme that is not unique to viruses—it is synthesized by many types of bacteria, including *Vibrio cholerae* and many streptococci. The enzyme cleaves *N*-acetylneuraminic acid residues from glycoproteins. Because glycoproteins containing *N*-acetylneuraminic acid are found in mucus, it has been hypothesized that the neuraminidases of the influenza virus aid in penetration of the mucus of the respiratory tract.

The proteins in the viral envelope are coded by viral genes. The lipids and carbohydrates of the envelope, in contrast, are derived from the host cell. The kinds of lipids and carbohydrates in the envelope thus depend on the type of host cell infected by the virus. The presence of lipids makes enveloped viruses sensitive to disinfection and damage by lipid solvents such as ether.

Viruses Have Three Basic Forms: Polyhedral, Helical, and Binal

Viruses have small genomes and are able to code for only a few structural proteins. This limitation results in viral coats that frequently consist of simple, repeating protein subunits. With this repeating structure and the energy restrictions associated with its assembly, viruses can assume only a few possible symmetrical forms that fall into three basic categories: **polyhedral, helical,** and **binal** (previously known as **complex**) (Figure 13.3). These three terms describe the architectural arrangement of capsids that make up the outer protein coat of the virion.

The electron microscope is invaluable for defining viral morphology. Even before the refinement of techniques for electron microscopy, Francis Crick and James D. Watson in 1956 predicted the shape and structure of plant viruses (viruses with plant hosts). They reasoned that because of the small amount of genetic information available in viruses, only a limited number of different molecules could be used to form the outer covering of a virion. The type of shape that could efficiently utilize such repeating building blocks was one with cubic symmetry. The underlying structure of viruses with cubic symmetrical forms is the icosahedron.

The icosahedron, the most common polyhedral form in viruses, has 20 faces, 30 edges, and 12 vertices. Each face on this geometrical structure is an equilateral triangle and results in a symmetrical framework. The animal viruses adenovirus, papovavirus, and herpesvirus are examples of viral nucleocapsids with an icosahedral shape.

Viral Structure and Function
Viral Structure: Structure and Shape • pp. 3–7

Many plant viruses and some bacterial and animal viruses have helical nucleocapsids. Examples of such viruses are the plant virus **tobacco mosaic virus (TMV),** the animal virus **rabies virus,** and the bacteriophage **M13.** TMV is rod-shaped and is composed of 2,130 protein subunits stacked in a helical fashion around a central core. The viral genome of single-stranded RNA is wound within the core and among rows of the subunits. The placement of the viral RNA within the protein coat protects the nucleic acid from harmful nucleases in the surrounding environment.

Viruses that have neither polyhedral (icosahedral) nor helical symmetry or have combinations of these forms are termed binal. Examples of binal viruses are the poxviruses and the T-even bacteriophages (**T2, T4,** and **T6**). Poxviruses have an indistinguishable capsid surrounding a nucleic acid core of double-stranded DNA. The poxviruses cause such diseases as smallpox (variola) and cowpox, characterized by pustular skin lesions called **pocks.**

The T-even bacteriophages have a complex structure that consists of three parts: head, sheath, and tail. The phage head has a hexagonal shape and is composed of protein subunits surrounding the viral genome. This phage head is attached to the tail portion via a narrow contractile sheath. The tail actually consists of six thin tail fibers that extend like folding legs from the sheath. These fibers are important for attachment to the bacterial surface during infection. Many bacteriophages differ from this structure and may lack a sheath (bacteriophages **T1** and **T5**), have short tails (bacteriophages **T3** and **T7**), or have no tail (bacteriophage φ**X174**). Other bacteriophages (bacteriophage **fd**) are filamentous and resemble long pieces of insulated wire. The wire represents their nucleic acid surrounded by a tubular protein coat.

Classification of Viruses

Many attempts have been made to develop systems for classifying viruses. Because all viruses must infect a host organism as a prerequisite for reproduction, early systems of viral classification were based on the type of host or the organ system infected: **tobacco mosaic virus, turnip yellow mosaic virus, cowpox virus, adenovirus,** and so on. The problem with this classification system was that many viruses were eventually found to infect multiple organs or have a wide host range.

Viruses sometimes are placed into three separate classes on the basis of their host: animal, plant, or bacteria. Some classification schemes include dividing viruses by the types of diseases they cause. However, such schemes have problems because viruses can produce different clinical signs and symptoms in the same host or in different hosts. Other classification schemes include dividing viruses by their nucleic acid relatedness, viral morphology, and chemical composition. While none of these schemes is completely without problems, virologists generally agree that most viruses can be separated on the basis of certain physical, chemical, and morphological characteristics. These characteristics—type of nucleic acid (DNA or RNA), symmetry of the nucleocapsid (helical, cubical, or binary), presence or absence of an envelope, and capsid size—were initially used by André Lwoff, Robert Horne, and Paul Tournier in 1962 to group viruses into several basic classes (the LHT system). The LHT system of classification does not attempt to show genetic relatedness among viral groups; instead it compares viruses on the basis of common similarities that can be readily observed or chemically measured.

Viral Structure and Function
Viral Structure: Taxonomy • pp. 8–9

In 1966 the International Committee on Nomenclature of Viruses (ICNV) was established to develop a systematic method for viral classification. Subcommittees of the ICNV were formed to specifically classify viruses infecting vertebrates, invertebrates, plants, and bacteria. The name ICNV was changed in 1973 to the International Committee on Taxonomy of Viruses (ICTV), and a fifth subcommittee to consider the classification of fungal viruses was established in 1975.

Bacteriophages Are Classified by Their Morphology and Nucleic Acid Content

Bacterial viruses (bacteriophages) are extensively studied particles that have been instrumental in studies of genetics and molecular biology (see transfer of genetic material, page 255, and recombinant DNA technology, page 281). There have been no specific guidelines for bacterial virus classification; most bacteriophages have been haphazardly named by scientists as new forms were

Viroids and Prions—Agents Smaller Than Viruses

Viruses were long considered to be the simplest infectious agents known. In 1961, however, William Raymer, a plant pathologist with the U.S. Department of Agriculture, discovered an infectious agent simpler than viruses in potatoes with the disease potato spindle tuber. After several years of intensive work, this agent was finally characterized and named a **viroid.** Viroids are several thousand times smaller than viruses and consist of only nucleic acid (Figure 13.4). The viroid originally found in potato spindle tuber disease had a molecular weight of 130,000 daltons in comparison with the 40 million daltons molecular weight of the TMV. The viroid nucleic acid apparently is protected from environmental nucleases by its tightly folded configuration. Viroids are unusually resistant to heat and ultraviolet radiation.

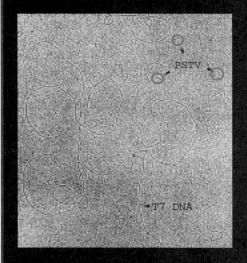

figure 13.4
Electron Micrograph of the Potato Spindle Tuber Viroid (PSTV), Comparing Its Size to the DNA of Bacteriophage T7 of *Escherichia coli* (×20,680).

Viroids are responsible for a number of plant diseases, including hop stunt, avocado sun blotch, cucumber pale fruit, citrus exocortis, potato spindle tuber, and tomato bunchy top. Because their nucleic acids are so small, viroids rely entirely on plant cell enzymes for replication. No viroid has yet been associated with organisms higher than plants.

Scrapie, a neurological disease of sheep, goats, and other animals characterized by twitching, excitability, intense itching, excessive thirst, weakness, and eventually paralysis, is caused by small infectious proteins, with no detectable nucleic acid. These **scrapie-associated fibrils (SAFs),** or **prions** (proteinaceous infectious particle) as they are now called, share the viroids' unusual resistance to heat and ultraviolet radiation. Prions appear to be an exception to the rule that all infectious agents contain nucleic acid as their genetic material (Figure 13.5). One hypothesis for their infectivity is that these particles may be encoded by a latent host gene that is activated upon infection of the host. Other slow, degenerative diseases such as kuru and Creutzfeldt-Jakob disease (CJD) in humans and transmissible encephalopathy in mink are caused by these proteinaceous agents.

CJD, a rare disease that normally is associated with old age, produces sponge-like holes in the brain and leads to depression, memory loss, and rapidly developing, devastating dementia. Although CJD may take up to 50 years to develop, once symptoms appear, death can occur within seven to nine months. Cattle are afflicted with a similar disease, bovine spongiform encephalopathy (BSE), or "mad cow disease," causing twitching, confusion, lethargy, and death. Scientific evidence suggests that humans may contract the disease through eating contaminated meat. BSE is especially a problem in Britain, where the disease first appeared in 1985 in a previously healthy Holstein dairy cow that ate protein meal prepared from sheep tissue, which may have been infected with scrapie. The cow became edgy, uncoordinated, and aggressive. By the end of 1995, researchers had identified 154,592 cattle with BSE on British farms. A public outcry for the British government to slaughter the country's 11 million to 13 million cattle arose in 1996 when several teenagers contracted CJD, which is rarely seen in young people. The teenagers were believed to have contracted the disease from eating contaminated beef. In response to this uproar, the British government agreed to destroy nearly five million cattle over a six-year period in an effort to wipe out mad cow disease.

a.

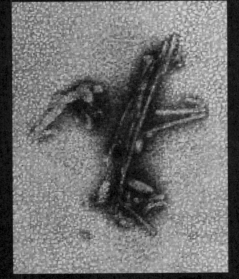

b.

figure 13.5
Electron Micrographs of Prions
a. Prions purified from clinically ill hamster brains infected with prion strain 263K; negatively stained with uranyl acetate (×115,760). b. Prions isolated from human Creutzfeldt-Jakob disease; negatively stained with phosphotungstic acid (×89,670).

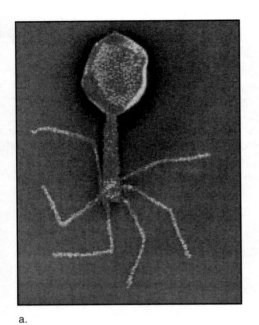
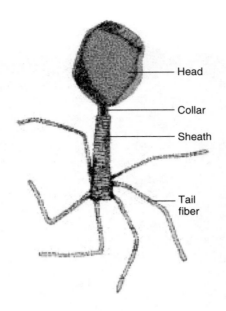
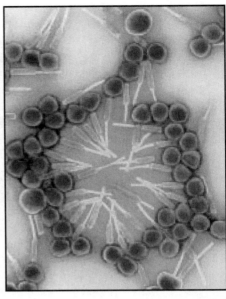

Head

Collar

Sheath

Tail
fiber

a.

b.

figure 13.6
Electron Micrographs of Bacteriophages
a. Bacteriophage T2 (family: *Myoviridae*) (colorized, ×270,000). b. Bacteriophage P1 (colorized, ×52,857). Both T2 and P1 are double-stranded DNA bacteriophages that infect *E. coli*.

discovered. As a general rule, phage morphology and the content of the phage genome and capsid have been used in such classification systems (Figure 13.6). For example, **SPO1** and **SPO2** are double-stranded bacteriophages that infect *Bacillus subtilis. Escherichia coli* is a host for many types of bacteriophages (frequently called **coliphages,** because they infect *E. coli*). The T-even coliphages (**T2, T4, T6**) are double-stranded DNA phages with binal symmetry consisting of a hexagonal head connected by a narrow sheath to long tail fibers. Coliphage φ**X174** contains a single-stranded circular DNA genome within an icosahedral capsid consisting of 12 capsomeres. Coliphage **fd** also contains single-stranded circular DNA, but it is filamentous with a helical symmetry. The DNA of bacteriophage λ is double stranded and linear in the virion but forms a circular structure within the infected host.

Recently the Bacterial Virus Subcommittee of the ICTV began to establish a system for the classification of bacterial viruses. Classification is based on the morphology and nucleic acid content of the virus (Table 13.2). Family names have been established for the more than 2,000 bacteriophages that have been discovered and characterized. The process is slow and tedious but provides us with an orderly system of nomenclature for bacteriophages.

Viruses Infect Other Microorganisms Besides Bacteria

Bacteriophages represent only one category of viruses that infect microorganisms. Other viruses infect cyanobacteria (cyanophages), fungi (mycoviruses), algae (phycoviruses), and protozoa. Cyano-

phages are similar to bacteriophages in structure and mode of infection. It has been suggested that such viruses may be useful in the biological control of algal blooms. Viruses that infect eucaryotic microorganisms (fungi, algae, and protozoa) frequently use their hosts as vectors for transmission to other organisms. The most extensively studied viruses of eucaryotic microorganisms have been the mycoviruses. All that have thus far been discovered contain double-stranded RNA. Viruses that infect fungi generally exist in a latent (present but not active) state and appear to be transmitted through hyphal connections and fungal spores. One mycovirus, **hypovirus,** causes reduced virulence (hypovirulence) when it is transmitted to the chestnut blight fungus *Cryphonectria parasitica.* Virus infection is associated with alterations of signal transduction pathways involved in the expression of fungal genes linked to virulence. This property makes hypovirus potentially useful as a biological agent for control of chestnut blight and other fungal diseases.

Plant Viruses Are Classified into 23 Virus Groups and Two Families

There are over 300 different plant viruses that have been categorized into 23 virus groups and two families by the Plant Virus Subcommittee of the ICTV (Table 13.3). An additional 200 viruses remain unclassified at this time.

Plant viruses do not fit easily into a basic taxonomic scheme and are grouped primarily according to the types of diseases they cause. All but two recognized groups of plant viruses contain RNA

table 13.2

Some Families of Bacteriophages

Family	Morphology	Type of Nucleic Acid[a]	Examples
DNA bacteriophages			
Inoviridae		Circular ss DNA	M13, fd
Microviridae		Circular ss DNA	φX174, G4, M12
Corticoviridae		Circular ds DNA	PM2
Myoviridae		Linear ds DNA	T2, T4, T6, P2
Pedoviridae		Linear ds DNA	T3, T7, P22
Plasmaviridae		Circular ds DNA	MVL2
Styloviridae		Linear ds DNA	λ, T1, T5
RNA bacteriophages			
Cystoviridae		Linear ds RNA	φ6
Leviviridae		Linear ss RNA	Qβ, R17, MS2, f2

[a]ss = single-stranded; ds = double-stranded.

table 13.3

Some Groups of Plant Viruses

Group	Morphology	Enveloped (E) or Naked[a] (N)	Approximate Size of Virion (nm)	Type of Nucleic Acid[b]	Representative Virus
DNA viruses					
Geminivirus		N	2–18	Circular ss DNA	Maize streak
Caulimovirus		N	50	Circular ds DNA	Cauliflower mosaic
RNA viruses					
Almovirus		N	18–58 × 18	Linear ss RNA	Alfalfa mosaic
Bromovirus		N	23	Linear ss RNA	Brome mosaic
Carlavirus		N	690 × 12	Linear ss RNA	Carnation latent
Closterovirus		N	600–2,000 × 12	Linear ss RNA	Beet yellows
Comovirus		N	30	Linear ss RNA	Cowpea mosaic
Cucumovirus		N	30	Linear ss RNA	Cucumber mosaic
Hordeivirus		N	110–160 × 23	Linear ss RNA	Barley stripe mosaic
Ilarvirus		N	26–35	Linear ss RNA	Tobacco streak
Luteovirus		N	25	Linear ss RNA	Barley yellow dwarf
Nepovirus		N	30	Linear ss RNA	Tobacco ringspot
Potexvirus		N	480–580 × 13	Linear ss RNA	Potato X
Potyvirus		N	680–900 × 12	Linear ss RNA	Potato Y
Rhabdovirus			130–150 × 45 430–500 × 110	Linear ss RNA	Lettuce necrotic yellow

table 13.3

Some Groups of Plant Viruses (continued)

Group	Morphology	Enveloped (E) or Naked[a] (N)	Approximate Size of Virion (nm)	Type of Nucleic Acid[b]	Representative Virus
Tobamovirus		N	300 × 18	Linear ss RNA	Tobacco mosaic
Tobanecrovirus		N	28	Linear ss RNA	Tobacco necrosis
Tobravirus		N	46–114 and 180–215 × 22	Linear ss RNA	Tobacco rattle
Tombusvirus		N	30	Linear ss RNA	Tomato bushy stunt
Tymovirus		N	30	Linear ss RNA	Turnip yellow mosaic

[a]Nonenveloped.
[b]ss = single-stranded; ds = double-stranded.

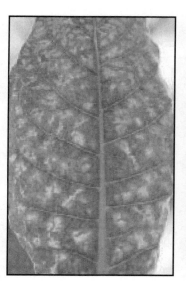
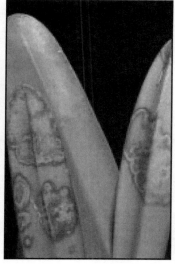

a.   b.

figure 13.7

Examples of Lesions from Virus Infection of Plants

a. Necrotric lesions caused by tobacco mosaic virus infection of the tobacco plant *Nicotiana glutinosa*. b. Leaf color changes caused by tobacco mosaic virus infection of an orchid.

as their genetic material. **Caulimovirus,** a virus that infects cauliflower, possesses double-stranded DNA as its genetic material. **Geminivirus** infects maize and has a single-stranded DNA genome.

Many plant viruses are transmitted by insect or arthropod vectors and can replicate in these vectors; other viruses are transmitted directly from plant to plant. Plant viruses appear to lack specific mechanisms for penetration of plant hosts. In most instances they enter the host as a result of physical damage to the plant cell due to insect injury, weather deterioration, or mechanical abuse from cultivation methods. The infection of plants by viruses leads to a number of different visible symptoms, including discoloration, molting, and yellowing of leaves; abnormal root growth; and reduced fruit production (Figure 13.7). Because viral infections cannot be cured, viral diseases cause major economic losses that amount to millions of dollars annually.

Animal Viruses Are Classified into 18 Families

Many of the viruses that infect vertebrates also infect invertebrates. It is not unusual, for example, for a virus carried by an arthropod (mites, ticks, or mosquitoes) to be transmitted to a vertebrate. The arthropod serves as a **vector,** or vehicle of transmission, for the virus. For this reason, a similar classification system exists for viruses infecting vertebrates and invertebrates.

The ICTV separates viruses infecting vertebrates and other similar hosts into 18 families on the basis of common characteristics (Table 13.4). These 18 viral families are divided into two main

table 13.4

Classification of Animal Viruses

Family	Morphology	Enveloped (E) or Naked[a] (N)	Approximate Size of Virion (nm)	Type of Nucleic Acid[b]	Representative Virus
DNA viruses					
Parvoviridae		N	22	Linear ss DNA	Kilham rat
Adenoviridae		N	70–90	Linear ds DNA	Human adeno 2
Iridoviridae		N	130–300	Linear ds DNA	Tipula iridescent
Hepadnaviridae		E	42	Circular ds DNA	Hepatitis B
Papovaviridae		N	45–55	Circular ds DNA	Polyoma
Herpesviridae		E	150–200	Linear ds DNA	Herpes simplex
Poxviridae		E	200–390	Linear ds DNA	Smallpox
RNA viruses					
Caliciviridae		N	40	Linear ss RNA	Norwalk
Picornaviridae		N	22–30	Linear ss RNA	Polio
Reoviridae		N	60–80	Linear ds RNA	Rotavirus
Arenaviridae		E	50–300	Linear ss RNA	Lassa fever
Filoviridae		E	800–900 × 80	Linear ss RNA	Ebola
Bunyaviridae		E	100	Linear ss RNA	California encephalitis
Coronaviridae		E	60–220	Linear ss RNA	Coronavirus OC43

table 13.4

Classification of Animal Viruses (continued)

Family	Morphology	Enveloped (E) or Naked[a] (N)	Approximate Size of Virion (nm)	Type of Nucleic Acid[b]	Representative Virus
Orthomyxoviridae		E	80–120	Linear ss RNA	Influenza
Paramyxoviridae		E	150–300	Linear ss RNA	Measles
Retroviridae		E	100	Linear ss RNA	Human immunodeficiency virus
Rhabdoviridae		E	70–80 × 130–240	Linear ss RNA	Rabies
Togaviridae		E	40–75	Linear ss RNA	Dengue

[a]Nonenveloped.

[b]ss = single-stranded; ds = double-stranded.

groups: DNA viruses and RNA viruses (Figure 13.8). This system provides perhaps the most systematic approach to vertebrate viral taxonomy at this time. The classification is by no means complete and will undoubtedly be revised as additional viral groups are recognized and characterized.

Some of the animal viruses such as **herpesvirus** and **rhabdovirus** have a wide host range, infecting a wide variety of animals. Other viruses have a narrow host range. For example, human beings are the only known natural host for the **poliovirus** and **rhinovirus** (picornavirus). The **Ebola virus** causes a highly fatal severe hemorrhagic disease in humans, but causes only inapparent infections with no detectable symptoms in African green monkeys, which can also be infected with the virus. Ebola viruses are morphologically and antigenically distinct from the rhabdoviruses (family: *Rhabdoviridae*), and are officially classified as members of a new family called *Filoviridae.* Animal viruses are responsible for many infectious diseases, including influenza (**influenza virus**); measles (**rubeola virus**); benign warts (**papovavirus**); rabies (**rhabdovirus**); encephalitis (**togavirus**); Dengue fever (**Dengue virus**); and acquired immune deficiency syndrome, or AIDS (**human immunodeficiency virus,** or **HIV**). These and other viral diseases are discussed in detail in Chapter 17.

Propagation and Assay of Viruses

Viruses are submicroscopic, intracellular, obligate parasites that lack many of the enzymes and cellular components (for example, ribosomes) to generate energy, synthesize proteins, and replicate their nucleic acid. Consequently, they require a living host that has these enzymes and cell constituents for replication. A suspension of virus particles cannot be observed under a light microscope, nor can these particles be propagated on a nutrient agar plate, as can most bacteria. The cultivation of viruses requires living host cells.

Viruses Require a Host for Propagation

Because viruses cannot replicate without a host, they also cannot be propagated in the laboratory without a suitable host organism (animal, plant, or bacterium). Extracellular virions do remain viable, but eventually they must find a suitable host for replication. This requirement for a host forms the basis for the cultivation of viruses.

Animal viruses may be cultivated in the laboratory in **animal tissue cultures.** These consist of animal cells that are propagated and maintained under laboratory conditions. Animal tissue cultures are established by treating a specific animal organ with an enzyme such as trypsin to disassociate the tissue mass into individual cells. The cell suspension is then placed into a flat-bottomed container (a flask, bottle, or Petri dish) and covered with a rich liquid medium for the maintenance of the animal cells. A typical maintenance medium usually contains amino acids, vitamins, ions, buffering agents, and animal serum. Antibiotics are also frequently added to such media to decrease or prohibit bacterial contamination. The cell suspension is usually incubated in an atmosphere containing 5% carbon dioxide. As the animal cells grow and divide, they attach to the surface of the container and eventually form a single, continuous layer (**monolayer**) of cells. Cultures initiated from the original host tissue are called **primary cultures.** Tissue cultures are maintained by periodically changing the liquid maintenance medium or, when the cells become too crowded (**confluent**), passing a portion of the cells into a new container to establish **secondary cultures.**

Cells from normal tissues do not grow indefinitely and eventually die after a finite number of passages. Such cells, however, can

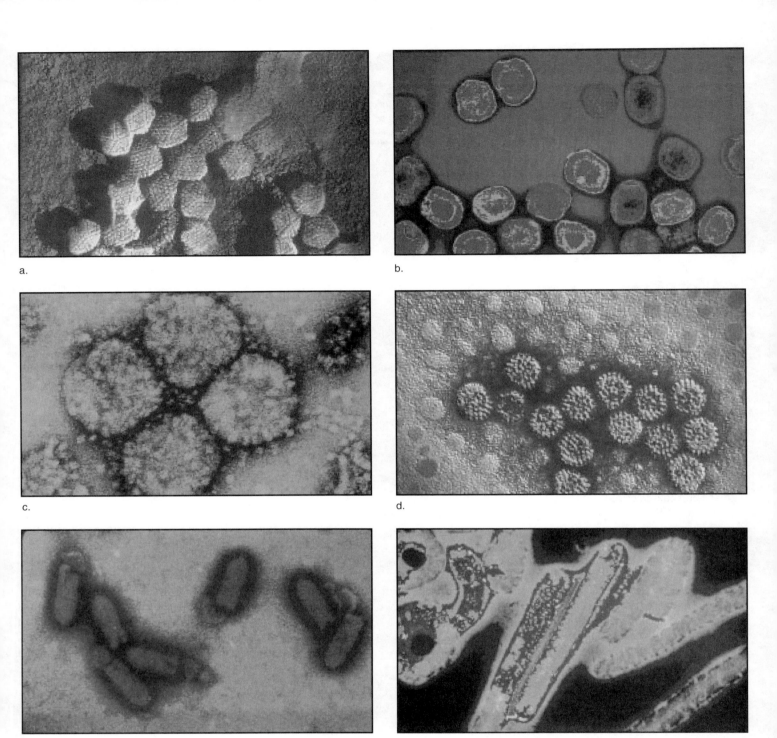

figure 13.8
Electron Micrographs of Some Animal Viruses

a. Adenovirus, a DNA virus (family: *Adenoviridae*) (colorized, ×300,000). b. Vaccinia virus, a DNA virus (family: *Poxviridae*). c. Coronavirus, an RNA virus (family: *Coronaviridae*) (colorized, ×500,000). d. Rotavirus, an RNA virus (family: *Reoviridae*) (colorized, ×48,500). e. Rabies virus, an RNA virus (family: *Rhabdoviridae*) (colorized, ×200,000). f. Ebola virus, an RNA virus (family: *Filoviridae*).

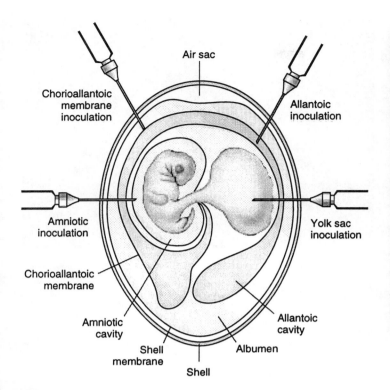

figure 13.9
Embryonated Egg and Sites for Virus Inoculation

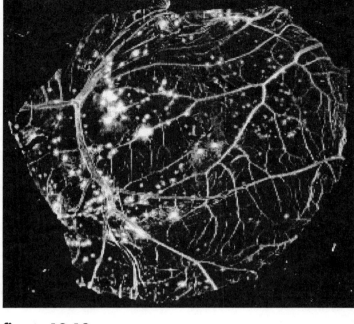

figure 13.10
Chicken Embryo Chorioallantoic Membrane Infected with Smallpox Virus
The opaque lesions on the transparent membrane are pocks.

be preserved by storage at ultralow temperatures in freezers or liquid nitrogen. Alternatively, certain types of cultures on occasion yield exceptional cells that acquire the ability to multiply indefinitely. These cells are used to establish **cell lines** that are immortal and grow continuously under proper maintenance. Examples of cell lines commonly used in research are HeLa cells (originally derived from cancerous cervical tissue of a woman named *H*enrietta *L*acks) and BHK cells (isolated from *b*aby Syrian *h*amster *k*idney tissue). These cells are widely used in research because they are readily available and easily propagated.

Viruses inoculated into tissue cultures infect, replicate, and eventually can cause cell lysis. Each virion initially infects only one cell. When this cell lyses, mature viruses are released, and they infect and lyse neighboring cells. Clear areas called **plaques** form where viruses have attacked cell cultures that are overlaid with soft nutrient agar. Because each plaque usually represents a single virion from the original inoculum, the number of plaques can be counted and multiplied by the dilution factor to quantitate the virus concentration in that inoculum.

Viruses also can be propagated in vivo by inoculating them directly onto animal or plant tissue. One animal model commonly used for animal viral studies is the chicken embryo. Embryonated eggs 6 to 12 days old are used for viral inoculations. Sites for inoculation include the chorioallantoic membrane, yolk sac, amniotic fluid, and allantoic cavity (Figure 13.9). The chorioallantoic membrane is inoculated by first disinfecting the shell surface and then drilling a small hole through the shell and the shell membrane.

The chorioallantoic membrane is collapsed by removing air from the air sac of the egg. Virus is deposited onto the collapsed chorioallantoic membrane, and the shell opening is resealed with wax or paraffin to prevent contamination. The embryonated egg is then incubated. As each virus infects cells and replicates, an opaque lesion called a pock appears on the transparent membrane (Figure 13.10). These visible lesions can be enumerated to determine the concentration of viruses in the original inoculum. Pock counting, although used extensively in the past for enumeration of viruses, has now been largely replaced by the plaque technique.

Bacteriophages are propagated in the laboratory on suitable host bacteria. The bacteriophages are first mixed with a suspension of the appropriate host bacteria in melted soft nutrient agar. This phage-bacteria suspension is then poured onto the surface of a Petri dish containing hardened agar. The plate is incubated, and the bacteriophages are allowed to infect and lyse the bacterial cells. Clear plaques form in areas of the bacterial lawn (a layer of confluent bacterial growth) where phages are present (Figure 13.11). Each plaque represents one original phage particle.

Viruses Can Be Assayed by Various Methods

Plaque or pock counting is one method used to quantitate viruses. Viruses can also be assayed by a variety of other methods, including the actual counting of virus particles and detection of virions by hemagglutination.

figure 13.11

Clear Plaques of Bacteriophage λ (left) and Bacteriophage T2 (right) on Lawns of *Escherichia coli.*

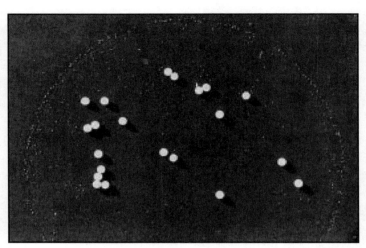

figure 13.12

Assay of Viruses by Electron Microscopy
Particles of poliovirus (small particles) are mixed with polystyrene latex spheres (large particles). The mixture is sprayed in droplets on a supporting membrane grid, dried, and shadowed. The resultant preparation is examined by electron microscopy, and the total number of virus particles is derived from the ratio of latex spheres to virions observed.

One of the first methods used to enumerate viruses was the direct counting of virus particles by electron microscopy (Figure 13.12). Virions are counted by mixing them with a known number of latex spheres and spraying the mixture onto a grid. The coated grid is examined by electron microscopy and the total number of virus particles is derived from the ratio of latex spheres to virions observed. Direct enumeration is rapid but does not distinguish infectious from noninfectious virus particles.

Viruses that possess hemagglutinin spikes (for example, influenza viruses) can be assayed by hemagglutination. The spikes attach to red blood cells and form bridges of virus particles between these cells. The maximum number of red blood cells that can be linked by a single virus particle is two because of the size of the cells. As additional bridges are constructed between virions and red blood cells, large aggregates develop. If the assay is performed in a small, clear tube or well, the aggregates sediment and form a film at the bottom. Red blood cells that do not aggregate simply fall to the bottom of the container, where they roll together and form a visible round red button. Since each virion is assumed to link two red blood cells, the total number of virus particles in a particular suspension can be approximated by diluting the original virus suspension and determining the dilution at which hemagglutination fails to occur. Like electron microscopy, hemagglutination assays do not distinguish between infectious and noninfectious virus particles.

Replication of Viruses

Virus replication is a multistep process that begins with attachment of the virion to the host cell and terminates with the production of progeny viral particles. The steps associated with virus replication are (1) **attachment** of the virion to the host (**adsorption**), (2) **penetra**-tion of the virus or its nucleic acid into the cell (and **uncoating** in animal and plant viruses), (3) **replication** of the viral nucleic acid and **synthesis** of viral proteins, (4) **assembly** and/or **maturation** of new virus particles, and (5) **release** of mature virus particles from the host cell (Figure 13.13). In most viruses, all of the steps except replication of the viral genome are similar. Because viruses may contain single- or double-stranded DNA or single- or double-stranded RNA, replication of the viral genome may occur in a variety of ways.

Virus Replication Begins with Infection of the Host

Virus-host interactions are very specific. The replication cycle for animal and bacterial viruses begins with adsorption, the attachment of the virus to a receptor on the cell surface. In bacteria, a variety of different molecular components can serve as receptors, including flagella, pili, outer membrane proteins, lipopolysaccharides, and teichoic acids. Bacteriophages have specialized structures for adsorption, such as the tail fiber in T-even phages. Phage attachment is immediately followed by injection of the phage nucleic acid into the host cell (Figure 13.14). Only the phage genome enters the cell. The remaining portions of the phage (the capsid, sheath, and tail) remain outside the host.

Most animal viruses lack specialized attachment structures and have attachment sites located throughout the virion's surface. However, enveloped viruses such as orthomyxoviruses and paramyxoviruses attach to the host cell through glycoprotein spikes. Adsorption occurs to specific receptors on the host cell. For example, orthomyxoviruses bind specifically to the sialic acid residues on the plasma membrane. Polioviruses bind only to cells of primates, and preferentially to cells of the central nervous system and cells lining the intestinal tract. Following adsorption, most enveloped viruses enter the cell by **endocytosis,** a process in which the virion is ingested

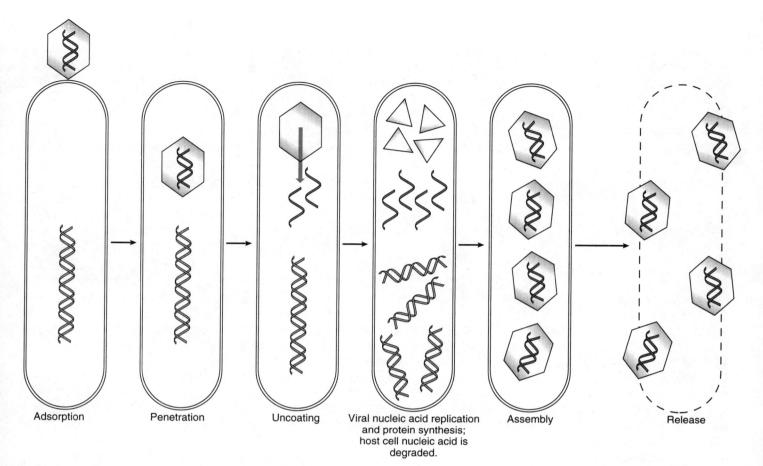

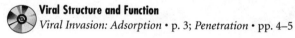

Adsorption Penetration Uncoating Viral nucleic acid replication and protein synthesis; host cell nucleic acid is degraded. Assembly Release

figure 13.13

Steps Associated with Virus Replication

Virus replication begins with adsorption of the virus to a host cell, followed by penetration of the virus or its nucleic acid into the cell (and uncoating in plant viruses). Viral nucleic acid is replicated and viral proteins are synthesized inside the host cell. New virus particles are assembled and mature viruses are released from the host cell.

Viral Structure and Function
Viral Invasion: Adsorption • p. 3; *Penetration* • pp. 4–5

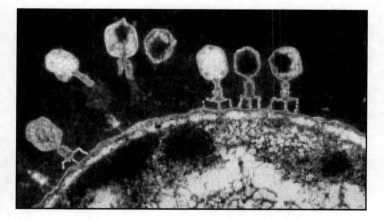

figure 13.14

Electron Micrograph of T4 Bacteriophages Attached to *Escherichia coli*

Bacteriophage attachment to receptors on the host cell surface is followed by injection of the phage nucleic acid into the cell (colorized, ×126,000).

into a phagolysosome (a vesicle inside the cytoplasm that fuses with a lysosome) and then later released into the cytoplasm. Some enveloped viruses enter by fusion of the virion envelope with the plasma membrane. Animal viruses that lack an envelope penetrate by endocytosis or by direct passage through the plasma membrane.

Plant viruses enter plant cells through openings in damaged cell walls, often formed by insects feeding on plant tissues. Inside the host cell, the virion is uncoated and its nucleic acid is released into the cytoplasm. The mechanism of uncoating is poorly understood but may involve host cell proteases.

Adsorption, penetration, and uncoating results in a period of the virus replication cycle in which infectivity is lost. During this period, known as the **eclipse,** no mature viral particles are present. In some viruses such as bacteriophage T4, the eclipse is characterized by a degradation of host DNA and a shift of the host metabolic machinery to synthesis of viral proteins. In the case of bacteriophage T4, viral genes are expressed in two stages: early proteins and late proteins. The early proteins are synthesized during the initial stages of viral infection and provide those viral-specific enzymes

Evidence That Bacteriophage Nucleic Acid, Not Protein, Enters the Host Cell During Infection

A major milestone in virology was the experiment of Alfred D. Hershey and Martha Chase in 1952 showing that bacteriophage nucleic acid, not the protein coat, different suspensions of *Escherichia coli*. Following infection, Hershey and Chase separated the infected cells from any unattached virions by low-speed centrifugation. radioactive label was lost after the blending step. In contrast, when ^{32}P-labeled phages were used for infection, most (65% to 80%) of the radioactive label remained within the blended cells. Second, the blended cells pro-

enters the host cell during infection (Figure 13.15). Hershey and Chase took bacteriophage T2 particles with radioactive ^{32}P and others with radioactive ^{35}S. Because all of the phosphorus in a bacteriophage is located in the nucleic acid, and sulfur is found only in the amino acids methionine and cysteine in the protein coat, this labeling was specific for these two phage components. The specifically labeled T2 particles were then used to separately infect two

They then subjected the infected host cells to violent agitation in a blender, a process that broke the phage tails and sheared off the empty coats, devoid of DNA, from the host cells. The remaining cells and injected phage material were assayed for progeny phage by the plaque technique.

Hershey and Chase's experiment yielded two significant results. First, they discovered that when ^{35}S-labeled phages were used to infect *E. coli*, 75% to 80% of the

duced normal phage progeny. These results showed that the protein portion of a bacteriophage remains outside the host cell during infection, whereas the nucleic acid enters the cell. Furthermore, because blended infected cells had lost their previously attached phage coats and tails but could still produce mature phage progeny, the experiment clearly showed that the phage nucleic acid, not the protein coat, carried the genetic information required for replication.

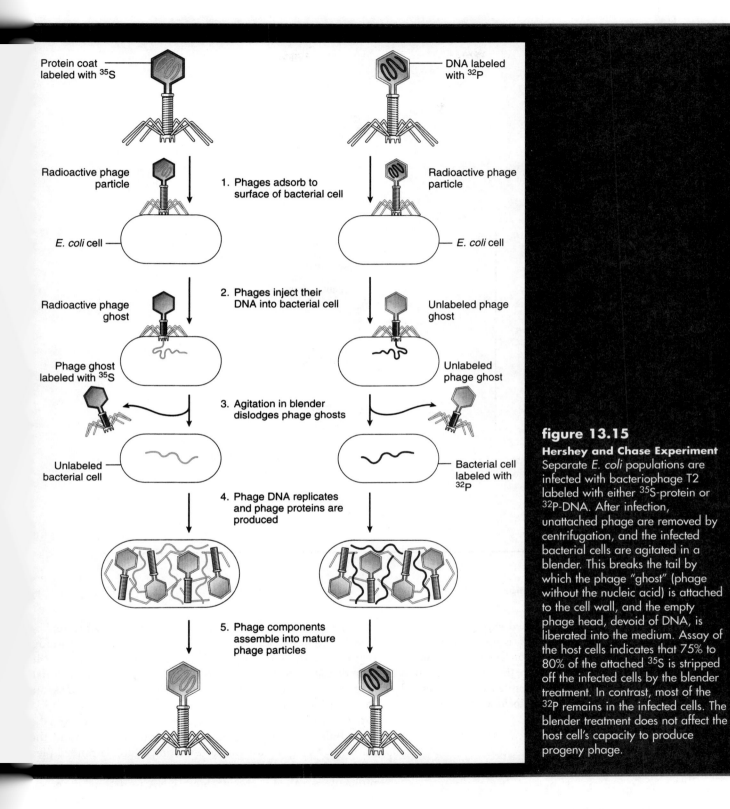

Protein coat labeled with ^{35}S

DNA labeled with ^{32}P

Radioactive phage particle

Radioactive phage particle

1. Phages adsorb to surface of bacterial cell

E. coli cell

E. coli cell

Radioactive phage ghost

2. Phages inject their DNA into bacterial cell

Unlabeled phage ghost

Phage ghost labeled with ^{35}S

Unlabeled phage ghost

3. Agitation in blender dislodges phage ghosts

Unlabeled bacterial cell

Bacterial cell labeled with ^{32}P

4. Phage DNA replicates and phage proteins are produced

5. Phage components assemble into mature phage particles

figure 13.15

Hershey and Chase Experiment
Separate *E. coli* populations are infected with bacteriophage T2 labeled with either ^{35}S-protein or ^{32}P-DNA. After infection, unattached phage are removed by centrifugation, and the infected bacterial cells are agitated in a blender. This breaks the tail by which the phage "ghost" (phage without the nucleic acid) is attached to the cell wall, and the empty phage head, devoid of DNA, is liberated into the medium. Assay of the host cells indicates that 75% to 80% of the attached ^{35}S is stripped off the infected cells by the blender treatment. In contrast, most of the ^{32}P remains in the infected cells. The blender treatment does not affect the host cell's capacity to produce progeny phage.

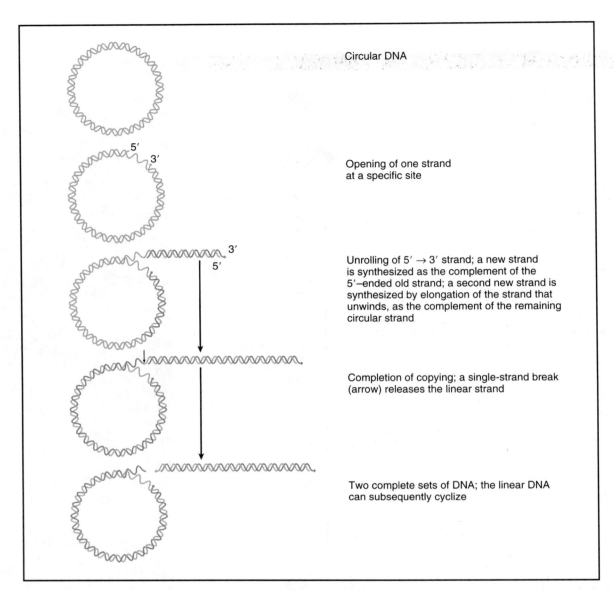

Circular DNA

Opening of one strand
at a specific site

Unrolling of 5′ → 3′ strand; a new strand
is synthesized as the complement of the
5′–ended old strand; a second new strand is
synthesized by elongation of the strand that
unwinds, as the complement of the remaining
circular strand

Completion of copying; a single-strand break
(arrow) releases the linear strand

Two complete sets of DNA; the linear DNA
can subsequently cyclize

figure 13.16
Rolling-Circle Mechanism of DNA Replication

necessary for the replication and continued expression of viral genes. The polymerases and other enzymes required for the transcription are either derived from the host or, in certain instances, are already present in the extracellular virion; these are injected into the cell with the viral nucleic acid. The late proteins are synthesized near the end of the infection process and include viral structural proteins and lytic enzymes.

 **Viral Structure and Function**
Viral Invasion • pp. 1–8

DNA Viruses Have Various Methods for Replication of DNA

The method of replication of DNA viral genomes depends on the type of genome. Most DNA viruses have double-stranded DNA that is either linear (poxvirus, herpesvirus, bacteriophage λ, and T-even phages) or circular (papovavirus and baculovirus).

In most cases, linear DNA is circularized before replication by the joining of short, complementary single-stranded regions on the ends of the DNA. The circularized double-stranded DNA is then replicated by a **rolling-circle mechanism** (Figure 13.16). An endonuclease nicks one strand of DNA, and the 5′ end of this strand is unwound and serves as a template for the synthesis of new DNA. The remaining circular DNA strand also is used as a template to elongate the strand that unwinds. As replication proceeds, a long double-stranded piece of DNA forms, with repetitive copies of the viral genome. This molecule is called a **concatamer** (DNA units linked end-to-end). The concatamer subsequently is cut by an endonuclease to form virion-sized genomes.

Bacteriophage T4 has a linear, double-stranded DNA genome but does not replicate by the rolling-circle mechanism. Instead, the DNA is replicated bidirectionally, as in bacteria. However, unlike

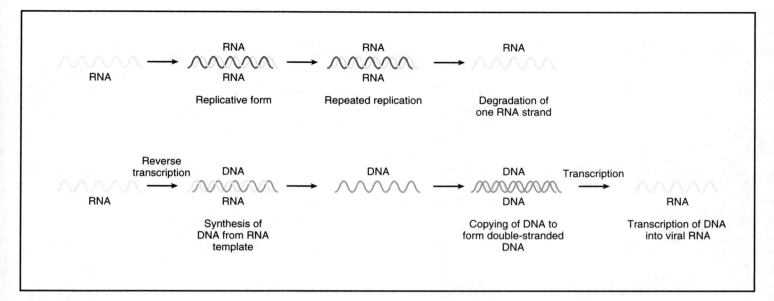

RNA → RNA / RNA (Replicative form) → RNA / RNA (Repeated replication) → RNA (Degradation of one RNA strand)

RNA →(Reverse transcription)→ DNA / RNA (Synthesis of DNA from RNA template) → DNA → DNA / DNA (Copying of DNA to form double-stranded DNA) →(Transcription)→ RNA (Transcription of DNA into viral RNA)

figure 13.17

Replication in Single-Stranded RNA Viruses

Single-stranded RNA viruses replicate their genomes by one of two modes. (a) The RNA is replicated to produce a replicative form, which becomes a template for the synthesis of RNA copies. (b) In retroviruses, the viral RNA genome serves as a template for the synthesis of a DNA molecule by reverse transcription. The DNA is copied to form double-stranded DNA, which then is transcribed into viral RNA.

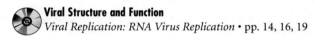

Viral Structure and Function
Viral Replication: RNA Virus Replication • pp. 14, 16, 19

bacterial DNA replication, bacteriophage T4 DNA replication occurs with repeated initiations so that a concatamer is formed. The concatamer subsequently is cleaved to form virion-sized genomes.

In the case of viruses that have single-stranded DNA, such as bacteriophage φX174, the DNA is converted to a double-stranded form, called the **replicative form,** by host DNA polymerase. The replicative form then replicates by the rolling-circle mechanism, but one of the DNA strands is discarded before new viral particles are assembled.

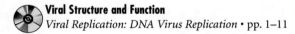

Viral Structure and Function
Viral Replication: DNA Virus Replication • pp. 1–11

RNA Viruses Have Various Methods for Replication of RNA

Double-stranded RNA viruses, such as reovirus, replicate in a manner similar to double-stranded DNA viruses, except that ribonucleotides instead of deoxyribonucleotides are used as the precursors. Single-stranded RNA viruses replicate in one of two manners. In most cases (togavirus, picornavirus, paramyxovirus, and rhabdovirus), the virion RNA is copied using a viral RNA replicase to form a complementary strand, which serves as a template to make additional copies of the genome. During replication the two complementary strands combine to form an intermediary replicative form. In retroviruses [Latin *retro,* backward] the single-stranded RNA genome (considered to be a plus strand) directly serves as a template for the synthesis of single-stranded DNA (minus strand DNA) using a viral reverse tran-

scriptase (RNA-dependent DNA polymerase) (Figure 13.17). This DNA is then copied to form double-stranded DNA, which may be used as a template for the synthesis of viral RNA or be integrated into the host genome. Many retroviruses are oncogenic, causing sarcomas, leukemias, and lymphomas in animals; it is this integration of viral-coded DNA into the host cell genome that causes cell transformation.

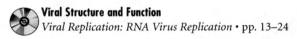

Viral Structure and Function
Viral Replication: RNA Virus Replication • pp. 13–24

Complete Virions Are Formed During Assembly

Viral components synthesized within the host cell must be packaged into complete virions prior to release. In the case of many bacteriophages, this assembly process is spontaneous and begins with the aggregation of capsomere subunits into complete capsids. Viral nucleic acid is then inserted into these empty phage heads, where the nucleic acid is condensed into a tightly packed mass. In complex viruses, the assembly process may involve several sequential steps, which eventually produce complete virions. It is known, for example, that the maturation and assembly of bacteriophage T4 takes place in three separate pathways involving synthesis of the head, tail, and tail fibers.

In enveloped animal viruses, assembly occurs by the wrapping of a portion of the host plasma membrane around the viral nucleoprotein core as it passes through the membrane to the outside of the cell. Prior to this step, viral-specified envelope proteins

One of the procedures often used to study phage growth as a function of time is the **one-step growth curve,** initially described by Max Delbrück and Emory Ellis

One-Step Growth Curve

(Figure 13.18). A heavy suspension of bacteria infected with bacteriophage is incubated for a few minutes to allow phage attachment to the bacteria. The suspension is then diluted several thousandfold and reincubated. Samples are removed from the suspension at different times and assayed for phage particles by the plaque method.

The results of such an experiment show that phage growth can be divided into several distinct phases. The first portion of phage growth is a **latent period** in which the number of plaque-forming units remains constant. During this period, the phages, which have infected the host cells, replicate and synthesize new material. Plating of a sample from the suspension during the latent period produces only one plaque per phage-infected bacterium. Although each infected bacterium may have several phage particles, these are immature at the time of plating. As a consequence, the progeny phages released from each bacterium are confined on the plate within the immediate area of the bacterium, resulting in the formation of a single plaque. In fact, samples taken at the very beginning of the growth curve produce no plaques, because immediately after entry into the host cell, the phage nucleic acid has not had an opportunity to replicate. This initial portion of the latent period, when no phage is produced, is known as the **eclipse period.**

As phage particles mature and are released from lysed bacterial cells, the number of detectable phages in the suspension dramatically increases. This increase, called the **rise period,** continues until all of the infected bacteria have lysed and released their contents of progeny phage. At this time the number of detectable phage particles reaches a plateau. The quantity of phage released from each bacterium can be calculated in a one-step growth curve by determining the ratio of phage particles at the beginning and end of the rise period. This ratio is called the **burst size** and is unique for any given phage-host interaction.

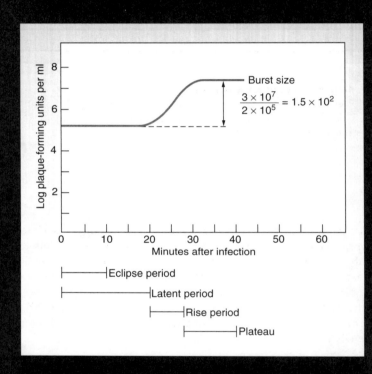

figure 13.18
A One-Step Growth Curve
A one-step growth curve consists of a latent period (which includes an eclipse period), a rise period, and a plateau. The burst size is determined by the ratio of phage particles at the beginning and end of the rise period. In this example, the burst size is 1.5×10^2.

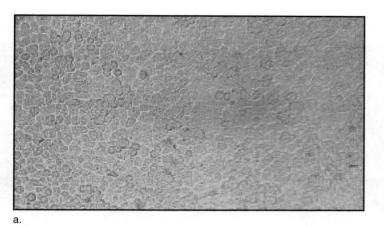
a.

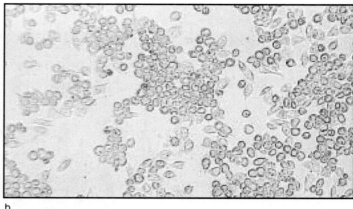
b.

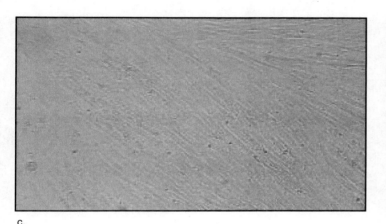
c.

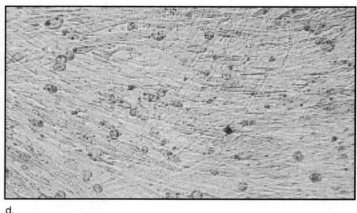
d.

figure 13.19

Examples of Cytopathic Effects

a. Normal human Hep-2 cell line. b. Human Hep-2 cell line infected with herpesvirus. The cytopathic effect is seen as discrete aggregations of cells. c. Normal human diploid cell line. d. Human diploid cell line infected with cytomegalovirus. The cytopathic effect is seen as rounded and enlarged cells with splitting of the cell layer and stranding.

migrate to the plasma membrane and replace the host proteins in the membrane. Thus the viral envelope consists of a combination of viral-specified proteins and host-specified lipids.

Viral Structure and Function
Viral Assembly: Viral Assembly • p. 2

Intact Virions Are Released from the Host After Assembly

The last step in virus replication is release of the intact virions from the host. The specific mechanism of release depends on the type of virus that has infected the cell. Bacteriophages are released from bacteria with plasma membranes typically disrupted by action of the enzyme lysozyme, one of the late proteins specified by the viral genome (filamentous phages and bacteriophage ϕX174 releases do not involve lysozyme).

Most phage release is an immediate process resulting in rapid cell lysis and death (although some bacteriophages such as M13 have a slow and nondestructive release). In contrast, the liberation of animal viruses is usually a slow process, often continuing for several hours. Animal viruses are either released through ruptures in the plasma membrane or, in the case of enveloped viruses, by a budding process from the host plasma membrane. In this latter instance, the viral envelope is actually derived from the host membrane, which has been modified by the insertion of viral-coded proteins. Because virus particles are gradually released from animal cells, the host cell may continue to metabolize during the process.

Viral Structure and Function
Viral Assembly: Virion Release • pp. 3–6

Viral Infections in Animal and Plant Cells Can Result in Cytopathic Effects

One of the consequences of viral infections in animal and plant cells is physical damage to the cells. Such morphological changes, which can be seen microscopically and macroscopically, are termed **cytopathic effects (CPEs).** Examples of CPEs are changes in the structure of the nucleolus; formation of inclusion bodies; and damage to the plasma membrane, with a tendency for cells to become rounded and fuse together to form giant cells, or polykaryocytes (Figure 13.19). CPEs occur early in the infection

One of the problems associated with viral diseases is linked to the nature of their replication. Because viruses are metabolically inert under extracellular the translation of viral mRNA (Figure 13.20). These compounds can also be chemically induced by exposing cells to double-stranded RNA, which suggests

Are Viral Diseases Treatable?

conditions and utilize the host metabolic machinery during replication, antimicrobial agents are generally ineffective in controlling viral infections. Antimicrobial agents could be used to inhibit viral replication within the host cell, but such inhibition would also have to be directed against cellular metabolism and consequently would also be detrimental to the host.

Different substances, however, have been used to control viral infections. These antiviral agents include dyes, interferons, and other chemical compounds. Two of these agents are particularly promising: **acyclovir** and **interferons.** Acyclovir, a nucleoside derivative, has been shown to be of limited effectiveness in controlling genital herpes. Interferons, glycoproteins first described by Alick Issacs and Jean Lindenmann in 1957, also have been used to interfere with viral replication. Interferons are naturally produced by mammalian cells during viral infection and inhibit viral replication, specifically

that viral double-stranded RNAs synthesized during infection may be the actual mediators of interferon induction.

Interferons are cell specific, not virus specific, and are most effective when they are produced by cells of the same species. This specificity of interferons presents problems in the industrial production of these antiviral agents. In the past, interferons were extracted with great expense and difficulty from human white blood cells. Recent advances in genetic engineering, however, have made it possible to genetically manipulate bacteria for the production of this compound. As a result, large quantities of interferon are now available for use in the treatment of viral diseases, including cancer.

Viral Structure and Function
Viral Disease: Viral Therapy • pp. 19–27

Microbial Pathogenesis
Nonspecific Host Defense: Cellular Defenses • p. 30

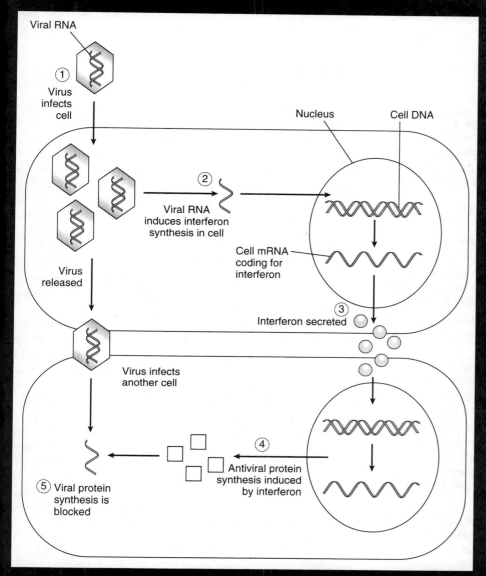

Viral RNA

① Virus infects cell

② Viral RNA induces interferon synthesis in cell

Virus released

Virus infects another cell

⑤ Viral protein synthesis is blocked

Nucleus

Cell DNA

Cell mRNA coding for interferon

③ Interferon secreted

④ Antiviral protein synthesis induced by interferon

figure 13.20

Mode of Action of Interferon

The general sequence of events associated with interferon production and activity follows. (1) Interferon production begins after virus infection of a cell. Double-stranded RNA viruses are particularly good inducers of interferon production. (2) The viral RNA induces interferon synthesis in the host cell. (3) This particular host cell is not protected by the interferon, but the interferon released from the infected cell moves to other uninfected cells and binds to their surfaces. (4–5) These uninfected cells, which now have interferon on their surfaces, are stimulated to produce at least two enzymes: a 2′, 5′-oligoadenylate synthetase that catalyzes the synthesis of an unusual polymer (2′, 5′-oligoadenylate) and a protein kinase. 2′, 5′-oligoadenylate activates an intracellular ribonuclease that degrades viral RNA. The protein kinase is activated only in the presence of double-stranded RNA, which, with the exception of the retroviruses, is formed as an intermediate in the replication of RNA viruses. The activated protein kinase catalyzes the phosphorylation of one of the factors (eIF2a) required for the initiation of protein synthesis. The phosphorylated eIF2a is inactive and, therefore, synthesis of all proteins, including viral proteins, ceases. There are three major classes of human interferons (IFN-α, IFN-β, and IFN-γ), which have as their major cell sources leukocytes, fibroblasts, and lymphocytes, respectively.

process and are believed to result from viral inhibition of host macromolecular synthesis. A visible consequence of CPEs are the plaques or pocks that appear from the viral infection of host cells, resulting from **lytic infections** (infections in which mature progeny virions are released from a lysed cell).

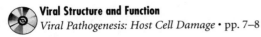
Viral Structure and Function
Viral Pathogenesis: Host Cell Damage • pp. 7–8

Other Consequences of Viral Infections

Lytic infections are only one effect of virus infection. Other possible consequences of virus-host cell interactions are **persistent infections, abortive infections, transforming infections,** and **lysogeny.**

Viruses Can Be Continuously Released from a Host Cell

Persistent infections are those in which viruses are continuously released from a cell that is not immediately killed. Under such conditions the host cell survives and continues to metabolize. An example of a persistent infection is infection of monkey kidney cells by **paramyxovirus SV5** (simian virus 5). Although SV5 causes lytic infection in many cells, it infects monkey kidney cells with practically no cell damage. The infected cells continue to grow and produce virus.

A similar but somewhat different situation occurs in the case of **defective interfering (DI)** viruses. DI viruses lack complete genomes and therefore are unable to multiply without assistance from other virions. However, when DI viruses and normal, infectious viruses simultaneously infect a cell, the result can be a reduction in cell damage and quantity of viruses released—a persistent infection. DI viruses arise from errors in viral replication and are believed to be involved in infections by **measles virus, Newcastle Disease Virus (NDV),** and **Western Equine Encephalitis (WEE) virus.**

Persistent infections also occur when the production of infectious viral particles is dampened by the presence of antibodies or antiviral agents. In some instances a virion may be less virulent in a particular host, resulting in a persistent rather than a lytic infection.

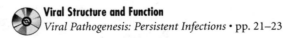
Viral Structure and Function
Viral Pathogenesis: Persistent Infections • pp. 21–23

There Can Be a Significant Reduction or Elimination of Virus Production in the Host

Not all viral infections lead to high-level production of complete, intact virions. Under certain conditions when there is interference in the viral multiplication cycle, virus production can be significantly reduced or completely eliminated. Such abortive infections occur when virions infect nonpermissive (not supporting productive viral infections) or not fully permissive cells, when there is a defect in components required for virus multiplication, or when antiviral agents interfere in the normal infection process.

Virus Infection Can Lead to Cell Transformation

Infections by certain types of DNA or RNA viruses can lead to transforming infections—those causing unregulated cell growth, or **cell transformation.** Transformed cells are distinguished from normal cells by changes in metabolism, the appearance of new antigens on the plasma membranes, altered morphology, and a loss in **contact inhibition.** Contact inhibition is a characteristic of animal cells in tissue culture. Normal cells in tissue culture move in a random amoeboid manner until the ruffled edges on their membranes touch. This contact slows down and inhibits further cell movement and division, resulting in a monolayer of cells. Transformed cells lose this contact inhibition and aggregate into masses of abnormal growth characteristic of **neoplasms,** or **tumors.**

Tumors may be **benign** or **malignant.** Benign (noncancerous) tumors arise when cells lose their ability to stop moving and grow upon contact with similar cell types, but still exhibit contact inhibition with other cell types. Malignant (cancerous) tumors, in contrast, consist of cells that do not respond to contact inhibition from either their own cell types or other cell types. Benign tumors, although rarely fatal, can grow large enough to interfere with normal host function. There are records of benign tumors weighing as much as 20 kg and displacing body organs. Malignant cells spread through the body via other tissues, blood, and the lymphatic system and therefore present a more serious problem to the host. Neoplasms, whether benign or malignant, are further categorized by their location in the organism. **Carcinomas** arise from epithelial tissue; **fibromas** from fibrous connective tissue; **melanomas** from pigment (melanin) cells; and **sarcomas** from connective tissue found in such areas as bone, muscle, and lymph nodes.

Viral Structure and Function
Viral Pathogenesis: Host Cell Damage • pp. 12–13

Oncogenic Viruses Cause Tumors

Both DNA viruses and RNA viruses are known to cause certain types of neoplasms in animals. Examples of **oncogenic** (tumor-causing) DNA viruses are papovaviruses, adenoviruses, and herpesviruses. **Simian virus 40 (SV40),** a papovavirus that was originally isolated from monkey kidney cells, causes tumors in the baby hamster. Adenoviruses of human or animal origin in many instances are oncogenic for newborn rodents. Certain types of herpesviruses are naturally oncogenic for animals and at least two of these viruses, **herpes simplex virus type 2** and **Epstein-Barr virus (EBV),** show possible evidence of involvement in human cancers. Two types of herpes simplex virus infect humans: **herpes simplex virus type 1** causes fever blisters and cold sores, and herpes simplex virus type 2 (or genital herpes, as it is commonly known) is primarily responsible for sexually transmitted genital infections (although herpes simplex virus type 1 can also cause genital infections). Epidemiological evidence has revealed not only that women with herpes simplex type 2 infections have a higher-than-average rate of cervical carcinoma, but also that some women having cervical carcinoma have high herpes simplex type 2 antibody titers. This evidence is only suggestive at this point, not definitive. Epstein-Barr virus, the causative agent of infectious mononucleosis, is another virus associated with human malignant disease. EBV has been found in tumor cells from patients with Burkitt's lymphoma, a neoplasm of lymphoid tissue found especially in children living in central Africa, and nasopharyngeal carcinoma.

Viral Structure and Function
Viral Disease: Enveloped DNA Virus • pp. 6–8

The retroviruses (RNA viruses) have been found to be oncogenic. One of these oncogenic retroviruses, **Rous sarcoma virus** (an oncornavirus), has been extensively studied. It was first isolated by Francis P. Rous and produces malignant tumors in birds. It also is one of the RNA viruses in which the enzyme reverse transcriptase was first discovered in 1970 by David Baltimore of the Massachusetts Institute of Technology, and Satoshi Mizutani and Howard M. Temin of the University of Wisconsin.

In recent years another retrovirus, the **human T cell lymphotrophic virus (HTLV),** has been strongly implicated in certain forms of human leukemia involving white blood cells called T cells. Robert Gallo of the National Cancer Institute has found HTLV antibodies in individuals with T-cell cancers. These and other findings suggest a clear association between HTLV and T-cell changes. At least three types of HTLVs have thus far been discovered. **HTLV-I** and **HTLV-II** are leukemia-lymphoma viruses. **HTLV-III** (now known as **human immunodeficiency virus,** or **HIV 1**) causes acquired immune deficiency syndrome (AIDS) (see AIDS, page 536). It has been suggested that the AIDS virus may have originated from a species of monkey (the African green) that carries a virus (**STLV-III,** for **simian T lymphotrophic virus type III**) that is remarkably similar to HIV 1. STLV-III does not cause illness in the African green monkey, but other monkeys and humans do get sick from it; AIDS is endemic (continuously present in the population) in central Africa, where the African green monkey is found. A second virus associated with AIDS, **HIV 2,** was discovered in 1986 in prostitutes in Senegal, West Africa. HIV 2 is related to a simian immunodeficiency virus (**SIV**) found in monkeys and appears to produce less severe disease than does HIV 1.

How do these oncogenic viruses transform cells? One theory states that cancer genes (**oncogenes**) on the chromosome cause cell transformation. It is easier to envision how DNA viruses could carry oncogenes in their genome and insert such cancer-causing genes directly into the host genome during infection. RNA viruses, however, present a problem with their RNA genome. For many years scientists questioned how genes in an RNA virus could be inserted into host DNA. It is now known that retroviruses contain reverse transcriptase. This enzyme transcribes viral RNA into DNA, which can subsequently be incorporated into the host DNA. This viral-coded DNA is sometimes known as a **provirus.** Reverse transcriptase, however, is not always associated with transformation; oncogenic RNA viruses possess reverse transcriptase, but not all viruses with reverse transcriptase are oncogenic. The enzyme nonetheless is important in cancer and explains the involvement of retroviruses in this disease.

Cancer Can Be Caused by Nonviral Factors

Viruses are not the only causative agents of cancer. Chemicals, radiation, and environmental factors are known to be intimately associated with different types of human cancers and may, in fact, induce oncogenes. Many of these carcinogens (cancer-causing agents) are commonly found in the environment and in industries. The addition of chemical cancer-causing agents to processed foods for preservation or flavor is particularly alarming and has come under close scrutiny in recent years. Governmental agencies have also monitored chemical pollution of the environment, especially where the chemicals are known tumor-inducing agents.

Cancer is a most-feared disease and is second only to cardiovascular disease as the greatest killer of our population. It is estimated that one out of every four people in the United States will develop cancer during their lifetime, with the majority of these individuals dying from the disease. The mortality rate of cancer in this country has nearly doubled in the last decade.

Despite these alarming statistics, there have actually been significant advances in the detection and treatment of human neoplasia (abnormal tissue growth) in the past few years. Acute lymphatic leukemia, at one time considered to be incurable, can now be treated with chemotherapy, with 50% of treated children living five years or more. Although no definitive vaccine or cure for cancer is available at this time, surgery, radiation therapy, and combination immunotherapy and chemotherapy regimens are often successful in arresting malignancies. As additional information is generated on the epidemiology of cancer—particularly on

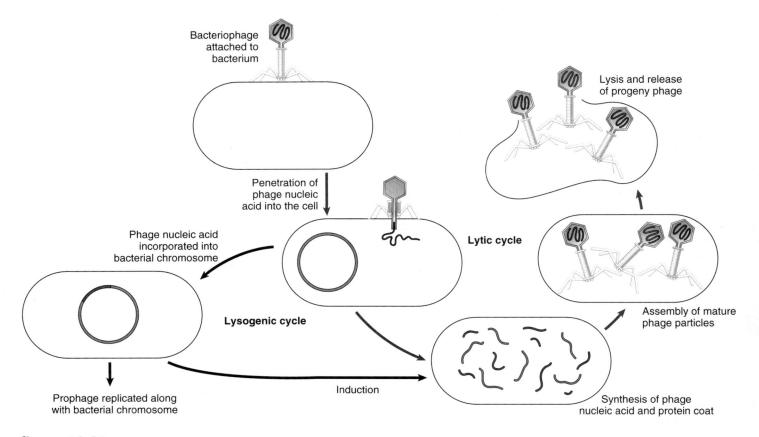

figure 13.21

Lysogeny

In a normal lytic cycle of infection, the bacteriophage replicates within the host cell, and progeny phage are released upon cell lysis. In a lysogenic cycle, the phage nucleic acid is incorporated into the bacterial chromosome and is replicated along with the chromosome. The prophage remains a part of the bacterial chromosome until it is induced to leave and enter a normal lytic cycle.

the role of viruses and other carcinogenic agents in the cause of different cancers—it should be possible to control and even eliminate many forms of this deadly disease.

A Bacteriophage Can Be Incorporated into the Host Chromosome in Lysogeny

A counterpart to transforming infections in eucaryotes is lysogeny in bacteriophage-bacteria interactions (Figure 13.21). Unlike normal lytic cycles of infection, in which bacteriophages replicate within the host cell and their progeny are released upon cell lysis, lysogeny involves incorporation of phage DNA into the host cell genome. This viral DNA, known as a **prophage,** is replicated along with the host DNA and vertically passed to daughter cells.

Not all bacteriophages are capable of lysogeny. Those that can enter such a relationship as well as participate in lytic infections are called **temperate,** to distinguish them from **virulent**

phages, which are capable only of lytic infections. It is difficult to determine if a bacterium carries a prophage. Bacteria containing prophages are called **lysogenic,** or **lysogens,** and can usually be identified as prophage carriers only when the prophage is released from the host genome and produces progeny phage particles upon resumption of the lytic cycle.

Lysogeny occurs with numerous types of bacteria and bacteriophages but has been extensively studied with the temperate bacteriophage λ, which infects *E. coli.* Bacteriophage λ has a shape similar to T-even bacteriophages, with a slender tail and a head filled with linear double-stranded DNA, but no tail fibers. Infection of a sensitive *E. coli* cell by this temperate phage results in one of two possible fates: a normal lytic cycle ensues, or the phage DNA is integrated into the bacterial genome during lysogeny. Whether or not lysogeny occurs is under the control of the infecting phage and depends on the activity of two repressors coded by a regulatory region on the phage genome. Should lysogeny be the choice, the phage DNA is circularized and integrated into the bacterial genome. Insertion of the phage nucleic acid always occurs in the same location on the host genome for any given *E. coli* cell. Whereas the phage genes are usually not expressed in this integrated form, the prophage is replicated with the bacterial DNA.

The prophage remains a part of the bacterial genome until it is **induced** to leave and enter into a normal lytic cycle. Induction occurs either spontaneously or artificially. Prophages can be artificially induced to enter a lytic cycle by exposure of the bacterial cells to a number of different agents that are known to alter DNA. Ultraviolet radiation, mitomycin C, and X rays are among these inducing agents.

An alternative to induction of a prophage is the **curing** of a lysogenic bacterium. Lysogenic bacteria are cured if their prophages are excised from the host genome and do not replicate to form progeny phage. Curing is accomplished by heavy irradiation or chemical treatment of the host cell. The cured cell no longer has a prophage and is susceptible to reinfection by the same phage or other phage types.

A bacterium that has entered into a lysogenic relationship with a particular phage cannot be reinfected with the same phage. This resistance is controlled by the same regulatory region on the phage genome that determines if lysogeny will occur. Occasionally a prophage may undergo mutations in its DNA that render it unable to produce progeny phage upon induction. These **defective prophages** can be recognized because curing of the lysogen may result in lysis, but with the release of incomplete, noninfectious phage particles. If, however, lysogenic bacteria containing such defective prophages are **superinfected** (infected with a different phage), the second phage acts as a **helper,** in some instances donating its genes to complement the missing genes in the defective prophage. The result is the release of a mixture of defective and normal progeny phage from the lysed cell during induction.

Lysogeny is a phenomenon that has important consequences for bacteria. Lysogens become resistant to superinfection by phages of the same type. More importantly, however, bacteria that integrate phage genes into their genome may assume new characteristics, a process known as **lysogenic conversion.** The pathogen *Corynebacterium diphtheriae,* for example, synthesizes a toxin that destroys epithelial cells lining the respiratory tract, resulting in a pseudomembrane characteristic of the disease diphtheria (see diphtheria, page 507). The toxin is not coded by the bacterial genome but by a gene (*tox* gene) on a temperate phage (**prophage β**). Cells of *C. diphtheriae* synthesize toxin only when they have undergone lysogenic conversion. If such cells are cured of their prophage, they no longer synthesize the toxin, and are incapable of causing disease. The expression of the *tox* gene is controlled by the metabolism and physiological state of the host bacterium. Toxin production is regulated by the exogenous Fe^{2+} supply; maximum toxin is produced only when the exogenous Fe^{2+} supply is low. Although it is not exactly known how Fe^{2+} regulates toxin production, one popular theory is that high exogenous Fe^{2+} concentrations induce the prophage to enter a lytic cycle, resulting in nonexpression of the *tox* gene.

Lysogenic conversions are common among toxin-producing bacteria. The scarlet-fever-causing erythrogenic toxin produced by *Streptococcus pyogenes* (see scarlet fever, page 498) and toxins produced by some strains of *Clostridium botulinum* (see botulism, page 517) are coded by prophages. In many cases lysogenic conversions are directly responsible for the virulence of pathogenic bacteria.

In 1957 two physicians, D. Carleton Gajdusek and Vincent Zigas, described a progressive degenerative disease confined to a small population in the eastern highlands of Papua New Guinea. This disease, characterized by cerebral ataxia (incoordination), neuronal loss, and a shivering-like tremor, was named **kuru** ("shivering," or "trembling," in the Foré language of the afflicted people).

Kuru was the first human degenerative disease shown to be caused by a prion, a finding that opened a new, exciting frontier in microbiology. Unlike conventional viral diseases, kuru has unique characteristics (Table 13P.1).

The kuru prion resembles viruses in its filterability (filterable in the 25-nm to 50-nm average pore diameter range), reaches high titers (up to 10^8 to 10^{10} infectious units per gram of tissue) in the brains of experimentally infected animals, and restriction of host range (humans are the only apparent natural hosts, although chimpanzees and other nonhuman primates have been experimentally infected). However, the kuru prion

table 13P.1

Properties of Kuru

- Long incubation period.
- Lack of immunogenicity or host immune response.
- Chronic progressive illness without remission or relapse.
- Induction of spongiform change, neuronal loss, and gliosis.
- Absence of specific viral particle by electron microscopy.
- Specific nucleic acid not yet identified, and resistance to procedures that attack nucleic acids (resistant to low pH, nucleases, ultraviolet irradiation at 237 nm, zinc hydrolysis, photochemical inactivation with psoralens, and chemical modification by hydroxylamine).
- Unaffected by immunosuppression, immunopotentiation, or most antiviral drugs; splenectomy or other factors that alter splenic function may vary the course of infection.
- No cytopathic effect in tissue culture.
- Unusual spectrum of resistance to certain physical and chemical treatments.

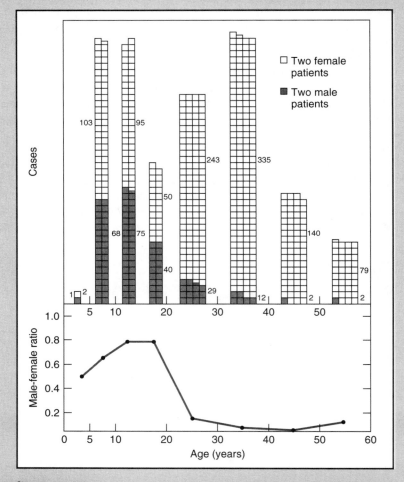

figure 13P.1

Age and Sex Distribution of the First 1,276 Kuru Patients Studied in Early Epidemiological Investigations

These early studies suggested that kuru was confined primarily to women and children. In recent years, age and sex patterns of the disease have completely changed; kuru is now found only among young adults (who were infected as children), not among the children.

has other, unconventional properties that are not associated with viruses. It is unusually resistant to ultrasonication, heat, ionizing radiation, and a variety of chemical agents. Furthermore, the kuru agent is resistant to procedures that attack nucleic acids: it has resistance to low pH, nucleases, ultraviolet irradiation at 237 nm, zinc hydrolysis, and chemical modification by hydroxylamine. This indicates that it does not possess nucleic acid.

Initial epidemiological studies showed that kuru was a disease confined primarily to the Foré women and children (Figure 13P.1). Further studies revealed that the disease was transmitted by ritual cannibalism among the tribes of this region. As a rite of mourning and respect for dead relatives and clansmen, women and children ate the viscera and highly infectious brains of the corpses. With missionary intervention in the late 1950s, cannibalism ceased among the Foré people and the incidence of kuru also decreased (Figure 13P.2). Since 1957 kuru has been disappearing gradually. Today it occurs only among the young adults (who were infected as children 40 years ago), not among the children. No one born in a village since the cessation of cannibalism has ever developed kuru. Because there is no other

known reservoir besides humans for the kuru prion, it is predicted that kuru will eventually be eliminated as a disease. However, it will always remain as a model of diseases caused by prions.

Sources

Gajdusek, D.C. ©The Nobel Foundation 1977. Unconventional viruses and the origin and disappearance of kuru. *Science* 197:943–960.

Prusiner, S.B. 1995. The prion diseases. *Scientific American* 72:48–57.

References

Alpers, M.P. 1979. Epidemiology and ecology of kuru. In *Slow transmissible diseases of the nervous system*. Vol. 1, *Clinical, epidemiological, genetic, and pathological aspects of the spongiform encephalopathies*. S.B. Prusiner, and W.J. Hadlow, eds. 67–90. New York: Academic Press.

Gajdusek, D.C., and V. Zigas. 1957. Degenerative disease of the central nervous system in New Guinea: the endemic occurrence of "kuru" in the native population. *New England Journal of Medicine* 257:974–978.

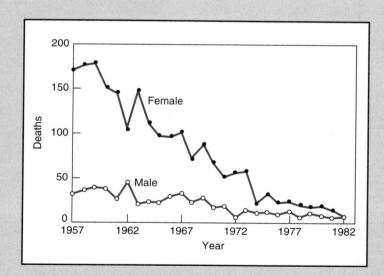

figure 13P.2
The Overall Incidence of Kuru Deaths in Male and Female Patients by Year Since Its Discovery in 1957

Summary

1. Viruses are intracellular parasites that metabolize and reproduce only within a host cell. All viruses have genetic material in the form of DNA or RNA surrounded by a protein coat (capsid). Some animal viruses also have a membranous envelope.

2. Viruses have three basic forms: polyhedral, helical, and binal. Animal and plant viruses display polyhedral or helical symmetry. The T-even bacteriophages have a binal structure that consists of three parts: a head composed of protein subunits surrounding the viral genome, a narrow sheath, and a tail consisting of thin tail fibers.

3. Bacteriophages are classified by their morphology and nucleic acid content. The T-even bacteriophages are binal phages containing double-stranded DNA. Coliphage φX174 contains a single-stranded circular DNA genome within an icosahedral capsid. Coliphage fd is a filamentous bacteriophage with a helical symmetry and single-stranded circular DNA.

4. The plant viruses include Caulimovirus, a double-stranded DNA virus that infects cauliflower, and Tobamovirus, a single-stranded DNA virus that causes tobacco mosaic disease.

5. Animal viruses are responsible for diseases such as severe hemorrhagic fever (Ebola virus), AIDS (human immunodeficiency virus), influenza (influenza virus), and measles (rubeola virus).

6. Animal and plant viruses may be cultivated in the laboratory in tissue cultures that are derived from cell lines. Viruses also can be propagated directly on animal or plant tissue.

7. Bacteriophages are propagated on lawns of suitable host bacteria. Clear plaques form in areas of the bacterial lawn where bacteriophages have infected and lysed the bacterial cells.

8. Virus replication consists of several steps: attachment of the virion to the host (adsorption), penetration of the virus or its nucleic acid into the cell (and uncoating in animal and plant viruses), replication of the viral nucleic acid and synthesis of viral proteins, assembly and/or maturation of new virus particles, and release of mature virus particles from the cell.

9. In addition to lytic infections, virus-host cell interactions can result in persistent infections, abortive infections, transforming infections, and lysogeny.

10. Lysogeny is the incorporation of bacteriophage DNA into the host cell genome. The incorporated bacteriophage DNA, or prophage, remains a part of the cell genome until it is induced to leave and enter into a normal lytic cycle. One consequence of lysogeny is the expression of the bacteriophage genes in the host bacterium, or lysogenic conversion.

EVOLUTION *and* BIODIVERSITY

Ebola virus, Dengue virus, and human immunodeficiency virus are all examples of emerging viruses that threaten the public health and kill thousands of people each year. Forty years ago these viruses either were not known or were not of major concern. Where did these viruses come from and what happened during the past four decades that resulted in this rapid rise in disease cases? Viruses, like procaryotes and eucaryotes, have evolved over the years and, in many cases, have become adapted to modern society. HIV is believed to have arisen from the simian T-lymphotrophic virus type III that infects African green monkeys. Ebola virus, one of the most deadly viruses known, is also carried by the African green monkey and can rapidly spread through a population as it did in Kikwit, Zaire, in the spring of 1995, causing massive hemorrhaging and multiple organ failure, and killing more than 90% of its victims. The Dengue virus, although known for many years, has recently emerged to cause vast epidemics of Dengue fever in Latin America. It seems that new viruses are discovered each year that are among the most dangerous infectious agents known. What appears to be new viruses in many cases are existing viruses that have adapted to changes in environmental conditions and new hosts. Viral genomes, which are significantly smaller than the genomes of procaryotes and eucaryotes, undergo mutations relatively easily. These mutations can lead to increased virulence and new diseases. Viruses may be the smallest infectious agents, but clearly are also among the most dangerous agents known to humankind.

Questions

Short Answer

1. Describe the basic structure of viruses.

2. Explain how viruses differ from other organisms.

3. Why are viruses called "obligate intracellular parasites"?

4. Prove (give evidence) that viruses are living.

5. Prove (give evidence) that viruses are nonliving.

6. Some viruses possess a membranelike envelope. Explain.

7. How do viroids differ from virions?

8. What criteria are used to classify viruses?

9. Why does the host figure so prominently in viral classification?

10. How can these obligate intracellular parasites be studied in the laboratory? What happens to the virus if it is not given a host?

11. How can viruses be enumerated?

12. Identify, in sequence, the steps associated with viral replication.

13. Briefly describe several methods of replication for viral nucleic acids.

14. Which viruses possess reverse transcriptase? What is the role of this enzyme?

15. What would be the fate of the viral progeny if the host cell were lysed prior to their maturation and release?

16. Compare and contrast the lytic and lysogenic life cycles of bacteriophages.

17. How does the life cycle of a plant or animal virus differ from the life cycle of a bacteriophage?

18. What is cell transformation and how is it evidenced?

Multiple Choice

1. T-even bacteriophages are:
   a. binal
   b. helical
   c. polyhedral

2. Which of the following requires host enzymes?
   a. assembly/maturation
   b. attachment (or adsorption)
   c. penetration (and uncoating for some viruses)

d. replication/synthesis
e. release

3. Which of the following is an example of a DNA virus?
   a. Ebola virus
   b. herpes simplex virus
   c. influenza virus
   d. human immunodeficiency virus

Critical Thinking

1. Describe early efforts to classify viruses. Discuss the current state of classification for viruses. Describe the system you would like to see in 10 or 20 years.

2. Given the high degree of host specificity, comment on the evolutionary links between viruses and their hosts. Research what we know about restriction endonucleases and transduction. Does this change your answer?

3. Identify several forms of cancer known or suspected to be caused by viral infections. What is necessary to prove the oncogenic role of a virus? What is known about the connection between some viruses and some forms of cancer?

4. Emerging diseases (for example, Ebola, Dengue fever, AIDS) are covered in the newspapers on a daily basis. Why are these diseases "emerging"? From a public health perspective, how would you prevent these diseases? What factors must you overcome to be successful?

 Supplementary Readings

Berns, K.I. 1990. Parvovirus replication. *Microbiological Reviews* 54:316–329. (A discussion of the replication of parvovirus.)

Birge, E.A. 1994. *Bacterial and bacteriophage genetics.* New York:Springer-Verlag. (An in-depth discussion of the genetics of bacteria and bacteriophages, including mechanisms for replication of phage nucleic acids.)

Bishop, J.M. 1989. Viruses, genes, and cancer. *American Zoologist* 29:653–666. (A review of the role of viruses and oncogenes in cancer.)

Diener, T.D. 1980. Viroids. *Scientific American* 244:66–73. (An excellent review article on viroids.)

Fields, B.N., and D.M. Knipe, ed. 1991. *Fundamental virology,* 2d ed. New York: Raven Press. (A comprehensive discussion of animal and human viruses.)

Gallo, R.C. 1987. The AIDS virus. *Scientific American* 256:47–56. (A review of the human immunodeficiency virus.)

Johnson, H.M., F.W. Bazer, B.E. Szente, and M.A. Jarpe. 1994. How interferons fight disease. *Scientific American* 70:68–75. (A review of the mode of action of interferons and their use in the treatment of infectious diseases and some forms of cancer.)

Karam, J.D., ed. *Molecular biology of bacteriophage T4.* Herndon, Va.: ASM Press. (An in-depth discussion of bacteriophage T4 and its value in research and teaching.)

Le Guenno, B. 1995. Emerging viruses. *Scientific American* 73:56–64. (A review of newly discovered hemorrhagic fever viruses, including Ebola virus, Hantavirus, and Marburg virus.)

Levy, J.A., H. Fraenkel-Conrat, and R. Owens. 1994. *Virology,* 3d ed. Englewood Cliffs, N.J.: Prentice-Hall. (A textbook of virology.)

Matthews, R.E.F. 1991. *Plant virology,* 3d ed. New York: Academic Press. (A textbook of plant viruses.)

Porterfield, J.S., ed. 1995. *Exotic viral infections.* London: Chapman & Hall. (A detailed description of diverse groups of viruses that cause a variety of human diseases.)

GLOSSARY

A

abortive infection An infection in which there is interference in the viral multiplication cycle, leading to a significant reduction or complete elimination of virus production.

abortive transduction Transduction in which the transducing phage DNA is not incorporated into the host chromosome, resulting in unilinear transmission of the phage DNA to only one of the two daughter cells formed at cell division.

accessory pigment A pigment other than chlorophyll that harvests light energy and transfers it to chlorophyll.

acidophile An organism that thrives at pHs as low as 1.

acquired immune deficiency syndrome (AIDS) An infectious disease syndrome caused by human immunodeficiency virus that results in a significant deficiency of CD4$^+$ cells and increased susceptibility to opportunistic infections and some forms of cancer.

acquired resistance Specific resistance of the body to a pathogen occurring only after host exposure to the pathogen or its products; also called specific resistance.

activated sludge process An aerobic sewage treatment process in which sewage is mixed with slime-forming bacteria in a large aeration tank to break down organic matter in the sewage.

activation energy (E_a) Energy required to initiate a chemical reaction.

active site The site on an enzyme that recognizes and binds to substrate.

active transport The energy-requiring, carrier-mediated movement of molecules across a membrane against a concentration gradient.

acute period The period of disease when signs and symptoms reach their peak.

Adansonian taxonomy *See* **numerical taxonomy.**

aerobe An organism that requires molecular oxygen for growth.

aerobic respiration Catabolic reactions producing ATP in which either organic or inorganic compounds are the primary electron donors and molecular oxygen is the terminal acceptor in electron transport.

aerotaxis The movement of organisms in response to oxygen.

agammaglobulinemia An immunodeficiency disease characterized by an inability or a decreased ability to synthesize γ-globulins.

agar A polysaccharide extract of red algae that is used as a solidifying agent in microbiological media.

agglutination The formation of visible clumps by the cross-linking of antigens and their corresponding antibodies.

agranulocyte A leukocyte that does not possess cytoplasmic granules; lymphocytes and monocytes are agranulocytes.

alga(pl. **algae**) A photosynthetic eucaryotic microorganism.

algicidal Having the property of killing algae.

algistatic Inhibiting algae.

alkalophile An organism that lives and grows between pH 8.5 and 11.5.

allosteric effector A substance that binds to the allosteric site of an allosteric enzyme, causing a change in the conformation of the enzyme active site and inhibition or activation of enzyme activity.

allosteric enzyme An enzyme with a binding site (active site) for the substrate and a different site (allosteric site) for binding an allosteric effector.

alpha (α) hemolysis Lysis of red blood cells characterized by incomplete zones of clearing, sometimes accompanied by a green discoloration, surrounding microbial colonies growing on blood agar.

alternative complement pathway An antibody-independent pathway for complement activation that bypasses the sequence of events from C1 to C2 in the classical complement pathway and involves properdin and two other serum proteins designated Factors B and D; also called the properdin pathway.

Ames test A test to screen mutagens by the incidence of back mutations in histidine-requiring auxotrophs of *Salmonella typhimurium.*

amino acid An organic compound of low molecular weight containing a carboxyl group and an amino group.

aminoglycoside One of a group of antimicrobial agents that reversibly bind to the procaryotic ribosome to inhibit protein synthesis. Streptomycin, gentamicin, and kanamycin are examples of aminoglycosides.

ammonification The formation of ammonia or ammonium ions from nitrogenous compounds by microbial action.

amphibolic pathway A metabolic pathway that functions in both anabolism and catabolism.

anabolism The synthesis of new substances from precursors, usually requiring energy.

anaerobe An organism that grows in the absence of molecular oxygen.

anaerobic respiration Catabolic reactions producing ATP in which either organic or inorganic compounds are the primary electron donors and an inorganic compound other than molecular oxygen is the terminal acceptor in electron transport.

anamnestic response The recall by the immune system of a prior response to a specific antigen; also called secondary response.

anaphylactic hypersensitive reaction A violent immune response to an antigen-IgE antibody reaction, characterized by increased permeability of capillaries, edema, and inflammation; also called type I hypersensitive reaction.

anaplerotic reaction A reaction that replenishes intermediates removed from metabolic pathways.

anoxygenic photosynthesis Photosynthesis that occurs in the absence of molecular oxygen and during which molecular oxygen is not produced.

antagonism The killing, inhibition, or injury of one microorganism by another.

antibiotic A chemical, produced by a microorganism, that inhibits or kills other microorganisms.

antibody A protein produced by the body in response to an antigen and directed specifically against antigenic determinant sites; also called immunoglobulin.

antibody-mediated hypersensitive reaction *See* **immediate hypersensitive reaction.**

antigen Any molecule that induces an antibody to be produced specifically against it and that is able to react with that particular antibody.

antigenic determinant *See* **epitope.**

antigen-presenting cell (APC) A cell that processes and presents antigen to T lymphocytes.

antimicrobial agent A chemical that inhibits or kills microorganisms.

antisense DNA or RNA A single-stranded DNA or RNA with a base sequence complementary to a targeted gene's RNA message that can bind the target RNA and inhibit it.

antiseptic An antimicrobial agent that is used on external body surfaces.

antiserum (pl. antisera) Serum that contains antibodies.

antitoxin An antibody against a toxin molecule, capable of reacting with and neutralizing the toxin.

aplanospore A nonmotile spore formed by algae during reproduction.

Archaea An evolutionarily distinct domain of procaryotes distinguished from the domain Bacteria by characteristics such as rRNA sequences, lack of muramic acid in the cell wall, and ether instead of ester bonds in membrane lipids.

Arrhenius plot A plot of the logarithm of the growth rate versus the inverse of the growth temperature.

arthrospore A fungal spore formed by fragmentation of vegetative hyphae and not resistant to heat or drying.

artificially acquired passive immunity Immunity that is acquired when antibodies formed in other hosts are introduced into a new host.

ascus (pl. asci) A saclike, ascospore-containing structure in fungi of the phylum *Ascomycota.*

aseptic technique The procedure for handling cultures in such a manner as to eliminate contamination by undesired microorganisms.

assimilatory nitrate reduction The reduction of nitrate to ammonia with the incorporation of the nitrogen into cellular materials.

assimilatory sulfate reduction The reduction of sulfate to hydrogen sulfide with the incorporation of the sulfur into cellular materials.

atmosphere The gaseous mass surrounding the earth.

atomic force microscope A type of microscope in which magnifications of several millionfold are achieved by using a minute probe to trace the outline of atoms on a specimen's surface.

attenuated vaccine A vaccine consisting of live microorganisms that have been rendered avirulent or with reduced virulence, but that still are antigenic; also called live, attenuated vaccine.

attenuation A regulatory mechanism involving the control of gene expression by termination of transcription.

autoclave An instrument for sterilizing materials by high temperature, pressure, and flowing steam.

autogamy A type of reproduction in which the micronucleus divides into two separate nuclei, which join to form a zygote nucleus. The cell then divides into two daughter cells.

autotroph An organism that uses carbon dioxide as a sole source of carbon.

auxotroph A mutant that has one or more growth factor requirements.

B

Babès-Ernst body *See* **metachromatic granule.**

bacillus (pl. bacilli) A cylindrical or cigar-shaped bacterial cell.

back mutation A subsequent mutation that reverses the effects of the original mutation.

Bacteria Name for domain of procaryotes other than those of the domain Archaea.

bactericidal Having the property of killing bacteria.

bacteriochlorophyll A photosynthetic pigment found in bacteria.

bacteriocin A protein produced by bacteria that kills other, closely related bacteria.

bacteriocinogenic plasmid A plasmid that carries genes for the synthesis of bacteriocins.

bacteriolytic Having the property of killing bacteria by lysis, or dissolution, of the cell.

bacteriophage A virus capable of infecting a bacterium; also called phage.

bacteriorhodopsin A light-harvesting purple pigment in *Halobacterium* that picks up protons and transports them across the bacterial plasma membrane.

bacteriostatic Having the property of inhibiting bacteria.

bacterium (pl. bacteria) A procaryotic microorganism.

bacteroid An irregular-shaped *Rhizobium* cell found in root nodules.

balanced growth Microbial growth in which there is an orderly increase in the DNA, RNA, and protein of the cell population.

basidiospore A sexual fungal spore produced by fungi of the phylum *Basidiomycota.*

basophil A granulocyte that takes up basic dyes.

batch culture Growth in a closed system, affected by nutrient limitation and waste product accumulation.

beta (β) hemolysis The complete lysis of red blood cells, characterized by clear zones surrounding microbial colonies growing on blood agar.

beta (β) oxidation The stepwise oxidation of fatty acid into 2-carbon fragments.

biliprotein A water-soluble accessory pigment for photosynthesis; also called phycobilin.

binary fission An asexual process of cell division in which a single cell divides into two separate and equal daughter cells.

binding protein   A soluble protein in the periplasm of gram-negative bacteria that binds to molecules and functions in their active transport across the membrane.

biochemical oxygen demand (BOD)   The quantity of oxygen required by microorganisms to oxidize organic matter in water; also known as biological oxygen demand.

bioenergetics   The study of energy transformations in living systems.

biofilm   Microorganisms attached to a surface by adhesive polysaccharides produced by the microbial cells.

biogeochemical cycle   The recycling of chemical elements through the biological and geologic components of the world.

biotechnology   The discipline dealing with the manufacture of commercially valuable products by the use of microorganisms.

B lymphocyte   A lymphocyte derived from the bone marrow and that can mature into antibody-secreting plasma cells; also called B cell.

bottom-fermenting yeast   Yeast that aggregates and settles during fermentation to produce a clarified beer low in alcohol content.

bright-field microscope   A type of microscope in which the specimen is viewed against a light background.

broad-spectrum antimicrobial agent   An antimicrobial agent that is effective against many different types of microorganisms.

broth   A liquid growth medium.

bulking   An activated sludge processing condition in which filamentous bacteria form loose flocs that do not rapidly settle, resulting in reduced clarification of wastewater.

butanediol fermentation   A fermentation in which the products are 2,3-butanediol, ethanol, carbon dioxide, and small quantities of lactate, succinate, acetate, and H_2.

C

calorie   The quantity of heat energy required to raise the temperature of 1 g of water 1°C.

calorimeter   A device to measure the quantity of energy within a chemical substance by the complete combustion of the substance.

Calvin (C$_3$) cycle   A sequence of chemical reactions used by autotrophs to fix carbon dioxide into organic compounds.

capping   In eucaryotes, the addition of 7-methylguanine at the 5' terminus of mRNA shortly after initiation of RNA synthesis, apparently to protect the RNA from degradation by nucleases.

capsid   The protein coat that surrounds the nucleic acid in viruses.

capsomere   An individual protein subunit of the capsid in viruses.

capsule   The layer of polysaccharide, protein, or glycoprotein external to the cell wall; also called slime layer.

carbohydrate   An organic compound composed of carbon, hydrogen, and oxygen in the approximate ratio of 1:2:1.

cardinal temperatures for growth   Minimum, maximum, and optimum temperatures for growth.

caries   A tooth disease characterized by destruction of the enamel, dentin, and/or cementum of the tooth by acid.

carotenoid   A lipid-soluble accessory pigment for photosynthesis.

carrier   A host that is infected with an infectious microorganism in the absence of disease, but that can spread the infectious agent to other susceptible hosts.

catabolism   The biochemical reactions associated with the breakdown of chemical compounds.

catabolite repression   The suppression of gene activity in the presence of glucose or some other readily utilizable energy source.

catalyst   A chemical agent that increases reaction rates without itself being changed.

cDNA library   A DNA library that contains cDNA constructed from mRNA.

cell envelope   The outer covering of a bacterium, consisting of the plasma membrane; the cell wall; and, in gram-negative bacteria, the periplasm and an outer membrane.

cell line   Culture of cells that, under proper maintenance, is immortal and grows continuously.

cell transformation   Unregulated cell growth in which there is a loss in contact inhibition and possibly also changes in cell morphology, the appearance of new antigens on the plasma membrane, and changes in cell metabolism.

cellular immunity   Immunity that is mediated by T lymphocytes and macrophages; also called cell-mediated immunity.

cell wall   The structure outside the plasma membrane that protects the cell and is responsible for shape and rigidity.

Centers for Disease Control and Prevention (CDC)   The federal agency responsible for the detection, monitoring, and control of diseases.

central dogma   The scheme of events describing the flow of genetic information from DNA to RNA to proteins.

chemical energy   Energy residing in the bonds of chemical compounds and released through the dissociation of these bonds.

chemiosmosis   The establishment of a proton gradient across a membrane and the synthesis of ATP as this gradient is dissipated from the transport of protons back across the membrane; also called proton motive force.

chemoautotroph   An organism that obtains its energy from the oxidation of chemical compounds and that uses carbon dioxide as a sole source of carbon.

chemoheterotroph   An organism that obtains its energy from the oxidation of chemical compounds and that requires organic forms of carbon.

chemolithotroph   An organism that obtains its energy from the oxidation of inorganic compounds; also called lithotroph.

chemoorganotroph   An organism that obtains its energy from the oxidation of organic compounds; also called organotroph.

chemostat   A continuous culture device with growth controlled by the flow rate of the system and the concentration of a limiting nutrient.

chemotaxis   The movement of organisms in response to a chemical stimulus.

chemotherapeutic agent   An antimicrobial agent that is selectively toxic for microorganisms but does not harm the host.

chemotroph   An organism that obtains its energy from the oxidation of chemical compounds.

chimera   A plasmid containing nucleic acid from two different organisms.

chlorobium vesicle   A specialized structure associated with photosynthesis in phototrophic bacteria of the families *Chlorobiaceae* and *Chloroflexaceae*; also called chlorosome.

chlorophyll   A photosynthetic, light-harvesting pigment having a porphyrin ring structure with magnesium as a central atom and phytol as a side chain.

chloroplast   The pigmented, membrane-enclosed organelle in algae and plants that is the site of photosynthesis.

chlorosome   *See* **chlorobium vesicle.**

chromatin   The readily stainable DNA-protein complex of the chromosomes in the nucleus of eucaryotic cells.

chromoplast   A pigmented plastid in algae and plants, responsible for the bright colors seen in flowers, fruits, and autumn leaves.

cilium (pl. **cilia**)   A short, hairlike structure found in large numbers on the cell surface of eucaryotic cells, and associated with locomotion.

citric acid cycle   *See* **TCA cycle.**

classical complement pathway   The antibody-dependent pathway for complement activation.

clonal selection theory   A theory that clones of B and T cells arise from a single cell that has been stimulated by an antigen.

clone   A population of cells derived from a single cell.

clustering of cases   A larger-than-normal number of disease cases in a particular geographic area.

co-agglutination   The formation of visible clumps by the cross-linking of antigens and corresponding antibodies that are linked by their Fc portions to the Protein A surface components of heat-killed *Staphylococcus aureus* cells.

coagulase   An enzyme produced by pathogenic staphylococci that causes clotting of plasma.

coccobacillus (pl. **coccobacilli**)   A plump, cigar-shaped bacterial cell.

coccus (pl. **cocci**)   A spherical bacterial cell.

codon   A sequence of three adjacent bases on mRNA that codes for an amino acid or the initiation or termination of protein synthesis.

coenocytic   Multinucleated (organism or cell).

coenzyme   An organic molecule of low molecular weight that binds to an enzyme and participates in the enzymatic reaction, often by accepting and donating electrons or functional groups.

cofactor   An inorganic or organic molecule of low molecular weight that binds to an enzyme and participates in the enzymatic reaction, often by accepting and donating electrons or functional groups.

cohort   The defined population group that is followed in prospective studies.

colicin   A bacteriocin produced by *Escherichia coli.*

coliform   A gram-negative aerobic or facultatively anaerobic non–spore-forming, rod-shaped bacterium that ferments lactose with gas production within 48 hours at 35°C.

colony (pl. **colonies**)   The visible population of cells arising from a single cell and growing on a solid culture medium.

colony stimulating factor (CSF)   A cytokine that stimulates division and differentiation of certain cells such as monocytes and macrophages.

col plasmid   A plasmid carrying genes for the synthesis of colicins.

co-metabolism   The metabolic transformation of a substance that does not serve as a source of nutrients to the microorganism.

commensalism   A symbiotic relationship in which one organism benefits and the other organism is unaffected.

common-source epidemic disease   A disease outbreak in which a group of people is exposed at one time to a specific disease agent.

communicable disease   A disease that can be transmitted by an infectious agent from one individual to another.

competence   The physiological state in which a bacterium is able to take up and incorporate donor DNA.

complement   A group of thermolabile proteins found in serum that interacts with antibodies to promote phagocytosis and lysis of bacteria.

complementary DNA (cDNA)   A DNA copy of mRNA.

complementary DNA library (cDNA library)   A DNA library that contains cDNA constructed from mRNA.

complex (undefined) medium (pl. **complex media**)   A culture medium, the exact composition of which is not known.

compound microscope   A microscope with two or more sets of lenses.

condenser   The part of the microscope that focuses light from the light source onto the specimen.

conidiophore   A fungal hypha with condiospores at the tip.

conidiospore, conidium (pl. **conidia**)   An asexual fungal spore, resistant to heat and drying.

conjugation   The joining of two cells with transfer of genetic material.

conjugative plasmid   A plasmid that carries a sequence of genes called the *tra* genes that are associated with conjugative transfer.

constitutive   Having continuous gene expression.

contact inhibition   The cessation of animal cell movement and division as a result of cell-to-cell contact.

continuous culture   A microbial culture with the volume and phase of growth maintained at a constant level by the addition of fresh medium and the removal of an equal volume of spent medium and old cells.

convalescent period   The period of disease when recovery occurs.

corepressor   A substance that acts with a repressor to prohibit gene expression.

coryneform   *See* **diphtheroid.**

cosmid   A plasmid vector that contains λ phage *cos* (cohesive end) sites incorporated into the plasmid DNA.

crista (pl. **cristae**)   The convoluted internal mitochondrial membrane.

cross-feeding   The phenomenon in which the growth of an organism is dependent on the provision of one or more nutrients or growth factors supplied by another organism; also called syntrophism.

cyclic photophosphorylation   The synthesis of ATP through cycling of electrons in light-dependent reactions of photosynthesis.

cyst   A dormant stage formed by some bacteria and protozoa that is resistant to dessication.

cytochrome   An electron transport molecule consisting of a porphyrin ring with a central iron atom conjugated to a protein.

cytogamy   The fusion of two cells without the exchange of nuclei.

cytokine   A low-molecular-weight protein that regulates important biological processes such as cell growth, cell activation, tissue repair, immunity, and inflammation.

cytokinesis   The separation of the cytoplasm of a dividing cell into two equal daughter cells following nuclear division.

cytopathic effect (CPE)   The visible morphological change to cells growing in tissue culture.

cytoplasmic membrane   *See* **plasma membrane.**

cytotoxic hypersensitive reaction   An exaggerated immune response caused by the interaction of antibodies with tissue cells and complement; also called type II allergic reaction.

D

dark-field microscope   A type of microscope in which the specimen appears light against a dark background.

death phase (of population growth curve)   The portion of the population growth curve where there is a net decrease in viable cell numbers; also called decline phase (of population growth curve).

decarboxylase   An enzyme catalyzing the removal of the carboxyl group from an amino acid, resulting in the formation of an amine or a diamine.

decimal reduction time (DRT)   The time required to kill 90% of the microorganisms in a suspension at a specific temperature; also called D value.

decline period   The period of disease when symptoms subside.

decline phase (of population growth curve)   *See* **death phase (of population growth curve).**

delayed hypersensitive reaction   An allergic reaction mediated by T lymphocytes.

deletion   The removal of DNA segments from the chromosome.

dendrogram   A diagrammatic matrix used to illustrate similarity levels in numerical taxonomy.

denitrification   The anaerobic conversion of nitrate into nitrogen gases.

deoxyribonucleic acid (DNA)   A type of nucleic acid that carries genetic information. DNA contains deoxyribose sugars (in contrast to RNA, which contains ribose sugars).

dermatomycosis   A fungal disease of the dermis.

diatom   A member of the algal division *Chrysophyta,* having two thin, overlapping shells of silica.

diauxic growth   A growth pattern in which there are two exponential phases of the population growth curve as the cells use one substrate and then the other.

differential medium   A culture medium that distinguishes different types of microorganisms by their metabolism of media components and subsequent colony appearance.

dikaryon   A fungus with paired but not fused nuclei, derived from different parent hyphae.

dimorphic   A fungus exhibiting both the mold and the yeast growth types under different environmental conditions.

dinoflagellate   An alga of the division *Pyrrophyta,* having a spinning type of motility as the result of its flagellation.

diphtheroid   A gram-positive pleomorphic bacterium that resembles *Corynebacterium diphtheriae* but is not virulent; also called coryneform.

diploid   Having two sets of chromosomes.

disease   A condition of ill health in a living organism that may be caused by an infectious agent (an infectious disease).

disinfectant   An antimicrobial agent that is used on nonliving surfaces.

disk diffusion method   A method to determine the antimicrobial susceptibility of a microorganism, using disks impregnated with known concentrations of antimicrobial agents.

dissimilatory nitrate reduction   The reduction of nitrate to nitrite, with nitrate used as an electron acceptor.

DNA fingerprinting   A technique for the identification of repetitive DNA sequences that occur in the genomes of humans and other eucaryotes.

DNA library   A collection of cloned DNA fragments from the genome of an organism.

domain   The highest level of classification, consisting of the Bacteria, the Archaea, and the Eucarya.

doubling time   *See* **generation time.**

dry weight   The weight of cells minus any moisture.

D value   *See* **decimal reduction time.**

E

ectomycorrhiza (pl. **ectomycorrhizae**)   A symbiotic association between a fungus and

plant roots in which the plant roots are surrounded but not penetrated by fungal hyphae.

ectosymbiosis   A symbiosis in which the microorganism may be attached but remains external to the host cell.

Einstein   *See* **photon.**

electromagnetic energy   Light energy that travels in photons.

electron microscope   A type of microscope in which magnifications of 100,000× or greater are achieved by replacing glass lenses with electromagnetic lenses and light with electrons.

electron transport chain   A series of electron carriers through which electrons are transported from a substrate to a final electron acceptor, typically resulting in ATP synthesis.

electroporation   The creation of small holes in the plasma membrane of a cell by electric shock to permit the entry of DNA.

Elek gel diffusion test   A test in which an antitoxin-toxin reaction for *Corynebacterium diphtheriae* is detected by precipitation on an agar plate.

elementary body (EB)   A small infectious body that is specialized for extracellular survival in the *Chlamydia* developmental cycle.

Embden-Meyerhof pathway   A sequence of chemical reactions in which one molecule of glucose is oxidized to two molecules of pyruvate; a glycolytic pathway.

empty magnification   An increase in magnification without an accompanying increase in resolution.

endemic disease   A disease that is continuously present in a population.

endergonic   A chemical reaction having a positive change in free energy and requiring input of energy to proceed.

endogenote   A recipient cell's genome in which the donor DNA can be integrated during the transfer of genetic material from one cell to another.

endomycorrhiza (pl. **endomycorrhizae**)   A symbiotic association between a fungus and plant roots in which fungal hyphae penetrate the plant roots.

endospore   A spore formed within a cell.

endosymbiont hypothesis   A theory that procaryotes living as endosymbionts inside eucaryotes evolved into chloroplasts and mitochondria.

endosymbiosis   A symbiosis in which the microorganism grows within the host cell.

endothermic   A chemical reaction proceeding with absorption of heat.

endotoxin   A toxin associated with the lipopolysaccharide portion of the outer membrane of gram-negative bacteria; the lipid A component of lipopolysaccharide is responsible for the toxicity of endotoxin.

energy   The capacity to do work.

enrichment culture   A culture medium that enhances the growth of specific types of microorganisms while often inhibiting the growth of other organisms.

enterohemorrhagic *Escherichia coli* (**EHEC**)   Strains of *E. coli* that produce a toxin closely related to Shiga toxin and can cause hemolytic-uremic syndrome, which is characterized by lysis of erythrocytes and kidney failure.

enteroinvasive *Escherichia coli* (**EIEC**)   Strains of *E. coli* that are invasive and cause hemorrhagic enterocolitis.

enteropathogenic *Escherichia coli* (**EPEC**)   Strains of *E. coli* that commonly cause diarrhea in newborn infants.

enterotoxigenic *Escherichia coli* (**ETEC**)   Strains of *E. coli* that synthesize heat-stable (stable toxin, ST) and heat-labile (labile toxin, LT) enterotoxins and cause traveler's diarrhea.

enterotoxin   An exotoxin that affects the small intestine.

enthalpy (H)   The total amount of energy released during a reaction.

Entner-Doudoroff pathway   A sequence of chemical reactions in which glucose is oxidized to 6-phosphogluconate and subsequently to pyruvate.

entropy (S)   Randomness or disorder in a system.

enzyme   A protein (or, in the case of ribozymes, RNA) catalyst found in living systems.

enzyme-linked immunosorbent assay (**ELISA**)   A laboratory technique used to detect antibodies or antigens in a sample through an enzyme that causes a color change in its substrate.

eosinophil   A granulocyte that takes up acid dyes, especially eosin.

epidemic disease   A disease that affects a large segment of the population within a region at one time.

epidemiology   The science dealing with the incidence, distribution, and control of disease in a population.

episome   Plasmid DNA that has been incorporated into the bacterial chromosome.

epitope   The portion of an antigen that determines immunologic specificity; also called antigenic determinant.

erysipelas   A skin disease characterized by invasion of the subcutaneous blood vessels, causing the appearance of red patches.

erythrocyte   A red blood cell.

estuary   A partially enclosed coastal body of water that separates marine waters from inland sources of fresh water.

Eucarya   The phylogenetic domain containing eucaryotes.

eucaryote   A cell or organism having a membrane-enclosed nucleus, specialized membrane-enclosed organelles, and a high level of internal structural organization not found in a procaryote.

eutrophic   Containing a high concentration of nutrients.

exergonic   A chemical reaction having a negative change in free energy and proceeding with liberation of energy.

exfoliatin   Staphylococcal exotoxin responsible for the pathogenesis of scalded skin syndrome.

exogenote   The donor DNA introduced into a recipient cell during the transfer of genetic material from one cell to another.

exon   Translatable portions of mRNA.

exosporium   The loose outer envelope that surrounds an endospore.

exothermic   A chemical reaction proceeding with the release of heat.

exotoxin   A toxic soluble protein produced by a microorganism and released into the environment.

exponential phase (of population growth curve)   The period of population growth in which the population is actively growing at a constant rate; also called logarithmic phase (of the population growth curve).

expression vector   A vector that contains not only the target gene but also regulatory sequences that can be used to control expression of the gene.

extrinsic membrane protein   A protein found in the lipid bilayer of the plasma membrane and that can be removed by changes in pH or ionic strength; also called peripheral membrane protein.

F

facilitated diffusion   The carrier-mediated movement of molecules across a membrane along a concentration gradient.

facultative anaerobe   An organism that grows in the presence or absence of oxygen, respiring in the presence of oxygen and fermenting in its absence.

fat   A triglyceride containing an ester of glycerol and three fatty acid molecules.

fatty acid   A straight-chain lipid having a carboxyl group at one end.

F⁺ cell   A cell that contains the F factor on a plasmid.

F⁻ cell   A cell that lacks the F factor.

F' cell   A cell in which the F factor and host genes are on a plasmid.

fecal coliform   A coliform that grows at a temperature of 44.5°C.

feedback inhibition   Inhibition by an end product of the activity of an enzyme in a metabolic pathway.

fermentation   The anaerobic oxidation-reduction of carbohydrates with organic compounds as electron donors and electron acceptors.

F factor   The fertility factor that is found in the donor bacterium during conjugation; also called sex factor.

fimbria (pl. **fimbriae**)   *See* **pilus**.

first law of thermodynamics   The law stating that energy can neither be created nor destroyed in any transformation.

flagellin   The protein subunit of a bacterial flagellum.

flagellum (pl. **flagella**)   A long, thin appendage used for cellular motility.

fluorescence microscope   A type of microscope in which objects absorb ultraviolet or near-ultraviolet light and emit visible light.

fomite   An inanimate object contaminated with an infectious microorganism.

food infection   A disease occurring when an infectious agent ingested with food or water establishes an active infection in the small intestine.

food intoxication   A disease occurring when food or water containing toxic products of microorganisms is consumed.

fractional sterilization   *See* **tyndallization.**

free energy (G)   The portion of energy released during a reaction that can be used for work; expressed as G° if determined under standard conditions of 1 atmosphere pressure and 1 molar concentration, and as G°', if determined under standard conditions and at pH 7.0.

fruiting body   A large, specialized structure containing spores and produced by some procaryotes (myxobacteria) and some fungi.

fungicidal   Having the property of killing fungi.

fungistatic   Inhibiting fungi.

fungus (pl. fungi)   A nonmotile eucaryotic microorganism that has a cell wall but does not contain chlorophyll.

furunculosis   An infection of the hair follicle, causing the formation of a boil or furuncle in the underlying subcutaneous tissue.

G

gametangium (pl. gametangia)   A specialized fungal reproductive structure located at the tip of the hypha and containing the gamete.

gamete   A haploid reproductive cell that unites with another gamete to form a diploid zygote.

gamma globulin (γ-globulin)   A protein fraction of blood rich in antibodies.

gamma (γ) hemolysis   No lysis of erythrocytes.

gas vacuole   An internal vacuole that retains gas and gives buoyancy to the cell.

gene   The segment of a chromosome that is transcribed into mRNA coding for a single polypeptide.

gene amplification   The process in which a cell produces large quantities of a specific gene product.

gene cloning   The insertion of a target gene into a vector for introduction into a cell, where the gene is amplified and expressed.

gene gun   A device that shoots DNA-coated microprojectiles into a cell without killing the cell.

generalized transduction   The transfer of random fragments of host DNA by transduction.

general recombination   Recombination involving a reciprocal exchange between two homologous DNA molecules; also called homologous recombination.

generation time   The time required for a population to double in number; also called doubling time.

gene therapy   The treatment of genetic diseases by replacement of dysfunctional genes.

genetic engineering   The deliberate modification of the genetic makeup of a cell or organism.

genetic recombination   The process through which genetic material from two separate cells is brought together.

genetics   The field of biology that deals with mechanisms responsible for the transfer of traits from one organism to another.

genome   One complete set of genes.

genomic library   A DNA library that contains DNA fragments from a digested genome.

genotype   The genetic composition of an organism.

genus (pl. genera)   The taxonomic category of related organisms, below family level and above species level.

germ-free animal   An animal that contains no microbial flora.

germicide   The general term used to describe antimicrobial agents that kill microorganisms.

germination   The outgrowth of spores to vegetative cells.

germ theory of disease   A theory that microorganisms cause disease.

gingivitis   Inflammation of the gum.

gluconeogenesis   The biosynthesis of glucose from noncarbohydrate compounds through reversal of the Embden-Meyerhof pathway.

glycocalyx   The matrix of polysaccharides on the surface of bacteria, instrumental in binding cells together in an aggregate mass to protect them from phagocytosis and assist them in attachment to a solid surface.

glycolysis   The oxidation of glucose to pyruvate; *see* Embden-Meyerhof pathway for an example.

glycoprotein   An organic compound consisting of carbohydrate and protein.

glyoxylate cycle   An anaplerotic pathway that channels 2-carbon compounds such as acetate and acetyl-CoA into the TCA cycle.

Golden Age of Microbiology   An era from 1876 to 1906 during which the causes of most bacterial diseases were discovered.

Golgi complex (Golgi apparatus)   The membrane-enclosed organelle associated with the packaging and secretion of substances from the cell interior through the membrane to the exterior.

Gram stain   A fundamental bacteriological staining technique to differentiate bacteria that retain the primary stain of crystal violet (gram-positive bacteria) from bacteria that are decolorized and take up the secondary stain of safranin (gram-negative bacteria).

granulocyte   A leukocyte possessing cytoplasmic granules; basophils, eosinophils, and neutrophils are granulocytes.

granum (pl. grana)   The chloroplast structure consisting of stacked layers of thylakoids.

greenhouse effect   An increase in land temperatures on the earth, resulting from increased levels of atmospheric carbon dioxide.

group translocation   The transport mechanism in which the substrate is chemically modified during movement across the membrane and the substrate can accumulate against a concentration gradient within the cell.

growth   The orderly increase in the cell mass of an organism.

growth factor   An organic nutrient required by microorganisms for growth, but not necessarily synthesized by them.

H

halophile   An organism that is osmophilic and has a specific requirement for sodium chloride.

haploid   Having one set of chromosomes.

hapten   A substance that combines with a specific antibody but cannot by itself induce the formation of antibodies.

haustorium (pl. haustoria)   The special absorptive hypha of a fungus.

hemagglutination   The agglutination of red blood cells.

hemolysin   An enzyme that breaks down red blood cells.

herd immunity   The immunization stage at which a large enough percentage of a susceptible population is immunized to significantly reduce or eliminate the spread of an infectious agent.

heterofermentation   Fermentation of glucose or other carbohydrates to a mixture of products.

heteropolysaccharide   A polysaccharide consisting of two or more types of sugars.

heterotroph   An organism that obtains its carbon from organic compounds.

hexose monophosphate shunt   *See* **pentose phosphate pathway.**

high-efficiency particulate air (HEPA) filter   A filter that removes 99.97% of particles 0.3 μm and larger from air.

high-frequency recombination (Hfr) cell   A cell in which the F factor is incorporated into the host chromosome, permitting the transfer of chromosomal genes to another cell.

high-frequency transduction   An increased frequency of specialized transduction through the production of lysate containing a high percentage of transducing bacteriophage.

Hill-Bendall scheme   The series of steps hypothesized to be responsible for electron transfer, ATP synthesis, and NADP reduction in the light reaction of photosynthesis.

histocompatibility antigen   *See* **human leukocyte antigen.**

histone   A positively charged protein associated with eucaryotic DNA.

homofermentation   Fermentation of glucose or other carbohydrates to a single product, lactate (lactic acid).

homologous recombination   *See* **general recombination.**

homopolysaccharide   A polysaccharide consisting of one type of sugar in a repeating structure.

hops   The dried petals from the vine *Humulus lupulus,* added to wort as a flavor enhancer and antimicrobial agent in beer brewing.

Human Genome Project   A concerted international effort to clone, map, and sequence the entire human genome.

human leukocyte antigen (HLA)   An antigen on the surface of human cells that is recognized by immune system cells and therefore is important in regulation of the immune response; also called histocompatibility antigen.

humoral immunity   Immunity associated with antibodies produced against antigens.

hyaluronidase   An enzyme that degrades hyaluronic acid.

hybridoma   A hybrid cell formed by the fusion of an antibody-producing lymphocyte and a rapidly dividing cancer cell and used continuously to manufacture identical antibodies.

hydrologic cycle   The cycling of water in the biosphere, beginning with the evaporation of water from oceans, lakes, and other surface bodies, followed by precipitation of atmospheric water and percolation of the water through the ground and back into the bodies of water.

hydrosphere   The aqueous envelope of the earth, including oceans, lakes, streams, and underground water.

hydrothermal vent   A natural vent on the sea floor that releases superheated water rich in hydrogen sulfide and other reduced inorganic compounds.

hypersensitivity   A state of abnormal susceptibility to an antigen, leading to an exaggerated immune response.

hypha (pl. **hyphae**)   A fungal filament.

I

idiotype   The variable region of an antibody molecule that determines its specificity.

immediate hypersensitive reaction   An allergic reaction involving IgE antibodies; also called antibody-mediated hypersensitive reaction.

immobilized enzymes (immobilized microbial cells)   Enzymes or microbial cells that are adsorbed onto a solid support (for example, cellulose particles or polyacrylamide beads). A substrate in solution is passed across the support and is changed into product by the immobilized enzymes or cells.

immunity   The specific resistance of a host to a pathogen.

immunization   The process or procedure by which a subject is rendered immune.

immunogenicity   The ability to stimulate antibody production.

immunoglobulin (Ig)   *See* **antibody.**

immunological tolerance   The inability to recognize antigens for antibody production.

immunology   The science that deals with the study of resistance of a host to infection.

impetigo   A bacterial skin disease characterized by pus-filled lesions that rupture and become encrusted.

incidence rate   The number of new cases of disease in a population during a specified time period; a type of morbidity rate.

inclusion body   An internal cell component that accumulates lipids, polysaccharides, or inorganic compounds; also called storage body.

incubation period   The time interval between infection and the first appearance of disease symptoms.

induced mutation   A mutation occurring as a result of chemical or radiation effects on the chromosome.

inducer   A substance that causes structural genes to be expressed.

induction   The process by which an enzyme is synthesized in response to the presence of a substance (the inducer).

industrial microbiology   The technology of using microorganisms to produce a product of commercial value.

infection   The presence of viable microorganisms in a host.

infectious disease   A disease that can be transmitted from one person, animal, or plant to another.

infectious dose, 50% end point (ID$_{50}$)   The quantity of pathogen required to infect successfully 50% of the inoculated animals within a given period of time.

inflammation   The host's nonspecific response to injury, irritation, or infection, characterized by dilation and increased permeability of the blood vessels in the affected area.

inhibitor   A chemical substance that prevents or slows an enzyme reaction by binding to the enzyme and preventing substrate binding.

innate resistance   Host resistance not directed against any particular pathogen; also called nonspecific resistance.

insertion The addition of DNA segments into the chromosome.

insertion sequence A genetic element inserted into portions of a procaryotic chromosome, and that can control gene expression.

integral membrane protein *See* **intrinsic membrane protein.**

interference contrast microscope A type of microscope in which contrast is achieved by destructive and/or additive interference of light waves.

interferon A glycoprotein produced by cells during viral infection and able to inhibit viral replication.

interleukin A cytokine that regulates growth and proliferation of lymphocytes.

interrupted mating The process in which conjugation between an Hfr cell and an F⁻ cell is interrupted at different times to permit mapping of the Hfr chromosome.

intrinsic membrane protein A protein embedded in the interior of the lipid bilayer of the plasma membrane, and that can only be removed by the use of detergents or nonpolar solvents; also called integral membrane protein.

intron A nontranslatable portion of mRNA.

ionosphere The uppermost layer of the atmosphere, above the stratosphere.

iris diaphragm The part of the microscope that controls the diameter of light leaving the condenser and striking the specimen.

isotype The constant-region determinant for an immunoglobulin class or subclass.

K

kappa (κ) chain One of two types of light chains occurring in an antibody molecule.

karyokinesis A process involving the division and separation of chromosomes in eucaryotes.

killed vaccine A vaccine that consists of dead microorganisms.

killer strain (of *Paramecium*) A paramecium that liberates toxic particles that are harmful to other, sensitive paramecia.

kilocalorie (kcal) The quantity of heat energy required to raise the temperature of 1 kg of water 1°C.

kinetic energy Energy of work or motion.

Kirby-Bauer test A disk diffusion test in which zones of inhibition are measured around disks to determine the susceptibilities of microorganisms to antimicrobial agents.

Koch's postulates A set of criteria for proving that a microorganism causes a particular disease.

Kornberg enzyme A synonym for DNA polymerase I, an enzyme that fills in the gaps of Okazaki fragments during DNA replication and also repairs ultraviolet light-inflicted DNA damage (named after Arthur Kornberg).

Krebs cycle *See* **TCA cycle.**

L

lagging strand The designation for the discontinuous daughter strand in DNA replication.

lag phase (of population growth curve) The period of population growth in which there is no increase in cell numbers.

lambda (γ) chain One of two types of light chains occurring in an antibody molecule.

laser-scanning confocal scanning microscope A type of microscope in which magnifications of several millionfold are achieved by scanning a cone of laser light across a specimen. The light is focused through a pinhole aperture to a specific point within the specimen and the imaging light from the specimen is focused through a second (confocal) pinhole to a detector.

latent infection An infection that does not immediately produce detectable or overt symptoms.

latex agglutination The formation of visible clumps by the cross-linking of antigens and corresponding antibodies that are attached to latex spheres.

leaching The extraction of metals from low-grade ores.

leader peptide In attenuation, a short peptide rich in tryptophan that is synthesized when tryptophan is abundant.

leading strand The designation for the continuous daughter strand in DNA replication.

leghemoglobin An oxygen-binding protein produced during symbiotic nitrogen fixation by *Rhizobium* and a legume; the heme portion of the protein is produced by the bacterium and the globin by the plant.

lethal dose, 50% end point (LD$_{50}$) The quantity of a pathogen required to kill 50% of the inoculated animals within a given period of time.

leucoplast A nonpigmented plastid found in plants, associated with the synthesis and storage of starch, proteins, and oils.

leukocidin A bacterial product that kills leukocytes.

leukocyte A white blood cell, such as a neutrophil, basophil, eosinophil, lymphocyte, or monocyte.

leukocytosis An abnormally high number of leukocytes.

leukopenia An abnormally low number of leukocytes.

L-form A bacterium that normally has a cell wall, but has lost the ability to synthesize the wall.

lichen A plantlike structure consisting of a fungus and an alga living in mutualistic symbiosis.

light microscope A type of microscope that uses light as its source of illumination. The four types of light microscopes are: bright-field, dark-field, fluorescence, and phase-contrast.

limnetic zone The zone of a lake to which light penetrates.

***Limulus* amoebocyte lysate (LAL) assay** An assay to detect endotoxin using extracts of amoebocytes from the horseshoe crab *Limulus polyphemus*.

lipid A fat or fatlike molecule that is insoluble in water but soluble in organic solvents.

lipopolysaccharide (LPS) A lipid-carbohydrate molecule consisting of three basic parts (O-specific side chain, core poly-saccharide, and Lipid A), found as part of the outer membrane of gram-negative bacteria.

lithosphere The solid portion of the earth.

lithotroph *See* **chemolithotroph.**

littoral zone The zone of a lake near to the shore.

live, attenuated vaccine *See* **attenuated vaccine.**

logarithmic phase (of population growth curve) *See* **exponential phase (of population growth curve).**

lophotrichous   A tuft of flagella on the cell.

L-phase variant   *See* **L-form.**

luciferase   The enzyme that catalyzes light formation in luminescent bacteria.

lymphocyte   An agranulocyte involved in antibody production and cell-mediated immunity.

lymphokine   A chemical mediator released by T lymphocytes.

lyophilization   A freeze-drying technique for long-term preservation of microorganisms.

lysogenic conversion   The expression of phage genes while the phage exists in a prophage state in the host chromosome.

lysogeny   The state in which a bacterium carries a prophage.

lysosome   A eucaryotic organelle containing hydrolytic enzymes.

lysozyme   An enzyme, commonly found in body secretions (tears and saliva) and egg white, that hydrolyzes the ß-1,4 linkages between *N*-acetylmuramic acid and *N*-acetylglucosamine in cell wall peptidoglycan.

lytic cycle   A virus life cycle that results in the release of virus upon lysis of the host cell.

M

macroorganism   An organism that can be seen with the unaided eye.

macrophage   A phagocytic cell.

macrophage activating factor (MAF)   A cytokine that alters macrophages immunologically and increases their phagocytic activity in cell-mediated immunity.

macrophage chemotactic factor (MCF)   A cytokine that attracts macrophages to the infection site in cell-mediated immunity.

macrophage migration inhibitory factor (MIF)   A cytokine that prevents macrophages from leaving the infection site in cell-mediated immunity.

magnetosomes   Intracellular crystal particles of the iron oxide magnetite (Fe_3O_4) that act as magnets and help bacteria orient their movement along magnetic fields.

magnetotaxis   The movement of organisms in response to a magnetic field.

major histocompatibility complex (MHC)   A cluster of genes coding for cell surface molecules that serves as a unique marker of the individual.

malting   A step in beer brewing involving the germination and crushing of barley grains to release amylases and proteases.

mast cell   A nonmotile connective tissue cell found next to capillaries.

matching coefficient (S_S)   The comparison of positive and negative characteristics among organisms in numerical taxonomy.

meiosis   Reduction division by which the chromosome number is halved in eucaryotic cells.

melting temperature (T_m)   The temperature at which there is a sharp increase in absorption of double-stranded DNA at 260 nm as the strands separate.

membrane attack complex (MAC)   The complement complex components (C5b–C9) that disrupt the plasma membrane and create a lytic transmembrane pore.

memory B lymphocyte   A B lymphocyte that mounts a rapid and enhanced secondary antibody response when challenged a second time with the same antigen.

mesophile   An organism with an optimum growth temperature of 20°C to 40°C.

messenger RNA (mRNA)   RNA that carries the genetic message from DNA and serves as a template for translation of the message into proteins.

metabolism   The catabolic and anabolic reactions in a cell.

metachromatic granule   An inclusion body containing polyphosphate granules and found in cells of *Corynebacterium* and other bacteria: also called Babès-Ernst body.

methyl-accepting chemotaxis protein (MCP)   Protein in the plasma membrane or periplasm that is involved in transmitting signals for movement of the flagellum; this protein is alternatively methylated or demethylated in response to the binding of chemoreceptors to specific chemicals; also called transducer.

methylotroph   An organism that uses 1-carbon compounds as its sole carbon and energy sources.

methyl red test   A laboratory test to differentiate between mixed acid fermenters and butanediol fermenters by use of a pH indicator, methyl red.

microaerophile   An organism that grows best at low oxygen concentrations.

microbial ecology   The field of science concerned with the interactions of microorganisms with the living and nonliving components of the environment.

microbiology   The study of organisms too small to be seen with the unaided eye, specifically viruses, bacteria, fungi, algae, and protozoa.

microorganism   An organism that normally cannot be seen without the aid of a microscope.

microscope   An instrument that uses lenses to magnify an object too small to be seen with the unaided eye.

microtubule   A hollow protein cylinder in a eucaryotic cell associated with the movement of chromosomes, flagella, and cilia.

mineralization   The conversion of organic matter to minerals and other inorganic materials.

minimal bactericidal concentration (MBC)   The lowest concentration of an antimicrobial agent that kills the test microorganism.

minimal inhibitory concentration (MIC)   The lowest concentration of an antimicrobial agent that inhibits growth of the test microorganism.

missense mutation   A mutation in which there is a change in the amino acid coded by the affected region of the chromosome.

mitochondrion (pl. mitochondria)   The membrane-enclosed organelle in a eucaryotic cell that is the site of respiration and ATP synthesis.

mitosis   The process in eucaryotic cells involving separation of replicated chromosomes and subsequent cytoplasmic division, resulting in two identical daughter cells.

mixed acid fermentation   The fermentation of glucose, resulting in the formation of lactate, succinate, and acetate, as well as ethanol, carbon dioxide, and H_2.

mixotroph   An organism that uses inorganic compounds as its energy source and organic compounds as its carbon source.

mold   A fungal growth type having a vegetative structure consisting of hyphae.

molecular approach   The method of procaryotic taxonomy in which genetic similarity is used to classify organisms.

monoclonal antibody   An antibody produced from a single hybridoma and its clones.

monocyte   An agranulocyte that has a single nucleus and is active in phagocytosis.

monolayer   A single layer of cells.

mononuclear phagocytic system   *See* **reticuloendothelial (RE) system.**

monotrichous   Having one flagellum on a cell.

Morbidity and Mortality Weekly Report (MMWR)   A weekly publication of the Centers for Disease Control and Prevention that contains up-to-date morbidity and mortality data on communicable diseases.

morbidity rate   *See* **prevalence rate, incidence rate.**

mortality rate   The number of deaths that result from a disease per unit population during a specified time period.

most probable number (MPN)   A statistical expression of cell density in a suspension.

multitrichous   Having more than one flagellum on a cell.

mutant   An organism that differs from its parent because of a change in the DNA.

mutation   An inheritable change in a chromosome.

mutualism   A symbiotic relationship in which organisms living together benefit one another.

mycelium (pl. **mycelia**)   A mass of hyphae.

mycorrhiza (pl. **mycorrhizae**)   A symbiotic association between a fungus and plant roots.

myeloma   A plasma tumor cell composed of cells derived from tissues of the bone marrow.

myxospore   A resistant cell formed by myxobacteria.

N

narrow-spectrum antimicrobial agent   An antimicrobial agent that is effective against specific microorganisms or groups of microorganisms.

natural history of disease   The sequence of events that occurs from the time a parasite infects a host to the time that the disease is resolved, either through recovery or death of the host.

naturally acquired active immunity   The production of antibodies in an individual in response to antigenic stimulation through natural infection.

naturally acquired passive immunity   Immunity that is acquired by the transfer of antibodies from one person to another person by natural means.

negative control   A regulatory system in which there is enzyme synthesis in the absence of the controlling factor.

negative stain   A stain in which the background rather than the specimen is stained; in electron microscopy, a stain in which the specimen is electron transparent (light) against an electron-dense (dark) background.

neurotoxin   A toxin that affects nerve tissues.

neutrophil   A granulocyte with multilobed nuclei that is the main phagocyte in the blood; also called polymorphonuclear leukocyte (PMN).

nitrification   The oxidation of ammonia to nitrite and of nitrite to nitrate.

nitrogenase   An oxygen-labile enzyme responsible for microbial nitrogen fixation.

nitrogen fixation   The reduction of nitrogen gas to ammonia.

nomenclature   The systematic naming of organisms.

noncommunicable disease   A disease that is not transmitted by an infectious agent (for example, alcoholism, mental disease, and diabetes).

nonconjugative plasmid   A plasmid that does not have *tra* genes, but can have *mob* (mobilization) genes that allow them to take advantage of the *tra* function of a conjugative plasmid for transfer between bacteria.

noncyclic photophosphorylation   The synthesis of ATP through the transfer of electrons eventually to NADP in light-dependent reactions of photosynthesis.

nongonococcal urethritis (NGU)   Inflammation of the urethra caused by a microorganism other than *Neisseria gonorrhoeae;* also called nonspecific urethritis (NSU).

nonhistone protein   A protein associated with eucaryotic DNA, differentiated from histone protein.

noninfectious disease   A disease that is not transmitted from one person, animal, or plant to another.

nonsense codon   *See* **termination codon.**

nonsense mutation   A mutation that results in the formation of a nonsense codon and premature termination of protein synthesis.

nonspecific resistance   *See* **innate resistance.**

nonspecific urethritis (NSU)   *See* **nongonococcal urethritis.**

normal flora   Organisms that normally colonize a host without causing disease.

Northern blot   A technique by which RNA fragments, separated by electrophoresis, are immobilized on a paper sheet and detected with a labeled nucleic acid probe.

nosocomial   Originating in a hospital; also called hospital-acquired.

nucleic acid   A class of molecules consisting of nucleotides joined by phosphodiester bonds (for example, DNA and RNA).

nucleic acid probe   A single-stranded nucleic acid segment with a base sequence that is complementary to a specific DNA or RNA sequence.

nucleocapsid   Viral nucleic acid surrounded by a capsid.

nucleoid   The region in a procaryotic cell that contains its genetic material.

nucleoside   A purine or pyrimidine base joined to a pentose.

nucleosome   The basic structural subunit of chromatin, containing approximately 200 base pairs and histone proteins.

nucleotide   A nucleoside containing one or more phosphate.

null cell   A cell that resembles a lymphocyte but lacks the surface characteristics of either B or T lymphocytes.

numerical aperture   The lens property, equivalent to n sin θ, where n is the refractive index of the medium between the lens and the specimen, and θ is one-half the angle of light entering the objective lens.

numerical taxonomy   The method of bacterial taxonomy in which observable characteristics carry equal weights in the comparison and classification of organisms; also called Adansonian taxonomy.

nutrient   A chemical substance used by an organism for cellular growth and activity.

O

objective lens   The lens that is closest to the specimen in a compound light microscope.

ocular lens   The lens that is nearest the eye in a compound light microscope.

Okazaki fragment   A short DNA fragment (1,000 to 2,000 nucleotides long in procaryotes) synthesized discontinuously on one strand of double-stranded DNA (named after Reiji Okazaki).

oligotrophic   Containing a low concentration of nutrients.

oncogene   A cancer gene in the chromosome.

one-step growth curve A graphic curve characterizing bacteriophage growth.

operator The region on the chromosome that controls expression of structural genes in an operon.

operon A unit on the chromosome under the control of an operator.

opportunistic pathogen An organism that normally is nonpathogenic but is capable of causing disease in a compromised host.

opsonin A substance that renders antigens more susceptible to phagocytosis.

opsonization The process by which an antigen is altered in such a manner that it is more readily engulfed by phagocytes.

optochin Chemical (ethylhydrocupreine hydrochloride) used for the identification of *Streptococcus pneumoniae*.

organotroph *See* **chemoorganotroph.**

organotropic Tissue or organ-specific.

osmophile An organism that requires an environment of high osmolarity for growth.

osmotolerant Tolerating high osmotic pressures.

outer membrane The exterior portion of the gram-negative envelope that consists of a phospholipid bilayer interspersed with proteins and lipoproteins.

oxidase test A test used to detect the presence of cytochrome c oxidase by the oxidation of *N,N*-dimethyl-*p*-phenylenediamine to a purple-blue product, indophenol.

oxidation A reaction involving loss of electrons.

oxidation-reduction A reaction involving the transfer of electrons from one molecule to another; also called redox reaction.

oxidation-reduction potential A measure of the tendency of a substance to donate or accept electrons, as determined relative to the standard hydrogen electrode; also called redox potential.

oxidative phosphorylation The synthesis of ATP from ADP and inorganic phosphate, coupled with a membrane-associated electron transport chain and the generation of a proton motive force across the membrane.

oxygenic photosynthesis Photosynthesis with the production of oxygen.

P

palindrome A double-stranded nucleic acid sequence that exhibits twofold symmetry around a central axis.

pandemic disease An epidemic disease that affects several countries or major portions of the world.

parasitism A symbiotic relationship in which one organism benefits and the other is harmed.

passive diffusion The movement of small molecules across a membrane down a concentration gradient.

Pasteur effect The inhibiting effect of oxygen upon glucose fermentation.

pasteurization A process of treating liquids with heat below the boiling point to kill most pathogenic and spoilage microorganisms.

pathogenicity The ability of an organism to infect and establish disease in a host.

penicillinase-producing *Neisseria gonorrhoeae* (PPNG) Strains of *N. gonorrhoeae* that produce ß-lactamase (penicillinase), an enzyme that breaks down the ß-lactam ring of penicillin.

pentose phosphate pathway A sequence of chemical reactions in which glucose-6-phosphate is oxidized to 6-phosphogluconate, which subsequently is decarboxylated to ribulose-5-phosphate; also called hexose monophosphate shunt, phosphogluconate pathway, and Warburg-Dickens pathway.

peptidoglycan The rigid layer of bacterial cell walls, consisting of *N*-acetylglucosamine, *N*-acetylmuramic acid, and a few amino acids.

periodontal disease A disease that affects the supporting structure of the tooth (gingiva, cementum, and supporting bone).

peripheral membrane protein *See* **extrinsic membrane protein.**

periplasm The region between the plasma membrane and the outer membrane in the cell envelope of gram-negative bacteria.

peritrichous Having flagella around the entire cell.

permease A membrane-bound protein carrier involved in the transport of molecules.

pertussis Whooping cough.

phage *See* **bacteriophage.**

phagemid A hybrid vector containing DNA from a filamentous bacteriophage and a plasmid.

phagocyte A cell that ingests bacteria, foreign particles, and other cells.

phagocytosis The process of ingestion and digestion by phagocytes of solid substances such as bacteria, foreign particles, and other cells.

phagolysosome The vacuole that forms from the fusion of a phagosome with a lysosome inside a phagocyte.

phagosome A phagocytic vesicle formed by the invagination of the plasma membrane of a phagocyte around a bacterium, virus, or other foreign material.

phase-contrast microscope A type of microscope that amplifies small differences in refractive indices to increase the contrast between the specimen and the surrounding medium.

phenol coefficient The ratio of the effectiveness of a chemical agent to that of phenol for a test organism.

phenom A category used to group similar organisms in numerical taxonomy.

phenotype Observable characteristics of an organism.

phosphogluconate pathway *See* **pentose phosphate pathway.**

phosphoketolase pathway A glycolytic pathway in which glucose is converted to pyruvate and ethanol, with xylulose-5-phosphate formed as an intermediate. Xylulose-5-phosphate is cleaved by phosphoketolase to acetyl phosphate and glyceraldehyde-3-phosphate, which then are further broken down to ethanol and pyruvate, respectively.

photoautotroph An organism that obtains its energy from light and uses carbon dioxide as its sole carbon source.

photoheterotroph An organism that obtains its energy from light and its carbon from organic compounds.

photolysis The light-dependent splitting of water.

photon A discrete packet of electromagnetic energy; also called Einstein.

photooxidation The light-dependent destructive oxidation of cellular structures or chemical compounds.

photophosphorylation ATP synthesis using light energy and electron transport.

photoreactivation The process by which a light-activated enzyme, photolyase, repairs pyrimidine dimers in DNA by cleaving the covalent linkages between the damaged pyrimidines.

photosynthesis The conversion of light energy into chemical energy either with (oxygenic) or without (anoxygenic) the production of oxygen. The chemical energy can be used to fix carbon dioxide into organic compounds.

photosystem An arrangement of chlorophylls and accessory pigments into groups of 250 to 400 molecules that gather electromagnetic energy and transfer excited electrons to a reaction center chlorophyll.

phototaxis The movement of organisms in response to light.

phototroph An organism that obtains its energy from light.

phycobilin *See* **biliprotein.**

phylogeny The study of comparative evolutionary relationships among organisms.

pilus (pl. **pili**) An appendage found on the surface of some procaryotes; pili are involved in conjugation and in attachment; also called fimbria.

plankton A free-floating aquatic community, composed of microscopic cyanobacteria, algae, plants, and/or animals.

plaque A clear area in a confluent lawn of bacteria or tissue culture cells caused by viral infection and cell lysis; a sticky film composed of microorganisms embedded in a polysaccharide/protein matrix on the surface of teeth.

plasma The fluid matrix of blood; plasma contains fibrinogen, antibodies, complement, and other components.

plasma cell An antibody-secreting cell formed from B lymphocytes.

plasma membrane The thin layer surrounding the cell cytoplasm, consisting primarily of phospholipids and proteins, that acts as a semipermeable barrier for the passage of molecules; also called cytoplasmic membrane or cell membrane.

plasmid Extrachromosomal DNA found in the cytoplasm of some procaryotes.

plasmodium (pl. **plasmodia**) Streaming protoplasmic mass, part of the life cycle of slime molds.

plastid A membrane-enclosed organelle found in algae and plants. There are three types of plastids: chloroplasts, chromoplasts, and leucoplasts.

platelet A small blood cell involved in blood coagulation and the transportation of serotonin; also called thrombocyte.

pleomorphic Having more than one distinct form.

pock An opaque lesion caused by a viral infection of the chorioallantoic membranes of embryonated eggs; a pustule on the surface of the skin.

point mutation A mutation involving a single base change in the chromosome.

polymerase chain reaction A laboratory technique to synthesize within a short period of time many copies of a DNA molecule. DNA is amplified by a cyclic repetition of three steps: (1) the original double-stranded DNA molecule is denatured at high temperature, (2) oligonucleotide primers are annealed to the DNA at low temperature, and (3) the primers are extended on the DNA template by a DNA polymerase.

polymorphonuclear leukocyte (PMN) *See* **neutrophil.**

polypeptide An organic compound composed of amino acids linked by peptide bonds, but of lower molecular weight than a protein.

polyribosome Two or more ribosomes joined together in a chain with mRNA.

pomace The skin, pits, and stems of grapes.

positive control A regulatory system in which the presence of a controlling factor turns on protein synthesis.

positive stain A stain in which the specimen is stained and appears dark against a light background.

potable Suitable to drink.

potential energy Stored energy or energy of position.

pour plate An agar plate that has been prepared by adding a dilute microbial suspension and melted agar into a sterile Petri dish.

prevalence rate The occurrence of disease in a population during a specified time period; a type of morbidity rate.

Pribnow box A consensus sequence (TATAAT) in DNA that is a binding site for RNA polymerase and located ten bases before the point of initiation of transcription.

primary metabolite A chemical compound associated with cell growth or function.

primary producer An organism capable of converting carbon dioxide to organic carbon.

prion An infectious particle containing protein but no nucleic acid; also called scrapie-associated fibril (SAF).

procaryote A cell or organism with no nuclear membrane, specialized membrane-enclosed organelles, or the extensive internal structural organization typically found in a eucaryotic cell.

prodromal period The period in the natural history of disease when the first signs and symptoms of disease appear.

profundal zone The zone of deep water in a lake beyond the depth of effective light penetration.

promoter A region on the chromosome, adjacent to the operator, to which RNA polymerase binds.

propagated epidemic disease A disease in which the disease agent is transmitted from one host to another either through direct contact or via a vector.

properdin pathway *See* **alternative complement pathway.**

prophage A temperate bacteriophage that is integrated into the host chromosome.

prospective study An observational epidemiological study that follows a group of people (a cohort) over a period of time to determine the rate at which a particular disease develops in relation to a specified characteristic.

protein An organic compound composed of amino acids linked by peptide bonds.

proton motive force *See* **chemiosmosis.**

protoplast A cell that has lost its cell wall but remains intact in an isotonic environment.

protoplast fusion A recombinant DNA technique in which protoplasts of two species are combined to produce a hybrid organism containing the chromosomes of both cells.

prototroph An organism with no additional requirements for growth.

protozoan (pl. **protozoa**) A motile eucaryotic microorganism that does not have a cell wall or chlorophyll.

pseudopodium (pl. **pseudopodia**) A cytoplasmic extension produced by amoebae during locomotion.

psychrophile An organism with an optimum growth temperature of 10°C to 20°C.

public health The science of protecting and improving community health through education and organized preventive medicine efforts.

pure culture A population of cells that arises from one cell.

purine A cyclic nitrogenous compound (for example, adenine and guanine) that is found in nucleic acids, many coenzymes, and certain antibiotics.

putrefaction The anaerobic microbial decomposition of meat proteins with the production of hydrogen sulfide, indole, mercaptans, ammonia, amines, and other foul-smelling compounds.

pyoderma An inflammatory skin infection caused by pus-forming bacteria.

pyogenic Pus-forming.

pyrimidine A cyclic nitrogenous compound (for example, cytosine, uracil, or thymine) that is found in nucleic acids, many coenzymes, and certain antibiotics.

pyrogen A substance that can cause a rise in body temperature.

Q

quellung reaction The apparent swelling of the bacterial capsule by the interaction of anti-capsular antibody and capsular antigen.

quinone An electron carrier that is a lipid-soluble substance of low molecular weight.

R

racking The procedure in wine making in which the wine is drawn from the sediment and added back to the top of the storage vat.

radioimmunoassay (RIA) A laboratory technique that uses a radioactively labeled antigen or antibody to compete with and measure the concentration of unlabled antigen or antibody in a sample.

reaction center A chlorophyll in the photosystem that receives electrons from other chlorophylls and accessory pigments and passes these excited electrons on to the transport chain.

reading frame The arrangement of nucleotides in mRNA so that a particular pattern of codons is established for translation.

reading frame shift A change in the reading of codons during translation so that an entirely new protein is formed.

reagin A tissue antibody produced in response to damaged tissue components resulting from infection by treponemes and some other infectious agents.

recalcitrance The total resistance of a chemical to microbial degradation.

recombinant DNA technology The techniques used to manipulate genes in living organisms to carry out genetic engineering.

redox potential *See* **oxidation-reduction potential.**

redox reaction *See* **oxidation-reduction reaction.**

reduction A reaction involving the uptake of electrons.

refractile (R) body A paramecium endosymbiont form that appears as tightly rolled ribbons and is believed to be associated with the toxic particles (paramecin) released by killer paramecia.

replica plating The technique in which replicate plates are inoculated from a master plate, using a pad of sterile velvet to transfer colonies of microorganisms.

replicative form A double-stranded nucleic acid that serves as an intermediate form in the replication of single-stranded viral nucleic acids.

replicon A stretch of DNA that is synthesized from a replication origin.

reporter gene A gene on a cloning vector that codes for an easily detectable trait.

repression The process by which enzyme synthesis is inhibited by the presence of a substance, the repressor.

repressor The regulator gene product that interacts with the operator to control gene expression.

reservoir of infection An animate or inanimate source of infectious agents.

resident flora A more or less constant group of organisms that is a part of the normal flora.

resistance plasmid (R plasmid) A plasmid that carries genes for antibiotic resistance and *tra* genes for conjugative transfer.

resolving power The ability to distinguish two objects as separate and distinct entities; also called resolution.

respiration Catabolic reactions producing ATP in which either organic or inorganic compounds are the primary electron donors and either molecular oxygen (aerobic) or another inorganic compound such as nitrate or sulfate (anaerobic) is the terminal electron acceptor.

restricted transduction *See* **specialized transduction.**

restriction endonuclease A nuclease that recognizes and, internally in the DNA, cleaves specific sequences known as palindromes.

reticulate body (RB) A large, noninfectious particle that is involved in intracellular multiplication in the chlamydia developmental cycle.

reticuloendothelial (RE) system The system of macrophages found in the spleen, thymus, lungs, lymph nodes, bone marrow, and liver; also called mononuclear phagocytic system.

retrospective study An observational epidemiological study in which comparisons are made between people with a particular disease (cases) and people without the disease (controls) with respect to a specified characteristic.

reverse transcriptase RNA-dependent DNA polymerase that uses RNA as a template to synthesize DNA.

rhizoid A rootlike fungal extension that anchors mycelia to the surface.

rhizosphere The region of soil closely surrounding the roots of a plant.

rhizosphere effect The presence of increased concentrations of microorganisms around plant roots as a result of organic matter excreted by the roots into the surrounding soil.

rho factor (ρ) The protein that unwinds the RNA-DNA hybrid in rho-dependent termination of transcription.

ribonucleic acid (RNA) A type of nucleic acid involved in protein synthesis. Three types of RNA exist in a cell: mRNA, rRNA, and tRNA. RNA contains ribose sugars (in contrast to DNA, which contains deoxyribose sugars).

ribosomal RNA (rRNA) RNA that is associated with ribosomes.

ribosome A cell component consisting of two subunits and containing proteins and rRNA. Ribosomes are the sites of protein synthesis.

ribozyme An RNA molecule that can catalyze a chemical reaction.

RNA primer A short segment (approximately 10 nucleotides long) of RNA that precedes or primes newly synthesized DNA.

RNA processing The modification of the RNA transcript before translation.

RNA splicing The excising of introns and rejoining of exons in mRNA after transcription and before translation.

rod A cylindrical bacterial cell.

rolling circle model A mode of DNA replication that begins with the cutting of one parental strand of the double helix; replication begins as the cut strand is rolled off the double helix.

rumen A special organ in ruminants in which cellulose is broken down by microorganisms.

ruminant A plant-eating mammal such as a cow, goat, or sheep that has a special organ called the rumen.

S

salmonellosis A gastrointestinal disease caused by *Salmonella;* also called *Salmonella* gastroenteritis.

saprophyte An organism living on dead or decaying organic mater.

scalded skin syndrome An epidermal disease of infants caused by *Staphylococcus aureus* and characterized by lesions resembling tissue that has been scalded with boiling water.

scanning tunneling microscope A type of microscope in which magnifications of several millionfold are achieved by shuttling electrons between a minute probe and a specimen's surface.

scrapie-associated fibril (SAF) *See* **prion.**

secondary metabolite A product (for example, an antibiotic) of a metabolic pathway that is not associated with primary cellular processes.

secondary response *See* **anamnestic response.**

second law of thermodynamics The law stating that all processes occur in such a manner that there is a total increase in entropy.

selective medium A culture medium that favors the growth of specific microorganisms while inhibiting the growth of undesired microorganisms.

semiconservative replication DNA replication, with each strand serving as a template for the synthesis of a new daughter strand.

sensitive strain (of *Paramecium*) A paramecium that is harmed by toxic particles released by killer strains of *Paramecium.*

sensitivity of a test The ability of a test to correctly identify those people who have a particular disease.

septicemia A systemic disease in which microorganisms actively multiply in circulating blood.

septic tank A type of anaerobic sewage treatment process commonly found in rural areas.

septum (pl. **septa**) A cross-wall.

serum (pl. **sera**) The fluid portion of blood remaining after plasma has clotted.

sewage The liquid waste material carried by a system of pipes and other conduits called sewers.

sex factor *See* **F factor.**

sexually transmitted disease (STD) A disease that is transmitted by sexual contact.

shigellosis Gastrointestinal disease caused by *Shigella* species; also called bacillary dysentery.

Shine-Dalgarno sequence A short, purine-rich region preceding the initiation codon on procaryotic mRNA that binds to the 16S rRNA of the 30S ribosomal subunit and serves to thread the mRNA into the ribosome.

shotgun cloning The enzymatic cleavage of an entire donor genome into small DNA fragments and the insertion of these fragments into cloning vectors.

shuttle vector A vector that is used to move DNA between two unrelated organisms.

siderochrome A siderophore that is a hydroxamate of low molecular weight.

siderophore An iron-binding compound that transports iron into the cell.

signature sequence A short, unique nucleotide sequence that is found in the 16S rRNA of certain groups of procaryotes.

silent mutation A mutation that has no effect on the amino acid coded by the affected area of the chromosome.

similarity coefficient (S_J) The comparison of positive characteristics among organisms in numerical taxonomy.

single-cell protein (SCP) Dried microbial cells that are used for food or feed.

slime layer *See* **capsule.**

SOS response An inducible repair system that excises and repairs DNA damage.

souring The formation of undesirable odors and tastes in meat resulting from volatile acids produced during microbial metabolism of meat proteins and carbohydrates.

Southern blot A technique by which DNA fragments, separated by electrophoresis, are immobilized on a paper sheet and detected with a labeled nucleic acid probe; named after Edward M. Southern.

specialized transduction The transfer of a specific portion of host DNA by transduction; also called restricted transduction.

species A taxonomic category just below genus level and describing organisms with a similar phenotype.

specificity of a test The ability of a test to correctly identify those people who do not have a particular disease.

specific resistance *See* **acquired resistance.**

spheroplast A cell that has lost a portion of its cell wall but remains intact in an isotonic environment.

spirillum (pl. **spirilla**) A spiral-shaped bacterial cell.

spontaneous generation A theory that living organisms can arise from nonliving matter.

spontaneous mutation A mutation that occurs naturally, usually as a result of errors in DNA replication or from mistakes during genetic recombination.

sporangiophore A fungal hypha with sporangia at the tip.

sporangiospore An asexual fungal spore formed within a sac called the sporangium.

sporangium (pl. **sporangia**) A specialized fungal reproductive structure containing sporangiospores; the outer envelope-like covering of an endospore.

spore The resistant resting body formed by some cells in response to unfavorable environmental conditions.

sporogenesis The process of spore formation.

spread plate An agar plate on which a dilute microbial suspension has been spread evenly across the surface to obtain isolated colonies.

staphylokinase A *Staphylococcus* protease that converts plasminogen in human serum to plasmin, thereby dissolving blood clots.

stationary phase (of population growth curve) The period of population growth in which there is no change in cell numbers.

steady state The state of growth in a continuous culture when cell numbers and nutrient levels in the culture vessel become constant.

sterilization   The killing of all viable organisms.

sterol   A type of lipid lacking fatty acids, routinely found in eucaryotic plasma membranes but rarely in procaryotic plasma membranes.

Stickland reaction   The sequence of chemical reactions in clostridia in which pairs of amino acids are fermented, with one amino acid serving as the electron donor and the other serving as the electron acceptor.

storage body   *See* **inclusion body.**

strain   A population of cells that are all derived from a common ancestor and retain the characteristics of the ancestor.

stratosphere   The layer of the atmosphere above the troposphere and extending up to approximately 50 km.

streak plate technique   A method used to obtain isolated colonies by streaking a mixed culture across the surface of an agar plate with an inoculating loop.

streptokinase   A *Streptococcus* protease that converts plasminogen in human serum to plasmin, thereby dissolving blood clots.

streptolysin O   An oxygen-labile hemolysin produced by *Streptococcus pyogenes*.

streptolysin S   An oxygen-stable hemolysin produced by *Streptococcus pyogenes*.

structure analog   A chemical compound that structurally resembles a cellular metabolite and competes with this metabolite in cellular enzymatic reactions.

substrate   The molecule on which an enzyme acts.

substrate-level phosphorylation   The addition of phosphate onto an organic compound.

subunit vaccine   A vaccine consisting of parts of a microorganism.

sulfonamide   An antimicrobial agent that is a structure analog of *p*-aminobenzoic acid.

superantigen   A bacterial protein that stimulates the immune system to produce large numbers of T lymphocytes.

suppressor mutation   A change in DNA that overcomes the effect of an original change in DNA, ultimately causing no alteration in the original gene.

surfactant   A surface-active compound.

swarmer cell   A flagellated daughter cell released from the parent cell.

symbiosis   A relationship between two or more organisms.

synchronous culture   A culture in which all the cells of the population are in the same stage of growth.

synergism   A symbiotic relationship in which different species of microorganisms living together benefit one another and grow better together than separately.

syngamy   Sexual reproduction involving union of two gametes to form a zygote.

synthetic drug   A man-made chemical used internally to inhibit or kill microorganisms.

synthetic (chemically defined) medium   A growth medium, the exact chemical composition of which is known.

syntrophism   *See* **cross-feeding.**

T

taxonomy   The systematic categorization of organisms into a coherent scheme.

TCA cycle   The sequence of chemical reactions in which pyruvate is oxidized to carbon dioxide and reduced coenzymes are produced; also called Krebs cycle and citric acid cycle.

T cytotoxic (T_C) cell   A CD8-containing T lymphocyte that interacts with and destroys cells containing antigens on their surfaces.

teichoic acid   An acidic polysaccharide of repeating subunits of glycerol or ribitol, joined by phosphodiester linkages, found in the cell wall and plasma membrane.

temperate phage   A bacteriophage that can become integrated into the host chromosome instead of immediately lysing the host.

termination codon   One of three codons (UAA, UAG, and UGA) that does not code for a specific amino acid and therefore signals the termination of protein synthesis; also called nonsense codon.

tests in parallel   Tests performed in which any test yielding a positive result is sufficient evidence for a disease state.

tests in series   Tests performed in which all tests must yield positive results to confirm a disease state.

thallus (pl. **thalli**)   The plantlike structure of a fungus or alga.

T helper (T_H) cell   A CD4-containing T lymphocyte that stimulates B lymphocytes to produce antibodies and is involved in cell-mediated immunity.

thermal death time (**TDT**)   The shortest time required to kill all of the microorganisms in a suspension at a specific temperature.

thermodynamics   The study of energy transformations.

thermophile   An organism with an optimum growth temperature of 40ºC or higher.

thrombocyte   *See* **platelet.**

thrush   A *Candida*-induced inflammation of the oral mucosa.

thylakoid   Membranous vesicles containing photosynthetic pigments.

T lymphocyte   A lymphocyte that is differentiated in the thymus and is important in humoral and cell-mediated immunity; also called T cell.

top-fermenting yeast   Yeast that rises to the surface of the beer during fermentation to produce beer that is uniform in turbidity and high in alcohol content.

toxoid   A toxin that has been treated to destroy its toxic activity but not its antigenic properties.

transcription   The synthesis of RNA from DNA.

transducer   *See* **methyl-accepting chemotaxis protein (MCP).**

transduction   The exchange of DNA by use of a bacteriophage.

transfection   The uptake of naked bacteriophage DNA through modified cell envelopes of competent bacteria; the insertion of cloning vectors into mammalian cells by endocytosis.

transferrin   An iron-binding protein found in the blood of vertebrates.

transfer RNA (**tRNA**)   RNA that carries amino acids to ribosomes during protein synthesis.

transformation   The insertion of naked extracellular DNA from a donor cell into a competent recipient cell.

transgenic animal or **plant**   An animal or plant that has obtained new genetic information from the insertion of foreign DNA.

transient flora   Organisms that inhabit a host for only a short period of time as part of the normal flora.

translation   The synthesis of protein from mRNA.

transmission of disease   The mechanism by which infectious agents are transferred from one host or object to a susceptible host.

transpeptidation   The penicillin-sensitive step in cell wall synthesis involving cross-linking of adjacent tetrapeptides.

transposon   A gene-containing element that can be moved among nucleic acids.

trickling filter   An aerobic sewage treatment process in which sewage is sprayed onto a bed of crushed rocks.

troposphere   The layer of the atmosphere closest to the earth and extending to an altitude of 8 to 12 km above the surface.

tube dilution method   A method in which tubes containing serial dilutions of an antimicrobial agent are inoculated with a test microorganism to determine antimicrobial susceptibility.

tubercle   A small nodular lung lesion formed in tuberculosis.

tuberculin   The *Mycobacterium tuberculosis* antigen used in the tuberculosis skin test.

tumor necrosis factor (**TNF**)   A cytokine that activates macrophages, granulocytes, and cytotoxic cells.

turbidostat   A continuous culture device in which the flow rate of fresh medium is automatically adjusted to maintain turbidity levels as measured by a light-sensing device.

tyndallization   A sterilization process in which material is heated to 100°C for 30 minutes on three consecutive days; also called fractional sterilization.

type I hypersensitive reaction   *See* **anaphylactic hypersensitive reaction.**

type II allergic reaction   *See* **cytotoxic hypersensitive reaction.**

U

uncoupler   A chemical agent that causes the membrane to be leaky to protons, thereby uncoupling ATP synthesis from proton movement across the membrane.

V

vaccine   A material administered to a subject to induce artificially acquired active immunity.

vacuole   A membrane-bound cell component.

valence   The number of antibody-binding sites on an antigen.

vector   A living organism that is an intermediary in the transfer of infectious agents; a vehicle for the introduction of a target gene into a cell during gene cloning.

vegetative cell   A cell that is engaged in growth, metabolism, and reproduction.

vehicle   An inanimate object capable of transmitting infectious agents.

viable count   A count of visible colonies growing on agar medium in a Petri dish.

viroid   Infectious RNA, devoid of a protein coat and several thousand times smaller than a virus.

virulence   A quantitative measure of pathogenicity; the capacity of a microorganism to overcome the body defenses of the host.

virulent phage   A bacteriophage that is capable of lytic infections.

virus   A submicroscopic filterable agent consisting of either RNA or DNA surrounded by a protein coat.

W

Warburg-Dickens pathway   *See* **pentose phosphate pathway.**

water activity (a_w)   The available water in an organism's surroundings; water activity is determined by measuring the relative humidity in the air space in a substance's environment.

western blot   A technique by which proteins are separated and immobilized on a paper sheet and detected by reaction with a labeled antibody.

white blood cell   *See* **leukocyte.**

wild type   The unaltered original genotype.

wobble   The ability of the third base on the 5' end of tRNA anticodon to pair with two or more bases at the 3' end of the mRNA codon.

wort   The liquid portion of malt, consisting of a dilute solution of sugars that is fermented to form beer.

Y

yeast   A unicellular eucaryotic fungal cell.

yeast artificial chromosome (**YAC**)   A vector that consists of a linear plasmid that is comprised partially of a yeast chromosome.

Z

zoonosis (pl. **zoonoses**)   An animal disease transmissible to humans.

zoospore   A flagellated spore formed by algae and some fungi during reproduction.

zygospore   A resistant fungal spore arising from a zygote.

zygote   A diploid cell resulting from the union of two haploid gametes.

molecular taxonomy, 310–11, 310f
subtractive, 278
Hybridoma, 475
Hydrocarbon-degrading microorganisms, **583–84**
Hydrogen
cellular content of, 84t, 570, 570t
characteristics of element, 647t
as electron donor, 80–81, 574–75
in photosynthesis, 186–87, 187f
function in cells, 84t
oxidation of, **172,** 573–74
Hydrogenase, 172, 574f
Hydrogenation reaction, 145
Hydrogen bacteria, 171t
Hydrogen bonds, 649–50, 650f
in base pairing, 216f, 218
Hydrogenobacter, 337
Hydrogenomonas, 172
Hydrogen-oxidizing bacteria, 336–37
Hydrogen peroxide, 93, 461
Hydrogen sulfide, 80
as electron donor, 333, 580
in photosynthesis, 187, 187f
as energy source, 80–81
formation from sulfate, 83, 83f
oxidation of, **171–72,** 573–74
Hydrogen sulfide production test, 324f
Hydrogen swell, 616
Hydrolase, in industrial processes, 623t
Hydrologic cycle, 586
Hydrophilic substance, 650–51
Hydrophobic substance, 651
Hydrothermal vent, 80, 80f, 340–41, 344
Hydroxamate, 88
β-Hydroxybutyryl-CoA, 160f
Hydroxylamine, 247, 248t
Hydroxyl free radical, 93, 461
Hyperchromicity, of denatured DNA, 217, 217f
Hypersensitive reaction, **479–81,** 479t
antibody-mediated, 479, 479t
delayed, 479, 479t
immediate, 479, 479t
type I, 469
Hyphae, 342, 361, 362f, 423
Hyphomicrobium, 19, 337, 337f
Hypochytriomycota, 366t, **369**

Hypolimnion, 587
Hypovirus, 390

Ice cream, 609t
Ich (fish disease), 369
Ichthyophthirius, 375t
ID$_{50}$, 447
Idiotype, 470
Idoxuridine (IUdR), 132, 132t, 540
Ig. *See* Immunoglobulin
i gene, 233–34
IL. *See* Interleukin
Ilarvirus, 392t
Illumination
critical, 24–25, 25f
Köhler, 24–25, 25f
in microscopy, **24–25,** 25f
α-Imino acid, 42
Immediate hypersensitive reaction, 479, 479t
type I, 479, 479t
type II, 479t, 480–81
type III, 479t, 480–81
Immobilized enzymes, 622–23
Immobilized microbial cells, 622–23, 623t
Immune complex, 481
Immune system, evolution of, 494
Immunity
cell-mediated, 468, **482–85**
humoral, **468–82**
Immunocompromised host, 429
Immunodiffusion test, 486
Immunoelectrophoresis, **486,** 487f
Immunofluorescence, 31
to detect antigens or antibodies, **489–90,** 489f
Immunogenicity, 468
Immunoglobulin (Ig), **469,** 470t. *See also* Antibody
bivalent, 470
evolution of, 494
formation in response to antigens, **477,** 477f
specificity of, 470
structure of, **469–71,** 470t, 471f
Immunoglobulin (Ig) genes, rearrangement of, **471–73,** 472f
Immunoglobulin A (IgA), **469,** 470t
secretory, 469
subclasses of, 470
Immunoglobulin D (IgD), **469,** 470t, 475
Immunoglobulin E (IgE), **469,** 470t

Immunoglobulin G (IgG), **469,** 470t, 480
subclasses of, 470
Immunoglobulin M (IgM), **469,** 470t, 475, 480, 494
Immunologic response, **475–81**
anamnestic, 477
primary, 477, 477f
secondary, 477, 477f
Immunologic tolerance, 473
Immunology, **7–8,** 468
Immunosuppression, 429, 479, 484–85
Impetigo, 328, 451t, 525t, 526, 526f
Incidence rate, 554
Incidence study, **561–63**
Incident-light excitation fluorescence microscope. *See* Epifluorescence microscope
Incineration, for sterilization, 121
Inclusion body, **65–66,** 71f
Incubation period, **446,** 446f
Incubatory carrier, 443
Indeterminate leprosy, 527
Indicator organism, for bacteria in water, **590–93**
Indirect ELISA, 490, 491f
Indirect fluorescent antibody test, 489f, 490
Indirect hemagglutination, 487
Induced mutation, 246
Inducer, 233–34, 234f
Induction
of prophage, 410f, 411
of protein, **233–34,** 234f, 236
Industrial processes, **619–23,** 619f, 633
conditions in industrial fermentors, **621**
culture methods, **621–23**
media for, **620,** 620t
microorganisms for, 11–12, **620–21**
Infant, disease rates among, 556
Infant botulism, 517
Infecting dose, 455, 516
Infection, 442
latent, **446–48**
Infection control program, 559
Infection thread, 419f, 420
Infectious abortion in cattle, 321
Infectious disease, 442
natural history of, **446–48,** 446f
Infectious hepatitis, 524, 524t
Inflammation, 453, 454t, **458–60,** 460f, 480
acute, 458, 460f

chronic, 458, 460f
subacute, 458, 460f
Inflammatory mediator, 458
Influenza, 443–44, 444t, 446, 500t, 513, 555, 557t
Influenza vaccine, 478, 513
Influenza virus, 386, 395, 395t, 500t, 513, 513f
antigenic shifts in, 513, 555
antiviral drugs, 132, 132t
Infusions, 13
Inhibitor, of enzyme, 143
Initiation codon, 230
Initiation complex, **229–32,** 231f, 233
Initiation factors, 232
Innate host resistance, **454–61**
Inoculating loop, 96, 97f, 121
Inorganic compounds, storage depots for, 65–66
Inorganic ions, content of cells, 81t
Inoviridae, 391t
Insect, bacterial symbionts of, **427,** 427f
Insertion, 246
Insertional inactivation, 281
Insertion sequence (IS), **260,** 261f
Insulin, genetically-engineered, 296–97, 296t, 298–300f, **300–301,** 301t
Interference
constructive, 28
destructive, 28
Interference contrast microscope, 30
Interferon, 132, 406, 407f, 456, 473, 474t, 484, 540
genetically-engineered, 296t, 296
Interleukin (IL), 473
Interleukin-1 (IL-1), 474t, 475
Interleukin-2 (IL-2), 474t, 475, 483
Interleukin-3 (IL-3), 474t
Interleukin-4 (IL-4), 474t
Interleukin-5 (IL-5), 474t
Interleukin-6 (IL-6), 474t
Interleukin-7 (IL-7), 474t
Interleukin-8 (IL-8), 474t
Interleukin-9 (IL-9), 474t
Interleukin-10 (IL-10), 474t
Interleukin-11 (IL-11), 474t
Interleukin-12 (IL-12), 474t
Interleukin-13 (IL-13), 474t
Interleukin-14 (IL-14), 474t
Intermittent carrier, 443
Internal cell structures, **65–68**
Internal membrane system, 52, 53f
Internet resources, 645–46

virulence of, iron and, **100,** 101t
N. meningitidis, 320t, 321, 500t, 512, 512t
carbon dioxide requirement, **135,** 135t
Neisseriaceae, 320t, 321
Nemalion, 355
Neomycin
commercial production of, 629t
mechanism of action of, 125t, 128, 128t, 629t
Neonatal respiratory disease, 499t, 503t, 506, 506t
Neoplasm. *See* Tumor
Nepovirus, 392t
Nested amplification, 291
Neufchâfatel cheese, 611t
Neumann, R.E., 314
Neuraminidase, 386, 513, 513f
Neurological syphilis, 535
Neurospora, 366t, 368
N. crassa, 14
Neurotoxin, 450, 451t, 517
Neutral fat, 47, 49f
Neutralization test, **487**
Neutron, 647
Neutrophils, 456, 457t
Newcastle disease virus, 408
Niacin, 85
Nicotinamide adenine dinucleotide. *See* NAD
Nicotinamide adenine dinucleotide phosphate. *See* NADP
nif genes, 297, 422, 434–35, 434f
NIH guidelines, for recombinant DNA research, 297
Nine-plus-two arrangement, of microtubules, 73, 74f
Nitrate
as electron acceptor, 150, 168, 168t
as nitrogen source, 82, **82,** 82f
in water supply, 578
Nitrate ammonification, 578
Nitrate reductase, 82, 82f, 170, 578
Nitrate reduction
assimilatory, 82, 170, 578
dissimilatory, 170, 578
Nitric oxide, 578
Nitrification, 172, 577f, **578,** 579, 599
Nitrifying bacteria, 53f, 171t, 172, 336, 336f, 573, 577f, 578
Nitrite, 573–74
as electron acceptor, 168t
as energy source, 80

in groundwater, 578
oxidation to nitrate, 172
Nitrite-oxidizing bacteria, 171t, **172,** 336
Nitrite reductase, 82, 82f
Nitrobacter, 92t, 171t, 172, 336, 578, 588
N. winogradskyi, 336f
Nitrococcus, 171t, 172, 336, 578
N. mobilis, 336f
N. oceanus, 53f
Nitrogen
cellular content of, 84t, 570, 570t
characteristics of element, 647t
function in cells, 84t
removal from sewage, 599
Nitrogenase, 82f, 320, 335, 420, 422–23, 422f
assay of, 423
oxygen-sensitivity of, 423
Nitrogenase complex, 422, 422f
Nitrogenase reductase, 422–23, 422f
Nitrogen cycle, 172, **576–79,** 577f
Nitrogen fixation, 12, **82–83,** 297, 343, 417f
abiotic, 576
crop yields and, **434–35,** 434f
by cyanobacteria, 334–35
energy required for, **422–23,** 422f
in nitrogen cycle, **576–77,** 577f
in nonleguminous crops, 435
nonsymbiotic, 576–77
scheme for, 422f
symbiotic, 320, **418–23,** 419–22f, 421t, 576
Nitrogen gas, 170, 578
atmospheric, 576
as nitrogen source, 82, **82–83**
Nitrogen source, 81–83, 620
Nitromersol (Metaphen), 122t, 124
Nitrosamine, 578, 615
Nitrosococcus, 171t, 172, 336, 578
N. oceanus, 336f
Nitrosofying bacteria, 336, 577f, 578
Nitrosolobus, 171t, 172, 336, 578
N. multiformis, 336f
Nitrosomonas, 92t, 171t, 172, 336, 578, 588
N. europaea, 336f
Nitrosospira, 172, 336
Nitrospina, 171t, 172, 336, 578
Nitrospira, 171t, 578
N. gracilis, 336f

Nitrous acid, 247, 248t
Nitrous oxide, 170, 578
NK cells. *See* Natural killer cells
Nocardia, 171t, 172, 342, 342t, 575–76, 581, 583
Nocardioforms, 328t, 342t, 638, 640–41
Nocardioides, 342t
Nocardiopsis, 342t
Nod factor, 420
nod genes, 420
Nomarski differential interference contrast microscope, 17f, 29–30f, 30
Nomenclature, 306, 306t
Noncommunicable disease, 442
Noncompetitive inhibitor, 143, 145
Nonconjugative plasmid, **260–61**
Nonculturable microbes, 347
Noncyclic photophosphorylation, **184–86**
Nongonococcal urethritis, 326, 327t, 444, 533t, **536**
Nonhistone proteins, 72
Noninfectious disease, 442
Nonmotile, gram-negative curved bacteria, 316t, **319,** 319f, 635
Nonphotosynthetic, nonfruiting gliding bacteria, 332t, 639–40
Nonpolar molecule, 649
Nonsense codon, 213, 231f, 232–33
Nonsense mutation, 246, 247f
Nonspecific resistance. *See* Innate host resistance
Nonsymbiotic nitrogen fixation, 576–77
Norfloxacin, 125t, 129
Nori, 355
Normal flora. *See* Microflora
Norwalk virus, 394t
Nosema, 375t
Nosepiece, 22, 22f
Nosocomial infection, **559,** 559t
Nostoc, 335f, 421t, 576, 587
Nostocaceae, 335, 335t
Notifiable disease, 554t
Novobiocin, 629t
Nuclear envelope, 72
Nuclease, **202,** 460
Nucleic acid. *See also* DNA; RNA
content of cells, 81t
degradation of, 202
functions in cells, **44–46**
metabolism of, 579
structure of, **44–46,** 46f

synthesis of, antibiotics that inhibit, 125, 125t, **128–29,** 128t
Nucleic acid hybridization. *See* Hybridization
Nucleic acid probe, **287–88,** 289f
pathogen identification with, **295,** 296f
Nucleocapsid, 386, 386f
Nucleoid, 18, 50f, **65,** 67f, 71f, 212
Nucleolus, 71f, 72, 228
Nucleoside, 44
Nucleoside-requiring bacteria, 84
Nucleosome, 223
Nucleotide, 44, 46f, 81t
Nucleus, 18, 71f, 72, 313t
Null cells. *See* Killer cells
Numerical aperture, 23–24, 24f
Numerical taxonomy, **308–9,** 308f, 309t
Nutrient broth, 95t
Nutrient deprivation, 70
Nutrient loss, 61
Nutrient transport, **85–89**
Nutritional requirements, **80–85**
Nuttall, 7t
Nyctotherus, 375t
Nystatin, 125t, 129–32
commercial production of, 629t
mechanism of action of, 126, 629t
structure of, 127f

O antigen, 58f, 60, 60f
Objective lens, 21–24, 22f, 24f, 29f
oil-immersion vs. dry, 24
Obligate anaerobe, 93
Obligate parasite, 418
Observational study, **561–63,** 561f
prospective, **561–63,** 562f, 563t
retrospective, **561–63,** 563t
Occupation, contribution to disease, 454
Ocean, 586
Oceanospirillum, 319
Ocular lens, 21–22, 22f, 29f
Oerskovia, 342t
Oil-immersion lens, 24
Oil spill, 11–12, 12f, **583–84**
Okazaki, Reiji, 221, 240
Okazaki fragments, 221–24, 222f, **240,** 241f
2',5'-Oligoadenylate, 407f
Oligomycin, 168t
Oligonucleotide, synthetic, 278–79, 279f

Xylulose-5-phosphate, 154,
155–56f, 159f, 191–92,
192f, 194, 195f

YAC. *See* Yeast artificial
chromosome
Yalow, Rosalyn, 490
Yaws, 318t
Yeast, 360, **361–62**
in beer production,
617–19, 619f
in distilled beverage
production, **619**

ethanol production by, **157**
lactose-fermenting, 609t
reproduction in, 365
on skin, 525
as source of single-cell
protein, 631–32, 632t
in wine production, **619**
Yeast artificial chromosome
(YAC), **285**
Yeast-mycelium dimorphism,
378, 378–79f
Yellow boy, 580
Yellow fever, 444–45t, 542f, 543t

Yellow fever vaccine, 478t
Yersin, Alexander J.E., 7t, 323, 509
Yersinia, 322, 322t, 324f
Y. pestis, 7t, 323, 323f,
444–45t, 451t
Yield of test, 561
Yogurt, 154, 331t, 609t, 610

Zernicke, Fritz, 28
Zidovudine. *See* Azidothymidine
Zigas, Vincent, 412
Zinc, microbial leaching of
ores, 582

Zinder, Norton, 254–55
Zone of inhibition, 133, 133f
Zoogloea, 595
Zoonosis, **443,** 444, 444f
Zoospore, 343, 352, 358f, 364,
369, 370f
Zooxanthellae, 350
Zovirax. *See* Acyclovir
Z-pathway, 184–85, 185f
Zygomycota, 360t,
365–69, 366t
Zygospore, 354f, 366
Zygote, 73–74, 362–63f, 364